Concept, Theories, and Management of Cryptocurrencies

Eduardo Tomé
Universidade Lusofona, Portugal

IGI Global
Scientific Publishing
Publishing Tomorrow's Research Today

Vice President of Editorial	Melissa Wagner
Director of Acquisitions	Mikaela Felty
Director of Book Development	Jocelynn Hessler
Production Manager	Mike Brehm
Cover Design	Jose Rosado

Published in the United States of America by
IGI Global Scientific Publishing
701 East Chocolate Avenue
Hershey, PA, 17033, USA
Tel: 717-533-8845
Fax: 717-533-7115
Website: https://www.igi-global.com E-mail: cust@igi-global.com

Library of Congress Cataloging-in-Publication Data

Names: Tome, Eduardo Luis de Campos, 1964- editor.
Title: Concept, theories, and management of cryptocurrencies / edited by Eduardo Tomé.
Description: Hershey, PA : IGI Global, [2025] | Includes bibliographical references and index. | Summary: "This book investigates the apparent new wonderful world of crypto currencies to understand what really happens in the market of cryptocurrencies and what are the main consequences of that evolution"-- Provided by publisher.
Identifiers: LCCN 2024048760 (print) | LCCN 2024048761 (ebook) | ISBN 9798369359860 (hardcover) | ISBN 9798369359877 (paperback) | ISBN 9798369359884 (ebook)
Subjects: LCSH: Cryptocurrencies. | Management.
Classification: LCC HG1710.3 .C68 2025 (print) | LCC HG1710.3 (ebook) | DDC 332.4/048--dc23/eng/20250108
LC record available at https://lccn.loc.gov/2024048760
LC ebook record available at https://lccn.loc.gov/2024048761
British Cataloguing in Publication Data
A Cataloguing in Publication record for this book is available from the British Library.

Table of Contents

Detailed Table of Contents

In this chapter, we will show that, despite the widespread (misconception) that they emerged with bitcoin (2009), cryptocurrencies emerged long before, with the development of private currencies. Their new appeal can be traced back to the emergence of the cypherpunk movement, but also to advances in cryptography. We will note that the longevity of cryptocurrencies, whose mortality rate is high, can be related to the theory of the liability of newness. At the same time, numerous of central bank digital currency (CBDC) projects have recently been launched. El Salvador's intention to make Bitcoin legal tender blurs the boundary between these two forms of digital currency. We will propose a taxonomy of the main forms of these assets and note that the longevity of cryptocurrencies, which have a high mortality rate, may be linked to their novelty. Finally, in this context, we will discuss the willingness and ability of CBDCs to supplant cryptocurrencies.

The study delves into the evolution of cryptocurrencies, tracing their journey from theoretical concepts to a globally recognized asset class. From the foundational ideas of early digital cash system to the groundbreaking emergence of Bitcoin, the study examines the key milestones that shaped the crypto landscape. The subsequent rise and fall in the crypto market, characterized by periods of exuberance and volatility, are analyzed to understand the underlying factors driving these dynamics. The study further explores the evolving regulatory landscape, highlighting the challenges and opportunities posed by the decentralized nature of cryptocurrencies. By examining the interplay between innovation, market volatility, and regulatory response, this study provide insights into the intellectual lineage, challenges, and context that shaped the crypto market development and the potential trajectory of cryptocurrencies in the future.

This chapter delves into the intricate and the over evolving realm of cryptocurrencies. It explores and explains cryptocurrencies, the history of them - the genesis, the working of them - the mechanics, the reason for their existence, and the types - the spectrum. Starting with an overview of the fundamental concepts, the chapter discusses and defines cryptocurrencies and their features, and the differences with fiat currencies. Then we trace the history of cryptocurrencies, highlighting significant milestones. Further, the chapter analyzes the rationale behind the existence of cryptocurrencies, discussing the use cases of several renowned cryptocurrencies and what decentralization actually brings about, explaining the distinct functionality and practical uses of prominent cryptocurrencies, through in-depth case studies of these currencies. We will also comprehend the fundamental workings of cryptocurrencies, such as consensus mechanisms, mining, etc. Lastly, the chapter explores the future prospects of cryptocurrencies, considering potential trends and challenges.

Cryptocurrencies were initially created for use in online payments. However, cryptocurrencies are rarely used for payments in practice. This chapter aims to show current state of cryptocurrencies in terms of their usage. It will evaluate usage of cryptocurrencies as money and as a financial instrument. In order for a commodity or digital document to be money, it must have the property of universality of application and a relatively stable value. At the moment, cryptocurrencies do not fulfill any of these requirements. Also, in addition to having the appropriate equipment (computer or smart phone), software support in the form of a digital wallet and an Internet connection, the user must have some experience in order to make the transaction without losses. On the other hand, it is clear that cryptocurrencies have the performance of financial instruments. The general conclusion is that cryptocurrencies are speculative instruments, which carry a significant level of risk. Investors' lack of education and lack of experience are the main dangers of investing in cryptocurrencies.

The rapid advancement of technology has revolutionized numerous aspects of our lives, and the financial industry is no exception. Digital financial technologies, often referred to as fintech, have emerged as a disruptive force, reshaping the way we engage with and manage our finances. This abstract explores the evolution, impact, and potential of digital financial technologies in enhancing financial inclusion, streamlining transactions, and promoting economic growth. Fintech encompasses a wide range of innovations, including mobile banking, digital wallets, peer-to-peer lending, crowdfunding platforms, blockchain-based cryptocurrencies, robo-advisors, and artificial intelligence-driven chatbots, among others. While digital financial technologies present numerous opportunities, they also pose challenges and risks. Cybersecurity threats, data privacy concerns, regulatory compliance, and the digital divide are some of the key issues that need to be addressed.

This chapter provides a comprehensive overview of the cryptocurrency ecosystem. It begins by tracing the market's origins, focusing on Bitcoin's 2009 launch and its transformative impact on digital transactions. Blockchain technology is explained in detail, covering its decentralized ledger system, including blocks, chains, nodes, and consensus mechanisms like Proof of Work and Proof of Stake. The chapter offers a historical perspective on mining, from early methods to advanced techniques. The workings of cryptocurrency exchanges are discussed, comparing centralized and decentralized platforms. The chapter examines cryptocurrency price determination through supply and demand dynamics and external influences such as economic trends and technological advancements etc. Market volatility and its implications for investors are analyzed, along with global regulatory approaches and their effects on the market. The chapter concludes with insights into future trends and emerging applications, offering a thorough understanding of the cryptocurrency market and its evolution.

corporate investment portfolios, providing insights for companies seeking to navigate the evolving crypto asset landscape.

Cryptocurrency is an innovative financial asset class that operates on the blockchain system. Despite its highly volatile nature, the number of investors has increased significantly in the past decade. This chapter aims to examine the factors that influence investors' intention and decision to invest in such a volatile asset. The empirical relationship between Investment behavior (BEH), Intention to invest in the cryptocurrency (INT), Risk perception (RP), Awareness (AWR), Social influence (SI), and Fear of Missing out (FOMO) are examined. Data was collected from the 94 cryptocurrency investors in India using purposive and snowball sampling. The results showed that AWR and PR have a positive but insignificant effect on cryptocurrency investors' intentions and investment decisions. On the other hand, FOMO and SI have a statistically positive and significant role in the investment process among cryptocurrency investors. The results provide practical implications for the regulatory authorities, investors, and academicians.

This paper aims for comprehensive analysis of the prevailing knowledge concerning portfolio diversification, hedge, and safe-haven characteristics in cryptocurrency investments. This study has reviewed studies, spanning various disciplines, to produce a systematic literature review and bibliometric analysis. The findings from this study show the expanding body of literature highlighting cryptocurrencies' potential to serve as a hedge against stocks, fiat currencies, geopolitical risks, and Economic Policy Uncertainty (EPU) risk. In addition to that, cryptocurrencies show properties of diversification and safe-havens, while stable coins exhibit an unstable peg with the US dollar. This paper also identified uncertainty as a significant factor influencing cryptocurrency returns. Furthermore, analysis suggests that investors should consider Gold, the European carbon market, CBOE Bitcoin futures, and crude oil as potential hedging instruments against unforeseen fluctuations in the cryptocurrency market.

The advent of cryptocurrency has transformed the global financial landscape, offering an alternative to traditional financial systems. Bitcoin, the first decentralized cryptocurrency, emerged in 2009, followed by a proliferation of various digital currencies. These developments have posed significant challenges to governments and regulatory bodies worldwide. The opaque nature of cryptocurrency regulation, combined with the decentralized structure of these assets, has led to a complex and often inconsistent regulatory environment. Given the growing importance of cryptocurrencies there is a clear need for cohesive and efficient regulatory considerations. This chapter focuses on the asserts the lack of true transparency in existing regulations, which is caused by divergent practices between jurisdictions and incompatible legal wordings as well as rapidly developing technology. This also raise concerns that the lack of a clear regulatory stance might generate more market turbulence, slow investment and foster illegal capital flow.

Cryptocurrencies have changed the financial industry and have the potential to make a considerable social impact. Since cryptocurrencies are a new phenomenon in the financial market, research on the social impact of cryptocurrencies remains in the initial stage. This chapter aims to present the current research stage on the social impact of cryptocurrencies. The findings from the review of the literature are structured to positive (financial inclusion, provision of access to credit, remittances, empowerment of individuals and communities, and philanthropic initiatives) and negative (high risk, illicit activities, and environmental harm). The chapter shows most of the findings are inconsistent and the conclusions vary. It is argued in the chapter that the negative impact of cryptocurrencies on the social fabric prevails due to the very meaning (nature) of cryptocurrencies.

In the first part we present the evolution of the volume of transactions, as a result of the continued intensification of the division of labor, as well as the sectoral and the spatial expansion of capitalist relations (internationalization). The contribution of financialization and the expansion of speculative capital portfolio movements is highlighted, especially in the late period of our days. Next, we proceed with the definition of the "potential monetary base". In the second part, we use the pre-defined terms in order to justify the evolution of money over three main phases - commodity money, tangible and intangible (digital) fiat-money. Moreover, the combined analysis of the two – volume of transactions and potential monetary base – is matched with international economic and political development. Finally, in the forth part, we evaluate the prospects of the new phase of monetary expansion (cryptocurrencies), given the technological possibilities of the virtual economy, and formulate the basic questions of institutional, economic and social nature.

Preface

INTRODUCTION

In the ever-expanding universe of digital finance, cryptocurrencies have emerged as both a technological marvel and a deeply disruptive economic force. Much of the existing literature focuses on how to enter the market, grasp the fundamentals of blockchain, or anticipate the "next big thing." However, what remains noticeably absent is a critical and structured exploration of the cryptocurrency market as a dynamic ecosystem—its evolution, underlying economic mechanisms, and the managerial frameworks shaping its trajectory.

This book, *Concept, Theories, and Management of Cryptocurrencies*, attempts to fill that gap. Our purpose is not to merely explain what cryptocurrencies are, but to delve into what they do—how they operate, mutate, and interact with both market and institutional forces. We take a layered approach: examining cryptocurrencies not just as a technological advancement, but as a socio-economic phenomenon with far-reaching implications.

One of the core challenges in the cryptocurrency landscape is the disjunction between information and knowledge. In a domain flooded with data—whitepapers, media narratives, speculative analyses—true understanding remains elusive. This book seeks to address that problem by providing structured, theory-driven insights that can inform users, analysts, policymakers, and managers alike.

Throughout these chapters, we look behind the scenes of what has been hailed as a revolutionary system. We question its promises, scrutinize its practices, and investigate the real consequences of its ongoing evolution. From foundational concepts to applied management theories, our contributors offer a panoramic yet incisive view of cryptocurrencies as a subject worthy of rigorous academic and professional analysis.

We hope this volume will serve as both a touchstone and a launchpad: a touchstone for understanding what cryptocurrencies have become, and a launchpad for further inquiry into what they might yet be.

ORGANIZATION OF THE BOOK

This edited volume opens with a foundational historical exploration in **Chapter 1**, which challenges the common misconception that digital currencies began with Bitcoin. The authors trace the roots of digital money to private currencies and the cypherpunk movement, presenting a taxonomy of digital currencies—virtual currencies, cryptocurrencies, tokens, and central bank digital currencies (CBDCs). The chapter also interrogates the longevity of these currencies through the lens of the "liability of newness" and addresses whether CBDCs might eventually overtake cryptocurrencies.

In **Chapter 2**, the historical thread continues with an in-depth look at the intellectual evolution and market trajectory of cryptocurrencies. The chapter documents key turning points, such as the rise of Bitcoin, subsequent market booms and busts, and the shifting regulatory responses across jurisdictions. It presents a balanced analysis of both technological and socio-economic forces shaping the crypto ecosystem and the lessons these bring for its future development.

Chapter 3 elaborates on the conceptual underpinnings, mechanics, and diversity of cryptocurrencies. Here, the authors unpack the technical principles—including mining and consensus mechanisms—and examine their real-world applications through detailed case studies. The discussion underscores the ideological and functional motivations for decentralized currency, providing a holistic view of the crypto asset class.

Turning toward the position of cryptocurrencies within existing financial structures, **Chapter 4** critically evaluates their current use cases. It distinguishes between cryptocurrencies as payment systems and as speculative financial instruments, ultimately concluding that they behave more like volatile assets than stable currencies. Key obstacles, such as usability and value stability, are presented as reasons for limited adoption as money.

Chapter 5 broadens the focus to digital financial technologies (fintech), situating cryptocurrencies within a wider landscape of innovations. The chapter explores technologies such as digital wallets, robo-advisors, and AI-driven financial tools, noting how fintech has enhanced inclusion and transaction efficiency. However, it also cautions against associated risks, including cybersecurity threats, data privacy issues, and uneven access.

Chapter 6 offers a market-focused perspective, charting the development of the cryptocurrency ecosystem. Starting with Bitcoin's inception, the authors discuss blockchain's architecture, mining evolution, and exchange structures. Price dynamics, market volatility, and regulatory interventions are dissected to reveal the complexities of valuation and investor behavior in this novel asset class.

In **Chapter 7**, the authors explore the current opportunities and unresolved challenges of cryptocurrency adoption. They detail the widespread global fascination with crypto assets, from mainstream coins like Bitcoin and Ethereum to newer entrants. Yet, while enthusiasm is high, the chapter warns of volatility, regulatory uncertainty, and technological barriers that inhibit broader mainstream adoption.

Chapter 8 turns to the intersection of crypto assets with business strategy and regulatory compliance. With a focus on the European regulatory environment, particularly the Markets in Crypto-Assets (MiCA) framework, the chapter examines how businesses are integrating crypto assets into portfolios and risk management. The implications of crypto-finance interconnectivity for corporate finance are analyzed in detail.

Chapter 9 presents an empirical study into the perceptions and behaviors of cryptocurrency investors, particularly in India. It identifies the psychological and social factors—such as Fear of Missing Out (FOMO) and social influence—that significantly shape investment decisions. The findings are positioned to inform policymakers and financial educators seeking to understand the drivers of retail crypto investing.

Chapter 10 investigates the potential for cryptocurrencies to serve as portfolio diversifiers, hedges, or safe-haven assets. Through a systematic literature review and bibliometric analysis, the chapter evaluates the hedging effectiveness of cryptocurrencies against traditional market risks, including economic policy uncertainty and geopolitical tensions. The findings suggest a nuanced role for crypto assets in risk management.

Chapter 11 addresses the fragmented global regulatory environment surrounding cryptocurrencies. It critiques the opacity and inconsistency of legal frameworks, which are often hindered by technological change and jurisdictional misalignment. The chapter argues for more coherent regulatory architecture to reduce market instability and discourage illicit activity while fostering innovation.

Chapter 12 address the broader societal implications of cryptocurrency adoption, moving beyond technical and economic dimensions to examine its social, cultural, and ethical impact. The analysis highlights how decentralized digital currencies can foster financial inclusion, particularly for the unbanked and underbanked populations globally. At the same time, the chapter presents a critical exploration of ethical dilemmas, including environmental concerns tied to crypto mining, the facilitation of illicit activities via anonymous transactions, and the potential to exacerbate economic inequalities. Through case studies and stakeholder perspectives, this chapter invites readers to reflect on how cryptocurrencies can be steered toward socially responsible innovation, emphasizing the importance of developing inclusive, ethical frameworks alongside technological advancement.

Chapter 13 presents a comprehensive analysis of the intersection between cryptocurrency misuse and digital forensic innovation, with a particular focus on dark web activities. It explores the increasingly sophisticated strategies employed by cybercriminals who leverage the anonymity of cryptocurrencies for illicit transactions, and underscores the urgent need for advanced forensic methodologies to counter these trends. The authors critically assess current limitations in host-based forensics—especially for mobile platforms—and advocate for updated, platform-relevant investigative tools. Emphasis is placed on AI and machine learning techniques, such as clustering heuristics and behavioral analysis, to trace transactions and unmask hidden actors on public blockchains. Additionally, the chapter discusses security vulnerabilities within forensic processes and calls for robust frameworks to support legal enforcement and cybercrime investigations in the age of digital currencies.

Chapter 14 introduces *BinancePy*, a Python-based trading bot that integrates the Binance API with the Relative Strength Index (RSI) indicator to automate cryptocurrency trading. Designed to reduce manual oversight while exploiting market inefficiencies, the bot operates on algorithmic logic to identify overbought and oversold conditions, thereby enabling timely and calculated trade execution. The chapter details the system's modular architecture—spanning data acquisition, signal generation, trade execution, and performance monitoring—and offers insights from initial backtesting that suggest profitability under specific market conditions. Serving as both a technical guide and a case study, this chapter offers a valuable resource for developers, traders, and fintech researchers interested in algorithmic trading and applied Python programming in decentralized markets.

Finally, **Chapter 15** offers a macroeconomic and historical lens on the evolution of money in relation to the rising prominence of virtual economies and cryptocurrencies. The first section traces the growth in transaction volume as an outcome of intensified labor division and global capitalist expansion, with particular emphasis on the effects of financialization and speculative capital flows. The authors then introduce and contextualize the concept of the "potential monetary base" across three key monetary phases: commodity money, fiat money (tangible and intangible), and digital currencies. A combined analysis of transaction volume and monetary base provides a framework to understand the dynamics of modern monetary development, aligned with international economic and political shifts. In its concluding segment, the chapter critically evaluates the emerging phase of cryptocurrency-driven monetary systems and raises pertinent institutional, regulatory, and socio-economic questions that challenge traditional financial paradigms.

CONCLUSION

As the editor of this volume, I am proud to present a curated collection of research that reflects the diverse, rapidly evolving, and deeply interconnected landscape of digital finance, cryptocurrency technologies, and virtual economic systems. Each chapter contributes a unique lens through which we can better understand not only the technological innovations driving the financial sector but also the complex ethical, regulatory, and socio-economic challenges they pose. From forensic investigations on the dark web to algorithmic trading bots and philosophical explorations of money's transformation, the book embodies the multidisciplinary spirit essential for navigating this digital frontier.

This work aims to serve as both a scholarly reference and a forward-looking guide for academics, practitioners, and policymakers. It is our hope that the insights offered within these pages will foster critical dialogue, spark new avenues of inquiry, and support more resilient and equitable frameworks for future financial innovation. As the digital economy continues to reshape global systems, it is imperative that we remain both vigilant and visionary—equipped with rigorous research, ethical grounding, and an openness to collaboration across domains.

Eduardo Tomé
Universidade Lusofona, Portugal

Chapter 1
A Brief History of Digital Currencies and Their Current Challenges (1989–2024):
Virtual Currencies, Cryptocurrencies, Tokens, and Central Bank Digital Currencies – Past and Future

Jean Michel Rocchi
Neoma Business School, France

Michel Ruimy
Institut d'Etudes Politiques de Paris, France

ABSTRACT

In this chapter, we will show that, despite the widespread (misconception) that they emerged with bitcoin (2009), cryptocurrencies emerged long before, with the development of private currencies. Their new appeal can be traced back to the emergence of the cypherpunk movement, but also to advances in cryptography. We will note that the longevity of cryptocurrencies, whose mortality rate is high, can be related to the theory of the liability of newness. At the same time, numerous of central bank digital currency (CBDC) projects have recently been launched. El Salvador's intention to make Bitcoin legal tender blurs the boundary between these two forms of digital currency. We will propose a taxonomy of the main forms of these assets and note that the longevity of cryptocurrencies, which have a high mortality rate, may

DOI: 10.4018/979-8-3693-5986-0.ch001

be linked to their novelty. Finally, in this context, we will discuss the willingness and ability of CBDCs to supplant cryptocurrencies.

INTRODUCTION

Money and banking have a long history, dating back to the first great civilizations (Goetzmann & Rouwenhorst, 2005). "Minting money" is a tangible manifestation of the power of monarchs and central states. Beyond its traditional functions as a unit of account, a store of value, and an intermediary for exchanges (a concept attributed to Aristotle), money also plays a role in social control.

Attacking money can be a strategic move to weaken an enemy, a technique known as unconventional warfare. During the American War of Independence, the British issued counterfeit American currency to cripple the economy of the rebellious colonies. Similarly, Emperor Napoleon employed this strategy during his early 19th-century European campaign, forging Austrian and Russian notes to purchase food and other supplies. In the 20th century, the Third Reich used Operation Bernhard to destabilize the British financial system during World War II, *''producing 500,000 British notes per month''* (Prime & Solomon, 2010).

Recent technological advancements in cryptography, coupled with the anarchist-inspired ideology of cypherpunks, have led to the emergence of libertarian instruments known as cryptocurrencies. This has prompted monetary authorities to develop new technological support for monetary transactions: central bank digital currencies (CBDCs).

This chapter will be organized as follows:

- The first section will delve into a literature review of ancient and modern forms of money, including coins, commodity money, private money, virtual currencies, cryptocurrencies, and CBDCs.
- The second section will explore the recent history of cryptography and cryptocurrencies.
- The third section will present a taxonomy of digital currencies.
- The fourth section will discuss the ecology of the populations of both cryptocurrencies and CBDCs.
- The fifth section will focus on the competition between CBDCs and cryptocurrencies.
- Section 6 will discuss the development of CBDCs around the world.
- Section 7 will traditionally be dedicated to discussion and areas for future research, concluding with concluding remarks.

LITERATURE REVIEW ON THE EVOLUTION OF CURRENCY

As Thomas Jefferson famously said, *"Money, not morality, is the principle of commercial nations."* Our literature review will systematically explore various forms of money and their associated technologies.

From Commodity Money to Metallic Money

Throughout history, technology has always had an influence on money, and the current phenomena are still an illustration of this: "*In Gutenberg's time, the technology of printing and the manufacture of high-quality paper spread throughout Europe. [...] In July 1661, the Swedish Bank in Stockholm issued the first banknote in Europe to compensate for a shortage of silver coins*" (Weatherford, pp. 129-130). Money has moved from commodity money to metallic money, then to paper money, which has become an exclusive attribute of nation-states (Weatherford, 1997; Ruimy & Rocchi, 2017). The first coins are thought to have been minted around the 7th century BC in the kingdom of Lydia (Dale, 2015): "*The Lydians are the first people known to us to have minted and used gold and silver coins*" (Herodotus, 1970). The first coins were made of an alloy of three quarters gold and one quarter silver - 'electron' in Greek or 'electrom' in Latin - (Thievaud, 1999). From a numismatic point of view, more than 2,000 electron coins have been catalogued to date, mainly in Asia Minor (Thievaud, 1999). But, money first took the form of a commodity: the Aztecs used cocoa beans. "*The natives of certain regions of India used almonds. The Guatemalans used corn, the Babylonians and Assyrians barley, the natives of the Nicobar Islands coconuts, while [...] Japan, Burma and other parts of South-East Asia, standardised measures of rice were traditionally used as commodity money.*" (Weatherford, 1997, pp.20). Elsewhere, some regions (China, North Africa, the Mediterranean) used salt, pastoral peoples (Siberian tribes, Hittites), living animals and in some geographical areas (Ireland and ancient Africa), human beings. '*'The Chinese issued the first paper banknote in 1040 AD*'' (Prime & Solomon, 2010). According to Redish (1993), "*Generally, throughout Europe, at least from the 13th century onwards, the monetary authorities proclaimed coins to be legal tender for given unit of account values.*" (p.779). Forgery was since the beginning a major concern for governments even if conversely it could be used as a weapon to weaken the economy of an enemy: '*'In 1470–1476, Milan sought to undermine the Venetians by forgery, and Frederich the Great used counterfeit notes during the Seven Years War.*'' (Prime & Solomon,2010).

Private Money Always Emerged as a Response to a Crisis of Confidence in Official Currencies

During the French Revolution, assignats, fiat currencies, were replaced by a "necessity currency" (Monneron medals) issued by a private bank of the same name. In the United States, the American Liberty Dollar range, a complementary silver currency, was created in 1998. Its reserve value was based on the weight of the precious metal it contained. However, in 2006, the US Treasury deemed it a counterfeit of the official currency, leading to the ban of its creator, Bernard von NotHaus (Ruimy & Rocchi, 2017). More recently, cryptocurrencies have gained prominence, characterized by their intangibility.

Virtual Currencies

The 1990s saw the emergence of virtual currencies, most of which were centralized and their use limited - at least in their early forms - in online messaging and virtual gaming environments. One of the first examples was the "Q coin," which could be purchased in "physical" stores in China for use on Tencent's online messaging platform. They are now widespread in massively multiplayer online games (MMOG), such as World of Warcraft, Second Life, etc. (Lehdonvirta & Castronova, 2014). Conversely, according to some researchers the first virtual currency ''flooz'' appeared in 1999 for the payment of internet merchants, but the promoter flooz.com enter into investigation for being used by organized crime and finally closed down August 26, 2001, also being a victim of the dot-com bubble burst. (Lisdorf, 2023).

From Cryptography Evolution to Cryptocurrencies Revolution

As Chen (2021) notes, "*Crypto*" *comes from cryptography, which emerged in the nineteenth century but whose practice dates back to Julius Caesar. Typically, this technique uses codes, symbols, and algorithms in order to protect important information from unwanted glances or unintended recipients*." Cryptocurrencies are linked to the culture *of Cypherpunks* (de Filippi, 2017). "*In 2008, the word 'crypto-currency' appeared with the publication of a document, under the name of Satoshi Nakamoto, justifying the Bitcoin system*" (Luchkin et al., 2020, p.426) Nevertheless many researchers considers that the first cryptocurrency was DigiCash which was launched in 1989. (De Filippi, 2018)

The Phenomenon of Convergence

As Guttmann (2003) points out, has *led to the gradual merging of e*-money and its successor, cybercash: ''*While electronic money ('e-money') is a broader concept referring to all computer-based fund-transfer mechanisms (for instance credit or debit cards, ACHs) and their access hardware (for example ATMs, POS terminals), cybercash is a more narrowly focused term applying to all fund transfer systems routed through the internet. The delineation between these two overlapping characterizations of the new money form is fluid. It is hard to distinguish clearly between 'electronic money' and 'cybercash', because the former has set the stage for the latter and is now gradually merging into it. Those omnipresent plastic cards, for instance, will soon be turned into smart cards which can be connected with any access ramp to the internet, whether personal computers (PCs), cell phones, or personal digital assistants (PDAs).*'' (p.9)

CBDC

As defined by Kiff et al. (2020), distinguishes itself from cryptocurrencies: "*Central bank digital currency is a digital representation of sovereign money that is issued by the monetary authority of a jurisdiction and appears on the liabilities side of the monetary authority's balance sheet*". While some researchers propose alternative terms like "sovereign digital currencies" (Zetzsche et al., 2020; Buckley et al., 2021), these have been met with mixed success. Mahdavieh (2022) employs a terminology that combines "*native government-backed cryptocurrencies*" and "*authority-backed native cryptocurrencies*," which could be misleading in categorizing all forms of money.

The Recent History of Cryptography and Cryptocurrencies

The technologies of asymmetric encryption with two keys – a secret (private) key and a shared (public) key – were discovered in 1976 by Whitfield Diffie and Martin Hellman. The RSA encryption system, developed in 1977 by Ronald Rivest, Adi Shamir, and Leonard Adelman, built upon this foundation. These technologies paved the way for the development of digital currencies and later cryptocurrencies in the 1980s (De Filippi, 2018).

In his book *Untraceable Electronic Mail, Return Addresses, and Digital Pseudonyms* David Chaum (1981) describes a methodology using public-key cryptography to mask both the identity of a participant and the contents of an e-mail and, in *Security Without Identification: Transaction Systems to Make Big Brother Obsolete* (1985), an electronic money system using cryptography. In 1989, he invented Digi-

Cash, an electronic money (centralised system) based on cryptographic protocols (Chaum, 1985, 1988, 1992). Subsequently, these electronic notes competed with other electronic payment services such as Netcash, Mondex, Cybercash... (Kutler, 1995). Even if many products and solutions were available: "*electronic money is of a much wider variety than traditional money: e-cash money, e-money, Cybercash, DigiCash, cyberbucks... that prescribers want to create and make develop*" (Weatherford, 1997, pp. 247), the DigiCash system is seen as the most effective way of guaranteeing a high level of security to such an extent that companies such as Microsoft were considering including it in their software. However, this private Dutch firm went bankrupt in 1998, putting an end to this technology (Tapscott & Tapscott, 2016)

While technology is a key aspect, the crux of the matter lies in how it's used and for whom. Timothy May, in his 1989 manifesto, "*Manifesto of Crypto-Anarchy*", emphasizes that advancements in cryptography should serve to enhance individual freedom. This freedom should empower individuals and limit government intervention and control over electronic transactions. Inspired by this idea, libertarians Éric Hughes and John Gilmore founded the Cypherpunk group in 1992.

In 1996, Douglas Jackson and Barry Downey launched e-Gold, an electronic money system linked to physical gold ownership. Users of their website could transfer ownership of gold to each other. However, the irreversible and anonymous nature of the transactions quickly made it attractive to criminal organizations. Following several accusations, the initiative was investigated by the FBI and ultimately ended. From the outset, the inherent difficulty of tracking the identity of anonymous users has made cryptocurrencies susceptible to being used *for illegal activities such as fraud and money laundering*.

The following year, Adam Back launched the Hashcash project, unrelated to cryptocurrencies. However, his innovative concept of "*proof of work*" played a crucial role in inspiring the future emergence of Bitcoin. (De Filippi, 2017)

In 1998, Dai, a member of the Cypherpunk movement, launched a project called B-money. The aim was to develop a decentralized and anonymous electronic payment system (De Filippi, 2017). The system was based on the concept of "*proof of work,*" meaning anyone who could demonstrate they had completed work would receive payment in virtual currency. Despite this, the system never saw the light of day. Interestingly, Nakamoto (Nakamoto, 2018) explicitly acknowledged its contribution to the advent of Bitcoin.

The same year, cryptographer Nick Szabo introduced his system called "bit gold." It has been suggested that Szabo and Nakamoto were actually the same person (De Filippi, 2017). Szabo's system aimed to time-stamp transactions, but it had a significant weakness: it remained vulnerable to Sybil attacks. In a short article titled "*God's Protocol,*" Szabo explained his philosophy. He believed that in the absence of a controlling authority or trusted third party, everything was implicitly in God's hands: ''*All parties would send their contributions to God. God would reliably determine the results and return the outputs. God being the ultimate in confessional discretion, no party would learn anything more about the other parties' inputs than it could learn from its own contributions and outcomes*'' (Tapscott and Tapscott, 2016).

In 2004, Hal Finney proposed a token inspired by both B-Money and Bit Gold. This token was based on the concept of "*reusable proofs of work,*" which meant that any work carried out on a computer would be rewarded with a token. While the system guaranteed the confidentiality of participants through cryptographic keys, it required a centralized server to ensure that players did not spend more than they had. However, these criticisms were addressed with the advent of Bitcoin five years later.

As explain Arslanian and Fisher (2019): '' *Bitcoin uses an algorithm called ECDSA (Elliptic Curve Digital Signature Algorithm) that also allows you to use your private key to generate a public key. That public key allows you to then generate your Bitcoin address. It is impossible for anyone who has your public key to guess your private key...*''(p.91).

Bitcoin (BTC) is a "viral" virtual currency (i.e. automatically duplicated), created in 2009 on a peer-to-peer basis by one or more computer scientists under the pseudonym Satoshi Nakamoto (Ruimy & Rocchi, 2017). "*We define an electronic document as a chain of digital signatures. Each owner transfers the coin to the next by digitally signing a hash of the previous transaction and the public key of the next owner and adding them to the end of the coin.*'' (Nakamoto, 2008). On January the 3rd, 2009, the first data recognised in a Bitcoin ledger ("Genesis Block") was created by Satoshi Nakamoto (Tapscott and Tapscott, 2016). Another milestone was reached on October the 5th, 2009 when Bitcoin was first sold in US dollars[1].

A significant step to recognition is the emergence of specialised markets (exchanges platforms) to trade bitcoins. The first announcement was initiated by dwdollar (2010) on February the 6th, 2010. In mining the ''Genesis Block'' he gained a reward of 50 bitcoins. The first evidence of a purchase of goods through Bitcoin is dated May 22, 2010: two pizzas for 10,000 Bitcoin, the equivalent of US$41 at the time. Nowadays, 'May 22' is celebrated by members of the global crypto community as 'Bitcoin Pizza Day'. Over the last decade, Bitcoin steadily began gaining momentum while Forbes announced '2013: Year of the Bitcoin'. "*In the early days of cryptoassets, buyers, sellers and users of these media (cryptographers, experienced geeks, developers, libertarians...) were a "niche" group of individuals. The landscape began to rapidly change in 2015 and 2016 as more and more individuals became interested in cryptocurrencies: from university students trading in their dorm rooms to early adopters who had chosen to diversify part of their portfolio into this new asset class. 2017 is a key year because it was a game changer for Bitcoin and the wider crypto ecosystem*" (Arslanian & Fisher, 2019, p.107).

On July 30, 2015, Vitalik Buterin launched Ethereum to address some of Bitcoin's limitations. Ethereum is not only a cryptocurrency but also an open-source blockchain platform that enables the issuance of 'smart contracts', which are digital contracts stored on a blockchain and automatically executed when specific conditions are met.

Stablecoins are cryptocurrencies whose value is linked to another asset (fiat currency, commodity, financial instrument) or to an algorithmic formula, ensuring a stable price. The first stablecoin was issued in token form on July 21, 2014, on the BitShares blockchain. Tether followed in 2015, and USD Coin, indexed to the US dollar, was introduced in 2018. Today, there are many stablecoins available, including Gemini Dollar, True USD, and Paxos Standard.

The authors have made an essentially subjective choice of the cryptocurrencies presented, as there are over 13,000 of them in existence in 2024 at the time of writing this chapter. Despite this, as shown in Figure 1 below, the global market by value is clearly dominated by Bitcoin, with Ethereum in second place.

According to the specialized website CoinMarketCap, as of April 5, 2025, there were nearly 13,240 cryptocurrencies with a total market capitalization of 2.45 trillion USD, dominated by Bitcoin and Ethereum, as illustrated in Figure 1.

Figure 1. Bitcoin (BTC) and Ethereum (ETH) dominance: Their market capitalization relative to the market capitalization of all other cryptocurrencies in the world on January 29, 2024

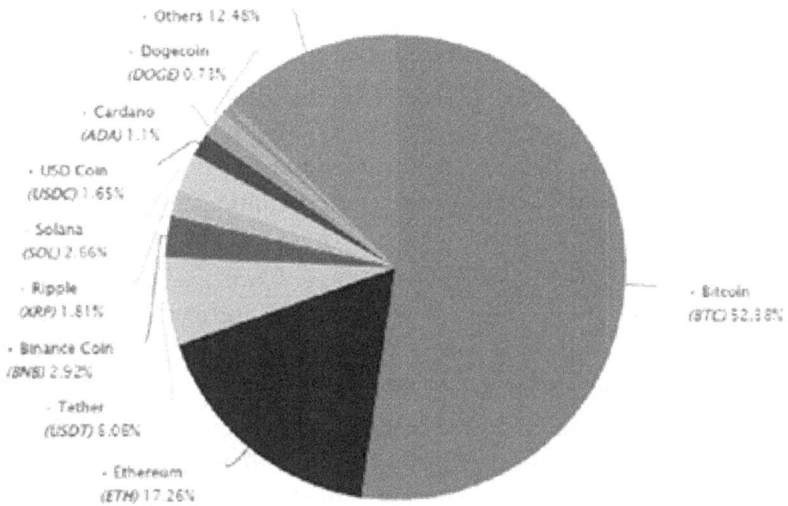

(Statista, 2024)

A PROPOSAL OF TAXONOMY OF DIGITAL CURRENCIES: VIRTUAL CURRENCIES, CRYPTOCURRENCIES, TOKENS, AND CBDCs

Private money has experienced a revival, particularly in the United States with the Liberty Dollar. Digital currencies, on the other hand, are a more recent phenomenon linked to Internet technology. We will explore their various forms: virtual currencies, cryptocurrencies, tokens, and CBDCs.

While the Authors' Choice of Cryptocurrency Terminology Serves a Practical Purpose, It Raises Some Questions

The term "cryptocurrency" is widely used in the market, from exchange platforms to final customers and even commercial and online banks. However, supervisory authorities, such as central banks and market regulators, use the term "cryptoassets" (Ferreira & Sandner, 2021; Hacibedel & Perez-Saiz, 2023) or, more rarely, "crypto-investments" because these media do not meet the traditional attributes of money. As a result, they are not recognized by these authorities, which fall outside their remit, while acknowledging their market exchange value and subjecting them to taxation. Kavuri & Milne (2021) propose a definition of *a cryptographic asset: "an asset on a blockchain that can be transferred between network participants and exchanged on cryptographic exchange platforms either at the prevailing market price, against other cryptoassets, or against conventional state fiat money."* One of their key characteristics is that their prices fluctuate based on the supply and demand dynamics of the platform (e.g., Bittrex, Coinbase, and Kraken in the United States, Upbit and Bithumb in Korea, Huobi in Singapore, OKX in Malta, Binance and Bitfinex in Hong Kong, and Bitstamp in the United Kingdom).

Virtual Currencies: Limited Acceptance

According to Lehdonvirta & Castronova (2014), the fundamental difference between virtual currencies and cryptocurrencies lies in their limited "*areas of acceptance*." Virtual currencies fail to meet the traditional criteria of a currency and are therefore outside the scope of regulation by monetary authorities, who classify them as "crypto-assets" (Ferreira & Sandner, 2021; Hacibedel & Perez-Saiz, 2023). According to the FATF (2014), a centralized characteristic feature of virtual currencies is their *single administrating authority. This third party controls the system and issues the currency, establishes its rules, maintains a central payment ledger, and has the authority to redeem it. The exchange rate for a convertible virtual currency can be either floating, determined by market supply and demand, or pegged, fixed by the administrator at a set value measured in fiat currency or another real-world store of value, such as gold or a basket of currencies. Currently, the vast majority of virtual currency payments transactions involve centralized virtual currencies. Examples include E-gold (defunct), Liberty Reserve dollars/euros (defunct), Second Life "Linden dollars", PerfectMoney, WebMoney "WM units", and World of Warcraft gold.* (p.5)

Hereafter, we propose a taxonomy and some examples of virtual currencies in Table 1.

Table 1. Significant examples of virtual currencies

	Real World and Platform	*Platform only*
Sectors	Messaging	Gaming
Nature	e.g. Tencent's "Q coin"	e.g. World of Warcraft, e.g. Second Life (''Linden Dollars'')
Issuing	Centralized	Centralized

Source: Authors

The Other Digital Currencies, Including Cryptocurrencies and CBDCs: A Large Acceptance Area

They have gained significant acceptance in various markets. While they share a common target audience, they differ in their characteristics, as illustrated in Table 2.

Table 2. A matrix of cryptocurrencies versus CBDC

	Centralized	**Decentralized**
Private issuer	e.g. DigiCash	e.g. Bitcoin, Ethereum
Central bank	e.g. Petro, e-CNY,eNaira	e.g. Bitcoin in El Salvador

Source: Authors

Tokens Versus Cryptocurrencies

A cryptocurrency is autonomous, based on its own technological platform. In contrast, tokens operate on a non-proprietary blockchain, such as NEO or Ethereum. To date, cryptocurrencies are primarily used for monetary purposes, including Bitcoin, Litecoin, ETH, and NEO. Tokens, on the other hand, have a wider range of applications, including security tokens, utility tokens, equity tokens, Musicoin, NFTs, and BNP. In Figure 2 hereafter, the authors provide an overview of various forms of currency, including official and unofficial, conventional and digital.

Figure 2. Types of currencies and equivalent: private and public, digital and traditional

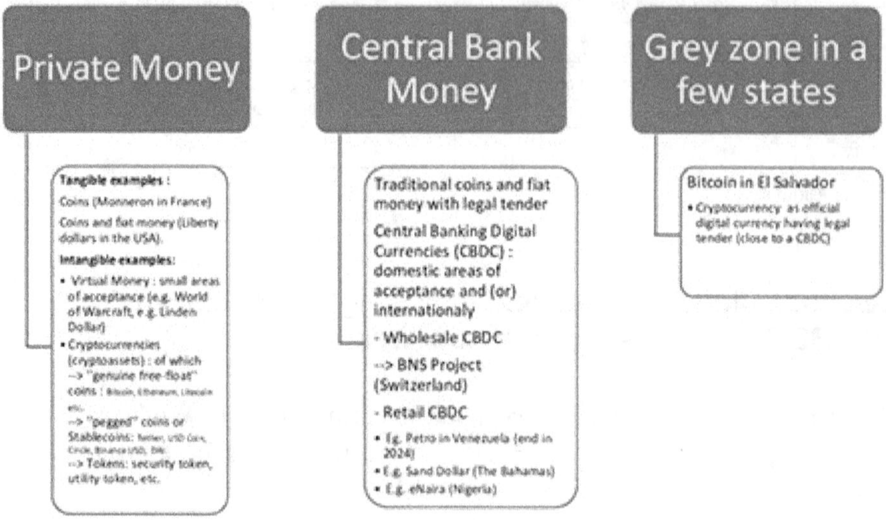

(Authors)

Cryptocurrencies' and CBDCs' Ecology of Population Analysis in a Nutshell

The success of cryptocurrencies will be analyzed in light of the organizational ecology of populations (Hannan and Freeman, 1977), particularly the variation, selection, and retention (VSR) model (Campbell, 1960, 1969). We will also consider the birth rate and "*organizationaldeath*" (Sutton, 1987). After examining the large population of cryptocurrencies, we will focus on the case of the CBDC population, which is still small and emerging. Due to its limited size, we will not study the virtual currency population, as we believe it is too small to yield significant and exploitable results.

Cryptocurrencies' Mortality Rate Analysis: The Evidence of a Liability of Newness

Pogudin et al. (2015) highlighted the high instability and high default rates associated with cryptocurrencies.

Lansky (2016) examined the number of extinct and surviving cryptocurrencies based on their lifespan. His findings revealed that cryptocurrencies tend to become extinct at the beginning of their existence. This concept of mortality is crucial in cryptocurrency analysis, as Lansky (2020) explains: *'A critical moment in the life of a cryptocurrency is its delisting from an exchange. This moment can be described as the death of a cryptocurrency' (p.62)* We concur with Lansky's analysis, suggesting that a cryptocurrency's delisting from an exchange platform constitutes an '*organizational death*' (Sutton, 1987). Lansky's (2020) study is consistent and reliable, covering a period from April 28, 2013, to April 6, 2018, as per data from coinmarketcap.com (2018), which examined over 2,500 cryptocurrencies. The findings on non-survival (delisting) are presented in Table 3.

Table 3. Probability of cryptocurrency delisting

Trading Period	1 Year	2 Years	3 Years	4 Years	5 Years
0 Years	35.1%	52.7%	61.6%	66.4%	70.9%
1 Year	27.1%	40.9%	48.2%	55.2%	
2 Years	18.9%	28.9%	38.6%		
3 Years	12.4%	24.3%			
4 Years	13.6%				

Source: Lansky, 2020.

According to Lansky, *the probability of a cryptocurrency being delisted decreases with its lifespan. For instance, a newly listed cryptocurrency has a 35% chance of being delisted within a year, while those traded for 3 or 4 years have a 12 to 13% chance of being delisted within the same timeframe. Interestingly, a newly listed cryptocurrency has a 71% probability of being delisted within 5 years''.* (Lansky, 2020, p. 62)

Regarding cryptocurrencies generated by Initial Coin Offerings (ICOs), Benedetti & Kostovetsky (2018) define an ICO as closed if it has shown no activity on its X account (formerly Twitter). Their study reveals that the mortality rate of ICOs within 120 days of fundraising from investors is 44%, significantly higher than the 35% mortality rate observed for all cryptocurrencies in the year following their IPO.

The high mortality rate and increased risk associated with young organizations, particularly cryptocurrencies, are consistent with the findings of the liability of newness theory (Stinchcombe, 1965). Stinchcombe defines the phenomenon of '*liability of newness' as follows: [a) New organizations, especially new types of organizations generally involve new roles, which have to be learned; ...b) the process of inventing new roles, the determination of their mutual relations and of structuring the field of rewards and sanctions so as to get the maximum performance, have high costs in time, worry, conflict, and temporary inefficiency; ...c) new organizations must rely heavily on social relations among strangers. This means that relations of trust are much more precarious in new than old organizations; ...d) one of the main re-*

sources of old organizations is a set of stable ties to those who use organizational services'' (pp.148-150)].

Analysis of the Cryptocurrencies Birth Rate

The growth in the birth rate of cryptocurrencies was exponential at the start of the 2013-2024 period, but then gradually tapered off. This is not surprising, as new entrants increased competition, leading to organizational mortality as shown in Table 4 below.

Table 4. Number of cryptocurrencies created (2013-2024)

Date	April 2013	Jan 2014	Jan 2015	Jan 2016	Jan 2017	Jan 2018	Jan 2019	Jan 2020	Jan 2021	Jan 2022	Jan 2023	March 2024
Number	7	67	501	572	636	1,359	2,086	2,403	4,154	8,714	9,002	13,217

Source: CoinGecko

Since 2013, CoinGecko has tracked 13,127 cryptocurrencies. As of March 2024, only 8,985 were considered "active," while 4,232 could be considered in *"organizational death"* (Sutton, 1987). This gives us a historical mortality rate of 32.23% over 11 years and 3 months.

The thousands of cryptocurrencies can be divided into three main categories: *Bitcoin,* the market leader and first modern cryptocurrency; *Altcoins* (or Alternatives to Bitcoin); and *Tokens*, cryptocurrencies using pre-existing blockchains.

As of March 2024, there are 724 exchange platforms, with Binance, Coinbase Exchange, Bybit, OKX, and Upbit leading the way.

A study by Feder et al. (2018), which is similar in temporal scope to Lansky (2020), found that a high mortality rate is not incompatible with a high birth rate. Young cryptocurrencies are more likely to fail due to increased competition, so high birth rates will contribute to the "organizational deaths" of tomorrow. Note the optimism bias in forums between start-up projects and those that actually materialize, as seen in Figure 3 below.

Figure 3. New currencies announced on the Bitcoin Forums each month (orange) compared to new currencies traded each month (black)

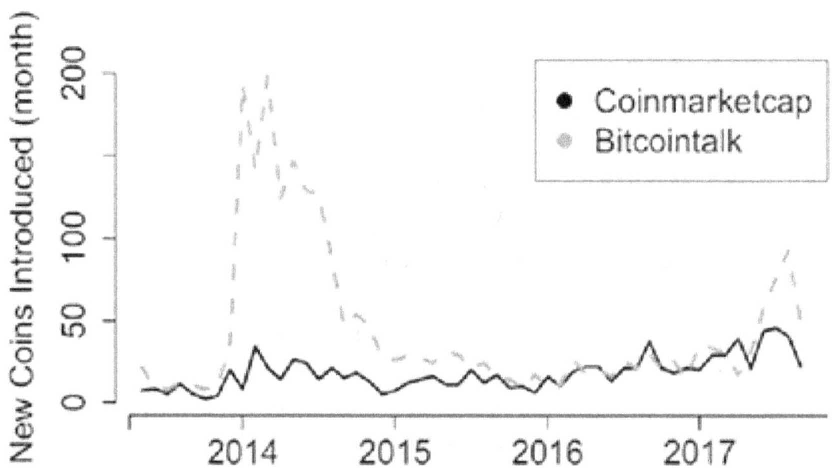

(Feder et al., 2018)

The *natural selection* between cryptocurrencies will be based on their ability to quickly join trading platforms, the volumes exchanged on them, and the evolution of their market capitalization. Retention will be a function of performance on these criteria, as described by Darwin's "*survival of the fittest*".

The sheer number of existing cryptocurrencies creates cut-throat competition. Governments' support for central bank digital currency (CBDC) and the launch of retail CBDCs have intensified this competition.

The Question of Mortality and the Birth of CBDCs

This matter remains difficult to understand. Only five CBDCs have been launched to date: the Petro in Venezuela, three in the Caribbean islands, and the eNaira in Nigeria. Several are still in the pilot phase. Petro's failure gave an apparent mortality rate of 20%, which is high. However, this figure is based on a small sample, and Venezuela is a pariah state with a large financial community. Many observers predicted its failure even before its launch. Therefore, the authors believe the mortality rate of CBDCs is likely to be lower than that of cryptocurrencies, due in part to the quality and reputation of the issuer. Time will tell whether this hypothesis is correct.

The birth rate of CBDCs appears to be high in the coming years, leading to numerous projects. According to de Sèze (2023), 90% of central banks are currently studying CDBCs. However, several factors will constrain this growth. There are approximately 200 states in the world, and not all will choose to issue a CBDC. Some states might even follow El Salvador's example and adopt Bitcoin as their digital currency.

If these optimistic hypotheses come to fruition, over one hundred CBDCs could emerge, competing with more than 13,200 cryptocurrencies. Of course, this scenario assumes that cryptocurrencies are not banned outright by all states, which is unlikely but not entirely impossible.

Nevertheless, as of March 14, 2024, the global crypto market capitalization surpassed 2.5 trillion dollars, with Bitcoin accounting for 1.44 trillion. A complete ban on cryptocurrencies would result in a significant loss of value for these assets. This would have three immediate consequences: a financial hardship for their holders, an induced financial crisis, and a loss of tax revenue from taxable assets for states often in need of financial resources. Such a decision seems highly unlikely at present.

Finally, in population ecology it is also sometimes customary to study pre-entry mortality (Carroll & Khessina, 2005), or ''*success in foundings attempts*'' versus the total amount of ''*founding attempts*'' i.e. the rate of failure prior to the launch itself, i.e. a rate of either technical failure, or giving up in the face of obstacles encountered during the study phase that seem difficult to overcome. For the time being, this phenomenon concerns Peru and Kenya, and the percentage of failures at pre-launch depends on what you compare it with: if you look at the CBDCs that have been launched, the figure is 40%; if you look at the currencies that have been pre-launched (pilot phase) the figure is around 10%, and only 3% if you look at all the projects that have been announced, whatever their stage of development. In conclusion, it would appear that few countries have been discouraged to date.

CBDCs AND CRYPTOCURRENCIES: COMPLEMENT OR SUBSTITUTION?

To date, the world's governments have taken three main positions on cryptocurrencies. The first is a ban, which would result in either no digital currencies at all or only CBDCs, with private and public forms excluded. El Salvador has taken a different approach, making Bitcoin its de facto official digital currency, a move that could be imitated by other countries. Finally, many countries plan to issue CBDCs in competition with cryptocurrencies, which are not recognized as digital currencies by the world's central banks but rather as simple crypto-assets with value and therefore taxable by governments. In this scenario, crypto-assets and CBDCs will coexist within this group of states.

Absolute or Implicit Ban of Cryptocurrencies

In one form or another, this debate has been clearly settled, since crypto-currencies are forbidden. As emphasizes Said (2019) many countries were quite early on clearly hostile to cryptocurrencies in various forms, adopting more or less consistent positions: ''*According to the Library of Congress, an "absolute ban" on trading or using cryptocurrencies applies in eight countries: Algeria, Bolivia, Egypt, Iraq, Morocco, Nepal, Pakistan, and the United Arab Emirates.*[...] *An "implicit ban" applies in another 15 countries, which include Bahrain, Bangladesh,* Colombia, the *Dominican Republic, Indonesia, Iran, Kuwait, Lesotho, Lithuania, Macau, Oman, Qatar, Saudi Arabia and Taiwan.* [...] *Various government agencies, departments, and courts have classified Bitcoin differently. China Central Bank banned the handling of bitcoins by financial institutions in China in early 2014. In Russia, though cryptocurrencies are legal, it is illegal to actually purchase goods with any currency other than the Russian ruble.*''(pp.5-6)

Countries that have banned cryptocurrencies (notably Russia) are not forbidden from issuing a government-backed CBDC, but in this case it will be the country's only digital currency and will not coexist with private digital forms.

The Salvadorian Conondrum: A Singularity (for the Moment)

On September 7th 2021, El Salvador was the first country in the world to grant legal tender to Bitcoin under the Bitcoin Law, as emphasizes Alvarez et al. (2023):''*According to this law, not only bitcoin must be accepted as a means of payment for taxes and outstanding debts, but also all businesses are required to accept bitcoin as a medium of exchange for all transactions*'' (pp.1) In a bid to encourage widespread adoption by the population, the Salvadorian government has launched an app called "Chivo Wallet", which allows the use of both dollars and bitcoins without transaction fees. To ensure that the app was downloaded by a large proportion of the population, a bonus of the equivalent of $30 in bitcoin was attached, a very substantial amount since it corresponded to 3.75 daily minimum wages in a country with a per capita GDP of $4,131.

This development raises many questions: has Bitcoin become a currency in El Salvador? The answer seems to be yes. But insofar as this recognition is limited to a single state, isn't it contrary to the universalist vocation of its creator's project (Nakamoto, 2008). What's more, Bitcoin has legal value in El Salvador, whereas it is only a cryptoasset in many countries, including the USA and is banned outright in other countries, notably China (Alekseenko, 2022): ''*There are different approaches worldwide on how to regulate cryptocurrency: legalization, partial ban, or absolute ban. China has chosen the third option''. (p.361).* Similarly, the anarchist-inspired Cypherpunks who inspired bitcoin could hardly have expected such a "political recuperation" of this cryptocurrency by a state.

Figure 4. From the bitcoin law to the bitcoin day

Martes
www.diarioelsalvador.com
$0.25
Diario El Salvador
4 Paso a paso para obtener la «wallet» Chivo

BITCOIN DAY

Desde hoy, El Salvador es el primer país que adopta el bitcóin como una moneda de curso legal.

El Gobierno ya compró 400 monedas, ha distribuido 200 cajeros y lanzó su propia billetera digital.

2 SALARIOS, PENSIONES Y PRECIOS SIGUEN EN DÓLARES

8 SALVADOREÑOS SE AHORRARÁN $400 MILLONES EN COMISIONES

10 PLATAFORMA INTERNACIONAL DA RESPALDO A LOS SERVICIOS

14 NEGOCIOS EN EL INTERIOR YA ACEPTAN PAGOS CON EL BITCÓIN

(El Salvador Diario, Issue of September 7th, 2021)

This initiative raises several questions. By giving Bitcoin the status of national currency, does this decision contradict the original project's objective of universalism? Is it a political recovery of an anarchist-inspired project, or is it merely an intermediate step for El Salvador before joining other national CBDC projects?

Central Bank Digital Currencies (CBDCs)

"The great struggle in history has been for the control of money. It is almost tautological to assert that controlling the production and distribution of money is to control the wealth, resources, and peoples of the world." (Weatherford, 1997, p. 246)

De Sèze (2023) proposes the following definition of CBDC'' *a liability of the central bank made available to economic agents in digital form and fully fungible with the other components of central bank money (banknotes and reserves, the latter being banks' deposits with the central bank). Issued by the central bank, CBDC is free from credit risk and can be exchangeable for banknotes and reserves.*''(p.91)

No country/region of the world is spared from the desire to develop a CBDC: "sand dollar" (Bahamas, 2020), e-Naira (Nigeria, 2021), Chinese digital yuan (e-CNY) with a pilot in 2019 but a real launch during the Winter Olympics in 2022. To date, CBDC is still at the project stage in many countries (Agur et al., 2019): "*Many are exploring the idea of issuing a central bank digital currency instead of restricting it to commercial banks.*".Kiff et al. (2020) underlines the difference in nature with cryptocurrencies: "*Central bank digital currency is a digital representation of sovereign money that is issued by the monetary authority of a jurisdiction and that appears on the liabilities side of the monetary authority's balance sheet*". According to Zhang and Huang (2021), "*the main motivations for CBDC are to promote the security, robustness and efficiency of payments, reduce issuance costs and increase the convenience of transactions*".

Since 2017, the Bank for International Settlements (BIS) has conducted regular surveys of central banks worldwide, inquiring about their involvement in the development of MNBCs. According to de Sèze (2023), by mid-January 2023, 91 central banks had reported work on MNBCs, with 35 focusing on wholesale MNBC and 87 on retail MNBC. Notably, 31 central banks had engaged in work on both wholesale and retail MNBCs, as exemplified by the central banks of China, Canada, and Bhutan.

To summarize, states have adopted three positions regarding cryptocurrencies: a ban, legal tender for Bitcoin (El Salvador), and coexistence and competition between CBDCs and cryptocurrencies, which are crypto-assets with a taxable value.

A Basic Taxonomy of CBDCs: Wholesale CBDCs versus Retail CBDCs and the Question of Remuneration

According to the definition of Das et al. (2023): ''*Wholesale CBDCs refer to digital forms of central bank reserves whose access is limited to banks and other financial institutions.*'' (p.6) In other words, this digital currency will be reserved for exchanges of high unit amounts between financial institutions and commercial banks, within the framework of the interbank payment system. The aim is to make transactions more efficient, or for these professionals to operate directly with the central bank and avoid an intermediary if necessary. Other objectives are to enhance the liquidity of the interbank system, reduce costs and risks, while increasing the traceability of transactions, and finally, to give the central bank full control over money supply issuance. The Banque Nationale Suisse (BNS), the Swiss Central Bank, is currently working on a wholesale CBDC project, as well as Central Banks of Bahrain, Canada (''project Jasper'') and Austria notably. According to Agur et al (2019), a wholesale CBDC would be much less destabilizing than a retail CBDC, as the latter would compete with bank deposits and could result in less credit being extended by commercial banks to economic agents.

Conversely as emphasizes Das et al. (2003): '*'Retail CBDCs refer to digital forms of central bank money that can be widely held and used by individuals.*'' (p.6) In other words, in this second scenario, the situation is very different, since all retail market players - or if you prefer, simply the public - will be able to use it in place of traditional payment methods or electronic payments of all kinds, such as credit card or e-money payments (e.g., digital yuan, eNaira). CBDC retail will be accessible via a mobile app, credit cards or any other payment system method. The aims are to provide a more modern, secure and convenient form of payment, to enhance the efficiency of the system, to reduce the use of cash, and to strengthen the central bank's control over monetary policy. According to Das et al. (2023) retail CBDCs have three main features: they provide a "*safe store of value*'', are an "*attractive means of payment*'' and lastly are a "*low cost solution*''. In terms of terminology some authors use Instead of "Retail CBDC" the expression "general purpose CBDC" or simply "rCBDC". '*'Most jurisdictions are considering issuing a non-remunerated CBDC*'' (Das et al., 2023, p.7). This is undoubtedly an important limitation, because while volatility is controlled and the value of the currency is guaranteed by the central bank, there is no possible protection against the general purpose CBDC negative impact of inflation or the opportunity cost of another investment. These are some reasons among others why the current situation could evolve in the future: "*Although at present the majority of central banks are exploring non-remunerated CBDCs, they could in the future also consider remuneration. A few central banks are already considering the possibility of remuneration.*" (Das et al., 2023, p.23).

Regarding rCBDCs, according to BIS's taxonomy (Auer & Böhme, 2020), there are two alternative models based on the central bank's position within the banking ecosystem.

There are two main types of retail CBDCs: a single-tier CBDC and an indirect CBDC.

- **Single-tier retail CBDC:** In this system, the central bank directly welcomes commercial bank customers and manages their transactions.
- **Indirect CBDC:** In this system, the CBDC is dedicated solely to commercial banks, which then issue indirect CBDCs.

The objectives of these CBDCs are to provide a modern, safer, and more convenient method of payment, improve payment system efficiency, and reduce the use of cash. All economic agents will be able to use CBDCs instead of traditional or electronic payment methods. CBDCs will be accessible via mobile applications, credit cards, or other payment systems.

Since 2024, the BIS project ("mBridge") of a multi-CBDC is gaining traction, aiming to address cross-border payment inefficiencies. This project involves the BIS Innovation Hub, central banks of Thailand, the UAE, China, and Hong Kong, and more recently, Saudi Arabia. Interoperability between different CBDCs is a key challenge for the future. (BISIH, 2024, a). It focuses on Asia and Middle East corridors and his currently in real-world testing. Nevertheless, there is the project Dunbar involving BIS Innovation Hub and the central banks of Australia, Malaysia Singapore and South Africa. It explores broader multi-currency collaboration, but it is more experimental. (Chu & Rathbun, 2025, BISIH, 2024, b).

THE DEVELOPMENT OF CBDCs AROUND THE WORLD

CBDCs are attracting interest on every continent, with many countries, including a large number of central banks, launching or developing them. While some countries have been more proactive in adopting this technological innovation, others have only gradually embraced it.

The Early Adopters Group: The Four Fully Launched CBDCs, and Advanced Pilots or Projects

Nigeria

The e-Naira, launched in October 2021, is Africa's first central bank digital currency. It has the same value as the fiat Naira, an equivalence guaranteed by the central bank. Unlike Bitcoin, which operates on a public blockchain, the e-Naira uses a centralized/private blockchain whose "Ledger" is provided by the central bank, which aims to control money creation. Banks and financial institutions can access the platform via APIs and issue e-Naira. There are two types of wallets: e-Naira Speed Wallet (combo) and e-Naira Speed App Lite.

The Bahamas

In October 2020, the Bahamas officially launched its CBDC, the "Sand Dollar," after a pilot project demonstrated satisfactory results in terms of financial inclusion, banking fees, and transaction efficiency. This CBDC utilizes Distributed Ledger Technology (DLT) and has been integrated with wireless network connectivity due to the frequent hurricanes in the region. While the Sand Dollar has certain limitations, such as its limited use to the national territory and the absence of remuneration, it offers several advantages. These include reduced operating costs, the potential for both wholesale and retail transactions, and a relatively stable price pegged to the US dollar.

The success of the Sand Dollar was more pronounced among merchants than individuals, as evidenced by a study by Branch et al. (2023). This success can be attributed to several local characteristics, including a high GDP per capita, a 90% smartphone penetration rate within the population (Laboure & Deffrennes, 2022), solid infrastructures, and clear regulations (Sisodia, 2024).

The Eastern Caribbean Central Bank (ECCB)

Established in October 1983, the Eastern Caribbean Central Bank (ECCB) is the monetary authority for eight island economies in the Eastern Caribbean: Anguilla, Antigua and Barbuda, the Commonwealth of Dominica, Grenada, Montserrat, Saint Kitts and Nevis, Saint Lucia, and Saint Vincent and the Grenadines. In 2017, the ECCB began exploring the issuance of a CBDC within the ECCU. Work on the development of DCash commenced in 2019, with the objectives of reducing cash usage within the ECCU by 50% over five years, promoting financial sector stability, and accelerating growth and development among member states, as stated by Timothy Antoine, the governor of the ECCB. DCash, the second Caribbean CDBC, was launched in March 2021.

Jamaica

Exploring the idea of an rCBDC since 2019, the Bank of Jamaica (BOJ) accelerated its development in 2020 (Noll, 2024) to launch it in July 2022 with the mobile payment provider, Lynk. JAM-DEX is the 3rd rCBDC in the Caribbean. The development of a rCBDC was included in the reform on retail payments and the transition to a digital economy on the basis that the BOJ wanted consumers and businesses to be part of a "*modern payment system, a digital alternative to cash*", which would lead to "*systemic efficiency and significant reductions in the costs of distributing and storing cash*" (Haynes, 2021). The three Caribbean rCBDCs are a failure because none of the initial objectives have been achieved for each of the projects: "*None of the Caribbean rCBDCs has so far achieved the expected objective. The combined average circulation of Sand Dollar, DCash and JAM-DEX has only reached 0.15% of the region's trading volume, making it difficult for economies to make the transition to a digital society. To stimulate the adoption of this medium, economic actors need more than just rCBDC technology, in particular the assurance of a widely accepted, easily accessible and user-friendly rCBDC. Thus, rCBDC may need to be integrated into existing payment systems*" (Noll 2014, p.6). This reminds us that it is not enough to introduce an innovation equipped with robust technology to change people's daily lives and the dominant practices of the business world.

Advanced pilots or projects, such as those in Sweden, are crucial in demonstrating the potential of real-time CBDCs and paving the way for their widespread adoption.

The Advanced Pilots or Projects

Sweden

The choice of "early adopter" countries like the Bahamas and Sweden for a retail CBDC stems from the convergence of pre-existing economic and societal data that supports their development. In Sweden, this initiative is influenced by cultural factors, including ''*a cashless society, a technologically savvy population, and a generally strong trust in institutions and new technologies* (Laboure & Deffrennes, 2022). Notably, Sweden was one of the first countries to adopt a cashless payment solution in 2012 with the Swish mobile payment system. Preparatory work for the e-Krona began in 2017, and the first tests were scheduled for February 2020.

China

As early as 2014, the People's Bank of China (PBoC) began working on CBDC projects using a private/centralized blockchain platform. The primary objectives are to replace cash, promote financial inclusion, and strengthen the national financial system. This will ultimately lead to greater internationalization of the yuan to compete with the dollar and euro. Tests on e-CNY, initiated in April 2020 in cities like Shenzhen, Suzhou, and Chengdu, culminated in the official launch of e-CNY in 2022 during the Winter Olympic Games. Despite these developments, ''*the impact on the money supply remains negligible*'', as noted by de Sèze (2023, p. 94).

Additionally, the Hong Kong Monetary Authority (HKMA) and the PBoC have collaborated to test the digital yuan for cross-border payments.

When it comes to regulation, there are three approaches: legalization, partial prohibition, or an outright ban. China has opted for the third option. (PBoC, 2021, 2022).

Mexico plans to launch a CBDC by 2025. This project aims to enable '*financial inclusion and expand fast, secure, and efficient payment options*''. (Hayashi & Toh, 2022).

India's "Digital Rupee" pilot project seeks to ''*promote a digital economy, efficient and less costly currency management, and protect the public from volatile private virtual currencies*''. (Hayashi & Toh, 2022; RBI, 2022).

Zimbabwe is Also Working on a CBDC Project

The Retail CBDC (ZIG), as described by John Mangudya, Governor of the Central Bank of Zimbabwe, quoted by cbdctracker.org, ''*represents the central bank's initial steps towards using the country's gold reserves to control the depreciation of the Zimbabwe dollar*''.

An Alternative and Complementary Explanation: The Kleptocracies' Group

"Kleptocracies" - Iran, Russia, Venezuela... - are "*corrupt organizations that rule by theft*" (Mahdavieh, 2022, p. 5). They are characterized by "*significant and highly exploited natural resources, degraded economic conditions - high inflation, lack of diversification... -, Western sanctions limiting their international trade and high corruption... which probably lead to the adoption of native cryptocurrencies - attributes common to all kleptocratic country - and illicit state behavior via a privatised blockchain*" (Mahdavieh, 2022).

Measures have been taken, notably by the United States, to counter the activity of these countries considered "hostile". "*Iran has developed a native cryptocurrency, but the United States has passed a law aimed at blocking illicit financing from Iran banning the use of digital currencies. Ditto for Venezuela in the preliminary stages of petro adoption.*" (Mahdavieh, 2022, p.17). While, in Iran, the interest of individuals in cryptocurrencies, and Bitcoin in particular, is explained by the means of accessing foreign currencies, the public authorities see it as a means of having a CBDC in the long term.

In October 2017, Russian President Vladimir Putin announced the state-sponsored "Crypto-Ruble" project. Testing began in 2021 for banks and in 2022 for individuals (Mahdavieh, 2022; Azhar & Hassan, 2022). This central bank-issued CBDC, under government authority, can be used by financial institutions and individuals. Since its value is equivalent to the ruble, it can be considered a "stablecoin" (Azhar & Hassan, 2022).

However, issuing CBDC doesn't guarantee success or public confidence. The "Petro" (Venezuela), launched in 2018, failed to fulfil its traditional currency roles due to hyperinflation. This led to the closure of crypto wallets in early 2024.

In this way, the CBDC can be diverted from its ultimate purpose. "*Thanks to blockchain technology, it is easy to increase corruption across socio-economic sectors through illicit state monopolies. The country's dependence on natural resource export revenues has led to instability in all three countries. Cryptocurrencies then appear as a potential solution to stabilise political and economic conditions while granting countless privileges to a corrupt government*" (Mahdavieh, 2022, p. 21)

Democracies (Significant OECD Countries)

Japan

In October 2020, The Bank of Japan announced the launch of a retail CBDC trial program. Phase 3 began in April 2023 and only private financial institutions are participating in this new test environment. The aim is to ensure the central bank is ready to put the digital yen into circulation if the Japanese government decides to do so. This country, like many other Asian neighbors, is seeking to catch up with China. (Laboure & Deffrennes, 2022; de Sèze, 2023)

United States

The CBDC issue was raised in September 2022 with the publication of a report commissioned by the White House. (*Technical Evaluation for a US Central Bank Digital Currency System*, The White House, Washington) While some people raise concerns about the potential loss of privacy and the exercise of control over the population, others believe that the currency should be controlled by the authorities. They argue that safeguards, such as security and control measures, should be included in future digital currencies to limit risks. CBDCs represent an original dividing line in the political landscape, with no clear consensus. Furthermore, it should be remembered that the US Congress has exclusive jurisdiction over the issuance of currency. Even if the central bank wished to issue a CBDC, it would need prior authorization from Congress. Therefore, while the technical aspects of CBDCs may be a concern for other countries, the primary political challenge in the United States is to respond quickly to the dynamic Chinese e-CNY offer, which could potentially weaken the dollar's pre-eminence on the international scene. (Waller, 2022; de Sèze, 2023)

England

If "Brexit" may appear to be the triggering event for the disappearance of the Sterling as an international reserve currency due to the weakness of the British economy, the launch of a "digital pound" could become an instrument of power for the United Kingdom, at the cost of many risks. In collaboration with the British Treasury, the Bank of England launched a consultation in February 2023 on the potential needs of a digital pound for the economy as well as its design. It seems that it will be several years before a decision is taken on its launch, as the future of the digital pound is also political. (Cunliffe, 2023). This is why it will probably not take place before the second half of the 2020s.

European Union/ECB

The implications of introducing a digital euro are well documented, with its history and objectives being extensively explored (Brunnermeier & Landau, 2022; Lagarde, C. & Panetta F. (2022); de Sèze, 2023). The European Central Bank published its first report on the digital euro in 2020, followed by a public consultation whose results were released in 2021. Following this publication, the ECB initiated an investigation phase involving the entire Eurosystem, aiming to launch the retail digital euro relatively quickly. Since November 2023, the ECB has officially entered the "preparatory phase" of the digital euro, which is expected to last two years. This phase will lead to the development of a first draft regulation covering the functional and operational aspects, technical requirements, and the membership model of the digital euro. In the meantime, the ECB plans to educate the public, consumers, businesses, and public administrations to ensure their readiness. Additionally, it will assess the compatibility of the technologies used for the digital euro with those already implemented in existing payment systems.

A Global Overview of Current CBDCs Initiatives: Launched, Pilots, and Projects

According to the Atlantic Council, it appears that by the end of June 2024, the following initiatives will be launched:

- 134 countries and monetary unions, representing 98% of global GDP, are exploring the implementation of a CBDC.

· Three countries have fully launched a CBDC: Bahamas, Jamaica, and Nigeria.
· Thirty-six pilot projects are underway, including the digital euro.
· Nineteen G20 countries are at an advanced stage of CBDC development.
· The founding members of BRICS (Brazil, Russia, India, China, South Africa) are in the pilot phase of exploring CBDCs. Some new members (Saudi Arabia, Iran, and the United Arab Emirates) are also exploring cross-border "wholesale" CBDCs.
· The largest CBDC pilot project, the e-CNY, encompasses 260 million wallets across 25 cities. Since 2022, it has been used in various contexts, including public transport, healthcare, and the purchase of crude oil. The future aims to develop its use by foreign tourists and expand cross-border applications.
· To date, two countries have cancelled their retail CBDC projects: Senegal and Ecuador. Additionally, given the collapse of the Venezuelan company Petro's price and the scandal surrounding its fall, we can consider that this initiative has definitively come to an end.

A global overview of existing (or closed) projects is available in Figure 5 below.

Figure 5. Today's central bank digital currencies status (as of June 2024)

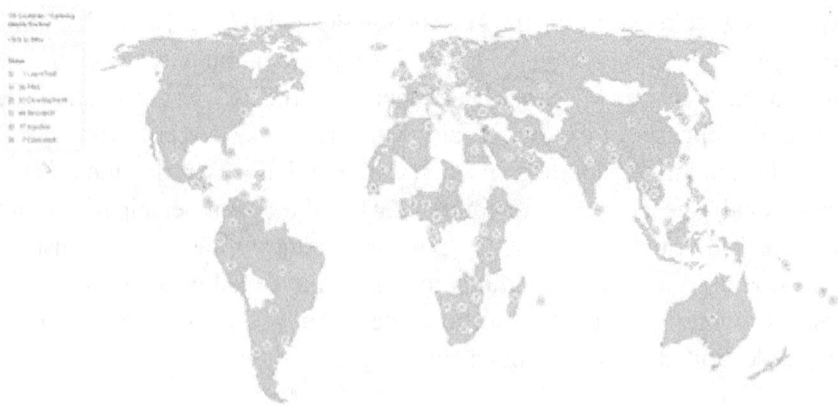

(https://www.atlanticcouncil.org/cbdctracker/)

Another source (https://cbdctracker.org) provides slightly different data. As of July 2024, there were 11 CBDCs launched, 21 pilot projects, 79 countries developing or researching a digital currency, and two cancelled projects (Peru and Kenya).

Table 5. Chronology of money, cryptography, and digital currencies

Name	Date	Country	Event
Bybit	2025	Dubai (UAE)	North Korea behind $1.5 billion hack of Bybit crypto exchange platform says FBI.
Project mBridge	2022-24	BIS-IH (Multi CDDC). Asia-Oceania.	Project of a multi-central bank currency (BIS + CBs of Thailand, UAE, China & Hong Kong, Saudi Arabia). Regional. Pilot stage
Project Dunbar	2024	BIS-IH (Multi-CBDC). WW.	BIS + CBs of Australia, Malaysia, Singapore and South Africa. Worldwide. Experimental.
ETFs	2024	USA	Bitcoin ETFs approval is boosting institutional investment.
	2024	Worldwide	>13,000 cryptocurrencies
Digital Dollar	2023	USA	Pilot
Digital Rupee	2023	India	Pilot
DREX	2023	Brazil	Pilot
3AC collapse	2022	Singapore	Estimated 3 billion loss of the crypto hedge fund Three Arrows Capital (3AC) falling into liquidation.
JAM-DEX	2022	Jamaica	In July launch of the national CBDC.
eNaira	2021	Nigeria	In October launched of the national CBDC.
Chivo Wallet	2021	El Salvador	''Bitcoin Law'': Bitcoin has legal tender.
D Cash	2021	ECBU (8 countries)	Launch of the CBDC of the ECCU (Caribbean).
MicroStrategy	2021	USA	MicroStrategy buys $1.9 billion in Bitcoin
Tesla	2021	USA	Tesla buys $1.5 billion in Bitcoin
Sand Dollar	2020	The Bahamas	Nationwide CBDC is officially launched.
e-CNY	2019	China	China's CBDC is fully launched in 2022 during Winter Olympics.
Initial Coin Offering	2018	Worlwide	ICO bubble burst.
BIS	2018	Worldwide	Report promoting further research on CBDCs.
	2018	Worldwide	1,359 cryptocurrencies
Petro	2018-2024	Venezuela	This CBDC launched in 2018, ended in 2024.
e.Krona	2017	Sweden	Testing
RSCoin	2016	Bank of England	Exploration of a CBDC framework.
"Sistema de Dinero Electrónico''	2015	Ecuador	Early state-backed digital payment system (not CBDC).
Ethereum	2013-2015		First Block in 2015.
Mr Gox	2014	Japan	The platform went bankrupt

continued on following page

Table 5. Continued

Name	Date	Country	Event
	2013	Worldwide	7 cryptocurrencies
Mt. Gox	2011	Japan	First Hack of the leading exchange platform
Altcoins	2011	Worldwide	Litecoin & Namecoin
Bitcoin	2009		Genesis Block
''token'' project	2004		Project of Hal Finney
Bit gold	1998		Nick Szabo's ''bit gold'' introduction
B-money	1998		Wei Dai Project
Hashcan	1997		Project (not of a cryptocurrencies)
eGold	1996	The USA	Private digital gold attempt.
DigiCash	1989	The Netherlands	International project (Bankruptcy).
	1989		May's Crypto-anarchy manifesto
Cryptography	1977		RSA Encryption system
Cryptography	1976		Diffie-Hellman key exchange
Aztec's cocoa beans	1200 – 1521 A.D.	Mexico	Commodity money has long survived in isolated parts of the world
	1040 A.D.	China	First paper banknote.
Electron coins	Circa 650 B.C.	Lydia	First coins ever minted (3/4 gold, ¼ silver)
Pure Gold	3rd millenium B.C.	Egypt	Gold has standardized weighs and values
Unit of value	Circa 3000 B.C.	Mesopotamia	Mesopotamian shekel
Commodity money	Circa 5000 B.C.		Ancient civilizations.

DISCUSSION AND AREAS FOR FUTURE RESEARCH

More and more studies are being carried out on crypto-assets, providing researchers with solid knowledge. The 13,000 cryptocurrencies listed, to date, by Coinbase constitute a wealth material, constantly being updated. However, this abundance can lead to a fragmentation of analyses, resulting in a pointillism of research that could get lost in too many monographs;

Nevertheless, the age of the currencies is beginning to lend itself to longitudinal analyses - a choice made for this study, but one that remains rare - and we feel that there is much to be done when it comes to analyses based on a historical perspective.

Similarly, we advise researchers to take a comparative look at crypto-currencies and CBDCs, whose boundaries seem clear-cut at first glance, but much less so on closer inspection. Moreover, it seems to the authors that these interactions lead to system analyses, or even to a quasi-cybernetic vision of the phenomenon.

Finally, we believe that these two groups (cryptocurrencies versus CBDCs) can also be analyzed through the prism of population ecology. In particular, we would like to study their biotic capacity, the factors that determine their birth and death, and of course their ability (or otherwise) to live in the same territory. This line of research could, for example, be based on the crisp-set QCA or fuzzy-set QCA methodologies (Ragin, 1987, 2000, Rocchi, 2022), using two representative samples of these populations.

CONCLUDING REMARKS

> *"From being a theoretical concept, CBDCs seem to have rapidly become an inevitable innovation [..] The challenge, in short, is to ensure that the introduction of CBDC will help to improve the global economy and achieve a more inclusive society." (Bilotta & Botti, 2021, p.193-196).*

Money dates back to the first great civilizations (Goetzmann, 2016). The form it has successively taken has always followed developments in technology: metal money, paper money, progress in computing, innovations in encryption techniques... Its latest transformation goes hand in hand with the ideology of the cypherpunks, whose philosophy is to promote individual freedom in the face of state control. With this in mind, the emergence of Bitcoin, which can be seen as a reaction to the financial crisis of 2007, had given impetus to the rise of cryptocurrencies.

While some states strictly prohibit cryptocurrencies, others have a more flexible approach, allowing them to derive tax revenue but also to use the underlying technology to develop their CDBC. Special case, El Salvador has given legal tender status to Bitcoin.

The development of digital currencies is in its early stages. While new encryption technologies have made it possible to create digital currencies, many cryptography specialists believe that no code, no matter how sophisticated, can avoid being discovered.

Over and above purely technological considerations, we need to ask ourselves whether or not users are committed to the system. The technology acceptance model (Davis, 1989) emphasizes the two primary factors of individuals' acceptance: *"perceived ease of use*" and *"perceived usefulness"*, while Gefen et al. (2003) in the context of online shopping are adding 'rust' as a variable. As emphasizes Lopez (2021), this analysis is complex, as perception of usefulness and trust is not the same in all parts of the world: "[...] *the success of a digital currency depends on the trust users have in it. So far consumers in Africa and Asia tend to trust telecommunications and social media companies for financial transactions more than regular banks, while in advanced economies, they tend to trust CBDC more than tech or credit card companies*." (p.191).

Some twenty years ago, Guttmann (2003) concluded his seminal book with a modesty that honored him and remains relevant today: "*The story of cybercash remains to be written. Still very much at the beginning of its life cycle, this innovation has yet to move beyond a subsidiary status. At this point it is impossible to tell how cybercash will evolve.*" (p.240) What's more, this uncertainty about their future is the only thing that cryptoassets and CBDCs have in common.

ACKNOWLEDGMENT

The author extend sincere gratitude to

- The Editor and the International Editorial Advisory Board (IEAB) of this book.
- All anonymous reviewers who provided very constructive feedback for thorough revision, improvement, extension, and fine-tuning of the chapter.
- Dr Ivan Topalovic who assisted to complete this task.

Disclaimer: The contents and views of this chapter are expressed by the authors in personal capacities. It is not necessary for the Editor and the Publisher to agree with these viewpoints, and they are not responsible for any duty of care in this regard.

REFERENCES

Agur, I., Ari, A., & Dell'Ariccia, G. (2019). Designing Central Bank Digital Currencies, IMF Working Paper 19/252.

Alekseenko, A. (2022). Ban of Cryptocurrencies in China and Judicial Practice of Chinese Courts. *China and WTO Review*, *8* (June), 361–388. DOI: 10.14330/cwr.2022.8.2.06

Alvares, F., Argente, D., & Van Patten, D. (2023). Are cryptocurrencies currencies? Bitcoin as legal tender in El Salvador, Science, 22 December, 22 Dec 2023, Vol 382, Issue 6677. DOI: DOI: 10.1126/science.add2844

Arslanian, H., & Fisher, F. (2019). *The Future of Finance, The Impact of Fintech, AI, and Crypto on Financial Services*. Palgrave Mac Millan., DOI: 10.1007/978-3-030-14533-0

Auer, R. & Böhme, R. (2020). The technology of retail central bank digital currency, *BIS Quarterly Review*, March.

Azhar, T. & Hassan, S. (2022). Current Challenges of Cryptocurrencies faced by governments, *Journal of Research and Reviews in Social Sciences Pakistan*, Vol 5 (1), Benedetti, H., and L. Kostovetsky. 2018. "Digital Tulips? Returns to Investors in Initial Coin Offerings."

Bilotta, N., & Botti, F. (2021). *The (Near) Future of Central Bank Digital Currencies*. Risks and Opportunities for the Global Economy and Society, Peter Lang AG. DOI: 10.3726/b18087

BISIH. (2024a). The Hong Kong Monetary Authority, Central Bank of Malaysia, Monetary Authority of Singapore, and South African Reserve Bank. 2022. "Project mBridge: Connecting Economies Through CBDC" Bank of International Settlements [online]. Accessed December 1, 2024.https:// www. bis. org/ publ/ othp59. htm

BISIH. (2024b). Reserve Bank of Australia, et al. 2022. "Project Dunbar -International Settlements Using Multi-CBDCs." Bank of International Settlements [online]. Accessed December 1, 2024. https:// www. bis. org/publ/ othp47. htm

Branch, S., Ward, L., & Allan Wright, A. (2023). The Evolution of SandDollar. *Inter Economics*, *58*(4), 178–184. DOI: 10.2478/ie-2023-0038

Brunnermeir, M., & Landau, J.-P. (2022). The digital euro: policy implications and perspectives, *Study Requested by the ECON Committee*, European Parliament, January. https://bankenverband.de/files/2022-12/report_digitaler_euro.pdf

Buckley, R. P., Arner, D. W., Zetzsche, D. A., & Didenko, A. N. Romburg, van. L., (2021). Sovereign Digital Currencies: Reshaping the Design of Money and Payments Systems, *Journal of Payments Strategy and Systems*, Volume 15, Number 1, pp.7-22. https://www.ssrn.com/link/UNSW-LEG.html

Buterin, V. (2013). "Ethereum White Paper: A Next Generation Contract & Decentralized Application Platform." http://www.the-blockchain.com/docs/Ethereum _white_paper-a_ next_generation_smart_contract_and_decentralized_application_platform-vitalik-buterin.pdf

Campbell, D. T. (1960). Variation and selective retention in creative thought as in other knowledge process. *Psychological Review*, *67*(6), 380–400. DOI: 10.1037/ h0040373 PMID: 13690223

Campbell, D. T. (1969). Variation and selective retention in sociocultural evolution. *General Systems*, *14*, 69–85.

Carroll, G. R., & Khessina, O. M. (2005). 'The ecology of entrepreneurship. In Alvarez, S. A., Agarwal, R., & Sorensen, O. (Eds.), *Handbook of Entrepreneurship Research* (pp. 167–200). Springer. DOI: 10.1007/0-387-23622-8_9

Chaum, D. (1983). Blind signatures for untraceable payments. *Advances in Cryptology Proceedings of Crypto*, *82*(3), 199–203.

Chaum, D. (1985, a). "Security without Identification: Transaction Systems to Make Big Brother Obsolete," *Communications of the ACM* 28, no. 10 (October 1), pp.1030–44, .DOI: 10.1145/4372.4373

Chaum, D. (1985, b). Cryptographic identification, financial transaction, and credential device. July 16. US Patent 4,529,870.

Chaum, David. (1992). Achieving electronic privacy. *Scientific American*, 267(2), 96{101.

Chaum, D. L. (1988). Blind signature systems. US Patent 4,759,063.

Chu, Y., & Rathbun, N. S. (2025). 'Monetary Sovereignty and Central Bank Digital Currencies: Competing Models for Future Cross-Border Payment Platforms'. *Global Policy*, •••, 1–12. DOI: 10.1111/1758-5899.13495

Cunliffe, J. (2023). ''The Digital Pound'', Bank of England, February, https://www.bankofengland.co.uk/speech/2023/february/jon-cunliffe-speech-at-uk-finance-update-on-central-bank-digital-currency

Dale, A. (2015). Walwet and Kukalim. Lydian coin legends, dynastic succession, and the chronology of Mermnad kings. *Kadmos*, *54*(1/2), 151–166. DOI: 10.1515/kadmos-2015-0008

Das, M., Mancini Griffoli, T., Nakamura, F., Otten, J., Soderberg, G., Sole, J., Tan, B. (2023). Implications of Central Bank Digital Currencies for Monetary Policy Transmission, International Monetary Fund, Fintech Note, September.

Davis, F. D. (1989). Perceived usefulness, perceived ease of use, and user acceptance of information technology. *Management Information Systems Quarterly*, *13*(3), 319–340. DOI: 10.2307/249008

De Filippi, P. (2014). Bitcoin: A regulatory nightmare to a libertarian dream.... *Internet Policy Review*, *3*(2), Hal-0102612. DOI: 10.14763/2014.2.286

De Filippi, P. (2018). *Blockchain et cryptomonnaies*. PUF. DOI: 10.3917/puf.filip.2018.01

Dwdollar (2010). New exchange (Bitcoin Market). Bitcointalk Forum. https: //bitcointalk.org/index.php?topic=20.msg265#msg265

FATF. (2014). Report: Virtual Currencies Key Definitions and Potential AML/CFT Risks, June. https://www.fatf-gafi.org/content/dam/fatf-gafi/reports/Virtual-currency-key-definitions-and-potential-aml-cft-risks.pdf

Feder, A., Gandal, N., Hamrick, J. T., Moore, T., & Vasek, M. (2018). "The Rise and Fall of Cryptocurrencies." In *The Workshop on the Economics of Information Security* (WEIS), chaired by R. Böhme. Innsbruck, Austria: University of Innsbruck.

Ferreira, A., & Sandner, P. (2021). Eu search for regulatory answers to crypto assets and their place in the financial markets' infrastructure. *Computer Law & Security Review*, *43*(November), 105632. Advance online publication. DOI: 10.1016/j.clsr.2021.105632

Gefen, D., Karahanna, E., & Straub, D. W. (2003). Trust and TAM in Online Shopping: An Integrated Model. *Management Information Systems Quarterly*, *27*(1), 51–90. DOI: 10.2307/30036519

Goetzmann, W. N. (2016). *Money Changes Everything: How Finance Made Civilization Possible*. Princeton University Press. DOI: 10.1515/9781400881307

Goetzmann, W. N., & Rouwenhorst, K. G. (2005). *The Origins of Value. The Financials Innovations that Created Modern Capital Markets*. Oxford University Press., DOI: 10.1093/oso/9780195175714.001.0001

Guttmann, R. (2003). *Cybercash: The Coming Era of Electronic Money*. Palgrave Macmillan. DOI: 10.1057/9781403914507

Hannan, M. T., & Freeman, J. (1977, March). The Population Ecology of Organizations. *American Journal of Sociology*, *82*(5), 929–964. DOI: 10.1086/226424

Haribedel, B., & Perez-Saiz, H. (2023, September). Assessing Macrofinancial Risks from Crypto Assets. *IMF Working Paper*, *29*(214), 1. Advance online publication. DOI: 10.5089/9798400255083.001

Hayashi, F. & Toh Y. L. (2022). Assessing the Case for Retail CBDCs: Central Banks' Considerations, *kcFED Payments System Research Breiefing*, Federal Reserve Bank of Kansas City, May 26.

Haynes, N. (2021). "A Primer on BOJ's Central Bank Digital Currency." *Jamaica Observer*, March 31

Hérodote. (1970). *Histoire, 1, 94*. Les Belles Lettres.

Herrera Anchustegui, I., & Hunter, T. (2018). Oil as Currency: Venezuela's Petro, a New 'Oil Pattern'? (2018). http://dx.doi.org/DOI: 10.2139/ssrn.3291272

Hughes, E. (1993). "A Cypherpunk's Manifesto," Activism.net, March 1993, https://www.activism.net/cypherpunk/manifesto.html

Kavuri, A. S., & Milne, A. (2021). Trading and regulation of cryptocurrencies, stablecoins and other. In *K* (pp. 147–162). Thomas Liaw, The Routledge Handbook of FinTech.

Kitco News. (2013). "2013: Year of the Bitcoin". Forbes, https://www.forbes.com/sites/ kitconews/2013/12/10/2013-year-of-the-bitcoin/#2f0b622e303c

Kiff, J., Alwazir, J., Davidovic, S., Farias, A., Khan, A., Khiaonarong, T., Malaika, M., Monroe, H., Sugimoto, N., Tourpe, H., & Zhou, P. (2020). A Survey of Research on Retail Central Bank Digital Currency, IMF Working Paper, June. file:///C:/Users/jeanm/Downloads/wpiea2020104-print-pdf.pdf

Kutler, J. (1995). "Digicash to test live Internet cash system with Mo. bank". *American Banker*, vol. 160, no. 204, 23 October, pp. 1

Laboure, M., & Deffrennes, N. (2022). *Democratizing Finance: The Radical Promise of Fintech*. Harvard University Press.

Lagarde, C., & Panetta, F. (2022). "Key Objectives of the Digital Euro". *The ECB blog*, juillet, https://www.ecb.europa.eu/press/blog/date/2022/html/ecb.blog220713~34e21c3240.fr.html

Lansky, J. (2016). Analysis of Cryptocurrencies Price Development. *Acta Informatica Pragensia*, *5*(2), 118–137. DOI: 10.18267/j.aip.89

Lansky, J. (2020). Cryptocurrency Survival Analysis. *The Journal of Alternative Investment Analysis*, (Winter), 55–63.

Lehdonvirta, V., & Castronova, E. (2014). *Virtual economies: Design and analysis*. MIT Press. DOI: 10.7551/mitpress/9525.001.0001

Lisdorf, A. (2023). Virtual Currency. In Lisdorf, A. (Ed.), *Still Searching for Satoshi. Unveiling the Blockchain Revolution*. Apress., DOI: 10.1007/978-1-4842-9639-4_1

Lopez, C. (2021). '' Digital Currency: A Global Regulatory Framework is Needed. In Bilotta, N., & Botti, F. (Eds.), *The (Near) Future of Central Bank Digital Currencies* (pp. 183–192). Risks and Opportunities for the Global Economy and Society, Peter Lang AG.

Luchkin, A. G., Lukasheva, O. L., Novikova, N. E., Melnikov, V. A., Zyatkova, A. V., & Yarotskaya, E. V. (2020). Cryptocurrencies in the Global Financial System: Problems and Ways to Overcome them, *Advances in Economics, Business and Management Research, volume 148,* Proceedings of the Russian Conference on Digital Economy and Knowledge Management (RuDEcK 2020)

Mahdavieh, R. (2022, June). State Adoption of Cryptocurrency: A Case Study Analysis of Iran, Russia, and Venezuela. *American Journal of Undergraduate Research*, *19*(1), 13–22. DOI: 10.33697/ajur.2022.055

Nakamoto, S. (2008). "Bitcoin: A Peer-to-Peer Electronic Cash System". *White Paper*. https://bitcoin.org/bitcoin.pdf

NewLibertyStandard. (2009). 2009 Exchange Rate. New Liberty Standard. http://newlibertystandard.wetpaint.com/page/2009+

Noll, F. (2024). Observations from the Retail CBDCs of the Caribbean, *kcFED Payments System Research Breiefing,* Federal Reserve Bank of Kansas City, April 10.

PBoC. (2022). ''Pressing Ahead with the Pilot Program of e-CNY R&D''. October, http://www.pbc.gov.cn/en/3688006/4671762/4688130/index.html

PBoC (People's Bank of China). (2021). ''Progress of Research & Development of e-CNY in China''. July. http://www.pbc.gov.cn/en/3688110/3688172/4157443/4293696/2021071614584691871.pdf

Prime, E. L., & Solomon, D. H. (2010). Australias Plastic Banknotes: Fighting Counterfeit Currency. *Angewandte Chemie International Edition*, *49*(22), 2–13. DOI: 10.1002/anie.200904538 PMID: 20358564

RBI (Reserve Bank of India). (2022), *Concept Note on CBDC*, October, https://rbi.org.in/Scripts/PublicationReportDetails.aspx?UrlPage=&ID=1218

Redish, A. (1993, November). Anchors Aweigh: The Transition from Commodity Money to Fiat Money in Western Economies. *The Canadian Journal of Economics. Revue Canadienne d'Economique*, *26*(4), 777–795. http://links.jstor.org/sici?sici=0008-4085%28199311%2926%3A4%3C777%3AAATTFC%3E2.0.CO%3B2-Q. DOI: 10.2307/135820

Rocchi, J.-M. (2022). Crisp Set vs Fuzzy Set Qualitative Comparative Analysis, Technical Differences, and Much More in Said Broumi (Ed.). Handbook of Research on Advances and Applications of Fuzzy Sets and Logic, IGI Global. pp.1-28

Rolle, J. (2022). "The Bahamas' Experience with the Sand Dollar". *Remarks at the Digital Euro Conference*. CBOB, November 7 https://www.centralbankbahamas.com/news/general-news/the-bahamas-experience-with-the-sand-dollar-remarks-by-governor-john-rolle

Rosales, A. (2019). Radical rentierism: Gold mining, cryptocurrency and commodity collateralization in Venezuela. *Review of International Political Economy*, *26*(6), 1311–1332. Advance online publication. DOI: 10.1080/09692290.2019.1625422

Rotta, T. N., & Paraná, E. (2022). Bitcoin as a digital commodity. *New Political Economy*, *27*(6), 1046–1061. DOI: 10.1080/13563467.2022.2054966

Ruimy, M., & Rocchi, J.-M. (2017). La monnaie à l'ère de la digitalization in Jean-Michel Rocchi (Ed.), MBA Finance, Eyrolles. (pp.817-852).

Said, A. (2019). The Economic Impact of Digital Fiat Currency (DFC): Opportunities and Challenges, 2nd Europe - Middle East - North African Regional Conference of the International Telecommunications Society (ITS): "Leveraging Technologies For Growth", Aswan, Egypt, 18th-21st February, 2019, International Telecommunications Society (ITS), Calgary. https://hdl.handle.net/10419/201744

de Sèze, N. (2023). Central bank digital currencies: A perspective of work across the world. *Revue d'Economie Financiere*, *149*(1), 91–105.

Sisodia, H. (2024). Case Study on the Sand Dollar CBDC of the Bahamas: Lessons, Challenges, and Insights. In Kaur, G., Lekhi, P., & Popli, S. (Eds.), *Exploring Central Bank Digital Currencie: Concepts, Frameworks, Models and Challenges* (pp. 298–314). IGI Global. DOI: 10.4018/979-8-3693-1882-9.ch018

Stinchcombe, A. L. (1965). Social structure and organizations. In March, J. (Ed.), *Handbook of Organizations* (pp. 142–193). Rand McNally.

Sutton, R. I. (1987). The Process of Organizational Death: Disbanding and Reconnecting. *Administrative Science Quarterly*, *32*(4), 542–569. DOI: 10.2307/2392883

Tapscott, A., & Tapscott, D. (2016). *Blockchain Revolution: How The Technology beyond Bitcoin is changing Money*. Business, and the World, Portfolio Penguin.

Thiveaud, J. M. (1999). Between myth and history, from electronic money to electronic wallets, e-cash, digicash, e-business.... *Revue d'Economie Financiere*, (53), 197–213.

Waller, J. (2022). The US Dollar and Central Bank Digital Currencies, October, https://www.federalreserve.gov/newsevents/speech/waller20221014a.htm

Weatherford, J. (1997). *The History of Money. From Sandstone to Cyberspace*. Crown Publishers.

Zetzsche, D. A., Buckley, R. P., Arner, D. W., Didenko, A. N., & van Romburg, L. J. (2020). Sovereign digital currencies: The future of money and payments? University of Hong Kong Faculty of Law Research Paper, (2020/053), 23-30.

ENDNOTES

1 New Liberty Standard, 2009

Chapter 2
Beyond Hype:
Understanding Cryptocurrencies Through Its History

Nidhiya Maria Thomas
https://orcid.org/0009-0000-0400-5595
Christ University, India

Natchimuthu Natchimuthu
https://orcid.org/0000-0002-2461-7801
Christ University, India

ABSTRACT

The study delves into the evolution of cryptocurrencies, tracing their journey from theoretical concepts to a globally recognized asset class. From the foundational ideas of early digital cash system to the groundbreaking emergence of Bitcoin, the study examines the key milestones that shaped the crypto landscape. The subsequent rise and fall in the crypto market, characterized by periods of exuberance and volatility, are analyzed to understand the underlying factors driving these dynamics. The study further explores the evolving regulatory landscape, highlighting the challenges and opportunities posed by the decentralized nature of cryptocurrencies. By examining the interplay between innovation, market volatility, and regulatory response, this study provide insights into the intellectual lineage, challenges, and context that shaped the crypto market development and the potential trajectory of cryptocurrencies in the future.

DOI: 10.4018/979-8-3693-5986-0.ch002

1. INTRODUCTION

The first decade of the twenty-first century was filled with economic downturns that affected people's trust in the financial systems and intermediaries. People believe that the interests of the financial system are not aligned with those of the public. This called for a decentralized financial system that offers autonomy, transparency, and security (Allen & Bryant, 2019). To leverage this, Satoshi Nakamoto published the concept of a peer-to-peer (P2P) transaction system based on blockchain technology (Nakamoto, 2008). This came to be known as cryptocurrency.

Cryptocurrencies are digital payment systems based on blockchain algorithms that leverage the security, transparency, and decentralized nature of blockchain technology (Narayanan & Clark, 2017). Bitcoin is the original cryptocurrency based on the P2P concept. The technological attraction made Bitcoin popular among the public, leading to the creation of altcoins, a term for cryptocurrencies other than Bitcoin (Jia et al., 2021). The absence of asset backing introduced volatility to the crypto market. However, this volatility also brought new growth potential and returns in the market, thereby emerging as a new asset class for investors (Milunovich, 2018).

The volatility, returns, and rapid growth of the market attracted research on various aspects of the crypto market, including volatility spillovers (S. Jiang et al., 2022; Özdemir, 2022; Phiri & Anyikwa, 2024; Zeng & Ahmed, 2023); the price prediction of cryptocurrencies(Khaniki & Manthouri, 2024; Koo & Kim, 2024; Patra & Mohanty, 2023), analysis of crypto as a safe-haven (Baur & Hoang, 2021; Corbet et al., 2020; He et al., 2024; Smales, 2022), and the future of blockchain and cryptocurrencies (Brasse & Hyun, 2023; Hossain, 2021; Morton, 2020). However, the literature focused a little on the history and evolution of the cryptocurrencies. This created a lack of information about the intellectual lineage, challenges, and context that shaped the crypto market development. This study addresses this gap by tracing the genesis of cryptocurrency as an obscured concept in the later decade of the 20th century to its current status as a global phenomenon.

The chapter is divided into the following sections. Section 2 discusses the intellectual lineage behind cryptocurrencies. Section 3 discusses the birth of Bitcoin. Section 4 talks about the growth of the crypto market. Section 5 discusses the bubble cycles in the crypto market. Section 6 points to the regulatory development in the field, and section 7 concludes the study.

2. THE DAWN OF DIGITAL CASH: DIGITAL CURRENCY PRECURSORS AND THEIR LIMITATIONS

The concept of digital currency has decades of intellectual lineage. The intellectual ferment for a digital currency started in the 1980s and laid the groundwork for the global phenomenon of cryptocurrencies (Figure 1). eCash by David Chaum, a paper by NSA on 'How to make a mint,' and the proposal of b-money by Wei Dai are some of the prominent pioneers of the digital money concept. However, the early concepts had their own limitations to their wide adoption, and cryptocurrencies emerged as an answer to these limitations.

2.1 eCash by David Chaum

The quest for security and anonymity for financial transactions dates decades back. David Chaum, a cryptographer, is a pioneer who addressed the significant obstacles to the digital payment system's security and anonymity. In 1983, he introduced the concept called 'blind signatures' in his paper 'Blind Signatures for Untraceable Payments.' Based on the concept, he then introduced e-cash, a replica of physical cash in the digital world (Chaum, 1983).

Digital signatures are cryptographic solutions to protect user identity. It allows the user to get the signature from the bank without actually revealing the message (Pointcheval & Stern, 1996). eCash was built upon the concept of blind signatures. eCash prevented the double spending problem and made the transaction untraceable using blind signatures (Chaum, 1992). Blinded coins can be obtained from a mint. When spending, the coins are partially unblinded to show the amount to the merchant. The merchant verifies the authenticity with the source and accepts it. Once received, it is fully unblinded and proves that it has never been used (Chaum, 2002). Even though it was complex, it provided anonymity and offline functionality to the public. However, the dependence on a central mint posed challenges to mainstream adoption.

2.2 How to Make a Mint

The US National Security Agency (NSA) published a paper titled 'How to Make a Mint: A Cryptography of Anonymous Electronic Cash' (Law et al., 1997). It delves into the theoretical aspects of an anonymous digital payment system. Unlike David Chaum's eCash, the NSA did not intend to create a physical electronic cash system. It proposed the concept of a system where the user can obtain untraceable digital currency from the bank and spend it anonymously (Law et al., 1997). The suggested electronic cash system also depends on the blind signature concept proposed in 1983.

The concepts discussed in the NSA paper, particularly the anonymous payment system and blind signature, paved the groundwork for cryptocurrency developers.

2.3 B-Money by Wei Dai

The b-money by Wei Dai is also a notable conceptual pioneer in the field, even though it was not directly implemented. Wei Dai proposed the concept of b-money in the year 1998 (Dai, 1998). Unlike the eCash by David Chaum, Wei Dai proposed a decentralized system. The b-money was based on the shared transaction ledger concept, eliminating the need for a third party. W. Dai also proposed two protocols for creating money. First, a channel that is open to manipulation by system keepers and a second channel based on a consensus mechanism to know the amount of money created periodically. W. Dai also introduced a concept similar to the Proof-of-Work mechanism. He proposed that users compete to create new money, solving the problem of expensive computation and securing the network (Dai, 1998).

The lack of details on the security and scalability in a real system challenged the functional implementation of the b-money concept. The uncertainty relating to the susceptibility of the money creation protocols to manipulation also contributed to the challenges. Even though the b-money did not materialize, its core concepts, like the proof-of-work, decentralization, and distributed ledger, significantly influenced the development of Bitcoin (Dai, 2008).

Despite the challenges, these concepts played a crucial role in laying the foundation for the future of digital currencies. The practicality of the blinded signature by David Chaum, the benefits of the digital payment system by the NSA, and the decentralization of digital payments by Wei Dai provided the springboard for further development in the field.

Figure 1. Key ideas found in bitcoin

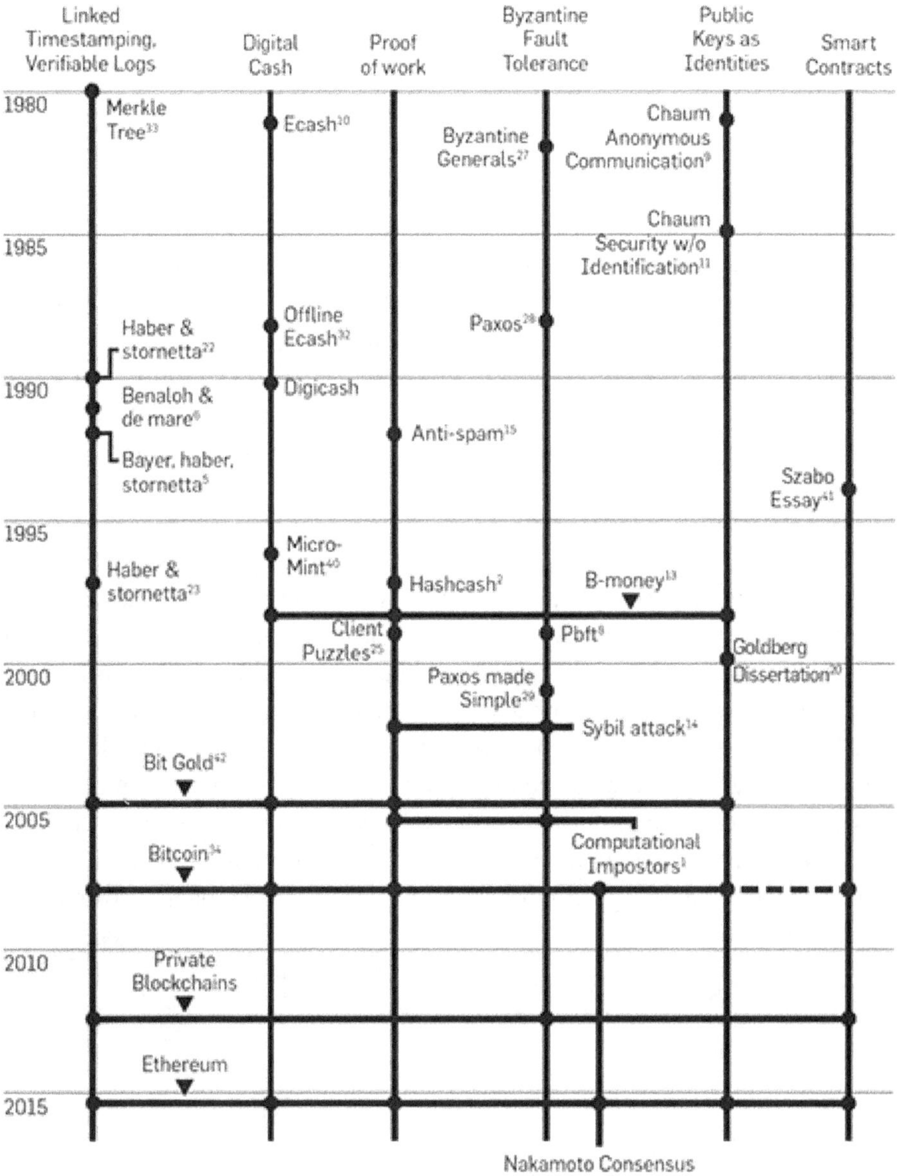

(Narayanan & Clark, 2017)

3. A PARADIGM SHIFT: THE BIRTH OF BITCOIN

The idea of Bitcoin was sawed in the fertile field tilled by the pioneering ideas of David Chaum and Wei Dai. However, the introduction of Bitcoin was a paradigm shift in the financial landscape as it addressed the limitations of scalability, double-spending prevention, and reliance on centralized authorities of the earlier concepts. Satoshi Nakamoto, a pseudonymous figure, published a whitepaper in 2008 titled 'Bitcoin: A Peer-to-Peer Electronic Cash System.' This article outlined the new approach to the digital currency system, introducing the decentralized, public ledger-based electronic cash system, Bitcoin (Nakamoto, 2008). Bitcoin combines the characteristics of blockchain technology, and mining offers a unique blend of transparency, security, and accessibility. Blockchain acts as a secure and transparent public ledger for transactions, while mining validates the transaction and secures the network. This section discusses the basic concepts of blockchain technology, decentralization, mining, and the launch of the Bitcoin genesis block.

3.1 Blockchain and Mining

Blockchain is a massive digital record that is constantly being updated across all the computers in the network. When a transaction occurs, the details are condensed into a block and added to this ledger. This creates a record of transactions and ownership. The blocks are added with a unique identification known as a hash (Zheng et al., 2017). The hash is mathematically derived from the data in the block, along with a link to the hash of the preceding block. This results in a chain of blocks. So, accessing or altering the information in one block requires alternating the linked blocks, which is computationally impossible. This way, blockchain ensures the security and anonymity of the transaction in a decentralized manner (Komalavalli et al., 2020).

Figure 2. The working of blockchain transaction

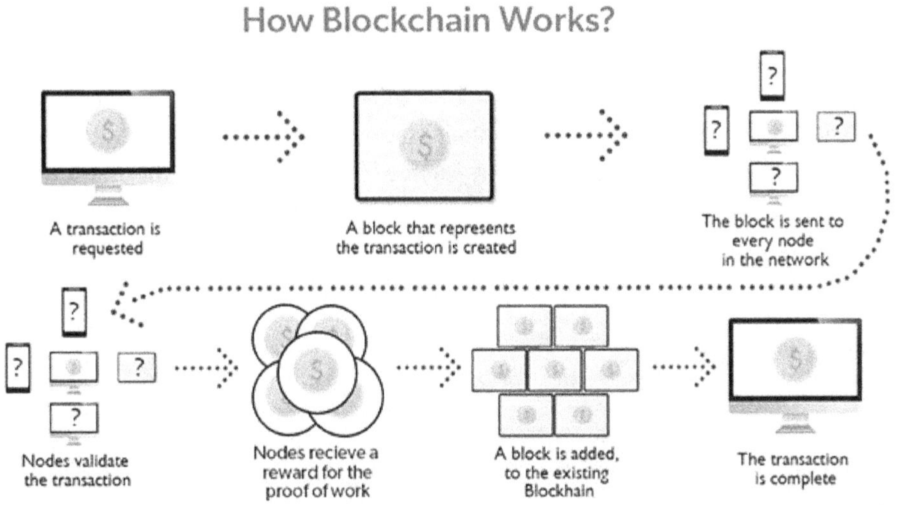

(Ujjawal, 2024)

Mining comes into the picture to add the block to the network. The miners compete to solve the mathematical puzzles of the transaction. The miner solves the puzzle, adds their verified block, and they are rewarded with newly minted Bitcoins. This is how new coins are added into circulation (Bhaskar et al., 2024). Miners verify the legitimacy of transactions and prevent fraud and double-spending. Therefore, mining requires high-powered computers, and they are at the high end of the energy consumption scale (J. Li et al., 2019).

3.2 The Genesis Block

Built upon the blockchain, the first-ever block on this chain is known as the genesis block. The genesis block was minted on 3 January 2009, marking the official launch of the Bitcoin transactions (McSweeney, 2024; Sambana, 2021). Along with the code, the genesis block has encrypted messages embedded in it. The message is believed to be an article about the financial crisis going on at the time and the potential of Bitcoin as an alternative financial system (Sambana, 2021).

The genesis block set the stage for the ever-growing Bitcoin network, where miners compete to validate the transactions and secure the expanding network of blockchain. The introduction of Bitcoin and the genesis block set a pivotal movement in the landscape of financial history. It has driven the focus of the people to the new decentralized finance and initiated conversations on the future of the financial system under the decentralized finance era.

4. BUILDING MOMENTUM: THE ASCENT OF THE CRYPTO MARKET

The development of the concept of Bitcoin was a climate-changing event in the finance world. However, the implementation and adoption of the new technology was slow and limited. Bitcoin was still in its infancy, and many questioned its viability in the real world. The pizza purchase by Laszlo Hanyecz using ten thousand Bitcoin became a milestone in Bitcoin history, making the first real-world functionality of Bitcoin. This section discusses the first real-world use of Bitcoin, the development of crypto exchanges, and the creation of altcoins

4.1 The Pizza Day

Laszlo was a programmer who wanted to test the application of Bitcoin technology. He offered ten thousand Bitcoins to anyone who was willing to buy him two pizzas in the Bitcoin Talk forum (Arslanian, 2022). Another forum user, Jeremy Sturdisvant, accepted the offer and bought Laszlo pizzas using his fiat money and got them delivered. On May 22, 2010, Laszlo sent ten thousand Bitcoins; thus, the historic transaction occurred. To mark this day, the Bitcoin community celebrates it as 'Bitcoin Pizza Day'(Wu & Wu, 2023).

The forty dollars worth of transactions then amounts to millions today, a stark reminder of Bitcoin volatility (Chaturvedi, 2024). However, the transaction was not just about food; it was the first documented Bitcoin transaction marking the functionality of Bitcoin as a currency. This seemingly insignificant event sparked public attention and initiated talks about the potential of digital currencies.

4.2 Cryptocurrency Exchanges

The need for an efficient and secure way to manage and trade the digital asset became significant. The need paved the way for developing cryptocurrency exchanges, which act as a marketplace for secured bargaining. Before the crypto exchanges, transactions were cumbersome, as they involved online peer-to-peer interaction and forums (Staff, 2024). The exchanges emerged as a platform for users to trade Bitcoin for fiat currencies and digital assets.

Mt.Gox was one of the early movers in the crypto exchanges. Mt. Gox was introduced in the year 2010. Mt.Gox provided a user-friendly interface for the people and dominated Bitcoin trading (Bolici & Rosa, 2016). However, security breaches and lack of operational efficiency led to the collapse of Mt. Gox in 2014 (W. Chen et al., 2019). Learning from the past, other exchanges emerged in the growing market. The major crypto exchanges currently are Binance, Coinbase, Kraken, etc

(Brasse & Hyun, 2023). As the crypto market matures, these exchanges offer a variety of trading features, including spot trading, margin trading, staking, etc., and they also provide educational resources to new investors (Bhaskar & Chuen, 2024). Recently, there has been a rise in decentralized exchanges (DEXs). They operate on blockchain technology and emerged as an alternative to the centralized exchange system. They offer greater security and control but are complex to operate and use (Makridis et al., 2023).

The crypto exchanges are evolving along with the crypto market. The emergence of crypto exchanges has facilitated price discovery, liquidity, and accessibility in the crypto market. However, there are challenges associated with this growth. The main threat to investors is the security risks of exchanges (Cheraghali et al., 2024). It is important to choose reputable exchanges with robust security measures. The regulatory landscape related to crypto exchanges is still evolving, which can create uncertainty for both the exchanges and users (Kavaloski, 2024).

4.3 Rise of the Altcoins

The successful adoption of Bitcoin opened the door for alternative cryptocurrencies, known as altcoins. Unlike Bitcoin, where the main focus was on peer-to-peer transactions, altcoins introduced a variety of functionalities and features (Cai & Pinto, 2024). For instance, Ethereum introduced the smart contracts function. They are self-executing contracts stored on the blockchain (Osterland & Rose, 2020). This feature can effectively automate various functions, paving the way for various decentralized applications (dApp) based on the Ethereum blockchain (Metcalfe, 2020). For users focusing on anonymity, the privacy-focused Monero coin, which utilizes cryptography to obscure transaction details, was introduced (Gomzin, 2022).

The functionality of altcoins extends beyond simple transactions. The widespread adoption of the Ethereum platform led to the popularity of Decentralized Finance (DeFi) applications, which enabled peer-to-peer lending, borrowing, and other financial services without an intermediary (Kaur et al., 2023). These developments in decentralized financial services enabled greater accessibility and autonomy for users. Another notable development based on altcoins is the Non-Fungible Tokens (NFTs). They are digital tokens representing the ownership of digital arts, collectibles, in-game items, etc (Ante, 2023b). This development opened a new avenue for creators and collectors within the digital art and gaming sphere.

The introduction of altcoins increased the competition in the crypto market, pushing the innovation in blockchain technology. These innovations attracted different investors with varied interests in the crypto market and enabled diversification opportunities. The altcoin, therefore, introduced a 'universe of choice' in the crypto space, signifying the ongoing evolution of digital assets and their potential in the financial environment.

5. BUBBLE DYNAMICS: UNDERSTANDING THE MARKET THROUGH ITS BOOM-BUST CYCLE

The introduction of altcoin made the crypto market popular and accessible among the public. However, the growth was not without a stumble. Along with periods of significant growth, the market also experienced significant price correction periods known as bubbles. Understanding the boom-bust cycle of the market can be crucial to understanding the market's development trajectory.

Cryptocurrencies are a nascent asset class; even then, they have witnessed several bubble periods. The rapid growth is often triggered by a specific event or trend and ends with a sharp decline in price. The bubble periods in the market, along with the events that triggered the growth and collapse of the bubble, are discussed in this section. There are four main bubble periods in the history of cryptocurrencies.

5.1 Bitcoin Bubble of 2011

The technological innovation behind Bitcoin created a frenzy in the market (Lee, 2022). Along with this attention, the introduction of crypto exchange, mainly Mt.Gox, created a user-friendly interface and easy access to the crypto market. This significantly increased the Bitcoin trading volume and market concentration, leading to a significant rise in the price. The media coverage depicts Bitcoin as a revolutionary currency without providing the technological complexity behind it, which attracted new investors, further inflating the price (Z. Li et al., 2019).

However, the rapid increase in the price of Bitcoin was halted when Mt.Gox was subjected to hacking, resulting in a substantial loss of Bitcoin. The security breach, along with the technical issues of Mt.Gox, shattered investors' confidence and triggered sell-offs, making the price of Bitcoin plummetM from $30 to $2 (Cheung et al., 2015).

5.2 Bitcoin Bubble of 2013

The European debt crisis hit the world in the year 2012. The economic distress in Cyprus and Greece increased the mistrust in the people. People began to see Bitcoin as a safe haven (Bouoiyour & Selmi, 2015). The spread of fear to all Eurozone countries increased the demand for Bitcoin (Kang et al., 2019). The introduction of altcoins like Litecoin offered functionality beyond Bitcoin's core function. This expanded the market appeal and attracted investors seeking diversification. Government recognition and legalization of cryptocurrency trading boosted investor confidence, increasing the price growth to 400 percent (Malhotra & Maloo, 2014).

The restrictions imposed by the Chinese government on the crypto exchanges created concerns about a potential crackdown. The trading suspension and bankruptcy filing of Mt.Gox further dampened investor confidence. These events triggered a prolonged plummet in the price of Bitcoin, creating a negative bubble in the market (Chaim & Laurini, 2019).

5.3 Crypto Bubble of 2017

In 2017, there was an increase in the Google search volume for crypto-related terms. The entry of institutional investors like Morgan Stanley, Mastercard, etc, into the crypto space signaled the potential of cryptocurrencies and the acceptance of cryptocurrencies by these institutional investors to the market (Huang et al., 2022). The scope of Web 3.0 demonstrates the impact of this new technology in improving business operation and management efficiency (Ghelani & Kian Hua, 2022). The fundraising mechanism based on issuing new cryptocurrencies called initial coin Offering (ICO) gained popularity among the public and entrepreneurs (Choi, 2022).

However, the boom of the ICO market also invited many fraudulent projects to the market. The investors who failed to do the due diligence on the project became victims of the scam. This created a domino effect in the market, where investors became wary of potential scams, decreasing the initial euphoria related to ICOs (de Andrés et al., 2022). This affected the price of Bitcoin and altcoins significantly. Along with the ICO scams, Facebook's banning of advertisements relating to cryptocurrencies added a blow to the boom (Burnie & Yilmaz, 2019).

5.4 Crypto Bubble of 2021

The pandemic, the shift in investor interest toward online assets, and increased institutional adoption were the main drivers of the 2021 bubble. Economic uncertainty created by the pandemic caused investors to seek alternative assets to hedge against inflation and volatility of traditional assets (Y. Jiang et al., 2021; Maitra et al., 2022). With its limited supply and decentralized nature, Bitcoin became an interesting option for investors. Influencers and celebrity endorsements also played a vital role in increasing the money flow into the crypto market. High-profile celebrities and influencers started promoting cryptocurrencies during the pandemic period, amplifying awareness and potential investments, particularly among young demographics (Ullah et al., 2022). This created hype and "fear of missing out" among the fans, leading to more short-term speculative investments rather than a research-based approach (Anaza et al., 2024; J.-N. Wang et al., 2023). The entry of institutional investors like Goldman Sachs, JP Morgan Chase, Fidelity Investments, etc, into the market created an air of credibility in the market (Castillo, 2018; Mason, 2021; Ponciano, 2021). The announcement by PayPal enabling their platform to buy, sell, and hold cryptocurrencies made mainstream adoption quick (Gould & Criscoe, 2020). The sense of innovation behind DeFi also fueled investment in the market (Maouchi et al., 2022). The period witnessed a significant bull run as Bitcoin reached its all-time high of USD 60000. The launch of the first US Bitcoin Exchange-Traded Funds (ETF) further fueled the bull run (X. Wang & Hui, 2024). However, the crypto market bull run began to wane with the shift in market narratives. Regulatory scrutiny increased, and internal and external market events created a wave of sell-offs, ultimately pushing the market into a long crypto winter.

The broader adoption of crypto trading increased crypto mining activities. Crypto mining is the process of verifying and adding transactions to the blockchain by solving computational problems. The high energy consumption relating to mining created concerns regarding the sustainability of the crypto market, see figure 3 (J. Li et al., 2019; Tayebi & Amini, 2024). A series of money laundering and illicit activities leveraging the anonymity and intractability of cryptocurrencies invited intense regulatory scrutiny from the government and policymakers (Dupuis & Gleason, 2020). Due to the borderless nature of cryptocurrencies, cross-border transactions of illegal money to less stringent jurisdictions further complicated the regulatory efforts. The uncertainty surrounding potential regulations made some investors take a cautionary approach, which dampened the overall market sentiment (Yen & Cheng, 2021).

Macroeconomic factors also played a role in this bubble bust. As a measure to combat inflation, governments raised interest rates. Cryptocurrencies, perceived as a riskier asset class, became less attractive to investors seeking a stable return. The rise in inflation also created uncertainty and risk aversion in the market (Conlon et al., 2021). This created a general sell-off in the market, impacting cryptocurrencies as well. Along with these external factors, internal factors also contributed to this bubble pop. Elon Musk's tweet criticizing the environmental impact of Bitcoin and the suspension of Tesla purchases using Bitcoin triggered a significant price drop, creating a domino effect in the cryptocurrency market (Ante, 2023a). The temporary fluctuation of Tether, a stable coin pegged against the US dollar, from the value of $1 also created concerns regarding stability and de-pegging (Grobys & Huynh, 2022). This further eroded investor confidence in the broader crypto market.

The complexity of some DeFi protocols and the risk associated with yield farming exposed investors to potential loss when the market corrected (Xu & Feng, 2023). The decline in the DeFi's total value locked (TVL) reflected this loss of confidence. The hype and celebrity endorsement created an unsustainable buying spree, pushing young investors to the market without fully understanding the risks (Ullah et al., 2022). Even though the entry of institutional investors in the market contributed to the bubble rise, some investors focused on short-term strategies for quick profits rather than long-term investment (KPMG, 2022). This contributed to the volatility during the pop.

The combination of regulatory pressure, internal market dynamics, and external personal influence created a perfect storm to pop the 2021 bubble. While the market showed signs of recovery, these bubbles act as a cautionary tale for investors to understand the market connectedness and the need for thorough market research.

Figure 3. Amount of carbon emission from data centers and crypto

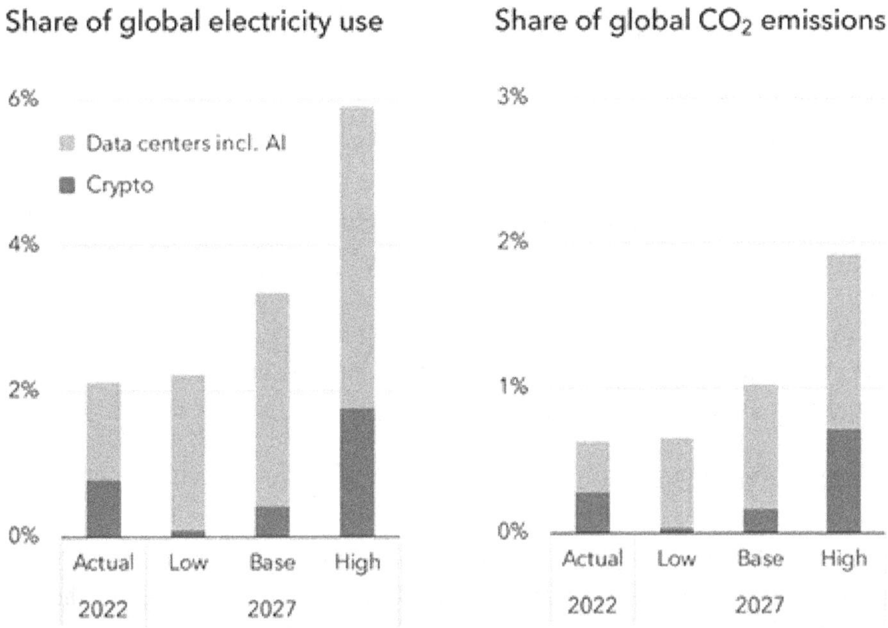

(Hebous & Vernon-Lin, 2024)

6. THE MARKET IN TRANSITION: VOLATILITY AND REGULATORY RESPONSE

The crypto market is often characterized by its volatile evolution and continues to navigate through a period of transition. As the market matures, governments around the world are grappling to strike a balance between fostering innovation and mitigating risk through effective regulation to enable stability and broader adoption. Therefore, this section delves into two aspects of this ongoing transition: the inherent volatility of cryptocurrencies and the regulatory response of the governments.

6.1 Understanding the Fluctuations

Cryptocurrencies are inherently volatile, meaning the price of cryptocurrencies can fluctuate drastically within a short period of time. Several factors can trigger this price swing. One of the key factors is the demand and supply dynamics. Most cryptocurrencies, especially Bitcoin, have a limited supply (Marthinsen & Gordon, 2022b; Meynkhard, 2019). This limited supply contrasts with the ever-changing demand of the market. When demand outpaces the supply, the price will rise and vice versa. As no regulatory mechanism or market force adjusts these sudden changes, the price fluctuates with small changes in the market demand (Marthinsen & Gordon, 2022b; Meynkhard, 2019).

For instance, in 2020, there was an increase in demand for Bitcoin by institutional investors due to the Bitcoin halving. This created a wave of increase in investor confidence as major companies like Tesla and MicroStrategy entered the market (Shen, 2024). This led to a supply crunch in the market, pushing the price of Bitcoin to 69000 USD in November 2021. However, the price rise was not sustainable. When the initial frenzy settled, profit-taking set in, and the news of China banning crypto mining reached the market; the price crashed (Chen & Liu, 2022). This illustrates how the price is sensitive to a minor shift in the demand-supply balance.

6.1.1 News and Events

News and events also play a significant role in the price fluctuation. Positive news and announcements can trigger a surge in investor confidence, like the news about the entry of institutional investors into the market. Likewise, negative news can create fear and panic in the market, like the news about the mining crackdown. Unlike traditional asset markets, the crypto market is highly sensitive to these news and events. A small shift can create large fluctuations in the market (Yao et al., 2024).

For instance, Dogecoin, a meme-based cryptocurrency, gained popularity in early 2001 with the hype in online communities like Reddit. During this period, Elon Musk created a series of tweets regarding Dogecoin (Vasishth et al., 2023). One tweet just read “Doge”. However, these light-hearted tweets created a huge wave of interest among retail investors, fueling a dramatic price surge. When the tweet dominance subsided, Doge's price dropped significantly, highlighting the news-driven sentiment shift, especially for coins that lack strong fundamentals (Vasishth et al., 2023).

The potential manipulation concerns of the market by coordinated groups or sharks exist due to the infancy stage of the market. These groups attempt to artificially inflate or deflate the price according to their needs by leveraging the lack of established safeguards in the market (Lund, 2022). The group may launch a buying spree to inflate the price and then quickly sell the holding for a significant profit. This leaves other investors holding the bag when the price correction occurs.

For instance, Avraham Eisenberg exploited the vulnerability of the Mango platform, a decentralized exchange, to inflate the price of MNGO contracts (Scharfman, 2024). He leveraged his position by buying and selling various cryptocurrencies at an inflated price to himself, creating an illusion of high demand. This attracted other investors to the market. Once the price reached his desired level. Eisenberg sold his holding, earning him a profit of a hundred million USD, leaving the market in a huge crash (Scharfman, 2024).

The mango market exploitation is a real example of how people can exploit the vulnerabilities in the crypto market. This calls for robust security measures and clearer regulations, along with the spread of market education.

6.2 Navigating the Regulatory Maze

Unlike traditional assets, cryptocurrencies operate in a complex landscape. The decentralized nature and the rapid pace of innovation make it difficult for governments to keep up with the regulatory regime. This section delves into the challenges and evolving regulatory approaches the government takes to navigate this regulatory maze.

6.2.1 Challenges

The very nature of cryptocurrencies poses a regulatory challenge to the government. The decentralization and borderless nature make transactions difficult to trace and control. International coordination and collaboration from the governments are required to regulate the crypto space that transcends geographical boundaries (Banerjee, 2020).

One of the instances that highlights this challenge is the Hydra market takedown. Hydra market is a notorious site selling illegal goods using cryptocurrencies like Bitcoin and Monero. The transactions using cryptocurrencies made it challenging for the government to track or take control of the transactions (Horton-Eddison et al., 2021; Scharfman, 2022). The takedown of the market called for coordination between the law enforcement agencies of the USA, Germany, and other countries. This highlights the need for international collaborations along with the need to develop regulations for cross-border transactions to regulate the crypto space effectively.

Another significant hurdle governments face is the pace of innovation in the crypto space. The regulatory frameworks struggle to keep up with the constant evolution of crypto products, services, and DeFi applications. The crypto space has evolved and shifted significantly by the time regulations are framed and implemented (Ducas & Wilner, 2017).

The rise of the play-to-earn game exemplifies the challenges of regulatory lag in the crypto space. The play-to-earn (P2E) game became a major trend in the crypto market in 2021. These games blurred the line between gaming and finance by allowing the players to earn cryptocurrencies by playing games. This caught regulators by surprise, as there are no established rules for these P2E games (Delfabbro & King, 2023). Uncertain classification and consumer protection were the main challenges faced by the government. The regulators struggled to classify the P2E games and their in-game tokens. Additionally, concern regarding the exploitation and addiction of the game, particularly for young audiences, called for consumer protection measures. However, the lack of established regulations made it difficult to hold the developers responsible. The lack of clear tax guidance also added to the uncertainty for both the players and the industry (McCaffrey, 2019). The regulatory response to this P2E game is an ongoing process. Some governments adopted a wait-and-see approach before implementing regulations. Some adopted a selective scrutiny approach, such as investigating games suspected of gambling and other deceptive practices. Some forward-thinking governments are developing frameworks tailored for P2E games, like rules for in-token classification, compliance with anti-money laundering, and introducing new tax classifications for game players (Packin, 2024).

6.2.2 Regulatory Measures

Despite these hurdles, governments actively explore ways to regulate the crypto market. These approaches vary according to the priorities of the government (Novak, 2019). Governments that are wary of consumer protection and illicit activities are taking a cautious stance on the regulations. They focus on stricter KYC, anti-money laundering compliance, or limiting trading activities. China, India, South Korea, and Russia are examples of countries that had taken a cautious approach to mitigate risk before embracing the opportunities associated with cryptocurrencies (De Araujo Consolino & Pedrosa-Garcia, 2018). On the other hand, governments that recognize the growth potential explore ways to foster innovation while mitigating risks through regulations. This involves creating a 'regulatory sandbox,' where startups test new crypto products in a controlled environment. Additionally, these governments establish clear registration and licensing requirements for crypto exchanges and other businesses to create a degree of legitimacy and transparency in the market. Singapore, UAE, Switzerland, and the USA are some countries that acknowledged the potential of cryptocurrencies while taking measures to mitigate the risk(Reshef Kera, 2020).

In conclusion, navigating the regulatory maze is a complex and ongoing process in the crypto space. The main challenge the government faces is to strike a balance between fostering innovation, consumer protection, and the development of a regulatory framework adaptable enough for future developments. Governments are constantly adapting their approaches in response to this evolving crypto landscape.

7. PRACTICAL IMPLICATIONS OF CRYPTOCURRENCY ADOPTION:

As cryptocurrencies continue to evolve, their role in economic stability, financial inclusion, and institutional adoption becomes increasingly relevant. The technological advancement in cryptocurrencies creates economic and financial transformation with implications for individuals, businesses, and government.

Implications for Individuals: The profound impact of cryptocurrency adoption is the scope of financial inclusion. According to the World Bank, approximately 1.4 billion people remain unbanked globally (Demirgüç-Kunt et al., 2022). This population lacks an accessible formal banking system. Creating a stable and developing crypto landscape can benefit these people by allowing them to store and transfer value without relying on traditional banking systems. Furthermore, cryptocurrencies can be a hedge for people in countries witnessing hyperinflation. For instance, citizens in countries like Argentina, Venezuela, and Turkey turned to Bitcoin and stablecoins to preserve their purchasing power (Fast, 2021; Marthinsen & Gordon, 2022a). The decentralized and borderless nature of cryptocurrencies provides them with financial autonomy in the restrictive economic environment.

Implications for Business: Businesses and corporations are integrating the change in customer preference with technological advancements. Corporations like Tesla, Microsoft, and Shopify have introduced cryptocurrency payment options, acknowledging the demand for digital assets as an alternative medium of transaction(Luo & Yu, 2024; Mironeanu et al., 2021). Through this shift, businesses can benefit from low transaction costs, fast-cross border transactions, and enhanced security (Mutambik et al., 2024). Beyond the payment option, blockchain-based smart contacts and self-executing agreements are revolutionizing the industry. For instance, real estate-based smart contracts are eliminating the need for traditional escrow facilities to facilitate secure and automated property transfer (Oza et al., 2024). These contracts eliminate the need for intermediaries in real estate transactions, supply chain management, and intellectual property right enforcement, streamlining processes and reducing costs (Cheng et al., 2023).

Implication for Government: Government and financial institutions are closely monitoring the developments in cryptocurrencies. The global bodies are challenged to balance innovation with consumer protection and financial stability. The illicit transactions and potential risk to monetary policies in the crypto market have led to a diverse regulatory response (Surjandy et al., 2024; Wasiuzzaman & Pg Hj Ahmad, 2025). Some nations like El Salvador embraced Bitcoin as legal tender, while others like China and India imposed restrictions on crypto activities (Parampathu, 2024; Xiong & Luo, 2024). However, one of the most significant trends in financial institutional adoption is the experiments with Central Bank Digital Currencies (CBDC). They act as a state-controlled alternative for decentralized cryptocurrencies. There are several piloting CBDCs, such as Digital Yuan, Digital Euro, and eNaira, to modernize financial infrastructure and maintain monetary sovereignty. CBDCs offer the advantage of digital transactions while retaining government oversight (H. Wang & Gao, 2024).

The adoption of cryptocurrencies is expanding in financial systems, commerce, and governmental policies. For individuals, digital assets offer a decentralized alternative to traditional financial systems, especially in regions with economic instability. Businesses take advantage of the efficiency and innovations associated with the crypto market. Governments grapple with the dual challenge of fostering innovations while ensuring stability. Cryptocurrencies are reshaping the global financial landscape by prompting ongoing debates about their role in the modern economy. The future trajectory of cryptocurrencies will depend on technological advancements, regulatory frameworks, and macroeconomic trends.

8. CONCLUSION

The digital currency landscape has witnessed a significant transformation in the past few decades, from the theoretical concept of a digital payment system to the global phenomenon of cryptocurrencies. The publication of the white paper on Bitcoin was a paradigm shift in digital currency history. The introduction of Bitcoin established a decentralized and permissionless form of digital transaction. The crypto market proliferated through a series of innovations and speculations. The frenzy created due to innovation and speculation led to a series of boom-and-bust cycles in the market, weeding out the cryptocurrencies that lacked fundamentals. This volatility and corrections highlight the inherent risk of the market and the need for a deeper understanding of these market dynamics.

Currently, the crypto market is in a transition in the regulatory landscape. Regulatory authorities around the world are facing a challenge to regulate a decentralized and rapidly evolving space without compromising the autonomy and innovations in the market. The governments are trying to establish a balance between fostering innovation, consumer protection, and the development of an adaptable regulatory framework for all future developments. These regulatory developments are crucial for the sustainable future of the cryptocurrencies.

The study helps policymakers understand various regulatory policies' effects on the financial landscape. Policymakers must balance the potential benefits of cryptocurrencies with the risks associated with volatility, market manipulation, and consumer protection. The study also highlights the importance of thorough market research and risk assessment for investors, as the market is inherently volatile and has the risk of market manipulation. Investors should understand the regulatory landscape of the market and employ diversification across asset classes.

For the researchers, the study provides a foundation for the various aspects of the crypto market. The study provides the breadth of the research activities conducted, and the researchers can delve into an in-depth study of these areas. Further research can focus on the sustainability and scalability of blockchain and cryptocurrencies and the developing regulatory landscape.

As the technologies based on blockchain and cryptocurrencies continue to evolve, it is clear that the journey of cryptocurrencies just commenced. However, whether cryptocurrencies evolve into a mainstream financial instrument or remain a niche asset class is yet to be determined. The development of appropriate regulatory frameworks to boost investor confidence, investor education to understand the complexities of the market, and innovations will play a special role in making cryptocurrencies the mainstream financial instrument. These developments will shape the role of cryptocurrencies in the financial ecosystem of tomorrow.

REFERENCES

Allen, B., & Bryant, S. K. (2019). The market for cryptocurrency: How will it evolve? *Global Economy Journal*, *19*(03), 1950019. Advance online publication. DOI: 10.1142/S2194565919500192

Anaza, N. A., Upadhyaya, B., Bennett, D., & Ruvalcaba, C. (2024). Is it FOMO or is it ME? The influence of personality traits on cryptocurrency consumption. *Psychology and Marketing*, *41*(1), 184–202. DOI: 10.1002/mar.21919

Ante, L. (2023a). How Elon Musk's Twitter activity moves cryptocurrency markets. *Technological Forecasting and Social Change*, *186*, 122112. DOI: 10.1016/j.techfore.2022.122112

Ante, L. (2023b). Non-fungible token (NFT) markets on the Ethereum blockchain: Temporal development, cointegration and interrelations. *Economics of Innovation and New Technology*, *32*(8), 1216–1234. DOI: 10.1080/10438599.2022.2119564

Arslanian, H. (2022). The History of Money. In Arslanian, H. (Ed.), *The Book of Crypto* (pp. 1–43). Springer International Publishing., DOI: 10.1007/978-3-030-97951-5_1

Banerjee, B. (2020). Digital Currencies and Cross-Border Policy Cooperation and Coordination. *G20 Digest, 2*(Special Issue), 23–34. https://ris.org.in/sites/default/files/2021-09/Biswajit Banerjee_2.pdf

Baur, D. G., & Hoang, L. T. (2021). A crypto safe haven against Bitcoin. *Finance Research Letters*, *38*, 101431. DOI: 10.1016/j.frl.2020.101431

Bhaskar, N. D., & Chuen, D. L. K. (2024). Bitcoin Exchanges. In D. B. T.-H. of D. C. (Second E. Lee Kuo Chuen (Ed.), *Handbook of Digital Currency* (pp. 537–551). Elsevier. DOI: 10.1016/B978-0-323-98973-2.00008-3

Bhaskar, N. D., Wanfeng, C., Haili, L., & Chuen, D. L. K. (2024). Bitcoin Mining Technology. In D. B. T.-H. of D. C. (Second E. Lee Kuo Chuen (Ed.), *Handbook of Digital Currency* (pp. 41–64). Elsevier. DOI: 10.1016/B978-0-323-98973-2.00002-2

Bolici, F., & Della Rosa, S. (2016). Mt.Gox Is Dead, Long Live Bitcoin! In Torre, T., Braccini, A. M., & Spinelli, R. (Eds.), *Empowering Organizations: Enabling Platforms and Artefacts* (pp. 285–296). Springer International Publishing., DOI: 10.1007/978-3-319-23784-8_22

Bouoiyour, J., & Selmi, R. (2015). Greece withdraws from Euro and runs on Bitcoin; April Fools Prank or Serious Possibility? *Grexit And Bitcoin*. https://mpra.ub.uni-muenchen.de/65317/

Brasse, A., & Hyun, S. (2023). Cryptocurrency Exchanges and the Future of Cryptoassets. In *The Emerald Handbook on Cryptoassets: Investment Opportunities and Challenges* (pp. 341–353). Emerald Publishing Limited. DOI: 10.1108/978-1-80455-320-620221022

Burnie, A., & Yilmaz, E. (2019). Social media and bitcoin metrics: Which words matter. *Royal Society Open Science*, *6*(10), 191068. DOI: 10.1098/rsos.191068 PMID: 31824713

Cai, J., & Pinto, G. (2024). Altcoins as safe havens for bitcoin investors. *Studies in Economics and Finance, ahead-of-p*(ahead-of-print). DOI: 10.1108/SEF-01-2024-0026

Chaim, P., & Laurini, M. P. (2019). Is Bitcoin a bubble? *Physica A*, *517*, 222–232. DOI: 10.1016/j.physa.2018.11.031

Chaturvedi, V. (2024). *Everything to Know About Bitcoin Pizza Day*. Quartz. https://qz.com/bitcoin-pizza-day-date-origin-history-cryptocurrency-1851481975

Chaum, D. (1983). Blind Signatures for Untraceable Payments. In Chaum, D., Rivest, R. L., & Sherman, A. T. (Eds.), *Advances in Cryptology* (pp. 199–203). Springer US., DOI: 10.1007/978-1-4757-0602-4_18

Chaum, D. (1992). Achieving Electronic Privacy. *Scientific American*, *267*(2), 96–101. https://www.jstor.org/stable/24939181. DOI: 10.1038/scientificamerican0892-96

Chaum, D. (2002). The Beginnings of Digital Money (1992). In *The Money Changers* (p. 4). Routledge., https://www.taylorfrancis.com/chapters/edit/10.4324/9781315071992-50/beginnings-digital-money-1992-david-chaum?context=ubx&refId=913eade8-aad5-4dea-8004-7a3979224feb

Chen, C., & Liu, L. (2022). How effective is China's cryptocurrency trading ban? *Finance Research Letters*, *46*, 102429. DOI: 10.1016/j.frl.2021.102429

Chen, W., Wu, J., Zheng, Z., Chen, C., & Zhou, Y. (2019). Market Manipulation of Bitcoin: Evidence from Mining the Mt. Gox Transaction Network. *IEEE INFOCOM 2019 - IEEE Conference on Computer Communications*, 964–972. DOI: 10.1109/INFOCOM.2019.8737364

Cheng, M., Chong, H.-Y., & Xu, Y. (2023). Blockchain-smart contracts for sustainable project performance: Bibliometric and content analyses. *Environment, Development and Sustainability*, *26*(4), 8159–8182. DOI: 10.1007/s10668-023-03063-w PMID: 37363021

Cheraghali, H., Molnár, P., Storsveen, M., & Veliqi, F. (2024). The impact of cryptocurrency-related cyberattacks on return, volatility, and trading volume of cryptocurrencies and traditional financial assets. *International Review of Financial Analysis*, *95*, 103439. DOI: 10.1016/j.irfa.2024.103439

Cheung, A., Roca, E., & Su, J.-J. (2015). Crypto-currency bubbles: An application of the Phillips–Shi–Yu (2013) methodology on Mt. Gox bitcoin prices. *Applied Economics*, *47*(23), 2348–2358. DOI: 10.1080/00036846.2015.1005827

Choi, T.-M. (2022). Financing Product Development Projects in the Blockchain Era: Initial Coin Offerings Versus Traditional Bank Loans. *IEEE Transactions on Engineering Management*, *69*(6), 3184–3196. DOI: 10.1109/TEM.2020.3032426

Conlon, T., Corbet, S., & McGee, R. J. (2021). Inflation and cryptocurrencies revisited: A time-scale analysis. *Economics Letters*, *206*, 109996. DOI: 10.1016/j.econlet.2021.109996

Corbet, S., Hou, Y. G., Hu, Y., Larkin, C., & Oxley, L. (2020). Any port in a storm: Cryptocurrency safe-havens during the COVID-19 pandemic. *Economics Letters*, *194*, 109377. DOI: 10.1016/j.econlet.2020.109377 PMID: 32834235

Dai, W. (1998). *B-Money*. https://bitcoinstan.io/prehistory/doc/1998_3.pdf

Dai, W. (2008). Bitcoin Whitepaper. In *List, Cryptography Mailing*. https://www.bitcoin.com/satoshi-archive/emails/wei-dai/1/

de Andrés, P., Arroyo, D., Correia, R., & Rezola, A. (2022). Challenges of the market for initial coin offerings. *International Review of Financial Analysis*, *79*, 101966. https://doi.org/https://doi.org/10.1016/j.irfa.2021.101966. DOI: 10.1016/j.irfa.2021.101966

De Araujo Consolino, A., & Pedrosa-Garcia, J. A. (2018). *Regulation of cryptocurrencies : evidence from Asia and the Pacific*. https://hdl.handle.net/20.500.12870/1212

del Castillo, M. (2018). *Fidelity Launches Institutional Platform For Bitcoin And Ethereum*. Forbes. https://www.forbes.com/sites/michaeldelcastillo/2018/10/15/fidelity-launches-institutional-platform-for-bitcoin-and-ethereum/

Delfabbro, P., & King, D. (2023). The evolution of young gambling studies: Digital convergence of gaming, gambling and cryptocurrency technologies. *International Gambling Studies*, *23*(3), 491–504. DOI: 10.1080/14459795.2023.2171469

Demirgüç-Kunt, A., Klapper, L., Singer, D., & Ansar, S. (2022). *The Global Findex Database 2021*. The World Bank. DOI: 10.1596/978-1-4648-1897-4

Ducas, E., & Wilner, A. (2017). The security and financial implications of blockchain technologies: Regulating emerging technologies in Canada. *International Journal (Toronto, Ont.)*, *72*(4), 538–562. DOI: 10.1177/0020702017741909

Dupuis, D., & Gleason, K. (2020). Money laundering with cryptocurrency: Open doors and the regulatory dialectic. *Journal of Financial Crime*, *28*(1), 60–74. DOI: 10.1108/JFC-06-2020-0113

Fast, R. (2021). Cryptocurrencies in hyperinflationary Venezuela. *Risk Governance and Control: Financial Markets and Institutions*, *11*(4), 62–67. DOI: 10.22495/rgcv11i4p5

Ghelani, D., & Kian Hua, T. (2022). Conceptual Framework of Web 3.0 and Impact on Marketing, Artificial Intelligence, and Blockchain. *International Journal of Information and Communication Sciences*, *7*(1), 10. DOI: 10.11648/j.ijics.20220701.12

Gomzin, S. (2022). How Monero Works. In Gomzin, S. (Ed.), *Crypto Basics* (pp. 119–137). Apress., DOI: 10.1007/978-1-4842-8321-9_6

Gould, A., & Criscoe, J. (2020). *PayPal Launches New Service Enabling Users to Buy, Hold and Sell Cryptocurrency*. Paypal Newsroom. https://newsroom.paypal-corp.com/2020-10-21-PayPal-Launches-New-Service-Enabling-Users-to-Buy-Hold-and-Sell-Cryptocurrency

Grobys, K., & Huynh, T. L. D. (2022). When Tether says "JUMP!" Bitcoin asks "How low?". *Finance Research Letters*, *47*, 102644. DOI: 10.1016/j.frl.2021.102644

He, C., Li, Y., Wang, T., & Shah, S. A. (2024). Is cryptocurrency a hedging tool during economic policy uncertainty? An empirical investigation. *Humanities & Social Sciences Communications*, *11*(1), 1–10. DOI: 10.1057/s41599-023-02532-x

Hebous, S., & Vernon-Lin, N. (2024). *Carbon Emissions from AI and Crypto Are Surging and Tax Policy Can Help*. International Monetary Fund. https://www.imf.org/en/Blogs/Articles/2024/08/15/carbon-emissions-from-ai-and-crypto-are-surging-and-tax-policy-can-help

Horton-Eddison, M., Shortis, P., Aldridge, J., & Caudevilla, F. (2021). Drug cryptomarkets in the 2020s: Policy, enforcement, harm, and resilience. *Global Drug Policy Observatory*. https://orca.cardiff.ac.uk/id/eprint/167557/1/Drug-Crypto-Markets_FINAL_June_2021.pdf

Hossain, M. S. (2021). What do we know about cryptocurrency? Past, present, future. *China Finance Review International*, *11*(4), 552–572. DOI: 10.1108/CFRI-03-2020-0026

Huang, X., Lin, J., & Wang, P. (2022). Are institutional investors marching into the crypto market? *Economics Letters*, *220*, 110856. DOI: 10.1016/j.econlet.2022.110856

Jia, A., Fan, M., Xu, X., Cui, D., Wei, W., Yang, Z., Ye, K., & Liu, T. (2021). *From Innovations to Prospects: What Is Hidden Behind Cryptocurrencies?* DOI: 10.1145/3379597.3387439

Jiang, S., Li, Y., Lu, Q., Wang, S., & Wei, Y. (2022). Volatility communicator or receiver? Investigating volatility spillover mechanisms among Bitcoin and other financial markets. *Research in International Business and Finance*, *59*, 101543. DOI: 10.1016/j.ribaf.2021.101543

Jiang, Y., Wu, L., Tian, G., & Nie, H. (2021). Do cryptocurrencies hedge against EPU and the equity market volatility during COVID-19? – New evidence from quantile coherency analysis. *Journal of International Financial Markets, Institutions and Money*, *72*, 101324. DOI: 10.1016/j.intfin.2021.101324

Kang, S. H., McIver, R. P., & Hernandez, J. A. (2019). Co-movements between Bitcoin and Gold: A wavelet coherence analysis. *Physica A*, *536*, 120888. DOI: 10.1016/j.physa.2019.04.124

Kaur, G., Habibi Lashkari, A., Sharafaldin, I., & Habibi Lashkari, Z. (2023). Introduction to Smart Contracts and DeFi. In Kaur, G., Habibi Lashkari, A., Sharafaldin, I., & Habibi Lashkari, Z. (Eds.), *Understanding Cybersecurity Management in Decentralized Finance. Financial Innovation and Technology* (pp. 29–56). Springer International Publishing., DOI: 10.1007/978-3-031-23340-1_2

Kavaloski, M. (2024). A Global Crypto Code of Conduct: Crafting and Internationally Centralized Regulatory Body for a Decentralized Asset. *Vand. J. Transnat'l L.*, *57*, 301.

Khaniki, M. A. L., & Manthouri, M. (2024). Enhancing Price Prediction in Cryptocurrency Using Transformer Neural Network and Technical Indicators. *ArXiv Preprint ArXiv:2403.03606*.

Komalavalli, C., Saxena, D., & Laroiya, C. (2020). Overview of Blockchain Technology Concepts. In S. Krishnan, V. E. Balas, E. G. Julie, Y. H. Robinson, S. Balaji, & R. B. T.-H. of R. on B. T. Kumar (Eds.), *Handbook of Research on Blockchain Technology* (pp. 349–371). Elsevier. DOI: 10.1016/B978-0-12-819816-2.00014-9

Koo, E., & Kim, G. (2024). Centralized decomposition approach in LSTM for Bitcoin price prediction. *Expert Systems with Applications*, *237*, 121401. DOI: 10.1016/j.eswa.2023.121401

KPMG. (2022). *Crypto: rise in institutional interest - Rapid loss of value is not isolated.* KPMG. https://kpmg.com/xx/en/home/insights/2022/12/crypto-rise-in-institutional-interest.html

Law, L., Sabett, S., & Solinas, J. (1997). How to make mint: The cryptography of anonymous electronic cash. *The American University Law Review*, *46*(4), 1131–1162. https://heinonline.org/HOL/P?h=hein.journals/aulr46&i=1145

Lee, S. C. (2022). Magical capitalism, gambler subjects: South Korea's bitcoin investment frenzy. *Cultural Studies*, *36*(1), 96–119. DOI: 10.1080/09502386.2020.1788620

Li, J., Li, N., Peng, J., Cui, H., & Wu, Z. (2019). Energy consumption of cryptocurrency mining: A study of electricity consumption in mining cryptocurrencies. *Energy*, *168*, 160–168. DOI: 10.1016/j.energy.2018.11.046

Li, Z.-Z., Tao, R., Su, C.-W., & Lobonţ, O.-R. (2019). Does Bitcoin bubble burst? *Quality & Quantity*, *53*(1), 91–105. DOI: 10.1007/s11135-018-0728-3

Lund, B. (2022). The Cryptocurrency "Pump-and-Dump." In *Handbook of Research on Cyber Law, Data Protection, and Privacy* (pp. 202–211). IGI Global. DOI: 10.4018/978-1-7998-8641-9.ch012

Luo, M., & Yu, S. (2024). Financial reporting for cryptocurrency. *Review of Accounting Studies*, *29*(2), 1707–1740. DOI: 10.1007/s11142-022-09741-w

Maitra, D., Ur Rehman, M., Ranjan Dash, S., & Hoon Kang, S. (2022). Do cryptocurrencies provide better hedging? Evidence from major equity markets during COVID-19 pandemic. *The North American Journal of Economics and Finance*, *62*, 101776. DOI: 10.1016/j.najef.2022.101776

Makridis, C. A., Fröwis, M., Sridhar, K., & Böhme, R. (2023). The rise of decentralized cryptocurrency exchanges: Evaluating the role of airdrops and governance tokens. *Journal of Corporate Finance*, *79*, 102358. DOI: 10.1016/j.jcorpfin.2023.102358

Malhotra, A., & Maloo, M. (2014). Bitcoin is it a Bubble? Evidence from Unit Root Tests. SSRN *Electronic Journal*. DOI: 10.2139/ssrn.2476378

Maouchi, Y., Charfeddine, L., & El Montasser, G. (2022). Understanding digital bubbles amidst the COVID-19 pandemic: Evidence from DeFi and NFTs. *Finance Research Letters*, *47*, 102584. Advance online publication. DOI: 10.1016/j.frl.2021.102584 PMID: 36406743

Marthinsen, J. E., & Gordon, S. R. (2022a). Hyperinflation, Optimal Currency Scopes, and a Cryptocurrency Alternative to Dollarization. *The Quarterly Review of Economics and Finance*, *85*, 161–173. DOI: 10.1016/j.qref.2020.12.007

Marthinsen, J. E., & Gordon, S. R. (2022b). The price and cost of bitcoin. *The Quarterly Review of Economics and Finance*, *85*, 280–288. DOI: 10.1016/j.qref.2022.04.003

Mason, E. (2021). *Bitcoin About-Face: JPMorgan Opens Crypto Trading To All Clients*. Forbes. https://www.forbes.com/sites/emilymason/2021/07/22/bitcoin-about-face-jpmorgan-opens-crypto-trading-to-all-clients/

McCaffrey, M. (2019). The macro problem of microtransactions: The self-regulatory challenges of video game loot boxes. *Business Horizons*, *62*(4), 483–495. DOI: 10.1016/j.bushor.2019.03.001

McSweeney, M. (2024). *Bitcoin's 'genesis' block of transaction was created 15 years ago*. Blockworks.Co. https://blockworks.co/news/bitcoin-genesis-block-fifteeth-birthday

Metcalfe, W. (2020). Ethereum, Smart Contracts, DApps. In *Blockchain and Crypt Currency* (pp. 77–93). DOI: 10.1007/978-981-15-3376-1_5

Meynkhard, A. (2019). Fair market value of bitcoin: Halving effect. *Investment Management and Financial Innovations*, *16*(4), 72–85. DOI: 10.21511/imfi.16(4).2019.07

Milunovich, G. (2018). Cryptocurrencies, Mainstream Asset Classes and Risk Factors: A Study of Connectedness. *The Australian Economic Review*, *51*(4), 551–563. DOI: 10.1111/1467-8462.12303

Mironeanu, A., Irimia, B., Săndulescu, V., & Teodoroiu, C. (2021). The impact of Tesla's bitcoin investment and its plans to accept it as payment method on the evolution of bitcoin. *Proceedings of the International Conference on Business Excellence, 15*(1), 58–74. DOI: 10.2478/picbe-2021-0007

Morton, D. T. (2020). The future of cryptocurrency: An unregulated instrument in an increasingly regulated global economy. *Loy. U. Chi. Int'l L. Rev.*, *16*, 129.

Mutambik, I., Almuqrin, A., Zhang, J. Z., & Alharbi, Z. H. (2024). Trust in Cryptocurrency Payments. *Journal of Organizational and End User Computing*, *36*(1), 1–36. DOI: 10.4018/JOEUC.353910

Nakamoto, S. (2008). *Bitcoin: A peer-to-peer electronic cash system*. Decentralized Business Review.

Narayanan, A., & Clark, J. (2017). Bitcoin's academic pedigree. *Communications of the ACM*, *60*(12), 36–45. DOI: 10.1145/3132259

Novak, M. (2019). Crypto-friendliness: Understanding blockchain public policy. *Journal of Entrepreneurship and Public Policy*, *9*(2), 165–184. DOI: 10.1108/JEPP-03-2019-0014

Osterland, T., & Rose, T. (2020). Model checking smart contracts for Ethereum. *Pervasive and Mobile Computing*, *63*, 101129. DOI: 10.1016/j.pmcj.2020.101129

Oza, V. J., Nikte, A., Bhanushali, V., & Rote, U. (2024). Smart Contracts and Tokenization: Revolutionizing Real Estate Transactions with Blockchain Technology. *2024 International Conference on Inventive Computation Technologies (ICICT)*, 1598–1604. DOI: 10.1109/ICICT60155.2024.10544886

Özdemir, O. (2022). Cue the volatility spillover in the cryptocurrency markets during the COVID-19 pandemic: Evidence from DCC-GARCH and wavelet analysis. *Financial Innovation*, *8*(1), 12. DOI: 10.1186/s40854-021-00319-0 PMID: 35132369

Packin, N. G. (2024). The Nexus of Gaming and NFTs: A Deep Dive Into the Future of Digital Interaction. *The Cambridge Handbook on Law and Policy for NFTs (Nizan Geslevich Packin, Ed.), Forthcoming*. https://ssrn.com/abstract=4787912

Parampathu, J. (2024). From securities to currencies: The regulatory consequences of adopting cryptocurrencies as legal tender. *Transnational Legal Theory*, *15*(2), 288–339. DOI: 10.1080/20414005.2024.2366140

Patra, G. R., & Mohanty, M. N. (2023). Price prediction of cryptocurrency using a multi-layer gated recurrent unit network with multi features. *Computational Economics*, *62*(4), 1525–1544. DOI: 10.1007/s10614-022-10310-1

Phiri, A., & Anyikwa, I. (2024). A multiscale analysis of returns and volatility spillovers in cryptocurrency markets: A post-COVID perspective. *The Investment Analysts Journal*, •••, 1–21.

Pointcheval, D., & Stern, J. (1996). *Provably secure blind signature schemes* (K. Kim & T. Matsumoto, Eds.; pp. 252–265). Springer Berlin Heidelberg. DOI: 10.1007/BFb0034852

Ponciano, J. (2021). *Goldman Sachs To Launch Crypto Trading Operation This Month After Bitcoin's Big Surge*. Forbes. https://www.forbes.com/sites/jonathanponciano/2021/03/01/goldman-sachs-to-launch-crypto-trading-operation-this-month-after-bitcoins-big-surge/

Reshef Kera, D. (2020). Sandboxes and Testnets as "Trading Zones" for Blockchain Governance. In Prieto, J., Pinto, A., Das, A. K., & Ferretti, S. (Eds.), *Blockchain and Applications* (pp. 3–12). Springer International Publishing., DOI: 10.1007/978-3-030-52535-4_1

Sambana, B. (2021). Blockchain Technology: Bitcoins, Cryptocurrency and Applications. *ArXiv Preprint ArXiv:2107.07964*. http://arxiv.org/abs/2107.07964

Scharfman, J. (2022). Additional Crypto Operations and Compliance Topics. In Scharfman, J. (Ed.), *Cryptocurrency Compliance and Operations* (pp. 205–221). Springer International Publishing., DOI: 10.1007/978-3-030-88000-2_11

Scharfman, J. (2024). Decentralized Finance (DeFi) Fraud and Hacks: Part 3. In Scharfman, J. (Ed.), *The Cryptocurrency and Digital Asset Fraud Casebook* (Vol. II, pp. 159–191). Springer Nature Switzerland., DOI: 10.1007/978-3-031-60836-0_6

Shen, M. (2024). *MicroStrategy Owns About 1% of All Bitcoin With Latest Purchase*. Bloomberg. https://www.bloomberg.com/news/articles/2024-03-19/microstrategy-owns-about-1-of-all-bitcoin-with-latest-purchase-mstr

Smales, L. A. (2022). Cryptocurrency as an alternative inflation hedge? *Accounting and Finance*.

Staff, C. (2024). *The Early Days of Crypto Exchanges*. Gemini. https://www.gemini.com/cryptopedia/crypto-exchanges-early-mt-gox-hack

Surjandy, F., I. P., & Heykal, M. (2024). The Impact of Government Support Factor on The Use of Cryptocurrency. *2024 International Conference on ICT for Smart Society (ICISS)*, 1–6. DOI: 10.1109/ICISS62896.2024.10751216

Tayebi, S., & Amini, H. (2024). The flip side of the coin: Exploring the environmental and health impacts of proof-of-work cryptocurrency mining. *Environmental Research*, *252*, 118798. DOI: 10.1016/j.envres.2024.118798 PMID: 38555086

Ujjawal, A. (2024). *How does the Blockchain Work?* Geeksforgeeks. https://www.geeksforgeeks.org/how-does-the-blockchain-work/

Ullah, S., Attah-Boakye, R., Adams, K., & Zaefarian, G. (2022). Assessing the influence of celebrity and government endorsements on bitcoin's price volatility. *Journal of Business Research*, *145*, 228–239. DOI: 10.1016/j.jbusres.2022.01.055

Vasishth, S., Sharma, S. K., Nayyar, A. K., & Vijayakuamar, K. (2023). Impact of Elon Musk's tweets on the price of Dogecoin using Sentiment Analysis. *2023 International Conference on Advances in Computing, Communication and Applied Informatics (ACCAI)*, 1–8. DOI: 10.1109/ACCAI58221.2023.10199593

Wang, H., & Gao, S. (2024). The future of the international financial system: The emerging CBDC network and its impact on regulation. *Regulation & Governance, 18*(1), 288–306. DOI: 10.1111/rego.12520

Wang, J.-N., Liu, H.-C., Lee, Y.-H., & Hsu, Y.-T. (2023). FoMO in the Bitcoin market: Revisiting and factors. *The Quarterly Review of Economics and Finance, 89*, 244–253. DOI: 10.1016/j.qref.2023.04.007

Wang, X., & Hui, X. (2024). Price-Volume Relationship in Bitcoin Futures ETF Market: An Information Perspective. *Discrete Dynamics in Nature and Society, 2024*(1), 1–14. DOI: 10.1155/2024/8066742

Wasiuzzaman, S., & Pg Hj Ahmad, A. M. S. L. (2025). Perception towards government advisory, perceived risk and willingness to invest in cryptocurrency. *Journal of Economics and Business, 133*, 106208. DOI: 10.1016/j.jeconbus.2024.106208

Wu, B., & Wu, B. (2023). Bitcoin: The Future of Money. In Wu, B., & Wu, B. (Eds.), *Blockchain for Teens* (pp. 77–134). Apress., DOI: 10.1007/978-1-4842-8808-5_3

Xiong, X., & Luo, J. (2024). In Leonardos, S., Alfieri, E., Knottenbelt, W. J., & Pardalos, P. (Eds.), *Global Trends in Cryptocurrency Regulation: An Overview* (pp. 71–92). Springer Nature Switzerland., DOI: 10.1007/978-3-031-68974-1_4

Xu, J., & Feng, Y. (2023). Reap the Harvest on Blockchain: A Survey of Yield Farming Protocols. *IEEE Transactions on Network and Service Management, 20*(1), 858–869. DOI: 10.1109/TNSM.2022.3222815

Yao, S., Sensoy, A., Nguyen, D. K., & Li, T. (2024). Investor attention and cryptocurrency market liquidity: A double-edged sword. *Annals of Operations Research, 334*(1–3), 815–856. DOI: 10.1007/s10479-022-04915-w

Yen, K.-C., & Cheng, H.-P. (2021). Economic policy uncertainty and cryptocurrency volatility. *Finance Research Letters, 38*, 101428. DOI: 10.1016/j.frl.2020.101428

Zeng, H., & Ahmed, A. D. (2023). Market integration and volatility spillover across major East Asian stock and Bitcoin markets: An empirical assessment. *International Journal of Managerial Finance, 19*(4), 772–802. DOI: 10.1108/IJMF-03-2021-0161

Zheng, Z., Xie, S., Dai, H., Chen, X., & Wang, H. (2017). An Overview of Blockchain Technology: Architecture, Consensus, and Future Trends. *2017 IEEE International Congress on Big Data (BigData Congress)*, 557–564. DOI: 10.1109/BigDataCongress.2017.85

Chapter 3
The Genesis, Mechanics, and Spectrum of "The New Age Gold" Cryptocurrencies

Mitrashis Basu Roy
VIT Bhopal University, India

D. Lakshmi
https://orcid.org/0000-0003-4018-1208
VIT Bhopal University, India

ABSTRACT

This chapter delves into the intricate and the over evolving realm of cryptocurrencies. It explores and explains cryptocurrencies, the history of them - the genesis, the working of them - the mechanics, the reason for their existence, and the types - the spectrum. Starting with an overview of the fundamental concepts, the chapter discusses and defines cryptocurrencies and their features, and the differences with fiat currencies. Then we trace the history of cryptocurrencies, highlighting significant milestones. Further, the chapter analyzes the rationale behind the existence of cryptocurrencies, discussing the use cases of several renowned cryptocurrencies and what decentralization actually brings about, explaining the distinct functionality and practical uses of prominent cryptocurrencies, through in-depth case studies of these currencies. We will also comprehend the fundamental workings of cryptocurrencies, such as consensus mechanisms, mining, etc. Lastly, the chapter explores the future prospects of cryptocurrencies, considering potential trends and challenges.

DOI: 10.4018/979-8-3693-5986-0.ch003

1 INTRODUCTION

1.1 Background

Imagining a world where paper currency and the concept of Dollars, Euros, Rubel, Rupees, etc have become a thing of the past, sounds absurd right? With new-age technology transforming the payment medium to paperless transactions, this world sounds too good to be true for looking into alternatives to fiat currencies. But what if someone says this is possible? And here, 'someone' happens to be unknown to any living being. 'Someone' might be a man or a woman, 'someone' might be a single person or a group of people, but the only known fact is that this someone is/are referred to as Satoshi Nakamoto, the founder of Bitcoin. With the potential to upend established economic structures and even the fundamental nature of money; cryptocurrencies have rapidly become a disruptive force in the financial sector. Presented in a whitepaper named, "Bitcoin: A Peer-to-Peer Electronic Cash System" in 2008 (Nakamoto, 2008), this idea was first introduced by Satoshi where Bitcoin posed to be a decentralized digital currency that leverages cryptographic principles for security and operates independently of any central authority. This happened to be the inception of Blockchain Technology suggesting a Distributed Ledger Technology architecture (El Ioini & Pahl, 2018), which paved the way for thousands of alternative cryptocurrencies, collectively known as altcoins, each aiming to enhance or differentiate the features introduced by Bitcoin (Soltani et al., 2022).

Cryptocurrency, at its core, is a virtual currency that uses cryptography to secure its transactions, making it nearly impossible to double-spend or counterfeit. Fueled by blockchain technology, cryptocurrencies enjoy their salient feature of decentralization. Blockchain architecture follows a distributed ledger methodology to track all the transactions over a network of computers, assuring transparency and immutability (El Ioini & Pahl, 2018). These peer-to-peer transactions allow us to eliminate the so-called 'middlemen' like the present financial institutions. Although cryptocurrencies promise to provide unrivaled financial sovereignty, typically lower transaction costs, and at the same time be of minimum risk, their unprecedented growth has spurred discussions about their acceptability, applications, potential advantages, and disadvantages. Some major downsides of cryptocurrency include ambiguity in regulations, market volatility, and the possibility of misuse during criminal operations. Despite these hurdles, driven by a desire for innovation and inclusivity, the graph of cryptocurrencies in 2024 is on the rise, or, as they say, "to the moon!"

1.2 Scope of Study

With a focus on their definition, operation('Mechanics'), history (Genesis'), and potential implications('Spectrum'), this chapter offers a thorough introduction to cryptocurrencies. We describe cryptocurrency, examine its salient features, and chart its development from Bitcoin to altcoins. We also look at why they were developed, discussing the drawbacks of conventional financial systems as well as their potential to democratize finance and lower transaction costs. Furthermore, we clarify the mechanics of cryptocurrencies: How do they work? What's the relation between cryptocurrencies and blockchain technology? Consensus Mechanisms? We answer each of them, using case studies of popular cryptocurrencies such as Ethereum, Bitcoin, and others.

2 UNDERSTANDING CRYPTOCURRENCIES AND ITS VIVID SPECTRUM

2.1 Defining Cryptocurrencies in a Nutshell

While explaining to a 5-year-old, cryptocurrency can be defined as digital magic money that they can spend on the internet, just like how they use paper currency or coins to buy their favorite snacks and toys. But I believe you are no five-year-old, so for you, cryptocurrencies can be termed as cryptic and digital stores of value (Bakhtiar, T. *et al.*, 2023) that leverage cryptographic techniques to provide secure transactions, cap the creation of units, and verify the credibility of any transfer of assets, like NFTs (H¨ardle et al., 2020). Owing to the features of blockchain, cryptocurrencies operate on a decentralized network, unlike traditional fiat currencies, issued and regulated by governments (H. White, 2015).

Their decentralized nature ensures that no central body or entity has control over the network, which otherwise would defeat the purpose of security and transparency. Although the Bitcoin network is the first blockchain and its currency—Bitcoin—often referred to as "digital gold" (A.Uddin et al., 2020)—is the first cryptocurrency to be introduced, thousands of alternative cryptocurrencies (altcoins) now exist, including the likes of Ethereum, Bitcoin Cash, XRP, etc., each with unique features and applications (Alfouderi et al., 2023). Figure 1 shows a visualization of the structure of the Bitcoin blockchain network (https://dailyblockchain.github.io/).

Figure 1. The structure of the bitcoin blockchain network in action

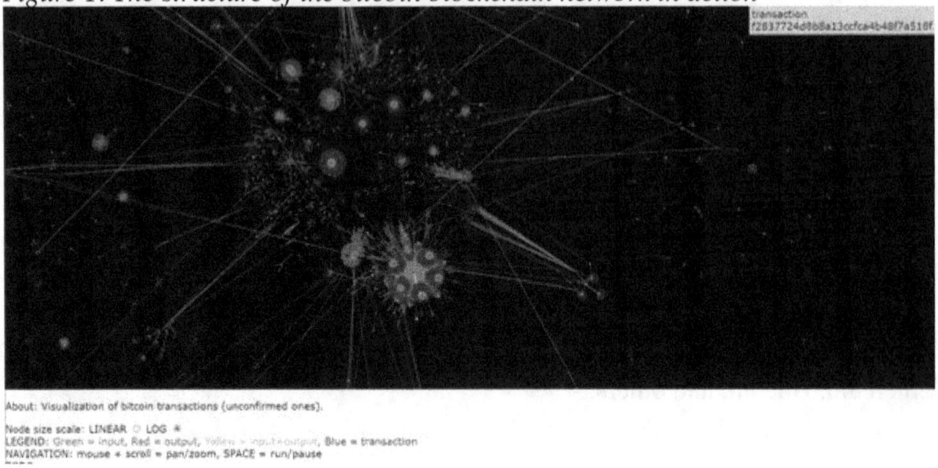

2.2 What Makes a Currency 'Crypto', the Features

The hype around cryptocurrencies is primarily because of how different they are from traditional currencies, making them a unique and appealing form of money-digital money. These features play a crucial role in how cryptocurrencies function. (A. F. M. Shahen Shah *et al.*, 2023)

2.2.1 Decentralization

De-: "away/down from," central: "authority" or "power," and -ization: "the action or process of." The action of being away from any authority or power—decentralization. The word perfectly summarizes its meaning. As aforementioned, cryptocurrencies operate on decentralized networks consisting of computers referred to as nodes. By its very nature, no centralized authority or single entity exercises control over the network, contributing to the other features of cryptocurrencies such as security and transparency (Heo, K., & Yi, S., 2023).

2.2.2 Security

Crypt: the use of cryptography techniques to secure and verify transactions, currency: a store of value. Similar to the word decentralization, cryptocurrency, in its very term, defines security as a prime feature of itself. Cryptocurrencies use advanced cryptographic techniques to secure transactions and control the creation of new units. Each record in the blocks of a blockchain is individually encrypted using a cryptographic technique, Hash. Hashes are a one-way mathematical function that generates a fingerprint of the input, but decrypting the fingerprint to get the original input is almost impossible. Thus, they are very secure. The Bitcoin blockchain uses SHA-256 cryptographic encryption; thus, the Bitcoin cryptocurrency is almost impossible to hack or counterfeit. The following code block and Figure 2 shows how even the slightest change in input can change the 64-bit encrypted text.

Let M be the record of the block which is to be tampered.

H(M) be the hash.

Let **M'** be the tampered record.

H(M)!= H(M')

As **H(M)** is stored in the successor block, the tamepering is easily identified.

Figure 2. Applying SHA256 on a text message

2.2.3 Transparency

All cryptocurrency transactions are recorded and can be tracked on its blockchain. Blockchain is a publicly accessible database/ledger; thus, the transactions are transparent and anyone can independently verify. Just as a strong foundation provides stability and support for a building, transparency in the user experience bolsters confidence and trust. You can see the Ethereum blockchain transactions in action *at*https://etherscan.io/ (Figure 3).

Figure 3. The transactions on the ethereum blockchain

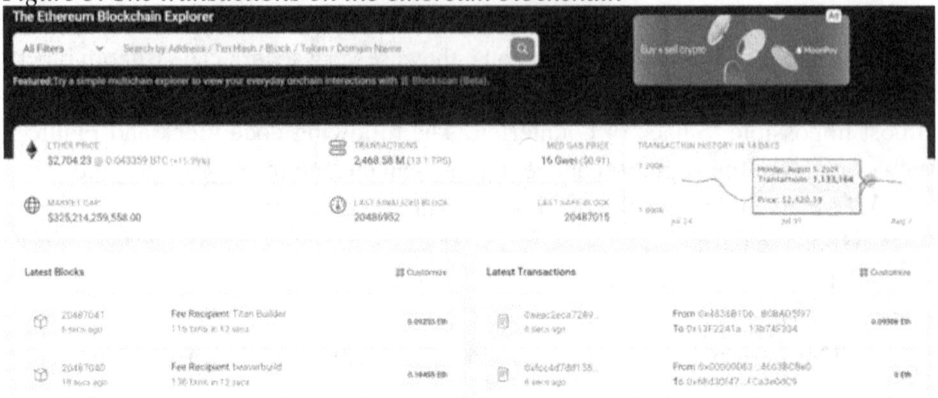

2.2.4 Immutability

A transaction cannot be mutated or deleted after it has been added to the blockchain. You can refer to Figure 2 to check for its immutable nature. This immutability comes with the assurance that the records are permanent and tamper-proof, maintaining the integrity of the financial system built on cryptocurrencies.

2.2.5 Pseudonymity

Cryptocurrency transactions are both visible and pseudonymous, which means that the parties' names are not connected to the transactions themselves. Instead, users may stay private while still using the network by operating through public addresses (Hazar, H. B., 2020). In Figure 3, you can see there is no mention of a name or any credentials that can be directly traced to a person; instead, it has the public addresses of the sender and receiver. Although multiple deanonymization attacks have been proposed, sophisticated cryptographic techniques are being leveraged to battle them (Biryukov & Tikhomirov, 2019).

2.2.6 Divisibility

Notice in Figure 3, that there is a transaction of 0.09306 eth. A txn in decimals? Exactly. Cryptocurrencies can be broken down into incredibly tiny bits, facilitating txn flexibility and divisibility. For example, BTC may be split into eight decimal places of transaction units (satoshis), or one hundred millionth of a BTC.

1 *Bitcoin* (*BTC*) = 100,000,000 *satoshis* (*sat*)

Similarly, ETH is divisible up to 18 decimal places, and the smallest of ETH is called *Wei*.

1 *ETH* = 1,000,000,000,000,000,000 *Wei* (10^18 *Wei*).

1 *Gwei* = 1,000,000 *Wei*.

Because of their ability to be divided, cryptocurrencies may be used for a variety of transaction sizes, from small-scale transfers to larger ones. This ability is one the its most distinguishing features when compared to fiat currencies.

2.3 Cryptocurrency Wallets: Your Digital Vault

Just like you carry around your wallet or purse to keep your money and do transactions out of it, cryptocurrencies too need to be stored in a special kind of wallet—crypto wallets (Suratkar, S. et al., 2020). Any crypto transactions, be they sending or receiving, can only be initiated if they are stored in these digital wallets. A digital wallet or crypto wallet can be defined as a software program that stores the user's public and private keys (Houy, S. et al., 2023). Using these keys the user can transact crypto assets. Additionally, it interacts with various blockchains enabling users to send and receive cryptocurrencies, manage, and monitor the user's crypto holdings. In the later part of this chapter, we will delve deeper into the inner workings of public and private keys and explore how they enable secure and efficient transactions.

Although cryptocurrency wallets can be divided into various types they are mainly classified based on their storage. Figure 4 shows the types of wallets for the same.

Figure 4. Types of wallets based on their storage

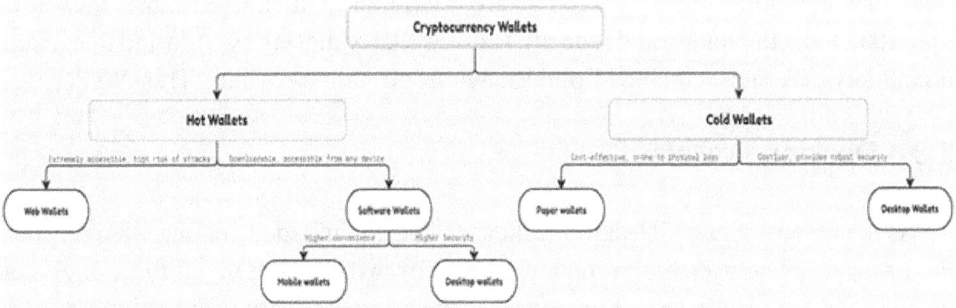

2.3.1 Hot Wallets

Hot wallets are highly accessible in nature and are designed for frequent online transactions. Although it is vulnerable to hacking attempts as it is connected to the internet at all times, they are typically free of cost, easily set up, and highly convenient to use, thus, there is a clear tradeoff between security and comfort. Hot wallets are divided into three types based on how they are installed (refer to *Figure 4*).

2.3.2 Web Wallets

Web wallets or Online wallets run on the cloud, thus, there is no need to download or install any applications on your computer or mobile devices. Mostly downloadable as web extensions, they can be accessed from any computing device via a web browser. There is an immense compromise on security owing to the fact that these wallets are hosted and controlled by third-party companies and you practically have no control over them, but they are the easiest to use and interact with. This issue is being addressed by new-age web wallets that offer the user full authority over the keys and funds. Metamask is the most famous web wallet, and other examples include MyEtherWallet, Brave Wallet, etc.

2.3.3 Mobile Wallets

Just like any other mobile application, mobile wallets can be installed on your smartphones and they operate similarly to their desktop counterparts. By doing so they compromise on certain features but their accessibility and convenience are much more than any other wallet type. They are often more vulnerable to loss, thus, it is important to install additional security features like wallet encryption and to backup private keys. Examples include Coinbase Wallet, Metamask Wallet, Trust Wallet, etc.

2.3.4 Desktop Wallets

As the name suggests, Desktop wallets can be downloaded and installed on your PC or laptop. The user has complete control over the wallet given the wallet and its holdings are locally stored on your system. Some primary offerings of desktop wallets include built-in exchange platforms, multi-chain and multi-currency support, etc. Although they are good to go, the security of these wallets can be compromised depending on the security features of your PC. The funds are vulnerable to security breaches like hacking or malware on your PC. Examples include Exodus, Atomic Wallet, Bitcoin Core, etc.

2.3.5 Cold Wallets

Any wallet that is not directly connected to the internet is a cold wallet. Unlike hot wallets, they are present in physical form and are not free. Being offline, they are much more secure against online threats; thus, they are used for the long-term storage of cryptocurrencies. Cold wallets are majorly divided into two types: Hardware wallets and Paper wallets.

2.3.6 Hardware Wallets

Hardware wallets might just look like your USB device, following the age-old plug-and-play system. They are physical electronic devices that generate public/ private keys through RNG (Random Number Generator) which are then stored in themselves. Unlike software wallets, which are connected to the internet, hardware wallets are designed to remain offline, except when the user connects them to a computer or mobile device to execute transactions. Moreover, hardware wallets are PIN-protected in case of any physical damage or loss. Although hardware wallets are inconvenient and less user-friendly, they are more secure than hot wallets. Ledger and Trezor are famous examples of hardware wallets.

2.3.7 Paper Wallets

As the name suggests, a paper wallet is a printed piece of paper with the crypto address and its private key in the form of QR codes. These codes, like any other QR codes, can be scanned to execute cryptocurrency transactions.

Figure 5. Example of a paper wallet for bitcoin

To create a paper wallet, you can check out https://www.bitaddress.org/. In Figure 5, the Bitcoin address can be used to receive Bitcoin, whereas the corresponding private key is used for spending. They are absolutely safe to use as there are no digital vulnerabilities, however, a significant downside is that paper wallets only store one pair of public/private keys, and hence they can be used only for the whole amount in one transaction. Also, paper wallets are vulnerable to physical damage like fire, water, etc.

2.3.8 Public and Private Keys

To understand how wallets work, one needs to understand the concept of public and private keys. Public keys are shared in public (obviously) to receive cryptocurrency from senders, whereas private keys are used to sign transactions and prove ownership of assets. Private keys are quite sensitive and should not be shared with anyone else, as they can grant others access to your holding. Refer to Figure 5 to understand how public and private keys work.

2.4 Traditional vs Crypto: The Difference Between Currencies

Fiat currencies and cryptocurrencies have paved the way for new-age financial activities in this ever-changing economic landscape (Khan, M. Z. et al., 2020). While traditional currencies like US dollars and Euros have been the cornerstone of global banking for centuries now, given that they are backed by governments and controlled by central banks, cryptocurrencies are products of the 21st century. No central bank or authority exercises power over this decentralized financial instrument. Let's look at several key differences between these two financial instruments in Table 1.

Table 1. Traditional currency vs cryptocurrency

Aspect	Traditional Currencies (Fiat)	Cryptocurrencies
Issuance & Control	Issued and controlled by central banks and governments	Decentralized, issued through mining or staking, with no central authority
Physical Form	Exists in both physical (cash) and digital forms	Entirely digital, no physical form
Regulation	Heavily regulated by government and financial institutions	Largely unregulated, with varying degrees of legal status globally
Transaction Speed	Transactions can be slow, especially cross-border, taking days	Generally faster, especially with certain cryptocurrencies like Ripple (XRP)
Transaction Costs	May involve high fees for cross-border transactions and intermediaries	Typically lower fees, especially for large transactions, as there are no intermediaries
Transparency	Transactions are private and not visible to the public	Transactions are transparent, recorded on a public ledger (blockchain)

continued on following page

Table 1. Continued

Aspect	Traditional Currencies (Fiat)	Cryptocurrencies
Security	Susceptible to counterfeiting, fraud, and theft	Highly secure due to cryptographic techniques, though the risk of hacking remains for digital wallets
Supply & Inflation	Controlled supply, can be increased by central banks, leading to inflation	Fixed or limited supply for most cryptocurrencies, which can act as a hedge against inflation
Accessibility	Widely accepted and used globally, with established infrastructure	Growing acceptance, but still limited in comparison to fiat currencies
Privacy	Users can have anonymity in transactions, though subject to government scrutiny	Pseudonymous, with transactions linked to public keys, not personal identities
Use Cases	Used for everyday transactions, trade, investment, and government reserves	Primarily used for investment, digital transactions, decentralized finance (DeFi), and certain goods/services

This evaluation underscores the fundamental differences among conventional and cryptocurrency-based systems. While conventional currencies are deeply embedded in the global economic device and offer stability and wide attractiveness, cryptocurrencies present a new paradigm with capacity benefits in terms of speed, cost, and decentralization, though additionally, they come with risks associated with law and security.

2.5 The Wide Spectrum of Cryptocurrencies, Its Types

Cryptocurrencies have developed from a single idea—Bitcoin—right into a substantial atmosphere of digital belongings with one-of-a-kind functions, technology, and use instances. This range within the cryptocurrency panorama may be extensively classified into 4 main sorts: Bitcoin, Altcoins, Tokens, and Stablecoins. Each of these types has specific characteristics that contribute to the richness of the cryptocurrency spectrum.

2.5.1 Bitcoin

Referred to as "digital gold', Bitcoin is the first and most famous cryptocurrency ever made. Introduced by Satoshi in 2009, BTC is a decentralized currency that does not require a government or an intermediary. BTC gave birth to the blockchain, which has currently revolutionized the digital ecosystem, sharing the podium with artificial intelligence, cloud computing, etc.

2.5.1.1 Key Features of Bitcoin

Decentralization: Bitcoin operates on a peer-to-peer network where each participating nodes have the ledgers installed in their computing system. The transactions of the BTC blockchain are tested by these nodes (miners) instead of a central authority.

Limited Supply: The total supply of bitcoin is capped at 21 million cash. This contributes to its limited supply, thus increasing its value over time.

Security: Bitcoin transactions are secured through a method referred to as mining, which entails fixing complex cryptographic puzzles. This procedure ensures the integrity of the blockchain and forestalls double-spending.

Global Acceptance: Bitcoin is extensively used as a form of payment and is often used as a benchmark for other cryptocurrencies.

Even in 2024, the price of BTC is breaking the charts despite its volatile nature. It remains the most valuable cryptocurrency to date and is garnering popularity with each passing date.

2.5.2 Altcoins

Any other cryptocurrency that is not bitcoin is an alternative coin, or "Altcoin." The term encompasses a wide range of digital assets that have been developed either from a fork of famous and durable cryptocurrencies or by developers to address specific issues and set themselves apart. Altcoins vary in their underlying technology, purpose, and market adoption, making the category highly diverse. Although they are different from each other considering their scripting language, consensus mechanism, transaction management, etc, there are certain features that are common for all of them.

- Peer-to-peer network involving a mining process
- Independent blockchain
- Replicate the characteristics of crypto - fungible, divisible, limited supply, etc.

2.5.2.1 Examples

Ethereum: Conceptualized by Vitalik Buterin in November 2013 and launched in July 2015, ethereum is the second-largest cryptocurrency by market capitalization as of today (August 2024). Currently, ethereum follows the PoS consensus protocol (earlier it followed PoW) functioning as a platform that enables developers to build decentralized applications, called DApps, by leveraging smart contracts that can be coded and stored on the blockchain directly.

Table 2. ETH vs BTC

Feature	Ethereum (ETH)	Bitcoin (BTC)
Purpose	Platform for DApps and smart contracts	Digital currency, store of value
Transaction Speed	Faster transactions (~15 seconds per block)	Slower transactions (~10 minutes per block)
Supply	No capped supply	Limited to 21 million coins
Consensus Mechanism	Transitioning from Proof of Work (PoW) to Proof of Stake (PoS)	Proof of Work (PoW)
Development Flexibility	High, with ability to create complex smart contracts	Limited, primarily used for currency transactions

Litecoin: Developed by Charlie Lee in October 2011, Litecoin is the earliest known altcoin. It is one of the few altcoins derived from BTC and the main purpose of litecoin was to improve upon the generation rate of BTC. The average time taken per transaction of LTC is 2.5 minutes whereas it is around 10 minutes for BTC. LTC stands in the top 10 cryptocurrencies by market capitalization.

Table 3. LTC vs BTC

Feature	Litecoin (LTC)	Bitcoin (BTC)
Transaction Speed	~2.5 minutes per block	~10 minutes per block
Supply Limit	84 million coins	21 million coins
Mining Algorithm	Scrypt (more accessible for consumer hardware)	SHA-256
Market Position	Often used for smaller transactions	Primarily used for larger transactions and as a store of value

Ripple: The Ripple blockchain, developed by Ripple Labs, was launched in 2012. Powered by its altcoin XRP the Ripple blockchain is a cross-border digital payment system used mainly as a global payment settlement, asset exchange, and remittance platform. It can seamlessly transfer both cryptocurrencies and fiat currencies, thus, it has found its adaptation in renowned banks and financial institutions. Unlike BTC, XRP is pre-mined with 100 billion XRP coins at its limit. As there is no mining required and the transaction validation hardly takes 5 seconds, the energy consumption and costs are relatively lower than BTC and other Altcoins.

Table 4. XRP vs BTC

Feature	Ripple (XRP)	Bitcoin (BTC)
Purpose	Cross-border payments, financial institution transfers	Decentralized digital currency
Transaction Speed	3-5 seconds per transaction	~10 minutes per transaction
Consensus Mechanism	Ripple Protocol Consensus Algorithm (RPCA)	Proof of Work (PoW)
Decentralization	More centralized, with Ripple Labs playing a significant role	Fully decentralized, no central control

Bitcoin Cash: The first hard fork of the BTC blockchain appeared in August 2017. This hard fork led to the birth of Bitcoin Cash (BCH). The primary goal of this hard fork was to increase the block size limit from 1 MB to 8 MB to address transaction time and scalability issues. The drawback of BCH is that it requires a higher cost to run a full node owning to its increased block size limit. This makes BCH vulnerable to centralization as only a few nodes would be able to afford such a high running cost.

Table 5. BCH vs BTC

Feature	Bitcoin Cash (BCH)	Bitcoin (BTC)
Block Size	8 MB to 32 MB (increased to allow more transactions)	1 MB (initially)
Transaction Speed	Faster due to larger block size	Slower due to smaller block size
Community Support	Strong, but smaller than Bitcoin's community	Largest and most active community in the cryptocurrency space
Use Case	Focus on everyday transactions	Store of value, larger transactions

2.5.3 Tokens

Tokens are a really intriguing type of currency. Unlike cryptocurrencies, they are digital assets built on pre-existing blockchains that perform specific functions within the project ecosystem and are not operational like typical cryptocurrencies (Schwiderowski, J. et al., 2024). Though a token can be used as a payment method within the project ecosystem, its primary purpose is its usage as a utility or asset to give the holder specific rights to participate in the blockchain network. Tokens and their underlying applications benefit from the technology and security of the native blockchain by leveraging their existing mining strength and tamper-proof nature. Unlike cryptocurrencies that need to be built from scratch, tokens are created using standard templates from blockchain platforms like Ethereum. Facilitated by the use of smart contracts, developers widely use smart contracts compliant with ERC20 standards due to their ease of implementation and wide adoption in the Ethereum platform. Tokens are different from cryptocurrencies in the following ways:

Table 6. Cryptocurrencies vs tokens

Aspect	Cryptocurrencies	Tokens
Blockchain	Operate on their own blockchain (e.g., Bitcoin).	Built on existing blockchains (e.g., Ethereum).
Function	Serve as digital currency or store of value.	Represent assets, rights, or access within a platform.
Creation	Created via mining or staking.	Created through smart contracts.
Primary Use	Used for transactions and investment.	Used within specific platforms or ecosystems.
Market Value	Traded on major exchanges with direct value.	Value often tied to platform success or specific use cases.
Regulation	Subject to financial regulations as assets or currencies.	Regulatory framework varies based on token type, like securities for security tokens.
Examples	Bitcoin (BTC), Ethereum (ETH).	Utility tokens, NFTs, stablecoins.

Tokens can further be divided into five main categories:

- Utility Tokens
- Security Tokens
- Governance Tokens
- Non-Fungible Tokens
- Stablecoins

Utility Tokens: Utility tokens offer the holder the right or license to use a product or service in a certain ecosystem. Issued during an ICO, these tokens can, in the future, be redeemed to access the product or services of the company or project. They're not meant as investments, but as tools to interact with the platform's ecosystem, either gaining certain voting rights within the ecosystem or facilitating the funding of the ICOs. These tokens can also encourage certain behaviors or reward users within the ecosystem. Decentralized platforms need utility tokens to work. Take a distributed cloud storage platform like Filecoin as an example. The Filecoin network uses FIL tokens to let users rent storage space in a distributed file storage system. People use the token to pay for and get storage services the network offers.

Security Tokens: Security tokens stand for ownership in outside assets, like companies real estate, or other investments. These tokens resemble traditional securities (such as stocks and bonds) and must follow securities rules. They give rights like dividends, profit-sharing, or voting on how a project is run. People use security tokens to turn ownership of assets into digital form and make them easier to buy and sell on blockchain systems. They can represent pieces of a company, bonds, or even small parts of real estate or valuable art. One of the best examples of security tokens is Harbor (R-token). Harbor turns real estate into tokens. R-tokens stand for parts of commercial properties. These tokens give investors a cut of the profits and value increase from the actual real estate.

Governance Tokens: As the name implies, governance tokens gives the owners exclusive decision-making power in a blockchain project or a decentralized autonomous organization (DAO). When people hold these tokens, they can vote on changes to the protocol how the project develops, and other key issues. Projects mainly use governance tokens to spread out control. People who own tokens can suggest changes, vote on ideas, and make group choices that shape the project's future. Governance tokens give users power by allowing them to have a say in a project's direction. This approach, which resembles democracy, helps to make sure the platform grows in a way that aligns with what the community wants instead of being under the control of just one entity. Uniswap has held its place as a renowned decentralized exchange whose governance token is UNI. People who own UNI can vote on crucial aspects of the protocol including fee structures, upgrades, and allocation of funds.

Non-Fungible Tokens: NFTs are distinctive and unique digital assets that can be owned only by a singular. They reflect exclusive ownership of a specific item present digitally including the likes of digital art, collectibles, in-game items, and other digital content. NFTs are unique and cannot be swapped on an equal basis, as opposed to fungible cryptocurrencies such as Bitcoin or Ethereum. Generated and stored on blockchain, their scarcity, origin, and ownership can be verified at any time. NFTs have transformed the realm of digital ownership, creating new opportunities for artists and content creators to commercialize their work. They also allow collectors to possess and exchange rare digital artifacts that were previously unavailable. Presently some NFT projects have reached tremendous heights in terms of prices, almost selling for millions of dollars, the costliest being $91.8 million! One of the oldest and iconic NFT project is Cryptopunks. There are 10,000 unique pixel art characters in total, highly sought after by collectors. Each CryptoPunk is a unique NFT with its own distinct features (Schaar, L., & Kampakis, S., 2022). This appreciation of NFT projects has contributed to them being looked upon as an alternate investment opportunity.

Stablecoins: The prices of cryptocurrencies are very volatile in nature, making them risky to invest in or trade with. This is where stablecoins come in. The prices of stablecoins are pegged to fiat currencies, like USD, or commodities, like gold (Lyons, R. K., & Viswanath-Natraj, G., 2023). This makes the price, as the name goes, stable. They offer the benefits of cryptocurrencies while being more stable and reliable. They have found their usage in decentralized finance (DeFi) for lending, borrowing, and yield farming, where stability is a must! Some famous examples of stablecoins include USDT and USDC, both of which are pegged to the value of the US dollar.

3 FROM GOLD TO CRYPTOCURRENCY, THE GENESIS OF "NEW AGE GOLD"

3.1 Currency Over the Years

From the very beginning of modern civilization, there has been a known history of money. Although 'money' and 'currency' are used interchangeably, they have different meanings. Money can be defined as a medium of exchange, and a store of value whereas, currency is a physical or tangible representation of money in the form of paper notes or coins. Figure 6 shows the evolution of currency over the years. Let's walk through the history of details.

Figure 6. Flowchart on evolution of currency

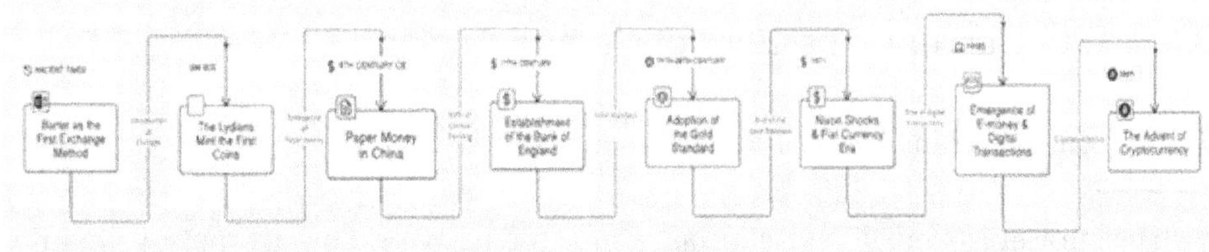

3.1.1 Ancient Times: Barter System

- **Event:** Barter as the First Exchange Method

The earliest form of trade was the barter system, where goods and services were exchanged directly without a standardized currency. This method was simple but inefficient, often leading to the "double coincidence of wants" problem. The barter system is the earliest form of trade known to human beings. In a barter system goods and services are exchanged with each other without any established currency. For example - Person X can trade a commodity with another commodity owned by person Y. This was simple but inefficient in certain ways, often leading to a double coincidence of wants, lack of common measure of value, etc.

3.1.2 ~600 BCE: Introduction of Coinage

- **Event:** The Lydians Mint the First Coins

The first metal coins were minted around 600 BCE in Lydians, in modern-day Turkey. Made using electrum, a naturally occurring alloy of gold and silver, the coins marked the beginning of the standardization of currency, thus simplifying trade and commerce. This then led to the modern-day adaptation of currencies.

3.1.3 9th Century CE: The Emergence of Paper Money

- **Event:** Paper Money in China

The first paper currency was issued in China during the Tang Dynasty, in the 9th century CE. Used initially as promissory notes, this eventually led to the replacement of heavy metal coinage with paper money as a standard medium of exchange. The concept of paper money was introduced in Europe by Marco Polo in the 13th century, which led to the establishment of the first known central bank of the world.

3.1.4 17th Century: The Birth of Central Banking

- **Event:** Establishment of the Bank of England

The current financial landscape as seen in today's world has its roots, primarily, in the vestiges of the first known central bank, the Bank of England, established in 1694. They soon started issuing standardized currency notes, marking the foundation of modern monetary systems. The 18th century saw governments across countries moving towards standardized paper currency.

3.1.5 19th-20th Century: The Gold Standard

- **Event:** Adoption of the Gold Standard

The amount of value held by paper currency and coins was not standardized until the 19th century. In the 19th century, the gold standard was widely adopted linking the value of a currency directly to the value of gold, wherein, for a certain unit of currency, a certain amount of gold could be bought. If there was a rise in the price of gold, the value and purchasing power of currencies would also increase accordingly. This, however, collapsed in the late 20th century after WWII when the US decided not to adhere to this standard.

3.1.6 1971: End of the Gold Standard

- **Event:** Nixon Shocks & Fiat Currency Era

During the reign of the USA's 37th president, President Richard Nixon, the inconvertibility of the US dollar to gold was discarded marking the end of the gold standard. This led to the uprising of fiat currencies, where money is backed by practically nothing but the decree of governments. This increased the reliance on central bank policies and monetary tools to maintain stability in the financial markets. Slowly internet gained prominence over the years which instilled the concept of digital transactions and E-money.

3.1.7 The 1990s: The Digital Currency Precursor

- **Event:** Emergence of E-money & Digital Transactions

With the advent of the internet, people started experiencing a virtual world, bringing about a gradual rise in digital banking and e-money. During this era, companies like PayPal emerged, which eased the rise of e-commerce, enabling hassle-free transactions over the internet. In 1999, mobile banking was introduced by European banks using SMS and hence referred to as SMS banking. Soon the world was gifted with what we now call "digital gold."

3.1.8 2009: The Advent of Cryptocurrency

- **Event:** Launch of Bitcoin

Decentralization, Blockchain, Web3, etc own its roots to an event in 2009, the launch of Bitcoin by Satoshi Nakamoto. This very incident became the cornerstone in challenging and attempting to change the financial institutions as we know it. In the next section, we will discuss the journey of Bitcoin and blockchain technology.

3.2 Bitcoin, the Excellence of Satoshi Nakamoto

Figure 7. Bitcoin and Satoshi Nakamoto's contributions

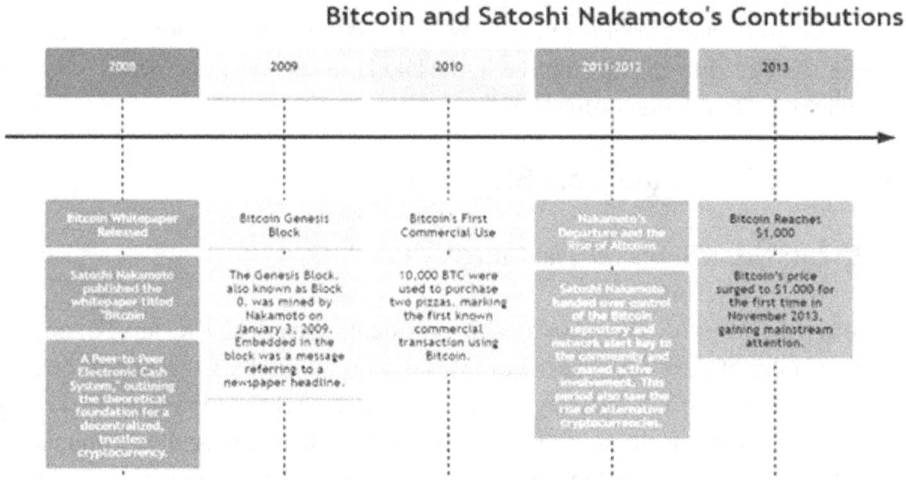

Imagine you are sending or receiving money overseas. You will typically do that through a bank that facilitates this service, and in return for this service, the bank will charge a significant amount of money. Digs deep in your pocket right? Moreover, these banks are controlled by central authorities, and in case of a financial crisis, like the event of 2008, these banks can declare bankruptcy, thus, the depositors will lose all the money that they thought was safe with the banks. Sounds like a robbery? And if you dare expect transparency in transactions where your privacy is maintained, that is not happening because this is no Utopia.

Bitcoin and blockchain technology never promise a Utopia, but they do try to solve the above issues. These were the key requirements that eventually brought about the birth of Bitcoin. Figure 7 encompasses the journey of BTC over the years.

2008 - The whitepaper of the Bitcoin blockchain, titled "Bitcoin: A Peer-to-Peer Electronic Cash System," was released by the anonymous Satoshi Nakamoto. This paper outlines the theoretical adaptation of the BTC decentralized network and its currency.

2009 - Nakamtot mines the first block or block 0 of the BTC blockchain; known as the Genesis Block. The address of this block is - ***0x000000000019d-6689c085ae165831e934ff763ae46a2a6c172b3f1b60a8ce26f***

This marked the official launch of the Bitcoin blockchain on the third of January, 2009. The fun fact is that this block embedded a newspaper article that hinted at the reason behind the BTC's creation.

2010 - Hungry? How about two pizzas? Price? Just 10,000 bitcoins! Sounds crazy? Well, this is exactly what happened in 2010 when a commercial transaction occurred where two pizzas were bought using 10k BTCs. The present-day value of 10k bitcoins is around 600 million dollars!
2011-2012 - This period marked a transition in the blockchain space where Satoshi Nakamoto took a back seat by handing over the BTC repository and network alert key to the community. This period also saw the rise of alternative coins—altcoins, with LTC being the first altcoin created in 2011.
2013 - November 2013, the altcoin hits $1,000 for the first time. This garnered BTC mainstream attention and sparked debates about its potential as a global currency; Digital Gold.

3.3 A Modern-Day Crypto Timeline

Figure 8. A modern-day crypto timeline

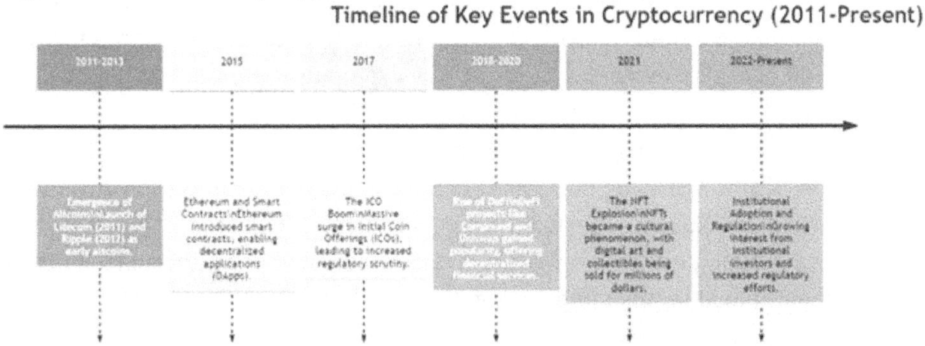

Although BTC and blockchain brought about a revolution in the modern-day financial industry, it was just the beginning. They led to several key events that are illustrated in Figure 8. From altcoins to NFTs and Web3, this sphere is ever evolving. Let's take a look at the modern-day crypto timeline -

2011-13 - As discussed in the earlier sections, this period marked the emergence of LTC in 2011 and XRP in 2012 as early altcoins. Both introduced changes in the consensus mechanism, transaction speed, etc to overcome the shortcomings of BTC and build applications by leveraging the features of blockchain technology. In 2013 Vitalik Buterin conceptualized Ethereum which was later launched in 2015.

2015 - The launch of ETH changed how we look at blockchain today. Earlier, blockchain was used to store transactions but with the advent of ETH the concept of smart contracts was introduced. Smart contracts are self-executing contracts with conditions directly written in the code. This allowed developers to build Decentralized applications (DApps) on the Ethereum blockchain, thus, expanding the use cases of blockchain beyond currency.

2017 - 2017 was the huge year of ICOs, where new cryptocurrency projects raised funds by selling participants and governance tokens (Li, J., & Mann, W., 2018). While it has also spawned some very legitimate projects from that time, it has been marred by scams and highly speculative investments, placing extra pressure on regulators.

2018-20 - Decentralized Finance or DeFi is the term coined for financial services constructed on blockchain technology, sans an intermediary. Among them, projects such as Compound and Uniswap (Lo, Y. C., & Medda, F., 2021) gained huge attention by providing ways for decentralized lending, borrowing, and trading (Saengchote, K., 2023).

2021 - Digital art, music, and other cool collectibles being sold for millions of dollars. NFTs. They became increasingly popular around this time, almost turning into a cultural cult. It has been dramatic in terms of shifting the perception of digital ownership and value. Cryptopunks, Bored Ape Yacht Club, Cryptokitties, etc are a few examples of NFTs that made people rich overnight.

2022-present - Although mass adaptation is yet far-fetched, recent developments suggest a growing interest in blockchain technology and cryptocurrencies from both institutional investors and governments around the world. With new industry regulations coming up, this era is witnessing innovation and regulation have combined in this quite narrow tight walk (Emmert, F., 2023).

4 WHY CRYPTOCURRENCIES EXIST AND HOW THEY SHAKE THINGS UP

This chapter has answered two major queries about cryptocurrencies till now, the spectrum and the genesis. But why do they exist and how do they contribute to a better decentralized ecosystem? Are they even legitimate? What are the use cases of some major cryptocurrencies? These questions and much more will be answered in this section.

4.1 Triumphing Over Traditional Financial Systems

With Bitcoin being the first to challenge the traditional banking system, this space has witnessed much more since its inception. The rise of DeFi, DeX, and DaO have established themselves as alternatives to banks solving issues pertaining to speed, efficiency, transparency, and much more. Cryptocurrencies like XRP allow near-instantaneous transactions, while platforms like Uniswap offer decentralized banking services. This alternative economy is slowly and steadily garnering attention (Aquilina, M. et al., 2024). Table 7 shows an in-depth comparison between traditional and decentralized financial systems, demonstrating how cryptocurrencies address the limitations of the prior.

Table 7. Conventional financial system vs cryptocurrencies

Attribute	Traditional Financial Systems	Cryptocurrencies
Transaction Speed	Can take several days, especially for cross-border transactions.	Near-instantaneous, with some networks processing transactions in seconds.
Transaction Fees	High fees due to multiple intermediaries (banks, clearinghouses, etc.).	Low fees, with many networks charging minimal amounts for transactions.
Accessibility	Requires a bank account and compliance with local regulations.	Accessible to anyone with an internet connection, no need for a bank account.
Transparency	Limited; financial institutions control access to transaction data.	High transparency; transactions are recorded on a public ledger (blockchain).
Security	Centralized systems vulnerable to hacks, fraud, and corruption.	Decentralized systems with cryptographic security make hacking very difficult.
Financial Inclusion	Excludes the unbanked population; difficult access in underbanked regions.	Provides financial services to the unbanked and underbanked globally.
Control	Controlled by central banks and financial institutions.	Controlled by users and decentralized networks, with no single point of control.
Inflation Resistance	Subject to inflation; central banks can print more money.	Often designed with a fixed supply (e.g., Bitcoin) to resist inflation.
Cross-Border Transactions	Complicated by currency exchange rates, regulatory compliance, and fees.	Simplified with borderless, peer-to-peer transactions across the globe.

4.2 Bitcoin: Digital Gold and Store of Value

As has already been previously mentioned in the chapter, BTC has a limited supply of 21 million, just like gold and other precious commodities. A mass adaptation of the BTC blockchain either through using it or investing in it, will, in turn, increase the value of bitcoin over a long period. This makes BTC the perfect equivalent of gold, which has, over the years, been used as a hedge against inflation and economic uncertainty. This deflationary nature of BTC along with the features of blockchain, makes it a lucrative option for both retail and institutional investors.

Bitcoin, being the first cryptocurrency, decides the volatility of the market to a great extent (Asena Deniz, E., & Teker, D., 2020). It serves as a benchmark for the entire crypto market, providing a reliable reference point for investors, traders, and other participants. Certain events like the 2017 Bull and Bear Run, the Covid-19 market crash, etc have greatly influenced the prices of BTC, impacting the whole of crypto markets.

4.2.1 BlackRock ETF Filing (June 2023)

BlackRock, a global investment company, filed for a Bitcoin ETF in June 2023. This news led to a surge in BTC's price from $25,000 to $31,000 within a few days, thus, radiating a positive sentiment in the crypto market. This led to some altcoins experiencing significant gains over that duration. However, the market corrected soon, thus, exhibiting the influence of BTC over crypto markets.

4.2.2 Covid-19 Market Crash (March 2020)

Covid-19 impacted the whole world including crypto markets. During this time the price of BTC dipped significantly within a very short period. This instilled fear among investors which led to panic selling. However, cryptocurrencies soon gained traction and spurred in value dramatically (Sarkodie, S. et al., 2022).

4.2.3 2017 Bull Run and Subsequent Crash

Throughout 2017, BTC rose from around $1,000 to $20,000. This led to a massive influx in the crypto market overall. Altcoins witnessed a massive surge in prices and overall growth. But, with the advent of 2018, the price of BTC dipped by almost 50% which led to a prolonged bull market. (Lahajnar, S., & Rozanec, A., 2020)

4.3 Investing and Trading Cryptocurrencies

'Buy low, sell high.' This is the mantra when it comes to any form of investing or trading. Similar to the stock market, investing and trading in the crypto market is perhaps the easiest and approachable way for us to generate wealth from cryptocurrencies. The principles of investing and trading are different, the prior believes in long-term profits whereas the former believes in short-term profits. There are certain differences between stock markets and crypto markets as elucidated in the Table 8.

Table 8. Stock market vs crypto market

Aspect	Stock Market	Crypto Market
Regulation	Highly regulated	Largely unregulated
Trading Hours	Set hours (e.g., 9:30 AM - 4:00 PM EST)	24/7 trading
Asset Type	Represents ownership in companies	Digital currencies and tokens
Volatility	Generally less volatile	Often highly volatile
Liquidity	Usually high for major stocks	Can vary widely
Market Cap	Larger (tens of trillions USD)	Smaller (around 6-7 trillion USD)
Investor Protection	Strong legal safeguards	Limited protections
Transaction Speed	Usually T+2 (trade date plus two days)	Near-instantaneous
Fundamental Value	Based on company performance	Often speculative
Market Participants	Mostly institutional investors	Mix of retail and institutional

4.3.1 Investing

Investors believe in the narrative that cryptocurrencies are still in their infancy, and it will take time to be accepted in the mainstream. Investors generally study decentralized organizations or the blockchain protocol, their functionalities, etc., depending on which they invest in their tokens or cryptocurrencies, respectively. Investors keep an eye out for potential ICOs, hard forks, and airdrops for investments. They also earn profit from either dividends or coin burns. BTC, ETH, LTC, SOL, etc. are among the most trusted cryptocurrencies that investors are currently betting on.

4.3.2 Trading

Unlike investing, trading is a short-term investment, where the frequency can vary from a very few seconds/minutes to a couple of weeks. Traders, typically with a higher risk appetite, do not ride on the intrinsic value of their assets but on the potential for percentage gains. They base their decisions on analyzing hourly price movements as well as historical price movements. Given the volatility of crypto markets, traders stand a chance to make or break huge profits. They too capitalize on airdrops, hard forks, and ICOs for immediate profits. The reason for the upsurge in the number of pump-and-dump schemes and meme coins can be traced back to the trading culture in cryptocurrencies. Examples include Dogecoin (Nani, A., 2022), Shiba Inu, PEPE, etc. These projects have no intrinsic value but are often traded in the market.

4.4 Sustaining the Ecosystem

Blockchain, as a technology, requires an honest and engaged community to ensure sustainable and sturdy growth in the ecosystem. In 2024, this ecosystem developed from cryptographic geeks talking about how awesome blockchain is to national and international hackathons where thousands of developers, users, and enthusiasts participate, enriching the community. This has led to a transition from Web 2 to Web 3 for many projects. The ecosystem also requires sustainable growth to ensure the safety of blockchains by providing tolerance from hacking techniques like 51% attacks, Byzantine fault attacks, etc. The different participants that directly or indirectly constitute the blockchain ecosystem are illustrated in Figure 9.

Figure 9. The participants of the blockchain ecosystem

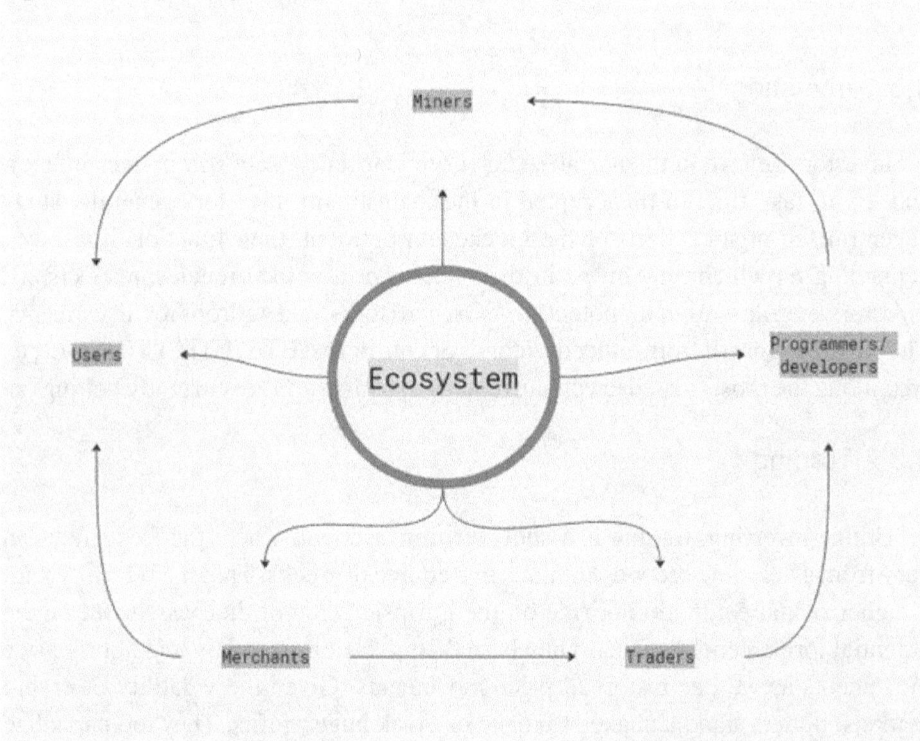

1) ***Programmers/Developers*** - Satoshi Nakamoto, Vitalik Buterin, and Charlie Lee are all developers, responsible for the creation of state-of-the-art blockchains. Programmers or developers are the foremost participants in a blockchain ecosystem where they are responsible for either developing the blockchain, like

determining the consensus mechanism, architecture, and interfaces, or developing DApps on the blockchain by leveraging smart contracts that can directly run on the blockchain. They play the role of an X-factor in developing, deploying, monitoring, and maintaining the blockchain as per requirements.

2) ***Miners*** - Now that a blockchain with a certain consensus mechanism has been built, someone needs to keep the chain running by validating and recording the transactions on the blockchain. This is exactly what the miners (in the case of PoW consensus) or forgers (in the case of PoS consensus) do. They contribute their effort and computing power to solve a cryptographic problem to validate and add transactions in a block. Based on the consensus mechanism, the miner who can mine the specific block is either pre-determined or the miners compete for the chance to mine a block. They are rewarded with either block rewards or gas fees charged on transactions. This contributes to the addition of new cryptocurrencies in the ecosystem which gradually keeps the ecosystem running.
3) ***Users*** - A blockchain user is the end-user of the blockchain protocol or the DApp. The applications are built keeping these group of participants in mind. A large user base ensures the security of the blockchain they are interacting with. For example, PancakeSwap is a renowned DeX where the end user can stake crypto to participate in governance, earn passive income through yield farming, provide liquidity to facilitate trades, etc. The end-user greatly benefits by interacting with this DeX, thus, the ecosystem around it grows stronger and more reliable.
4) ***Merchants*** - Merchants include business entities that accept cryptocurrency as a form of payment for their goods and services. They facilitate the circulation of cryptocurrencies, giving them fiat currency-like adaptability. Examples include Pizza Hut and Burger King in Venezuela; Baskin Robbins in certain US states like Idaho and Montana; Expedia, etc.
5) ***Traders*** - Crypto traders are indirect participants in the ecosystem, but they play a key role in making the community thrive. They speculate and buy/sell crypto via a DeX. The urge to actively participate and make money in this market garners a lot of people from different backgrounds, thus, increasing the participation in a certain cryptocurrency that is being traded or invested. Using a DeX, which is typically designed to compare and contrast trades in cryptocurrencies, contributes to creating a community for that certain DeX, thus, increasing the adaptation of blockchain technology and cryptocurrencies overall.

This community, largely driven by cryptocurrencies, has contributed to modern ecosystems like Metaverses and Web3 by leveraging Artificial Intelligence, Augmented Reality, and Virtual Reality. The advent of these advancements has led to considerable growth in social networking, data security, and decentralized networks (Cao, L., 2022).

4.5 Case Studies

4.5.1 Ethereum: Smart Contracts and DApps

When Ethereum was conceptualized in 2013, it aimed to revolutionize how we perceive blockchain technology and its applications. It was keen on expanding the possibilities of blockchain beyond simple financial transactions. While Bitcoin posed as a digital currency, Ethereum aimed to be an entirely decentralized platform where anyone could build their decentralized application by deploying smart contracts on the blockchain directly. This pretty much solidified Ethereum as the second-largest cryptocurrency by market capitalization and the most-adopted decentralized, layer-one platform for building DApps.

This inherent limitation in Bitcoin's scripting language was purposeful for security but greatly limited its potential use cases. Ethereum fixed this by including a more dynamic Turing-complete programming language, Solidity, which provides the power of self-executing smart contracts with complex logic. This flexibility was needed to build everything from decentralized finance (DeFi) applications to gaming to supply-chain management applications.

4.5.1.1 Use Cases

- ***Smart Contracts***:

Automating Agreements: Smart contracts on Ethereum can automatically execute when the predefined conditions in the code are met. Have look at the code below where, depending on the user input, the contract will execute once the condition is satisfied.

```
□// SPDX-License-Identifier: MIT

pragma solidity ^0.8.0;

contract SimpleCondition {

uint256 public threshold = 100;
```

```
string public message;

// Function to set the message if the condition is met

function setMessage(uint256 number) public {

// Condition: The number must be greater than the threshold

if (number > threshold) {

message = "Condition met: Number is greater than the thresh-
old!";

} else {

message = "Condition not met: Number is too small.";}}}

□
```

Here, if the input number is greater than 0, the contract would execute and print, "Condition met: Number is greater than the threshold!" Otherwise, the else section would be executed. This self-executing nature is highly crucial for DeFi applications, wherein the application would transact cryptocurrencies automatically when the conditions in the smart contracts are met.

Decentralized Finance: Ethereum has proved itself to be the cornerstone of the rise in the DeFi ecosystem. Traditional financial services such as lending, borrowing, investing, and trading are being done day in and day out with the intervention of any intermediaries. Most of the famous Defi projects, including the likes of Aave, a lending platform, and Curve, a decentralized exchange specializing in trading and investing in stablecoins, are built and operate on the Ethereum blockchain. This makes the whole process much more secure, transparent, and user-authoritative in nature.

- ***Decentralized Applications (DApps)***:

Gaming and NFTs: Games are always fun, isn't it? How about you play your favorite games and earn money? Well, not the fiat ones, but crypto. This is made possible with the current developments in the GameFi space. Ethereum has fueled the current advent of GameFi, introducing blockchain-based games and NFTS, which function as an in-game unique asset for players. For example, Axie Infinity is a popular game where you own axies, inspired by Pokémon, which you can trade, own, lend, or even sell to redeem AXS (Mazur, M., & Polyzos, E., 2024).

Supply chain management: A supply chain has a lot of stakeholders, ranging from suppliers to retailers and countless intermediaries. The sensitive data regarding these transactions can easily be tampered with as they are stored in a centralized database. This is where Ethereum's smart contracts can be leveraged. They can be used to create transparent, tamper-proof records of supply chain transactions (Kechagias, E. P. et al., 2023). Businesses like IBM have tested Ethereum for the purpose of tracking product origin and movement, ensuring authenticity and reducing fraud.

4.5.2 Polkadot: Interoperability and Scalability

A twist in the story. A co-founder of Ethereum leaves the foundation and develops Polkadot to address the issue of interoperability between different blockchains. The name? Dr. Gavin Wood. With the rise of independent networks, the fragmentation in the blockchain ecosystem posed a serious challenge in creating a unified, decentralized web. Polkadot took it into their hands to solve this issue, to ensure integrity and efficiency (Johnson, S. et al., 2019).

Polkadot found its purpose not only in interoperability but also in scalability. Scalability issues have plagued most first-generation blockchains, including Ethereum. Large numbers of transactions typically generated network congestion and led in exorbitant costs, making them unsuitable for large-scale applications.

4.5.2.1 Use Cases

- ***Interoperable Blockchain Ecosystem:***

Cross-Chain Communication: The one-of-a-kind architecture of Polkadot basically allows for the different blockchains to function in their independence while retaining the ability to talk and exchange data with each other over its central relay chain. This enables developers to come up with blockchains that can specialize in an area but still interact with others, making it possible to develop complex multi-chain applications.

Customizable Parachains: Projects can create their own parachains to be functional for specific use cases, like privacy-focused transactions, high-speed trading, or gaming. These chains, as they are independently existing chains, benefit from Polkadot's security, letting developers innovate without starting from scratch.

- ***Scalability for Large-Scale dApps:***

Higher Throughput: Due to the architecture of Polkadot, it offers a great deal of throughput, given that there might well be several transactions being processed at the same time on different parachains. This makes Polkadot suitable for use cases with loads that are high and require fast and efficient processing, like decentralized finance platforms or large-scale gaming applications.

Governance and Upgradability: Polkadot features an on-chain governance system, allowing holders to vote with their tokens on network upgrades and changes. Thus, it will adapt better to different technological advances in the area of users' needs. Thereby, network evolution is ensured without hard forks, which may turn out to be potentially disruptive in other blockchain ecosystems.

4.5.3 Chainlink:Bridging Real-World Data with Blockchain

Ever heard of the Oracle problem? It refers to the challenges in getting reliable and real-world data into your blockchain. This problem made it difficult to create smart contracts that relied on off-chain information because, although blockchains are inherently secure and decentralized, they cannot access external data directly. The external data might vary from as significant as price feeds to as trivial as weather data. This is exactly what Chainlink has solved, making its token LINK one of the most relevant utility tokens out there.

Founded by Sergey Nazarov and Steve Ellis in 2017, Chainlink Oracles aims to solve this problem. They act as a network of secure and reliable external data points referred to as the oracles. The decentralization among oracles ensures that there is no single point of failure and that the data being accessed maintains its integrity.

4.5.3.1 Use Cases

- ***Decentralized Finance***

Price Feeds for DeFi Protocols: Currently, Chainlink's most popular use case is offering price feeds in a decentralized manner for DeFi protocols. For example, lending and trading platforms like Aave and Synthetix, respectively, utilize Chainlink oracles to receive the true prices of assets in a securely vaulted, lent, and traded form of cryptocurrencies.

Stablecoins: Chainlink oracles maintain the peg of stablecoins, among many others. Pricing information is used to ensure that stablecoins, such as DAI or USDC, mirror their underlying value.

- **Insurance and Real-World Data Integration**:

Parametric insurance: With parametric insurance, settlement happens ex-ante because of the occurrence of certain predefined events—such as a natural disaster or a flight delay. Oracles from Chainlink feed the requisite real-world data—for example, about the weather or the status of the flight—to execute a smart contract.

Supply Chain Automation: This involves using Chainlink to automate and secure supply chain processes. Real-time data such as temperature or location will be fed into smart contracts to ensure end-to-end handling of goods, ensuring parties have transparent and immutable records of transactions.

5 CONCLUSION

While this ends our foray into the world of cryptocurrencies, manifestly speaking, that is something we have all witnessed: the birth and lightning development of one of the most disruptive technologies in the history of finance. It has grown from a niche technological experiment in mysterious inception with Bitcoin to the diverse ecosystem we see today, challenging traditional conceptions of money and value.

In this chapter, we have covered the following three basic facets of cryptocurrencies:

First, we defined what they are: digital assets built on blockchain technology that decentralize traditional currencies. We have gone over their core characteristics—from immutability and transparency to their capabilities for creating financial inclusions and doing borderless transactions. This background is essential in understanding the position occupied by cryptocurrencies within the modern world of finance.

Our journey throughout the history of the cryptocurrency world revealed that it was one of rapid and many times tumultuous evolution. From the 2008 publication of the Bitcoin whitepaper to thousands of alternative coins and tokens, the growth in the crypto space has been remarkable, punctuated by bull runs, market crashes, and technological breakthroughs. This gives a historical context for tenacity and flexibility within the crypto ecosystem.

We then turned to why cryptocurrencies exist at all, what the underlying motivations and problems they are trying to solve are. From providing financial services to unbanked people to serving as a hedge against inflation and government control, cryptocurrencies represent much more than a technological innovation – they stand for a vision of financial freedom and decentralization.

No doubt, as we take a reflective look back through the journey we have taken and learned, it is highly evident that already, in our financial landscape, there can be nothing other than the everlasting mark of cryptocurrencies. They challenged conventional notions of currency, opening up debates about the real nature of money, which has given way to new prospects for financial inclusions and innovations.

The journey of cryptocurrencies, however, does not stop here. The space is fast-changing, with new developments happening almost every other day—challenges included. Discussions and developments on regulatory frameworks, mainstream adoption, and integration into existing financial systems are at stake.

Although we have not delved into any deep technical mechanism underlying them or made any leading forecast about their future, it shall not be forgotten that the effects of cryptocurrencies transcend what is visible to us today. The backing blockchain technology and philosophy of decentralization hold within them the potential to affect many other sectors other than finance.

While it's yet to be seen if at all cryptocurrencies will ever be "The New Age Gold," what there is undeniably is the truth that they changed the way we think about money, value, and financial systems. They opened up new ways of thinking about and engaging with money in the digital age.

As this chapter closes, always remember that the world of cryptocurrencies is very dynamic. The knowledge learned here forms just a good base for understanding this revolutionary technology. Staying informed and adaptable, however, will turn out to be vital in going through this exciting and complex landscape.

Already, the chapter written about cryptocurrencies in the annals of the history of finance is an important one. Their story doesn't end here. As it unfolds, it's going to be central in shaping the future of money and financial systems across the world.

REFERENCES

Alahmad, M., Alfouderi, A. D. E. L., Alonaizi, A. H. M. A. D., & Aldhamen, M. (2023). Comparison Study of the Top 5 Leading Cryptocurrencies based on General Consensus Protocol: Bitcoin, Ethereum, Tether, XRP and Bitcoin Cash. *WSEAS Transactions on Computer Research*, *11*, 23–32.

Akther, U. (2020). Bitcoin—A hype or digital gold? Global evidence. *Australian Economic Papers*, *59*(3), 215–231. DOI: 10.1111/1467-8454.12178

Aquilina, M., Frost, J., & Schrimpf, A. (2024). Decentralized finance (DeFi): A functional approach. *Journal of Financial Regulation*, *10*(1), 1–27. DOI: 10.1093/jfr/fjad013

Asena Deniz, E., & Teker, D. (2020). Crypto currency applications in financial markets: Factors affecting crypto currency prices. *Pressacademia Procedia*, *11*(1), 34–37. DOI: 10.17261/Pressacademia.2020.1235

Bakhtiar, T., Luo, X., & Adelopo, I. (2023). Network effects and store-of-value features in the cryptocurrency market. *Technology in Society*, *74*, 102320. DOI: 10.1016/j.techsoc.2023.102320

Biryukov, A., & Tikhomirov, S. (2019, June). Deanonymization and linkability of cryptocurrency transactions based on network analysis. In *2019 IEEE European symposium on security and privacy (EuroS&P)* (pp. 172-184). IEEE. DOI: 10.1109/EuroSP.2019.00022

Cao, L. (2022). Decentralized ai: Edge intelligence and smart blockchain, metaverse, web3, and desci. *IEEE Intelligent Systems*, *37*(3), 6–19. DOI: 10.1109/MIS.2022.3181504

El Ioini, N., & Pahl, C. (2018). *A Review of Distributed Ledger Technologies.*, DOI: 10.1007/978-3-030-02671-4_16

Emmert, F. (2023). The regulation of cryptocurrencies in the United States of America. *European Journal of Law Reform*, *25*(1-2), 1–2. DOI: 10.5553/EJLR/138723702023025001002

Hazar, H. B. (2020). Anonymity in cryptocurrencies. In *Eurasian Economic Perspectives: Proceedings of the 26th and 27th Eurasia Business and Economics Society Conferences* (pp. 171-178). Springer International Publishing.

Heo, K., & Yi, S. (2023). (De) centralization in the governance of blockchain systems: Cryptocurrency cases. *Journal of Organization Design*, *12*(3), 59–82. DOI: 10.1007/s41469-023-00138-w

Houy, S., Schmid, P., & Bartel, A. (2023). Security aspects of cryptocurrency wallets—A systematic literature review. *ACM Computing Surveys*, *56*(1), 1–31. DOI: 10.1145/3596906

Johnson, S., Robinson, P., & Brainard, J. (2019). Sidechains and interoperability. *arXiv preprint arXiv:1903.04077.*

Kechagias, E. P., Gayialis, S. P., Papadopoulos, G. A., & Papoutsis, G. (2023). An ethereum-based distributed application for enhancing food supply chain traceability. *Foods*, *12*(6), 1220. DOI: 10.3390/foods12061220 PMID: 36981145

Khan, M. Z., Ali, Y., Sultan, H. B., Hasan, M., & Baloch, S. (2020). Future of currency: A comparison between traditional, digital fiat and cryptocurrency exchange mediums. *International Journal of Blockchains and Cryptocurrencies*, *1*(2), 206–224. DOI: 10.1504/IJBC.2020.109003

Lahajnar, S., & Rozanec, A. (2020). The correlation strength of the most important cryptocurrencies in the bull and bear market. *Investment Management and Financial Innovations*, *17*(3), 67–81. DOI: 10.21511/imfi.17(3).2020.06

White, L. H. (2015). The market for cryptocurrencies. *The Cato Journal*, *35*, 383.

Li, J., & Mann, W. (2018). Initial coin offering and platform building. SSRN *Electronic Journal*, 1-56.

Lo, Y. C., & Medda, F. (2021). Uniswap and the Emergence of the Decentralized Exchange. *Journal of financial market infrastructures, 10*(2), 1-25.

Lyons, R. K., & Viswanath-Natraj, G. (2023). What keeps stablecoins stable? *Journal of International Money and Finance*, *131*, 102777. DOI: 10.1016/j.jimonfin.2022.102777

Mazur, M., & Polyzos, E. (2024). Non-fungible tokens (NFTs). In *The Elgar Companion to Decentralized Finance, Digital Assets, and Blockchain Technologies* (pp. 280-297). Edward Elgar Publishing.

Nakamoto, S. (2008). *Bitcoin: A peer-to-peer electronic cash system.* Bitcoin: A Peer-to-Peer Electronic Cash System. https://bitcoin.org/bitcoin.pdf

Nani, A. (2022). The doge worth 88 billion dollars: A case study of Dogecoin. *Convergence (London)*, *28*(6), 1719–1736. DOI: 10.1177/13548565211070417

Saengchote, K. (2023). Decentralized lending and its users: Insights from Compound. *Journal of International Financial Markets, Institutions and Money*, *87*, 101807. DOI: 10.1016/j.intfin.2023.101807

Sarkodie, S. A., Ahmed, M. Y., & Owusu, P. A. (2022). COVID-19 pandemic improves market signals of cryptocurrencies–evidence from Bitcoin, Bitcoin Cash, Ethereum, and Litecoin. *Finance Research Letters*, *44*, 102049. DOI: 10.1016/j.frl.2021.102049 PMID: 35475023

Schaar, L., & Kampakis, S. (2022). Non-fungible tokens as an alternative investment: Evidence from cryptopunks. *The Journal of The British Blockchain Association.*

Schwiderowski, J., Pedersen, A. B., & Beck, R. (2024). Crypto tokens and token systems. *Information Systems Frontiers*, *26*(1), 319–332. DOI: 10.1007/s10796-023-10382-w

Shah, A. S., Karabulut, M. A., Akhter, A. S., Mustari, N., Pathan, A. S. K., Rabie, K. M., & Shongwe, T. (2023). On the vital aspects and characteristics of cryptocurrency—A survey. *IEEE Access : Practical Innovations, Open Solutions*, *11*, 9451–9468. DOI: 10.1109/ACCESS.2023.3240103

Soltani, R., Zaman, M., Sampalli, S., & Joshi, R. (2022). Distributed Ledger Technologies and Their Applications: A Review. *Applied Sciences (Basel, Switzerland)*, *12*(15), 7898. DOI: 10.3390/app12157898

Suratkar, S., Shirole, M., & Bhirud, S. (2020, September). Cryptocurrency wallet: A review. In *2020 4th international conference on computer, communication and signal processing (ICCCSP)* (pp. 1-7). IEEE. DOI: 10.1109/ICCCSP49186.2020.9315193

Härdle, W. K., Harvey, C. R., & Reule, R. C. (2020). Understanding cryptocurrencies. *Journal of Financial Econometrics*, *18*(2), 181–208.

Chapter 4
The Place of Cryptocurrencies in the Financial System Between Money and Financial Assets

Nenad Tomić
https://orcid.org/0000-0003-1565-3197
University of Kragujevac, Serbia

ABSTRACT

Cryptocurrencies were initially created for use in online payments. However, cryptocurrencies are rarely used for payments in practice. This chapter aims to show current state of cryptocurrencies in terms of their usage. It will evaluate usage of cryptocurrencies as money and as a financial instrument. In order for a commodity or digital document to be money, it must have the property of universality of application and a relatively stable value. At the moment, cryptocurrencies do not fulfill any of these requirements. Also, in addition to having the appropriate equipment (computer or smart phone), software support in the form of a digital wallet and an Internet connection, the user must have some experience in order to make the transaction without losses. On the other hand, it is clear that cryptocurrencies have the performance of financial instruments. The general conclusion is that cryptocurrencies are speculative instruments, which carry a significant level of risk. Investors' lack of education and lack of experience are the main dangers of investing in cryptocurrencies.

DOI: 10.4018/979-8-3693-5986-0.ch004

INTRODUCTION

Cryptocurrencies are form of digital money which operates independently of a central bank (Poongodi et al., 2021). They are initially created for use in online payments. Even the very title of Bitcoin white paper says that it is meant to be a system for sending electronic cash on peer-to-peer basis (Nakamoto, 2008). However, their use in payments is just a small fragment of their overall economic impact. Cryptocurrencies have a significant impact on the market because they provide an alternative to traditional financial systems, enabling the direct exchange of value between individuals without intermediaries (Shin & Rice, 2022). In addition, cryptocurrencies promote decentralization, transparency and security of transactions through blockchain technology, providing financial inclusion to people who do not have access to traditional banking services. Also, the technologies behind cryptocurrencies, such as smart contracts and decentralized finance (DeFi), pave the path for various forms of decentralized business and finance in the future.

Blockchain is the foundational technology behind cryptocurrencies. It is designed for functioning in an environment in which there is no central institution that can confirm the credibility of the data and participants do not trust each other (Bamakan, Motavali & Bondarti, 2020). This technology allows participants to perform transactions in order to introduce new data to a ledger. Transactions should not be understood solely as payments, but as events that lead to a change in involved participants. Blockchain consists of a series of blocks, in which transactions are preserved. The content of each block must be in accordance with the balances which are results of previously built-in blocks. This means that the Entity X could not use funds already consumed in a previously accepted transaction p. In case it tries, the transaction q would be rejected and could not become part of a new block. The creation of new blocks is performed without third party mediation. Since there is no mutual trust among participants, it is necessary to ensure the mechanism that the data will be proven and confirmed. A mechanism that checks the veracity of new transactions and performs their packaging in blocks is called a consensus protocol (Schneider, 1990).

This chapter aims to show current state of cryptocurrencies in terms of their usage. It consists of four main parts. The first part elaborates theoretical background of cryptocurrencies. It presents blochain as the technology behind them, then explains their economic foundation in the form of synthetic commodity money and later evaluates them as money and as financial instruments. The second part is dedicated to aspects of their use. It discusses topics of payments, financial inclusion, investment activities and creation of business ecosystem. In focus of the third part of the paper are pronounced forms of misuse of cryptocurrencies. The last part analyzes trends in global regulation of cryptocurrencies and government response in form of central bank digital currencies (CBDCs).

THEORETICAL BACKGROUND

Blockchain Technology

The principle of execution of transactions in blockchain is based on cryptography. Each user has at least one account created with use of asymmetric cryptography. The hash value of the user's public key represents his account number, while the private key is used for signing transactions. When making a transaction, the sender applies the selected hash function to it and signs the resulting value with a private key. This signature authenticates the transaction. Other users, called miners in this case, need to confirm the integrity of the executed transaction and the participant who proposed it. This means that the digital signature should match the sender's signature, i.e. it must be possible to decrypt it using sender's public key. Then the hash value of the transaction should match the one signed by the user. After confirmation, one of the miners (depending on the algorithm) packs the transactions into a block and proposes a new block to other miners (Ismail & Materwala, 2019). Other miners check whether the block size is within the limits of the allowed values, whether according to the time stamp it follows the previous block, as well as all hash values. This process is called consensus algorithm, and its design depends on the applied protocol.

Figure 1 shows the mechanism of appending blocks into a blockchain. Each block has two parts: a header and a body (Narayan et al., 2016, p. 32). A header consists of the sequence number, the version of the protocol used to mine the block, a time stamp in UNIX format used to determine the chronological order of the block, the root of the Merkle tree of the hash values of the transactions that will be embedded in the block, the weight factor of the mining, the hash value of the previous block and the hash record of the block itself. A body contains the transactions that the miner wants to confirm. The arrow connecting two blocks is hash pointer. It is a graphical tool used in structured databases to link the hash value to the original data record from which the value was derived.

Figure 1. Mechanism of appending blocks into a blockchain

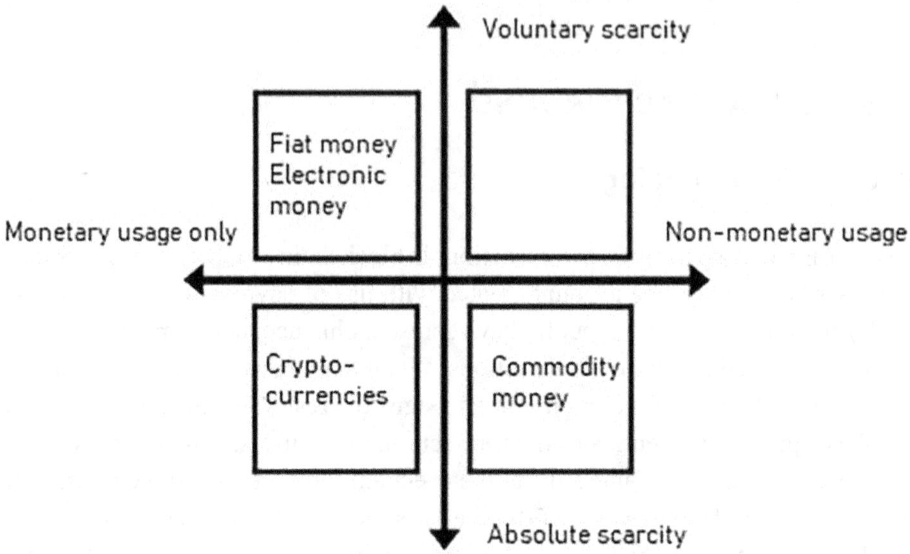

(Tran et al., 2023)

Thanks to the hash value contained in each block, the content of Block N depends on the content of Block N-1. By initiating a transaction, a simple script is actually run to prevent double spending and counterfeiting. The script first checks whether in all previous transactions there is one or more of them through which the payer came into possession of the funds that are the subject of the new transaction. If such transactions do not exist, the payer can try to convince the system that he still has funds. A malicious individual tries to change the content of Block N-1, in order to perform a transaction in Block N for which he does not have funds, but then the hash value of Block N-1 changes. In other words, Block N contains not only data related to new transactions, but also a summary of data from the previous block (the hash value of the previous block). In order for a malicious individual to succeed in his intention, he must change not only a transaction in Block N-1, but also change its hash value that will be found in Block N (Oliveira et al. 2020). A very large number of miners ensure that those who behave maliciously will be prevented from their intention to change the ledger. The reason is simple: the miners share between themselves only those transactions that are valid and those blocks that have been confirmed. The hash values of earlier blocks prevent the change of previously entered data. That is why the blockchain is an append-only database technology.

Consensus protocols ultimately prevent malicious behavior through a system of incentives. Analyzing the design and performance of consensus protocols requires a lot of time and detail. However, what is common to all of them is that participants - miners - receive some kind of reward for being the first to mine a valid block. Since each solution becomes valid only when it is confirmed by other miners, individuals are not motivated to offer blocks containing fraudulent transactions. In the so-called proof-of-work protocol, which is used by most other cryptocurrencies besides Bitcoin, block mining is actually computationally intensive. In the case of malicious behavior, individuals not only miss out on a potential reward, but also directly suffer financial losses.

Synthetic Commodity Money

Blockchain technology forms a technical basis of cryptocurrencies. In a functional sense, their foundation lies in the concept of synthetic commodity money. The model in question was formulated in the seventies of the 20th century, as a hybrid form that simultaneously has the characteristics of both commodity money and fiat money (Coase, 1972, p. 144). The basic characteristics that distinguish commodity money from fiat money are non-monetary usage and absolute scarcity.

Every form of money has a basic monetary application. It is used in payments as a medium of exchange between a person who makes payment - payer and a person who receives funds - payee. Commodity money is characterized by the fact that, in addition to monetary, it also has a non-monetary usage. Forms of non-monetary application vary from religious and ceremonial to practical. Shells of specific mollusc species, the so-called cowries were used for centuries in the coastal area of the Indian Ocean and the western shores of the Pacific Ocean, because they had ceremonial importance in rituals. On the other hand, salt has been used as money for centuries because it had a great practical application in extending the shelf life of food. North American Indians were paid with buck and deer skins until the arrival of European colonizers. Skins had practical uses as clothing and primitive armor against arrows. The use of buck skins in payments had such an effect on Europeans that the word buck has since become synonymous with money (Weatherford, 1997, p. 23). Later, some forms of coinage mix practical and ceremonial use.

Fiat money (banknotes and coins) has no non-monetary usage. Its sole purpose is the realization of the payment process, because the only value it carries is monetary. As it does not represent goods from the environment, but an artificially created product whose value is given by a state symbol, cash does not satisfy any human need. That is why in case of withdrawal of money from use, or hyperinflation, banknotes and coins become worthless.

Commodity money is characterized by absolute scarcity. As it is a commodity from the environment, which is more or less processed to obtain a final form, the availability of commodity money depends on the final stock of its basic form. Thus it was possible to produce as many skins as many bucks were hunted. The inhabitants of the Yap archipelago were in an even more unfavorable position, because the stone used to make the slabs with a hole in the middle was not on the island, but was brought from Palau and Guam, hundreds of kilometers away. Minting money from precious metals was possible only if the state had mines with adequate supplies. The lack of gold ore was a key reason why the Greek polis minted silver coins only.

With fiat money, the situation is somewhat different. Its material basis has an insignificant share in its total value due to the absence of non-monetary application. Therefore, it is relatively cheap to suddenly increase the supply of fiat money, because the nominal value, which is attributed to it, can change out of proportion to the change in production costs. That is why the scarcity of fiat money is said to be limited voluntarily, not absolutely.

Synthetic commodity money is characterized by absolute scarcity and the absence of non-monetary usage (Selgin, 2015). The first characteristic is shared with commodity money, while the second one is shared with fiat money. It is a medium of exchange that has a rapidly increasing marginal cost of production, or in some way production of additional units is voluntarily disabled. At the same time, such a means of exchange has no other application, except for making payments. Figure 2 shows the relationship between commodity money, cash, electronic money and cryptocurrencies in terms of scarcity and non-monetary applicability.

Figure 2. Relationship between commodity money, cash, electronic money and cryptocurrencies in terms of scarcity and non-monetary applicability

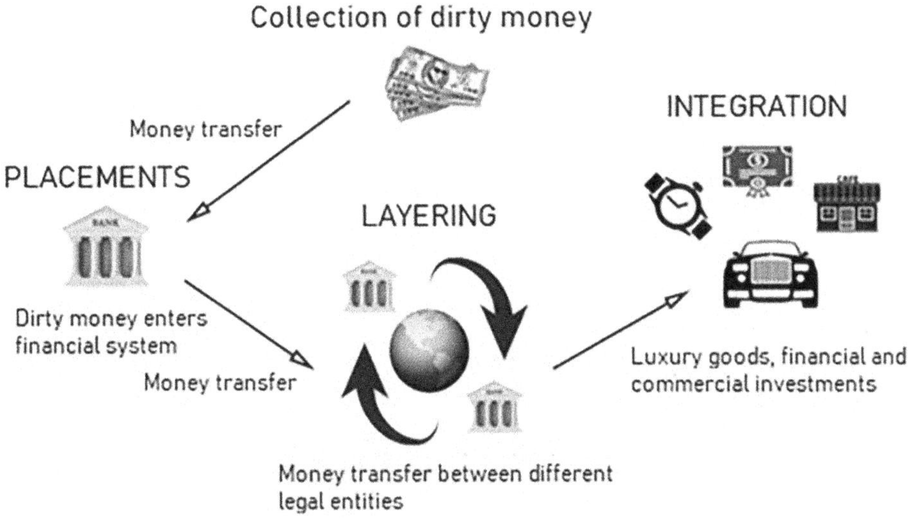

(Tomić, 2020b)

Before cryptocurrencies, synthetic commodity money could already be encountered in practice after the Gulf War in 1991. Due to the sanctions imposed on them, the Iraqi authorities were forced to develop their own money printing technology. The previous Iraqi dinars, printed in Switzerland, were declared invalid. However, due to national tensions within Iraq itself, the northern part of the country, inhabited by Kurds, was isolated from economic life. That is why in this part of Iraq, the replacement of the old "Swiss" dinar with the new "Saddam" dinar was not carried out. In northern Iraq, the old dinar remained in use for a decade, becoming the first operational example of synthetic commodity money. Its further production was prevented by developing circumstances, but payments remained the only sphere of application.

Most cruptocurrencies follow this model. Their supplies is either set at maximum level from the very beginning or increase at a decreasing rate reaching some maximum level at a known time in the future. Both solutions represent patterns of absolute scarcity, with inability of central authority, if existing, to suddenly increase supply. The intention of this design was to support stability of their value through predictability. However, the use of cryptocurrencies had some totally different aspects.

Cryptocurrencies as Money

In order for a commodity (physical form) or digital document (electronic form) to be money, it must have the property of universality of application and a relatively stable value (Claeys, Demertzis & Efstathiou, 2018). It does not have to be accepted always and everywhere, but it must allow payment at a large number of points of sale. A deposit, which is an intangible form of money in a current account, can be accessed electronically via a payment card, but its use for payment may not be accepted in all scenarios. There are merchants who do not own a POS terminal for card payments, and even those who do may temporarily experience traffic overload or loss of connection. And yet deposit money is a legally recognized form of money in every country, because it enables payment in the vast majority of cases. In some European countries, such as Sweden, the merchant is not obliged to accept payment in cash, if he has ensured the conditions for the use of payment cards. In short, both forms of money have a foothold in institutions as well as in the conditions of use and habits of consumers. Without all three components, it is impossible to establish a new form of money.

At the moment, cryptocurrencies do not fulfill any of these requirements. Although there are countries where certain cryptocurrencies are accepted as an official means of payment, globally the institutional basis is still non-existent. The positions of central banks towards them vary from those who warn citizens of possible abuses, to those who have openly prohibited their application (Dabrowski & Janikowski, 2018). There is no support from the state in case of fraud nor the legal framework for a consumer to independently prosecute the perpetrator. Furthermore, it can be said that algorithms of key cryptocurrencies lead a more stable monetary policy than all central banks, because they are known and predictable. That is true, but one should not forget that monetary policy is part of the broader context of national economic policy. Timing the same algorithm for all conditions prevents the cryptocurrency from adapting to change in market conditions, which inevitably leads to either excessive inflation or deflation. It can be concluded that cryptocurrencies do not have a foothold in institutions.

Conditions of use in payments are not ideal either. Provided that both parties are approximately well-informed about what cryptocurrencies are and how they work, they need to have some IT background to be able to use them. With the development of contactless payment cards, the last difficulty (although trivial) of their application has been eliminated. This is not the case with cryptocurrencies, because in addition to having the appropriate equipment (computer or smart phone), software support in the form of a digital wallet and an Internet connection, the user must have some experience in order to make the transaction without losses. For those users who have the knowledge to do everything the right way, the ultimate obstacle remains - the speed of the system. All key cryptocurrency systems are seriously lagging behind card systems, not only in terms of speed of reaching the finality of transactions, but also in terms of throughput. This means that, paradoxically, the mass use of cryptocurrencies in payments at the moment would be the worst possible thing for their future. Even with a small increase in the volume of use, the accumulation of unexecuted transactions, the extension of the average waiting time, and the consequent increase in the fees would follow (Ward, 2023). Even a partial solution in terms of constant fees and increased throughput would not help, as it would still eliminate their use in retail where instant confirmation of payment is required. They would not be suitable even for most online payments, especially when instant delivery of purchased content is required (when it comes to electronic distribution channels, granting access to subscription content, etc.). Therefore, they would only be suitable for payments where instant finality is not important. Finding an individual who meets all of the above requirements for use actually narrows down the pool of potential users significantly, making it more difficult to obtain money status. The means of payment used by 2% of the community cannot be money (Jonker, 2019).

Consumer habits are directly influenced by the conditions of use. To say that habits depend entirely on them would be oversimplifying the situation, but it is definitely impossible to penetrate a critical mass of users without essential ease and speed of use. The average user would be willing to learn how to use a new means of payment only if he is forced to do so, either by law or by the inability to use the means he is used to. In this regard, the potential mass use of cryptocurrencies in payments is often linked to the withdrawal of cash from use. However, it is forgotten that such an arrangement should first of all have an institutional basis, and that it should not depend on consumer habits. In order for users to massively turn to the use of cryptocurrencies in payments, they need to have some kind of incentive. Currently, such an incentive does not exist, but, compared to card payments, there are actually too many open questions and risks.

The basic functions of money are a medium of exchange, a unit of account, and a store of value (Mankiw, 2015, p. 82). By analyzing them on the example of Bitcoin, it can be concluded that cryptocurrencies do not fulfill any of them. The same analysis can be applied on virtually any other cryptocurrency that does not belong to the group of stablecoins.

Money is distinguished from other goods as a medium of exchange. Only those commodities that can be exchanged for any other commodity or service can be considered money. If it does not have this property, the commodity in question is not money. Therefore, cryptocurrencies are not money, because they do not have the property of general acceptance. The vast majority of merchants do not want to accept payments in cryptocurrencies, either out of fear of pronounced volatility, or because of a lack of knowledge needed to manage them. Some of the better-known cryptocurrencies can be used in payments at certain merchants, but this does not mean that they are mediums of exchange. Their limited application in payments suggests their potential to fulfill this function, but not at the current level of organization and functioning.

In order for money to satisfy the function of a unit of account, it is necessary for its value to be stable (Furtula & Marković, 2010, p.12). Sudden and frequent changes of its value expressed in other currencies reduce the possibility of its use as a unit of account. In this case, goods and services change their value too often and suddenly, which makes it difficult for merchants to do business and for customers to choose. All cryptocurrencies are characterized by an unstable value expressed in one of the convertible currencies (US dollar is most often used one). Bitcoin leads the way in the dynamics and intensity of changes, since as the most popular cryptocurrency it is a frequent subject of purchase and sale transactions. The situation is not more stable with other popular cryptocurrencies either. Of course, there are stablecoins, but they are most often tied to the dollar. Therefore, they are not a good choice for consumers and traders from countries whose national currency shows a high volatility against the dollar. This further means that they show stability only for users in the USA (or some other countries whose currencies are tied to dollar). That also means that the law of the optimal currency area also applies to cryptocurrencies (Mundell, 1961).

The volatility of cryptocurrencies can be considered a key cause of their failure to fulfill the function of store of value (Ammous, 2018). To illustrate the intensity and dynamics of Bitcoin volatility, the period September 2023 - February 2024 can be taken. According to data from *Yahoo! finance*[1], the monthly rate of return in September 2023 was 3.9%, in October 28.5%, in November 8.8%, in December 11.7%, in January 2024 0.7% and in February 22.8%. A random selection identified a period during which Bitcoin had no decline on a monthly basis, but a cumulative growth of over 100% in just six months. Also, fluctuations on a daily basis can be very pronounced. Even during January 2024, which is one of the most stable months in the last few years, there were identified dates when the change in value was almost 10%. Individuals or companies, who want to make their wealth stable and predictable, will not choose to store value in money that carries pronounced unpredictability of value in such a short period of time. Using the example of Bitcoin, it can be concluded that cryptocurrencies do not fulfill any of the three basic functions of money.

ECONOMIC IMPLICATIONS

Payments and Remittances

In the environment for which cryptocurrencies are nominally intended - e-commerce - payment cards and card-based payment applications have an unbeatable advantage. Payment cards have the advantage of being present in payment transactions for decades. Customers use them intuitively and trust them. This is not the case with cryptocurrencies, because in addition to having the appropriate equipment (computer or smart phone), software support in the form of a digital wallet and an internet connection, the customer must have some experience in order to complete the transaction without losses. For those who have the knowledge to do everything correctly, the final obstacle remains - the performance of the system. All cryptocurrencies seriously lag behind card systems, not only in the speed of achieving transaction finality, but also in terms of throughput and scalability. This means that, paradoxically, the mass use of cryptocurrencies in payments at this time would be the worst possible thing for their future. Even a small increase in the volume of transactions would lead to an accumulation of unexecuted transactions, an increase in the average waiting time and, consequently, an increase in the cost of executing payments.

Another big obstacle in the field of payments is that the number of businesses that accept cryptocurrencies as a means of payment is still extremely small. Although they are often presented as the future of money and a tool for decentralizing the economy, their application in everyday business encounters numerous obstacles that slow down their wider use. One of the main reasons businesses avoid cryptocurrencies is the high volatility of their value. The prices of all key cryptocurrencies can change drastically in a very short period of time. For business owners, this kind of volatility represents a big risk: the value of payments received in cryptocurrency can drop significantly before the funds are converted into fiat money, which can directly affect the profitability and stability of the business. In addition, unclear or insufficiently developed legislation is a significant obstacle. In many countries, it is still not clearly defined how cryptocurrencies are treated in the tax and legal system, which causes entrepreneurs uncertainty and fear of potential legal problems. Even where regulation exists, it changes frequently, further discouraging businesses from relying on digital currencies as a legitimate means of payment.

However, there are some aspects of their use where their impact is significantly higher than in the case of retail e-commerce. While financial inclusion and system of remittances wille be discussed in following part, here should be addressed property of inflation resistance. In modern business conditions, many economies are faced with high and unpredictable inflation rates. The purchase of foreign currencies with a stable value is often unavailable to citizens, who face the danger that inflation will derogate the accumulated value. Therefore, citizens of such countries often decide to purchase cryptocurrencies. It was previously stated that the key cryptocurrencies show high volatility. However, this problem does not imply inflationary pressure. On the contrary, since most cryptocurrencies have an algorithm for creating new units of value which is known in advance, a large number show deflationary characteristics. In this sense, they are a good alternative for storing value.

The consequence of the global drop in the price of oil, which was the most important export product of Venezuela, was the growing inflation during 2017. Due to the general decline in the value of its currency bolivar, in February 2018 the government decided to issue the first national cryptocurrency - the Petro. Although the white paper was published, key information about the technical aspects of the cryptocurrency and how the value is determined remained unclear. In various versions and translations of the documents, it was stated that it was a token on the blockchain platform Ethereum or NEM. Also, it was not specified how the value is supposed to be linked to the price of one barrel of oil. There were claims that the Petro was actually an attempt to avoid international sanctions, as the cryptocurrency allowed Venezuela to access international financial flows without the mediation of banks and financial institutions. Since the USA has already imposed financial sanctions on Venezuela, the trading of Petro was additionally prohibited (Osborne, 2018). In the long term, crypto exchanges did not accept Petro, so it remained a locally used cryptocurrency, without clear data on the scope of use or how to determine the value. At the beginning of 2024, the project was completely suspended.

Another example is the crypto exchange Golix, founded in Zimbabwe in 2015. Zimbabwe was notorious for its high inflation rates, which made it difficult for the local population to plan economic activities and store value. Golix offered a solution by allowing most of the known cryptocurrencies to be purchased directly with the local currency. This offered a local alternative for storing value. Since 2018, Golix has been targeted by the central bank, which has had it banned. Although it has resumed operations after legal disputes, users have been increasingly having difficulty withdrawing money, and it is assumed that the founders stole some of the funds. Although this experiment failed, it showed one way in which bad monetary policy decisions can be circumvented at the local level.

Financial Inclusion

Financial services are exclusive all over the world (Birkenmaier & Fu, 2018). Different services set more or less rigorous requirements, which the potential user should fulfill. For example, in order to open a current account in the bank and obtain a debit card, the client needs to be employed in order to be able to pay for the monthly maintenance of the account. However, obtaining a credit card requires permanent employment and a certain level of income, since this type of service implies the approval of a credit line. The conditions do not end here, so it is often necessary for the client to provide a guarantor, who will return the debt in case of non-fulfillment of obligations. From the above, it is clear that obtaining a credit card is more exclusive than opening a current account, because it excludes a whole range of potential users: temporary employees, students, and often retired persons, if they are applying for the first time. Criteria also exist for services offered by other financial institutions, only that they are mostly related to the level of the user's income.

Another reason for the exclusivity of financial services is insufficiently developed infrastructure (Tomić & Todorović, 2018, p.315). In developing countries, it is often the case that the infrastructure of financial institutions does not follow the population density. Densely populated rural areas do not have enough users, which is why the opening of bank branches and the installation of ATMs are missing, which further repels potential users. In this way, the entire population remains excluded from the banking system, which later spills over into other financial services.

Globally, significantly more people have access to mobile telephony and the Internet than to financial services. The vast majority of these people are located in developing countries, which of course does not mean that the phenomenon is not present in developed economies, among individuals from the social margins, ex-convicts and people without valid personal documents. In developed countries, a significant number of migrants also lack access to financial services. According to a 2017 World Bank report, an estimated 1.7 billion adults do not have a bank account (Demirgüç-Kunt et al., 2018). There is no exact data on what percentage of this population has access to mobile telephony and the Internet, but it is believed to be the majority. Therefore, it is estimated that cryptocurrencies could help achieve financial inclusion.

Cryptocurrencies enable individuals excluded from traditional finance to access some forms of financial services. Good internet signal coverage and the increasing technical potential of modern mobile phones enable the use of financial applications constantly and practically everywhere. With the help of a digital wallet, which can be downloaded and stored on a mobile phone, individuals without bank accounts can transfer and store monetary value. The use of mobile phones to facilitate the transfer of money over long distances is already common in African countries. A well-known example is the M-Pesa system, popular among migrants from East Africa who send money to family members in their homeland (Espinoza, 2014). A current account is not required to use this mobile wallet, as the account is linked to the user's phone number. However, this payment system which primarily serves for remittances needs a network of agents, who will support withdrawals. Cryptocurrencies do not have this problem, as all monetary value is in electronic form.

Another advantage is the price. Sending money through traditional channels such as banks and money remitters is expensive. In addition, a certain time is required to reach the finality of the transaction. Cryptocurrencies are a faster and cheaper way to transfer value, especially in international transactions. That's why this kind of system is very useful for migrants who want to send remittances to their families (El Hajj & Farran, 2024). Cryptocurrencies also serve as potential financial instruments, offering residents of countries with underdeveloped capital markets or high inflation an alternative to store value and generate returns (Setyawan Winotoatmojo & Ananda, 2024).

Good example for this claim is El Salvador. The law adopted in June 2021 made Bitcoin legal tender in El Salvador, on par with the US dollar. The national currency, the colon, was replaced by the dollar in 2001 in order to achieve the country's financial stability. However, dollarization further impoverished El Salvador, undermining their already weak export potential. In 2020, over 23% of GDP was remittances from expats. That is why the introduction of Bitcoin is seen as a means of facilitating remittance payments and increasing attractiveness for foreign investors. The law stipulated that all merchants in El Salvador are required to accept Bitcoin as a means of payment, unless they have access to the technology that supports the transactions (Burke, 2022). The government of El Salvador has also established a system that allows the conversion of Bitcoin to US dollars to reduce the risk of volatility for traders. ATM terminals were installed, the national Chivo digital wallet was designed and national reserves in Bitcoin were formed, the value of which rapidly appreciated at the beginning of 2024 (Ward, 2024).

Cryptocurrencies can serve financial inclusion only by addressing the key barriers and challenges their use entails. In order for them to be used as means of payment, their clear regulation is needed. As it will be presented later, in most national economies, cryptocurrencies are regulated as a financial instrument. Regulating cryptocurrencies as a means of payment should serve to increase security, both perceived and objective one, based on appropriate security protocols and procedures in case of misuse. A higher perception of security will create user confidence in the system, leading to higher usage. With adequate regulation, the key obstacles to the wider use of cryptocurrencies for financial inclusion are the technical literacy of the target population group and need for continuous education.

Investment Activities

In order to precisely understand the application of cryptocurrencies for investment purposes, it is necessary to define what investment is. One of the accepted definitions says that an investment is an investment of financial means, time and other resources in order to achieve future returns or benefits. An example of a nonfinancial investment is the purchase of an apartment or tourist capacity for renting. It includes investing money in the purchase of real estate and later renting it out, in order to generate income. During the time it creates returns, the real estate has stable value, slightly depreciating or even appreciating, depending on the market situation. An example of a financial investment is the purchase of a bond or a share of a company. Bonds yield interest, while profitable companies yield dividends. During all that time, the value of the principal investment remains the same (for bonds) or may depreciate or appreciate slightly, depending on the market situation (shares).

Cryptocurrencies do not fit this definition. Investing money is accompanied by gaining ownership of a certain amount of coins, which offer appreciation in value as the only way to make a return. Cryptocurrencies do not earn interest or dividends. On the example of the initial coin offering (ICO), it can be shown that they can bring a part of the project's return (Roosenboom, van der Kolk, & de Jong 2020). It is the only situation when investing in cryptocurrencies really represents an investment. Unfortunately, there is no guarantee that an investment in an ICO can yield a share of the project return, nor that any cryptocurrency will appreciate after purchase. In practice, this means that instead of a return, investors will very often record a loss. Therefore, when investing in cryptocurrencies, one cannot speak of investments in the classical sense, but of speculative investments.

Speculative investments aim at making quick profits based on frequent price changes of traded financial instruments (Milka, 2021). They are characterized by a high degree of risk and pronounced uncertainty. Most often, they are not the result of an analysis of the fundamental value of the traded asset and long-term models, but rather an assessment of market changes. The subject of trading in traditional investment are shares and bonds of less creditworthy companies, often in the process of restructuring, which can bring high returns, but also cause a loss of the investment. Due to the high level of risk, speculative investment is justified only if it is undertaken by an experienced investor who has knowledge in risk management and protection strategies.

In the case of cryptocurrencies, the situation is completely reversed. A large number of investors do not have knowledge about the assets they are investing in, nor do they have a risk management strategy. Most investors in the cryptocurrency market have never invested in traditional financial instruments and are not prepared to react in different situations (Sharma et al., 2024). The first big rise in the price of Bitcoin attracted a large number of individuals eager to make a quick profit. Even during periods of growth in the value, daily and weekly oscillations can have an inverse movement. Furthermore, the whole cryptocurrency market tends to follow the same trend, which means that the value of the most frequent cryptocurrencies usually rises and falls simultaneously (Hong, 2016). In such circumstances, the only salvation for investors is to convert assets into stablecoins. The problem is that the market is young, so even experienced investors from traditional markets cannot correctly assess when to enter and exit the market. In the case of investors who just wanted a quick profit based on a few short-term trades, a negative market return can cause nervousness and panic.

The rise in the price of Bitcoin, Ethereum and other cryptocurrencies created speculative bubbles in the market. In economic theory, the situation that followed is called the "greater fool theory" (Liu & Conclon, 2018, p. 38). According to this concept, investors buy an asset at a high price only because they believe they will later sell it to someone else at an even higher price, regardless of the asset's underlying value. At the same time, they are aware that the asset is already overvalued (Allen, Morris & Pastlewaite, 1993). Investors hope that buying and selling will happen in the upward phase of the trend, ie. that the asset will not lose value. A sufficient number of interested investors will over time provide returns for investors who have bought the cryptocurrency in the begining. However, the inevitable drop in demand will be reflected in the inability to sell. Declining prices will cause losses to investors who bought the cryptocurrency last, or may leave them with a large amount of cryptocurrency in their possession in the long run.

General recommendations for reducing risk when investing in cryptocurrencies are similar to investing in traditional payment instruments. The basic measure is a careful selection of investment instrument. Following other investors just because they started early is not a good option, as there is a chance that the investor will join during a downtrend, when most of the others are selling the cryptocurrency. Bitcoin and Ethereum may not always be a good choice, although the markets of these two are the deepest. On the other hand, investing in a new cryptocurrency with a low initial value is certainly speculation, with a high chance that the entire value of the investment will be lost. Another important aspect is diversification (Platanakis, Sutcliffe & Urquhart, 2018). Investing in only one cryptocurrency carries its specific risk. The best diversification when investing in cryptocurrencies is to use other financial instruments, which have less volatility, as a backup option. In the case of market shocks, the entire cryptocurrency market tends to move in the same direction, so diversification within the market does not reduce risk sufficiently.

The third important aspect is the existence of an investment strategy. An investor must know what his goal is and he should have a plan on how to achieve it. Investing money because others are doing it, without a clear plan of action and portfolio management strategy sooner or later leads to a sure loss. The key is for the investor to have worked out situations if the investment in the selected portfolio turns out to be good, but also if it turns out to be a bad choice. The buy-and-hold strategy may simply not yield results in practice, regardless of how convinced the investor is that the value of cryptocurrencies will grow over a long enough period of time.

A negative example of this is the cryptocurrency Luna (TERRA). In April 2022, it was the eighth largest cryptocurrency by market capitalization, at around US$40 billion. The Terra project was supposed to be a whole blockchain ecosystem, so in addition to its own cryptocurrency, it also included a stablecoin TerraUSD (UST) (Lee, Lee & Lee, 2023). Although its value adjusted to the US dollar, the trouble was that unlike Tether, TerraUSD was not backed by dollar reserves, but by the cryptocurrency Luna. The algorithm reacted according to a complex formula that in the event of a drop in the value of TerraUSD, it would start selling the cryptocurrency Luna, in order to use convertible money as support to stabilize the exchange rate of the stablecoin. However, the algorithm failed, so at the beginning of May 2022, the TerraUSD rate fell to $0.91. Then the algorithm, in order to stabilize the TerraUSD exchange rate, started overproducing Luna cryptocurrency, whose value fell uncontrollably (Asadov, Yildirim & Masih, 2023). In just one week, the first true hyperinflation of a cryptocurrency occurred, as the number of Lunas in circulation increased from 725 million to 6.9 trillion (Kaloudis, 2022). The value, on the other hand, dropped to one-hundredth of a cent, practically destroying the entire project. It is estimated that in a few days, investors lost over 40 billion US dollars invested in Luna and about 18 billion invested in TerraUSD.

Based on the previous example and the explanation of the requirement to have an investment plan, one more important fact is reached. Investing in cryptocurrencies requires constant information and monitoring of the market. Cross-checking the data obtained on technology portals and following the posts of other investors on social networks, helps the investor to get a bigger picture of what is really going on. This leads to the following conclusion - it is impossible to (successfully) invest in the cryptocurrency market, if one does not understand how it works. In this sense, not only the understanding of blockchain technology (which is mandatory) helps, but it is necessary to monitor the development of specific communities. In the case of the failed Terra ecosystem, having two connected cryptocurrencies was a huge asset, until it became a huge burden. Those investors who followed the situation managed to save part of their investment, while the inert ones lost everything. So, in the cryptocurrency market, there is a buy-and-hold strategy, but not the ability to invest money and forget about it during the next period.

Finally, in terms of the amount, investing in cryptocurrencies must have a different character from the traditional one. Individuals can deposit all their savings in a bank with a high degree of certainty, knowing that they have deposit insurance. With a slightly lower degree of certainty (which is still high enough), they can buy shares of an investment fund that invests in low-risk assets (say, government securities). Investing in cryptocurrencies should go up to the limit of the amount that the investor is willing to lose. The risks are disproportionately higher compared to the risks of investing in traditional instrument, which means that the potential loss is 100%

of the invested funds. In this sense, the best advice is to invest only after sufficient education, monitoring the market situation and making crypto investment part of a wider portfolio, which may bring a high return, but is not decisive in case of loss.

Business Ecosystem

The cryptocurrency business ecosystem represents a complex network of actors, technologies and services that together enable the exchange of value, the development of digital products and services, as well as the creation of completely new business models. At the center of this ecosystem are cryptocurrencies themselves, while platforms and services are being developed around them. Payments made in cryptocurrencies run mentioned elements of the ecosystem. The most famous cryptocurrency that appears as the backbone of an ecosystem with a whole network of services is Ethereum. A large number of smart contracts and decentralized finance (DeFi) applications are based on this currency. In addition, non-fungible tokens (NFT) represent another product of blockchain technology and a close relative of cryptocurrencies.

A smart contract is a software code linked to the blockchain, which serves to confirm, control and connect the intended actions, signed by the interested participants. Smart contracts are concluded online, recorded in the corresponding blockchain, where the nodes involved in the work ensure that the provisions are fulfilled when the conditions are met (Albizri & Appelbaum, 2021). As a computer program, it simultaneously expresses the content of the contractual agreement and manages the implementation of that content, based on the conditions fulfilled by the contractors themselves or third parties (Idelberger et al. 2016). Agreed contractual provisions are converted into executable computer instructions. As can be concluded, smart contracts are not "smart", because they do not involve machine learning that can lead to different outcomes in case of changed conditions, but rather automated contracts. The goal of smart contracts is to simplify the contracting process, reduce transaction costs through the elimination of intermediaries and increase trust between the contracting parties. The benefits of smart contracts are greater in more complex and expensive arrangements. Thus, cross-border payments can be made with a lower risk of default by one of the participants.

Decentralized applications (Decentralized Applications - DApps) are applications that run on the Ethereum blockchain. They use smart contracts as the basis for executing their logic and functionality. They are decentralized, meaning that data and operations are performed on multiple nodes in the Ethereum network, instead of on a centralized server. Thanks to this, they are resistant to censorship and reduce the risk of abuse of power by central authorities. They also give users more control over their data and digital assets. They can include different types of applications, such as financial applications, games, marketplaces or contracting platforms. DApps are often open-source and support a development community that contributes to their further improvement. Open access to code enables innovation and collaboration, which can lead to faster progress and the creation of better solutions.

One of the spheres of application of blockchain technology are so-called non-fungible tokens (NFTs). They appeared much later than the cryptocurrencies. Although the name resembles cryptocurrencies because of the word token, in practice NFTs do not represent electronic money, but a digital certificate of ownership of an asset (Nadini et al., 2021). Thanks to the performance of the blockchain, digital ownership can be recorded, verified and ultimately changed if necessary within an online community, without the involvement of a centralized institution. More importantly, NFTs, unlike cryptocurrencies, are designed so that they are non-fungible, that is, each of these tokens confirms the ownership of only one holder over one unique form of digital asset (Bao & Rouband, 2022, 215). They effectively behave like tokens whose total supply is 1 and is immutable. Therefore, owning one NFT excludes the possibility of other users to own it, because it is indivisible, so there is no possibility of co-ownership. It is irreplaceable, because by exchanging it, the owner cannot get another token that has the same value, for the simple reason that the other token will not refer to the same piece of digital asset. The only way for the owner to stay with the same value they already own is to not exchange the token.

MISUSES OF CRYPTOCURRENCIES

The use of cryptocurrencies is much more common in illegal activities than in e-commerce payments. The pseudonymity feature makes it possible to hide the true identity of the users involved in the transaction. This made it possible to use cryptocurrencies to pay for criminal activities and illegal goods, i.e. to transfer large sums of money without leaving a written trace, for the purposes of money laundering or financing terrorist activities.

Trade in Illegal Goods and Services

The widespread use of cryptocurrencies has made them a preferred means of payment in the trade of illegal products. In parallel with the Internet, the dark part of the Internet (dark web) was developed. It is accessed through special browsers that, by redirecting traffic, enable hiding the IP address of the user accessing the server. The network that communicates with the dark web is called TOR (The Onion Routing). In symbiosis with TOR, cryptocurrencies enable almost completely anonymous communication, content sharing and payment, creating ideal conditions for the illegal community over the Internet.

On the basis of this symbiosis, marketplaces of illegal products and services were created on the dark web. Intoxicants, weapons, juvenile pornography, stolen financial credentials, fake documents and other goods that are considered illegal only in some jurisdictions were traded in such markets Intoxicants, weapons, juvenile pornography, stolen financial credentials, fake documents and other goods that are considered illegal only in some jurisdictions were traded in such markets. An infamous example of such a market was the website *Silk Road*, a copy of the well-known auction site eBay (Van Hout & Bingham, 2013). The growing popularity of Bitcoin during 2012 was used to popularize the marketplace, which in turn made Bitcoin even more attractive. In October 2013, after a long-term surveillance, the FBI arrested William Ulbricht on charges that he is the owner and organizer of the website. Ulbricht was known to the public as Dread Pirate Roberts, which was the pseudonym he used to introduce himself on the site. The total turnover of the site exceeded one billion US dollars at the current value of Bitcoin. Defendant Ulbricht was sentenced to double life imprisonment without the possibility of parole for money laundering, drug trafficking, incitement to murder and hacking, and the site was shut down.

The closure of Silk Road had a significant impact on the development of the dark web, both in terms of increased attention from the authorities and the public, and in the development of technologies to combat online crime. However, other marketplaces have appeared trying to fill the void. Some of the famous ones are *AlphaBay*, *Hansa* and *Wall Street Market*. However, these markets were also later closed by the authorities. The dark web continued to evolve, with new marketplaces and platforms for illegal activity appearing and disappearing. It became more difficult to maintain large marketplaces in the long term, so smaller decentralized platforms emerged instead. Cryptocurrencies also evolved, so Monero (XMR) appeared alongside Bitcoin. Its advantage is the application of the so-called stealth address and ring signature, which allow the application of one-time addresses to hide transaction information. Although it is only 48th in terms of market capitalization on March 1, 2024, Monero is the most popular currency on the dark web after Bitcoin.

Blackmailing and Ransome

Ransomware is a form of malicious software whose purpose is to disable access to a computer's operating system or to encrypt data, after which the victim is asked to pay a ransom. Attacks involving ransomware are becoming increasingly prevalent in the digital world and pose a serious threat to individuals and organizations. Basically, malicious software blocks access to the system or encrypts data, which prevents the normal use of infected devices. The attackers then offer a key to decrypt the data or promise to restore access to the system after paying a ransom, which is usually demanded in cryptocurrency.

Attack methodology can vary. One approach involves the use of phishing messages distributed via e-mail, which contain malicious attachments. The messages appear to be legitimate, and may contain some element that the potential victim is familiar with, in order to be enticed to open the malicious attachment. After infecting a computer system, ransomware can quickly spread to connected systems and devices, often causing widespread damage. Another approach involves finding security flaws in the system. This primarily refers to buggy protective elements or outdated systems that do not recognize a certain type of attack. The first group of attacks is aimed at mass targets, while the second usually targets a smaller group of users or a single individual. In this case, it is most often a mass service provider institution or a company. After a single computer is infected, the ransomware spreads throughout the organization targeting the system block.

Although a ransom payment is required to eliminate the damage, the victim has no guarantee that his data will be decrypted or the functionality of the system will be restored (Beaman et al., 2021). If the data is encrypted, user finds only one unlocked document on the desktop that states the amount, term and currency in which the ransom is requested. Virtually all redemptions in the last ten years have been requested in Bitcoin.

In recent years, ransomware attacks have become sophisticated, targeting organizations and institutions of critical infrastructure, including electronic payment providers. Such targets are particularly attractive to attackers because of the potential financial gain they can make due to the importance of the affected systems to day-to-day operations. The consequences of such attacks can be devastating, including loss of important data, financial losses, business interruption, as well as reputational damage to the affected organization. In light of these risks, understanding the nature of ransomware and developing effective strategies for prevention and response become key elements for preserving the security and stability of electronic payment systems (O'Kane, Sezer, & Carlin, 2018., p. 321).

In addition to ransomware, online blackmail with Bitcoin ransom is used by spam e-mails, in which users are directly threatened with the publication of personal and confidential information. Attackers usually state that they have been following the user for a long time and are in possession of their sensitive data. To make the attack look more believable and personalized, it appears to the user that the e-mail was sent from his personal address - which is just another trick used by attackers. It is an automated mass attack, phishing type.

Money Laundering

Money laundering is the process of introducing money acquired through illegal activities into the legal financial flows (Levi & Reuter, 2011). Criminal activities such as drug trafficking, smuggling of excise goods, illegal arms trade, white slave trade, extortion and racketeering generate a large amount of money in cash form. Legal activities can also produce "dirty money" through faking business performances and avoiding paying taxes (Reuter & Turman, 2004). The problem for the owner of this kind of money is its transportation, storage and use in legal activities. A large number of countries, through anti-money laundering laws, have a procedure for determining the origin of assets. This means that dirty money needs to be "laundered" so that it appears to come from legal activity. Laundering takes place through three key stages.

After acquiring money from illegal activities, the first stage of hiding its origin is introducing it into legal flows. This is achieved by depositing smaller amounts in a bank or more often in several banks by different depositors, in order to avoid the suspicion of paying a large amount of money at once. This represents the placement phase. The next stage is layering. It is necessary to hide the trail of money through a network of transactions between connected individuals and legal entities, so that it appears to be legal and normal transactions. The integration phase includes the centralization of financial resources that now appear to originate from legal activities and their investment in legal businesses (OECD, 2009).

Cryptocurrencies have increased the possibilities of money laundering, especially in the area of money transfers across borders. Direct transactions between individuals avoid the oversight that exists over the traditional financial system. The advantage especially existed in the beginning, when there was no obligation to apply KYC (know your customer) and AML (anti money laundering) measures. A number of jurisdictions have now introduced certain measures that must be met by crypto exchanges that offer services to clients in their territory. Even so, malicious individuals were left with plenty of room to transfer illegal money. One way is online betting and gambling. A large number of online casinos are located in tax havens, i.e. offshore centers. As a rule, these casinos do not check the origin of the money that is invested, and allow the payment of winnings even if the player has not used the money in the game. In practice, this means that for a small amount of commission, the online casino can "launder" the invested dirty money.

Other dangers are apps called mixers and tumblers. They serve to create a parallel network of transactions in which essentially several users transfer money to themselves, from origin address to destination address. Since the money is transferred with the aim of hiding the trace, the output record will look different, i.e. it will appear that one user receives money from other users, while his money is transferred from his account to accounts of other random user. In this way, it is more difficult to trace the origin of the money, and it is even more difficult to determine the existence of a connection between an entity and the account. Even without the application itself, opening a large number of accounts and transferring money between them, as a rule, makes it progressively more difficult to connect people to accounts.

ICO projects can also be used for money laundering purposes. A criminal group can launch a fake ICO, with the aim of legitimizing illegally acquired money by investing its own funds through members or third parties

Terrorism Financing

Anti-money laundering measures are often effective in the fight against terrorism financing. In both cases, it is necessary to suppress the transfer of large amounts of money. The purpose is different, because in the case of money laundering, the funds are transferred to be included in legal flows, and in the case of terrorism financing, they are used for extremely illegal activity. Terrorist cells usually use the funds to procure illegal weapons, explosives, transportation, accommodation and other logistics. While part of the payments can be made in the official currencies of the countries in which they operate, purchases of illegal products and services are often paid for in electronic money and cryptocurrencies.

Therefore, cryptocurrencies in the financing of terrorism are used for the collection and transfer of funds, but also for payments. Sponsors of terrorist cells often have legitimate businesses, making it difficult to transfer funds while avoiding being linked to the group itself. Cryptocurrencies with the previously mentioned performance represent an adequate tool used by sponsors in recent years. While it is generally accepted that cryptocurrencies still represent a minority source of funding, the UN warns that in just a few years their share in total funds of terrorist groups has grown from 5% to around 20% (Shukla, 2022). The first group linked to cryptocurrency financing was ISIS at the height of its power in 2016. Although the group has been destroyed in the Levant, its factions still exist in Africa, where, according to Bloomberg, they are massively using cryptocurrencies for financing (Hill, 2024). During 2020, US authorities seized around 300 cryptocurrency accounts in two actions linked to open campaigns led by the Al-Qassam Brigades and Al-Qaeda groups[2]. After the escalation of the conflict in the Middle East, allegations emerged that Hamas was also financing part of its operations through cryptocurrencies (Berwick, 2023).

Cryptocurrencies undoubtedly provide more opportunities for use in illegal activities than traditional financial services. Therefore, one should be prepared for their more intensive application in the future, combined with innovative techniques for erasing traces of communication. That is why it is essential that national legislations and security services cooperate internationally and approach these challenges as a common problem.

GOVERNMENT RESPONSES TO CRYPTOCURRENCIES

Legal Regulation

The legal regulation of innovative processes, products and services is characterized by the existence of the so-called legislative gap. The method of performing new processes, as well as the application of new products, cannot be predicted in advance. Therefore, legislators cannot determine in advance their impact on the environment, nor the number and type of stakeholders whose rights and opportunities should be regulated. That is why there is a legislative gap, as a time interval between the start of the application of an innovative process, product or service and the moment of their regulation (Crane, 2021). Such a gap was also present in the case of cryptocurrencies. The emergence of Bitcoin did not motivate national legislatures to start dealing with this innovation. Greater interest came only after the creation of a deep secondary market. That is why the legal regulation of cryptocurrencies should be viewed from two perspectives: one is the regulation of cryptocurrencies as financial instruments, while the other is the regulation of cryptocurrencies in payments, primarily with the aim of preventing money laundering.

The first forms of regulation of cryptocurrencies as financial instruments concern the obligation to pay tax on capital gains realized through trading. It can be immediately noticed that this kind of regulation negates the theoretical essence of cryptocurrencies, because it is not viewed as electronic money, but as a financial instrument, i.e. as an asset. The above is a consequence of the application of cryptocurrencies in practice, which is many times higher in investments than in payments. The first country to start charging capital gains tax on cryptocurrency trading is Germany. The Ministry of Finance there issued guidelines in 2013, which determined that cryptocurrencies should be treated as assets, not currencies. Under those guidelines, the sale, exchange and trade of cryptocurrencies may result in capital gains tax liabilities. The guidelines were later further elaborated and clarified. The United States of America (USA) did the same in 2014, and in the following years similar regulations would be passed by a large number of countries around the world.

Specifics regarding exemptions from capital gains charges exist in numerous national regulations. Thus, in the German system there is a minimum amount (600 euros) below which capital gains are not taxed, and long-term capital gains (when the cryptocurrency holding period is longer than one year) are also not taxed. Other jurisdictions apply different tax rates to short-term and long-term capital gains.

Consensus exists in the largest number of regulations regarding the method of determining capital gains, because as a rule, the first in first out (FIFO) method is applied.

The first regulation of cryptocurrencies with the aim of preventing money laundering and terrorist financing was carried out in the USA in 2013. The Ministry of Finance's agency in charge of combating money laundering and terrorist financing (Financial Crimes Enforcement Network - FinCEN) issued guidelines that included the obligations of entities that carry out transactions with cryptocurrencies to identify their users (the so-called know your customer - KYC policy, otherwise typical of banks). The first legal solution in this area was passed in Japan in 2017, through the Law on Virtual Currencies.

Globally, the most well-known regulation in this area is the Fifth EU Directive on the Prevention of Money Laundering and the Financing of Terrorism, which refers to cryptocurrencies and prepaid cards (European Commission, 2018). The essence of the directive is the requirement that crypto exchanges and digital wallet providers register for business in the EU territory, and that they further implement the KYC policy, through mandatory registration and identification of users. In this way, the pseudonymous possession of cryptocurrencies becomes personalized, which makes it difficult to use them in money laundering.

Central Bank Digital Currencies

With the growth of the cryptocurrency market, the inevitable question of the application of this concept by states for the reform of payment transactions arose. Government digital money is emerging not only as a real need due to the digitization of business, but also as an opportunity for states to prevent the possibility of private cryptocurrency systems en masse among consumers. It should be immediately clear that the creation of real cryptocurrencies based on blockchain technology by states is not impossible, but it would not be desirable. As already stated, blockchain is designed for situations where there is a certain number of participants who do not trust each other in the process of making decisions. When reaching a consensus, the participants are equal, i.e. their votes are worth the same. In practice, it would mean that the state would lose the ability to control the conduct of monetary policy in such a system. It is clear that it would be extremely disadvantageous for the state to implement a monetary system that it will not be able to control later. A digital money system in which the state would maintain a leadership position and make all decisions would not be a true blockchain system. Fortunately, cryptographic techniques have for decades offered the possibility of implementing an electronic money system primarily based on blind signatures (Chaum, 1983). CBDC should be viewed in that light, as a form of electronic money that was developed back in the nineties of the XX century, only that the issuer would be a central bank instead of private entities.

The two key motivations for introducing CBDC are monetary policy and payment control. The ability to conduct monetary policy depends on the implemented solution for storing value. CBDC can be stored on a card or mobile application (device-based solution), or on a separate current account with a centralized institution, such as an organizational unit of the central bank (register-based solution). In addition, the ability to conduct monetary policy would be affected by the status of cash and deposit money after the introduction of electronic money. The survival of cash as an alternative retains the same degree of limitations that central banks face today. In the case of implementing a card/application system, there would be no revolutionary changes. A fundamental change would occur in the case of implementing a current account-based CBDC. Central banks could influence the entire money supply through interest rates, which would increase the possibilities for monetary policy. In the event of a general decline in demand and a deep recession, central banks could respond with a negative interest rate policy (Bofinger, 2018). In the case of cash or a device-based CBDC, consumers could respond to falling interest rates by converting their deposits into cash or transferring them to an app, thereby remaining outside the reach of monetary policy. Without cash and autonomously stored CBDCs, spending would be the only way for holders to prevent long-term asset loss

The two key motivations for introducing CBDC are monetary policy control and payment control. The ability to conduct monetary policy depends on the status of cash and deposit money after the introduction of electronic money and implemented solution for storing value. The survival of cash as an alternative retains the same degree of limitations that central banks face today. In case that electronic money substitutes cash, the differences arise from an approach for storing value. CBDC can be stored on a card or mobile application (device-based solution), or on a separate current account with a centralized institution, such as an organizational unit of the central bank or commercial bank (register-based solution). In the case of implementing a card/application system, there would be no revolutionary changes. A fundamental change would occur in the case of implementing a current account-based CBDC. Central banks could influence the entire money supply through interest rates, which would increase the possibilities for monetary policy. In the event of a general decline in demand and a deep recession, central banks could respond with a negative interest rate policy (Bofinger, 2018). In the case of cash existence or a device-based CBDC, consumers could respond to negative interest rates by converting their deposits into cash or transferring them to an app, thereby remaining outside the reach of monetary policy. Without cash and autonomously stored CBDCs, spending would be the only way for holders to prevent long-term asset loss.

The state can easily monitor each individual customer by centralizing payment information. The motive may be the control the payment system, in order to prevent money laundering, terrorist financing and criminal activities. Large amounts of data from telecommunications companies and banks have already been taken over by states under the pretext of combating terrorism (Hsinchun, Roger & Veda, 2012). But, a dictatorial authority could merge a customer's payment account with data from internet searches, social network communication, and movement tracks, in order to deduce that he poses a threat to national security. This conclusion does not have to be inherently malicious. Automatic data processing isn't always reliable. Consequently, an individual's conduct may inadvertently be construed as dangerous. Blocking an individual consciously due to anti-state conduct raises an entirely different issue of subjective evaluations of undesirable behavior, thereby creating ample room for abuses. By halting the source of funds for a day or more, the state conveys a clear message to the disloyal individual and any others who might work against the authorities' interests.

CONCLUSION

Cryptocurrencies are announced as money that operates on democratic principles and is resistant to government attempts to influence its performance. However, so far they have not taken the place of electronic money in practice, because their application in payments is insignificant. Not only is it difficult to find a merchant who is willing to accept payment with cryptocurrencies, but after a short analysis it is easy to conclude that even those who are ready to accept this means of payment do so as a promotional move, and not out of economic necessity. Several authors have concluded by analyzing the balance of all Bitcoin accounts that a very small number of users have ever paid anything with it. Paradoxically, the only area where cryptocurrencies really serve the purpose of money is illegall, when they are used to mobilize funds for terrorist financing, money laundering, or payment for illegal products and services. It can be concluded that cryptocurrencies have not fulfilled the functions of money and do not behave like money in practice.

On the other hand, it is clear that cryptocurrencies have the performance of financial instruments. Both end users and national regulations treat them that way. Users often buy different cryptocurrencies and sell them through specialized exchanges, betting on their value in the coming period. Moreover, they usually do not have any information about the cryptocurrency itself, who the issuer is, whether the supply is fixed or can be changed, and whether it is part of a wider project or not. In the second decade of the XXI century, it was possible to earn a return many times higher than the stake thanks to the immature market. While rates of return have reduced significantly after 2021, there is still room for a big profit, but also a big loss. The text mentions the example of the cryptocurrency Luna, which is the best illustration of this claim. In addition, since 2014, states have already started taxing investment returns as capital gains, thereby introducing cryptocurrencies as a financial instrument. The general conclusion is that cryptocurrencies are speculative instruments, which carry a significant level of risk. Investors' lack of education and lack of experience are the main dangers of investing in cryptocurrencies.

The market has gone in the wrong direction. Instead of a system that will compete with payment cards without infrastructure restrictions and with lower commissions, the money of the dark web was born. Instead of a system free from the influence of the state and corporate restraints, a financial instrument was created on the value of which a few individuals can have a decisive influence. Cryptocurrencies are not democratic systems, and their use today represents the negation of everything from the Bitcoin manifesto.

REFERENCES

Albizri, A., & Appelbaum, D. (2021). Trust but Verify: The Oracle Paradox of Blockchain Smart Contracts. *Journal of Information Systems*, *35*(2), 1–16. DOI: 10.2308/ISYS-19-024

Allen, F., Morris, S., & Pastlewaite, A. (1993). Finite Bubbles with short sale constraints and asymmetric information. *Journal of Economic Theory*, *61*(2), 206–229. DOI: 10.1006/jeth.1993.1067

Ammous, S. (2018). Can cryptocurrencies fulfil the functions of money? *Quarterly Review of Economics and Finance*. *The Quarterly Review of Economics and Finance*, *70*, 38–51. DOI: 10.1016/j.qref.2018.05.010

Asadov, A., Yildirim, R., & Masih, M. (2023). Toward greater stability in stablecoins: Empirical evidence from an analysis of precious metals. *Borsa Istanbul Review*, *23*(5), 1152–1172. DOI: 10.1016/j.bir.2023.07.004

Bamakan, S. M. H., Motavali, A., & Bondarti, A. B. (2020). A survey of blockchain consensus algorithms performance evaluation criteria. *Expert Systems with Applications*, *154*, 113385. DOI: 10.1016/j.eswa.2020.113385

Bao, H., & Rouband, D. (2022). Non-Fungible Token: A Systematic Review and Research Agenda. *Journal of Risk and Financial Management*, *15*(5), 215. DOI: 10.3390/jrfm15050215

Beaman, C., Barkworth, A., Akande, T. D., Hakak, S., & Khan, M. K. (2021). Ransomware: Recent advances, analysis, challenges and future research directions. *Computers & Security*, *111*, 102490. DOI: 10.1016/j.cose.2021.102490 PMID: 34602684

Berwick, A. (2023). Hamas Needed a New Way to Get Money From Iran. It Turned to Crypto. *Wall Street Journal*, November 12

Birkenmaier, J., & Fu, Q. (2018). Household Financial Access and Use of Alternative Financial Services in the U.S.: Two Sides of the Same Coin? *Social Indicators Research*, *139*(3), 1169–1185. DOI: 10.1007/s11205-017-1770-6

Bofinger, P. (2018). Digitalisation of money and the future of monetary policy, *Vox – CEPR Policy portal*

Burke, Q. J. (2022). The Great Bitcoin Experiment: A Social Analysis of Cryptocurrency in El Salvador. *Senior Scholar Papers*. Paper 567

Chaum, D. (1983). Blind signatures for untraceable payments. *Advances in Cryptology Proceedings of Crypto*, *82*, 199–203.

Claeys, G., Demertzis, M., & Efstathiou, K. (2018). Cryptocurrencies and monetary policy. Policy Department A at the request of the Economic and Monetary Affairs Committee, June

Coase, R. H. (1972). Durability and monopoly. *The Journal of Law & Economics*, *15*(1), 143–149. DOI: 10.1086/466731

Crane, E. (2021). Ted Cruz says Senate can't regulate crypto without knowing 'what in the hell' it is. *NY Post*, August 10

Dabrowski, M., & Janikowski, L. (2018). Virtual currencies and central banks monetary policy: challenges ahead. *In-depth analysis requested by the ECON committee*, Brussels: European parliament

Demirgüç-Kunt, A., Klapper, L., Singer, D., Ansar, S., & Hess, J. (2018). *The Global Findex database 2017: Measuring financial inclusion and the fintech revolution*. World Bank Group. DOI: 10.1596/978-1-4648-1259-0

El Hajj, M., & Farran, I. (2024). The Cryptocurrencies in Emerging Markets: Enhancing Financial Inclusion and Economic Empowerment. *Journal of Risk and Financial Management*, *17*(10), 467. DOI: 10.3390/jrfm17100467

Espinoza, J. (2014). Mobile Money: The Battle for Africa. *Wall street journal*, September 3

European Commission (2018) Directive (EU) 2018/843 of the European Parliament and of the Council of 30 May 2018 amending Directive (EU) 2015/849 on the prevention of the use of the financial system for the purposes of money laundering or terrorist financing, and amending Directives 2009/138/EC and 2013/36/EU, Official Journal of European Union, L series

Furtula, S., & Marković, D. (2010). *Monetarni system Evropske unije*. Kragujevac: Ekonomski fakultet u Kragujevcu

Hill, M. (2024). Islamic State Is Increasingly Using Crypto to Fund Africa Militant Goals. *Bloomberg*, March 11

Hong, K. (2016). Bitcoin as an alternative investment vehicle. *Information Technology and Management*, *18*(4), 265–275. DOI: 10.1007/s10799-016-0264-6

Hsinchun, C., Roger, C., & Veda, S. (2012). Business intelligence and analytics: From big data to big impact. *Management Information Systems Quarterly*, *36*(4), 1171–1172.

Idelberger, F., Governatori, G., Riveret, R., & Sartor, G. (2016). Evaluation of Logic-Based Smart Contracts for Blockchain Systems, *RuleML2016*, Stony Brook, NY

Ismail, L., & Materwala, H. (2019). A Review of Blockchain Architecture and Consensus Protocols: Use Cases, Challenges, and Solutions. *Symmetry*, *2019*(11), 1198. DOI: 10.3390/sym11101198

Jonker, N. (2019). What drives the adoption of crypto-payments by online retailers? *Electronic Commerce Research and Applications*, *35*, 100848. DOI: 10.1016/j.elerap.2019.100848

Kaloudis, G. (2022). The Collapse of UST and LUNA Was Devastating, but There Is Still Hope for Crypto. *coindesk.com*, May 15

Lee, S., Lee, J., & Lee, Y. (2023). Dissecting the Terra-LUNA crash: Evidence from the spillover effect and information flow. *Finance Research Letters*, *53*, 103590. DOI: 10.1016/j.frl.2022.103590

Levi, M., & Reuter, P. (2011). Money Laundering. In Tonry, M. (Ed.), *The Oxford handbook of crime and public policy* (pp. 289–375). Oxford University Press.

Liu, F., & Conlon, J. (2018). The simplest rational greater-fool bubble model. *Journal of Economic Theory*, *175*, 38–59. DOI: 10.1016/j.jet.2018.01.001

Mankiw, G. (2015). *Macroeconomics* (9th edition), New York, NY: MacMillan education

Milka, P. (2021). Speculation in the cryptocurrency market. *The Review of Economics Finance & Investments*, *1*(1), 24–33. DOI: 10.53752/refi.2020.1.12

Mundell, R. A. (1961). A Theory of Optimum Currency Areas. *The American Economic Review*, *51*(4), 657–665.

Nadini, M., Alessandretti, L., Di Giacinto, F., Martino, M., Aiello, L. M., & Baronchelli, A. (2021). Mapping the NFT revolution: Market trends, trade networks, and visual features. *Scientific Reports*, *11*(1), 1–11. DOI: 10.1038/s41598-021-00053-8 PMID: 34686678

Nakamoto, S. (2008). Bitcoin: A peer-to-peer electronic cash system, available at: https://bitcoin.org/bitcoin.pdf, retrieved August 10, 2024

Narayanan, A., Bonneau, J., Felten, E., Miller, A., & Goldfeder, S. (2016). *Bitcoin and cryptocurrency technologies*. Princeton university press.

O'Kane, P., Sezer, S., & Carlin, D. (2018). Evolution of ransomware. *IET Networks*, *7*(5), 321–327. DOI: 10.1049/iet-net.2017.0207

OECD. (2009). *Money laundering awareness handbook for tax examiners and tax auditors*. OECD.

Oliveira, M. T., Reis, L. H. A., Medeiros, D. S. V., Carrano, R. C., Olabarriaga, S. D., & Mattos, D. M. F. (2020). Blockchain reputation-based consensus: A scalable and resilient mechanism for distributed mistrusting applications. *Computer Networks*, *179*, 107367. DOI: 10.1016/j.comnet.2020.107367

Osborne, C. (2018). Trump bans Venezuela's cryptocurrency Petro in the US. *ZDNet*, March 20

El Hajj, M., & Farran, I. (2024). The Cryptocurrencies in Emerging Markets: Enhancing Financial Inclusion and Economic Empowerment. *Journal of Risk and Financial Management*, *17*(10), 467. DOI: 10.3390/jrfm17100467

Platanakis, E., Sutcliffe, C., & Urquhart, A. (2018). Optimal vs naïve diversification in cryptocurrencies. *Economics Letters*, *171*, 93–96. DOI: 10.1016/j.econlet.2018.07.020

Poongodi, M., Nguyen, T. N., Hamdi, M., & Cengiz, K. (2021). Global cryptocurrency trend predictionusing social media. *Information Processing & Management*, *58*(6), 102708. DOI: 10.1016/j.ipm.2021.102708

Reuter, P., & Turman, E. M. (2004). *Chasing dirty money*. Institute for International Economics.

Roosenboom, P., van der Kolk, T., & de Jong, A. (2020). What determines success in initial coin offerings? *Venture Capital*, *22*(2), 161–183. DOI: 10.1080/13691066.2020.1741127

Schneider, F. (1990). Implementing Fault-Tolerant Services Using the State Machine Approach: A Tutorial. *ACM Computing Surveys*, *22*(4), 299–319. DOI: 10.1145/98163.98167

Selgin, G. (2015). Synthetic commodity money. *Journal of Financial Stability*, *17*, 92–99. DOI: 10.1016/j.jfs.2014.07.002

Setyawan, A. A., Winotoatmojo, H. P., & Ananda, N. K. (2024). Cryptocurrency and Financial Inclusion: Bridging the Gap in Emerging Countries. *Dinasti International Journal of Economics. Finance & Accounting*, *5*, 510–516.

Sharma, R. K., Khan, S., Singh, R., & Birari, A. (2024). Speculative investment decisions in cryptocurrency: A structural equation modelling approach. *Journal of Decision Systems*, •••, 1–22. DOI: 10.1080/12460125.2024.2410030

Shin, D., & Rice, J. (2022). Cryptocurrency: A panacea for economic growth and sustainability? A critical review of crypto innovation. *Telematics and Informatics*, *71*, 101830. DOI: 10.1016/j.tele.2022.101830

Shukla, S. (2022). UN Says Crypto Use in Terror Financing Likely Soaring. Bloomberg, October 31

Tomić, N. (2020b). *Organizacija savremenog platnog prometa*. Kragujevac: Ekonomski fakultet Univerziteta u Kragujevcu

Tomić, N., & Todorović, V. (2018). Challenges of transition to cashless society. In Babić, V. (Ed.), *Contemporary issues in Economics, business and management – EBM 2018* [proceedings of the international scientific conference]. Faculty of Economics.

Tomić, N., Todorović, V., & Jakšić, M. (2017). Misuses of electronic payment systems, Contemporary Issues in Economics, Business and Management - EBM 2016, Stojanović-Aleksić, V. (ed.), Faculty of Economics University of Kragujevac, 245-253

Tran, V. D., Ata, S., Tran, T. H., Lam, D. K., & Pham, H. L. (2023). CrowdFund: CrowdFunding decentralized implementation on Ethereum blockchain. *Sustainability*, *15*(21), 15545. DOI: 10.3390/su152115545

Van Hout, M. C., & Bingham, T. (2013). „Silk Road", the virtual drug marketplace: A single case study of user experience. *The International Journal on Drug Policy*, *24*(5), 385–391. DOI: 10.1016/j.drugpo.2013.01.005 PMID: 23465646

Ward, S. V. (2023, December 23). Bitcoin Fees Surge Reinforcing The Network's Antifragility. *Forbes*.

Ward, S. V. (2024, February 5). El Salvador Embraces Future With Bitcoin As Bukele Secures Historic Victory. *Forbes*.

Weatherford, J. (1997). *The history of money*. Crown Publisher Inc.

ENDNOTES

1 Retrieved on February 23, 2024

2 https://www.justice.gov/opa/pr/global-disruption-three-terror-finance-cyber-enabled-campaigns Retrieved August 10, 2024

Chapter 5
Digital Financial Technologies

Arohi Anand
https://orcid.org/0009-0004-4870-1567
Sarala Birla University, India

Animesh Karn
https://orcid.org/0000-0002-0359-8496
Amity University, Ranchi, India

ABSTRACT

The rapid advancement of technology has revolutionized numerous aspects of our lives, and the financial industry is no exception. Digital financial technologies, often referred to as fintech, have emerged as a disruptive force, reshaping the way we engage with and manage our finances. This abstract explores the evolution, impact, and potential of digital financial technologies in enhancing financial inclusion, streamlining transactions, and promoting economic growth. Fintech encompasses a wide range of innovations, including mobile banking, digital wallets, peer-to-peer lending, crowdfunding platforms, blockchain-based cryptocurrencies, robo-advisors, and artificial intelligence-driven chatbots, among others. While digital financial technologies present numerous opportunities, they also pose challenges and risks. Cybersecurity threats, data privacy concerns, regulatory compliance, and the digital divide are some of the key issues that need to be addressed.

DOI: 10.4018/979-8-3693-5986-0.ch005

INTRODUCTION

FinTechs utilize a range of innovative technologies, such as cryptocurrencies, blockchain, artificial intelligence, and machine learning, to enhance and streamline financial services. Although these technologies have distinct purposes and applications, they are often grouped as "emerging technologies" or "disruptive technologies" due to their potential to revolutionize various industries, including finance, healthcare, and transportation (Zohren & Roberts, 2018). They are also commonly referred to as "digital technologies" or "digital innovations" since they involve digital data and processing. In the context of FinTechs, they are collectively known as "digital financial technologies" or "digital financial innovations", highlighting their digital nature and their ability to disrupt and innovate the traditional financial industry (Jajodia & Krotov, 2019).

The rise of digital financial technologies has been facilitated by the widespread use of smartphones, improved internet connectivity, and the availability of digital payment systems. Fintech encompasses a wide range of innovations, including mobile banking, digital wallets, peer-to-peer lending, crowdfunding platforms, cryptocurrencies based on blockchain technology, robo-advisors, and AI-driven chatbots (O'Reilly, 2019). These technologies aim to address inefficiencies, enhance convenience, and improve accessibility in financial services. One of the significant impacts of digital financial technologies is the advancement of financial inclusion. Traditional banking services often fail to reach underserved populations, especially in developing countries or remote areas. However, fintech has bridged this gap by enabling access to financial services through mobile devices. Mobile banking applications provide secure and affordable ways for individuals to manage their finances, transfer money, access credit, and save for the future (Böhme et al., 2015).

Additionally, digital payment platforms have simplified transactions, reducing reliance on cash and increasing financial security. Furthermore, fintech has democratized access to capital through its integration into lending and investment. Peer-to-peer lending platforms connect borrowers directly with lenders, eliminating intermediaries and expanding the availability of credit. Similarly, crowdfunding platforms allow entrepreneurs to raise funds from a broader pool of investors, promoting innovation and entrepreneurship. These digital lending and investment platforms utilize algorithms and data analytics to assess creditworthiness, making the process more efficient and reducing reliance on traditional credit scoring methods (Christidis & Devetsikiotis, 2016).

Blockchain technology and cryptocurrencies have also gained significant attention. Blockchain offers secure and transparent transactions by eliminating the need for intermediaries. Cryptocurrencies like Bitcoin and Ethereum provide alternative forms of digital money, enabling borderless and near-instantaneous transactions.

Additionally, blockchain-based smart contracts have the potential to automate and streamline various financial agreements, such as insurance claims or supply chain financing (Dwyer, 2015).

Artificial intelligence (AI) has emerged as a game-changer in the financial industry. AI-powered chatbots and virtual assistants enhance customer support by providing personalized recommendations, answering queries, and assisting in financial planning. Algorithms are used by robo-advisers to provide automated investing recommendations based on individual preferences and risk tolerance. These AI-driven tools reduce costs, improve efficiency, and enhance the overall customer experience. Despite the opportunities presented by digital financial technologies, there are also challenges and risks. Cybersecurity threats, data privacy concerns, regulatory compliance, and the digital divide are some of the key issues that need to be addressed. Additionally, continuous adaptation and regulation are necessary to ensure consumer protection and financial stability in the face of rapid technological advancement (Sgroi, et al., 2019).

Digital financial technologies have the potential to reshape the financial landscape by promoting financial inclusion, streamlining transactions, and driving economic growth. The incorporation of mobile banking, digital payments, blockchain, artificial intelligence, and other fintech developments has created new ways for consumers and organizations to obtain financial services and manage their finances more efficiently. However, it is crucial to address the associated challenges and risks to fully harness the potential of these technologies for the benefit of society.

CRYPTOCURRENCIES

In the later part of 1980's a movement took place which brought a dynamic change in the digital system. This movement was known as the *Cypherpunk Movement*. One of the original programmers, Eric Hughes, an American mathematician and computer programmer, explained about this movement in his book, *A Cypherpunk's Manifesto* (Hughes, 1993). Eric Hughes is considered one of the founders of the cypherpunk movement, alongside, Timothy C. May and John Gilmore. He coined the motto: *Cypherpunks Write Code*. The cypherpunks want encrypted and secure digital communications, as well as anonymous transactions. Unlike credit card transactions, where both the payer and the receiver can be recognized, cypherpunks envisioned a digital currency in which people could send and receive money without being tracked—similar to paying in cash at local stores.

The Cryptocurrency Timeline

Cryptocurrency is a type of digital or virtual currency that utilizes cryptography for security measures. It operates independently from central banks and allows for direct transfers between individuals without the involvement of intermediaries like banks or payment processors. In 1983, David Chaum introduced the concept of digital cash through his research paper, *Blind Signatures for Untraceable Payments* (Chaum, 1983). He later founded DigiCash, an electronic cash company, to commercialize his ideas. However, DigiCash filed for bankruptcy in 1998. That same year, Wei Dai discussed the idea of a cryptographic-based form of money on the cypherpunks mailing list, which shares many similarities with modern-day cryptocurrencies. Satoshi Nakamoto, an unnamed person or group, issued a whitepaper in 2008 outlining Bitcoin, a decentralized digital money that works without a central authority (Nakamoto, 2008).

The first Bitcoin transaction occurred in 2009, and the Bitcoin network was launched. Satoshi left the project in 2010 without revealing much about their identity. Subsequently, other cryptocurrencies like Litecoin and Namecoin were created in 2011, and Ethereum was introduced in 2013, allowing for the development of decentralized applications on its blockchain (Jobes, 2019). The value of Bitcoin reached an all-time high of nearly $20,000 in 2017, drawing significant attention to cryptocurrencies and blockchain technology. Since then, numerous new cryptocurrencies and blockchain projects have emerged, offering diverse applications beyond just currency, such as supply chain management and digital identity verification. Blockchain technology, the foundation of cryptocurrencies, has also found adoption in various industries beyond finance, including healthcare, logistics, and voting systems.

Early Digital Currency Movements

In 1996, E-Gold, an electronic currency tied to gold ownership, was created by Douglas Jackson and Barry Downey (Jobes, 2019). This digital currency allowed users to transfer gold ownership between website users, inadvertently becoming a tool for money laundering and illegal activities. The thoughts that eventually evolved to Bitcoin are credited to cryptocurrency pioneer Nick Szabo. His Bit Gold concept made use of blockchain principles such as peer-to-peer networks, mining, ledgers, and cryptography. Bit Gold aimed to eliminate centralized currency distributors and authorities, reflecting the properties of real gold. Despite being unsuccessful, Bit Gold inspired future digital currencies. Wei Dai introduced B-money, an anonymous and distributed electronic payment system, in 1998. Though it differed from Bitcoin, it also aimed to provide anonymity, privacy, and security. However, B-money was not successful (Zohren & Roberts, 2018).

Types of Cryptocurrencies

A notable feature of cryptocurrencies is that they are generally not generated by a central entity, which can potentially make them less susceptible to government intervention or regulation. They operate on a decentralized public ledger known as blockchain, which maintains and updates records of all transactions held by currency holders. There is a vast array of cryptocurrencies available, with new ones being introduced frequently. In general, they can be categorized into four groups: payment cryptocurrencies, utility tokens, stablecoins, and central bank digital currencies (Hayek et al., 2018).

Payment Cryptocurrency. It is the first significant type of cryptocurrency. Bitcoin, the most well-known cryptocurrency, was the first successful example of a digital payment cryptocurrency. A payment cryptocurrency serves as both a medium of exchange and entirely peer-to-peer electronic cash to enable transactions. Bitcoin, Litecoin, Monero, Dogecoin, and Bitcoin Cash are examples of payment cryptocurrencies.

Bitcoin (BTC). The world's inaugural cryptocurrency, Bitcoin, originated from a 2008 white paper and remains the most widely recognized form of digital currency. It operates on its own blockchain, where transactions are verified and new Bitcoins are generated by a decentralized network of miners, with a predetermined maximum limit. By January 2022, Bitcoin held the highest market capitalization in the cryptocurrency realm, reaching $896 billion.

Ether (ETH). Ether is the cryptocurrency native to the Ethereum blockchain. Similar to Bitcoin, Ether operates on its independent blockchain. Unlike Bitcoin, however, Ether has no predetermined supply cap, allowing for the potential creation of an unlimited number of coins. Ethereum also introduces smart contracts, which are self-executing programs that trigger automatically when specific conditions are met on the Ethereum blockchain.

Solana (SOL). SOL is the native coin of the same-named platform. It, like Ethereum and Bitcoin, operates on a blockchain technology. Solana's network can handle 50,000 transactions per second, making this platform particularly appealing to investors wishing to trade swiftly.

Ripple. Ripple is a cryptocurrency created to make money transfers abroad and remittances easier. It is used by financial companies and banks to transfer funds across borders and operates on a distributed blockchain network.

XRP. XRP, which operates on the Ripple network, has been dubbed a "cryptocurrency for banks" since it is specifically designed to meet the needs of the financial services industry. XRP was created to simplify international payments by acting as a bridge between two separate currencies, allowing for cheaper and faster global transfers.

Cardano. Dubbed as a third-generation cryptocurrency, it is the native coin of the Cardano blockchain. Cardano splits its blockchain into two layers to increase transaction speeds and implements native tokens to ensure a better experience for ADA holders.

Stablecoin. A stablecoin is a cryptocurrency that has its value tied to another money, commodity, or financial instrument. Stablecoins seek to provide an alternative to the excessive volatility of other cryptocurrencies such as Bitcoin (BTC), which has rendered crypto assets unsuitable for everyday transactions. They are intended to lessen volatility in comparison to unpegged cryptocurrencies such as Bitcoin. Stablecoins seek price stability by holding reserve assets as collateral or by employing algorithmic algorithms that are designed to regulate supply. Tether (USDT), USD Coin (USDC), bitCNY (BITCNY), TrueUSD (TUSD), Dai (DAI), Paxos Standard (PAX), Paxos Gold (PAXG), and Gemini Dollar (GUSD) are some examples of stablecoins.

Tether. Tether is a stablecoin that is connected to an external asset to provide a less volatile price. In this situation, each coin is backed by an equivalent quantity of US dollars, preventing it from experiencing the same market volatility as other cryptocurrencies. However, there is significant controversy about whether it is genuinely backed by the dollar.

USD Coin. USD Coin, like Tether, is a stablecoin linked to the US dollar that cannot be mined. USD Coin, on the other hand, offers more transparent funding and better auditing methods than Tether. The goal is to reduce some of the risk associated with cryptocurrency by allowing users to withdraw their coins and receive the corresponding amount of cash in exchange.

Utility Token. Utility tokens form a distinct subset within the cryptocurrency realm, offering users a plethora of functionalities across blockchain platforms and decentralized applications (dApps). These tokens are tailored to specific ecosystems, enabling users to execute actions within particular networks. Unlike conventional cryptocurrencies such as Bitcoin (BTC), utility tokens have a designated purpose within the framework of a crypto project's ecosystem, rather than functioning as real-world mediums of exchange. Primarily, utility tokens are confined to specific smart contract protocols and are not intended for broader economic transactions. An illustrative instance is the Basic Attention Token (BAT) of Brave. BAT exclusively facilitates content creator tipping through the Brave browser or integrated BAT wallets on platforms like Twitter. Additional utility token exemplars encompass Chainlink

(LINK), 0x (ZRX), Binance Coin (BNB), Zilliqa (ZIL), Aurora (AOA), MATIC, UNI, MANA, ENJ, and AR. These tokens exemplify the utility token concept, each serving a distinct role within its associated ecosystem.

Binance Coin. Binance Coin is the native cryptocurrency of Binance, which will be the world's largest cryptocurrency exchange by 2021. Users that pay with BNB have lower transaction fees for this exchange. As a result, Binance Coin has grown in popularity, becoming one of the largest cryptocoins on the market. Binance eliminates or "burns" a predetermined percentage of the currencies in circulation to ensure their value remains steady.

Chainlink. Chainlink is a decentralized database network that gives real-world data to blockchain smart contracts. Chainlink enables blockchains to communicate securely with external data feeds, events, and payment mechanisms, delivering the vital off-chain information required by complicated smart contracts to become the dominant form of digital agreement.

Central Bank Digital Currency (CBDC). Central bank digital currencies represent a digital form of currency issued by a nation's central bank. While like cryptocurrencies, CBDCs have a value that's pegged to the country's fiat currency, as determined by the central bank. The introduction of CBDCs aids financial inclusivity and streamlines the execution of monetary and fiscal policies. These currencies utilize blockchain-based tokens to symbolize a digital rendition of a specific nation's fiat currency, maintaining a centralized nature under the governance of the country's relevant monetary authority.

Cryptocurrencies offer a wide range of benefits, from fast and secure trans- actions to the ability to operate outside of traditional financial systems. While there are many different types of cryptocurrencies, each with their own unique characteristics and use cases, they all share the common goal of transforming the way we think about money and financial transactions.

Use of cryptocurrencies is, however, associated with its own set of risks including malware infections, hacker attacks, lack of legal framework and legal risks, bankruptcy and closing of exchanges, profitability, technical problems, absence of guarantee for damages and virtual money market crash (Liu et al., 2019). To protect oneself from cryptocurrency risks, one can research about exchanges, know how to store cryptocurrency safely, use a hybrid strategy when it comes to digital wallet security, use two strong passwords and engage with trustworthy cryptocurrency wallets, exchanges, brokerages and mobile apps (Brody & Bunnell, 2019). It is also important to keep one's keys to oneself.

BLOCKCHAIN

Blockchain is a dispersed, distributed digital ledger that facilitates the recording of transactions and the tracking of assets across a network of computers (Morris, 2018). The asset could be a concrete object like real estate, a house, or a vehicle, or it could be intangible like digital money, intellectual property rights, and so on. It allows for the secure and transparent recording and sharing of information without the involvement of intermediaries such as banks or other financial entities. In a blockchain, each block contains several transactions that are confirmed and added to the chain in chronological order. Once added to the chain, a block cannot be modified or removed, making it an immutable record of all network transactions (Zhang, 2019).

The Blockchain Process

Blockchain technology utilizes principles from cryptography, a field within mathematics and computer science. It employs digital signatures to uniquely sign each transaction, such as transferring assets between individuals. These signatures are kept private but can be verified by anyone (Brody & Bunnell, 2019). For instance, if user A sends assets to user B, the sender's identity can be confirmed, but the signature cannot be co-opted for unauthorized transactions. Through this cryptographic approach, the system establishes responsibility and deters identity fraud. In essence, actions like asset transfers or data updates on the blockchain are tied to their originator and cannot be disowned or shifted afterward (Reiff, 2019). The basic process of blockchain can be broken down into the following steps:

- **Transaction:** A user initiates a transaction by sending a digital asset (such as cryptocurrency) from one address to another.
- **Verification:** The transaction is broadcast to the network of nodes (computers) on the blockchain. These nodes use complex algorithms to verify the transaction, ensuring that it is valid and has not been double-spent.
- **Block Creation:** Once the transaction is verified, it is combined with other verified transactions to create a block. This block contains a unique code called a *hash*, which serves as a digital fingerprint of the block.
- **Blocks Addition:** The new block is added to the blockchain, where it becomes part of a permanent, unalterable record of all transactions on the network.
- **Consensus:** Before a block is added to the chain, the nodes on the blockchain must agree that it is valid. This process is known as consensus, and it is usually achieved through a proof-of-work or proof-of-stake algorithm.

- **Mining:** Some blockchain networks, such as Bitcoin, use a process called mining to verify transactions and add new blocks to the chain. Miners use powerful computers to solve complex mathematical problems and earn rewards in the form of cryptocurrency.
- **Ledger Updation:** Once a block is added to the chain, the ledger is updated with the new transaction information, and the process begins again with a new transaction.

Overall, the process of blockchain is designed to be secure, transparent, and decentralized, allowing for the exchange of digital assets without the need for intermediaries like banks or financial institutions.

Blockchain in Real-Time: A Case Study

Blockchain technology has gained significant attention across industries due to its potential to revolutionize various processes, enhance transparency, and ensure secure transactions (Kshetri, 2018). This case study explores a real-time application of blockchain technology in the supply chain industry. By leveraging blockchain, a global logistics company aimed to streamline its supply chain operations, improve transparency, and mitigate the risks associated with counterfeit products.

Background

The logistics company, referred to as XYZ Logistics, operates a vast supply chain network spanning multiple countries. It faced challenges in ensuring the authenticity and traceability of goods throughout the supply chain. Counterfeit products and tampering incidents not only affected the company's reputation but also posed significant risks to consumer safety. XYZ Logistics sought to address these issues by implementing blockchain technology.

Implementation

XYZ Logistics partnered with a blockchain solutions provider to design and deploy a blockchain-based supply chain management system. The system involved the integration of various stakeholders, including suppliers, manufacturers, distributors, and retailers, onto a blockchain platform. The platform utilized a permissioned blockchain network, ensuring that only authorized participants could access and verify the data.

Key Features

The key features of the new blockchain-augmented supply chain management system were:

1. **Product Digitization:** Each product within the supply chain was assigned a unique digital identity that contained relevant information such as manufacturing details, quality certifications, and logistics data. This digital identity was stored on the blockchain, enabling real-time tracking and verification.
2. **Smart Contracts:** Smart contracts were used to automate and enforce contractual agreements between the stakeholders. These self-executing contracts helped streamline processes such as payments, quality inspections, and delivery confirmations, reducing the need for manual intervention.
3. **Real-Time Tracking:** The blockchain system incorporated Internet of Things (IoT) devices, such as sensors and RFID tags, to track the location and condition of products in real-time. Data from these devices was securely recorded on the blockchain, providing a transparent and tamper-proof audit trail.
4. **Verification and Authentication:** Participants within the supply chain could verify the authenticity and integrity of products by accessing the blockchain. They could validate the digital identities of products, ensuring that they were not counterfeit or compromised during transit.

Benefits and Outcomes

By implementing blockchain technology, XYZ Logistics achieved several significant benefits:

1. **Enhanced Transparency:** The blockchain system provided a transparent view of the entire supply chain, enabling stakeholders to track products at every stage. This transparency reduced information asymmetry and improved trust among participants.
2. **Improved Security:** The immutable nature of blockchain ensured that the recorded data was tamper-proof. This feature significantly reduced the risks of counterfeit products, as any attempts to manipulate the data would be immediately detected.
3. **Efficient Processes:** The automation of contracts and real-time tracking capabilities streamlined the supply chain processes, reducing delays and optimizing inventory management. Payments were executed automatically upon successful delivery, reducing administrative overheads.

4. **Customer Trust and Safety:** With the ability to verify product authenticity, consumers gained confidence in the products they purchased. Counterfeit and substandard goods were effectively eliminated, ensuring consumer safety and satisfaction.

Conclusion

By leveraging blockchain's transparency, security, and automation features, XYZ Logistics successfully improved the traceability and authenticity of products, leading to enhanced trust among stakeholders and better customer experiences. The case study exemplifies the transformative potential of blockchain technology in various industries.

Advantages of the Blockchain Technology

Blockchain technology offers several advantages, including (Zhang et al., 2019):

Decentralization. Blockchains run on a decentralized network, which means that no central authority, such as a government or financial institution, controls them. Instead, transactions are validated and recorded by a network of nodes (computers) that collaborate to ensure the system's integrity.

Transparency. Transactions recorded on a blockchain are openly accessible to all participants within the network. This transparency acts as a safeguard against fraudulent activities and guarantees that all involved parties can place their confidence in the accuracy of the ledger's information.

Security. Blockchains use advanced cryptographic techniques to secure transactions and prevent fraud. Once a block is added to the chain, it cannot be altered or deleted, making it an immutable record of all transactions on the network.

Trust. The transparent and immutable nature of the blockchain can help build trust between parties, as it provides a secure and reliable record of transactions. This can be particularly useful in applications like peer-to-peer lending and crowdfunding.

Privacy. While transactions on a blockchain are transparent, the identity of the person making the transaction is not directly tied to their real-world identity. Instead, users are identified by a unique address or public key.

Efficiency. Transactions on a blockchain can be processed quickly and at a low cost, particularly when compared to traditional banking systems.

Disadvantages of the Blockchain Technology

Despite its numerous advantages, blockchain technology comes with certain disadvantages that require careful consideration (Dasgupta & Shetty, 2018):

Complexity. Among these is its inherent complexity, which can prove challenging for individuals lacking technical proficiency to comprehend and navigate.

Scalability. As the size of the blockchain grows, the amount of data that needs to be processed also increases. This can lead to slower transaction times and higher transaction fees.

Energy Consumption. The process of bitcoin mining and validating transactions on the blockchain necessitates a substantial amount of processing power, which consumes a significant amount of energy. This has sparked concerns regarding blockchain technology's environmental impact.

Lack of Standardization. There are currently no widely accepted standards for blockchain technology, which can make it difficult to integrate with existing systems and applications.

Limited Privacy. While transactions on the blockchain are transparent, the identities of users are often non-anonymous raising concerns about privacy and confidentiality, particularly in applications like healthcare and financial services.

Regulation. As blockchain technology becomes more widely adopted, governments and regulatory bodies are likely to introduce new regulations and policies. This could create additional costs and complexity for businesses and users.

While blockchain technology offers significant advantages, it also has some drawbacks that need to be carefully considered in the development and implementation of blockchain-based applications.

ARTIFICIAL INTELLIGENCE AND MACHINE LEARNING

Artificial Intelligence (AI) and Machine Learning (ML) are two related technologies that have grown in popularity in recent years. They are frequently used in conjunction to develop intelligent systems capable of learning from data and making decisions based on that learning. Artificial intelligence is a broad field that includes a variety of technologies and techniques such as natural language processing, computer vision, and robotics. It is focused with developing intelligent systems capable of doing tasks ordinarily performed by humans, such as interpreting language, recognizing things, and making judgments (Sgroi et al., 2019).

Machine learning, on the other hand, is a subset of artificial intelligence focused with the development of algorithms and models that can learn from data. ML algorithms are meant to examine big datasets to detect patterns and relationships in the data and then utilize that information to create predictions or judgments. One of the primary benefits of artificial intelligence and machine learning is their capacity to automate formerly manual operations. This has the potential to result in considerable cost savings and enhanced efficiency across a wide range of businesses, from manufacturing to healthcare (Gans & Leigh, 2017).

The ability of artificial intelligence and machine learning to learn and adapt over time is another advantage. These technologies can become more accurate and effective at executing their tasks as they are exposed to more data and experience.

Role of AI and ML in FinTech Industry

Artificial intelligence and machine learning play a significant role in FinTech in various ways. Artificial intelligence is used in finance to enable data patterns to be automatically recognized, examined, and modified. Nevertheless, even with imperfect data quality, artificial intelligence in FinTech can still offer insightful forecasts about exchange rates, investments, and short- or long-term trends (Cusumano & Yoffie, 2019). Some of the essential roles artificial intelligence and machine learning play include:

Fraud Detection. AI and ML are used to identify fraudulent transactions by analyzing vast amounts of data in real-time. This helps prevent fraudulent activities and protect financial assets of customers.

Risk Management. AI and ML help financial institutions to manage and mitigate risks by analyzing and processing large data sets. This can help identify potential risks before they happen, leading to better decision making and improved financial stability. The most relevant and perhaps most promising are AI-based credit scores. Credit rating, in essence, measures a customer's ability and willingness to pay back loans. Many pieces of information, including total income, credit history, transaction analyses, employment history, etc., are used by AI to determine credit ratings. A mathematical model for calculating credit scores is based on statistical techniques that take a lot of data into account. Artificial intelligence-based credit scores provide sensitive, individual credit score judgments based on a number of extra real-time indicators as a result, potentially enabling more individuals with incomes to access loans.

Customer Service. AI-powered chatbots and virtual assistants are used by financial institutions to provide quick and efficient customer service. They can answer frequently asked questions, provide guidance on products and services, and help customers resolve issues.

Personalized Marketing. AI and ML are used to analyze customer data and provide personalized marketing offers and recommendations. This can help financial institutions to tailor their products and services to specific customer needs and preferences. The use of data and artificial intelligence by banks to assess a person's financial health is one such example. Banks desire to extend loans and provide investment avenues but also desire to set fair fees. By looking at their credit scores, they may prevent overcharging dependable customers and undercharging risky ones. They can analyze their own consumer data and draw insights thanks to artificial intelligence. Artificial intelligence can infer many types of linkages from these portfolios. For instance, a person's employment and residence are obvious sources of information, but there is also the idea that even small facts, like their email provider, might indicate whether they are high net-worth individuals.

Investment Management. AI and ML algorithms are used to analyze market data and predict future trends in the stock market, helping investors to make better investment decisions.

To summarize, artificial intelligence and machine learning play a critical role in improving the efficiency and accuracy of financial processes, providing better customer service, and enhancing risk management in FinTech.

CLOUD COMPUTING

Cloud computing has been increasingly adopted in the FinTech industry, providing benefits such as cost-effectiveness, scalability, and security (Deng et al., 2018). Here are some examples of how cloud computing is being used in FinTech:

Data Storage and Processing. Cloud computing offers FinTech companies a cost-effective and scalable way to store and process large amounts of financial data. This is particularly useful for companies dealing with big data analytics, such as credit card companies and investment firms.

Infrastructure as a Service (IaaS). FinTech companies can use cloud-based IaaS platforms to host their applications and services, instead of building and maintaining their own infrastructure. This enables them to reduce costs and scale their services as needed.

Software as a Service (SaaS). FinTech companies can leverage cloud-based SaaS applications for various functions such as accounting, payments, and customer relationship management. This provides them with the flexibility to access software on a subscription basis, rather than purchasing and installing software on their own servers.

Security and Compliance. Cloud computing providers offer a range of security and compliance features, including encryption, firewalls, and intrusion detection. FinTech companies can leverage these features to ensure the safety of their data and compliance with regulations.

Collaboration and Communication. Cloud based collaboration and communication tools can enable FinTech companies to work more efficiently with their teams, partners, and clients. This can include tools for video conferencing, instant messaging, and document sharing.

Cloud computing has transformed the way FinTech companies operate, making it easier and more cost-effective for them to manage and process financial data, deliver services, and stay compliant with regulations (Zhang et al., 2019).

THE INTERNET OF THINGS (IOT) AND BIG DATA ANALYTICS

The Internet of Things (IoT) and big data analytics are transforming the FinTech industry by providing companies with powerful insights and tools to better understand and serve their customers (Christidis & Devetsikiotis, 2016). Here are some examples of how IoT and big data analytics are being used in FinTech:

Smart Devices and Wearables. Smart devices and wearables, driven by the IoT technology platform, are becoming increasingly popular for making transactions and payments. These devices collect valuable data on consumer behavior and preferences, which can be analyzed to provide insights into customer needs and preferences.

Predictive Analytics. FinTech companies can use big data analytics to analyze vast amounts of data from various sources, including social media, mobile devices, and transaction data, to identify patterns and trends. These insights can be used to make informed decisions about product development, marketing, and customer engagement.

Fraud Detection. Big data analytics can be used to detect and prevent fraud in real-time. By analyzing transaction data and identifying patterns that indicate fraudulent behavior, FinTech companies can stop fraud before it occurs.

Personalized Financial Advice. IoT and big data analytics can be used to provide personalized financial advice to customers. By analyzing a customer's financial behavior, FinTech companies can offer targeted advice on how to save money, invest wisely, and manage debt.

Risk Management. FinTech companies can use IoT devices and big data analytics to monitor risk in real-time. By analyzing data from various sources, including social media and news feeds, they can identify potential risks and take proactive measures to mitigate them.

Square: A Case of Leveraging Big Data Analytics for FinTech

Use of big data analytics has helped Square to establish itself as a leader in the FinTech lending space. Square offers loans to small businesses through its lending arm, Square Capital. Using machine learning algorithms and predictive analytics, Square developed a proprietary scoring model that considers hundreds of variables including sales history, social media activity, and customer reviews, to determine a business's creditworthiness. The use of big data analytics has also enabled Square to reduce the risk of default among its borrowers. By analyzing this vast amount of data, Square is able to make lending decisions more quickly and accurately than traditional lenders, which typically rely on a smaller set of financial metrics.

The combination of IoT and big data analytics is providing FinTech companies with powerful insights into customer behavior and preferences, allowing them to better understand and serve their customers (Fleder, & Hosanagar, 2009). This, in turn, is helping to drive innovation and improve the overall customer experience in the financial industry.

NON-FUNGIBLE TOKENS (NFTS)

Non-fungible tokens (NFTs) have emerged as a revolutionary digital asset class, transforming the way we perceive ownership and value in the digital realm. Unlike fungible assets, such as currency or stocks, which are interchangeable, NFTs are unique and indivisible (Mazur & Polyzos, 2024). They represent ownership of a specific digital or physical item, recorded on a blockchain. This digital ledger ensures transparency, security, and immutability, making it virtually impossible to counterfeit or alter recorded ownership.

In 2021, the Non-fungible Token (NFT) craze exploded, with many digital artists and creators using the Ethereum blockchain to create and sell unique digital assets (Kräussl & Tugnetti, 2024). Essentially, an NFT is a digital certificate of authenticity and ownership. The technology behind NFTs is built on blockchain platforms, with Ethereum being the most prominent, although other blockchains like Solana, Tezos, and Flow are also gaining traction. The decentralized nature of the Ethereum platform made it an ideal platform for NFTs, as it allowed creators to verify the authenticity of their digital assets and sell them directly to buyers without needing intermediaries.

The uniqueness of each NFT is defined by metadata that links it to a specific digital asset, such as an image, video, audio file, or even a physical object. This metadata is stored on the blockchain, providing a verifiable record of ownership and provenance (Kshetri, 2018). The rise of NFTs has disrupted various industries, including art, music, gaming, and collectibles, creating new avenues for creators and collectors alike.

Uses of Non-Fungible Tokens

NFTs have found diverse applications across numerous sectors, showcasing their versatility and potential (Hughes et al., 2019).

Digital Art and Collectibles. NFTs have revolutionized the art world, enabling artists to tokenize their digital creations and sell them directly to collectors. This eliminates the need for intermediaries and provides artists with greater control over their work and royalties. Platforms like OpenSea and Rarible have become marketplaces for digital art and collectibles, fostering a vibrant ecosystem for creators and collectors. For example, Beeple's "Everydays: The First 5000 Days" sold for $69 million, demonstrating the immense value that digital art can command in the NFT market.

Gaming: NFTs are transforming the gaming industry by introducing play-to-earn models and enabling in-game asset ownership. Players can own unique in-game items, such as characters, weapons, and virtual land, which can be traded or sold as NFTs. This creates a more immersive and rewarding gaming experience, where players can earn real-world value for their in-game achievements. Games like Axie Infinity utilize NFTs to represent in-game characters and items, allowing players to earn cryptocurrency by playing the game.

Music: NFTs are empowering musicians to monetize their work in new ways, bypassing traditional record labels and streaming services. Artists can sell exclusive songs, albums, and merchandise as NFTs, providing fans with unique digital collectibles and experiences. Artists like Kings of Leon have released albums as NFTs, offering fans exclusive content and perks.

Real Estate: NFTs are being explored as a means of tokenizing real estate assets, simplifying the process of buying, selling, and transferring property ownership. This could potentially reduce transaction costs and increase transparency in the real estate market.

Supply Chain Management: NFTs can be used to track and verify the provenance of goods, ensuring authenticity and transparency in supply chains. By recording the movement of products on a blockchain, NFTs can help prevent counterfeiting and fraud.

Ticketing: NFTs are being used to create secure and verifiable event tickets, reducing fraud and scalping. Digital tickets can be programmed with unique features, such as exclusive access to content or experiences.

Advantages of Non-Fungible Tokens

NFTs offer several advantages that contribute to their growing popularity (Rehman et al., 2021).

Authenticity and Provenance: NFTs provide a verifiable record of ownership and provenance, ensuring the authenticity of digital assets. This is particularly valuable for digital art and collectibles, where counterfeiting can be a significant issue.

Decentralization and Transparency: NFTs are stored on a blockchain, which is a decentralized and transparent ledger. This eliminates the need for intermediaries and provides a secure and immutable record of transactions.

Ownership and Control: NFTs give creators and collectors greater control over their digital assets. Artists can sell their work directly to collectors, retaining a larger share of the profits. Collectors can own unique digital items and trade them freely on the secondary market.

New Revenue Streams: NFTs create new revenue streams for creators and businesses. Artists can earn royalties from secondary sales of their work, and businesses can monetize digital assets in innovative ways.

Community Building: NFTs can foster a sense of community among creators and collectors. Exclusive NFT drops and events can create a sense of belonging and exclusivity.

Disadvantages of Non-Fungible Tokens

Despite their numerous advantages, NFTs also have certain disadvantages (Valeonti et al., 2021).

Environmental Concerns: Some blockchain platforms, particularly Ethereum, consume significant amounts of energy, raising environmental concerns. However, newer blockchains and scaling solutions are addressing these issues.

Volatility and Speculation: The NFT market is highly volatile and speculative, with prices fluctuating significantly. This can make NFTs a risky investment.

Copyright and Intellectual Property Issues: The legal framework surrounding NFTs is still evolving, and there are concerns about copyright and intellectual property infringement.

Security Risks: Like any digital asset, NFTs are vulnerable to security risks, such as hacking and phishing. Users must take precautions to protect their digital wallets and private keys.

Accessibility and Understanding: The technical complexity of NFTs can be a barrier to entry for some users. Understanding blockchain technology and digital wallets requires a certain level of technical knowledge.

Non-fungible Tokens represent a paradigm shift in the way we perceive ownership and value in the digital age. Their unique properties, such as authenticity, transparency, and decentralization, have opened up new possibilities for creators, collectors, and businesses across various industries. While NFTs offer numerous advantages, they also come with certain disadvantages, such as environmental concerns and security risks. As technology continues to evolve, it is crucial to address these challenges and establish a robust regulatory framework to ensure the long-term sustainability and growth of the NFT market. The continued development of layer 2 solutions, and more energy efficient blockchains will help to mitigate environmental impacts. As technology becomes more accessible and user-friendly, NFTs have the potential to transform the way we interact with digital assets and create new opportunities for innovation and creativity.

THE ROAD AHEAD: FUTURE DIRECTIONS IN DIGITAL FINANCIAL TECHNOLOGIES

The landscape of digital financial technologies is in a state of constant evolution, with new innovations emerging regularly that promise to further disrupt and redefine the financial industry. As we look ahead, it's clear that the trends discussed in this chapter—cryptocurrencies, blockchain, AI and machine learning, cloud computing, IoT, big data analytics, and NFTs—will continue to play pivotal roles. However, their future trajectories and convergence will likely shape the next wave of financial innovation.

Enhanced Integration and Interoperability

One of the most significant developments on the horizon is the enhanced integration and interoperability of different digital financial technologies. Currently, many of these technologies operate in silos, with limited interaction between them. In the future, we can expect to see greater efforts to create seamless connections between these technologies, allowing for more holistic and efficient financial solutions. For instance, the convergence of AI and blockchain could lead to more sophisticated fraud detection systems that not only identify suspicious transactions but also trace their origins and destinations with greater accuracy and transparency. Similarly, the integration of IoT and big data analytics could enable real-time, personalized financial advice based on an individual's spending habits and financial goals.

Prominence of Decentralized Finance (DeFi)

Decentralized Finance (DeFi) is poised to gain further prominence, driven by advancements in blockchain technology and smart contracts. DeFi platforms offer a range of financial services, such as lending, borrowing, and trading, without the need for traditional intermediaries.[1] As blockchain technology matures and scalability issues are addressed, DeFi has the potential to become more accessible and user-friendly, attracting a broader audience. The development of more robust regulatory frameworks will also be crucial in fostering trust and encouraging wider adoption of DeFi solutions.

Central Bank Digital Currencies and the Future of Money

Central Bank Digital Currencies (CBDCs) are likely to play a transformative role in the future of money. As more central banks explore the issuance of their own digital currencies, we can anticipate significant changes in how money is created, distributed, and used. CBDCs could enhance the efficiency of payment systems, reduce transaction costs, and promote financial inclusion. However, they also raise important questions about privacy, security, and the role of central banks in the digital[2] age. The successful implementation of CBDCs will require careful consideration of these factors and a balanced approach that leverages the benefits of digital technology while mitigating potential risks.

AI-Driven Personalization and Automation

Artificial intelligence and machine learning will continue to drive greater personalization and automation in financial services. AI-powered robo-advisors will become more sophisticated, offering tailored investment advice and financial planning based on individual circumstances and goals. Chatbots and virtual assistants will provide seamless customer support, handling complex queries and transactions with greater efficiency. AI algorithms will also play a crucial role in risk management, fraud detection, and credit scoring, enabling financial institutions to make more informed decisions.

The Expanding Role of Big Data and Analytics

Big data and analytics will become even more critical in the financial industry, providing valuable insights into customer behavior, market trends, and risk factors. Financial institutions will leverage advanced analytics techniques to personalize products and services, optimize pricing, and enhance customer experience. The ability to analyze vast amounts of data in real-time will also enable more proactive risk management and fraud prevention. However, the use of big data in finance also raises important ethical and privacy considerations, necessitating robust data governance frameworks.

NFTs and the Tokenization of Assets

Non-fungible tokens (NFTs) have demonstrated their potential to revolutionize ownership and value in the digital realm. In the future, we can expect to see the tokenization of a wider range of assets, including real estate, intellectual property, and even traditional financial instruments. This tokenization could increase liquidity, reduce transaction costs, and democratize access to investment opportunities. NFTs may also play a growing role in areas such as identity verification, supply chain management, and digital rights management.

Challenges and Considerations

Despite the immense potential of digital financial technologies, several challenges and considerations must be addressed. Cybersecurity remains a paramount concern, as the increasing reliance on digital systems makes the financial industry a prime target for cyberattacks. Robust security measures, including encryption, multi-factor authentication, and blockchain technology, are essential to protect sensitive financial data and ensure the integrity of transactions.

Regulatory frameworks must also evolve to keep pace with the rapid pace of technological change. Regulators face the challenge of fostering innovation while mitigating risks and ensuring consumer protection. Striking the right balance is crucial to creating a regulatory environment that encourages responsible innovation and promotes the stability of the financial system.

Furthermore, the digital divide remains a significant barrier to the widespread adoption of digital financial technologies. Efforts must be made to ensure that the benefits of these technologies are accessible to everyone, regardless of their socio-economic status or geographic location. Financial literacy programs and initiatives to improve digital inclusion can play a vital role in bridging this gap.

CONCLUSION

The future of digital financial technologies is bright, with the potential to transform the financial industry in profound ways. The continued advancement and convergence of cryptocurrencies, blockchain, AI and machine learning, cloud computing,

IoT, big data analytics, and NFTs will drive greater efficiency, transparency, and accessibility in financial services. However, realizing this potential requires addressing key challenges related to cybersecurity, regulation, and digital inclusion. By embracing responsible innovation and working collaboratively, stakeholders can shape a future where digital financial technologies benefit individuals, businesses, and society as a whole.

REFERENCES

Böhme, R., Christin, N., Edelman, B., & Moore, T. (2015). Bitcoin: Economics, technology, and governance. *The Journal of Economic Perspectives*, *29*(2), 213–238. DOI: 10.1257/jep.29.2.213

Brody, D., & Bunnell, T. (2019). *Blockchain, cryptocurrencies, and smart contracts: Innovations and legal issues*. Wolters Kluwer Law & Business.

Chaum, D. (1983). Blind signatures for untraceable payments. In Chaum, D., Rivest, R. L., & Sherman, A. T. (Eds.), *Advances in Cryptology* (pp. 199–203). Springer., DOI: 10.1007/978-1-4757-0602-4_18

Christidis, K., & Devetsikiotis, M. (2016). Blockchains and smart contracts for the internet of things. *IEEE Access : Practical Innovations, Open Solutions*, *4*, 2292–2303. https://ieeexplore.ieee.org/abstract/document/758150. DOI: 10.1109/ACCESS.2016.2566339

Cusumano, M. A., & Yoffie, D. B. (2019). Competing in the age of ai: Strategy and leadership when algorithms and networks run the world. *Harvard Business Review*.

Dasgupta, S., & Shetty, S. (2018). Blockchain and cybersecurity: Issues and challenges. *IEEE Potentials*, *37*(2), 38–43.

Deng, H., Garcia, M. L., & Kaminsky, P. (2018). Blockchain-based platform for industrial iot: A case study. *IEEE Transactions on Industrial Informatics*, *14*(7), 3204–3212.

Dwyer, G. P. (2015). The economics of bitcoin and similar private digital currencies. *Journal of Financial Stability*, *17*, 81–91. DOI: 10.1016/j.jfs.2014.11.006

Fleder, M., & Hosanagar, K. (2009). Blockbuster culture's next rise or fall: The impact of recommender systems on sales diversity. *Management Science*, *55*(5), 697–712. DOI: 10.1287/mnsc.1080.0974

Gans, J. S., & Leigh, A. (2017). Artificial intelligence and healthcare. *Harvard Business Review*, *95*(1), 50–60.

Hayek, M., Kondor, D., & Vayanos, D. (2018). Liquidity in the time of covid-19: A preliminary report. *Journal of Financial Economics*, *21*(3), 1–35.

Hughes, A., Park, A., Kietzmann, J., & Archer-Brown, C. (2019). Beyond Bitcoin: What blockchain and distributed ledger technologies mean for firms. *Business Horizons*, *62*(3), 1–9. DOI: 10.1016/j.bushor.2019.01.002

Hughes, E. (1993). *A Cypherpunk's Manifesto*. Archived from the original on March 24, 2021. Retrieved January 20, 2025, from https://nakamotoinstitute.org/library/cypherpunk-manifesto/

Jajodia, S., & Krotov, V. (2019). *Blockchain and healthcare: The coming disruption*. CRC Press.

Jobes, M. (2019). *Fintech: Financial technology beginner guide cherrytree style*. Independently published.

Kräussl, R., & Tugnetti, A. (2024). Non-Fungible Tokens (NFTs): A Review of Pricing Determinants, Applications and Opportunities. *Journal of Economic Surveys*, *38*(2), 555–574. DOI: 10.1111/joes.12597

Kshetri, N. (2018). Blockchain's roles in meeting key supply chain management objectives. *International Journal of Information Management*, *39*, 80–89. DOI: 10.1016/j.ijinfomgt.2017.12.005

Liu, W., Du, Y., & Deng, X. (2019). An adaptive machine learning-based dynamic prediction model for stock price trend forecasting. *Expert Systems with Applications*, *128*, 1–12.

Mazur, M., & Polyzos, E. (2024). Non-fungible tokens (NFTs). In *The Elgar Companion to Decentralized Finance, Digital Assets, and Blockchain Technologies*. Edward Elgar Publishing., DOI: 10.4337/9781035307760.00019

Morris, D. Z. (2018). *The blockchain: A guide for legal and business professionals*. Thomson Reuters.

Nakamoto, S. (2008). *Bitcoin: A peer-to-peer electronic cash system*. https://bitcoin.org/bitcoin.pdf

O'Reilly, T. (2019). *WTF?: What's the future and why it's up to us*. HarperCollins.

Rehman, W., Zainab, H., Imran, J., & Bawany, N. Z. (2021). NFTs: Applications and Challenges. In *22nd International Arab Conference on Information Technology (ACIT)* (pp. 1-7). IEEE. DOI: 10.1109/ACIT53391.2021.9677260

Reiff, N. (2019). *Investing in blockchain: Cryptocurrency, fintech, and beyond*. Skyhorse Publishing.

Sgroi, D., Proto, E., & Oswald, A. J. (2019). Artificial intelligence and life satisfaction. *Proceedings of the National Academy of Sciences of the United States of America*, *116*(20), 9788–9795.

Valeonti, F., Bikakis, A., Terras, M., Speed, C., Hudson-Smith, A., & Chalkias, K. (2021). Crypto Collectibles, Museum Funding and OpenGLAM: Challenges, Opportunities and the Potential of Non-Fungible Tokens (NFTs). *Applied Sciences (Basel, Switzerland)*, *11*(21), 9931. DOI: 10.3390/app11219931

Zhang, G. P. (2019). *Neural networks for time series forecasting with r: An intuitive step by step blueprint for beginners*. Createspace Independent Publishing Platform.

Zhang, Y., Wen, Y., Chen, Y., & Li, J. (2019). Blockchain based cloud manufacturing: A case study of 3D printing service. *Robotics and Computer-integrated Manufacturing*, *56*, 335–344.

Zohren, S., & Roberts, S. (2018). Blockchain for financial market infrastructures. *Annual Review of Financial Economics*, *10*(1), 311–328.

ADDITIONAL READING

Arnold, M. (2021). *FT Guide to digital financial services*. Pearson. This guide provides a comprehensive overview of the FinTech landscape, covering various aspects from digital banking and payments to blockchain and AI, explaining the application of these in the retail and institutional financial services industry.

Atzori, M. (2015). Blockchain technology and decentralized governance: Is the state still necessary? [IJEGR]. *International Journal of Electronic Government Research*, *11*(1), 1–18.

Davenport, T. H., & Ronanki, R. (2018). *Artificial intelligence for the real world*. Harvard Business Review Press. This book provides a practical guide to implementing AI in business, including financial services, focusing on real-world applications and strategies.

European Union Agency for Cybersecurity (ENISA). (Various years). *Threat Landscape Reports*. ENISA publishes regular reports on cybersecurity threats, many of which discuss threats relevant to FinTech, such as those targeting blockchain, digital wallets, and online banking. These reports offer valuable insights into security challenges and mitigation strategies.

Marr, B. (2016). *Big data in practice: How 45 successful companies used big data analytics to deliver extraordinary results*. John Wiley & Sons. This book offers practical insights into how big data analytics is applied in various industries, with relevant examples for the financial sector.

Narayanan, A., Bonneau, J., Felten, E., Miller, A., Goldfeder, S., & Clark, J. (2016). *Bitcoin and cryptocurrency technologies: A comprehensive introduction*. Princeton University Press. This book offers a comprehensive technical introduction to Bitcoin and cryptocurrencies, covering the underlying technology, economics, and potential applications.

OECD. (2020). *The tokenisation of assets and potential implications for financial markets*. OECD Publishing. This report by the OECD delves into the concept of asset tokenization using blockchain, offering insights into its potential to reshape financial markets and the associated regulatory considerations.

Russell, S. J., & Norvig, P. (2020). Artificial intelligence: A modern approach (4th ed.). Pearson Education Limited. While a general AI textbook, it provides fundamental knowledge of AI and machine learning concepts that are crucial to understanding their applications in FinTech.

Tapscott, D., & Tapscott, A. (2016). *Blockchain revolution: How the technology behind bitcoin is changing money, business, and the world.*[1] Portfolio Penguin. This book explores the broader implications of blockchain technology across various industries, including finance, supply chain management, and governance.

World Bank. (2023). *Fintech and the future of finance*. World Bank. This publication by the World Bank explores the implications of fintech and the digital transformation of financial services for market outcomes on one side, and regulation and supervision, on the other, and how these interact.

KEY TERMS AND DEFINITIONS

Artificial Intelligence (AI): The simulation of human intelligence processes by computer systems. In FinTech, AI is used for fraud detection, risk management, and customer service.

Blockchain: A distributed digital ledger that records transactions across many computers. It is known for its security, transparency, and immutability.

Central Bank Digital Currency (CBDC): A digital version of a country's national currency, issued directly by the central bank.

Cloud Computing: The practice of using a network of remote servers hosted on the internet to store, manage, and process data, rather than a local server or a personal computer.

Cryptocurrency: A digital or virtual currency that uses cryptography for security. It operates independently of a central bank. Examples include Bitcoin and Ethereum.

FinTech: A term used to describe technology-driven innovation in financial services, encompassing a wide range of applications from mobile banking to cryptocurrencies.

Machine Learning (ML): A subset of AI that enables systems to learn from data and improve from experience without being explicitly programmed.

Non-Fungible Token (NFT): A unique digital asset that represents ownership of a specific item or piece of content. NFTs are not interchangeable.

Stablecoin: A type of cryptocurrency designed to have its value pegged to a relatively stable asset, such as the US dollar, to minimize price volatility.

Utility Token: A type of cryptocurrency token that provides access to a product or service within a specific blockchain ecosystem.

Chapter 6
Understanding the Cryptocurrency Market

Reena Dogra
https://orcid.org/0000-0002-9388-1059
Himachal Pradesh University, India

Aprajita Kimta
https://orcid.org/0009-0009-8492-3040
Himachal Pradesh University, India

ABSTRACT

This chapter provides a comprehensive overview of the cryptocurrency ecosystem. It begins by tracing the market's origins, focusing on Bitcoin's 2009 launch and its transformative impact on digital transactions. Blockchain technology is explained in detail, covering its decentralized ledger system, including blocks, chains, nodes, and consensus mechanisms like Proof of Work and Proof of Stake. The chapter offers a historical perspective on mining, from early methods to advanced techniques. The workings of cryptocurrency exchanges are discussed, comparing centralized and decentralized platforms. The chapter examines cryptocurrency price determination through supply and demand dynamics and external influences such as economic trends and technological advancements etc. Market volatility and its implications for investors are analyzed, along with global regulatory approaches and their effects on the market. The chapter concludes with insights into future trends and emerging applications, offering a thorough understanding of the cryptocurrency market and its evolution.

DOI: 10.4018/979-8-3693-5986-0.ch006

INTRODUCTION

The cryptocurrency market has developed rapidly, emerging as one of the fastest-growing financial markets worldwide (Conrad et al., 2018). The origins of cryptocurrencies trace back to 2009, when an anonymous individual or group using the pseudonym Satoshi Nakamoto introduced Bitcoin. This marked the birth of the decentralized digital currency movement, with Bitcoin designed as a peer-to-peer electronic cash system to facilitate transactions without intermediaries (Judmayer et al., 2017). Initially, the cryptocurrency market was dominated by Bitcoin, but it has since expanded to include thousands of alternative cryptocurrencies with distinct functions and uses (Aysan et al., 2021). Cryptocurrencies are built on blockchain technology, a decentralized ledger that records all transactions across a network of computers. This technology ensures transparency, security, and immutability, which are critical for fostering trust in digital currencies (Yermack, 2015). Since Bitcoin's inception, the cryptocurrency market has expanded rapidly, both in terms of the number of cryptocurrencies and their market capitalization. As of November 2021, the market capitalization of cryptocurrencies exceeded $3 trillion, reflecting their growing importance and acceptance (CoinMarketCap, 2021). The significance of cryptocurrencies in today's financial landscape is multifaceted. Cryptocurrencies facilitate faster and cheaper cross-border transactions compared to traditional financial systems, making them particularly valuable for global commerce (Chuen et al., 2017). Institutional adoption of cryptocurrencies has grown significantly, with companies like Tesla and MicroStrategy integrating cryptocurrencies into their operations. Furthermore, the cryptocurrency market operates 24/7 across global exchanges, enabling seamless trading and liquidity for participants worldwide (Corbet et al., 2019). Overall, the cryptocurrency market represents a dynamic and rapidly evolving sector. Its continued growth and maturation will likely depend on ongoing innovations, regulatory developments, and broader economic trends shaping global markets (Fahlenbrach & Frattini, 2022).

BLOCKCHAIN TECHNOLOGY

Blockchain technology is a rapidly evolving field in IT and computing, characterized by its encrypted and distributed database system for recording data. The term 'blockchain' was first coined by David Chaum in 1982 as part of his work on cryptographic protocols (Chaum, 1982), and further developed by Stuart Haber and W. Scott Stornetta in 1992, who introduced a method for securing digital documents using timestamps (Haber & Stornetta, 1992). The concept gained popularity with the creation of Bitcoin by Satoshi Nakamoto in 2009, who developed the first digital currency using blockchain technology. Since then, the tools, technologies, and protocols related to blockchain have been expanding (Yermack, 2015). Blockchain operates as a distributed database that records transactions, validated and maintained by a global network of computers. Instead of relying on a central authority like a bank, transaction records are overseen by a large community, ensuring that no single individual has control or the ability to alter or erase transaction history. Blockchain enables all participants in the network to view each other's entries, preventing any single central entity from gaining control over the network (Conrad et al., 2018). Unlike conventional centralized databases, the information on a blockchain is immutable due to its decentralized structure and the consensus guarantees provided by its participants. When a transaction is initiated, it is sent to the network, where computer algorithms verify its authenticity. After the transaction is confirmed, it is connected to previous transactions, creating a continuous chain known as the blockchain (Nakamoto, 2008). Blockchain technology relies on a decentralized network, functioning as a peer-to-peer system. Consequently, blockchain technology is a fraud-resistant system with the potential to revolutionize the financial sector in a transparent and advanced manner (Yermack, 2015). It offers many benefits more efficiently than traditional business processes, with its applications expanding across various sectors and locations. These benefits are illustrated in Figure 1.

Figure 1. Benefits of blockchain technology

Types of Blockchain Technology

1. **Public Blockchains:** Public blockchains are accessible to anyone, allowing individuals to participate in the decision-making process by becoming nodes. However, users may or may not receive benefits for their involvement. No single entity owns the ledgers, and they are publicly available to all network participants (Nakamoto, 2008). Public blockchains are non-restrictive and distributed ledger systems that do not require any permissions. Anyone with access can be authorized to retrieve data from the blockchain. This type of blockchain also

grants authorization for verifying both current and past records. Examples of this type of blockchain include Bitcoin, Ethereum, and Litecoin (Buterin, 2013).

2. **Private Blockchains:** Private blockchains are restricted and have controlled access. They require permission from system administrators for transactions (Pilkington, 2016). These blockchains operate within closed systems and networks, typically within organizations or enterprises where membership is selective. The controlling organization manages the security, authorizations, permissions, and accessibility. Consequently, private blockchains function similarly to public blockchains but within a smaller, more restrictive network. Examples include Hyperledger, Corda, and Multichain (Androulaki et al., 2018).
3. **Hybrid Blockchains**: A hybrid blockchain combines features of both public and private blockchains, offering better control to achieve broader objectives. It integrates aspects of centralized and decentralized systems while maintaining a closed nature (Zheng et al., 2017). Hybrid blockchains prioritize integrity, transparency, and security. In hybrid blockchains, the main benefits include maximum customization with a blend of private permission-based and public permission-less systems. Only a specific portion of data or records from the blockchain is made public, while the rest remains confidential within the private network. The hybrid blockchain system is flexible, allowing users to easily join a private blockchain with multiple public blockchains, enhancing both security and transparency across the blockchain network. Examples include the IBM Blockchain Platform and Dragonchain.
4. **Consortium Blockchain**: Consortium blockchains are semi-decentralized systems that enable organizations to jointly manage the blockchain network. They can function within a single organization or involve multiple entities collaborating to exchange information or perform mining activities (Weber et al., 2016). Examples include the Energy Web Foundation and R3.

Blockchain Architecture

Blockchain technology operates on the principle of a decentralized database, where the database exists on multiple computers, with each copy being identical to the others Blockchain architecture can be primarily divided into three layers Applications, Decentralized Ledger, and Peer-to-Peer Network. The Applications layer is at the top of the network followed by the Decentralized Ledger, which maintains transaction records with transparency and integrity, with the Peer-to-Peer Network forming the bottom layer (Narayanan et al. 2016).

Figure 2. Layers of blockchain architecture

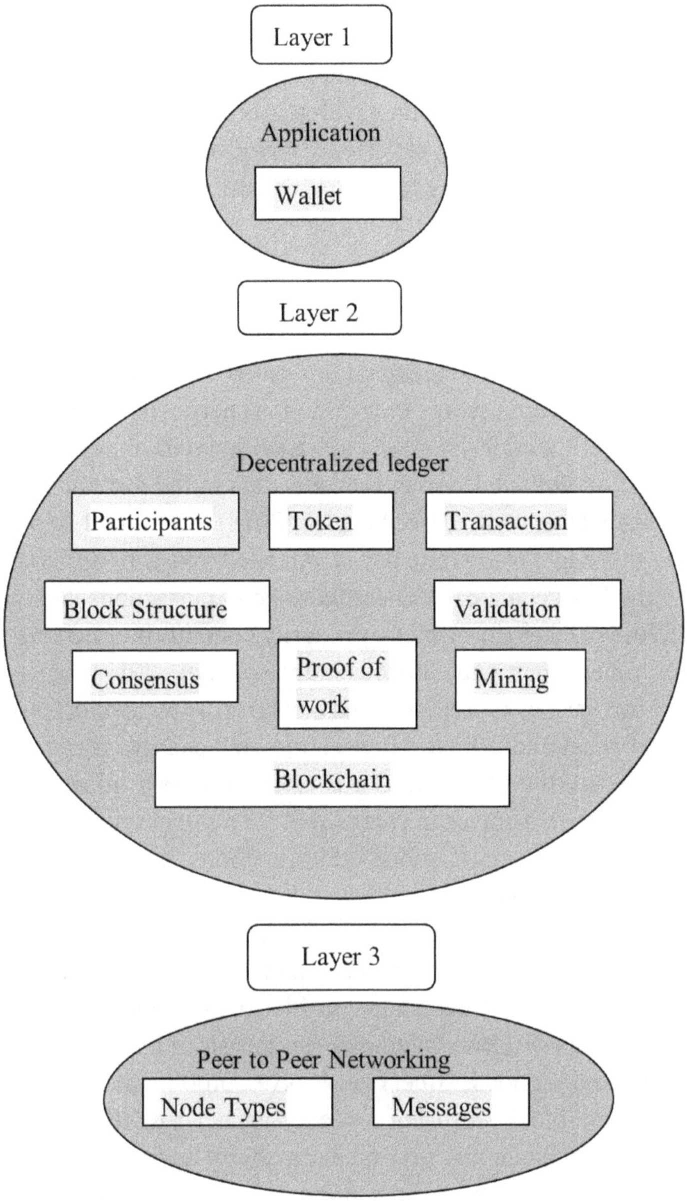

1. **Applications**

The application layer offers blockchain-based applications for end users. It can be installed on computers or mobile devices or hosted on a third-party platform, providing flexibility and accessibility for users (Sarmah, 2018; Paul et al., 2021). Additionally, these applications often include features for managing digital assets, performing transactions, and integrating with other blockchain services. This ensures a comprehensive and user-friendly experience for individuals and businesses looking to leverage blockchain technology for secure and efficient operations (Judmayer et al., 2017).

2. **Decentralized Ledger**

A decentralized ledger is a shared and replicated database synchronized among network members. It keeps records of transactions between participants within the network. This ledger functions similarly to a traditional database but differs in that it stores information in the header and records data in the form of tokens or cryptocurrencies (Narayanan et al. 2016, Sarmah, 2018). The initial step in recording transactions in the ledger is to group newly validated transactions into a block. Any participant in the blockchain can collect these new transactions and create blocks to be added to the blockchain. A block primarily contains transactions, along with a hash pointer, timestamps, and a nonce (Judmayer et al., 2017).

Nodes perform various functions based on their role in the blockchain network. When a node proposes and validates transactions and engages in mining to achieve consensus and secure the blockchain, it is referred to as a miner (Giudici et al., 2020; Tredinnick, 2019, Narayanan et al. 2016). Nodes can also perform tasks such as simple payment verification, among other functions, depending on the specific blockchain being used (Nakamoto, 2008).

Proof of Work (PoW) is a consensus mechanism widely used in blockchain networks such as Bitcoin. It involves miners competing to solve complex mathematical puzzles to validate transactions and add new blocks to the blockchain (Judmayer et al., 2017; Sovbetov, 2018). Bitcoin employs hashcash as its proof of work mechanism for verifying transactions. Miners must solve a proof of work puzzle to validate transactions within a block, ensuring its acceptance across the network. Proof of work is expensive to sustain and may face scalability and security challenges due to its reliance on miners' incentives. An alternative and more advanced solution for this is known as "Proof of Stake" (PoS) (Narayanan et al. 2016)

Proof of Stake (PoS) is an alternative consensus mechanism adopted by some cryptocurrencies, including Ethereum 2.0. In PoS, participants validate and create new blocks based on the number of coins they hold and are willing to "stake" as collateral. This approach aims to achieve consensus more efficiently and with lower energy consumption compared to PoW (Chen, 2021; Sovbetov, 2018). Proof-of-stake aims to reduce network congestion and address environmental sustainability concerns associated with the proof-of-work protocol (Li & Wang, 2017; Woebbeking, 2021).

3. **Peer to peer network**

Blockchain utilizes P2P network technology to provide a decentralized ledger for digital assets. In a blockchain P2P network, all the nodes or computers are connected to one another. Each node maintains a complete copy of the ledger, which is compared to other nodes to ensure data accuracy (Nakamoto, 2008; Sarmah, 2018). This is the opposite of a centralized system like a bank, where transactions are privately stored and managed. The P2P architecture is crucial for blockchains, as it allows cryptocurrencies like Bitcoin to be transferred globally without any intermediary or central server. The creator of Bitcoin, Satoshi Nakamoto, referred to it as a "peer-to-peer electronic cash system". Key benefits of using P2P networks in blockchain include cost-effectiveness, scalability, and resilience, as the loss of a single node does not bring down the entire network. However, P2P networks also have drawbacks like slower performance, data vulnerability, and high computational power requirements (Dwyer, 2015; Sovbetov, 2018).

How Blockchain Works

Blockchain technology functions as a decentralized digital ledger that records and verifies transactions across a network of computers. Each transaction is bundled into a block and linked sequentially to the previous one, creating a secure and immutable chain of records (Nakamoto, 2008; Sarmah, 2018). Figure 3 represents the working of a blockchain.

Figure 3. Working of a blockchain

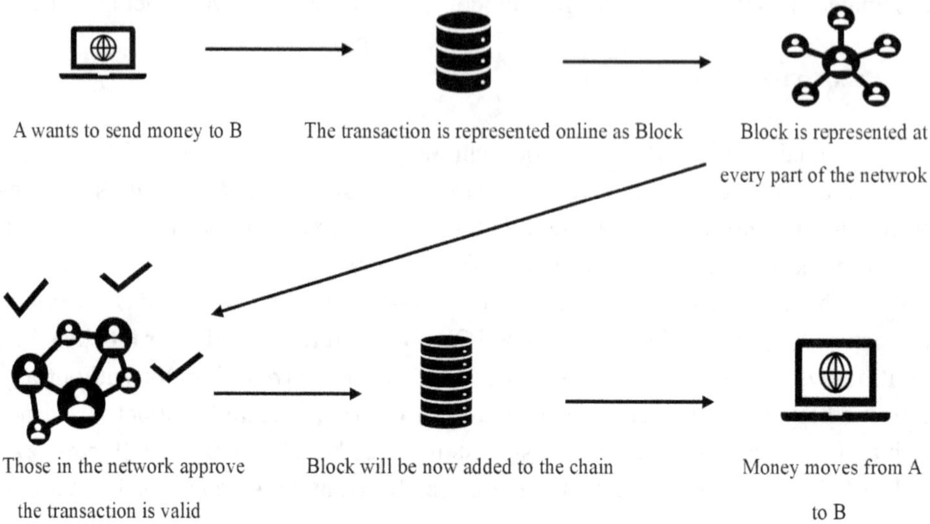

Let us understand how blockchain works with an example suppose A wants to send Bitcoins to B. This transaction is broadcast to a decentralized network of computers, known as nodes, for validation. Each node independently verifies the transaction details to ensure that person A has the sufficient balance and that the transaction follows the network's rules.

Once validated, this transaction, along with other recent transactions, is grouped into a block. A miner or validator node then competes to solve a complex mathematical puzzle, a process known as mining (in proof-of-work systems) or staking (in proof-of-stake systems). The first node to solve the puzzle gets to add the new block to the existing blockchain.

The newly created block includes a reference to the previous block. Once added, the block is broadcast to the entire network, and all nodes update their copy of the blockchain to include this new block. This makes the transaction from Person A to Person B permanent and immutable, ensuring transparency and security. If anyone tries to alter the transaction, the change would be invalidated by the network, as it would not match the cryptographic hash of the previous block.

Advantages of Blockchain

1. The decentralized nature of blockchain technology enables a database to be shared without the need for a central authority.
2. Blockchains offer complete, consistent, and current data with high accuracy.

3. Users have the ability to manage their information and transactions.
4. Blockchain operates on a decentralized network, making it resistant to security breaches that typically target centralized system.
5. Blockchains ensure transparency and immutability in transactions, as all recorded transactions cannot be altered or deleted.
6. Users within a blockchain can easily track the history of transactions, as each transaction is digitally stamped.
7. Multiple copies of data can be stored in the blockchain, allowing users to avoid centralizing sensitive data.

Disadvantages of Blockchain

1. Blockchains are costly and resource-intensive because every node in the network must perform redundant tasks to achieve consensus.
2. In blockchain, a transaction is confirmed only after all nodes in the network successfully verify it. This process can be slow because each new block must be verified by all nodes to authenticate the transaction.
3. One drawback of blockchain is its complexity, which makes it challenging for the average person to understand. The technology involves intricate concepts and processes that have not been simplified enough for widespread consumer adoption and mainstream use.

MINING OF CRYPTOCURRENCY

Cryptocurrency mining serves as the backbone of blockchain networks, ensuring the validity and trustworthiness of transactions in a decentralized manner. Cryptocurrency mining is the process of validating transactions and creating new coins on a blockchain network (Narayanan et al., 2016; Nakamoto, 2008). Miners use powerful computers to solve complex mathematical problems, which allows them to add new blocks to the blockchain and earn rewards in the form of newly minted cryptocurrency. This process not only secures the network against fraud but also decentralizes control, as anyone with the necessary hardware and software can participate (Dwyer, 2015; Sarmah, 2018). Since the emergence of Bitcoin, mining technology has evolved through four generations: Central Processing Units (CPUs), Graphics Processing Units (GPUs), Field-Programmable Gate Arrays (FPGAs), and Application-Specific Integrated Circuits (ASICs). Each successive generation has brought improvements in mining efficiency (Judmayer et al., 2017; Narayanan et al., 2016). In 2011, GPU-based devices began to replace CPU-based ones. FPGA devices entered the market in January 2012, and by 2014, they had become the dominant technology. Although ASIC devices were introduced in early 2013, their adoption lagged behind FPGAs due to the higher initial costs involved (Narayanan et al., 2016).

Generations of Mining

CPU Mining: The first generation of Bitcoin mining was performed on general-purpose computers using their central processing units (CPUs). CPU mining involved running simple code that searched for valid nonces in a linear manner. However, this method is extremely slow on general-purpose computers. Today, CPU mining is not profitable due to the high difficulty levels. Anyone attempting to mine using a CPU likely does not understand how Bitcoin mining works and would be disappointed by the lack of earnings (Judmayer et al., 2017).

GPU Mining: GPU mining refers to the process of using graphics processing units (GPUs) for Bitcoin mining. As CPUs proved too slow for effective mining, miners turned to GPUs, which are designed for high data processing capacity and parallel processing, making them well-suited for computing multiple hashes simultaneously with different nonces. GPUs are widely available and can be easily set up (Narayanan et al., 2016; Sovbetov, 2018). Additionally, GPUs can be overclocked to operate faster than their intended speed, which boosts mining efficiency and potentially increases profits, though it also raises risks such as overheating or errors. Errors from overclocking can be mitigated by verifying solutions on a CPU, and miners frequently adjust overclocking settings to optimize profitability (Sarmah, 2018). Multiple GPUs can be connected to a single motherboard and CPU, enabling miners to create efficient setups capable of managing numerous GPUs simultaneously (Judmayer et al., 2017).

FPGA Mining: FPGA mining refers to the practice of using Field-Programmable Gate Arrays (FPGAs) for cryptocurrency mining. Miners initially turned to FPGAs around 2011 as they offered better performance than GPUs on certain operations crucial for mining, such as bit manipulation. Unlike GPUs, FPGAs could potentially utilize all of their transistors for mining tasks and were easier to cool in mining setups (Judmayer et al., 2017). Despite these advantages, FPGA mining faced several challenges. FPGAs were pushed beyond their typical operational limits for continuous mining, leading to reliability issues like errors and malfunctions (Narayanan et al., 2016). Additionally, programming and setting up FPGAs required specialized knowledge, which was less widely available compared to GPU mining setups. Ultimately, FPGA mining was short-lived as the arrival of Application-Specific Integrated Circuits (ASICs) offered even greater efficiency (Narayanan et al., 2016).

ASIC Mining: ASIC mining refers to the process of using Application-Specific Integrated Circuits (ASICs) to mine cryptocurrencies. These specialized hardware devices are designed specifically for the efficient mining of a particular cryptocurrency algorithm, offering high processing power and energy efficiency compared to general-purpose CPUs or GPUs. Mining today is predominantly powered by Bitcoin ASICs, which are specialized chips specifically designed, manufactured, and optimized for mining Bitcoins (Judmayer et al., 2017). Initially, early generations of Bitcoin ASICs faced challenges, often failing to meet performance expectations due to technical issues. Over time, these ASICs have matured, and more reliable models are now available (Sarmah, 2018).

Key Tasks Involved in Bitcoin Mining

1. **Listen for transactions:** Miners listen for new transactions broadcasted on the network. They validate these transactions by ensuring that signatures are correct and that the outputs being spent have not already been spent.
2. **Maintain blockchain and listen for new blocks:** Miners keep an up-to-date copy of the entire blockchain. This involves requesting and receiving all historical blocks when they join the network and continuously listening for and validating new blocks.
3. **Assemble a candidate block:** With an updated blockchain, miners can start building their own blocks. They collect valid transactions they have heard about and assemble them into a new block that extends the most recent block in the blockchain.
4. **Find a nonce that makes the block valid:** This is the most computationally intensive part of mining. Miners need to find a special number called a nonce that, when added to their block, results in a hash that meets the Bitcoin network's difficulty criteria.
5. **Hope the block is accepted:** Once a miner finds a valid block, they broadcast it to the network. The block will only become part of the consensus chain if other miners accept it and begin mining on top of it, rather than on a competitor's block.
6. **Profit:** If a miner's block is accepted, they receive a block reward. They also collect transaction fees from the transactions included in their block.

Mining new cryptocurrency typically involves solving complex mathematical problems to validate transactions and add them to a blockchain. Cryptocurrency mining, like Bitcoin, begins with miners monitoring the network for new transactions. They verify these transactions by confirming the signatures and ensuring that the outputs being spent have not been previously used. Simultaneously, miners maintain an updated copy of the blockchain, which involves receiving historical blocks and continuously validating new ones (Narayanan et al., 2016). With an updated blockchain, miners assemble candidate blocks by collecting validated transactions and organizing them into a new block linked to the latest one in the chain. The most crucial step is finding a correct nonce (special number). This nonce, when added to their block, results in a hash that meets the network's difficulty criteria. This process requires significant computational power and involves extensive trial and error (Bonneau et al., 2015). Once a miner successfully finds the correct nonce, they broadcast the valid block to the network. Other miners verify the block and, if accepted, they use it for further block creation. As a reward for this effort, the miner receives a certain number of newly created Bitcoins, known as the block reward, along with transaction fees from the included transactions in the block (Narayanan et al., 2016). This newly mined Bitcoin is then credited to the miner's wallet, increasing the total supply of Bitcoin in circulation.

In essence, Bitcoin mining involves validating transactions, maintaining the blockchain, assembling new blocks, solving complex computational problems to find valid nonces, and earning rewards when blocks are successfully added to the blockchain.

EXCHANGE OF CRYPTOCURRENCIES

A cryptocurrency exchange is a digital marketplace that allows users to buy, sell, and trade various cryptocurrencies, with Binance being the world's largest by trading volume (Sovbetov, 2018). The value of Bitcoin and other cryptocurrencies is often represented by their exchange rates against traditional currencies. Most Bitcoin users do not mine the cryptocurrency themselves; instead, they buy bitcoins using fiat money. Online exchanges, where users can trade bitcoins for other currencies, play a crucial role in the cryptocurrency ecosystem (Dwyer, 2015). A cryptocurrency exchange operates much like a stock exchange, enabling investors to buy and sell digital currencies like Bitcoin, Ethereum, or Tether. These platforms function through digital marketplaces accessible via mobile apps or desktop interfaces (Sovbetov, 2018). In Bitcoin's history, there have been a few major exchange platforms. Mt. Gox, which launched in July 2010, was the first Bitcoin exchange and dominated the USD exchange market for several years. However, as Mt. Gox experienced various technical problems and legal issues, trading at BitStamp, BTCe, and BiFinex (collectively referred to as the Big 3) began to rise. By the latter half of 2013, the Big 3 had captured more than 50 percent of the Bitcoin-USD exchange market share. Mt. Gox ultimately suspended all transactions in February 2014 due to a severe security breach (Narayanan et al., 2016). Since then, the cryptocurrency exchange landscape has continued to evolve rapidly. Newer platforms such as Coinbase, Binance, and Kraken have risen, offering a wider range of cryptocurrencies and trading pairs. These exchanges have played pivotal roles in shaping the global cryptocurrency market, providing advanced trading features, security measures, and regulatory compliance to meet growing demand and investor expectations (Sovbetov, 2018; Dwyer, 2015).

Types of Cryptocurrency Exchange

Centralised Exchange (CEX)

Centralized exchanges (CEXs) operate in a manner similar to conventional equity stock exchanges. As their name suggests, centralized exchanges are governed by a single authoritative entity that monitors and controls all activities on the platform. centralized nature allows for a structured and controlled trading environment, where the exchange itself acts as an intermediary between buyers and sellers (Chan et al., 2020). This setup provides a layer of security and trust for users, as the exchange takes on the responsibility of facilitating trades, ensuring liquidity, and maintaining market order. One of the primary benefits of centralized exchanges is their ability to offer high liquidity. This high liquidity is crucial for traders, especially those dealing with large volumes of assets, as it ensures that they can enter and exit positions without significantly affecting the market price (Auer & Claessens, 2021). Popular Crypto Exchanges are Binance, Coinbase Exchange, Kraken and KuCoin.

Advantages of Centralized Cryptocurrency Exchanges

1. **High Liquidity:** Centralized exchanges provide high liquidity by having a large number of active participants and trading activity, which allows users to buy and sell assets promptly without significant price variations.
2. **User-Friendly Interfaces:** CEXs are designed to be accessible to both new and experienced traders, offering intuitive interfaces and comprehensive trading tools.
3. **Range of Services:** They often provide additional financial services such as futures trading, margin trading, staking, lending, and more, catering to various investment strategies.
4. **Customer Support:** Centralized exchanges typically offer robust customer support, providing assistance for technical issues, account-related queries, and other concerns.

Disadvantages of Centralized Cryptocurrency Exchanges

1. **Security Risks:** Centralised exchange holds users funds in custodial wallets, making them attractive targets for hackers. Several high-profile hacks have resulted in significant losses for users.
2. **Transaction Fees:** Trading on centralised exchanges often incurs fees for transactions, withdrawals, and sometimes even deposits. These fees can be relatively high compared to decentralized exchanges (DEXs).
3. **Privacy Concerns:** Users are typically required to undergo Know Your Customer (KYC) and Anti-Money Laundering (AML) procedures, which involve providing personal information. This reduces anonymity compared to DEXs.

Decentralised Exchange (DEX)

Decentralized exchanges (DEXs) represent a paradigm shift in how cryptocurrencies are traded, operating on blockchain technology without a central authority overseeing transactions (Buterin, 2013; Pilkington, 2016). Unlike centralized exchanges (CEXs), which rely on intermediaries to facilitate trades and manage user funds, DEXs allow users to interact directly with each other through smart contracts deployed on the blockchain (Sarmah, 2018; Chan et al., 2020). One of the primary advantages of DEXs is peer-to-peer trading. This means that users can execute trades directly with one another without relying on a central authority to match orders (Morton, 2020; Riley, 2021). Another defining characteristic of DEXs is decentralized control and governance. Unlike CEXs, where decisions are made by a central entity, DEXs operate in a distributed manner where decisions are typically governed by the community of users. Users can trade anonymously on these platforms, as they often do not require users to undergo Know Your Customer (KYC) or Anti-Money Laundering (AML) verification procedures. Since users retain control of their funds and transactions occur directly on the blockchain, DEXs are less susceptible to large-scale hacks or thefts that target centralized custodial wallets (Sovbetov, 2018; Giudici et al., 2020). Overall, decentralized exchanges represent an innovative approach to cryptocurrency trading, offering increased transparency, privacy, and community-driven governance compared to traditional centralized exchanges (Morton, 2020). As the cryptocurrency ecosystem continues to evolve, DEXs play a crucial role in providing alternative trading solutions that empower users and promote decentralization in financial markets. Examples of DEXs include Uniswap, PancakeSwap, and Kyber, etc.

Advantages of Decentralized Exchanges

1) **Security:** DEXs do not hold user's funds in centralized wallets, significantly reducing the risk of large-scale hacks or thefts targeting centralized exchanges.
2) **Privacy:** Many DEXs allow users to trade anonymously, as they typically do not require Know Your Customer (KYC) or Anti-Money Laundering (AML) verification. This enhances user privacy and reduces exposure to identity theft or data breaches.
3) **Direct Control:** Users retain control of their funds throughout the trading process. Trades are executed directly between users' wallets via smart contracts, eliminating the need for intermediaries and reducing counterparty risk.

Disadvantages of Decentralized Cryptocurrency Exchanges

1) **Liquidity Challenges:** Decentralised exchange may face liquidity issues, particularly for less popular trading pairs. This can result in higher price volatility and difficulty in executing large trades at desired prices.
2) **Complexity:** Some decentralised exchange platforms have complex user interfaces and trading mechanisms, which can be challenging for beginners to navigate. Users may need to familiarize themselves with new concepts like wallet management, smart contracts, and decentralized governance.
3) **Transaction Speed and Costs:** Transactions on DEXs can be slower and more costly compared to centralized exchanges due to the need to interact with smart contracts and pay blockchain network fees. This can affect the overall user experience, especially during periods of high network congestion.
4) **Limited Customer Support:** DEXs generally offer minimal or decentralized customer support compared to centralized exchanges. Resolving issues or disputes may require relying on community forums, which can lead to delays in assistance.

Figure 4. Centralised & decentralised exchange

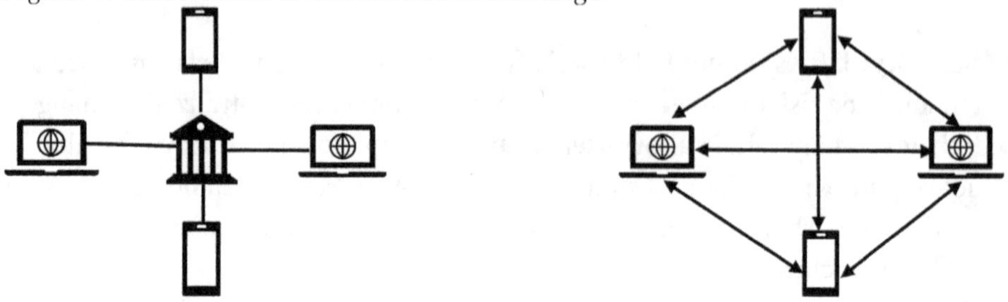

HOW EXCHANGE WORKS

Centralized Exchange

Let's consider an example in a centralized exchange setting: A, B, and C are involved in trading Bitcoin on a platform like Coinbase. A, B, and C each create accounts on Coinbase and deposit their assets. A deposits $2,000 in fiat currency, while B deposits 1 Bitcoin. When A wants to buy Bitcoin, they place a buy order on Coinbase. B, looking to sell their Bitcoin, places a sell order. Coinbase matches A's buy order with B's sell order, managing the transaction and ensuring the secure transfer of Bitcoin from B to A, and the corresponding fiat amount from A to B. C, also a user on Coinbase, can only view their own transactions and account balance. The centralized nature of the exchange means that Coinbase oversees all transactions and asset management, providing a trusted, user-friendly platform but also representing a single point of failure.

Decentralized Exchange

In a decentralized exchange scenario, A, B, and C use a platform like Uniswap to trade cryptocurrencies without relying on a central authority. Each participant uses their own digital wallets to manage their funds. A, B, and C connect their wallets to Uniswap. A want to buy Bitcoin, so they initiate a transaction to exchange $2,000 worth of Ethereum for Bitcoin. B, who wants to sell Bitcoin, creates a corresponding trade offer. Instead of a central authority managing the transaction, Uniswap's smart contract technology automatically matches A's buy order with B's sell order, facilitating the exchange directly between their wallets. All three participants can view and verify the transaction on the blockchain, ensuring transparency and security. In this decentralized system, there is no single point of control, reducing the risk of a central failure and enhancing user autonomy.

Price Determination of Cryptocurrency

Cryptocurrency prices refer to the current market value of various digital currencies like Bitcoin and Ethereum. These prices fluctuate constantly based on supply and demand dynamics, market sentiment, regulatory news, technological advancements, and broader economic factors. When demand for a cryptocurrency exceeds its supply, prices tend to rise, and when supply exceeds demand, prices fall (Narayanan et al., 2016). Market sentiment, driven by public perception and investor confidence, also plays a crucial role; positive news can boost prices, while negative news can cause declines (Giudici et al., 2020). Additionally, government regulations and policies significantly impact cryptocurrency prices, with regulatory news often causing substantial price volatility (Riley, 2021). Cryptocurrency prices are influenced by a variety of factors that make them highly volatile and unpredictable. Technological advancements within the blockchain space, such as improvements in security and scalability, can enhance a cryptocurrency's utility and drive up its price (Li & Whinston, 2020). Moreover, the entry of institutional investors into the cryptocurrency market can lead to significant price increases due to large-scale investments (Judmayer et al., 2017).

Global economic events and geopolitical developments also play a role; for instance, economic instability or currency devaluation in a country can drive people to invest in cryptocurrencies as a store of value. Furthermore, media coverage and social media trends can rapidly sway investor sentiment, leading to swift price movements (Morton, 2020). The development of new applications and use cases for cryptocurrencies, such as decentralized finance (DeFi) platforms and non-fungible tokens (NFTs), also contribute to their valuation (Yadav et al., 2022). Overall, the cryptocurrency market is complex and influenced by a variety of interrelated factors, making price predictions challenging and the market highly dynamic (Giudici et al., 2020). Understanding cryptocurrency price behavior is essential for gaining insight into the market dynamics of the cryptocurrency industry.

IMPACT OF SUPPLY AND DEMAND ON CRYPTOCURRENCY'S PRICE

Price and Demand

The price of crypto is significantly influenced by its demand in the market. Cryptocurrency prices and demand are highly volatile. Demand for cryptocurrency increases due to factors such as growing adoption, positive regulatory news, or macroeconomic trends, and its price tends to rise (Ciaian et al., 2016). This is because the supply of cryptocurrency is fixed and limited. When more people seek to buy cryptocurrency, the increased demand against the relatively inelastic supply drives prices upward. Conversely, if demand decreases due to negative news, regulatory crackdowns, or market sentiment shifts, the price of cryptocurrency generally falls (Sovbetov, 2018). Positive developments, such as major companies adopting cryptocurrencies, can drive prices up, while negative events like security breaches or regulatory crackdowns can lead to price drops (Chen, 2021). This dynamic of supply and demand is fundamental to volatility and price movements in the cryptocurrency market.

Price and Supply

The relationship between the supply of a cryptocurrency and its price is a fundamental aspect of its market dynamics, governed largely by the principles of supply and demand (Li & Wang, 2017). When the supply of a cryptocurrency is limited or decreases, and demand remains steady or increases, the price typically rises due to scarcity. Conversely, if the supply of a cryptocurrency is abundant or increases significantly, and demand does not increase, the price is likely to fall (Sovbetov, 2018). Market perception and investor sentiment play crucial roles even with a fixed supply. If confidence in the cryptocurrency's future diminishes, demand falls, leading to a decline in price (Li & Whinston, 2020). Technological developments, regulatory changes, and macroeconomic factors also interplay with supply dynamics to influence prices for instance, improvements in blockchain technology or favorable regulatory news can boost demand, thus raising prices even if supply remains constant. On the other hand, regulatory crackdowns or technological flaws can decrease demand, leading to a fall in prices (Chen, 2021). Ultimately, the balance between supply and demand is influenced by external factors.

Impact of Macroeconomic Variables on Bitcoin Price

Macroeconomic variables have significant influence on cryptocurrency prices. Factors such as global economic stability indicators like GDP growth and inflation rates, regulatory developments, currency market dynamics, geopolitical events, market liquidity, and technological advancements collectively shape investor sentiment and drive demand for digital assets (Chan et al., 2020; Li & Whinston, 2020). Understanding these macroeconomic dynamics is crucial for predicting and navigating the volatile price movements of cryptocurrencies.

1. **Inflation Rate:** Inflation rates play a crucial role in shaping the demand for cryptocurrencies like Bitcoin, often regarded as digital gold due to their perceived store of value properties. As traditional fiat currencies experience higher inflation rates, investors seek alternative assets that can preserve purchasing power over time (Dwyer, 2015; Giudici et al., 2020). The increased demand for cryptocurrencies during periods of inflation can drive up their prices. Additionally, the transparency and unchangeable nature of blockchain technology supporting cryptocurrencies increase their appeal as reliable stores of value during times of economic uncertainty and currency devaluation.
2. **Monetary Policies:** Central bank decisions regarding interest rates and quantitative easing can significantly influence investor sentiment toward cryptocurrencies. When central banks lower interest rates and implement expansionary monetary policies, investors often seek higher returns in assets that are perceived as less vulnerable to central bank manipulation and inflationary pressures—like cryptocurrencies (Sovbetov, 2018; Li & Wang, 2017). This shift in investor behavior can drive up cryptocurrency prices. Moreover, these monetary easing measures can lead to increased fiat currency supply, potentially devaluing them over time. This dynamic not only boosts the appeal of decentralized cryptocurrencies such as Bitcoin as stores of value but also underscores their role as inflation hedges in uncertain economic environments.
3. **Geopolitical Events:** Political instability, trade disputes, or sanctions often provoke volatility in traditional markets and lead investors to seek refuge in decentralized assets like cryptocurrencies. These digital assets are perceived as independent of government policies and immune to geopolitical risks that affect traditional financial assets (Woebbeking, 2021). A recent example is the geopolitical tensions surrounding the Russia-Ukraine conflict in early 2022. As the conflict escalated, traditional financial markets experienced significant volatility and declines. Investors, concerned about the impact of sanctions on Russia and the broader geopolitical instability, began seeking alternatives to

traditional assets. During this period, Bitcoin and other cryptocurrencies saw a notable increase in demand, which drove prices up.

4. **Regulatory Developments:** Changes in cryptocurrency regulations significantly impact adoption and market sentiment. Positive regulatory shifts typically boost prices as they enhance investor confidence, increase market liquidity, and foster institutional participation. Conversely, negative regulatory news or uncertainty can lead to price declines as it creates doubts about legality, usability, and long-term viability (Judmayer et al., 2017; Li & Whinston, 2020). For example, when China imposed a ban on Initial Coin Offerings (ICOs) and cryptocurrency exchanges in 2017, it triggered a significant market downturn and dampened investor confidence globally (Motsi-Omoijiade, 2018).
5. **Technological Advancements:** Innovations in blockchain technology are constantly pushing the boundaries of what cryptocurrencies can achieve. With new scalability solutions and enhanced security measures, cryptocurrencies are becoming more functional and attractive to a wider audience. Faster transaction speeds and lower costs make them more practical for everyday use, while improved privacy features address growing concerns about data security (Tredinnick, 2019). These developments can significantly increase the adoption and value of cryptocurrencies across various industries.
6. **Market Sentiment and Speculation:** Cryptocurrency markets are highly sensitive to investor sentiment, media influence, and speculative activity (Liu & Serletis, 2019). Positive developments or media coverage, such as endorsements by influential figures or major corporations adopting cryptocurrencies, can create a positive feedback loop of increased buying interest and price appreciation. Conversely, negative sentiment, market manipulation, or regulatory uncertainty can trigger sell-offs and price volatility (Woebbeking, 2021). A notable example of this dynamic occurred in 2021 when Tesla CEO Elon Musk announced that Tesla would accept Bitcoin as payment for its cars. This endorsement by a high-profile figure led to a surge in Bitcoin's price (Gupta & Chaudhary, 2022). However, the opposite effect was also evident when Elon Musk later reversed this decision, citing environmental concerns over Bitcoin mining's energy consumption, which triggered a significant sell-off, leading to a sharp decline in Bitcoin's price.
7. **Global Economic Stability:** Economic downturns or financial crises can drive interest in alternative assets such as cryptocurrencies, especially during periods of distrust in traditional financial systems. The decentralized nature of cryptocurrencies offers potential resilience against economic instability and capital controls, appealing to investors seeking portfolio diversification and wealth preservation strategies outside traditional financial markets (Sovbetov, 2018). A prominent example of this occurred during the economic turmoil caused by

the COVID-19 pandemic in 2020. As the pandemic spread globally, it triggered a significant economic downturn, leading to widespread market volatility and uncertainty. Bitcoin, in particular, was perceived as "digital gold" due to its limited supply and decentralized nature (Li & Whinston, 2020).

Market Volatility

Cryptocurrency markets are known for their high volatility compared to traditional financial markets. Market volatility refers to the rapid and significant changes in the prices of cryptocurrencies within a short period. Understanding why cryptocurrencies are more volatile, the historical context of major price swings, and the impact of volatility on investment decisions and trading strategies is essential for anyone looking to navigate this dynamic market.

Reasons for High Volatility

1. **Market Size and Liquidity:** Cryptocurrencies operate in a relatively small market compared to traditional assets like stocks and bonds. The market capitalization of all cryptocurrencies combined is still a fraction of that of the global stock market. This smaller market size means that large trades can disproportionately impact prices, leading to significant fluctuations (Giudici et al., 2020).
2. **Speculation and Investor Sentiment:** A large portion of cryptocurrency trading is driven by speculation rather than fundamental value. News, rumors, and market sentiment can cause rapid changes in price. Positive news, such as regulatory approval or institutional adoption, can drive prices up quickly, while negative news, such as security breaches or regulatory crackdowns, can lead to sharp declines (Sovbetov, 2018).
3. **Regulatory Environment:** Cryptocurrencies operate in a rapidly evolving regulatory landscape. Announcements from governments and financial authorities regarding the legality and regulation of cryptocurrencies can cause immediate and significant market reactions (Riley, 2021). For example, China's repeated bans on cryptocurrency trading and mining have led to substantial price drops.
4. **Technological Developments:** Innovations and updates within the cryptocurrency ecosystem, such as hard forks or the launch of new platforms and protocols, can influence prices. The anticipation of these events can drive up prices, while unexpected technical issues can lead to declines (Narayanan et al., 2016).

Historical Analysis of Major Price Swings

The history of cryptocurrency markets is marked by significant price swings and market crashes. Some notable examples include:

1. **Genesis Block Creation (2009):** Bitcoin's inception began with the mining of its Genesis block on January 3, 2009. This event marked the birth of the world's first cryptocurrency, laying the foundation for the decentralized digital currency revolution.
2. **Early Adopter Purchases (2010):** In May 2010, programmer Laszlo Hanyecz conducted the first documented real-world transaction using Bitcoin, purchasing two pizzas for 10,000 BTC. Known as "Bitcoin Pizza Day," this event demonstrated Bitcoin's potential as a medium of exchange and highlighted its emerging value.
3. **Mt. Gox Hack (2011):** In June 2011, Mt. Gox, the largest Bitcoin exchange at the time, suffered a catastrophic hack, resulting in the theft of approximately 850,000 bitcoins valued at $450 million. This breach severely undermined confidence in the cryptocurrency market and caused a significant drop in Bitcoin's price.
4. **Silk Road Shutdown (2013):** Silk Road was an online black market known for facilitating money laundering and illegal drug transactions through Bitcoin. Silk Road, considered the first darknet market, was established in 2011 and ultimately shut down by the FBI in 2013. The closure led to a temporary price decline amid increased regulatory scrutiny and negative media coverage.
5. **COVID-19 Pandemic (2020):** The onset of the COVID-19 pandemic in March 2020 led to a sharp sell-off across global financial markets, including cryptocurrencies. Bitcoin dropped from around $10,000 to below $4,000 in a matter of days. However, it quickly rebounded and entered a new bull run, reaching an all-time high of nearly $65,000 in April 2021.
6. **Tesla's Bitcoin Investment (2021):** In February 2021, Tesla announced a $1.5 billion Bitcoin purchase and declared it would accept the cryptocurrency as payment for its products. This endorsement from a major global company boosted Bitcoin's credibility as an institutional-grade asset, leading to a significant price increase.
7. **Bitcoin ETF Launch (2024):** The launch of a Bitcoin Exchange-Traded Fund (ETF) in 2024 marked a pivotal moment for mainstream cryptocurrency adoption. It significantly boosted Bitcoin's credibility as a legitimate investment, attracting a broader range of investors. This development further legitimized Bitcoin as an asset, contributing to its increasing acceptance and integration into the financial mainstream.

These events underscore the dynamic and often unpredictable nature of the cryptocurrency market. Each milestone, from technical advancements and regulatory changes to institutional endorsements, has played a crucial role in shaping Bitcoin's journey and its impact on the broader financial landscape.

Impact of High Volatility on Investors and Traders

1. **Opportunities for Profit:** High volatility presents opportunities for substantial profits. Traders can take advantages of price swings through strategies such as day trading, swing trading, and arbitrage. The potential for quick gains attracts many to the market, despite the associated risks.
2. **Increased Risk:** Another aspect of high volatility is increased risk. Prices can move against traders just as quickly as they can move in their favor, leading to significant losses.
3. **Emotional Decision-Making:** Volatility can lead to emotional decision-making among investors and traders. Fear and greed often drive market behavior, leading to panic selling during downturns and irrational exuberance during bull runs. These fluctuations in emotions can lead to less optimal investment choices.
4. **Long-Term Investment Strategies:** For long-term investors, high volatility can be both a challenge and an opportunity. While short-term price swings can be unsettling, long-term investors who hold through volatility have historically been rewarded, as evidenced by Bitcoin's overall upward trajectory despite periodic crashes.
5. **Hedging and Risk Management:** To manage the risks associated with high volatility, investors and traders employ various hedging strategies. These may include diversifying their portfolios, using stop-loss orders to limit potential losses, and engaging in options and futures trading to hedge against price movements.

In conclusion, market volatility is an intrinsic aspect of the cryptocurrency market, driven by factors such as market size, speculation, regulatory changes, technological developments, and manipulation. Historical analysis reveals significant price swings and market crashes, highlighting the need for investors and traders to navigate this market with caution. While high volatility offers opportunities for profit, it also presents substantial risks, necessitating sound risk management strategies and a long-term perspective.

REGULATORY ASPECTS OF CRYPTOCURRENCY MARKETS

The regulatory landscape for cryptocurrencies varies widely across the globe, reflecting the diverse perspectives and approaches of different governments towards this emerging asset. Regulations can significantly impact market operations, investor behavior, and technological innovation in the cryptocurrency space. Understanding these regulatory frameworks is crucial for anyone involved in the crypto market

United States

In the United States, the regulatory environment for cryptocurrencies is complex and involves multiple agencies. Key regulatory bodies include the Securities and Exchange Commission (SEC), the Commodity Futures Trading Commission (CFTC), and the Financial Crimes Enforcement Network (FinCEN).

1. **AML and KYC Requirements:** The U.S. has stringent Anti-Money Laundering (AML) and Know Your Customer (KYC) requirements. Cryptocurrency exchanges and service providers must comply with these regulations to prevent money laundering and illicit activities. These rules require exchanges to verify the identities of their users and report suspicious transactions, which adds a layer of security but also increases operational costs and complexity.
2. **Securities Regulation:** The SEC has been actively involved in regulating the cryptocurrency market, particularly focusing on Initial Coin Offerings (ICOs) and tokens that qualify as securities. The SEC's primary concern is protecting investors and ensuring transparency. This has led to numerous enforcement actions against projects that fail to comply with securities laws, impacting the innovation landscape as projects must carefully navigate regulatory requirements to avoid legal issues.
3. **Commodity Regulation:** The CFTC classifies Bitcoin and other cryptocurrencies as commodities. This classification allows for the trading of cryptocurrency futures and other derivatives on regulated exchanges. The CFTC's oversight aims to prevent market manipulation and ensure fair trading practices.

European Union

The European Union (EU) has taken a more harmonized approach to cryptocurrency regulation through directives and regulations that apply across member states.

1. **Fifth Anti-Money Laundering Directive (5AMLD):** The 5AMLD, which came into effect in January 2020, extends AML and KYC obligations to cryptocurrency exchanges and wallet providers. This directive requires these entities to register with financial authorities and adhere to strict customer verification processes.
2. **Markets in Crypto-Assets (MiCA) Regulation:** The MiCA regulation, proposed in 2020, aims to create a comprehensive regulatory framework for cryptocurrencies within the EU. MiCA covers various aspects, including stablecoins, security tokens, and utility tokens. It seeks to provide legal certainty, protect consumers, and foster innovation by creating a clear and consistent regulatory environment.
3. **Data Privacy:** The General Data Protection Regulation (GDPR) also impacts cryptocurrency businesses operating in the EU. Companies must ensure that they handle user data in compliance with GDPR, which includes securing consent for data collection and offering users the right to access and delete their data.

China

China has adopted a highly restrictive approach to cryptocurrencies, aiming to control financial risks and maintain regulatory oversight

1. **Ban on trading and ICOs:** In September 2017, China banned cryptocurrency exchanges and Initial Coin Offerings (ICOs). This ban aimed to curb speculative trading, protect investors, and prevent financial instability. As a result, many Chinese cryptocurrency exchanges moved their operations overseas.
2. **Ban on mining:** In 2021, China extended its restrictions to cryptocurrency mining, citing environmental concerns and the need to maintain financial stability. The crackdown led to a significant drop-in global Bitcoin mining activity and forced miners to relocate to more crypto-friendly jurisdictions.

Other Countries

1. **Japan:** Japan is one of the most progressive countries in terms of cryptocurrency regulation. The Financial Services Agency (FSA) oversees the industry, and since 2017, Japan has recognized Bitcoin as legal. Exchanges must register with the FSA and comply with stringent AML and KYC requirements. Japan's proactive regulatory approach has fostered a thriving cryptocurrency market while ensuring investor protection.

2. **Singapore:** Singapore has positioned itself as a global hub for cryptocurrency and blockchain innovation. The Monetary Authority of Singapore (MAS) regulates the sector under the Payment Services Act (PSA), which provides a clear legal framework for digital payment tokens. The PSA includes provisions for AML and KYC compliance, ensuring a balance between innovation and regulatory oversight.
3. **Switzerland:** Switzerland is renowned for its crypto-friendly regulatory environment. The Swiss Financial Market Supervisory Authority (FINMA) has issued clear guidelines for ICOs and classifies tokens into three categories: payment tokens, utility tokens, and asset tokens. Switzerland's regulatory clarity and support for blockchain technology have made it an attractive destination for crypto startups.
4. **India:** India's regulatory stance on cryptocurrencies has been ambiguous. The Reserve Bank of India (RBI) imposed a banking ban on crypto transactions in 2018, which was lifted by the Supreme Court in 2020. India does not have a specific law governing cryptocurrencies. However, there have been indications that the government is working on legislation to regulate cryptocurrencies more comprehensively.

IMPACT OF REGULATION ON MARKET OPERATIONS AND INNOVATION

Regulations have a profound impact on the cryptocurrency market, influencing both market operations and innovation:

1. **Market Operations**: Regulations determine the level of transparency, security, and stability in the market. Stringent AML and KYC requirements enhance security and investor confidence but can increase operational costs for businesses. Bans and restrictions, as seen in China, can disrupt market activities and drive operations to more favorable jurisdictions (Global Legal Insights, n.d.; Blockchain India, n.d.).
2. **Innovation**: Regulatory clarity fosters innovation by providing a clear framework within which businesses can operate. Conversely, regulatory uncertainty or overly restrictive measures can hamper innovation, leading talented individuals and projects to seek more favorable environments.

In conclusion, the regulatory aspects of cryptocurrency markets are diverse and evolving. Different countries have adopted distinct approaches, reflecting their priorities and concerns. While some jurisdictions provide a supportive environment that fosters innovation and market growth, others impose stringent regulations that can limit market activities.

FUTURE SCOPE OF CRYPTOCURRENCIES

The cryptocurrency market has evolved significantly since the inception of Bitcoin in 2009. As we look to the future, several emerging trends and potential developments are poised to shape the landscape of digital currencies. Key among these is the growth of new applications such as non-fungible tokens (NFTs) and Metaverse projects, the increasing institutional adoption of cryptocurrencies, and ongoing challenges related to security and regulatory frameworks.

Emerging Trends and Applications

1. **Non-Fungible Tokens (NFTs)**: NFTs have taken the digital world by storm, representing unique digital assets authenticated using blockchain technology. Unlike cryptocurrencies such as Bitcoin, which are fungible and identical to each other, NFTs are one-of-a-kind. NFTs utilize blockchain technology to provide a secure and transparent way to verify ownership and authenticity. Each NFT is minted with a unique identifier that distinguishes it from any other token. NFTs are unique cryptographic tokens on a blockchain that cannot be duplicated. This uniqueness has found applications in digital art, gaming, music, and virtual real estate. Cryptocurrencies play a crucial role in the NFT ecosystem by facilitating transactions, providing a means for buying, selling, and trading NFTs on various platforms. Additionally, cryptocurrencies often serve as the primary medium of exchange within NFT marketplaces, enabling seamless and borderless transactions. The NFT market is still in its infancy, but its potential for growth is vast, as it opens up new revenue streams for content creators and redefines ownership in the digital age.
2. **Metaverse Projects**: The Metaverse is another frontier where cryptocurrencies are set to play a pivotal role. The concept of a Metaverse refers to a shared virtual space where physical and digital realities merge, allowing users to interact and engage in a persistent digital environment. Cryptocurrencies and blockchain technology are fundamental to the Metaverse's economy, enabling transactions, ownership, and the creation of virtual goods and services. Platforms like Decentraland and Sandbox are early examples where users can buy, sell, and trade virtual real estate and assets using cryptocurrencies. As the Metaverse expands, it will likely drive the demand for digital currencies and blockchain solutions (Forbes, 2023).

3. **Expansion of Decentralized Finance (DeFi) Platforms**: DeFi is revolutionizing the financial sector by providing decentralized alternatives to traditional financial services. DeFi platforms use smart contracts to offer services such as lending, borrowing, trading, and yield farming without intermediaries. Cryptocurrencies are integral to the DeFi ecosystem, acting as collateral for loans, facilitating transactions, and providing liquidity within DeFi protocols. As more users and developers engage with DeFi, the ecosystem continues to expand, offering increasingly advanced financial products and services.
4. **Innovations in DeFi Security**: While DeFi offers numerous benefits, it also presents security challenges. Recent trends show a focus on enhancing DeFi security through improved smart contract audits, insurance protocols to cover potential losses, and the development of more secure decentralized exchanges (DeFi Pulse, 2023). These advancements aim to build trust and stability in the DeFi ecosystem, encouraging broader adoption.
5. **Development of Central Bank Digital Currencies (CBDCs)**: Central banks worldwide are exploring the issuance of digital currencies as a complement to physical cash. CBDCs are digital forms of a country's fiat currency, designed to offer the benefits of cryptocurrencies while maintaining regulatory oversight. Countries such as China, with its digital yuan, and the European Union, with the digital euro initiative, are leading the way in CBDC development (World Economic Forum, 2023). The adoption of CBDCs could streamline payments, reduce transaction costs, and enhance financial inclusion. CBDCs could serve as a gateway for more people to become familiar with digital currencies, potentially increasing awareness and adoption of cryptocurrencies like Bitcoin and others (World Economic Forum, 2023).
6. **Emergence of Green Cryptocurrencies**: In response to environmental concerns, several projects are focusing on creating eco-friendly cryptocurrencies. For example, Ethereum's transition to a proof-of-stake (PoS) consensus mechanism with Ethereum 2.0 significantly reduces its energy consumption. Other cryptocurrencies, such as Cardano and Algorand, have also adopted PoS models to minimize their environmental footprint. Additionally, projects like Chia Network are exploring innovative approaches to sustainable blockchain technology.
7. **Asset Tokenization**: Tokenization involves converting real-world assets, such as real estate, stocks, and commodities, into digital tokens on a blockchain. This process offers increased liquidity, fractional ownership, and easier transferability of assets. Cryptocurrencies play a pivotal role in the tokenization process by enabling seamless transactions and providing a medium for trading these digital assets. It facilitates the buying, selling, and transferring of tokenized assets across decentralized platforms. Tokenization has the potential to revolutionize

various industries by democratizing access to investment opportunities and streamlining asset management.

8. **Increasing Institutional Adoption**: Over the past few years, institutional adoption of cryptocurrencies has been on the rise. Major financial institutions, hedge funds, and publicly traded companies have begun to invest in and integrate cryptocurrencies into their operations. This trend is significant because it adds a layer of legitimacy and stability to the market. For instance, companies like Tesla and MicroStrategy have added Bitcoin to their balance sheets, and financial giants like Fidelity and BlackRock are offering cryptocurrency investment products to their clients. The involvement of such entities could lead to greater market liquidity, reduced volatility, and broader acceptance of cryptocurrencies as a mainstream asset class.

Ongoing Challenges and Potential Solutions

1. **Security Concerns:** Security remains a significant challenge for the cryptocurrency market. Hacks, scams, and frauds are prevalent, posing risks to investors and undermining trust in digital currencies The decentralized nature of cryptocurrencies makes them particularly vulnerable to cyberattacks (Pinjarkar et al., 2024). Innovations in blockchain technology, such as the development of more secure consensus algorithms and the implementation of robust smart contract audits, are crucial to enhancing security. Additionally, educating users about safe practices and improving regulatory oversight can help mitigate these risks (Paul et al., 2021).
2. **Regulatory Hurdles:** Regulatory frameworks for cryptocurrencies vary widely across jurisdictions, creating uncertainty and complexity for market participants (Pinjarkar et al., 2024). Some countries have embraced cryptocurrencies, while others have imposed strict regulations or bans. Clear and consistent regulations can provide legal clarity, protect investors, and prevent illicit activities. Collaboration between governments, regulatory bodies, and industry stakeholders is essential to developing balanced regulations that promote innovation while ensuring security and compliance (Singh et al., 2021).
3. **Volatility:** The volatile nature of cryptocurrency prices can deter mainstream adoption and limit their utility as a medium of exchange or store of value. Stablecoins, which are pegged to fiat currencies or commodities, offer a potential solution by providing price stability. These stablecoins can facilitate transactions and reduce exposure to price fluctuations, making them more attractive for everyday use and financial services (Paul et al., 2021).

4. **Environmental Impact:** The energy-intensive mining process of cryptocurrencies like Bitcoin has raised concerns about their environmental impact, particularly regarding carbon emissions (Singh et al., 2021). Transitioning to more energy-efficient consensus mechanisms, such as proof-of-stake (PoS), and promoting sustainable mining practices are potential solutions to mitigate these environmental concerns (Pinjarkar et al., 2024).

Addressing these ongoing challenges requires a multifaceted approach involving technological innovation, regulatory clarity, education, and industry collaboration. By tackling these issues, the cryptocurrency market can evolve towards greater stability, security, and mainstream acceptance in the global economy.

CONCLUSION

The cryptocurrency market has grown rapidly and has a significant impact on the global financial system, offering both opportunities and challenges. Since the introduction of Bitcoin, the market has expanded to include many different digital assets, each with its own unique features. The decentralized nature of cryptocurrencies provides an alternative to traditional financial systems, bringing innovation but also introducing elements of instability. Several factors drive the cryptocurrency market, including technological progress, changes in regulations, and overall economic conditions. The rise of decentralized finance and increased acceptance of cryptocurrencies by major investors have strengthened their role in today's economy. However, the market faces risks such as regulatory uncertainty, security issues, and price volatility.

Cryptocurrencies are set to play a significant role in the future of finance. Their potential to enhance financial inclusion and reshape traditional financial systems makes them a crucial area of focus. To understand the cryptocurrency market, one needs to examine various aspects, including the technology behind it, market trends, and its broader economic impact. The future of cryptocurrencies will likely be shaped by ongoing innovation, evolving regulations, and their interactions with traditional financial systems.

In summary, the cryptocurrency market is at a crucial point, with the potential to bring significant changes. It requires careful consideration and strategic management. By thoroughly understanding its components and underlying drivers, we can better navigate this complex but promising area and make the most of its benefits while managing its risks.

REFERENCES

Androulaki, E., Barger, A., Bortnikov, V., Cachin, C., Christidis, K., De Caro, A., & Yellick, J. (2018, April). Hyperledger fabric: a distributed operating system for permissioned blockchains. In *Proceedings of the thirteenth EuroSys conference* (pp. 1-15).

Auer, R., & Claessens, S. (2021). Cryptocurrency and the future of monetary policy. *The Journal of Economic Perspectives*, *35*(2), 123–146.

Aysan, A. F., Demir, E., Gozgor, G., & Lau, C. K. M. (2021). Effects of the cryptocurrency market on global economic conditions: Evidence from Bitcoin. *Economic Modelling*, *94*, 283–292.

Buterin, V. (2013). Ethereum White Paper: A Next-Generation Smart Contract and Decentralized Application Platform.

Chan, Q., Ding, W., Lin, C., & Rossi, A. G. (2020). An inside look into cryptocurrency exchanges. *Available atSSRN* 3759062. http://dx.doi.org/DOI: 10.2139/ssrn.3759062

Chen, Y. (2021). Empirical analysis of bitcoin price. *Journal of Economics and Finance*, *45*(4), 692–715. DOI: 10.1007/s12197-021-09549-5

Chuen, D. L. K., Guo, L., & Wang, Y. (2017). Cryptocurrency: A new investment opportunity? *Journal of Alternative Investments*, *20*(3), 16–40. DOI: 10.3905/jai.2018.20.3.016

Ciaian, P., Rajcaniova, M., & Kancs, D. A. (2016). The economics of Bit-Coin price formation. *Applied Economics*, *48*(19), 1799–1815. DOI: 10.1080/00036846.2015.1109038

Conrad, C., Custovic, A., & Ghysels, E. (2018). Long-and short-term cryptocurrency volatility components: A GARCH-MIDAS analysis. *Journal of Risk and Financial Management*, *11*(2), 23. DOI: 10.3390/jrfm11020023

Corbet, S., Lucey, B., & Yarovaya, L. (2019). The future of cryptocurrencies: A research agenda. *Finance Research Letters*, *29*, 469–478.

Dwyer, G. P. (2015). The economics of Bitcoin and similar private digital currencies. *Journal of Financial Stability*, *17*, 81–91. DOI: 10.1016/j.jfs.2014.11.006

Energy Web Foundation. (2020). Blockchain for Energy Transition.

Fahlenbrach, R., & Frattini, F. (2022). Innovation and regulation in the cryptocurrency market. *Journal of Financial Stability*, *60*, 101021.

Giudici, G., Milne, A., & Vinogradov, D. (2020). Cryptocurrencies: Market analysis and perspectives. *Economia e Politica Industriale*, *47*(1), 1–18. DOI: 10.1007/s40812-019-00138-6

Gupta, H., & Chaudhary, R. (2022). An empirical study of volatility in cryptocurrency market. *Journal of Risk and Financial Management*, *15*(11), 513. DOI: 10.3390/jrfm15110513

IBM. (2019). IBM Blockchain Platform Overview.

Judmayer, A., Stifter, N., Schindler, P., & Weippl, E. (2017). Blocks and chains: Introduction to Bitcoin, cryptocurrencies, and their consensus mechanisms. *Synthesis Lectures on Information Security, Privacy, and Trust*, *9*(1), 1–123. DOI: 10.1007/978-3-031-02352-1

Li, X., & Wang, C. A. (2017). The technology and economic determinants of cryptocurrency exchange rates: The case of Bitcoin. *Decision Support Systems*, *95*, 49–60. DOI: 10.1016/j.dss.2016.12.001

Li, X., & Whinston, A. B. (2020). Analyzing cryptocurrencies. *Information Systems Frontiers*, *22*(1), 17–22. DOI: 10.1007/s10796-019-09966-2

Liu, J., & Serletis, A. (2019). Volatility in the cryptocurrency market. *Open Economies Review*, *30*(4), 779–811. DOI: 10.1007/s11079-019-09547-5

Morton, D. T. (2020). The future of cryptocurrency: An unregulated instrument in an increasingly regulated global economy. *Loy. U. Chi. Int'l L. Rev.*, *16*, 129.

Motsi-Omoijiade, I. D. (2018). Financial intermediation in cryptocurrency markets–regulation, gaps and bridges. In *Handbook of Blockchain, Digital Finance, and Inclusion, Volume 1* (pp. 207-223). Academic Press. https://doi.org/DOI: 10.1016/B978-0-12-810441-5.00009-9

Nakamoto, S. (2008). Bitcoin: A peer-to-peer electronic cash system.

Narayanan, A., Bonneau, J., Felten, E., Miller, A., & Goldfeder, S. (2016). *Bitcoin and cryptocurrency technologies*.

Oman, Z. U., & Suryanarayana, K. A Study on Latest Trends and Growth of Crypto Currencies and Its Regulatory Aspect in India. https://doi:DOI: 10.14445/23939125/IJEMS-V9I12P103

Paul, A. K., Qu, X., & Wen, Z. (2021). Blockchain–a promising solution to internet of things: A comprehensive analysis, opportunities, challenges and future research issues. *Peer-to-Peer Networking and Applications*, *14*(5), 2926–2951. DOI: 10.1007/s12083-021-01151-0

Paul, P., Aithal, P. S., Saavedra, R., & Ghosh, S. (2021). Blockchain technology and its types—A short review. [IJASE]. *International Journal of Applied Science and Engineering*, *9*(2), 189–200. DOI: 10.30954/2322-0465.2.2021.7

Pilkington, M. (2016). *Blockchain Technology: Principles and Applications*. Research Handbook on Digital Transformations.

Pinjarkar, L., Agrawal, P., Gupta, G. K., Kaur, G., Sheikh, F., & Perwez, S. (2024, September). Blockchain security in cryptocurrency: Challenges, solutions, and future prospects. In *AIP Conference Proceedings* (Vol. 3242, No. 1). AIP Publishing.

Riley, J. (2021). The current status of cryptocurrency regulation in China and its effect around the world. *China and WTO Review*, *7*(1), 135–152. DOI: 10.14330/cwr.2021.7.1.06

Sarmah, S. S. (2018). Understanding blockchain technology. *Computing in Science & Engineering*, *8*(2), 23–29. DOI: 10.5923/j.computer.20180802.02

Singh, S., Hosen, A. S., & Yoon, B. (2021). Blockchain security attacks, challenges, and solutions for the future distributed iot network. *IEEE Access : Practical Innovations, Open Solutions*, *9*, 13938–13959. DOI: 10.1109/ACCESS.2021.3051602

Sovbetov, Y. (2018). Factors influencing cryptocurrency prices: Evidence from bitcoin, ethereum, dash, litcoin, and monero. *Journal of Economics and Financial Analysis*, *2*(2), 1–27. DOI: 10.1991/jefa.v2i2.a16

Tredinnick, L. (2019). Cryptocurrencies and the blockchain. *Business Information Review*, *36*(1), 39–44. DOI: 10.1177/0266382119836314

Weber, I., Zhu, L., & Schmidt, C. (2016). A Data-Centric Perspective on Business Process Management in the Cloud. *Future Generation Computer Systems*.

Winnowicz, K., Au, C. D., & Stein, D. (2021). Crypto Regulation within the European Union. *Available atSSRN* 4194771.

Woebbeking, F. (2021). Cryptocurrency volatility markets. *Digital Finance*, *3*(3), 273–298. DOI: 10.1007/s42521-021-00037-3 PMID: 34368626

Yadav, S. P., Agrawal, K. K., Bhati, B. S., Al-Turjman, F., & Mostarda, L. (2022). Blockchain-based cryptocurrency regulation: An overview. *Computational Economics*, *59*(4), 1659–1675. DOI: 10.1007/s10614-020-10050-0

Yaga, D., Mell, P., Roby, N., & Scarfone, K. (2019). Blockchain technology overview. *arXiv preprint arXiv:1906.11078*.

Yermack, D. (2015). Is Bitcoin a real currency? An economic appraisal. *Handbook of Digital Currency*, 31-43.

Zheng, Z., Xie, S., Dai, H., Chen, X., & Wang, H. (2017). An Overview of Blockchain Technology: Architecture, Consensus, and Future Trends. *IEEE International Congress on Big Data*. DOI: 10.1109/BigDataCongress.2017.85

Chapter 7
Opportunities and Current Issues With Cryptocurrency

Komal Bhardwaj
https://orcid.org/0000-0002-9378-5542
Maharishi Markandeshwar University (Deemed), Ambala, India

Garima
https://orcid.org/0000-0002-1793-8084
Maharishi Markandeshwar University (Deemed), Ambala, India

Preety Sharma
https://orcid.org/0009-0005-9918-8449
Maharishi Markandeshwar University (Deemed), Ambala, India

Arshan Kler
https://orcid.org/0000-0001-8337-0215
Chandigarh Group of Colleges, Jhanjeri, India

ABSTRACT

Nowadays, over the world, cryptocurrency has become a contentious issue in financial industry. In fact, cryptocurrencies like Bitcoin, which are backed by blockchain technology, are revolutionizing the global financial paradigm. Every country is experiencing this fever, which is drawing interest from individuals in every walk of life. It is not just affecting one area. Some are attracted to the possibility of financial gain, while others are fascinated by the underlying technology and how it can affect different industries. Such kind of exuberance has never been seen like this before due to the world's infatuation with cryptocurrencies, which range from more recent entries like Shiba Inc. to more well-known ones like Bitcoin and Ethereum. This

DOI: 10.4018/979-8-3693-5986-0.ch007

paper investigates the opportunities presented by the cryptocurrency like bitcoin ecosystem and its digital money as alternatives to traditional currencies and the key challenges that cryptocurrencies must overcome to achieve widespread adoption.

INTRODUCTION

The massive growth of information and communication technologies has paved a new way of doing financial transactions by replacing the physical currency with digital currency. The vogue of virtual currency had started just after the global meltdown in the year 2008. Many nations across the globe have legalised the use of cryptocurrencies such as Japan, Australia, European Union, United States, China and others. The reason that can be attributed for the immense popularity of crypto is the ease and convenience offer to users as an alternative mode of paying physical cash.

Cryptocurrencies are virtual or digital currencies in which a decentralised system that used encryption verifies transactions, maintains records and regulate the generation of new units and safeguard transactions via the use of cryptographic technology Nakamoto, (2009), Haque, & Shoaib (2023). The most widely accepted definition of cryptocurrencies is digital financial assets for which cryptography decentralized technology ensures ownership and ownership transfers (Swan, 2015; Giudici, Milne & Vinogradov, 2020). They are employed to pay for actual products and services in the real world. (Dostov and Shust, 2014; Guadamuz and Marsden, 2015). Furthermore, cryptocurrencies mark a substantial shift from the conventional framework for financial system management, design, and regulation. (Shahzad et al., 2018). Blockchain is the technology causing cryptocurrencies to proliferate. (Hashemi et al., 2019). Han et al. (2019). A blockchain is made up of several blocks, each of which has a set of transactions and is connected to the others in an arrangement akin to a chain. Blockchain-based currencies represent a pioneering advancement in the fields of technology and finance. Tapscott & Tapscott (2017). A network of users validates transactions and is rewarded with additional bitcoin units in exchange for their work. Moreover, cryptocurrencies are decentralised, no financial institution or centralised authority controls them. Separate public and private keys are used to secure transactions, private keys being used for accessing and managing a user's cryptocurrency holdings and public keys being used for accepting payments. In order to validate transactions and create new units of a cryptocurrency, users must solve challenging mathematical puzzles known as mining. Some cryptocurrencies require specialised gear (i.e., a high-end GPU-equipped computer) to mine because this process is computationally intensive. Cryptocurrencies can be bought, sold, or traded peer-to-peer on online exchanges, and they are frequently used as a medium of exchange. Cryptocurrencies come in a wide variety, each with special features and technological characteristics. As a whole, cryptocurrencies refer to the thousands of distinct digital currencies that now exist. In particular, a plethora of different cryptocurrencies founded on the blockchain technology concept emerged following the launch of the bitcoin cryptocurrency, all aiming to reach a critical mass of users that would enable broader adoption. The following are the current market capitalization figures on a global scale: Litecoin, Dogecoin, Ethereum, XRP, Tether, Bitcoin Cash, Stellar, and so on. Bitcoin is the most well-known illustration of a completely decentralised, peer-to-peer cryptocurrency. One of the primary drawbacks of the decentralized payment method is the market's susceptibility to large price swings.

Wallace (2011) stated that Nakamoto was the first person who mined and introduced the first 50 units into circulation in 2009, after that Bitcoin continues to be a favourite among miners and investors. It started the cryptocurrency "revolution," which gave rise to a number of well-known coins, such as Tether, XRP, Ethereum, and Litecoin. However people began to invest large sums of money in cryptocurrency in 2017, despite the fact that it had no history of producing revenue. There was an investment of crores of money in crypto and other coins.

LITERATURE REVIEW

Cryptocurrencies have emerged as a significant innovation in the financial landscape, presenting both exciting opportunities and considerable challenges. This literature review synthesizes current research to provide a comprehensive overview of these aspects.

Blockchain technology is a distributed ledger system that makes it possible to record transactions between numerous parties in a safe and transparent manner. It is composed of a series of blocks, each carrying a collection of transactions, and is based on cryptographic concepts. Cryptographic hashes are used to connect these blocks, guaranteeing the integrity and immutability of the data recorded on the blockchain. (Nakamoto, 2008). According to Sas & Khairuddin (2019) customers' responses to blockchain technology establish guidelines for businesses to manage their resources, recommend laws that should be put in place to facilitate the shift, and highlight specific fixes for the technology's acknowledged limitations. Subsequently there is always risk associated with cryptocurrencies, including the possibility of large losses and unanticipated price spikes. For example, the value of Bitcoin peaked in April 2021 and then dropped by over 50% the following month, hitting a 4-month low. According to a World Bank (2018) analysis, cryptocurrencies can also increase the effectiveness and transparency of international transactions. Cryptocurrency may lower intermediation costs, speed up transactions, and improve financial inclusion for people and businesses in developing nations, according to the paper. Rancic and

Stankovic (2019) looked at the possibility of using cryptocurrencies to lower the expenses and risks associated with financing cross-border trade. The study discovered that, especially for small and medium-sized businesses, cryptocurrencies can greatly lower transaction costs and enhance the speed and security of cross-border trade finance. A study by Demir et al. (2018) looked at how cryptocurrencies can help displaced and refugee populations access financial services. According to the report, cryptocurrencies can be a useful tool for financial inclusion, especially for groups that have trouble gaining access to conventional financial institutions. The United Nations Development Programme (UNDP) also noted in a 2019 report that cryptocurrencies have the potential to lower transaction costs, expand financial inclusion, and spur economic growth in poor nations. Tolossa & Khawrin (2022). An array of organizations, nations, and consortiums have now integrated blockchain into their systems to reap its benefits. (Makhdoom et al., 2019, Hewa et al., 2020). Furthermore, there is always a threat that is directly tied to the volatility of the cryptocurrency market and the contagion effect, which can expose the entire financial system to a disruptive process, illustrates a serious risk to the global economy. Sas & Khairuddin (2019). However, blockchain technology is decentralized and transactions are verified and approved by network members collectively, there is no need for a central authority. (Swan, 2015). Although blockchain technology has great potential, there are a few issues that need to be resolved before it can be widely used. One of the main issues is scalability, since the blockchain systems in use today find it difficult to effectively manage large volumes of transactions. (Easley et al., 2019). Another significant concern is privacy because of the possibility that blockchain's transparency would reveal private information. (Kosba et al., 2016). Furthermore, there are substantial obstacles related to the application of blockchain technology due to regulatory and legal concerns, including jurisdictional concerns and data protection rules. (Vukolić, 2017). Additionally, blockchain technology offers a plethora of prospects in a variety of industries. Blockchain has the potential to improve transparency, lower costs, and streamline cross-border transactions in the banking sector. (Yli-Huumo et al., 2016). Blockchain can enhance the efficiency, legitimacy, and traceability of supply chain management. (Tran et al., 2019).

STATEMENT OF PROBLEM

The use of cryptocurrencies has created new avenues for asset storage and transaction. Many think it's significantly superior to conventional fiat and gold. In 2023, almost $222.70 million people in India joined the cryptocurrency wagon. (The Economic Times, Oct 01, 2023). Moreover, fundamental technologies of cryptocurrencies, blockchain and Web 3.0, have already been adopted by numerous businesses and are anticipated to form the basis of the next major Metaverse movement.

RESEARCH METHODOLOGY

The design of the current study employs a qualitative descriptive research approach. When a thorough analysis of an issue or subject is sought, qualitative research is recommended.

Through library research techniques, data sources are gathered by utilising offline and online resources such as books, scientific journals, and news articles written by reputable sources. After data analysis, conclusions are made based on the goals of the study.

OBJECTIVES

To investigate the opportunities presented by the cryptocurrency.
To find out the key challenges that cryptocurrencies must overcome to achieve widespread adoption.

CHALLENGES PRESENT IN CRYPTOCURRENCY

Legality and Regulation Challenges: Regulations have a significant impact on the adoption of Cryptocurrencies. At a glance financial authorities and governments are finding it difficult to create policies that combine consumer protection with innovation. Mainly Central bank has complete control over all policies and the result of a nation's monetary policy whereas in case of cryptocurrencies, it is permitted to create an account and allows for numerous accounts. However in Indian government has levied a 30% tax on all cryptocurrency transactions, but finance minister said that taxing cryptocurrencies does not imply that it is legal. Furthermore, in order to promote confidence, stability, and broad adoption, it is imperative to resolve regulatory ambiguities and create a clear regulatory framework.

Technological Barriers: Cryptocurrencies use cutting-edge blockchain technology, yet there are technological obstacles in adoption of existing blockchain networks as it hampered by issues such as high transaction fees and slow processing times. Three important areas still need improvement: transaction speed, scalability, and user-friendliness. To stimulate broad adoption, it is imperative to improve network scalability, lower transaction costs, and streamline the user experience. Technological advancements can improve accessibility and bridge the gap by creating wallets that are easy to use, integrating seamlessly with the current financial infrastructure, and having intuitive interfaces.

Security and privacy Concerns: Security concerns surrounding cryptocurrencies are important for both people and organizations. Moreover cryptocurrencies having decentralized feature and having low susceptibility and security (Kshetri, 2017). There are a lot of obstacles to overcome due to security issues like frauds, hackers, and the possibility of losing private keys. However to build confidence and encourage broader adoption, hardware wallets, multi-factor authentication, strong security measures, and educational campaigns promoting ethical cryptocurrency storage and use are essential.

Expensive: Energy consumption is the other major expense a miner must pay, in addition to the initial equipment cost. (Hayes, 2017). The findings indicate that the rewards obtained from solving a block have not outweighed the expenses incurred by mining the virtual money. (O'Dwyer & Malone, 2014). (Vranken, 2017 found that the significant energy consumption and sophisticated computer requirements associated with the mining of these virtual currencies are cryptocurrency ranges from 10MW to 3-6 GW.

Volatility and market risk: According to the efficient market theory, historical data indicates the values of a given asset. However, cryptocurrency is considered an inefficient type of commodity since investors are unable to forecast future prospects due to the lack of historical data. According to Dwyer, 2015 the monthly average volatility returns for cryptocurrency, such as Bitcoin, are significantly higher than gold. On the other hand, the monthly highest volatilities for gold and other currencies are higher than the lowest monthly volatilities for Bitcoin. Furthermore Cheung et al. 2015 reported three significant bubble bursts in Bitcoin between 2011 and 2013, lasting between 66 and 106 days.

Scalability: The primary issues with cryptocurrencies' scalability are their poor transaction rates, expensive fees, and constrained computing capacity. Blockchain has a storage scalability problem that prevents or hinders participation, especially from nodes with low memory. Sanka & Cheung (2021). It is challenging for the nodes to hold that much data that, by the Satoshi blockchain rule, cannot be erased. Moreover as the number of transactions increases, the network can become congested, leading to slower transaction times and higher fees.

OPPORTUNITIES PRESENT IN CRYPTOCURRENCY

Financial Inclusion and Economic Empowerment: Cryptocurrencies have the potential to improve financial inclusion particularly in areas with restricted access to conventional banking services, no matter where they are, anyone can safely save, send, and receive money with digital currencies. Through circumventing conventional middlemen, cryptocurrencies enable people to engage in international trade, carry out cross-border transactions, and obtain financial services that were previously inaccessible to them. Increasing financial inclusion may boost impoverished communities, spur economic expansion, and open up new business prospects.

Secure Technology: A cryptocurrency can potentially offer greater security compared to conventional money by leveraging advanced cryptographic protocols, multi-factor authentication, decentralized ledger technology, and reduced susceptibility to physical theft. Many cryptocurrency platforms implement Multi-Factor Authentication which involves requiring users to provide two or more forms of verification, such as a password and a one-time code sent to their mobile device.

Investment and trading: Investment opportunities exist with cryptocurrencies such as Ethereum (ETH), Bitcoin (BTC), and others. Many people invest in and hoard cryptocurrencies in the hopes that their value will increase over time. Users can purchase, sell, and exchange different cryptocurrencies on trading sites. But it's critical to comprehend the dangers and unpredictability of cryptocurrency trading. Giudici et al. (2020) Many people invest in cryptocurrencies like Bitcoin (BTC), Ethereum (ETH), and altcoins. Trading platforms allow buying, selling, and trading.

Investment Diversification: Cryptocurrency investment diversification presents special chances to improve a portfolio. With their decentralized networks and huge return potential, cryptocurrencies like Ethereum and Bitcoin lessen reliance on established financial institutions. By distributing risk across several asset classes, their low connection with traditional assets can increase diversification. The cutting-edge blockchain technology underlying cryptocurrencies also opens fresh growth prospects outside of the financial sector. Investors must, however, manage this new asset class's significant volatility, regulatory uncertainties, and security threats. Investors might possibly profit from cryptocurrencies' tremendous growth potential while reducing risks by carefully investing a modest portion of their portfolio to them.

Cross-Border Transactions: In comparison to conventional banking systems, Böhme et al. (2015) discovered that cryptocurrencies can drastically cut down on the time and expense of cross-border remittances. According to the survey, bitcoin transactions are quicker, less expensive, and more convenient for users—especially in nations where remittance costs are high. Since cryptocurrencies are more affordable, quicker, and secure than established financial systems, they offer tremendous potential for cross-border transactions. Cryptocurrency transactions can be finished swiftly and affordably, in contrast to traditional techniques that frequently need several middlemen, exorbitant fees, and drawn-out processing times. Because cryptocurrencies are decentralized, there is no need for central authorities, which lowers the possibility of political unrest and volatility in the value of currency exchanges. This makes cryptocurrencies especially appealing for cross-border value transfers and international remittances, as they offer a smooth method of doing so. Furthermore, increased trust and efficiency in cross-border transactions are fostered by the openness and security of blockchain technology, which promotes greater financial inclusion and global economic integration.

Smart contracts: By automating and securely safeguarding intricate agreements without the need for middlemen, smart contracts present revolutionary prospects inside the Bitcoin ecosystem. These self-executing contracts function on blockchain platforms like Ethereum, guaranteeing accuracy, trust, and transparency by having the terms explicitly encoded into code. Smart contracts speed up procedures, reduce the chance of fraud and human mistake, and lower transaction costs by doing away with the requirement for third-party verification. They make a wide range of applications possible, including supply chain management, real estate, and intellectual property rights, as well as decentralized finance (DeFi). By offering a safe, unchangeable, and automated method of managing and carrying out contractual agreements, smart contracts' efficiency and dependability have the potential to completely transform a number of industries and promote innovation and economic expansion.

Blockchain Technology: Blockchain technology can be viewed as a sort of next-generation software for business process improvement from a business standpoint. Blockchain technology and other collaborative technologies claim to be able to drastically reduce the "cost of trust" by streamlining business operations between enterprises. Because of this, compared to the majority of conventional internal investments, it might deliver noticeably better returns for each dollar invested. The underlying technology behind cryptocurrencies is blockchain and its developers can work on new projects or contribute to already-existing ones to create decentralized applications.

New Business Models: Innovative business models leveraging the unique attributes of blockchain technology are made possible by cryptocurrencies. Tokenization of assets is a prominent example, enabling companies to issue digital tokens representing ownership of real or virtual assets, thereby enhancing liquidity and accessibility (Catalini & Gans, 2016). Decentralized Autonomous Organizations (DAOs) utilize smart contracts to create organizational structures without centralized authority, promoting more transparent operations and democratic decision-making (Buterin, 2013). Additionally, new fundraising mechanisms such as Security Token Offerings (STOs) and Initial Coin Offerings (ICOs) provide firms with novel ways to raise capital on a global scale (Adhami, Giudici, & Martinazzi, 2018). These models streamline processes and reduce costs while fostering community involvement and engagement, driving innovation across various sectors, including real estate, finance, entertainment, and the arts (Schär, 2021).

Decentralized Finance: DeFi offers decentralized alternatives to conventional financial services, marking a significant change in the economic environment. (Kumar et al., 2020). By holding certain cryptocurrencies in a wallet to support the network, investors earn rewards. Decentralized Finance (DeFi) offers financial services without the use of conventional middlemen like banks and brokers, presenting a revolutionary opportunity within the cryptocurrency ecosystem. DeFi systems, based on blockchain technology, facilitate activities such as lending, borrowing, trading, and earning interest through decentralized applications (dApps) (Schär, 2021). This increases accessibility to financial services by providing affordable, transparent, and efficient options, especially for the underbanked or unbanked populations (Adhami, Giudici, & Martinazzi, 2018). DeFi also promotes innovation through programmable financial instruments, enabling the creation of complex financial products and automated processes (Mik, 2021). By leveraging the security, transparency, and immutability of blockchain technology, DeFi has the potential to transform the financial landscape into a more robust and inclusive system (Narayanan et al., 2016).

DISCUSSION

The emergence of cryptocurrencies, especially Ethereum and Bitcoin, has completely changed the way we consider online transactions. These virtual currencies have a number of advantages, including lower transaction costs, quicker settlement times, and more transaction transparency. (Jiang & Zhang, 2021). High transaction fees, which can range from 2% to 5% of the transaction value, are frequently assessed by traditional payment systems. On the other hand, transactions using cryptocurrency can be completed for as little as a few cents each, which is a much lower price. (Liao, 2021). Small enterprises with narrow profit margins can especially benefit from this. Additionally, transactions involving cryptocurrencies can be completed nearly immediately, giving firms more liquidity and flexibility. (Böhme et al., 2015).

However, adopting cryptocurrencies comes with a number of difficulties. One of the primary issues that must be resolved is the presence of regulatory and legal obstacles. Governments find it challenging to control and oversee cryptocurrencies due to their decentralized nature, which causes uncertainty and confusion among investors and businesses. (Chen & Zhang, 2019). An additional significant obstacle related to cryptocurrencies is security concerns. Wallets that store digital money online are susceptible to theft and hacking. Both people and companies who invest in cryptocurrencies may suffer large losses as a result of this. The possibility of fraud and frauds also exists, which might undermine trust in the technology and prevent its uptake. (Swan, 2015).

Lastly, another issue that needs to be addressed is a lack of knowledge about cryptocurrencies. Since cryptocurrency is a complicated technology, understanding it completely calls for a certain level of technical expertise. Businesses and individuals that are not familiar with the technology may find this to be a barrier to adoption. (Nakamoto, 2008). In conclusion, even if cryptocurrencies have many advantages, there are a number of obstacles that must be removed before they can be widely used. Among the primary issues that must be resolved are security worries, regulatory and legal obstacles, and a lack of knowledge about cryptocurrencies. However, with the correct answers, both individuals and companies may be able to reap the rewards of cryptocurrency adoption.

In recent years, there has been a growing interest in the use of cryptocurrencies in global trade. A World Trade Organization study found that using cryptocurrencies in international trade might lower transaction costs, boost transparency, and enable quicker and safer transactions. (WTO, 2021). Since as was mentioned in the previous section, a number of factors affect cryptocurrency acceptance in this situation.

Another important element that may influence the acceptance of cryptocurrencies in global trade is knowledge and comprehension of them. A hurdle to adoption may arise from the fact that many firms are still ignorant of cryptocurrencies and their potential advantages. Thus, initiatives to raise knowledge and comprehension of cryptocurrencies may aid in encouraging their use in global trade. (Kshetri, 2018).

Another important problem that may prevent cryptocurrencies from being widely used in international trade is security concerns. Because cryptocurrencies are decentralized and rely on online wallets, they are susceptible to cyberattacks and other security lapses. Businesses must therefore have faith that their transactions are safe and shielded from online attacks. (WTO, 2021).

Finally, businesses wishing to use cryptocurrencies in international trade must also take into account how well they integrate with current systems. For transactions to be carried out successfully and efficiently, cryptocurrency must be easily linked with current accounting and payment systems. (Kshetri, 2018). In summary, although integrating cryptocurrency into global trade has many advantages, a number of issues must be carefully taken into account to guarantee its successful implementation. To enable the broad use of cryptocurrencies in global trade, a number of important issues must be resolved, including regulatory and legal frameworks, security concerns, knowledge and comprehension of cryptocurrencies, transaction costs, and interface with current systems. But because of security concerns, some businesses are still hesitant to embrace cryptocurrencies, even with the potential advantages. According to a Deloitte survey, 44% of participants said security was their top concern, making it the largest obstacle to bitcoin adoption. (Deloitte, 2020).

In conclusion, key elements that may influence the adoption of cryptocurrencies are the attitudes and views of businesses about it. Businesses' trust in cryptocurrency's dependability and security is a major factor in its uptake; yet, security issues still need to be resolved to guarantee broad acceptance.

CONCLUSION

Cryptocurrencies are virtual or digital currencies in which a decentralised system that used encryption verifies transactions, maintains records and regulate the generation of new units and safeguard transactions via the use of cryptographic technology and every country is experiencing this fever, which is drawing interest from individuals in every walk of life. It is not just affecting one area. Some are attracted to the possibility of financial gain, while others are fascinated by the underlying technology and how it can affect different industries. In fact, cryptocurrencies like Bitcoin, which are backed by blockchain technology, are revolutionising the global financial paradigm. Blockchain is a revolutionary contemporary distributed ledger technology that offers numerous advantages, including immutability, efficiency, speed, autonomy, transparency, auditability, privacy, and cost savings. However, cryptocurrency has the ability to completely transform a number of different industries by solving enduring problems and opening up fresh avenues for creativity. But still there are certain difficulties in developing an infrastructure for digital currencies in terms of legalities, security, Technological barriers, market volatility, scalability, performance, and different cost scenarios. However, opportunities in cryptocurrency like Financial Inclusion, Cross-Border Transactions, diversification, decentralized finance, new business model and the emergence of DeFi apps, emphasizes its potential significance. However, to fully fulfill crypto potential and clear the path for a transparent, safe, and decentralized finance, researchers and practitioners must work together to overcome these issues.

REFERENCES

Adhami, S., Giudici, G., & Martinazzi, S. (2018). Cryptocurrency: A new asset class? *Journal of Corporate Finance*, *50*, 225–241.

Böhme, R., Christin, N., Edelman, B., & Moore, T. (2015). Bitcoin: Economics, technology, and governance. *The Journal of Economic Perspectives*, *29*(2), 213–238. DOI: 10.1257/jep.29.2.213

Buterin, V. (2013). Ethereum: The World Computer. Ethereum White Paper.

Catalini, C., & Gans, J. S. (2016). Some Simple Economics of the Blockchain. National Bureau of Economic Research Working Paper No. 22952.

Chen, H., & Zhang, Y. (2019). Blockchain-based decentralized cryptocurrency exchanges. *Electronic Commerce Research and Applications*, *35*, 100830.

Deloitte. (2020). Global Blockchain Survey 2020. Retrieved from https://www2.deloitte.com/content/dam/Deloitte/cn/Documents/financial-services/deloitte-cn-fs-global-blockchain-survey2020-en-201007.pdf

Demir, I. (2018). Blockchain Technology for Social Impact: Opportunities and Challenges Ahead. *Journal of Economic and Social Policy*, *20*(1), 1–18.

Dostov, V., & Shust, P. (2014). Cryptocurrencies: An unconventional Challenge to The AML/CFT Regulators? *Journal of Financial Crime*, *21*(3), 249–263. DOI: 10.1108/JFC-06-2013-0043

Easley, D., O'Hara, M., & Basu, S. (2019). From mining to markets: The evolution of bitcoin transaction fees. *Journal of Financial Economics*, *134*(1), 91–109. DOI: 10.1016/j.jfineco.2019.03.004

Giudici, G., Milne, A., & Vinogradov, D. (2020). Cryptocurrencies: Market analysis and perspectives. *Economia e Politica Industriale*, *47*(1), 1–18. DOI: 10.1007/s40812-019-00138-6

Guadamuz, A., & Marsden, C. (2015). Blockchains and Bitcoin: Regulatory Responses to Cryptocurrencies. *First Monday*, *20*(12). Advance online publication. DOI: 10.5210/fm.v20i12.6198

Han, X., Yuan, Y., & Wang, F. Y. (2019, November). A blockchain-based framework for central bank digital currency. In 2019 IEEE International conference on service operations and logistics, and informatics (SOLI) (pp. 263-268). IEEE.

Haque, M. A., & Shoaib, M. (2023). The digital currency in India: Challenges and prospects. BenchCouncil Transactions on Benchmarks. *Standards and Evaluations*, *3*(1), 100107.

Hashemi Joo, M., Nishikawa, Y., & Dandapani, K. (2019). Cryptocurrency, a Successful Application of Blockchain Technology. *Managerial Finance*, *46*(6), 715–733. DOI: 10.1108/MF-09-2018-0451

Hayes, A. S. (2017). Cryptocurrency value formation: An empirical study leading to a cost of production model for valuing bitcoin. *Telematics and Informatics*, *34*(7), 1308–1321. DOI: 10.1016/j.tele.2016.05.005

Hewa, T., Gür, G., Kalla, A., Ylianttila, M., Bracken, A., & Liyanage, M. (2020). The role of blockchain in 6G: Challenges, opportunities and research directions. *2020 2nd 6G Wireless Summit (6G SUMMIT)*, 1-5.

Jiang, L., & Zhang, X. (2021). Cryptocurrency as an Investment Tool: A Critical Review. *Frontiers in Blockchain*, *4*, 31.

Kethineni, S., Cao, Y., & Dodge, C. (2017). Use of Bitcoin in Darknet Markets: Examining Facilitative Factors on BitcoinRelated Crimes. *American Journal of Criminal Justice*, *43*(2), 141–157. DOI: 10.1007/s12103-017-9394-6

Kosba, A., Miller, A., Shi, E., Wen, Z., & Papamanthou, C. (2016). Hawk: The blockchain model of cryptography and privacy-preserving smart contracts. In *Proceedings of the 2016 ACM SIGSAC Conference on Computer and Communications Security* (pp. 839-851). ACM. DOI: 10.1109/SP.2016.55

Kumar, R., Jangir, S., Kumar, V., & Kaushal, R. (2020). Staking in Proof-of-Stake Blockchain. In *2020 International Conference on Computer Science, Engineering and Applications (ICCSEA)* (pp. 1-6). IEEE.

Liao, M. (2021). A survey of blockchain technology applied to digital asset trading. *Journal of Business Research*, *136*, 509–516.

Makhdoom, I., Abolhasan, M., Abbas, H., & Ni, W. (2019). Blockchain's adoption in IoT: The challenges, and a way forward. *Journal of Network and Computer Applications*, *125*, 251–279. DOI: 10.1016/j.jnca.2018.10.019

Mik, E. (2021). Decentralized Finance: The future of finance or just another hype? *Financial Innovation*, *7*(1), 8.

Nakamoto, S. Bitcoin: A peer-to-peer ElectronicCash system, 2009, Available online: https://bitcoin.org/bitcoin.pdf

Narayanan, A., Bonneau, J., Felten, E., Miller, A., & Goldfeder, S. (2016). *Bitcoin and Cryptocurrency Technologies: A Comprehensive Introduction*. Princeton University Press.

O'Dwyer, K. J., & Malone, D. (2014). Bitcoin mining and its energy footprint. *25th IET Irish Signals and Systems Conference and China-Ireland International Conference on Information and Communications Technologies (ISSC/CIICT 2014)*. 26-27 June 2014, Limerick, Ireland.

Rancic, M., & Stankovic, J. (2019). "The Use of Cryptocurrencies in Trade Finance." Facta Universitatis, Series. *Economics and Organization*, *16*(2), 151–166.

Sanka, A. I., & Cheung, R. C. (2021). A systematic review of blockchain scalability: Issues, solutions, analysis and future research. *Journal of Network and Computer Applications*, *195*, 103232. DOI: 10.1016/j.jnca.2021.103232

Sas, C., & Khairuddin, I. E. (2019). Risks and Opportunities in the Cryptocurrency Market. Ovidius University Annals. *Economic Sciences Series*, *19*(2), 879–883. DOI: 10.1145/2838739.2838821

Schär, F. (2021). Decentralized Finance: On Blockchain- and Smart Contract-based Financial Markets. *Review - Federal Reserve Bank of St. Louis*, *103*(3), 115–136.

Shahzad, F., Xiu, G., Wang, J., & Shahbaz, M. (2018). An Empirical Investigation on the Adoption of Cryptocurrencies Among the People of Mainland China. *Technology in Society*, *55*, 33–40. DOI: 10.1016/j.techsoc.2018.05.006

Swan, M. (2015). *Blockchain: Blueprint for a new economy*. O'Reilly Media.

Tapscott, A., & Tapscott, D. (2017). How blockchain is changing finance. *Harvard Business Review*, *1*(9), 2–5.

Tolossa, D., and Khawrin, M. (2022). The opportunities and challenges of cryptocurrencies: a systematic review. Vidya-A journal of gujarat university, *1*(1), 48-53.

Tran, A. B., Ouyang, M., Ma, X., & Yuan, M. L. (2019). Blockchain for IoT: The challenges and opportunities. *IEEE Internet of Things Journal*, *6*(2), 2521–2540.

United Nations Development Programme. (2019). "Blockchain and Distributed Ledger Technology in the UN System." UNDP Report.

Verma, K., & Jain, A. (2022). *What Is Digital Rupee? How Is It Different From Cryptocurrency?* Forbes Advisor.

Vranken, H. (2017). Sustainability of bitcoin and blockchains. *Current Opinion in Environmental Sustainability*, *28*, 1–9. DOI: 10.1016/j.cosust.2017.04.011

Vukolić, M. (2017). Rethinking permissioned blockchains. In *Proceedings of the ACM Workshop on Blockchain, Cryptocurrencies and Contracts* (pp. 3-7). ACM. DOI: 10.1145/3055518.3055526

Wallace, B. 2011, "The Rise and Fall of Bitcoin," Wired, November 23, retrieved at https://www.wired.com/magazine/2011/11/mf_bitcoin

World Bank. (2018). "Remittance Prices Worldwide." World Bank Report.

Yli-Huumo, J., Ko, D., Choi, S., Park, S., & Smolander, K. (2016). Where is current research on blockchain technology?—A systematic review. *PLoS One*, *11*(10), e0163477. DOI: 10.1371/journal.pone.0163477 PMID: 27695049

Chapter 8
Bridging Finance, Regulation, and Portfolio Management With Crypto Assets:
A Business Perspective

Maicol Ochoa Arrellano
Universidad Europea, Spain

Leslie Rodríguez-Valencia
Universidad Europea, Spain

Santos Andrés Gutiérrez Figueroa
https://orcid.org/0009-0004-6821-7406
Universidad Europea, Spain

Asaf Levi Alfaroviz
Universidad Europea, Spain

ABSTRACT

This chapter provides a comprehensive overview of the evolving role of crypto assets in modern financial markets. It begins by introducing the fundamental concepts of tokens and crypto assets, highlighting their unique characteristics and the emergence of the field of token engineering. The chapter then delves into the latest European regulations governing these assets, particularly the EU Regulation on Markets in Crypto Assets (MiCA) and examines their impact on companies. The chapter further explores the relationship between crypto assets and the traditional financial system, analyzing the interconnections between leading cryptocurrencies, stablecoins, and

DOI: 10.4018/979-8-3693-5986-0.ch008

traditional assets. It also discusses the implications of these relationships for corporate risk management and investment strategies. Finally, the chapter examines the potential benefits and risks of incorporating crypto assets, such as Bitcoin, into corporate investment portfolios, providing insights for companies seeking to navigate the evolving crypto asset landscape.

1. INTRODUCTION

In recent years, decentralized networks, including Bitcoin, Ethereum, and Solana, have attracted substantial interest from corporations. One of the primary reasons behind this growing interest is the substantial market capitalization that these systems have been able to accumulate in a relatively short period of time (CoinMarketCap, 2024). With respect to companies, decentralized networks have gained significant appeal as a result of their ability to provide secure, transparent, and tamper-proof transactions. The growing interest of companies in decentralized networks can be attributed to the increased need for secure and efficient financial systems, as well as the need to reduce transaction costs and processing times. Furthermore, these networks possess the potential to transform digital interactions, providing considerable advantages over the web2 approach. As a result, many companies are investing in decentralized networks and exploring new use cases for blockchain technology. The novel functions that companies can gain access to, as well as the investment prospects presented by these new blockchain initiatives, are both quite appealing to companies nowadays. Nevertheless, the adoption of this technology may pose challenges since businesses may struggle to maximize its full potential. Furthermore, little is known about the underlying causes and dynamics of the value of these crypto-economic systems.

Proposals have been put forward to investigate decentralized networks from a complexity perspective, with the assumption that they exhibit complex behaviors (Stoisic et al., 2019; Serena et al., 2022; Bielinskyi & Serdyuk, 2021; Gidea et al., 2020). In these crypto tokenized economies, which resemble other complex systems, characteristics such as the presence of simple elements, information transfer within the network, non-linear dynamics, evolution, learning, and notably the absence of central control can be observed (Mitchell, 2009). Furthermore, these systems are adaptive, dynamic, and multi-scale in nature (Voshmgir & Zargham, 2020).

The coordinating ability of decentralized networks is impressive in terms of directing resource allocation among a variety of stakeholders. This approach is especially applicable to the management of physical and financial resources, such as the distribution of tokens to motivate participants in the ecosystem (Voshmgir & Zargham, 2020). Although promising, designing such systems is challenging.

The challenges posed by the characteristics of these systems make it difficult to study their origins and dynamics, especially when it comes to comprehending the flow of value within the network. To address this uncertainty, researchers and practitioners have categorized various platforms based on the fundamental properties of these systems. In the following section, we will discuss some of them. Additionally, recognizing the need to enhance the current designs of decentralized platforms or improve operational decision-making, numerous valuation models have been developed, with a focus on the essential crypto-economic properties that influence the value of various elements of the system. These models are designed to provide a more comprehensive understanding of the value of decentralized systems and support decision-making processes. In this chapter, we will present one of the latest theories in token engineering that explores how system components receive value.

It has quickly been understood that tokens play a fundamental role in these systems. To devise improved designs and establish more effective incentive mechanisms, considerable attention has been directed towards this fundamental aspect of any token-based economy. As a result, a fresh field of study has arisen, with the objective of developing tools and models to engineer these systems, which is referred to as token engineering (Kifokeris et al., 2023; Maier, 2023).

In the context of a crypto-economic system, tokens are used as the fundamental unit of value that is exchanged among the system's stakeholders. These tokens are unique to decentralized ecosystems, and they serve as a representation of the system's state, granting the token holder the authority to modify the system's state. The term "state" pertains to a distinct set of data recorded on the distributed ledger that is processed by all the nodes forming part of the network (Li et al., 2019; Voshmgir, 2020). Unlike traditional financial assets such as stocks or bonds, tokens be utilized for a wide range of purposes. This makes it more intricate to determine the "fair value" of these tokens when compared to traditional financial assets (Kaal et al., 2021). We shall devote a specific section to examining the financial distinctions between the two assets, in order to enable the corporation to comprehend the differences.

The European Union's Regulation on Markets in Crypto Assets (MiCA) offers a foundational definition and framework for these assets, highlighting their diverse nature and broad utility. This chapter explores the intricate taxonomy of crypto assets, categorizing them into utility tokens, asset-referenced tokens (stablecoins), and e-money tokens, as defined by MiCA, while also considering security tokens under MiFID II (Markets in Financial Instruments Directive II) and the pending regulation of NFTs.

The complexities of classifying crypto assets extend beyond traditional definitions, as demonstrated by various regulatory authorities and academic proposals. For instance, FINMA's categorization based on economic function and the intricate five-level taxonomy proposed by Alzhrani et al. (2022) exemplify the nuanced nature of these digital entities. This discussion delves into the regulatory implications, intrinsic characteristics, and economic functions of crypto assets, aiming to elucidate the distinctions between utility tokens and security tokens, and to outline the regulatory landscape shaped by MiCA and MiFID II. This comprehensive analysis provides a critical understanding of the evolving role of crypto assets in modern financial markets.

The primary objective of this chapter is to provide an overview of crypto assets and their implications for corporations and companies. In order to offer a comprehensive perspective, we have chosen to address four key aspects of crypto assets from a corporate standpoint. The structure of the chapter has been designed to facilitate this approach. The second part of the chapter will provide a foundational understanding of tokens and crypto assets, laying the foundation for understanding where the value of these assets originates. In the third section, attention will be directed towards the latest regulations governing these aspects and their impact on companies. The fourth section will draw comparisons between crypto assets and the traditional financial system to assist companies in understanding how they can utilize these assets. In the fifth section, the most recent literature on incorporating crypto assets into a company's portfolio will be introduced, and in the discussion section, we will examine our findings and emphasize several key recommendations on this topic.

2. DEVELOPING CRYPTO-ECONOMIC SYSTEMS THROUGH THE ISSUANCE OF TOKENS: CRYPTO ASSETS

Cryptoeconomic systems are sophisticated socioeconomic frameworks that utilize blockchain networks and comparable decentralized technologies. They represent an adaptable network with multi-scale spatio-temporal dynamics. These systems are characterized by (i) autonomous individual actors, (ii) economic policies integrated into software (the protocol or smart contract code), and (iii) emergent properties resulting from the interactions of those actors with the entire network, according to the rules established by the software (Voshmgir an Zargham, 2020).

Cryptoeconomic systems provide a public infrastructure that facilitates socioeconomic interactions and coordination, in the absence of intermediaries or traditional organizations. They represent an institutional infrastructure upon which socioeconomic collaboration is enabled. These systems enable secure and transparent record-keeping without requiring intermediaries like banks, as highlighted by Burniske (2018). In essence, crypto-economic systems enable participants to engage in financial activities while maintaining control over their assets, thereby disintermediating traditional financial systems (Pernice et al., 2020). For instance, Ethereum is a platform that allows developers to build dApps, which can facilitate everything from financial transactions to supply chain management, thereby demonstrating the practical applications of crypto-economic systems in corporate environments.

One of the defining features of crypto-economic systems is the use of tokens, which can represent various forms of value, including currencies, assets, or access to services (Cong et al., 2018). These tokens are often utilized within decentralized applications (dApps) that operate on blockchain networks, allowing users to interact directly with one another without relying on traditional financial institutions (Shanaev et al., 2020). The value of these tokens is influenced by factors such as supply and demand, network effects, and the underlying utility they provide to users (Stylianou et al., 2021).

Tokens, are digital representations of assets that provide additional functionalities beyond mere currency. They can be classified into utility tokens, which grant access to specific services or products within a blockchain ecosystem, and security tokens, which represent ownership rights in underlying assets, such as equity (Morozova, 2020; Shanaeva et al., 2020). The distinction between coins and tokens is significant; while coins typically function as a payment medium, tokens often confer specific rights or utilities to their holders (Chen et al., 2020).

Moreover, the governance of crypto-economic systems is typically "decentralized", meaning that decisions are made collectively by participants rather than a central authority (Grau, 2021). This decentralization fosters a sense of community and trust among users, as they can verify transactions and maintain the integrity of the system through consensus mechanisms (Hayes, 2017). Although it is known that many decentralized platforms are not truly decentralized, as major decisions are made by a small group of developers, this is a risk that companies should be aware of, even though it is beyond the scope of this chapter.

Crypto assets represent a novel class of digital assets that leverage blockchain technology for secure and decentralized transactions. They can be categorized into various types, including cryptocurrencies, stablecoins, and tokens. In the subsequent section, we will present the most recent MiCA regulation, which focusses significantly on this subject. Nevertheless, cryptocurrencies, such as Bitcoin and Litecoin, primarily serve as mediums of exchange and stores of value, while security tokens like Ether produces future cashflow when staked. Stablecoins in contrast, aim to maintain a stable value relative to traditional currencies through backing or algorithmic mechanisms (Baer et al., 2023; European Systemic Risk Board, 2023). The term "crypto asset" encompasses all these forms, highlighting their reliance on cryptographic techniques and distributed ledger technology (Kostoula, 2023). We refer to tokens when discussing the functionalities they have within a crypto-economic system, while crypto assets are essentially tokens that we analyze from a more economic and financial perspective.

Let us now proceed to discuss tokens in greater detail. Since their inception, various theories have been proposed to classify them into different categories based on their characteristics. The taxonomic work on tokens necessitates an understanding of what tokens precisely represent within the system they belong to and how these tokens impact the business model of the blockchain project utilizing them. Proposals such as Euler's (Euler, 2018) inspired Olivera et al. (2018) to devise a token classification method tailored for developers of blockchain-based systems. Employing the morphological box technique to recognize patterns in various parameter combinations (supply, layer, incentive system, etc.), they identified classes of tokens referred to as archetypes. Each of these archetypes or token classes shares the same parameters and, consequently, the same business model, as depicted in Table 1 (Oliveira et al., 2018).

Table 1. Different types of token archetypes (classes) proposed by Oliveira et al.

Archetype	Main Purposes	Description
CryptoCurrency	Currency	A token with the ambition to become a widespread digital form of currency. (Cryptocurrency ; Asset-/Usage-/Work-Based ; Currency ; Digital ; Schedulebased / one-time fixed / discretionary ; Use Platform / Stay Long-Term ; Spendable ; Tradable ; (Non-)/Destroyable ; (Non-)/Expirable ; Fungible ; Blockchain Native ; New Chain New Code / New Chain Forked Code)
Equity Token	Earnings, Store of Wealth	A token which confers to its holder a right to equity-related earnings, such as profitsharing, application rents or platform fees. (Tokenised Security ; Asset-/Usage-Based ; Toll / Earnings ; Physical/Digital/ Legal ; Schedule-based / one-time fixed / discretionary ; Enter Platform / Use Platform / Stay Long-Term ; Non-Spendable ; (Non-)/ Tradable ; (Non-)/Destroyable ; (Non-)/Expirable ; (Non-)/Fungible ; Blockchain Native / Protocol / dApp ; New/Forked Code , New / Forked Chain / on top of Protocol)
Funding Token	Store of Wealth, Funding	A token which is perceived as a long-term investment from the holder's perspective, and as a financing vehicle for the project's team and/or the community (bounties). (Tokenised Security / Utility Token ; Usage-/Work-Based ; Right / Value Exchange / Toll ; Physical/Digital ; Schedule-based / one-time fixed / discretionary ; Enter Platform / Use Platform / Stay Long-Term / Leave Platform ; (Non-)/Spendable ; Tradable ; (Non-)/Destroyable ; (Non-)/Expirable ; (Non-)/Fungible ; Blockchain Native / Protocol / dApp ; New/Forked Code , New / Forked Chain / on top of Protocol)
Consensus Token	Validation Reward, Store-of Wealth	A token which is used as a reward to nodes which ensure data validation and consensus. (Utility Token ; Work-Based ; Right / Reward ; Digital ; Schedule-based / one-time fixed ; Enter Platform / Use Platform / Stay Long-Term / Leave Platform ; (Non-)/Spendable ; Tradable ; (Non-)/Destroyable ; (Non-)/Expirable ; (Non-)/Fungible ; Blockchain Native / Protocol ; New/Forked Code , New / Forked Chain)

continued on following page

Table 1. Continued

Archetype	Main Purposes	Description
Work Token	Work Reward	A token which is used as reward to users who complete certain actions or exhibit certain behaviour. (Utility Token ; Work-Based ; Right / Reward ; Digital ; Schedule-based / one-time fixed ; Enter Platform / Use Platform / Stay Long-Term / Leave Platform ; (Non-)/Spendable ; Tradable ; (Non-)/Destroyable ; (Non-)/Expirable ; (Non-)/Fungible ; Blockchain Native / Protocol / dApp ; New/Forked Code , New / Forked Chain / on top of protocol)
Voting Token	Voting Right	A token which confers a voting right to its holder. (Utility Token ; Asset-/Usage-Based ; Right ; Physical / Digital ; Schedule-based / one-time fixed / Discretionary ; Use Platform / Stay Long-Term ; Non-Spendable ; (Non-)/Tradable ; (Non-)/Destroyable ; (Non-)/Expirable ; (Non-)/Fungible ; Blockchain Native / Protocol / dApp ; New/Forked Code , New / Forked Chain / on top of protocol)
Asset Token	Voting Right, Asset Ownership	A token which represents asset ownership. (Utility Token / Tokenised Security ; Asset-Based ; Right / Toll ; Physical / Digital / Legal ; one-time fixed / Discretionary ; Enter Platform / Use Platform / Stay Long-Term ; Spendable ; (Non-)/Tradable ; (Non-)/Destroyable ; (Non-)/ Expirable ; (Non-)/Fungible ; Blockchain Native / Protocol / dApp ; New/Forked Code , New / Forked Chain / on top of protocol)
PaymentToken	Payment	A token which is used as internal payment method in the application. (Utility Token ; Usage-Based ; Right / Value Exchange; Digital ; schedule-based / one-time fixed; Enter Platform / Use Platform / Stay Long-Term ; Spendable ; Tradable ; (Non-)/Destroyable ; (Non-)/ Expirable ; Fungible ; Blockchain Native / Protocol / dApp ; New/ Forked Code , New / Forked Chain / on top of protocol)

Note: Table 1 taken from Oliveira, L., Zavolokina, L., Bauer, I., & Schwabe, G. (2018, December). To token or not to token: Tools for understanding blockchain tokens. ICIS.

We can argue that this classification method is focused on the system's design, emphasizing parameters that represent the supply side rather than the demand side. This classification is oriented towards the design of a crypto-economic system from the developer's perspective. For this reason, it focuses on technical elements that can be engineered by the developers themselves.

In their recent work, Sumanov and Polanski (2023) broaden the scope of classification by incorporating the demand side, positing that a token's value may be attributed to the user's engagement with the token and the resulting behaviors. They argue that a token's value can be influenced by the user's interaction with it and the subsequent behaviors that arise from this interaction. By incorporating this perspective, researchers and practitioners can gain a more comprehensive understanding of the elements that contribute to a token's value and make more informed decisions when designing the crypto-economic system that suits their needs, thus optimizing behaviors within the network.

While the origins of value (OoV's) represent general sources that explain the value possession through a token and are chosen in a way that they do not intersect, the value capture mechanisms (VCM) are essentially sets of possibly multiple origins of value whose value can be extracted through a specific behavior pattern (Sumanov & Polanski, 2023).

Origins of Value (OoVs) are the fundamental sources of value that drive the demand for a token. They represent the different ways in which a token can provide value to its holders. For example, the "Future Cashflow" OoV represents the value a token derives from its ability to unlock a future income stream, such as rewards for participating in a protocol. Another OoV is "Governance", which captures the value a token provides by granting the holder the ability to influence the management of limited resources within the ecosystem. By understanding the specific OoVs that a token is designed to provide, the token's purpose and functionality can be clearly defined, allowing for more effective design and implementation.

Sumanov and Polanski utilize Equation 1 to capture and quantify the value of a token.

Equation 1

$$U=Q(p,x,s,t)-L(p,x,s,t)$$

Where Q represents the utility of holding x tokens at a specific price p, given the state of a blockchain, s, and over a period of time, t. We might think that there are only positive elements in holding a token; however, from the holder's perspective, there are also risks and costs associated with holding a token, represented by L. Thus, fundamentally, it is a maximization problem. Assuming the market is in its optimal state, a positive U implies that from the holder's perspective, it is beneficial to hold the token, and if U is negative, holding the token is not beneficial.

Table 2. The origins of value and value erosion of a token

Number	Origin of Value	Description
1	Value Transfer	Value is gained based on the involvement in transactions (settlements)
2	Future Cashflow	Future income stream exposed by the token, related to the use of the token in the protocol
3	Governance	Value begotten by exertion of influence on the management/distribution of limited resources
4	Access	Value begotten by purely granting access to a resource, but not compounding it with any additional utility

Number	Origin of Value	Description
5	Representation	Value is extrinsically sourced and comes from representing a unit of some other asset
6	Hedonic Value	The value is begotten by social contract, e.g., as a result of popularity or other context not captured by the regular economic models
7	Risk Exposure	Generalized loss (in the probabilistic sense) corresponding to deliberate exposure to certain risks(of alienation or depreciation) acting as a necessary condition for activation of other origins of value
8	Conditional Action	Generalized loss corresponding to a need to carry out certain specific actions so that value is begotten (e.g., perform work)

Note: Table 2 taken from Sumanov, V., & Polanski, S. (2023). Token Classification Framework by Consideration of Origins of Value and Mechanisms of Manifestation Thereof. Retrieved the 20th of September 2023 from https://github.com/powerpool-finance/powerpool-research/blob/main/Papers/Value_Capturing_Mechanisms_.pdf

In their paper the authors describe 8 origins of value and loss as shown in Table 2. These value origins are atomic and multiple ones can exist in a token. For this reason, the authors refer to the mechanisms that capture the value as the mechanisms that determine how a token's value manifests. Value capture mechanisms (VCM's) can be graphically represented using a connected network of OoVs, where the OoVs are the nodes, and the edges are the interactions between them. For example, the "work token" VCM captures the value of a token that is staked and then used to perform tasks or services within the ecosystem. The holder is rewarded with future cashflows for successfully completing these tasks. This VCM combines the origins of value for Future cashflow and conditional Action, where the reward is contingent on the holder performing the required work.

The authors present 10 value capture mechanisms in their work, as illustrated in Figure 1. It is crucial to emphasize that a token can have multiple VCMs simultaneously, as seen in the case of Ethereum's native token, Ether, which shares two VCMs: consensus and value transfer (Sumanov & Polanski, 2023).

Figure 1. Value capture mechanisms proposed by Sumanov and Polanski

Note: Figure taken from Sumanov, V., & Polanski, S. (2023). Token Classification Framework by Consideration of Origins of Value and Mechanisms of Manifestation Thereof. Retrieved the 20th of September 2023 from https://github.com/powerpool-finance/powerpool-research/blob/main/Papers/Value_Capturing_Mechanisms_.pdf

Companies can apply the theory by following the workflow outlined by Sumanov & Polanski (2023). If a firm wishes to devise a new token-based system to motivate and coordinate agents within its ecosystem, it would initially identify the essential components of the system:

1. Interacting agents: The agents are the company's customers, suppliers, and service providers who will participate in the ecosystem.
2. Principal value and information flows: The main value flow is the execution of tasks or services by the agents for the company and its customers. Information flows include task assignments, performance metrics, and token rewards/ penalties.
3. Key system metrics: The company wants to maximize the number and value of tasks successfully executed, while minimizing failed tasks and disruptions.

Next, the company would determine the correct (incentivized) and incorrect (disincentivized) agent behaviors needed to achieve the system goals. This leads to the identification of relevant origins of value, such as future cashflow (rewards for task completion) and conditional action (tasks must be executed to earn rewards).

The company would then group these origins of value into appropriate value capturing mechanisms (VCM). In this case, a work token VCM would be suitable, as it combines future cashflow and conditional action.

Finally, the company would select an implementation pattern for the token, likely based on an existing work token archetype, and define the necessary technical properties (e.g., mintability, tradability, delegability) to operationalize the desired VCMs.

The key advantages of this framework are:

1) It starts with the demand-side considerations (origins of value) rather than technical details, ensuring the token design is purpose-driven.
2) The hierarchical structure (OoVs -> VCMs -> Implementation Patterns) provides a clear, modular way to reason about token design.
3) The visual representation of OoV dependencies helps identify appropriate VCMs and detect the need for new ones.
4) The formal treatment of token value as an optimization problem bridges theory and practice.

By following this structured approach, the company can create a token system tailored to its specific ecosystem needs and incentive mechanisms.

This methodology helps to understand how a company can design a crypto-economic system to achieve its objectives. This example clarifies what a token is and why it can be considered an asset from an economic and financial perspective.

Given that we have a clearer grasp of the concept of a crypto economic system and the role of tokens or crypto assets within it, let us delve into the latest European regulations surrounding this topic and examine their impact on businesses.

3. THE TAXONOMY OF CRYPTO ASSETS UNDER THE MiCA REGULATION AND ITS EFFECT ON COMPANIES

In generic terms, crypto assets correspond to "a digital representation of value or rights that can be transferred and stored electronically, using distributed ledger technology or similar technology." This is determined by Article 3(5) of the EU Regulation on Markets in Crypto Assets (MiCA). However, achieving uniformity in this definition requires a conceptual journey through various assimilations of the inherent nature of these digital entities.

Regardless of the numerous existing typologies in the taxonomy of crypto assets, with the entry into force of MiCA, we observe the regulation of three types of crypto assets: utility tokens, asset-referenced tokens (stablecoins), and e-money tokens. Security tokens fall under the MiFID II regulation, while NFTs remain, for the moment, pending regulation.

Beyond the legacy taxonomy of utility and security tokens, the taxonomy of these assets is considerably more complex. For example, the Swiss Financial Authority (FINMA) categorizes them into three types based on their underlying economic function: payment tokens (means of payment or transferring value), utility tokens, and asset tokens (securities under Swiss financial market laws) (FINMA, 2018). 3).

However, attributing the taxonomy of a crypto asset is a much more difficult task. Some authors have identified up to 30 nested dimensions and 42 characteristics (Xu et al., 2017, p. 246) within blockchains that host these digital assets, such as decentralization, blockchain configuration, storage and computation, or other architectural designs and deployment. Recently, Alzhrani et al. (2022, p. 5) proposed a five-level taxonomy comprising a system, subsystem, component, aspect, and finally, the characteristic level.

Among the proposals for digital asset taxonomies is a token design decision tree related to blockchain application development (Oliveira et al., 2018, p. 7), characterized by thirteen aspects such as: layer, purpose, standard, fungibility, underlying asset, ownership of the underlying asset, transferability, expiration date, flow, offerings, supply, and issuance.

Therefore, a token can be considered in terms of its layer: native or secondary, where the former is specific to the platform on which they are implemented as a core component of the platform, mainly as a cryptocurrency, while the latter supports the application's functions. Whereas the purpose refers to the utility, stability or technical safety characteristics, the regulation refers to the standard's technical qualification; fungibility to its ability to be exchanged for another identical token; the underlying asset to whether the token represents an asset and its ownership (total or fractional) if applicable; transferability, expiration, and flow (linear or circular) consider the circulation of a token; while offerings, supply, and issuance encompass the economic foundation of the token and its revenue models (Arslanian & Fischer, 2019, p. 141).

Numerous Web3 projects have oriented their native tokens to provide digital access to an application or service via blockchain-based infrastructure, for example, to pay transaction fees on the network, protocol governance, or participant rewards. This occurs illustratively with the native token of the Ethereum network (ETH) and those of the Solana (SOL), XRP Ledger (XRP), Cardano (ADA), Avalanche (AVAX), or Algorand (ALGO) networks, as well as operational tokens on different blockchains like Enjin (ENJ), 1Inch Network (1INCH), or Uniswap (UNI).

From a regulatory perspective at least, the tendency of most entities or corporations that list their assets on various exchange platforms seems to be towards utility tokens. But not because the exact nature of these digital assets is solely utilitarian, but because, under the current regulation, they do not meet the requirements to be considered securities.

According to MiCA, for a token to be considered a security, it must possess intrinsic characteristics representative of typically underlying financial assets, such as company shares or profit flows, or a right to dividends or interest payments. The security token, from an economic function perspective, is analogous to shares, bonds, or derivatives (listed market instruments), partial or total ownership of real estate or private equity assets.

The European Securities and Markets Authority (ESMA) estimates that the elements that are required for a crypto asset to be recognized as a security include the following: "grants rights similar to shares, bonds, or other securities (e.g., those incorporating a derivative)" (ESMA, 2024, p. 8). Additionally, "under Article 4(1)(44) of MiFID II, three criteria must be met for a crypto-asset to be deemed a security: it must be part of a 'class of securities,' be (ii) negotiable on the capital market, and (iii) not be a payment instrument"(ESMA, 2024, p. 8). In this sense, ESMA clarifies that payment instruments are "explicitly excluded from the definition of securities in MiFID II. The definition of 'payment instrument' in PSD2 does not fully coincide with the concept of a payment instrument in MiFID II... The latter appears closer to the notion of funds in PSD2, while the former refers to devices (physical or digital) used to perform payment transactions and should thus be understood broadly (i.e., encompassing both liquid payment methods and non-cash payment instruments)" (ESMA, 2024, p. 10).

Furthermore, the token must represent a contractual right that gives rise to a financial commitment, and its value must depend solely on exchange rate fluctuations, commodity prices, stock indices, interest rates, returns or performance of underlying assets, or a combination of these elements, or grant some right of participation in the issuer's capital or profits or voting rights over the issuing entity.

However, one might think that a token's potential to offer benefits to its holders due to participation in liquidity pools or staking could lead to their classification as securities. The mentioned benefits do not fit the assumptions of Article 4.1.43) of MiFID II if, additionally, they do not combine a deposit with one or more financial derivatives, or with references to one or more underlying assets, or if there is no commitment from the issuer to offer a guaranteed or minimum return or is subject to protection against the issuer's insolvency.

On the other hand, tokens that offer the function of liquidity pool provider could be interpreted as a deposit system under Article 2.1.3) of Directive 2014/49/EU. However, for this to be the case, it must in some way constitute a deposit system representing funds received by a credit institution in the course of its banking activities, or generate interest for the holder or be subject to the return of an amount equal to the deposited sum.

According to ESMA, crypto assets that fit the definition of securities must possess "the existence of an unenforceable profit expectation", without necessarily entailing ownership or governance rights (ESMA, 2024, p. 30). Based on this, ESMA points out that "crypto assets can be recognized as securities if they grant rights similar to shares, bonds, or other securities (e.g., securities incorporating a derivative)" (ESMA, 2024, p. 10).

Moreover, the European Banking Authority (EBA) interprets security tokens to be those that "typically provide rights (e.g., in the form of ownership rights and/or rights similar to dividends). For example, in the context of capital raising, asset tokens may be issued in the context of an ICO that allows companies to raise capital for their projects by issuing digital tokens in exchange for fiat money or other crypto assets" (EBA, 2019, p. 4). At the same time, it considers utility tokens as those that "typically allow access to a specific product or service often provided via a DLT platform but are not accepted as a means of payment for other products or services..." (EBA, 2019, p. 7).

In this respect, if the token does not comply with the description of a tradable security specified by ESMA and the EBA, as it does not entitle its holders to any right to participate in the issuer's profits, nor to receive dividends or any other form of economic participation merely by holding the tokens, and its potential value is subject solely to market speculation and demand (not in any underlying asset or cash flow), then its classification will be that of a utility token.

Additionally, it must be ruled out that the token does not fit the e-money definition in Article 2.2 of Directive 2009/110/EC, which is positive when the token is not issued at the nominal value of legal tender, nor backed by a redemption obligation by the issuer. Although the token is stored electronically, it does not function to be used for making digital payments between a payer and a payee.

Determining the token's taxonomy is the essential circumstance to address its regulatory regime, which will be determined by its intrinsic characteristics. If the tokens are designed to be used or consumed in some way, they are very likely utility tokens under MiCA. In contrast, if the token's intrinsic function is designed to serve as or represent financial assets, we are dealing with a security token regulated under MiFID II.

According to the MiCA regulation, tokens may contain intrinsic features designed to serve as a store of value or medium of exchange for any type of good, service, or asset in general. In this category would be stablecoins and e-money tokens, which can be issued, under strict requirements, both by companies and entities such as central banks or other governmental departments, commercial banks, and organizations authorized for this purpose.

It is important to remember that blockchains are distributed transactional platforms that rely on peer-to-peer networks which, unlike traditional business models, do not require intermediaries and owe their complex computational capacity to the functions of the smart contracts they operate on (Zheng et al., 2020, p. 6). Although systems built on blockchain can be autonomous, in everyday business activity they may need to communicate with other centralized or distributed systems. Therefore, the interoperability that enables this communication between a blockchain system and other blockchain or non-blockchain systems is only possible with the intervention of oracles (Xu et al., 2019) and other gateways and interfaces.

Accordingly, the introduction of crypto assets into the portfolio of any retail or corporate investor becomes more cost-effective. These assets can be interconnected and disconnected from conventional assets, placing them within a new class of investment assets (Corbet et al., 2019, p. 6).

4. A CORPORATE VIEW OF THE RELATIONSHIP BETWEEN THE MAIN CRYPTO ASSETS AND OTHER FINANCIAL MARKETS

The relationship between the leading cryptocurrencies Bitcoin (BTC), Ethereum (ETH), and the stablecoin Tether (USDT) with traditional financial assets has become increasingly intertwined in recent years. From a corporate perspective, understanding these interconnections is crucial for navigating the convergence of the crypto and traditional financial markets.

Numerous studies have examined the correlation dynamics between cryptocurrencies and traditional assets. Some results indicate that BTC and ETH have exhibited a high and sustained positive correlation, especially since 2020 (Salehi and Rafsanjani, 2024). This suggests that these two major cryptocurrencies are subject to common risk factors and are increasingly behaving as risk assets, like equities.

On the other hand, stablecoins, such as Tether (USDT), play a crucial role in bridging the crypto and traditional financial ecosystems. Evidence shows that stablecoins account for over 60% of all crypto transactions, serving as a mean to store value and facilitate cash-in/cash-out activities within the crypto system (ESMA, 2024). In particular, Tether dominates the stablecoin market, accounting for 70% of market capitalization and 90% of trading volumes (ESMA, 2024).

Interestingly, there are further results also revealing certain BTC correlation with gold, a traditional inflation hedge, which has been positive and intermittent over the same period (Flow Traders, 2023). This aligns with the narrative of BTC emerging as an alternative store of value asset, potentially offering protection against currency debasement (Flow Traders, 2023; Two Sigma, 2021).

The strong correlations among cryptocurrencies and their growing ties to traditional assets like equities and gold indicate that the crypto market is becoming more integrated with the broader financial system (Flow Traders, 2023). This has important implications for corporate risk management and investment strategies, as crypto exposure can no longer be considered a completely uncorrelated asset class. The correlations between the leading cryptocurrencies Bitcoin (BTC), Ethereum (ETH), and the stablecoin Tether (USDT) with traditional assets like stocks and gold have important implications for corporate investment strategies:

1. **Increased Correlation Between Cryptocurrencies and Stocks:** notably, ETH has a significantly higher correlation with major stock indexes like the S&P 500 and Nasdaq 100 compared to BTC (ESMA, 2024). This suggests that ETH is increasingly behaving as a risk asset, like equities. Corporations must carefully assess the diversification benefits of including ETH in their investment portfolios, as its growing ties to the stock market reduce its potential as an uncorrelated asset.
2. **Bitcoin as a Potential Hedge:** In contrast, BTC has exhibited a weaker correlation with stocks and a negative correlation with the US dollar index (ESMA, 2024). This aligns with the narrative of BTC emerging as a potential hedge or store of value asset, like gold (Cryptopotato, 2023; Cryptoslate, 2023). Corporations may consider incorporating BTC exposure as part of a diversification strategy to mitigate risks in their traditional asset portfolios.

3. **Stablecoins and Corporate Treasury Management:** The dominance of Tether in the stablecoin market and its growing interconnectedness with traditional assets like gold, WTI, and Brent crude oil (Baur and Hoang, 2021) highlight the need for corporations to carefully assess their exposure to stablecoins. Corporations should develop robust policies and procedures to manage the risks associated with these crypto-fiat hybrid instruments, which can have significant implications for their treasury management and financial reporting.
4. **Evolving Market Structure and Liquidity Dynamics:** The highly concentrated nature of the crypto market, with a few exchanges accounting for most of the trading volume (Foroutan and Lahmiri, 2024), and the uneven distribution of liquidity across crypto assets, can pose challenges for corporate treasury management and risk mitigation strategies. Corporations must closely monitor these market structure and liquidity dynamics to effectively manage their crypto-related exposures.

Given the correlations mentioned above, it would be irresponsible, from a corporate point of view, not to mention the relationship or impact that other macroeconomic factors have on major crypto assets, just as they have on traditional financial assets.

In that sense, we find it interesting providing several key insights into how global interest rate environments influence the correlation between cryptocurrencies and traditional financial assets. In summary, we can say that the key points are:

1. **Opportunity Cost:** When interest rates are low, cryptocurrencies like Bitcoin (BTC) and Ethereum (ETH) become more attractive to investors due to the lower opportunity cost of holding non-yielding assets. Conversely, when rates rise, the appeal of cryptocurrencies diminishes as investors can earn higher returns from safer assets like bonds (Coindesk, 2023; Piguet Galland, 2024).
2. **Risk Sentiment:** Changes in interest rates can influence overall market sentiment. When central banks raise rates to combat inflation, it signals a more restrictive monetary policy and can dampen risk appetite. In such environments, investors may move away from riskier assets like cryptocurrencies and stocks toward safer havens (Coindesk, 2023).
3. **Inflation Expectations:** If central banks raise rates to curb rising inflation, it can erode the purchasing power of fiat currencies. In response, some investors may turn to cryptocurrencies as a hedge against inflation, potentially driving up their prices. However, if inflation expectations are well-anchored, the increase in rates can lead to a decline in cryptocurrency prices due to the higher opportunity cost (Coindesk, 2023).

4. **Historical Trends:** Periods of low interest rates have been associated with price appreciation in cryptocurrencies, while rapid rate hikes have led to declines, reflecting broader market trends. For example, the Fed's interest rate hikes in 2018 coincided with a significant drop in Bitcoin's price, which cascaded across the broader cryptocurrency market (Cointelegraph, 2024; Piguet Galland, 2024).
5. **Sensitivity to Rates:** Cryptocurrencies, being highly volatile assets, are particularly sensitive to changes in the interest rate environment. When rates rise, liquidity tends to leave the crypto market, leading to price drops (Cointelegraph, 2024).

In summary, interest rates impact the correlation between cryptocurrencies and traditional assets by influencing investor behaviour, market sentiment, and inflation expectations. As the crypto market becomes more integrated with the broader financial system, understanding the role of interest rates in this relationship is crucial for navigating the evolving landscape.

Finally, we consider the role played by the US Treasury and US debt as another aspect of interest from a corporate view. Changes in the U.S. Treasury's balance, particularly the Treasury General Account (TGA), can significantly impact the crypto market during economic downturns:

1. **TGA Balance and Liquidity:** When the TGA balance is lower, it injects more funds into the economy, potentially boosting liquidity and stimulating riskier investments like cryptocurrencies (CTO Labs, 2024). During economic downturns, the Treasury may maintain a lower TGA balance to provide additional stimulus.
2. **Quarterly Refinancing Announcements (QRA):** The U.S. Treasury Secretary's QRA, which outlines the government's three-month borrowing needs, can influence financial markets, including cryptocurrencies (CTO Labs, 2024). If the Treasury reduces its gross issuance or maintains a lower TGA balance, it could boost economic activity and rally risk assets, including cryptocurrencies.
3. **Correlation with Bitcoin:** A lower TGA balance, which can occur during economic downturns, may have a positive correlation with Bitcoin prices (CTO Labs, 2024). As the TGA balance decreases, it could potentially stimulate economic activity and make riskier investments like Bitcoin more attractive to investors.
4. **Funding Rates and Demand:** However, during economic downturns, Bitcoin funding rates have turned negative, signalling reduced demand and trader caution in the market (CTO Labs, 2024). Negative funding rates might indicate waning enthusiasm for Bitcoin, despite potential positive macroeconomic factors like a lower TGA balance.

5. **Volatility and Liquidity Concentration:** Economic downturns can lead to increased volatility and liquidity concentration in the crypto market (Phemex, 2022). The most-traded assets like Bitcoin and Ethereum exhibit significantly better liquidity compared to less-traded cryptocurrencies, posing challenges for risk management strategies.

On the other hand, it is worth noting that the impact of U.S. debt on the crypto asset market varies depending on the type of cryptocurrency:

Bitcoin (BTC) and Ethereum (ETH)

- Bitcoin and Ethereum, as the two largest cryptocurrencies by market capitalization, are sensitive to macroeconomic factors like U.S. debt levels.
- Rising U.S. debt can lead to concerns about inflation and economic instability, which may drive investors to seek alternative assets like Bitcoin as a hedge (Markets.com, 2024).
- However, during periods of high U.S. debt and economic uncertainty, investors may also move funds into safer assets like cash, potentially reducing demand for cryptocurrencies (Markets.com, 2024).

Tether - USDT

- Stablecoins like Tether are designed to maintain a stable value pegged to fiat currencies like the U.S. dollar.
- As a result, stablecoins are less directly impacted by U.S. debt levels compared to other cryptocurrencies.
- However, if high U.S. debt leads to a weakening of the U.S. dollar, it could potentially affect the perceived stability and value of dollar-pegged stablecoins (BitTime, 2024).

Altcoins and DeFi Tokens

- Altcoins and decentralized finance (DeFi) tokens are more speculative and volatile compared to Bitcoin and Ethereum.
- These assets may be more sensitive to broader economic conditions and investor sentiment, which can be influenced by factors like U.S. debt levels.
- During periods of economic uncertainty driven by high U.S. debt, investors may become more risk-averse, leading to a decline in demand for altcoins and DeFi tokens (Nasdaq, 2023).

- It is important to note that the relationship between U.S. debt and crypto asset prices is complex and can be influenced by various other factors, such as regulatory changes, technological advancements, and overall market sentiment. Investors should carefully consider these factors when making investment decisions in the crypto asset market.

In summary, the convergence of the crypto and traditional financial markets presents both opportunities and challenges for corporations. On the one hand, the growing correlations between cryptocurrencies and traditional assets may allow corporations to incorporate crypto exposure into their investment and risk management strategies. However, the high interconnectedness of the crypto market and its potential for contagion effects require careful consideration and robust risk assessment.

Corporations should closely monitor the evolving relationship between cryptocurrencies, stablecoins, and traditional assets, as well as the market structure and liquidity dynamics within the crypto ecosystem. This knowledge can inform strategic decision-making, such as:

1. **Asset Allocation and Portfolio Diversification:** Corporations may need to reevaluate the role of cryptocurrencies and stablecoins within their investment portfolios, considering their evolving correlations with traditional assets and the potential diversification benefits or risks.
2. **Treasury Management and Liquidity Risk:** Corporations should assess their exposure to stablecoins, particularly Tether, and develop robust policies and procedures to manage the risks associated with these instruments. Additionally, corporations should consider the implications of uneven liquidity distribution in the crypto market for their treasury operations.
3. **Regulatory Compliance and Risk Mitigation:** As the crypto-traditional finance convergence continues, corporations must stay abreast of evolving regulatory frameworks and ensure compliance with relevant laws and regulations. This may involve enhancing internal controls, implementing robust risk management practices, and collaborating with regulatory authorities.
4. **Operational Integration and Technological Adoption:** Corporations may explore opportunities to integrate crypto-based technologies, such as blockchain, into their business processes to enhance efficiency, transparency, and security. However, this should be done with a clear understanding of the associated risks and the evolving regulatory landscape.

5. INCORPORATING CRYPTO ASSETS IN CORPORATE PORTFOLIOS

The emergence of Bitcoin and other cryptocurrencies, and their rapid success as investment options for hundreds of thousands of people, leads us to question how the inclusion of Bitcoin and other cryptocurrencies affects the risk-return balance of a portfolio. Bitcoin has emerged as a novel investment option, capturing significant interest from both the investors and media. Despite this attention, the investment advantages of Bitcoin remain relatively unexplored. Thus, this research investigates the potential benefits and risk of incorporating Bitcoin into a conventional benchmark portfolio comprising stocks and bonds according to researchers in the area.

Valuation plays a key role in many areas such as portfolio management, acquisition analysis (mergers and acquisitions), and corporate finance. Therefore, Corporate portfolio management (CPM) proves essential for the strategic management of a company's range of projects, programs, or investments to fulfill its broader business aims. (Pidun, et al., 2011) (Rodríguez-Valencia, et al., 2023). The primary goals of CPM are to optimize the balance between risk and return, improve resource utilization, and foster overall corporate growth and profitability. (Rochet & Villeneuve, 2005)

There is an ever-growing literature examining the relationship of Bitcoin with other financial assets, with influential work by Platanakis & Urquhart (2020) demonstrates that, regardless of the asset allocation strategies and levels of risk aversion, Bitcoin offers significant advantages, leading to substantially higher risk-adjusted returns. Dwyer (2015) shows that the average monthly volatility of Bitcoin is higher than that of gold or a set of foreign currencies while Urquhart (2016) shows that Bitcoin returns are inefficient, which is supported by Nadarajah and Chu (2017) and Bariviera (2017). Grobys and Sapkota (2019) show no evidence of significant momentum profits in cryptocurrency markets.

Calculating the return of the different financial assets available for investment is fundamental in building a portfolio. There are numerous definitions of return for financial assets, and each type of asset (fixed income, variable income, derivatives, etc.) has its own forms of valuation. Another parameter to consider is the risk of assets and portfolios. The most commonly accepted definition in financial markets states that "the risk of an asset is the degree of uncertainty in achieving the expected return on financial investments." This definition implies that risk reflects any variation in said return, whether the return obtained is higher or lower than expected. (Grauer, 1986)

There are several ways to evaluate these potential variations in an asset's return, with variance being the most commonly used statistical measure. Variance is a measure that expresses the sum of the squared deviations of an asset's return from its expected or historical return.

It is observed that the risk of a portfolio is the sum of the risks of the individual assets weighted by their squared weights, plus the summation of the product of the weights of each pair of assets multiplied by the covariance between them. In this breakdown of the covariance calculation, we see the importance of the correlation between asset returns in portfolio diversification. This idea already appears in the early works of Modern Portfolio Theory, initiated by Harry Markowitz (1952). Among finance professionals, the importance of seeking uncorrelated profitable assets to build portfolios began in the 1970s, when the knowledge of Modern Portfolio Theory started to spread. The search for low correlation explains the trends of:

H. Markowitz's model is also known as the Mean-Variance Decision Model, the principal objective was the graphical and analytical demonstration (linear programming) of the relationship between the investor's expectations (their attitude towards risk) and the selection of an optimal portfolio, always considering the two parameters of expected return and existing risk in the market. (Markowitz, 2014). However, Portfolio theory is highly sensitive to estimation risk that may overstate (understate) returns (risk). This means that optimal portfolios constructed via the classical Markowitz mean-variance optimization can be unstable with a weak out-of-sample performance and this phenomenon has been well-substantiated in the portfolio theory literature. (Kolm, et al., 2014; Levy & Levy, 2014; Carroll, et al., 2017).

The integration of alternative investments into traditional stock-bond portfolios has been extensively examined in the literature, yielding mixed outcomes. Gorton & Rouwenhorst (2006), Hillier at al. (2006), and Gao & Nardari (2018) all find that adding commodities to a benchmark portfolio adds value.

The analysis of the positive effects that cryptocurrencies like Bitcoin can have on investors' portfolios should determine if, based on optimization models, this class of assets should be included in the composition of efficient portfolios. this has already been researched by various authors who generally conclude that cryptocurrencies improve (shift upwards and to the left) the efficient frontier for investors. Brière et al., (2015) demonstrate that Bitcoin's correlation with other assets is exceptionally low, significantly enhancing the risk-adjusted returns of portfolios when included. Gangwal (2016) presents an early analysis highlighting the positive impact of incorporating Bitcoin into portfolios at a basic level. One of the most thorough pioneering studies on this topic was conducted by Katjazi and Moro (2019), utilizing monthly data from January 31, 2012, to January 31, 2017. They examined various asset classes, including gold, equities, fixed income, money markets, commodities, real estate, and alternative investments via a hedge fund index. Their analysis focused on the effects of adding Bitcoin from the viewpoint of investors in the USA, the Eurozone, and China. Lamothe-López et al., (2024) demonstrate investing in cryptocurrencies, especially Bitcoin, has enhanced the risk-return profile for investors over recent years. However, it is uncertain whether this positive impact will continue in the future, as the correlation between Bitcoin and other similar assets with traditional investments may rise, and their returns might "normalize." Indeed, Nguyen (2022) shows that during periods of increased uncertainty, such as the COVID-19 pandemic, the correlation between Bitcoin's performance and the S&P 500 index significantly intensified.

Wu and Pandey (2014) argue that while Bitcoin may not be practical as a currency, it can substantially enhance portfolio efficiency. Kajtazi and Moro (2019) recently analyzed the impact of Bitcoin in portfolios comprising US, European, and Chinese assets, corroborating previous findings that Bitcoin boosts portfolio performance by increasing returns rather than reducing risk. However, these studies only cover a brief period and often exclude the significant growth in Bitcoin trading volume and price in 2017, as well as the subsequent market upheaval in 2018.

Subsequently, Bakry et al. (2021) carried out an intriguing analysis from the perspective of an American investor. They utilized variables similar to those in Katjazi and Moro's (2019) study and added additional indicators such as the Baltic Exchange Dry Index (BDI), a reliable measure of real economic activity, and the DJUBENS (Dow Jones-UBS Energy Spot Subindex), related to the energy sector. Their analysis employed the mean-variance optimization model proposed by Markowitz (1952), aiming to maximize the Sharpe ratio. The authors concluded that Bitcoin serves as an asset class with a positive diversification effect on portfolios, as the risk-return performance of portfolios including this cryptocurrency surpasses that of portfolios without it.

Additionally, the study by Ho Kim (2022) also confirms the positive effects of including cryptocurrencies in investors' portfolios. Lastly, we should mention the study by Liu (2019), which analyzes the characteristics for investors of portfolios composed solely of cryptocurrencies. Evidently, it does not make sense for an investor to invest only in crypto assets, but analyzing the effects of diversification within the universe of these investments is useful.

In conclusion, incorporating Bitcoin into traditional portfolios can offer significant diversification benefits and enhance risk-adjusted returns. Research on Bitcoin's investment advantages remain relatively unexplored despite its growing popularity. While further research is needed to address the limitations of previous studies and to explore longer-term effects, the existing evidence suggests that cryptocurrencies can play a valuable role in modern investment strategies.

6. DISCUSSION

The rapid evolution of crypto-economic systems, characterized by the issuance of tokens and the utilization of blockchain technology, has significantly transformed the landscape of modern financial markets. As corporations increasingly engage with decentralized networks such as Bitcoin and Ethereum, it is essential to critically examine the implications of these developments for corporate strategy, investment practices, and regulatory compliance.

At the core of crypto-economic systems is the concept of tokens, which serve as the fundamental unit of value exchanged among stakeholders within a decentralized network. Tokens come in various forms, including currencies, assets, or access to services, and their classification into utility tokens and security tokens is crucial for understanding their role in corporate finance. Utility tokens provide access to specific services or products within a blockchain ecosystem, while security tokens confer ownership rights in underlying assets, such as equity. This distinction is vital for companies as they navigate the complexities of tokenization and its implications for their business models.

The classification and regulation of crypto assets are pivotal in understanding their role and potential in modern financial markets. MiCA and MiFID II provide essential frameworks for defining and regulating these assets, distinguishing between utility tokens, asset-referenced tokens (stablecoins), e-money tokens, and security tokens. The complexity of categorizing crypto assets is evident through various regulatory perspectives, such as economic function-based categorization and academic taxonomies that consider multiple dimensions and characteristics.

Utility tokens, primarily used for accessing digital applications and services, differ fundamentally from security tokens, which represent financial assets and entail regulatory obligations under MiFID II. The emergence of liquidity pools and staking mechanisms introduces further nuances in classifying these assets, raising questions about their regulatory treatment.

Moreover, the role of blockchain technology in facilitating the transfer, storage, and functionality of crypto assets underscores the need for robust regulatory frameworks to ensure transparency, security, and investor protection. As crypto assets continue to evolve, their integration into investment portfolios and the broader financial ecosystem will depend on clear regulatory definitions and frameworks, ensuring they serve their intended economic functions while safeguarding market integrity.

The integration of crypto assets into corporate investment strategies presents both opportunities and challenges. On one hand, the potential for enhanced portfolio diversification is significant. Research indicates that incorporating cryptocurrencies, particularly Bitcoin, into traditional investment portfolios can improve risk-adjusted returns and shift the efficient frontier upward. The low correlation of Bitcoin with traditional assets, such as stocks and bonds, positions it as a valuable addition to a diversified portfolio, particularly in times of economic uncertainty. However, the volatility and speculative nature of cryptocurrencies necessitate a cautious approach to their inclusion in corporate investment strategies.

The relationship between crypto assets and traditional financial markets is becoming increasingly intertwined. Studies have shown that major cryptocurrencies like Bitcoin and Ethereum exhibit significant correlations with traditional assets, such as equities and commodities. This convergence raises important questions about the role of cryptocurrencies as alternative investments and their potential to act as hedges against inflation or economic instability. For instance, Bitcoin has been posited as a digital gold, serving as a store of value during periods of economic turmoil. However, the increasing correlation between cryptocurrencies and traditional assets may diminish their effectiveness as uncorrelated diversifiers in the future.

A future line of research might be the development of more sophisticated valuation models for crypto assets that can account for their unique characteristics and the complex dynamics within crypto-economic systems. Such models could provide corporations with more robust tools for evaluating the potential risks and rewards of incorporating crypto-assets into their investment strategies.

By addressing these research gaps, scholars and practitioners can provide corporations with the insights and tools necessary to harness the potential of crypto assets while mitigating the associated risks. This will be crucial for corporations seeking to remain competitive and adaptable in the rapidly evolving financial landscape.

REFERENCES

Alzhrani, F. E., Saeedi, K. A., & Zhao, L. (2022). A Taxonomy for Characterizing Blockchain Systems. *IEEE Access : Practical Innovations, Open Solutions, 10*, 110568–110589. DOI: 10.1109/ACCESS.2022.3214837

Arslanian, H., & Fischer, F. (2019). A High-Level Taxonomy of Crypto-assets. In H. Arslanian & F. Fischer, The Future of Finance (pp. 139–156). Springer International Publishing. DOI: 10.1007/978-3-030-14533-0_12

Baer, K., de Mooij, R., Hebous, S., & Keen, M. (2023). *Taxing cryptocurrencies, WP/23/143, July 2023*. International Monetary Fund.

Bakry, W., Rashid, A., Al-Mohamad, S., & El-Kanj, N. (2021). Bitcoin and Portfolio Diversification: A Portfolio Optimization Approach. *Journal of Risk and Financial Management, 14*(7), 1–24. DOI: 10.3390/jrfm14070282

Bankrate. (2024). Federal Reserve impact on stocks, crypto, and other investments. https://www.bankrate.com/investing/federal-reserve-impact-on-stocks-crypto-other-investments/

Bariviera, A. (2017). The inefficiency of Bitcoin revisited: A dynamic approach. *Economics Letters, 161*, 1–4. Advance online publication. DOI: 10.1016/j.econlet.2017.09.013

Baur, D. G., & Hoang, L. (2021). The Bitcoin gold correlation puzzle. *Journal of Behavioral and Experimental Finance, 32*, 100561. DOI: 10.1016/j.jbef.2021.100561

Bielinskyi, A. O., Serdyuk, O. A., Semerikov, S. O., & Soloviev, V. N. (2021). *Econophysics of cryptocurrency crashes: a systematic review* (Vol. 3048). DOI: 10.31812/123456789/6974

BitTime. (2024). The potential impact of Tether (USDT) on the future of cryptocurrencies. https://support.bittime.com/hc/en-us/articles/9379605185295-The-Potential-Impact-of-Tether-USDT-on-the-Future-of-Cryptocurrencies

Bolt, W., & van Oordt, M. R. C. (2020). On the value of virtual currencies. *Journal of Money, Credit and Banking, 52*(4), 841–861. DOI: 10.1111/jmcb.12619

Briere, M., Oosterlinck, K., & Szafarz, A. (2015). Virtual currency, tangible return: Portfolio diversification with bitcoin. *Journal of Asset Management, 16*(6), 365–373. DOI: 10.1057/jam.2015.5

Burniske, C. (2018). *Cryptoassets: The innovative investor's guide to Bitcoin and beyond*. McGraw-Hill Education.

Carroll, R., Conlon, T., Cotter, J., & Salvador, E. (2017). Asset allocation with correlation: A composite trade-off. *European Journal of Operational Research*, *262*(3), 1164–1180. DOI: 10.1016/j.ejor.2017.04.015

Chen, J., Lin, D. C., & Han, C. H. (2020, March). Volatility effect on the adoption and valuation of tokenomics. In *Proceedings of the 35th Annual ACM Symposium on Applied Computing* (pp. 294-300). DOI: 10.1145/3341105.3373891

CoinDesk. (2023). Crypto's interest in rates. https://www.coindesk.com/markets/2023/09/13/cryptos-interest-in-rates/

CoinMarketCap. (2024). CoinMarketCap. Retrieved June 20, 2024, from https://coinmarketcap.com/

Cointelegraph. (2024). Impact of Fed interest rates on crypto holders. https://cointelegraph.com/explained/impact-of-fed-interest-rates-on-crypto-holders

Cong, L. W., Li, Y., & Wang, N. (2018). Tokenomics: Dynamic adoption and valuation. *Review of Financial Studies*, *34*(3), 1105–1155. DOI: 10.1093/rfs/hhaa089

Corbet, S., Lucey, B., Urquhart, A., & Yarovaya, L. (2019). Cryptocurrencies as a financial asset: A systematic analysis. *International Review of Financial Analysis*, *62*, 182–199. DOI: 10.1016/j.irfa.2018.09.003

Crypto.com. (2021). Macroeconomic factors that impact the crypto market. https://crypto.com/research/macroeconomic-factors-that-impact-crypto-market

Cryptopotato. (2023). Ethereum is more correlated to stocks than Bitcoin: IntoTheBlock. https://cryptopotato.com/ethereum-is-more-correlated-to-stocks-than-bitcoin-intotheblock/

Cryptoslate. (2023). Bitcoin and gold are becoming increasingly correlated in conservative investment strategies. https://cryptoslate.com/bitcoin-and-gold-are-becoming-increasingly-correlated-in-conservative-investment-strategies/

Dwyer, G. P. (2015). The economics of Bitcoin and similar private digital currencies. *Journal of Financial Stability*, *17*, 81–91. DOI: 10.1016/j.jfs.2014.11.006

EBA. (2019). Report with advice for the European Commission on crypto-assets (p. 30). European Banking Authority EBA. https://www.eba.europa.eu/sites/default/files/documents/10180/2545547/67493daa-85a8-4429-aa91-e9a5ed880684/EBA%20Report%20on%20crypto%20assets.pdf

ESMA. (2024). Consultation paper on the draft guidelines on the conditions and criteria for the qualification of crypto-assets as financial instruments (ESMA75-453128700–52; p. 39). European Securities and Market Authority.

Euler, T. (2018). *The Token Classification Framework: A multi-dimensional tool for understanding and classifying crypto tokens*. Untitled Inc.

European Securities and Markets Authority (ESMA). (2024). Risk article: Crypto assets, market structures, and EU relevance. https://www.esma.europa.eu/sites/default/files/2024-04/ESMA50-524821-3153_risk_article_crypto_assets_market_structures_and_eu_relevance.pdf

European Systemic Risk Board. (2023). Crypto-assets and decentralised finance. ESRB Report.

FINMA. (2018). Guidelines for enquiries regarding the regulatory framework for initial coin offerings (ICOs) (p. 11). Swiss Financial Market Supervisory Authority FINMA. https://www.finma.ch/~/media/finma/dokumente/dokumentencenter/myfinma/1bewilligung/fintech/wegleitung-ico.pdf?sc_lang=en&hash=C9899ACF22747D56C800C6C41A7E28AB

Flow Traders. (2023). Navigating the convergence of crypto and traditional financial markets. https://www.flowtraders.com/media/1kymgo0i/navigating-the-convergence-of-crypto-and-traditional-financial-markets.pdf

Foroutan, P., & Lahmiri, S. (2024). Connectedness of cryptocurrency markets to crude oil and gold: An analysis of the effect of COVID-19 pandemic. *Financial Innovation*, *10*(1), 68. DOI: 10.1186/s40854-023-00596-x

Gangwal, S. (2016). Analyzing the effect of adding Bitcoin to portfolio. International Journal of Economics and Management Engineering, 3519-3532.

Gao, X., & Nardari, F. (2018). Do commodities add economic value in asset allocation? New evidence from time-varying moments. *Journal of Financial and Quantitative Analysis*, *53*(1), 365–393. DOI: 10.1017/S002210901700103X

Gidea, M., Goldsmith, D., Katz, Y., Roldan, P., & Shmalo, Y. (2020). Topological recognition of critical transitions in time series of cryptocurrencies. *Physica A*, *548*, 123843. DOI: 10.1016/j.physa.2019.123843

Gorton, G., & Rouwenhorst, K. (2006). Facts and fantasies about commodity futures. *Financial Analysts Journal*, *62*(2), 47–68. DOI: 10.2469/faj.v62.n2.4083

Grau, C. (2021). Stochastic valuation of revenue-collecting tokens in cryptoeconomic organizations. SSRN Electronic Journal. https://doi.org/DOI: 10.2139/ssrn.3641234

Grauer, R. R. (1986). Normality, solvency, and portfolio choice. *Journal of Financial and Quantitative Analysis*, *21*(3), 265–278. DOI: 10.2307/2331041

Grobys, K., & Sapkota, N. (2019). Cryptocurrencies and momentum. *Economics Letters*, *6-10*, 6–10. Advance online publication. DOI: 10.1016/j.econlet.2019.03.028

Harvey, C. R., Abou Zeid, T., Draaisma, T., Luk, M., Neville, H., Rzym, A., & Van Hemert, O. (2022). An investor's guide to crypto. Available at *SSRN* 4124576.

Hayes, A. (2017). Cryptocurrency value formation: An empirical analysis leading to a cost of production model for valuing Bitcoin. *Telematics and Informatics*, *34*(7), 1308–1321. DOI: 10.1016/j.tele.2016.05.005

Hillier, D., Draper, P., & Faff, R. (2006). Do precious metals shine? An investment perspective. *Financial Analysts Journal*, *62*(2), 98–106. DOI: 10.2469/faj.v62.n2.4085

Kaal, W. A., Evans, S. R., & Howe, H. A. (2021). Digital Asset Valuation. *Rich. JL & Tech.*, *28*, 657.

Kajtazi, A., & Moro, A. (2019). The Role of Bitcoin in Well Diversified Portfolios: A comparative Global Study. *International Review of Financial Analysis*, *61*, 143–157. DOI: 10.1016/j.irfa.2018.10.003

Kifokeris, D., Dounas, T., Tezel, A., & Moon, S. (2023). What is the potential value of tokens and token engineering for the architecture, engineering, and construction industry? A positional paper.

Kim, J. H. (2022). Analyzing diversification benefits of cryptocurrencies through backfill simulation. *Finance Research Letters*, *50*, 103238. DOI: 10.1016/j.frl.2022.103238

Kolm, P., Tütüncü, R., & Fabozzi, F. (2014). 60 Years of portfolio optimization: Practical challenges and current trends. *European Journal of Operational Research*, *234*(2), 356–371. DOI: 10.1016/j.ejor.2013.10.060

Kostoula, T. (2023). Valuation of cryptoassets in EU insolvency: Challenges and prospects. *INSOL International Insolvency Review*, *32*(1), 8–40. DOI: 10.1002/iir.1490

Labs, C. T. O. (2024). Bitcoin's future: US Treasury refinancing and the crypto market. https://www.ctol.digital/news/bitcoins-future-us-treasury-refinancing-crypto-market

Lamothe-López, P., Lamothe-Fernández, P., & Rodríguez-Valencia, L. (2024). Cryptocurrencies - Financial Technologies of the Future. In P. Lamothe-López, P. Lamothe-Fernández, & L. Rodríguez-Valencia, The Inclusion of Bitcoin and Other Cryptocurrencies in Investors' Portfolios. doi:DOI: DOI: 10.5772/intechopen.1003990

Levy, H., & Levy, M. (2014). The benefits of differential variance-based constraints in portfolio optimization. *European Journal of Operational Research, 234*(2), 372–381. DOI: 10.1016/j.ejor.2013.04.019

Li, X., Wu, X., Pei, X., & Yao, Z. (2019, March). Tokenization: Open asset protocol on blockchain. In 2019 IEEE 2nd International Conference on Information and Computer Technologies (ICICT) (pp. 204-209). IEEE.

Liu, W. (2019). Portfolio diversification across cryptocurrencies. *Finance Research Letters, 29*, 200–205. DOI: 10.1016/j.frl.2018.07.010

Maier, M. (2023). *Web3 and Token Engineering. in 6G and Onward to Next G: The Road to the Multiverse*. IEEE., DOI: 10.1002/9781119898566

Markets.com. (2024). Tether's impact on the cryptocurrency market. https://www.markets.com/education-centre/tether-on-cryptocurrency-market/

Markowitz, H. (1952). Portfolio Selection. *The Journal of Finance, 7*(1), 77–91.

Markowitz, H. (2014). Mean–variance approximations to expected utility. *European Journal of Operational Research, 234*(2), 346–355. DOI: 10.1016/j.ejor.2012.08.023

Mitchell, M. (2009). *Complexity: A guided tour*. Oxford university press. DOI: 10.1093/oso/9780195124415.001.0001

Morozova, T., Akhmadeev, R., Lehoux, L., Yumashev, A. V., Meshkova, G. V., & Lukiyanova, M. (2020). Crypto asset assessment models in financial reporting content typologies. *Entrepreneurship and Sustainability Issues, 7*(3), 2196–2212. DOI: 10.9770/jesi.2020.7.3(49)

Nadarajah, S., & Chu, J. (2017). On the inefficiency of Bitcoin. *Economics Letters, 150*, 6–9. DOI: 10.1016/j.econlet.2016.10.033

Nasdaq. (2023). The Tether price connection: USDT's impact on the crypto market. https://www.nasdaq.com/articles/the-tether-price-connection%3A-usdts-impact-on-the-crypto-market

Nguyen, K. Q. (2022). The correlation between the stock market and Bitcoin during COVID-19 and other uncertainty periods. *Finance Research Letters, 46*, 102284. DOI: 10.1016/j.frl.2021.102284 PMID: 35431674

Oliveira, L., Zavolokina, L., Bauer, I., & Schwabe, G. (2018, December). To token or not to token: Tools for understanding blockchain tokens. ICIS.

Phemex. (2022). How interest rates affect cryptocurrency. https://phemex.com/blogs/how-interest-rates-affect-cryptocurrency

Pidun, U., Rubner, H., Krühler, M., Untiedt, R., & Nippa, M.Boston Consulting Group. (2011). Corporate portfolio management: Theory and practice. *The Bank of America Journal of Applied Corporate Finance*, *23*(1), 63–76. DOI: 10.1111/j.1745-6622.2011.00315.x

Piguet Galland. (2024). Rate hikes vs crypto hype. https://www.piguetgalland.ch/en/news/rate-hikes-vs-crypto-hype

Platanakis, E., & Urquhart, A. (2020). Should investors include Bitcoin in their portfolios? A portfolio theory approach. *The British Accounting Review*, *52*(4), 100837. Advance online publication. DOI: 10.1016/j.bar.2019.100837

Rochet, J., & Villeneuve, S. (2005). Corporate portfolio management. *Annals of Finance*, *1*(3), 225–243. DOI: 10.1007/s10436-005-0018-7

Rodríguez-Valencia, L., Lamothe-Fernández, P., & Alaminos, D. (2023). The market value of SMEs: A comparative study between private and listed firms in alternative stock markets. *Annals of Finance*, *19*(1), 95–117. DOI: 10.1007/s10436-022-00420-z

Salehi, A., & Rafsanjani, M. K. (2024). Risk analysis of blockchain technology in financial markets. Physica A: Statistical Mechanics and its Applications. https://www.sciencedirect.com/science/article/pii/S0378437124004126

Serena, L., Ferretti, S., & D'Angelo, G. (2022). Cryptocurrencies activity as a complex network: Analysis of transactions graphs. *Peer-to-Peer Networking and Applications*, *15*(2), 839–853. DOI: 10.1007/s12083-021-01220-4

Shanaev, S., Sharma, S., Shuraeva, A., & Ghimire, B. (2020). The marginal cost of mining, Metcalfe's law and cryptocurrency value formation: Causal inferences from the instrumental variable approach. SSRN Electronic Journal. https://doi.org/ DOI: 10.2139/ssrn.3432431

Stosic, D., Ludermir, T. B., & Stosic, T. (2019). Exploring disorder and complexity in the cryptocurrency space. *Physica A*, *525*, 548–556. DOI: 10.1016/j.physa.2019.03.091

Stylianou, K., Spiegelberg, L., Herlihy, M., & Carter, N. (2021). Cryptocurrency competition and market concentration in the presence of network effects. *Ledger*, *6*, 1–20. DOI: 10.5195/ledger.2021.226

Sumanov, V., & Polanski, S. (2023). Token Classification Framework by Consideration of Origins of Value and Mechanisms of Manifestation Thereof. Retrieved September 20, 2023, from https://github.com/powerpool-finance/powerpool-research/blob/main/Papers/Value_Capturing_Mechanisms_.pdf

Two Sigma. (2021). Risk analysis of crypto assets. https://www.twosigma.com/articles/risk-analysis-of-crypto-assets/

Urquhart, A. (2016). The inefficiency of Bitcoin. *Economics Letters*, *148*, 80–82. DOI: 10.1016/j.econlet.2016.09.019

Voshmgir, S. (2020). *Token Economy: How the Web3 reinvents the internet* (Vol. 2). Token Kitchen.

Voshmgir, S., & Zargham, M. (2020). Foundations of Cryptoeconomic Systems. WU Vienna University of Economics and Business. Working Paper Series / Institute for Cryptoeconomics / Interdisciplinary Research No. 1.

Wu, C., Pandey, V., & Dba, C. (2014). The value of Bitcoin in enhancing the efficiency of an investor's portfolio. *Journal of Financial Planning*, *27*(9), 44–52.

Xu, X., Weber, I., Staples, M., Zhu, L., Bosch, J., Bass, L., Pautasso, C., & Rimba, P. (2017). A Taxonomy of Blockchain-Based Systems for Architecture Design. *2017 IEEE International Conference on Software Architecture (ICSA)*, 243–252. DOI: 10.1109/ICSA.2017.33

Zheng, Z., Xie, S., Dai, H.-N., Chen, W., Chen, X., Weng, J., & Imran, M. (2020). An Overview on Smart Contracts: Challenges, Advances and Platforms. *Future Generation Computer Systems*, *105*, 475–491. DOI: 10.1016/j.future.2019.12.019

KEY TERMS AND DEFINTIONS

Crypto-Economic Systems: Sophisticated socioeconomic frameworks that utilize blockchain networks and comparable decentralized technologies.

Tokens: The fundamental unit of value that is exchanged among the stakeholders in a crypto-economic system.

Crypto Asset: A digital representation of value or rights that can be transferred and stored electronically, using distributed ledger technology or similar technology.

Token Engineering: A field of study focused on developing tools and models to engineer crypto-economic systems.

Utility Tokens: Tokens that grant access to specific services or products within a blockchain ecosystem.

Security Tokens: Tokens that represent ownership rights in underlying assets, such as equity or real estate.

Stablecoins: Cryptocurrencies that aim to maintain a stable value relative to traditional currencies through backing or algorithmic mechanisms.

:

Value Capture Mechanisms (VCMs): Sets of possibly multiple origins of value whose value can be extracted through a specific behavior pattern.

MiCA (Markets in Crypto-Assets): The EU regulation that defines and regulates different types of crypto assets.

MiFID II (Markets in Financial Instruments Directive): The EU regulation that governs the classification of security tokens.

Chapter 9

Empirical Analysis of Cryptocurrency Investors' Perception:

Insights into Investment Behaviour and Market Dynamics

Shradha Attri
https://orcid.org/0000-0002-5649-1318
Central University of Himachal Pradesh, India

Sanjeev Gupta
https://orcid.org/0000-0002-9032-9437
Central University of Himachal Pradesh, India

Sachin Singh
https://orcid.org/0009-0009-5522-2093
Central University of Himachal Pradesh, India

ABSTRACT

Cryptocurrency is an innovative financial asset class that operates on the blockchain system. Despite its highly volatile nature, the number of investors has increased significantly in the past decade. This chapter aims to examine the factors that influence investors' intention and decision to invest in such a volatile asset. The empirical relationship between Investment behavior (BEH), Intention to invest in the cryptocurrency (INT), Risk perception (RP), Awareness (AWR), Social influence (SI), and Fear of Missing out (FOMO) are examined. Data was collected from the 94 cryptocurrency investors in India using purposive and snowball sampling. The results showed that AWR and PR have a positive but insignificant effect on crypto-

DOI: 10.4018/979-8-3693-5986-0.ch009

currency investors' intentions and investment decisions. On the other hand, FOMO and SI have a statistically positive and significant role in the investment process among cryptocurrency investors. The results provide practical implications for the regulatory authorities, investors, and academicians.

1. INTRODUCTION

The emergence of Bitcoin was a paradigm shift in the financial system. In 2008, the pseudonymous Satoshi Nakamoto published a white paper, "Bitcoin: A Peer-to-Peer Electronic Cash System", in which the solution for two traditional financial and banking problems was provided: first, the double-spending problem and second, intermediaries in the financial system (Nakamoto, 2008). The global financial crisis of 2007-08 exposed vulnerabilities in the traditional financial system, leading to a quest for alternatives leveraging advanced technology. Bitcoin uses a peer-to-peer system without the involvement of intermediaries. The fundamental technology behind cryptocurrency is blockchain. In January 2009, the first genesis block in the Bitcoin blockchain was generated (J. Wu, 2021). Bitcoin was first used in a commercial transaction in 2010 to buy two Papa John's pizzas for 10,000 Bitcoin (Krishnan et al., 2020). Decentralised mechanisms with blockchain in the cryptocurrency system distinguish its operation from the traditional financial system.

Blockchain's inclusion in cryptocurrency provides numerous advantages over the traditional financial system. A distributed ledger technology (DLT) records all the transactions in a secure, transparent, and immutable manner across the network of computers by the nodes (Babich & Hilary, 2018; Renduchintala et al., 2022). Because of the hash value and consensus mechanism in the system, the blockchain's immutability ensures that there will be no tampering throughout the entire blockchain system (Folkinshteyn & Lennon, 2017; Härdle et al., 2020). No single entity has control over the entire network, which means cryptocurrency is decentralised. This implies that the level of risk and corruption in the system can be reduced due to a consensus mechanism among the nodes. Proof-of-work (PoW) and Proof-of-stake (PoS) are the two common consensus mechanisms used in the cryptocurrency system (Conti et al., 2017; Nakamoto, 2008).

There is no inherent or fundamental value in cryptocurrency. The value is determined by the demand and supply, investor sentiment, regulatory news and macroeconomic trends (Güler, 2023; Kyriazis et al., 2022; Smutny et al., 2021). However, cryptocurrency provides a new investment avenue for investors (Hong, 2017). The disconnect between the traditional and cryptocurrency markets allows investors to diversify their portfolios and mitigate risk to some extent (Brière et al., 2015; Harb et al., 2022; Singh et al. 2025a). Previous studies have examined Bitcoin as a safe haven, a hedge, and a diversifier (Baur et al., 2017; Klein et al., 2018; Yan et al., 2022). Investment in the cryptocurrency market is very risky due to its inherent volatility, but the market capitalisation of the cryptocurrency market is still growing (Attri et al. 2025). Bitcoin acquired 56.2% of the market capitalisation, followed by Ethereum. Table 1 shows the market capitalisation of the top ten cryptocurrencies.

Table 1. Top cryptocurrency by market capitalisation

Cryptocurrency	Market capitalisation
Bitcoin	$ 1.04 Trillion
Ethereum	$ 279.56 Billion
Tether	$ 114.55 Billion
BNB	$ 62.95 Billion
Solana	$ 56.51 Billion
USDC	$ 33. 56 Billion
Ripple	$ 26.21 Billion
Toncoin	$ 13.34 Billion
Dogecoin	$ 12. 64 Billion
Cardano	$ 10.86 Billion

Source: https://coinmarketcap.com/

The entire market capitalisation of cryptocurrency has witnessed tremendous growth in the last decade. Social influence or herd behaviour is one of the prominent reasons for the substantial increase in the cryptocurrency market growth. Previous studies examined the factors affecting cryptocurrency investment and found that perceived ease of use, perceived usefulness, attitude, subjective norms, perceived behavioural control, perceived risk, security, performance expectancy, effort expectancy, financial literacy and facilitating conditions significantly affect the behavioural intention that ultimately forms the actual behaviour of the investor (Alomari & Abdullah, 2023; Kumari et al., 2023; R. Wu et al., 2022). Previous literature demonstrates high volatility in the cryptocurrency market (Akyildirim et al., 2020; Katsiampa, 2019; Yi et al., 2018). Figure 1 illustrates that the volatility in the Bitcoin return series was substantial from 2019 to 2020, mainly due to the global COVID-19 pandemic. However, investors are still investing in cryptocurrency despite it being a highly volatile asset class.

Figure 1. Bitcoin return series (EViews)

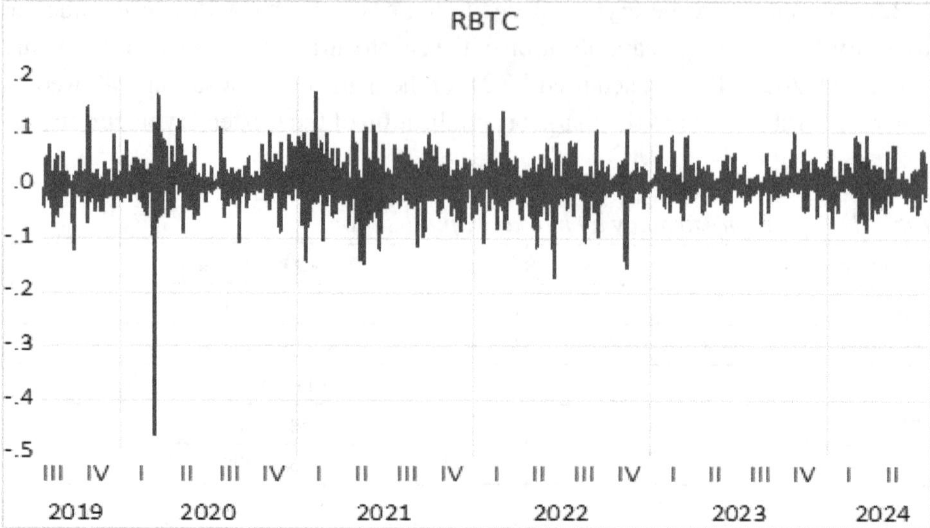

So, there is a need to understand the perception and behaviour of investors and find out the reasons why investors prefer to invest in cryptocurrency. The present study examined the role of social influence, FOMO, risk perception and awareness in cryptocurrency investment. An individual is mainly influenced by the immediate peer group, which can lead to herd behaviour among investors. The chance of higher returns in a shorter period can make investors feel like they've missed out on an opportunity or something that others have experienced. It's necessary to understand the social influence and FOMO since these may be key reasons for investing in the market.

2. LITERATURE REVIEW

Numerous studies have been conducted to understand the substantial increase in the number of investors and the potential drivers and barriers to the adoption of cryptocurrency (Al-Amri et al., 2019; Dickson & Mahwera, 2022; Jonker, 2019; Li et al., 2022). Walton & Johnston, (2018) combined the two theories of psychology, the theory of planned behaviour (TPB) and the technology acceptance model (TAM), to study the perception of bitcoin adoption among South African cryptocurrency investors and found that perceived benefit, attitude, subjective norm and perceived behavioural control have a significant effect on the investor's intention to use Bitcoin and the most commonly found barrier in Bitcoin adoption is its volatile and complex nature. A study conducted among Malaysian Muslim investors to examine the factors affecting investment in the cryptocurrency market found that compatibility, awareness, and facilitating conditions have a positive and significant impact on investment in the cryptocurrency market, whereas trust, profitability, and perceived ease of use have no significant effect on investors' decisions. (Ayedh et al., 2020). The factors influencing cryptocurrency adoption for remittance were studied, along with the potential challenges in the United Arab Emirates (UAE). It was suggested that service providers should prioritise risk management. Two main approaches to reduce the risk were recommended: implementing security measures by providing custodial and non-custodial wallets and employing trust-building strategies such as the payment card industry (PCI) (Jegerson et al., 2023). In previous studies of cryptocurrency adoption and investment behaviour, the most commonly used theories were the Theory of Reasoned Action (TRA), the Theory of Planned Behaviour (TPB), the Technology Acceptance Model (TAM), and the Unified Theory of Acceptance and Use of Technology (UTAUT).

2.1. Theory of Planned Behaviour (TPB)

The theory of planned behaviour (TPB) is the psychological approach to understanding human behaviour. TPB is the extension of the Theory of Reasoned Action (TRA) by Fishbein et al., 1967 in which behavioural intention is formed by two components: Attitude and subjective norms. TPB theory describes three main components of human behaviour: attitude, subjective norms, and perceived behavioural control. These three components make up the intention towards a particular behaviour. To investigate the investment behaviour of cryptocurrency investors, the study employs the TPB to explain the theory, which aids in assessing users' behavioural intentions. In the conceptual framework, the intention to invest in cryptocurrency is influenced by awareness, social influence, risk perception, and fear of missing out (FOMO). The intention ultimately shapes the actual investment behaviour towards cryptocurrencies.

2.1.1. Awareness

Awareness refers to the level of knowledge one possesses about a matter. The level of awareness varies among the investors. To be financially literate, one must have an understanding and knowledge of the financial market (Lusardi, 2019). Kumari et al., (2023) examined the impact of awareness, personal innovativeness and subjective financial literacy on the intention to adopt blockchain-based cryptocurrencies and found the moderating role of technology awareness and subjective literacy on the intention of the user. The investors must have both basic and advanced technical knowledge and understanding of the market, as cryptocurrency is a highly volatile and potentially lucrative market (Mikhaylov, 2020). The level of awareness is required because of the market's nature. It is highly valued and provides quick returns, which can lead the general public to invest in the market due to social influence or greed for high returns in the short run, which is called fear of missing out (FOMO). Therefore, it is necessary to have financial knowledge, awareness, and literacy about the cryptocurrency market.

2.1.2. Social Influence

Social influence refers to the external factors that shape an individual's perceptions and behaviour. These can include peer influence, social media, cultural and societal norms, and external information sources. Word-of-mouth influences the most among other external factors (Lam & Mizerski, 2005). The impact of social influence can be either positive or negative. Alomari & Abdullah, 2023 investigated the moderating role of financial literacy on the behavioural intention towards cryptocurrency usage among 344 Saudi Arabian public university students and found that financial literacy moderates the relationship between social influence, performance expectancy, security and behavioural intention. Substantial literature supports the idea that social pressure is one of the main reasons for cryptocurrency investment (Ebizie et al., 2022; Kala et al., 2023; Putra & Darma, 2019). Individuals often adhere to what is typically accepted within society to be accepted. One such common phenomenon is cryptocurrency investment, which can lead to herding behaviour and result in behavioural biases in the investment process (Cristofaro et al., 2022).

2.1.3. Fear of Missing Out (FOMO)

Fear of Missing Out (FOMO) is a psychological phenomenon in which an individual is apprehensive that others are experiencing gains or higher returns and that they are not part of such opportunities (Kala et al., 2023; Przybylski et al., 2013). Due to the high volatility, the market has witnessed sudden fluctuations in the prices of cryptocurrencies (Aggarwal, 2019). This has led to herd behaviour in the market, giving the general public the feeling of missing out on quick profits in the short term, resulting in FOMO in the cryptocurrency market. FOMO can lead to greedy behaviour or herding behaviour among individuals, which can have subsequent adverse effects (Gupta & Shrivastava, 2022).The prices of cryptocurrencies are primarily driven by investors' sentiments. This impulsive behaviour is mainly driven by social influence among the investors. Güler, (2023) analysed investor sentiment behaviour in cryptocurrency during COVID-19 and found that investors' rational and irrational sentiments impact the bitcoin return, which is attributed to FOMO among the crypto investors.

2.1.4. Risk Perception

Risk is a fundamental characteristic of the cryptocurrency market (Anser et al., 2020). The way investors perceive risk in cryptocurrency largely influences their investment decisions (Sukumaran et al., 2022). The higher the risk, the higher the potential gain, which also means a tremendous potential for heavy losses as there is no intrinsic value or fundamental for the cryptocurrency market. Most investors tend to have a risk-averse attitude during the investment process (Singh et al. 2025b). Risk perception is impacted by various external factors, such as awareness, knowledge, personal experience, social influence, attitude, herd behaviour, and cultural context (Almansour et al., 2023; Kala et al., 2023; Manzoor et al., 2023). Regulatory authorities must address the risks associated with cryptocurrency. Investor perception plays a crucial role in any behaviour, especially in investment decisions, as they involve the investor's hard-earned money. Heavy losses in cryptocurrency investments can adversely affect a nation's financial stability. Therefore, it's essential to understand and navigate the risks present in the cryptocurrency market.

2.1.5. Behavioural Intention

Behavioural Intention is the user's/investor's mental state when carrying out an action with a specific goal. Intention to do a task is formed by motivation. The formation of intention is affected by multiple internal and external factors. The intention to invest in the cryptocurrency market is mainly influenced by attitude, perceived behavioural control, security, awareness, social influence, risk perception, and FOMO (Galang Prasetyo & Kurniasari, 2023; Pham et al., 2021; Pilatin & Dilek, 2023). Self-awareness and rational behaviour by the investor are essential for translating intention into actual behaviour. Intention formed due to herd behaviour is not a rational decision by the investor, and such behaviour might result in heavy losses.

2.1.6. Investment Behaviour

Investment behaviour refers to the actions and decisions made by investors with the expectation of future high returns. Investment behaviour is mainly influenced by the investor's intention to invest or not, which is affected by multiple internal and external factors. Investors' ability and capability to invest in cryptocurrency are affected by social influence, herd behaviour, past experiences, future expectations, and greed for quick profits (Nurbarani & Soepriyanto, 2022; Patras et al., 2023; Sukumaran et al., 2022; Osakwe, 2024). Cryptocurrency investments should be made after thoroughly understanding the market, as they could lead to significant losses without considering the basics (Attri et al., 2025).

3. RESEARCH METHODOLOGY

The present chapter uses Structural Equation Modelling (SEM) to analyse the conceptual framework of the study. Descriptive statistics were estimated in SPSS. The adapted instrument was used to collect the data. Data from 94 crypto investors were collected by using purposive and snowball sampling.

3.1. Scale Development and Measures

An adapted instrument was used to collect the data. The instrument consists of three main sections. The first section includes the demographic profile of the respondents. The second section asks questions about the investors' investment profile. The third section consists of 26 items related to awareness (4 items), risk perception (4 items), social influence (4 items), Fear of Missing out (FOMO) (5 items), intention to invest in cryptocurrency (4 items), and investment behaviour (5 items). The scale used in the present study is adapted from various previous studies: the scale for Awareness (Alomari & Abdullah, 2023); risk perception (Chen et al., 2022); FOMO (Kala et al., 2023); social influence (Alomari & Abdullah, 2023); intention to invest in cryptocurrency (Cristofaro et al., 2022); investment decision (Salman, 2020).

3.2. Data Collection

Purposive and snowball sampling were used to collect data from crypto investors in India. 120 questionnaires were distributed to the respondents through online and offline mediums, out of which 94 were completed and eligible for final analysis. Descriptive analysis was conducted in IBM SPSS Statistics 25, and for structural and measurement models, SmartPLS 4 software was used.

3.3. Data Analysis

This section provides a comprehensive overview of the demographic profile of the respondents along with the structural and measurement model of the study.

3.3.1. Demographic Statistics

Table 2 shows the demographic profile of the respondents. A greater discrepancy was found among males and females in the context of investment in cryptocurrency, as the majority of the respondents in the study are male (62.8%). Suggesting that females are more risk averse as cryptocurrency is a highly volatile asset class; this can be due to the wealth effect. Most of the respondents are 29- to 38-year-olds, as this age group has higher earnings and is more likely to invest in highly volatile assets in expectation of higher returns. Private sector employees with master's degrees are more likely to invest in the crypto market. 43.6% of the respondents are from the income class group.

Table 2. Demographic profile of the respondents (N=94)

Respondent Profile	Frequency	Percent
Age		
18-28	34	36.2
29-38	42	44.7
39-48	9	9.6
48 and above	9	9.6
Gender		
Male	59	62.8
Female	35	37.2
Occupation		
Private sector employee	44	46.8
Public sector employee	31	33.0
Self-employed	12	12.8
Student	7	7.4
Educational Background		
Up to high school/Diploma	19	20.2
Bachelor's Degree	8	8.5
Master's Degree	47	50.0
Ph.D. and above	20	21.3
Income		
Up to 2,50,000	23	24.5
2,50,001-5,00,000	21	22.3
5,00,000-7,50,000	9	9.6
7,50,001 and above	41	43.6

Source: IBM SPSS Statistics 25

3.3.2. Investor's Investment Profile

Table 3 contains detailed information about the investors' experience in the cryptocurrency market, the trading applications they use for investment, and their cryptocurrency portfolios. Most of the respondents have been investing in cryptocurrency for more than five years. Novice investors should avoid investing in such a high-volatility asset class without any knowledge of technical analysis. The two most used crypto trading applications by the respondents are WazirX and CoinDCX. The most familiar and traded cryptocurrencies among the respondents are Bitcoin and Ethereum, which have acquired more than half of the market capitalisation of the cryptocurrency market, with Bitcoin alone acquiring 56.2%[1] of the market.

Table 3. Investor's investment profile

Investment Experience **How long you have been investing in cryptocurrencies:**		
	No. of Respondents	Percent
Less than 1 year	22	23.4
1 to 2 years	20	21.3
3 to 5 years	19	20.2
6 to 8 years	25	26.6
8 years and more	8	8.5
Trading Application for Cryptocurrency Investment Which application do you use for investments and trading in cryptocurrency?		
Binance	14	14.9
WazirX	17	18.1
Coinswitch	13	13.8
CoinDCX	17	18.1
Zebpay	33	35.1
Cryptocurrency investment Which cryptocurrencies have you invested in?		
Bitcoin	48	51.1
Ethereum	16	17.0
Tether	14	14.9
Ripple XRP	4	4.3
Cardano	9	9.6
Dogecoin	3	3.2

Source: IBM SPSS Statistics 25

3.3.3. Measurement Model Assessment

Table 4. Internal consistency reliability and convergent validity

	Reliability			Convergent validity
	Cronbach's alpha	Composite reliability (rho_a)	Composite reliability (rho_c)	Average variance extracted (AVE)
AWR	0.869	0.887	0.910	0.718
BEH	0.857	0.867	0.898	0.638
FOMO	0.840	0.847	0.887	0.612
INT	0.828	0.829	0.886	0.659
RP	0.815	0.847	0.876	0.640
SI	0.832	0.846	0.887	0.663

Note: AWR- Awareness; BEH- Investment Behaviour; FOMO- Fear of Missing Out; INT- Intention to invest in cryptocurrency; RP- Risk Perception; SI- Social Influence
Source: SmartPLS 4

Reliability of scale indicates consistent outcomes under the same conditions (Hair et al., 2019). Cronbach alpha shows the internal consistency of the scale adapted for the study. Cronbach alpha value ranges from 0.60 to 0.95 (Hair et al., 2019). In the present study, the Cronbach alpha and composite reliability values lie between the set boundaries. Table 4 shows that Cronbach alpha values lie between 0.815 and 0.847, which indicates that the scales are reliable and have established internal consistency. Cronbach alpha is considered as the lower bound, and composite reliability (roh _c) is the upper bound for internal consistency. Composite reliability (roh_a) shows the true reliability and lies between Cronbach alpha and composite reliability (rob_c). In the present study, both composite reliability (roh_a and roh_c) are reliable and establish the internal consistency of the scale.

Average Variance Extracted (AVE) indicates the accuracy of the items used to measure the construct. AVE is used to measure the convergent validity of the scale. All the items must explain 50% of the variance in the construct, which means AVE must be greater than 0.50. AVE is more than 0.50 for all the constructs.

Table 5. Discriminant validity- Fornell-Larcker criterion

	AWR	BEH	FOMO	INT	RP	SI
AWR	**0.848**					
BEH	0.613	**0.799**				
FOMO	0.604	0.702	**0.782**			
INT	0.697	0.746	0.721	**0.812**		
RP	0.812	0.658	0.675	0.724	**0.800**	
SI	0.637	0.703	0.789	0.720	0.667	**0.814**

Source: SmartPLS 4

Table 6. Discriminant validity-cross-loading

	AWR	BEH	FOMO	INT	RP	SI
AWR1	**0.858**	0.468	0.511	0.65	0.676	0.589
AWR2	**0.906**	0.637	0.581	0.666	0.724	0.6
AWR4	**0.857**	0.502	0.491	0.556	0.703	0.468
AWR6	**0.764**	0.46	0.456	0.458	0.657	0.485
BEH2	0.405	**0.775**	0.467	0.547	0.593	0.438
BEH3	0.538	**0.866**	0.637	0.59	0.548	0.646
BEH4	0.313	**0.768**	0.464	0.479	0.369	0.527
BEH5	0.498	**0.857**	0.641	0.704	0.569	0.629
BEH6	0.651	**0.719**	0.56	0.618	0.52	0.543
FOMO1	0.404	0.714	**0.719**	0.593	0.452	0.604
FOMO2	0.46	0.494	**0.731**	0.479	0.436	0.669
FOMO3	0.558	0.516	**0.821**	0.558	0.586	0.631
FOMO4	0.512	0.434	**0.771**	0.525	0.671	0.538
FOMO5	0.441	0.565	**0.86**	0.64	0.502	0.645
INT1	0.604	0.622	0.578	**0.821**	0.605	0.607
INT2	0.476	0.654	0.595	**0.796**	0.529	0.638
INT3	0.602	0.494	0.553	**0.828**	0.584	0.457
INT4	0.583	0.636	0.608	**0.803**	0.63	0.616
RP1	0.68	0.447	0.47	0.511	**0.737**	0.492
RP2	0.495	0.459	0.434	0.425	**0.75**	0.442
RP3	0.706	0.536	0.496	0.574	**0.862**	0.595
RP4	0.689	0.625	0.697	0.735	**0.845**	0.58
SI1	0.488	0.55	0.61	0.506	0.372	**0.786**

continued on following page

Table 6. Continued

	AWR	BEH	FOMO	INT	RP	SI
SI2	0.454	0.446	0.616	0.485	0.551	**0.808**
SI3	0.542	0.702	0.739	0.621	0.567	**0.844**
SI4	0.568	0.565	0.601	0.689	0.644	**0.819**

Source: SmartPLS 4

Discriminant validity refers to the distinctiveness of each construct and the relationship between the constructs. It can be measured with cross-loading, Heterotrait-Heteromethod Correlation (HTMT), and Fornell-Larcker criteria. The present study uses the Fornell-Larcker criteria and cross-loading to measure discriminant validity. In Table 5, the Fornell-Larcker criterion indicates that a construct should account for the variance of its own indicators rather than the variance of other constructs.

Cross-loading criteria in Table 6 indicate the significant factor matrix for each construct, making each construct distinct from the others. All the items cross-loading are above 0.7, indicating that each construct is significantly distinguishable from the others.

3.3.4. Structural Model Assessment

Table 7. Total indirect effects

	Original sample	Sample mean	Standard deviation	t-statistics	p-values
RP -> INT -> BEH	0.166	0.159	0.104	1.604	0.109
SI -> INT -> BEH	0.173	0.175	0.080	2.163	0.031
AWR -> INT -> BEH	0.158	0.168	0.104	1.514	0.130
FOMO -> INT -> BEH	0.194	0.196	0.086	2.248	0.025

Source: SmartPLS 4

Table 7 shows that FOMO and social influence significantly impact cryptocurrency investment, as an investment in the crypto market is primarily driven by herd behaviour in society. The general public's desire to earn more in a shorter period influences them to invest in this highly volatile asset class. The risk perception has been found to have a somewhat positive impact on investment behaviour in cryptocurrency markets. This impact, however, may not be statistically significant, potentially due to the prevalence of social influence and FOMO among investors and the significant influence of peer pressure in motivating individuals to invest in the cryptocurrency market. The level of awareness among investors does not seem to influence their investment decisions within this market significantly. This suggests that factors other than awareness and risk perception are potentially more influential in shaping investment behaviour in the cryptocurrency market.

Table 8. Total effect

	Original sample	Sample mean	Standard deviation	t-statistics	p-values	Direction/ relation	Decision
AWR -> BEH	0.158	0.168	0.104	1.514	0.130	Positive	Insignificant
AWR -> INT	0.212	0.224	0.137	1.542	0.123	Positive	Insignificant
FOMO -> BEH	0.194	0.196	0.086	2.248	0.025	Positive	Significant
FOMO -> INT	0.259	0.261	0.112	2.320	0.020	Positive	Significant
INT -> BEH	0.746	0.752	0.048	15.487	0.000	Positive	Significant
RP -> BEH	0.166	0.159	0.104	1.604	0.109	Positive	Insignificant
RP -> INT	0.223	0.212	0.136	1.635	0.102	Positive	Insignificant
SI -> BEH	0.173	0.175	0.080	2.163	0.031	Positive	Significant
SI -> INT	0.232	0.233	0.106	2.193	0.028	Positive	Significant

Source: SmartPLS 4

Table 8 confirms the decision and direction of the variables regarding the structural relationship in the study. All four constructs have a positive impact on intention, and intention, in turn, has a positive impact on investment behaviour in the cryptocurrency market. The awareness and risk perception of the investor has an insignificant effect on the investment decision, which may be attributed to FOMO and social influence. The direct and indirect effects of FOMO and social influence on intention to invest and investment decisions in the cryptocurrency market are statistically significant. The coefficient of determination (R^2) value indicates how much the exogenous variable explains the endogenous variable. R^2 for the model is 0.557, which describes latent variables that can explain 55.7% of the investment behaviour in the cryptocurrency market.

Figure 2. Path analysis results (SmartPLS 4)

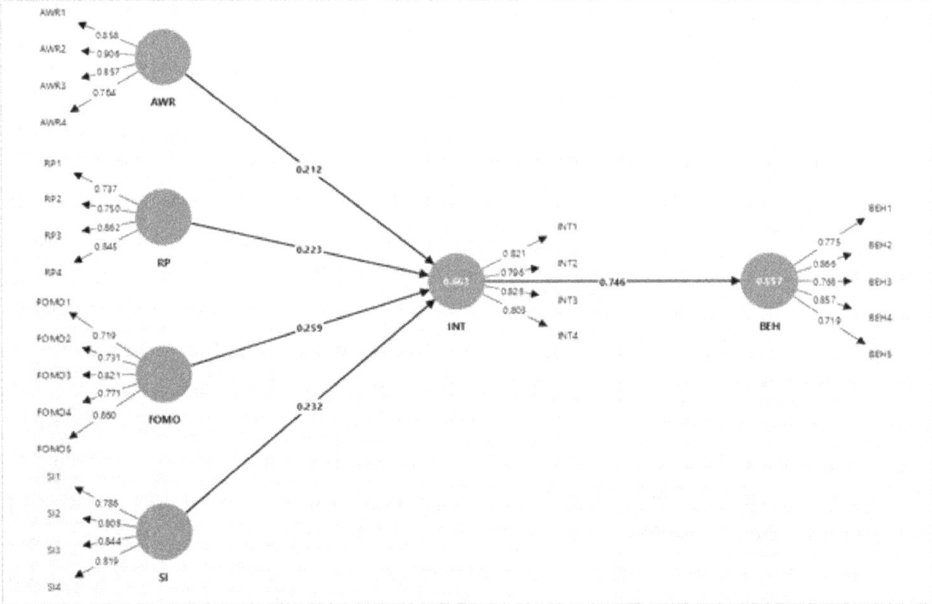

4. CONCLUSION

The present chapter aims to identify the factors influencing investors' investment decisions in the cryptocurrency market. Although the cryptocurrency market has been around for almost a decade, comprehensive regulation is needed, which raises concerns about investor interest and their hard-earned money. This can ultimately adversely affect the financial stability of the economy, which raises serious issues for many economies at present. Therefore, the present study identifies and assesses the factors influencing investors' investment decisions. The theory of planned behaviour (TPB) was used as the conceptual framework for the study. The data collected through the adapted questionnaire was analysed in SPSS to get the demographic and investment profile of the investors. For reliability and validity, the collected data were analysed in the SmartPLS 4 software. The study discovered that the level of awareness and risk perception has no effect on investors' intentions and investment decisions. This could be due to peer pressure or investors' greed to be part of the cryptocurrency market due to the prospect of rapid and substantial returns. The results show that social influence significantly impacts investors' decision-making in the cryptocurrency market. Peer pressure creates FOMO, leading investors to participate in the crypto market. Additionally, risk perception plays a crucial role in the investor's intention when making an investment decision in a highly volatile asset.

4.1 Implications

The findings of the study suggest practical implications for investors, academicians, and regulatory authorities. Novice investors should avoid investing in the cryptocurrency market without a basic understanding due to its high volatility. The study shows that awareness levels do not play a role in investment decisions, especially in the cryptocurrency market. Instead, investors are mainly influenced by social pressure and fear of missing out. This highlights the need to raise awareness about cryptocurrency among the general public, as many people are investing without considering the risks involved. So, novice investors can get help or investment advice from experts in the crypto market. The findings indicate the necessity of implementing a robust and comprehensive regulatory framework for cryptocurrency investments. The increasing number of investors in the cryptocurrency market underscores the importance of safeguarding their interests and funds. It is imperative for the government and central banks to formulate comprehensive regulations for crypto investments to prevent any adverse impact on the financial stability of the economy. Therefore, there is a pressing need for global and national cryptocurrency regulation. The collapse of cryptocurrency alone is unlikely to cause systemic risk comparable to the 2008 financial crisis. However, if institutional adoption continues to grow and crypto becomes deeply embedded in global finance, future collapses could have more severe repercussions. A sudden collapse of the crypto market could trigger liquidity crises, investor losses, and broader economic disruptions, underscoring the necessity for a balanced regulatory approach rather than avoidance. Integrating subjects like decentralised finance, cryptocurrency, stablecoin blockchain, and non-fungible tokens (NFTs) in the curriculum at school, college and university levels so that financial knowledge is provided from the beginning, and students must be financially aware and financially literate so they can make informed decisions about saving, investing and managing money along with new career opportunities, foster innovation and entrepreneurship, advance financial inclusion, raises awareness of regulatory and ethical issues in the country.

4.2 Limitations and Future Directions

The present study was conducted in a few cities to gather data from a limited number of crypto investors. For future research, it would benefit the researcher to collect data from a larger and more diverse group of crypto investors to gain a more comprehensive understanding of cryptocurrency investment behaviour. Conducting a global study would offer a broader perspective on cryptocurrency investors' perceptions worldwide. Future studies could also delve into the dual properties (Asset or Currency) of cryptocurrency.

REFERENCES

Aggarwal, D. (2019). Do bitcoins follow a random walk model? *Research in Economics*, *73*(1), 15–22. DOI: 10.1016/j.rie.2019.01.002

Akyildirim, E., Corbet, S., Lucey, B., Sensoy, A., & Yarovaya, L. (2020). The relationship between implied volatility and cryptocurrency returns. *Finance Research Letters*, *33*, 101212. Advance online publication. DOI: 10.1016/j.frl.2019.06.010

Al-Amri, R., Zakaria, N. H., Habbal, A., & Hassan, S. (2019). Cryptocurrency adoption: Current stage, opportunities, and open challenges. *International Journal of Advanced Computer Research*, *9*(44), 293–307. DOI: 10.19101/IJACR.PID43

Almansour, B. Y., Elkrghli, S., & Almansour, A. Y. (2023). Behavioral finance factors and investment decisions: A mediating role of risk perception. *Cogent Economics & Finance*, *11*(2), 2239032. Advance online publication. DOI: 10.1080/23322039.2023.2239032

Alomari, A. S. A., & Abdullah, N. L. (2023). Factors influencing the behavioral intention to use Cryptocurrency among Saudi Arabian public university students: Moderating role of financial literacy. *Cogent Business & Management*, *10*(1), 2178092. Advance online publication. DOI: 10.1080/23311975.2023.2178092

Anser, M. K., Zaigham, G. H. K., Imran Rasheed, M., Pitafi, A. H., Iqbal, J., & Luqman, A. (2020). Social media usage and individuals' intentions toward adopting Bitcoin: The role of the theory of planned behavior and perceived risk. *International Journal of Communication Systems*, *33*(17), e4590. Advance online publication. DOI: 10.1002/dac.4590

Attri, S., Gupta, S., & Singh, S. (2025). Risk Forecasting Using Artificial Intelligence and Machine Learning: Evidence From Stock and Cryptocurrency Markets. In *Artificial Intelligence for Financial Risk Management and Analysis* (pp. 187–196). DOI: 10.4018/979-8-3373-1200-2.ch009

Attri, S., Gupta, S., & Singh, S. (2025). Risk Forecasting Using Artificial Intelligence and Machine Learning: Evidence From Stock and Cryptocurrency Markets. In Artificial Intelligence for Financial Risk Management and Analysis (pp. 187–196). https://doi.org/DOI: 10.4018/979-8-3373-1200-2.ch009

Ayedh, A., Echchabi, A., Battour, M., & Omar, M. (2020). Malaysian Muslim investors' behaviour towards the blockchain-based Bitcoin cryptocurrency market. *Journal of Islamic Marketing*, *12*(4), 690–704. DOI: 10.1108/JIMA-04-2019-0081

Babich, V., & Hilary, G. (2018). Distributed ledgers and operations: What operations management researchers should know about blockchain technology. *Manufacturing & Service Operations Management*, *22*(2), 223–240. DOI: 10.1287/msom.2018.0752

Baur, D. G., Hong, K. H., & Lee, A. D. (2017). Bitcoin: Medium of exchange or speculative assets? *Journal of International Financial Markets, Institutions and Money*. Advance online publication. DOI: 10.1016/j.intfin.2017.12.004

Brière, M., Oosterlinck, K., & Szafarz, A. (2015). Virtual currency, Tangible Return: Portfolio Diversification with Bitcoin. *Journal of Asset Management*, *16*(6), 365–373. DOI: 10.1057/jam.2015.5

Chen, X., Miraz, M. H., Gazi, M. A. I., Rahaman, M. A., Habib, M. M., & Hossain, A. I. (2022). Factors affecting cryptocurrency adoption in digital business transactions: The mediating role of customer satisfaction. *Technology in Society*, *70*, 102059. Advance online publication. DOI: 10.1016/j.techsoc.2022.102059

Conti, M., Kumar, E. S., Lal, C., & Ruj, S. (2018). A survey on security and privacy issues of bitcoin. *IEEE Communications Surveys and Tutorials*, *20*(4), 3416–3452.

Cristofaro, M., Giardino, P. L., Misra, S., Pham, Q. T., & Hiep Phan, H. (2022). Behavior or culture? Investigating the use of cryptocurrencies for electronic commerce across the USA and China. *Management Research Review*, *46*(3), 340–368. DOI: 10.1108/MRR-06-2021-0493

Dickson, P., & Mahwera, D. A. (2022). Financial Institutions Readiness Towards Cryptocurrency Adoption: A Case of Banks in Tanzania. *Journal of Business and Management Review*, *3*(10), 740–753. DOI: 10.47153/jbmr310.4672022

Ebizie, P. I., Nkamnebe, A. D., & Ojiaku, O. C. (2022). Factors Influencing Cryptocurrency Adoption Among Nigerian University Fintech Entrepreneurs: An UTAUT perspective. *British Journal of Marketing Studies*, *10*(3), 25–37. DOI: 10.37745/bjms.2013/vo10.n3pp2537

Fishbein, M., Ajzen, I., & Tra, T. (1967). *Theory of reasoned action.*

Folkinshteyn, D., & Lennon, M. (2017). Braving Bitcoin: A technology acceptance model (TAM) analysis. *Journal of Information Technology Case and Application Research*, *18*(4), 220–249. DOI: 10.1080/15228053.2016.1275242

Galang Prasetyo, T., & Kurniasari, F. (2023). *The Influence of Subjective Norms, Financial Literacy, Trust, and Government Regulation on Behavioral Intention to Invest in Crypto Assets. January*, 1–24. DOI: 10.20944/preprints202301.0400.v1

Güler, D. (2023). The Impact of Investor Sentiment on Bitcoin Returns and Conditional Volatilities during the Era of Covid-19. *Journal of Behavioral Finance, 24*(3), 276–289. DOI: 10.1080/15427560.2021.1975285

Gupta, S., & Shrivastava, M. (2022). Herding and loss aversion in stock markets: Mediating role of fear of missing out (FOMO) in retail investors. *International Journal of Emerging Markets, 17*(7), 1720–1737. DOI: 10.1108/IJOEM-08-2020-0933

Hair, J. F., Black, W. C., Babin, B. J., & Anderson, R. E. (2019). Multivariate Data Analysis. In *Mathematics of Computation* (7th ed., Vol. 50, Issue 181). Annabel Ainscow. DOI: 10.2307/2007941

Harb, E., Bassil, C., Kassamany, T., & Baz, R. (2022). Volatility Interdependence Between Cryptocurrencies, Equity, and Bond Markets. *Computational Economics*. Advance online publication. DOI: 10.1007/s10614-022-10318-7 PMID: 36187467

Härdle, W. K., Harvey, C. R., & Reule, R. C. G. (2020). Understanding Cryptocurrencies. *Journal of Financial Econometrics, 1*(19), 1–28. DOI: 10.1093/jjfinec/nbz033

Hong, K. H. (2017). Bitcoin as an alternative investment vehicle. *Information Technology and Management, 18*(4), 265–275. DOI: 10.1007/s10799-016-0264-6

Jegerson, D., Khan, M., & Mertzanis, C. (2023). Adoption of cryptocurrencies for remittances in the UAE: The mediation effect of consumer innovation. *European Journal of Innovation Management. Sdg, 10*. Advance online publication. DOI: 10.1108/EJIM-09-2022-0538

Jonker, N. (2019). What drives the adoption of crypto-payments by online retailers? *Electronic Commerce Research and Applications, 35*(April), 100848. DOI: 10.1016/j.elerap.2019.100848

Kala, D., Chaubey, D. S., & Al-Adwan, A. S. (2023). Cryptocurrency investment behaviour of young Indians: Mediating role of fear of missing out. *Global Knowledge, Memory and Communication*, (February). Advance online publication. DOI: 10.1108/GKMC-07-2023-0237

Katsiampa, P. (2019). An empirical investigation of volatility dynamics in the cryptocurrency market. *Research in International Business and Finance, 50*, 322–335. DOI: 10.1016/j.ribaf.2019.06.004

Klein, T., Pham Thu, H., & Walther, T. (2018). Bitcoin is not the New Gold – A comparison of volatility, correlation, and portfolio performance. *International Review of Financial Analysis, 59*, 105–116. DOI: 10.1016/j.irfa.2018.07.010

Krishnan, S., Balas, V., Julie, E. G., Harold, R. Y., Balaji, S., & Kumar, R. (2020). *Handbook Of Research On Blockchain Technology*. Elsevier.

Kumari, V., Bala, P. K., & Chakraborty, S. (2023). An Empirical Study of User Adoption of Cryptocurrency Using Blockchain Technology: Analysing Role of Success Factors like Technology Awareness and Financial Literacy. *Journal of Theoretical and Applied Electronic Commerce Research*, *18*(3), 1580–1600. DOI: 10.3390/jtaer18030080

Kyriazis, N., Papadamou, S., Tzeremes, P., & Corbet, S. (2022). The differential influence of social media sentiment on cryptocurrency returns and volatility during COVID-19. *The Quarterly Review of Economics and Finance*, *xxxx*, 1–11. DOI: 10.1016/j.qref.2022.09.004 PMID: 36281469

Lam, D., & Mizerski, D. (2005). The effects of locus of control on word-of-mouth communication. *Journal of Marketing Communications*, *11*(3), 215–228. DOI: 10.1080/1352726042000333180

Li, C., Zhang, Y., & Xu, Y. (2022). Factors Influencing the Adoption of Blockchain in the Construction Industry: A Hybrid Approach Using PLS-SEM and fsQCA. *Buildings (Basel, Switzerland)*, *12*(9), 1349. Advance online publication. DOI: 10.3390/buildings12091349

Lusardi, A. (2019). Financial literacy and the need for financial education: Evidence and implications. *Swiss Journal of Economics and Statistics*, *155*(1), 1–8. DOI: 10.1186/s41937-019-0027-5

Manzoor, A., Jan, A., Shafi, M., Ashraf Parry, M., & Mir, T. (2023). Role of perceived COVID-19 disruption, personality traits and risk perception in determining the investment behavior of retail investors: a hybrid regression-neural network approach. *Journal of Economic and Administrative Sciences*. DOI: 10.1108/JEAS-01-2023-0026

Mikhaylov, A. (2020). Cryptocurrency market analysis from the open innovation perspective. *Journal of Open Innovation*, *6*(4), 1–19. DOI: 10.3390/joitmc6040197

Nakamoto, S. (2008). *Bitcoin: A Peer-to-Peer Electronic Cash System*. 1–9. DOI: 10.2139/ssrn.3977007

Nurbarani, B. S., & Soepriyanto, G. (2022). Determinants of Investment Decision in Cryptocurrency: Evidence from Indonesian Investors. *Universal Journal of Accounting and Finance*, *10*(1), 254–266. DOI: 10.13189/ujaf.2022.100126

Osakwe, C. N. (2024). *An integrative model for understanding cryptocurrency investment-related behaviours : A comparison between millennials and pre-millennials. November 2022*, 1–19. DOI: 10.1002/ijfe.3031

Patras, W., Rasool, A., & Idrees, M. (2023). Assessment of Investors' Investment Behaviour: Mediating Effect of Risk Tolerance: a Case of Pakistan Stock Exchange. *Journal of Social Research Development*, *4*(2), 305–315. DOI: 10.53664/JSRD/04-02-2023-07-305-315

Pham, Q. T., Phan, H. H., Cristofaro, M., Misra, S., & Giardino, P. L. (2021). Examining the Intention to Invest in Cryptocurrencies. *International Journal of Applied Behavioral Economics*, *10*(3), 59–79. DOI: 10.4018/IJABE.2021070104

Pilatin, A., & Dilek, Ö. (2023). Investor intention, investor behavior and crypto assets in the framework of decomposed theory of planned behavior. *Current Psychology, Cc*. DOI: 10.1007/s12144-023-04307-8

Przybylski, A. K., Murayama, K., Dehaan, C. R., & Gladwell, V. (2013). Motivational, emotional, and behavioral correlates of fear of missing out. *Computers in Human Behavior*, *29*(4), 1841–1848. DOI: 10.1016/j.chb.2013.02.014

Putra, I. G. N. A. P., & Darma, G. S. (2019). Is Bitcoin Accepted in Indonesia? *International Journal of Innovative Science and Research Technology*, *4*(2), 424–430. www.ijisrt.com424

Renduchintala, T., Alfauri, H., Yang, Z., Di Pietro, R., & Jain, R. (2022). A Survey of Blockchain Applications in the FinTech Sector. *Journal of Open Innovation*, *8*(4), 185. DOI: 10.3390/joitmc8040185

Salman, M. (2020). *The impact of heuristic availability bias on investment decision-making: Moderated mediation model. September*, 1–12. DOI: 10.1002/bsd2.148

Singh, S., Singh, M., & Attri, S. (2025a). Mapping stock market dynamics: A tripartite neural network approach using modified grid search for stock market prediction. *Expert Systems with Applications*, *278*(February), 127243. https://doi.org/10.1016/j.eswa.2025.127243

Singh, S., Singh, M., & Attri, S. (2025b). Dynamic volatility linkages among crude oil, exchange rate, interest rate, gold and equity markets: An empirical Asian perspective. *Managerial Finance*. Advance online publication. DOI: 10.1108/MF-01-2025-0016

Smutny, Z., Sulc, Z., & Lansky, J. (2021). Motivations, barriers and risk-taking when investing in cryptocurrencies. *Mathematics*, *9*(14), 1–22. DOI: 10.3390/math9141655

Sukumaran, S., Bee, T. S., & Wasiuzzaman, S. (2022). Cryptocurrency as an Investment: The Malaysian Context. *Risks*, *10*(4), 86. Advance online publication. DOI: 10.3390/risks10040086

Walton, A., & Johnston, K. (2018). *Exploring Perceptions Of Bitcoin Adoption : The South African Virtual Community Perspective*. 165–182. DOI: 10.28945/4080

Wu, J. (2021). *Essays on Bitcoin and Cryptocurrencies*. https://scholarworks.wmich.edu/dissertations/3812

Wu, R., Ishfaq, K., Hussain, S., Asmi, F., Siddiquei, A. N., & Anwar, M. A. (2022). Investigating e-Retailers' Intentions to Adopt Cryptocurrency Considering the Mediation of Technostress and Technology Involvement. *Sustainability (Basel)*, *14*(2), 641. Advance online publication. DOI: 10.3390/su14020641

Yan, Y., Lei, Y., & Wang, Y. (2022). Bitcoin as a Safe-Haven Asset and a Medium of Exchange. *Axioms*, *11*(8), 415. DOI: 10.3390/axioms11080415

Yi, S., Xu, Z., & Wang, G. J. (2018). Volatility connectedness in the cryptocurrency market: Is Bitcoin a dominant cryptocurrency? *International Review of Financial Analysis*, *60*, 98–114. DOI: 10.1016/j.irfa.2018.08.012

ENDNOTES

1 https://coinmarketcap.com/currencies/bitcoin/

Chapter 10
Exploring Portfolio Diversification, Hedging, and Safe-Haven Traits in Cryptocurrency Investments

Gurwinder Kaur Dua
https://orcid.org/0009-0003-3269-1969
Post Graduate Government College, India

ABSTRACT

This paper aims for comprehensive analysis of the prevailing knowledge concerning portfolio diversification, hedge, and safe-haven characteristics in cryptocurrency investments. This study has reviewed studies, spanning various disciplines, to produce a systematic literature review and bibliometric analysis. The findings from this study show the expanding body of literature highlighting cryptocurrencies' potential to serve as a hedge against stocks, fiat currencies, geopolitical risks, and Economic Policy Uncertainty (EPU) risk. In addition to that, cryptocurrencies show properties of diversification and safe-havens, while stable coins exhibit an unstable peg with the US dollar. This paper also identified uncertainty as a significant factor influencing cryptocurrency returns. Furthermore, analysis suggests that investors should consider Gold, the European carbon market, CBOE Bitcoin futures, and crude oil as potential hedging instruments against unforeseen fluctuations in the cryptocurrency market.

DOI: 10.4018/979-8-3693-5986-0.ch010

1. INTRODUCTION

The paper by Nakamoto (2008) laid the groundwork for the cryptocurrency market, which is now recognized as a decentralized form of digital currency that disrupts traditional financial systems (Almeida 2021). The cryptocurrency market has experienced rapid growth and continues to evolve (Białkowski 2020; Fang et al. 2021; Li et al. 2021). It captivates the interest of individual and institutional investors, regulators, and the media, making it a significant topic of research across various academic disciplines (Angerer et al. 2020).

Investors face the challenge of effectively managing their portfolios, and empirical studies highlight the importance of understanding the relationships between cryptocurrencies and other assets (Bouri et al. 2022), as well as their interrelationships (Kumar et al. 2022) and volatility characteristics (Klinkova and Grabinski 2017; Wang et al. 2022) in portfolio management. Consequently, insights into the diversification, hedging, and safe-haven attributes of these assets are crucial, especially given the nascent nature of the cryptocurrency market.

In light of this, and considering the rapid accumulation of empirical evidence regarding cryptocurrencies, it is essential to compile and synthesize the existing quality knowledge while identifying gaps in the literature to guide future research (Angerer et al. 2020; Corbet et al. 2019). To achieve this, we undertake a systematic literature review. Our objectives are twofold: (1) to enhance understanding of the current academic literature on portfolio diversification, hedging, and safe-haven properties in cryptocurrency investments; and (2) to present key research findings that are valuable to investors, policymakers, academics, businesses, and society at large.

Our contributions to the literature are multifaceted. First, we provide the most comprehensive and up-to-date systematic literature review, accompanied by a bibliometric analysis that consolidates knowledge on portfolio diversification, hedging, and safe-haven properties in cryptocurrency investments.

Second, our review identifies and elucidates the existing academic knowledge related to these properties in cryptocurrency investments, complementing broader literature reviews conducted by Almeida (2021) and others (Almeida and Gonçalves 2022; Angerer et al. 2020; Bariviera and Merediz-Solà 2021; Corbet et al. 2019; Flori 2019b; Hairudin et al. 2020; Haq et al. 2021; Jalal et al. 2021; Kyriazis et al. 2020).

Third, we employ more inclusive keywords in our Web of Science (WoS) search, allowing us to consider contributions from peripheral studies on portfolio diversification, hedging, and safe-haven properties in cryptocurrency investments.

Finally, we enhance previous reviews by integrating bibliometric analysis with a critical examination of existing literature. We also identify research gaps and future directions regarding the use of crypto assets in investment strategies. Our findings are significant for researchers, investors, analysts, and regulators, providing structured networking for research outlets and literature strands, along with time-trended information pertinent to future studies on the diversification, hedging, and safe-haven properties of cryptocurrency investments.

Simultaneously, we offer investors and analysts a valuable compilation of practical insights to inform their investment strategies, while our synthesis provides regulators with guidance for effectively overseeing cryptocurrency markets.

Existing research also suggests that cryptocurrencies possess diversification and safe-haven characteristics, which vary with time and market conditions. Additionally, stablecoins may function as safe havens and diversifiers, contributing to market efficiency, though they exhibit an unstable peg to the US dollar. A notable finding from the literature is that uncertainty significantly influences cryptocurrency returns. Furthermore, we recommend that investors consider Gold, along with the European carbon market and CBOE Bitcoin futures, in their investment strategies.

2. METHODOLOGY

This research has opted for a comprehensive review process. Drawing on the studies by Almeida and Gonçalves (2022), Jiang et al. (2021), Liang et al. (2016), Linnenluecke et al. (2020), Milian et al. (2019), and Yue et al. (2021), this research has considered the Web of Science (WoS) database to ensure the integrity of the sample.

Our objective was to encompass the entire timeline from the publication of the first article on cryptocurrencies to the present day. We used Nakamoto's (2008) seminal article, which introduced cryptocurrencies, as our reference point. Consequently, we searched the WoS database for articles published from January 1, 2009, to November 25, 2021, to capture all relevant literature on cryptocurrencies. Our approach involved using broader keywords related to portfolio diversification, hedging, and safe-haven properties in cryptocurrency investments, setting our research apart from other reviews such as those by Flori (2019a), Haq et al. (2021), Jalal et al. (2021), and Kyriazis et al. (2020). The selected keywords included "Cryptocurrencies," "Bitcoin," "Portfolio diversification," "Investment," and "Alternative investment," leading to the following research equation: "cryptocurrency OR Bitcoin AND diversification AND portfolio AND invest AND alternative."

To enhance the quality of our research, we focused exclusively on English-language journal articles listed in the 2021 Academic Journal Guide by the Association of Business Schools. Additionally, all articles had to address cryptocurrencies from the perspective of investors or investments, while also considering methodologies.

We did not impose any restrictions on the fields of study, allowing us to enrich our research on portfolio diversification, hedging, and safe-haven properties in cryptocurrency investments with relevant peripheral studies. Our final sample comprised 175 articles.

Following the methodologies outlined by Bartolacci et al. (2020), Ding et al. (2014), Galvao et al. (2019), Rialti et al. (2019), Sadeghi Moghadam et al. (2021), and Van Eck and Waltman (2017), we conducted comprehensive literature review (Bartolacci et al. 2020; Rialti et al. 2019; Van Eck and Waltman 2017; Caputo et al. 2019).

3. LITERATURE FINDINGS ON HEDGING PROPERTIES, SAFE-HAVEN PROPERTIES AND PORTFOLIO DIVERSIFICATION OF CRYPTOCURRENCY INVESTMENTS

3.1 Do Cryptocurrencies Have Hedging Properties?

The literature review indicates that cryptocurrencies, particularly Bitcoin, exhibit hedging properties against various assets and risks. Key findings include:

- **Hedging Against Stocks and Fiat Currencies:** Cryptocurrencies have been shown to hedge effectively against stock market fluctuations and fiat currencies (Fang et al. 2020; Hsu et al. 2021).
- **Gold and Geopolitical Risks:** Bitcoin and other cryptocurrencies can serve as hedges against gold and geopolitical uncertainties (González et al. 2021; Colon et al. 2021).
- **Economic Policy Uncertainty:** Cryptocurrencies also provide a hedge against Economic Policy Uncertainty (EPU) and the volatility caused by events like the COVID-19 pandemic (Yen and Cheng 2021; Demir et al. 2020a).
- **Bitcoin's Unique Position:** Bitcoin is highlighted for its effectiveness as a hedge in both normal and stressed market conditions, evolving from a speculative asset to a more stable investment tool (Bhuiyan et al. 2021; Vo et al. 2021).

Overall, the findings suggest that cryptocurrencies, particularly Bitcoin, are increasingly recognized for their potential to diversify portfolios and serve as hedging instruments in various economic contexts. This underscores the importance of further interdisciplinary research to explore these dynamics in the evolving landscape of cryptocurrency investments.

The advantages of utilizing cryptocurrencies differ based on regional and country-specific assets, as well as emerging asset classes like forex and equities (Omane-Adjepong and Alagidede 2020). In developed stock markets, Monero and Dash are recognized as effective diversifiers (Jeribi and Ghorbel 2021), while Ethereum stands out as the most effective short-term diversifier. In the long run, cryptocurrencies such as Bitcoin, Ripple, Litecoin, Stellar, Monero, and Dash also exhibit strong diversification characteristics (Bouri et al. 2020b; Jiang et al. 2021a).

The literature indicates that Bitcoin offers notable diversification benefits for investors (Corbet et al. 2020a; Mensi et al. 2019; Scharnowski 2021). High-frequency trading evidence shows advantages in pairs like BTC-XRP and BTC-LTC, as well as in crypto-portfolio diversification with BTC-ETH, BTC-ETC, or BTC-EOR (Wang and Ngene 2020). Additionally, Bitcoin can enhance diversification for traditional equity indices, particularly the Dow Jones Islamic index and sustainable indices like the FTSE 4 Good index (Uddin et al. 2020). These diversification benefits are evident in both short and long-term periods (Uddin et al. 2020). Furthermore, including Bitcoin in portfolios denominated in Chinese Yuan, Japanese Yen, and US Dollar has been shown to improve risk-adjusted returns, underscoring Bitcoin's diversification potential (Bedi and Nashier 2020). However, for portfolios in China, Gold may serve as a superior diversifier compared to Bitcoin. While Bitcoin can yield higher returns than Gold, it also increases risk, making it a more suitable diversifier for risk-seeking Chinese investors (Pho et al. 2021).

The literature also emphasizes that Bitcoin is relatively detached from most financial assets, which enhances its ability to provide diversification benefits (Bhuiyan et al. 2021). There is limited and time-varying connectedness between Bitcoin and traditional assets, further supporting its diversification capabilities (Mensi et al. 2020b; Zeng et al. 2020). Additionally, Bitcoin is recognized as a good diversifier for BRICS economies (Jeribi and Ghorbel 2021) and for indices like the FTSE and Nikkei, which exhibit negative dynamic dependence (Fakhfekh et al. 2021). The absence of risk spillover effects from Economic Policy Uncertainty (EPU) to Bitcoin suggests that Bitcoin can serve as a diversifier during extreme EPU shocks (Wang et al. 2019).

However, during periods of instability and market shocks, the effectiveness of diversification appears to diminish (Guo et al. 2021). Prior to China's ICO ban in 2017, incorporating cryptocurrencies into portfolios could yield diversification benefits. Yet, following the announcement, evidence indicates that these benefits dissipated (Zhang and Gregoriou 2021). Furthermore, co-movements between cryptocurrencies and stock indices have generally been positive and intensified during the COVID-19 pandemic, leading to a failure of cryptocurrencies to provide diversification benefits (Goodell and Goutte 2021b). The deterioration of diversification benefits in crypto portfolios during the COVID-19 period has also been noted (Demiralay and

Golitsis 2021). Additionally, the close integration among major cryptocurrencies has undermined diversification possibilities (Naeem et al. 2021b), with jumps in one cryptocurrency increasing the likelihood of jumps in others, thereby reducing diversification benefits (Bouri et al. 2020c).

Moreover, evidence suggests that employing a Hierarchical Risk Parity approach can enhance crypto portfolio management, offering superior diversification properties and better handling volatility and tail risk compared to traditional risk-based strategies (Burggraf 2021).

3.2. Do Cryptocurrencies Offer Diversification Benefits?

The potential for cryptocurrencies to enhance diversification is a significant topic within the cryptocurrency literature. Research indicates that incorporating cryptocurrencies into traditional investment portfolios—comprising stocks, currencies, and commodities—can enhance diversification benefits and returns while simultaneously reducing portfolio volatility (Ma et al. 2020). Additionally, cryptocurrencies can help mitigate liquidity risk (Ghabri et al. 2020). For example, integrating cryptocurrencies like Bitcoin, Ethereum, and Litecoin into an equity portfolio provides diversification advantages compared to a portfolio consisting solely of equities (Bouri et al. 2020a; Kumah and Mensah 2020). The cross-correlation between cryptocurrencies and traditional assets is variable and generally weak, supporting the notion that cryptocurrencies, particularly Bitcoin and Ethereum, serve as effective financial diversifiers (Charfeddine et al. 2020). However, achieving optimal diversification requires a careful balance of digital and traditional assets (Charfeddine et al. 2020).

Incorporating cryptocurrencies into portfolios of small-cap stocks also enhances risk diversification and returns (Matkovskyy et al. 2021). These diversification benefits are evident across various stock indexes, including global, developed, emerging, and U.S. markets (Jiang et al. 2021a; Kumah and Odei-Mensah 2021).

When considering investments in gold, cryptocurrencies such as Cardano, Tether, and Tezos also appear to offer diversification advantages (González et al. 2021; Hsu et al. 2021). Investors in emerging markets may find that holding cryptocurrencies like Bitcoin or Ripple can provide diversification during periods of market distress, helping to reduce risks associated with emerging equities and foreign currency fluctuations (Omane-Adjepong and Alagidede 2020). However, the effectiveness of these cryptocurrencies as diversifiers can vary based on regional and country-specific assets, as well as across emerging asset classes like forex and equities (Omane-Adjepong and Alagidede 2020).

In developed stock markets, Monero and Dash are also recognized as effective diversifiers (Jeribi and Ghorbel 2021). In the short term, Ethereum appears to be the most effective diversifier, while in the long term, cryptocurrencies such as Bitcoin,

Ripple, Litecoin, Stellar, Monero, and Dash exhibit similar characteristics (Bouri et al. 2020b; Jiang et al. 2021a).

The literature consistently highlights Bitcoin's diversification benefits for investors (Corbet et al. 2020a; Mensi et al. 2019; Scharnowski 2021). Evidence suggests that high-frequency trading pairs like BTC-XRP and BTC-LTC, as well as crypto-portfolio diversification involving BTC-ETH, BTC-ETC, or BTC-EOR, yield positive results (Wang and Ngene 2020). Furthermore, Bitcoin can enhance diversification for traditional equity indices, particularly the Dow Jones Islamic index and sustainable indices like the FTSE 4 Good index (Uddin et al. 2020). These diversification benefits are observed over both short and long-term periods (Uddin et al. 2020). Additionally, Bitcoin's inclusion in portfolios denominated in Chinese Yuan, Japanese Yen, and U.S. Dollar has been shown to improve risk-adjusted returns, underscoring its diversification potential (Bedi and Nashier 2020). However, for portfolios in China, gold may serve as a superior diversifier compared to Bitcoin. While Bitcoin can yield higher returns than gold, it also increases risk, making it a more suitable diversifier for risk-seeking Chinese investors (Pho et al. 2021).

The literature on Bitcoin's diversification properties indicates that it is relatively insulated from most financial assets, allowing it to provide significant diversification benefits (Bhuiyan et al. 2021). There is limited and time-varying connectedness between Bitcoin and traditional assets, further supporting its role as a diversifier (Mensi et al. 2020b; Zeng et al. 2020). Additionally, Bitcoin is recognized as a good diversifier for BRICS economies and indices like the FTSE and Nikkei, which exhibit negative dynamic dependence (Jeribi and Ghorbel 2021; Fakhfekh et al. 2021). The absence of risk spillover effects from Economic Policy Uncertainty (EPU) to Bitcoin suggests that Bitcoin may serve as a diversifier during extreme EPU shocks (Wang et al. 2019).

However, during periods of market instability and shocks, the effectiveness of diversification may diminish (Guo et al. 2021). Prior to China's ban on Initial Coin Offerings (ICOs) in 2017, including cryptocurrencies in a portfolio could yield diversification benefits. Post-announcement, however, evidence indicates that these diversification advantages may dissipate (Zhang and Gregoriou 2021).

3.3. Are Cryptocurrencies Safe Havens?

The literature also explores the safe-haven characteristics of cryptocurrencies. Findings indicate that Bitcoin, Stellar, and Ripple are effective safe havens for US stock indices, similar to Litecoin and Monero. Conversely, Ethereum, Dash, and Nem are identified as good safe havens for sectors such as financial services, telecommunications, utilities, and information technology (Bouri et al. 2020d). Additionally, Bitcoin, Ethereum, Ripple, and Litecoin are considered safe havens for metal and agricultural commodities, although they are less effective for energy commodities (Naeem et al. 2021a). Although Ethereum is the least correlated cryptocurrency with oil price returns, making it a potential safe-haven against oil (Jareño et al. 2021), it appears to be a weak safe-haven for the S&P 500, STOXX 600, DAX, and FTSE 250 indices (B˛edowska-Sójka and Kliber 2021). Cardano, Tether, and Tezos may also serve as safe-havens when considering investments in gold (González et al. 2021).

In the case of Bitcoin, evidence suggests it can be regarded as a strong safe-haven for crude oil, but it is a weak safe-haven for the S&P 500 index (Corbet et al. 2020b), FTSE 250, and DAX indices (B˛edowska-Sójka and Kliber 2021). Additionally, Bitcoin may act as a safe-haven during extreme economic policy uncertainty (EPU) shocks (Jareño et al. 2020; Wang et al. 2019).

Conversely, there is evidence indicating that Bitcoin lacks safe-haven properties during the COVID-19 pandemic (Disli et al. 2021), particularly for investments in energy assets like crude oil and gas (Ghorbel and Jeribi 2021b). Furthermore, cryptocurrencies in general are not typically considered safe-havens against stock markets (Conlon et al. 2020; Goodell and Goutte 2021b; Jiang et al. 2021a; Thampanya et al. 2020) or gold (Corbet et al. 2020b).

Nonetheless, research shows that the safe-haven capabilities of cryptocurrencies fluctuate over time and under varying market conditions (B˛edowska-Sójka and Kliber 2021; Conlon et al. 2020; Guo et al. 2021; Hsu et al. 2021; Jareño et al. 2020; Raheem 2021; Umar et al. 2021; Wang et al. 2020). In periods of heightened uncertainty, cryptocurrencies can serve as effective safe-haven instruments (Hsu et al. 2021; Jareño et al. 2020). For example, during the volatile and uncertain times of the COVID-19 pandemic, Bitcoin and Ethereum were utilized as short-term safe-havens against the stock market (Corbet et al. 2020a; López-Cabarcos et al. 2021; Mariana et al. 2021).

When uncertainty looms in the cryptocurrency market, investors may turn to gold, which demonstrates stable and reliable safe-haven characteristics against cryptocurrency volatility (Hassan et al. 2021). The European carbon market may also be considered a safe-haven for the cryptocurrency market (Yang and Hamori 2021).

3.4. The Impact of Uncertainty on Cryptocurrency Investments

This literature review also sheds light on the influence of uncertainty on cryptocurrency investments. Evidence indicates a strong causal relationship between social media uncertainty (Twitter-Based Economic Uncertainty (TEU) and Twitter-Based Market Uncertainty (TMU)) and cryptocurrency returns (Bitcoin, Ethereum, Bitcoin Cash, and Ripple) (Aharon et al. 2022). When examining Bitcoin's price reactions to fiat currency uncertainty, it is found that such uncertainty generates additional demand for Bitcoin, although this demand does not directly determine Bitcoin prices

(Jin et al. 2021). Moreover, uncertainty effects are identified as determinants of net directional spillovers among cryptocurrency returns (Ji et al. 2019a). Additionally, uncertainty and trading volume are crucial factors for cryptocurrency market integration (Bouri et al. 2021c), confirming that uncertainty indeed influences cryptocurrency returns (Colon et al. 2021).

Furthermore, a positive correlation exists between Bitcoin and trade policy uncertainty in the USA, indicating that Bitcoin returns can be significantly affected by trade policy uncertainty (Gozgor et al. 2019). During extreme events, Bitcoin returns appear to be negatively correlated with changes in trade policy uncertainty (Gozgor et al. 2019).

This literature review also emphasizes that EPU does not lead to increased volatility in the cryptocurrency market, suggesting that high-risk crypto investors are largely unaffected by the economic environment (Papadamou et al. 2021). However, an increase in EPU does enhance the attractiveness of cryptocurrencies (Balli et al. 2020), which in turn leads to higher Bitcoin returns (Wang et al. 2020).

Moreover, evidence shows that following a spike in U.S. EPU, both the trading volume and volatility of Bitcoin increased. In contrast, the same cannot be said for the United Kingdom's EPU or the global economic policy uncertainty (GEPU) (Nguyen Quang et al. 2020). Consequently, the impact of the UK EPU on the BTC/GBP pair is less significant than that of the U.S. EPU on the BTC/USD pair (Wang et al. 2020). Additionally, China's EPU significantly affects cryptocurrencies like Litecoin and Bitcoin (Yen and Cheng 2021).

3.5. The Influence of Sentiment and News on Cryptocurrency Investment

This literature review examines the effects of sentiment and news on cryptocurrency investments. It has been found that investor attention is significantly affected by the performance of major cryptocurrencies like Bitcoin, Ethereum, and Litecoin (Lin, 2021). Additionally, emotions play a role in influencing Bitcoin's return volatility and trading volume (Ahn and Kim, 2021). The flow of information indicates that cryptocurrency returns can impact investor sentiment (Akyildirim et al., 2021a). Notably, Bitcoin appears to dominate sentiment connectedness, likely due to its widespread recognition. Furthermore, the volatility of sentiment connectedness is observed to be greater than that of return connectedness, suggesting that there are times when investor interest in the cryptocurrency market is renewed (Akyildirim et al., 2021a).

Negative sentiment has been identified as a predictor of Bitcoin returns, realized volatility, price jumps, and trading volumes. For instance, research shows that sentiment from former President Trump's tweets can influence Bitcoin prices

(Huynh, 2021). Additionally, tweets about Bitcoin and related Google searches can lead to herding behavior in these markets, while Economic Policy Uncertainty (EPU) patterns and the interconnectedness of foreign exchange and equity markets can dampen such herding effects (Philippas et al., 2020).

In terms of news sentiment within the cryptocurrency market, positive news tends to correlate with increased returns and trading volumes (Naeem et al., 2020). Unlike traditional currencies, which typically see returns rise after positive news and fall after negative news, Bitcoin shows a positive reaction to both, indicating a strong enthusiasm for the cryptocurrency that persists regardless of news sentiment. This effect is particularly pronounced during bubble periods. However, negative news related to cyber-attacks and fraud can lead to declines in Bitcoin's returns and volatility (Rognone et al., 2020). Interestingly, Bitcoin returns may decrease following positive news related to unemployment and durable goods announcements (Corbet et al., 2020c), while an increase in negative news surrounding these topics can lead to higher Bitcoin returns (Corbet et al., 2020c). Notably, the GBP and Consumer Price Index (CPI) do not appear to have a significant relationship with Bitcoin returns (Corbet et al., 2020c).

Informed trading is evident in the Bitcoin market, particularly before negative market events and significant positive developments. Specifically, informed traders tend to establish their positions two days prior to positive news and one day before negative news (Feng et al., 2018).

3.6. The Role of Stablecoins in Cryptocurrency Investment

Stablecoins play a crucial role in the cryptocurrency market (Hoang and Baur, 2021). Their issuance contributes to the efficiency of cryptocurrency markets and aids in price discovery. Stablecoins can also serve as safe havens (Wang et al., 2020), with USD-pegged stablecoins generally outperforming gold-pegged ones (Wang et al., 2020). However, their effectiveness varies with market conditions; in stable markets, they primarily act as diversifiers (Wang et al., 2020). For example, Tether can function as a diversifier or safe haven when investing in gold (González et al., 2021). Additionally, Tether's negative correlation with stock indices positions it as a significant safe haven during adverse market conditions (Goodell and Goutte, 2021b). Despite its potential as a safe haven, Tether's reliability has fluctuated over time, particularly due to short-term historical losses linked to its unstable peg to the US dollar (Conlon et al., 2020). Moreover, research indicates that stablecoins are not perfect substitutes for one another (Ante et al., 2021) and exhibit considerable price volatility (Hoang and Baur, 2021). Bitcoin also influences stablecoin volatility due to the high correlation in their returns, volumes, and volatility (Hoang and Baur,

2021). Consequently, a decline in past Bitcoin volatility tends to coincide with an increase in stablecoin volatility (Grobys et al., 2021).

3.7. The Cryptocurrency Market

Research suggests that during times of crisis, investors should consider reducing their exposure to Bitcoin in favor of Litecoin, Ethereum, and Ripple to mitigate risk and preserve returns (Mensi et al., 2020a). However, during the COVID-19 pandemic, Bitcoin experienced significant growth, with its prices rising alongside the number of COVID-19 fatalities (Corbet et al., 2020c; Goodell and Goutte, 2021a). Moreover, research indicates that COVID-19 did not affect the relationship between cryptocurrency hedge funds and Bitcoin and Ethereum (Khelifa et al. 2021). Bitcoin and Ethereum are the primary cryptocurrencies utilized by fund managers in the cryptocurrency space (Khelifa et al. 2021). In times of market stress, crypto assets can be categorized as speculative assets, primarily acting as tail contagion transmitters (with Bitcoin fitting this category), or as technical assets, which serve as tail contagion revivers (where Ethereum is classified) (Ahelegbey et al. 2021). Additionally, during bullish market phases, Bitcoin appears to be a significant driver of risk among cryptocurrencies (Nguyen et al. 2020). Interestingly, while Bitcoin shows a strong positive correlation with its forks during periods of low volatility, this correlation turns negative during high volatility periods (Bazán-Palomino 2020).

Regarding policy influences, it has been observed that cryptocurrency returns (including Bitcoin, Ethereum, Litecoin, and Ripple) tend to rise during periods of tightening Chinese monetary policy, whereas U.S. monetary policies do not significantly impact cryptocurrency returns (Nguyen et al. 2019).

Further findings suggest that the launch of Bitcoin futures did not correlate with the crash of the Bitcoin spot market in 2017 (Hattori and Ishida 2021). The effects of the 2017 Bitcoin bubble on the P2P market varied by currency and country, with the U.S. dollar being a notable exception due to its global trading prevalence (Holub and Johnson 2019). Although there is no direct link between Bitcoin futures and the 2017 bubble collapse, a negative correlation exists between Bitcoin returns and the introduction of Bitcoin futures (Liu et al. 2020). Additionally, the advent of Bitcoin futures has altered the mean and tail dependencies between stock and cryptocurrency markets (Lahiani et al. 2021), and it has been suggested that futures markets may induce convergence shifts among cryptocurrencies (Apergis et al. 2020).

In the specific context of Ethereum on the BitMEX swap, the introduction of the swap has led to decreased price volatility for Ether, increased spot trading volume, and improved market efficiency. Furthermore, the day-of-week effect has diminished while the hour-of-the-day effect has intensified, indicating greater participation from informed institutional traders in Ether spot markets (Alexander et al. 2020). It has also been identified that extreme positive and negative returns in cryptocurrencies are influenced by trading volume, with a Granger causality observed from trading volume to the returns of Bitcoin, Ripple, Ethereum, Litecoin, Nem, Dash, and Stellar at both ends of the return distribution (Bouri et al. 2019).

However, other studies suggest that when accounting for structural breaks, there is no causal link between the growth of COVID-19 and cryptocurrency returns (Sahoo 2021). Evidence also points to asymmetry in return spillover behaviors across different quantiles, suggesting that during market turmoil, investors should adopt trading strategies that consider the magnitude and flow of return spillovers within the cryptocurrency market (Bouri et al. 2021b).

When examining Bitcoin's energy consumption, findings reveal a relationship between Bitcoin's energy use and its returns and trading volumes (Huynh et al. 2021). However, contrary to the notion that energy plays a crucial role in cryptocurrencies, evidence shows a weak connection between energy commodities and cryptocurrencies (Ji et al. 2019b).

Several studies contribute methodologically, indicating that machine learning algorithms (MLAs) should be employed for better forecasting of Bitcoin futures prices and volatility, as they outperform traditional models like ARIMA and random walk in predicting Bitcoin futures prices (Akyildirim et al. 2021b). Additionally, the non-homogeneous hidden Markov (NHHM) model with four states is recommended, emphasizing the presence of a predictor with state-dependent, time-varying predictive power (Koki et al. 2022).

Finally, for forecasting the Value-at-Risk (VaR) of Bitcoin, Litecoin, and Ethereum, the Laplace GAS specification, which accounts for volatility and asymmetric responses to both positive and negative volatility, demonstrates superior performance across most levels (Liu et al. 2020).

Volatility remains a key characteristic of the cryptocurrency market, which is also addressed in this literature review. The introduction of Bitcoin futures has been associated with increased volatility, liquidity, and kurtosis in the Bitcoin spot market, while simultaneously exerting a downward effect on Bitcoin returns and skewness (Jalan et al. 2021). Investors looking to invest in cryptocurrencies characterized by higher idiosyncratic volatility may achieve greater profits, as this volatility is positively correlated with cryptocurrency returns (Zhang and Li, 2020). The literature review also indicates that the volatility connectedness within the cryptocurrency market, as well as between cryptocurrencies and other asset classes, fluctuates depending on time and market conditions (Ahmed, 2021; Bouri et al., 2021a; Gemici and Polat, 2020; Xu et al., 2021). For example, Bitcoin tends to positively impact developed markets across various market conditions, while emerging markets exhibit an asymmetric response to Bitcoin's volatility (Ahmed, 2021). Additionally, the volatility connectedness between cryptocurrencies and traditional currencies is not static; it tends to emerge during periods of economic and financial instability (Andrada-Félix et al., 2020). During the COVID-19 pandemic, Bitcoin, Ethereum, and Ripple acted as net transmitters of returns and volatility, whereas fiat currencies like the Euro, Yuan, and GBP were net receivers. However, the overall return and volatility connectedness is dynamic and changes over time (Umar et al., 2021).

Moreover, research shows that Bitcoin's past realized volatilities (RV) and jumps play a significant role in predicting its future realized volatility (Qiu et al., 2021). Bitcoin's volatility is a major contributor to the overall volatility in the cryptocurrency market (Dimpfl and Elshiaty, 2021). The spillover patterns of volatility in the cryptocurrency market vary, as the return and volatility structures differ among various cryptocurrencies (Sensoy et al., 2021). Notably, larger cryptocurrencies like Bitcoin, Ethereum, and Litecoin both receive and transmit volatility spillovers within the market (Polat and Günay, 2021). Interestingly, even low-capitalized cryptocurrencies can act as transmitters of volatility connectedness, as seen with Maidsafe Coin (Yi et al., 2018).

3.8. Cryptocurrency Portfolios

When it comes to constructing cryptocurrency portfolios, research indicates that portfolios composed solely of cryptocurrencies can benefit from strategic selection compared to naive portfolios, resulting in improved Sharpe ratios and average returns (Tavares et al., 2020). Given the speculative nature of the cryptocurrency market, all investors—both professional and individual—should focus on optimizing their cryptocurrency portfolios to enhance performance by minimizing variance (Schellinger, 2020). For instance, professional portfolio managers might aim to create a global minimum variance portfolio, while individual investors, with fewer resources, may prefer investing in market cap portfolios of coins rather than tokens due to their superior Omega ratios (Schellinger, 2020).

However, there is evidence suggesting that constructing a portfolio consisting exclusively of cryptocurrencies may entail significant risks, as Bitcoin and altcoin prices are highly correlated (Demir et al., 2020b; Yang et al., 2020). Further findings indicate that employing a two-sided Weibull distribution for estimating Value-at-Risk (VaR) in a cryptocurrency portfolio that includes Bitcoin, Ripple, Dash, and Litecoin outperforms other benchmark methods, as it effectively captures the unique characteristics of cryptocurrencies' time series, such as volatility clustering, heavy tails, skewness, and extreme volatility (Silahli et al., 2021). Additionally, an algorithm based on vine copulas for estimating VaR and Expected Shortfall (ES) in a cryptocurrency portfolio has demonstrated strong performance (Trucíos et al., 2020). Furthermore, the Black-Litterman model with variance-based constraints (VBCs) has shown superior performance compared to traditional benchmarks, addressing the challenges portfolio theory faces when applied to cryptocurrency portfolios, particularly due to higher estimation errors in parameters (Platanakis and Urquhart, 2019).

3.9. Future Research Directions

In the realm of cryptocurrency literature that explores cryptocurrencies as diversifiers, hedgers, and safe havens, there are notable gaps that warrant further investigation. Specifically, there is a need to explore the potential role of stablecoins as diversifiers, hedges, or safe havens (Wang et al., 2020), as well as to analyze the volatility of stablecoins in greater depth (Grobys et al., 2021). Additional research is also necessary to determine whether the stability of stablecoins is time-varying and to assess if new-generation stablecoins exhibit greater stability compared to their predecessors (Hoang and Baur, 2021). Future research is crucial for exploring the relationships between cryptocurrencies and various asset classes, including equities, bonds, currencies, and commodities (Bouri et al. 2021a; Cao and Xie 2021; Demiralay and Bayracı 2020; González et al. 2021; Hsu et al. 2021). Specifically, there is a need to investigate these relationships in less examined stock markets, such as those in Africa (Kumah and Odei-Mensah 2021) and Islamic markets (Aloui et al. 2021), as well as to consider broader commodity (Kumah and Mensah 2020) and currency markets (López-Cabarcos et al. 2021). Future studies should also analyze a larger sample of cryptocurrencies (Charfeddine et al. 2020; Jiang et al. 2021a).

Moreover, it is essential to further assess the environmental sustainability of various cryptocurrencies beyond Bitcoin, as they exhibit different characteristics, including varying carbon footprints and energy consumption levels, which influence their relationships with energy and utility companies (Corbet et al. 2021). This analysis will aid green investors in determining whether to include cryptocurrencies in their portfolios.

Despite the increasing contributions to cryptocurrency literature, additional research is needed to explore the potential for hedging Bitcoin and other cryptocurrencies with different assets (Majdoub et al. 2021) and to analyze their hedging capabilities against other markets, particularly during economic downturns (Kinkyo 2020; Jareño et al. 2021). The diversification and safe-haven properties of cryptocurrencies also warrant further investigation (González et al. 2021). For example, researchers should examine the time-variant safe-haven properties of cryptocurrencies (Jareño et al. 2020) and the factors driving the variability in their safe-haven and hedging properties concerning certain stock indices, such as those in the US (Bouri et al. 2020d). Additionally, the diversification benefits in both emerging and advanced economies should be explored in the context of cryptocurrency regulation (Akhtaruzzaman et al. 2020).

Given the multitude of cryptocurrencies available, it is important to investigate the overall causal relationships among them (Kim et al. 2021) and to delve deeper into cryptocurrency futures and options (Qiao et al. 2020). There is also a need to examine the relationship between spillover risk and market capitalization (Moratis 2021) and to analyze the interconnections between liquidity changes and price volatility to better understand cryptocurrency price behavior (Katsiampa et al. 2019).

Future studies should also focus on the effects of liquidity and transaction costs on optimal portfolio rebalancing and diversification involving cryptocurrencies (Ma et al. 2020). Investigating the asymmetric effects during bull and bear market periods and their implications for portfolio management is also crucial (Demir et al. 2020b). Furthermore, the literature emphasizes the need to understand how size, frequency, and timing of jumps and co-jumps influence correlations within the cryptocurrency market (Mensi et al. 2020a).

Additional research is necessary to understand why and how cryptocurrencies respond differently to various types of uncertainty (Colon et al. 2021). Future studies should consider the impacts of monetary and fiscal policy uncertainty on cryptocurrency returns and volatility (Bedi and Nashier 2020; Bhuiyan et al. 2021; Gozgor et al. 2019) and analyze how cryptocurrencies with high and low market capitalizations react to changes in Twitter-Based Economic Uncertainty (TEU) and Twitter-Based Market Uncertainty (TMU) (Aharon et al. 2022), as well as shifts in the Economic Policy Uncertainty Index (EPU) and other uncertainty indices (Al-Yahyaee et al. 2019; Jareño et al. 2020; Wang et al. 2021). It is also important to assess whether uncertainty is priced across different cryptocurrency markets (Aharon et al. 2022).

Research should further explore the non-linear responses of Bitcoin to high-frequency news sentiment (Rognone et al. 2020) and the potential bidirectional relationship between investor sentiment and cryptocurrencies, particularly Bitcoin (López-Cabarcos et al. 2021). There is also a need to investigate investor sentiment using various proxies, including Google Search trends, VIX, Tweets, surveys, and their impact on cryptocurrency price dynamics (Pho et al. 2021).

The increasing application of machine learning techniques in this field is evident; however, future research should focus on developing more advanced deep learning algorithms and machine learning methods, such as XGBoost (Huynh 2021; Huynh et al. 2020a; Sun et al. 2020). There are indications to further utilize methodologies such as inverse volatility (IV), l2-norm constrained minimum variance (NMV), minimum variance (MV), l2-norm constrained maximum decorrelation (NMC), risk parity (RP), and maximum diversification (MD) for assessing portfolio construction with cryptocurrency allocations (Huynh et al. 2020b). Additionally, it is crucial to analyze the shifts in the efficient frontier within a three-dimensional framework (mean–variance–skewness), incorporating Bitcoin as a component of the investment opportunity set (Kwon 2020).

Other analytical techniques, including Value-at-Risk (VaR) assessments using a rolling time window approach (Chemkha et al. 2021) and the multivariate factor stochastic volatility model (MFSVM) (Shi et al. 2020), are also recommended for exploring portfolio profit and loss dynamics (Chemkha et al. 2021) and for investigating the interplay between cryptocurrencies and traditional assets (Shi et al. 2020).

4. CONCLUSIONS

Our findings reveal that Finance Research Letters is the most cited journal, aligning with the results of Aysan et al. (2021), but differing from the conclusions of Almeida and Gonçalves (2022). We identify Asia as the leading continent in contributions to the literature on portfolio diversification, hedging, and safe-haven properties in cryptocurrency investments, with China being the most cited country and a major contributor. This contrasts with the findings of Almeida and Gonçalves (2022), García-Corral et al. (2022), Jiang et al. (2021b), and Yue et al. (2021), which suggest that Europe has made more contributions and citations. Trinity College Dublin emerges as the institution with the highest citation count on this research topic.

Our results indicate that (1) cryptocurrencies can serve as hedges against stocks, fiat currencies, geopolitical risks, and Economic Policy Uncertainty (EPU) risk, although these properties fluctuate over time; (2) cryptocurrencies exhibit diversification and safe-haven characteristics, but these vary with time and market conditions; (3) investors should consider Gold, the European carbon market, CBOE Bitcoin futures, and crude oil as hedges against unexpected fluctuations in the cryptocurrency market; (4) uncertainty is a significant factor influencing cryptocurrency returns; (5) stablecoins may function as safe havens and diversifiers, contributing to market efficiency, although they demonstrate an unstable peg to the US dollar; (6) individual investors might prefer investing in coins with larger market capitalizations rather than tokens, due to their superior Omega ratio.

This study is valuable for researchers, investors, analysts, regulators, and academics. Our findings offer researchers and academics a structured framework for networking within research outlets and literature strands, providing time-trended information relevant for future studies on portfolio diversification, hedging, and safe-haven properties of cryptocurrency investments. Additionally, it presents investors and analysts with a crucial compilation of practical insights to enhance their investment strategies, while also offering regulators guidance for effective cryptocurrency market regulation.

A limitation of our research is the reliance on a single database (WoS). However, based on our quality criteria (ABS journal guide list), there were no significant contributions from other databases (Scopus). Future updates are necessary to maintain relevance in identifying research trends and unresolved inquiries, as well as to debate current and future research directions. By clustering our literature, we have clarified existing findings and potential future avenues; further (sub) clustering could yield new insights with significant scientific contributions.

For future research directions, particularly in light of the recent UST stablecoin collapse and the Russia-Ukraine War, we emphasize the need to investigate whether the stability of stablecoins is time-varying and their potential roles as diversifiers, hedges, or safe havens. Moreover, a critical examination of the underlying events and their causes should be conducted in the context of the 2022 crash of Bitcoin and other cryptocurrencies. The relationship between value conservation and returns may be significantly discordant in crypto markets, affecting volatility (Appel and Grabinski 2011). As Klinkova and Grabinski (2017) argue, the resulting market instability can lead to chaotic behaviour, which presents mathematical challenges and differs markedly from randomness in investment modelling.

REFERENCES

Aharon, D. Y., Demir, E., Chi, K. M. L., & Zaremba, A. (2022). Twitter-Based Uncertainty and Cryptocurrency Returns. *Research in International Business and Finance*, *59*, 101546. DOI: 10.1016/j.ribaf.2021.101546

Ahelegbey, D. F., Giudici, P., & Mojtahedi, F. (2021). Tail Risk Measurement in Crypto-Asset Markets. *International Review of Financial Analysis*, *73*, 101604. DOI: 10.1016/j.irfa.2020.101604

Ahmed, W. M. A. (2021). Stock Market Reactions to Upside and Downside Volatility of Bitcoin: A Quantile Analysis. *The North American Journal of Economics and Finance*, *57*, 101379. DOI: 10.1016/j.najef.2021.101379

Ahn, Y., & Kim, D. (2021). Emotional Trading in the Cryptocurrency Market. *Finance Research Letters*, *42*, 101912. DOI: 10.1016/j.frl.2020.101912

Akhtaruzzaman, M., Sensoy, A., & Corbet, S. (2020). The Influence of Bitcoin on Portfolio Diversification and Design. *Finance Research Letters*, *37*, 101344. DOI: 10.1016/j.frl.2019.101344

Akyildirim, E., Aysan, A. F., Cepni, O., & Pinar Ceyhan Darendeli, S. (2021a). Do Investor Sentiments Drive Cryptocurrency Prices? *Economics Letters*, *206*, 109980. DOI: 10.1016/j.econlet.2021.109980

Akyildirim, E., Cepni, O., Corbet, S., & Uddin, G. S. (2021b). Forecasting Mid-Price Movement of Bitcoin Futures Using Machine Learning. *Annals of Operations Research*, •••, 1–32. PMID: 34316087

Al-Yahyaee, K. H., Rehman, M. U., Mensi, W., & Idries, M. W. A.-J. (2019). Can Uncertainty Indices Predict Bitcoin Prices? A Revisited Analysis Using Partial and MultivariateWavelet Approaches. *The North American Journal of Economics and Finance*, *49*, 47–56. DOI: 10.1016/j.najef.2019.03.019

Alexander, C., Choi, J., Massie, H. R. A., & Sohn, S. (2020). Price Discovery and Microstructure in Ether Spot and Derivative Markets. *International Review of Financial Analysis*, *71*, 101506. DOI: 10.1016/j.irfa.2020.101506

Almeida, J. (2021). Cryptocurrencies and Financial Markets–Extant Literature and Future Venues. *European Journal of Economics Finance and Administrative Sciences*, *109*, 29–40.

Almeida, J., & Gonçalves, T. C. (2022). A Systematic Literature Review of Volatility and Risk Management on Cryptocurrency Investment: A Methodological Point of View. *Risks*, *10*(5), 107. DOI: 10.3390/risks10050107

Aloui, C., Hamida, H., & Yarovaya, L. (2021). Are Islamic Gold-Backed Cryptocurrencies Different? *Finance Research Letters*, *39*, 101615. DOI: 10.1016/j.frl.2020.101615

Andrada-Félix, J., Fernandez-Perez, A., & Sosvilla-Rivero, S. (2020). Distant or Close Cousins: Connectedness between Cryptocurrencies and Traditional Currencies Volatilities. *Journal of International Financial Markets, Institutions and Money*, *67*, 101219. DOI: 10.1016/j.intfin.2020.101219

Angerer, M., Hoffmann, C. H., Neitzert, F., & Kraus, S. (2020). Objective and Subjective Risks of Investing into Cryptocurrencies. *Finance Research Letters*, *40*, 101737. DOI: 10.1016/j.frl.2020.101737

Ante, L., Fiedler, I., & Strehle, E. (2021). The Influence of Stablecoin Issuances on Cryptocurrency Markets. *Finance Research Letters*, *41*, 101867. DOI: 10.1016/j.frl.2020.101867

Apergis, N., Koutmos, D., & Payne, J. E. (2020). Convergence in Cryptocurrency Prices? The Role of Market Microstructure. *Finance Research Letters*, *40*, 101685. DOI: 10.1016/j.frl.2020.101685

Appel, D., & Grabinski, M. (2011). The origin of financial crisis: A wrong definition of value. *Portuguese Journal of Quantitative Methods*, *2*, 33–51.

Aysan, A. F., Demirta¸s, H. B., & Saraç, M. (2021). The Ascent of Bitcoin: Bibliometric Analysis of Bitcoin Research. *Journal of Risk and Financial Management*, *14*(9), 427. DOI: 10.3390/jrfm14090427

Balli, F., de Bruin, A., Md, I. H. C., & Naeem, M. A. (2020). Connectedness of Cryptocurrencies and Prevailing Uncertainties. *Applied Economics Letters*, *27*(16), 1316–1322. DOI: 10.1080/13504851.2019.1678724

Bariviera, A. F., & Merediz-Solà, I. (2021). Where Do We Stand in Cryptocurrencies Economic Research? A Survey Based on Hybrid Analysis. *Journal of Economic Surveys*, *35*(2), 377–407. DOI: 10.1111/joes.12412

Bartolacci, F., Caputo, A., & Soverchia, M. (2020). Sustainability and Financial Performance of Small and Medium Sized Enterprises: A Bibliometric and Systematic Literature Review. *Business Strategy and the Environment*, *29*(3), 1297–1309. DOI: 10.1002/bse.2434

Bazán-Palomino, W. (2020). How Are Bitcoin Forks Related to Bitcoin? *Finance Research Letters*, *40*, 101723. DOI: 10.1016/j.frl.2020.101723

Bedi, P., & Nashier, T. (2020). On the Investment Credentials of Bitcoin: A Cross-Currency Perspective. *Research in International Business and Finance*, *51*, 101087. DOI: 10.1016/j.ribaf.2019.101087

B˛edowska-Sójka, B., & Kliber, A. (2021). Is There One Safe-Haven for Various Turbulences? The Evidence from Gold, Bitcoin and Ether. *The North American Journal of Economics and Finance*, *56*, 101390. DOI: 10.1016/j.najef.2021.101390

Bhuiyan, R. A., Husain, A., & Zhang, C. (2021). A Wavelet Approach for Causal Relationship between Bitcoin and Conventional Asset Classes. *Resources Policy*, *71*, 101971. DOI: 10.1016/j.resourpol.2020.101971

Białkowski, J˛. (2020). Cryptocurrencies in Institutional Investors' Portfolios: Evidence from Industry Stop-Loss Rules. *Economics Letters*, *191*, 108834. DOI: 10.1016/j.econlet.2019.108834

Bouri, E., Chi, K. M. L., Lucey, B., & Roubaud, D. (2019). Trading Volume and the Predictability of Return and Volatility in the Cryptocurrency Market. *Finance Research Letters*, *29*, 340–346. DOI: 10.1016/j.frl.2018.08.015

Bouri, E., Gabauer, D., Gupta, R., & Tiwari, A. K. (2021a). Volatility Connectedness of Major Cryptocurrencies: The Role of Investor Happiness. *Journal of Behavioral and Experimental Finance*, *30*, 100463. DOI: 10.1016/j.jbef.2021.100463

Bouri, E., Kristoufek, L., & Azoury, N. (2022). Bitcoin and S&P500: Co-Movements of High-Order Moments in the Time-Frequency Domain. *PLoS One*, *17*(11), e0277924. DOI: 10.1371/journal.pone.0277924 PMID: 36413562

Bouri, E., Lucey, B., & Roubaud, D. (2020a). Cryptocurrencies and the Downside Risk in Equity Investments. *Finance Research Letters*, *33*, 101211. DOI: 10.1016/j.frl.2019.06.009

Bouri, E., Lucey, B., & Roubaud, D. (2020b). The Volatility Surprise of Leading Cryptocurrencies: Transitory and Permanent Linkages. *Finance Research Letters*, *33*, 101188. DOI: 10.1016/j.frl.2019.05.006

Bouri, E., Roubaud, D., & Syed, J. H. S. (2020c). Do Bitcoin and Other Cryptocurrencies Jump Together? *The Quarterly Review of Economics and Finance*, *76*, 396–409. DOI: 10.1016/j.qref.2019.09.003

Bouri, E., Saeed, T., Vo, X. V., & Roubaud, D. (2021b). Quantile Connectedness in the Cryptocurrency Market. *Journal of International Financial Markets, Institutions and Money*, *71*, 101302. DOI: 10.1016/j.intfin.2021.101302

Bouri, E., Syed, J. H. S., & Roubaud, D. (2020d). Cryptocurrencies as Hedges and Safe-Havens for US Equity Sectors. *The Quarterly Review of Economics and Finance*, *75*, 294–307. DOI: 10.1016/j.qref.2019.05.001

Bouri, E., Vo, X. V., & Saeed, T. (2021c). Return Equicorrelation in the Cryptocurrency Market: Analysis and Determinants. *Finance Research Letters*, *38*, 101497. DOI: 10.1016/j.frl.2020.101497

Burggraf, T. (2021). Beyond Risk Parity–A Machine Learning-Based Hierarchical Risk Parity Approach on Cryptocurrencies. *Finance Research Letters*, *38*, 101523. DOI: 10.1016/j.frl.2020.101523

Cao, G., & Xie, W. (2021). The Impact of the Shutdown Policy on the Asymmetric Interdependence Structure and Risk Transmission of Cryptocurrency and China's Financial Market. *The North American Journal of Economics and Finance*, *58*, 101514. DOI: 10.1016/j.najef.2021.101514

Caputo, A., Marzi, G., Maley, J., & Silic, M. (2019). Ten Years of Conflict Management Research 2007-2017: An Update on Themes, Concepts and Relationships. *International Journal of Conflict Management*, *30*(1), 87–110. DOI: 10.1108/IJCMA-06-2018-0078

Charfeddine, L., Benlagha, N., & Maouchi, Y. (2020). Investigating the Dynamic Relationship between Cryptocurrencies and Conventional Assets: Implications for Financial Investors. *Economic Modelling*, *85*, 198–217. DOI: 10.1016/j.econmod.2019.05.016

Chemkha, R., BenSaïda, A., Ghorbel, A., & Tayachi, T. (2021). Hedge and Safe Haven Properties during COVID-19: Evidence from Bitcoin and Gold. *The Quarterly Review of Economics and Finance*, *82*, 71–85. DOI: 10.1016/j.qref.2021.07.006 PMID: 34898971

Colon, F., Kim, C., Kim, H., & Kim, W. (2021). The Effect of Political and Economic Uncertainty on the Cryptocurrency Market. *Finance Research Letters*, *39*, 101621. DOI: 10.1016/j.frl.2020.101621

Conlon, T., Corbet, S., & McGee, R. J. (2020). Are Cryptocurrencies a Safe Haven for Equity Markets? An International Perspective from the COVID-19 Pandemic. *Research in International Business and Finance*, *54*, 101248. DOI: 10.1016/j.ribaf.2020.101248 PMID: 34170988

Conlon, T., Corbet, S., & McGee, R. J. (2021). Inflation and Cryptocurrencies Revisited: A Time-Scale Analysis. *Economics Letters*, *206*, 109996. DOI: 10.1016/j.econlet.2021.109996

Corbet, S., Hou, Y. G., Hu, Y., Larkin, C., & Oxley, L. (2020a). Any Port in a Storm: Cryptocurrency Safe-Havens during the COVID-19 Pandemic. *Economics Letters*, *194*, 109377. DOI: 10.1016/j.econlet.2020.109377 PMID: 32834235

Corbet, S., Katsiampa, P., & Chi, K. M. L. (2020b). Measuring Quantile Dependence and Testing Directional Predictability between Bitcoin, Altcoins and Traditional Financial Assets. *International Review of Financial Analysis*, *71*, 101571. DOI: 10.1016/j.irfa.2020.101571

Corbet, S., Larkin, C., & Lucey, B. (2020c). The Contagion Effects of the COVID-19 Pandemic: Evidence from Gold and Cryptocurrencies. *Finance Research Letters*, *35*, 101554. DOI: 10.1016/j.frl.2020.101554 PMID: 38620241

Corbet, S., Lucey, B., Urquhart, A., & Yarovaya, L. (2019). Cryptocurrencies as a Financial Asset: A Systematic Analysis. *International Review of Financial Analysis*, *62*, 182–199. DOI: 10.1016/j.irfa.2018.09.003

Corbet, S., Lucey, B., & Yarovaya, L. (2021). Bitcoin-Energy Markets Interrelationships—New Evidence. *Resources Policy*, *70*, 101916. DOI: 10.1016/j.resourpol.2020.101916

Demir, E., Bilgin, M. H., Karabulut, G., & Doker, A. C. (2020a). The Relationship between Cryptocurrencies and COVID-19 Pandemic. *Eurasian Economic Review*, *10*(3), 349–360. DOI: 10.1007/s40822-020-00154-1

Demir, E., Simonyan, S., García-Gómez, C. D., & Chi, K. M. L. (2020b). The Asymmetric Effect of Bitcoin on Altcoins: Evidence from the Nonlinear Autoregressive Distributed Lag (NARDL) Model. *Finance Research Letters*, *40*, 101754. DOI: 10.1016/j.frl.2020.101754

Demiralay, S., & Bayracı, S. (2020). Should Stock Investors Include Cryptocurrencies in Their Portfolios after All? Evidence from a Conditional Diversification Benefits Measure. *International Journal of Finance & Economics*, *26*(4), 6188–6204. DOI: 10.1002/ijfe.2116

Demiralay, S., & Golitsis, P. (2021). On the Dynamic Equicorrelations in Cryptocurrency Market. *The Quarterly Review of Economics and Finance*, *80*, 524–533. DOI: 10.1016/j.qref.2021.04.002

Dimpfl, Thomas, and Dalia Elshiaty. 2021. Volatility Discovery in Cryptocurrency Markets. Journal of Risk Finance. ahead-of-print.

Ding, Ying, Ronald Rousseau, and DietmarWolfram. 2014. Measuring Scholarly Impact. Cham: Springer.

Disli, M., Nagayev, R., Salim, K., Rizkiah, S. K., & Aysan, A. F. (2021). In Search of Safe Haven Assets during COVID-19 Pandemic: An Empirical Analysis of Different Investor Types. *Research in International Business and Finance*, *58*, 101461. DOI: 10.1016/j.ribaf.2021.101461 PMID: 36540341

Fakhfekh, M., Jeribi, A., Ghorbel, A., & Hachicha, N. (2021). Hedging Stock Market Prices with WTI, Gold, VIX and Cryptocurrencies: A Comparison between DCC, ADCC and GO-GARCH Models. *International Journal of Emerging Markets*.

Fang, F., Chung, W., Ventre, C., Basios, M., Kanthan, L., Li, L., & Wu, F. (2021). Ascertaining Price Formation in Cryptocurrency Markets with Machine Learning. *European Journal of Finance*, •••, 1–23.

Fang, T., Su, Z., & Yin, L. (2020). Economic Fundamentals or Investor Perceptions? The Role of Uncertainty in Predicting Long-Term Cryptocurrency Volatility. *International Review of Financial Analysis*, *71*, 101566. DOI: 10.1016/j.irfa.2020.101566

Feng, W., Wang, Y., & Zhang, Z. (2018). Informed Trading in the Bitcoin Market. *Finance Research Letters*, *26*, 63–70. DOI: 10.1016/j.frl.2017.11.009

Flori, A. (2019a). Cryptocurrencies in Finance: Review and Applications. *International Journal of Theoretical and Applied Finance*, •••, 22.

Flori, A. (2019b). News and Subjective Beliefs: A Bayesian Approach to Bitcoin Investments. *Research in International Business and Finance*, *50*, 336–356. DOI: 10.1016/j.ribaf.2019.05.007

Galvao, A., Mascarenhas, C., Marques, C., Ferreira, J., & Ratten, V. (2019). Triple Helix and Its Evolution: A Systematic Literature Review. *Journal of Science and Technology Policy Management*, *10*(3), 812–833. DOI: 10.1108/JSTPM-10-2018-0103

García-Corral, F. J., Cordero-García, J. A., de Pablo-Valenciano, J., & Uribe-Toril, J. (2022). A Bibliometric Review of Cryptocurrencies: How Have They Grown? *Financial Innovation*, *8*(1), 1–31. DOI: 10.1186/s40854-021-00306-5 PMID: 35024296

Gemici, E., & Polat, M. (2020). Causality-in-Mean and Causality-in-Variance among Bitcoin, Litecoin, and Ethereum. *Studies in Economics and Finance*, *38*(4), 861–872. DOI: 10.1108/SEF-07-2020-0251

Ghabri, Y., Guesmi, K., & Zantour, A. (2020). Bitcoin and Liquidity Risk Diversification. *Finance Research Letters*, *40*, 101679. DOI: 10.1016/j.frl.2020.101679

Ghorbel, A., & Jeribi, A. (2021a). Investigating the Relationship between Volatilities of Cryptocurrencies and Other Financial Assets. *Decisions in Economics and Finance*, *44*(2), 817–843. DOI: 10.1007/s10203-020-00312-9

Ghorbel, A., & Jeribi, A. (2021b). Volatility Spillovers and Contagion between Energy Sector and Financial Assets during COVID-19 Crisis Period. *Eurasian Economic Review*, *11*(3), 449–467. DOI: 10.1007/s40822-021-00181-6

González, M. O., Jareño, F., & Skinner, F. S.González. (2021). Asymmetric Interdependencies between Large Capital Cryptocurrency and Gold Returns during the COVID-19 Pandemic Crisis. *International Review of Financial Analysis*, *76*, 101773. DOI: 10.1016/j.irfa.2021.101773

Goodell, J. W., & Goutte, S. (2021a). Co-Movement of COVID-19 and Bitcoin: Evidence from Wavelet Coherence Analysis. *Finance Research Letters*, *38*, 101625. DOI: 10.1016/j.frl.2020.101625 PMID: 36569647

Goodell, J. W., & Goutte, S. (2021b). Diversifying Equity with Cryptocurrencies during COVID-19. *International Review of Financial Analysis*, *76*, 101781. DOI: 10.1016/j.irfa.2021.101781

Gozgor, G., Tiwari, A. K., Demir, E., & Akron, S. (2019). The Relationship between Bitcoin Returns and Trade Policy Uncertainty. *Finance Research Letters*, *29*, 75–82. DOI: 10.1016/j.frl.2019.03.016

Grabinski, M., & Klinkova, G. (2019). Wrong use of averages implies wrong results from many heuristic models. *Applied Mathematics*, *10*(7), 605–618. DOI: 10.4236/am.2019.107043

Grabinski, M., & Klinkova, G. (2020). Scrutinizing distributions proves that IQ is inherited and explains the fat tail. *Applied Mathematics*, *11*(10), 957–984. DOI: 10.4236/am.2020.1110063

Grobys, K., Junttila, J., Kolari, J. W., & Sapkota, N. (2021). On the Stability of Stablecoins. *Journal of Empirical Finance*, *64*, 207–223. DOI: 10.1016/j.jempfin.2021.09.002

Guo, X., Lu, F., & Wei, Y. (2021). Capture the Contagion Network of Bitcoin–Evidence from Pre and Mid COVID-19. *Research in International Business and Finance*, *58*, 101484. DOI: 10.1016/j.ribaf.2021.101484 PMID: 34518717

Hairudin, A., Sifat, I. M., Mohamad, A., & Yusof, Y. (2020). Cryptocurrencies: A Survey on Acceptance, Governance and Market Dynamics. *International Journal of Finance & Economics*, *27*(4), 4633–4659. DOI: 10.1002/ijfe.2392

Haq, I. U., Maneengam, A., Chupradit, S., Suksatan, W., & Huo, C. (2021). Economic Policy Uncertainty and Cryptocurrency Market as a Risk Management Avenue: A Systematic Review. *Risks, 9*(9), 163. DOI: 10.3390/risks9090163

Hassan, M. K., Hasan, M. B., & Rashid, M. M. (2021). Using Precious Metals to Hedge Cryptocurrency Policy and Price Uncertainty. *Economics Letters, 206*, 109977. DOI: 10.1016/j.econlet.2021.109977

Hattori, T., & Ishida, R. (2021). Did the Introduction of Bitcoin Futures Crash the Bitcoin Market at the End of 2017? *The North American Journal of Economics and Finance, 56*, 101322. DOI: 10.1016/j.najef.2020.101322

Hoang, L. T., & Baur, D. G. (2021). How Stable Are Stablecoins? *European Journal of Finance*, •••, 1–17.

Holub, M., & Johnson, J. (2019). The Impact of the Bitcoin Bubble of 2017 on Bitcoin's P2P Market. *Finance Research Letters, 29*, 357–362. DOI: 10.1016/j.frl.2018.09.001

Hsu, S. H., Sheu, C., & Yoon, J. (2021). Risk Spillovers between Cryptocurrencies and Traditional Currencies and Gold under Different Global Economic Conditions. *The North American Journal of Economics and Finance, 57*, 101443. DOI: 10.1016/j.najef.2021.101443

Huynh, A. N. Q., Duong, D., Burggraf, T., Hien, T. T. L., & Bui, N. H. (2021). Energy Consumption and Bitcoin Market. *Asia-Pacific Financial Markets, 29*(1), 79–93. DOI: 10.1007/s10690-021-09338-4

Huynh, T. L. D. (2021). Does Bitcoin React to Trump's Tweets? *Journal of Behavioral and Experimental Finance, 31*, 100546. DOI: 10.1016/j.jbef.2021.100546

Huynh, T. L. D., Hille, E., & Nasir, M. A. (2020a). Diversification in the Age of the 4th Industrial Revolution: The Role of Artificial Intelligence, Green Bonds and Cryptocurrencies. *Technological Forecasting and Social Change, 159*, 120188. DOI: 10.1016/j.techfore.2020.120188

Huynh, T. L. D., Nasir, M. A., Vo, X. V., & Nguyen, T. T. (2020b). 'Small Things Matter Most': The Spillover Effects in the Cryptocurrency Market and Gold as a Silver Bullet. *The North American Journal of Economics and Finance, 54*, 101277. DOI: 10.1016/j.najef.2020.101277

Iqbal, N., Fareed, Z., Wan, G., & Shahzad, F. (2021). Asymmetric Nexus between COVID-19 Outbreak in the World and Cryptocurrency Market. *International Review of Financial Analysis, 73*, 101613. DOI: 10.1016/j.irfa.2020.101613 PMID: 38620823

Jalal, R. N. U. D., Alon, I., & Paltrinieri, A. (2021). A Bibliometric Review of Cryptocurrencies as a Financial Asset. *Technology Analysis and Strategic Management*, •••, 1–16.

Jalan, A., Matkovskyy, R., & Urquhart, A. (2021). What Effect Did the Introduction of Bitcoin Futures Have on the Bitcoin Spot Market? *European Journal of Finance*, *27*(13), 1251–1281. DOI: 10.1080/1351847X.2020.1869992

Jareño, F., González, M. O., López, R., & Ramos, A. R. (2021). Cryptocurrencies and Oil Price Shocks: A NARDL Analysis in the COVID-19 Pandemic. *Resources Policy*, *74*, 102281. DOI: 10.1016/j.resourpol.2021.102281 PMID: 34658484

Jareño, F., González, M. O., Tolentino, M., & Sierra, K. (2020). Bitcoin and Gold Price Returns: A Quantile Regression and NARDL Analysis. *Resources Policy*, *67*, 101666. DOI: 10.1016/j.resourpol.2020.101666

Jeribi, A., & Ghorbel, A. (2021). Forecasting Developed and BRICS Stock Markets with Cryptocurrencies and Gold: Generalized Orthogonal Generalized Autoregressive Conditional Heteroskedasticity and Generalized Autoregressive Score Analysis. *International Journal of Emerging Markets*.

Ji, Q., Bouri, E., Chi, K. M. L., & Roubaud, D. (2019a). Dynamic Connectedness and Integration in Cryptocurrency Markets. *International Review of Financial Analysis*, *63*, 257–272. DOI: 10.1016/j.irfa.2018.12.002

Ji, Q., Bouri, E., Roubaud, D., & Kristoufek, L. (2019b). Information Interdependence among Energy, Cryptocurrency and Major Commodity Markets. *Energy Economics*, *81*, 1042–1055. DOI: 10.1016/j.eneco.2019.06.005

Jiang, S., Li, X., & Wang, S. (2021). Exploring Evolution Trends in Cryptocurrency Study: From Underlying Technology to Economic Applications. *Finance Research Letters*, *38*, 101532. DOI: 10.1016/j.frl.2020.101532

Jiang, Y., Lie, J., Wang, J., & Mu, J. (2021a). Revisiting the Roles of Cryptocurrencies in Stock Markets: A Quantile Coherency Perspective. *Economic Modelling*, *95*, 21–34. DOI: 10.1016/j.econmod.2020.12.002

Jiang, Y., Wu, L., Tian, G., & Nie, H. (2021b). Do Cryptocurrencies Hedge against EPU and the Equity Market Volatility during COVID-19?–New Evidence from Quantile Coherency Analysis. *Journal of International Financial Markets, Institutions and Money*, *72*, 101324. DOI: 10.1016/j.intfin.2021.101324

Jin, X., Zhu, K., Yang, X., & Wang, S. (2021). Estimating the Reaction of Bitcoin Prices to the Uncertainty of Fiat Currency. *Research in International Business and Finance*, *58*, 101451. DOI: 10.1016/j.ribaf.2021.101451

Katsiampa, P., Corbet, S., & Lucey, B. (2019). High Frequency Volatility Co-Movements in Cryptocurrency Markets. *Journal of International Financial Markets, Institutions and Money*, *62*, 35–52. DOI: 10.1016/j.intfin.2019.05.003

Khelifa, S. B., Guesmi, K., & Urom, C. (2021). Exploring the relationship between cryptocurrencies and hedge funds during COVID-19 crisis. *International Review of Financial Analysis*, *76*, 101777. DOI: 10.1016/j.irfa.2021.101777 PMID: 36569817

Kim, M. J., Canh, N. P., & Park, S. Y. (2021). Causal Relationship among Cryptocurrencies: A Conditional Quantile Approach. *Finance Research Letters*, *42*, 1–8. DOI: 10.1016/j.frl.2020.101879

Kinkyo, T. (2020). Hedging Capabilities of Bitcoin for Asian Currencies. *International Journal of Finance & Economics*, *27*(2), 1769–1784. DOI: 10.1002/ijfe.2241

Klinkova, G., & Grabinski, M. (2017). Due to Instability Gambling is the best Model for most Financial Products. *Archives of Business Research*, *5*(3), 255–261. DOI: 10.14738/abr.53.3029

Koki, C., Leonardos, S., & Piliouras, G. (2022). Exploring the predictability of cryptocurrencies via Bayesian hidden Markov models. *Research in International Business and Finance*, *59*, 101554. DOI: 10.1016/j.ribaf.2021.101554

Kumah, S. P., & Mensah, J. O. (2020). Are cryptocurrencies connected to gold? A wavelet-based quantile-in-quantile approach. *International Journal of Finance & Economics*, *27*(3), 3640–3659. DOI: 10.1002/ijfe.2342

Kumah, S. P., & Odei-Mensah, J. (2021). Are Cryptocurrencies and African stock markets integrated? *The Quarterly Review of Economics and Finance*, *81*, 330–341. DOI: 10.1016/j.qref.2021.06.022

Kumar, A., Iqbal, N., Mitra, S. K., Kristoufek, L., & Bouri, E. (2022). Connectedness among major cryptocurrencies in standard times and during the COVID-19 outbreak. *Journal of International Financial Markets, Institutions and Money*, *77*, 101523. DOI: 10.1016/j.intfin.2022.101523

Kwon, J. H. (2020). Tail behavior of Bitcoin, the dollar, gold and the stock market index. *Journal of International Financial Markets, Institutions and Money*, *67*, 101202. DOI: 10.1016/j.intfin.2020.101202

Kyriazis, N., Papadamou, S., & Corbet, S. (2020). A Systematic Review of the Bubble Dynamics of Cryptocurrency Prices. *Research in International Business and Finance*, *54*, 101254. DOI: 10.1016/j.ribaf.2020.101254

Lahiani, A., jeribi, A., & Jlassi, N. B. (2021). Nonlinear Tail Dependence in Cryptocurrency-Stock Market Returns: The Role of Bitcoin Futures. *Research in International Business and Finance*, *56*, 101351. DOI: 10.1016/j.ribaf.2020.101351

Li, R., Li, S., Yuan, D., & Zhu, H. (2021). Investor Attention and Cryptocurrency: Evidence from Wavelet-Based Quantile Granger Causality Analysis. *Research in International Business and Finance*, *56*, 101389. DOI: 10.1016/j.ribaf.2021.101389

Liang, X., Yang, Y., & Wang, J. 2016. Internet Finance: A Systematic Literature Review and Bibliometric Analysis. Proceedings of the International Conference on Electronic Business (ICEB) 38. Available online: https://aisel.aisnet.org/iceb2016/38 (accessed on 14 November 2022).

Lin, Z. Y. (2021). Investor Attention and Cryptocurrency Performance. *Finance Research Letters*, *40*, 101702. DOI: 10.1016/j.frl.2020.101702

Linnenluecke, M. K., Marrone, M., & Singh, A. K. (2020). Conducting Systematic Literature Reviews and Bibliometric Analyses. *Australian Journal of Management*, *45*(2), 175–194. DOI: 10.1177/0312896219877678

Liu, R., Wan, S., Zhang, Z., & Zhao, X. (2020). Is the Introduction of Futures Responsible for the Crash of Bitcoin? *Finance Research Letters*, *34*, 101259. DOI: 10.1016/j.frl.2019.08.007

Liu, W., Semeyutin, A., Chi, K. M. L., & Gozgor, G. (2020). Forecasting Value-at-Risk of Cryptocurrencies with RiskMetrics Type Models. *Research in International Business and Finance*, *54*, 101259. DOI: 10.1016/j.ribaf.2020.101259

López-Cabarcos, M. Á., Pérez-Pico, A. M., Piñeiro-Chousa, J., & Ševi'c, A. (2021). Bitcoin Volatility, Stock Market and Investor Sentiment. Are They Connected? *Finance Research Letters*, *38*, 101399. DOI: 10.1016/j.frl.2019.101399

Ma, Y., Ahmad, F., Liu, M., & Wang, Z. (2020). Portfolio Optimization in the Era of Digital Financialization Using Cryptocurrencies. *Technological Forecasting and Social Change*, *161*, 120265. DOI: 10.1016/j.techfore.2020.120265 PMID: 32863444

Majdoub, J., Ben Sassi, S., & Bejaoui, A. (2021). Can Fiat Currencies Really Hedge Bitcoin? Evidence from Dynamic Short-Term Perspective. *Decisions in Economics and Finance*, *44*(2), 789–816. DOI: 10.1007/s10203-020-00314-7

Mariana, C. D., Ekaputra, I. A., & Husodo, Z. A. (2021). Are Bitcoin and Ethereum Safe-Havens for Stocks during the COVID-19 Pandemic? *Finance Research Letters*, *38*, 101798. DOI: 10.1016/j.frl.2020.101798 PMID: 33100925

Matkovskyy, R., Jalan, A., Dowling, M., & Bouraoui, T. (2021). From Bottom Ten to Top Ten: The Role of Cryptocurrencies in Enhancing Portfolio Return of Poorly Performing Stocks. *Finance Research Letters*, *38*, 101405. DOI: 10.1016/j.frl.2019.101405

Mensi, W., Al-Yahyaee, K. H., Idries, M. W. A.-J., Vo, X. V., & Kang, S. H. (2020a). Dynamic Volatility Transmission and Portfolio Management across Major Cryptocurrencies: Evidence from Hourly Data. *The North American Journal of Economics and Finance*, *54*, 101285. DOI: 10.1016/j.najef.2020.101285

Mensi, W., Rehman, M. U., Maitra, D., Al-Yahyaee, K. H., & Sensoy, A. (2020b). Does Bitcoin Co-Move and Share Risk with Sukuk and World and Regional Islamic Stock Markets? Evidence Using a Time-Frequency Approach. *Research in International Business and Finance*, *53*, 101230. DOI: 10.1016/j.ribaf.2020.101230

Mensi, W., Sensoy, A., Aslan, A., & Kang, S. H. (2019). High-Frequency Asymmetric Volatility Connectedness between Bitcoin and Major Precious Metals Markets. *The North American Journal of Economics and Finance*, *50*, 101031. DOI: 10.1016/j.najef.2019.101031

Milian, E. Z., Spinola, M. M., & Carvalho, M. M. (2019). Fintechs: A Literature Review and Research Agenda. *Electronic Commerce Research and Applications*, *34*, 100833. DOI: 10.1016/j.elerap.2019.100833

Moghadam, S., Reza, M., Safari, H., & Yousefi, N. (2021). Clustering Quality Management Models and Methods: Systematic Literature Review and Text-Mining Analysis Approach. *Total Quality Management & Business Excellence*, *32*(3-4), 241–264. DOI: 10.1080/14783363.2018.1540927

Mokni, K. (2021). When, Where, and How Economic Policy Uncertainty Predicts Bitcoin Returns and Volatility? A Quantiles-Based Analysis. *The Quarterly Review of Economics and Finance*, *80*, 65–73. DOI: 10.1016/j.qref.2021.01.017

Moratis, G. (2021). Quantifying the Spillover Effect in the Cryptocurrency Market. *Finance Research Letters*, *38*, 101534. DOI: 10.1016/j.frl.2020.101534

Naeem, M., Bouri, E., Boako, G., & Roubaud, D. (2020). Tail Dependence in the Return-Volume of Leading Cryptocurrencies. *Finance Research Letters*, *36*, 101326. DOI: 10.1016/j.frl.2019.101326

Naeem, M. A., Farid, S., Balli, F., & Syed, J. H. S. (2021a). Hedging the Downside Risk of Commodities through Cryptocurrencies. *Applied Economics Letters*, *28*(2), 153–160. DOI: 10.1080/13504851.2020.1739609

Naeem, M. A., Qureshi, S., Rehman, M. U., & Balli, F. (2021b). COVID-19 and Cryptocurrency Market: Evidence from Quantile Connectedness. *Applied Economics, 54*(3), 280–306. DOI: 10.1080/00036846.2021.1950908

Nakamoto, S. 2008. Bitcoin: A Peer-to-Peer Electronic Cash System. Available online: https://bitcoin.org/en/bitcoin-paper (accessed on 10 October 2022).

Nguyen, L. H., Chevapatrakul, T., & Yao, K. (2020). Investigating Tail-Risk Dependence in the Cryptocurrency Markets: A LASSO Quantile Regression Approach. *Journal of Empirical Finance, 58*, 333–355. DOI: 10.1016/j.jempfin.2020.06.006

Nguyen, T. V. H., Nguyen, B. T., Nguyen, K. S., & Pham, H. (2019). Asymmetric Monetary Policy Effects on Cryptocurrency Markets. *Research in International Business and Finance, 48*, 335–339. DOI: 10.1016/j.ribaf.2019.01.011

Okorie, D. I., & Lin, B. (2020). Crude Oil Price and Cryptocurrencies: Evidence of Volatility Connectedness and Hedging Strategy. *Energy Economics, 87*, 104703. DOI: 10.1016/j.eneco.2020.104703

Omane-Adjepong, M., & Alagidede, I. P. (2020). Dynamic Linkages and Economic Role of Leading Cryptocurrencies in an Emerging Market. In *Asia-Pacific Financial Markets* (Vol. 27). Springer. DOI: 10.1007/s10690-020-09306-4

Papadamou, S., Kyriazis, N. A., & Tzeremes, P. G. (2021). Non-Linear Causal Linkages of EPU and Gold with Major Cryptocurrencies during Bull and Bear Markets. *The North American Journal of Economics and Finance, 56*, 101343. DOI: 10.1016/j.najef.2020.101343

Philippas, D., Philippas, N., Tziogkidis, P., & Rjiba, H. (2020). Signal-Herding in Cryptocurrencies. *Journal of International Financial Markets, Institutions and Money, 65*, 101191. DOI: 10.1016/j.intfin.2020.101191

Pho, K. H., Ly, S., Lu, R., Van Hoang, T. H., & Wong, W. K. (2021). Is Bitcoin a Better Portfolio Diversifier than Gold? A Copula and Sectoral Analysis for China. *International Review of Financial Analysis, 74*, 101674. DOI: 10.1016/j.irfa.2021.101674

Platanakis, E., & Urquhart, A. (2019). Portfolio Management with Cryptocurrencies: The Role of Estimation Risk. *Economics Letters, 177*, 76–80. DOI: 10.1016/j.econlet.2019.01.019

Polat, O., & Günay, E. K. (2021). Cryptocurrency Connectedness Nexus the COVID-19 Pandemic: Evidence from Time-Frequency Domains. *Studies in Economics and Finance, 38*(5), 946–963. DOI: 10.1108/SEF-01-2021-0011

Qiao, X., Zhu, H., & Hau, L. (2020). Time-Frequency Co-Movement of Cryptocurrency Return and Volatility: Evidence fromWavelet Coherence Analysis. *International Review of Financial Analysis*, *71*, 101541. DOI: 10.1016/j.irfa.2020.101541

Qiu, Y., Wang, Y., & Xie, T. (2021). Forecasting Bitcoin Realized Volatility by Measuring the Spillover Effect among Cryptocurrencies. *Economics Letters*, *208*, 110092. DOI: 10.1016/j.econlet.2021.110092

Quang, N., Binh, T. H. L., & Phuc, C. N. (2020). Influences of Uncertainty on the Returns and Liquidity of Cryptocurrencies: Evidence from a Portfolio Approach. *International Journal of Finance & Economics*, *27*(2), 2497–2513. DOI: 10.1002/ijfe.2283

Raheem, I. D. (2021). COVID-19 Pandemic and the Safe Haven Property of Bitcoin. *The Quarterly Review of Economics and Finance*, *81*, 370–375. DOI: 10.1016/j.qref.2021.06.004

Rialti, R., Marzi, G., Ciappei, C., & Busso, D. (2019). Big Data and Dynamic Capabilities: A Bibliometric Analysis and Systematic Literature Review. *Management Decision*, *57*(8), 2052–2068. DOI: 10.1108/MD-07-2018-0821

Rognone, L., Hyde, S., & Sarah Zhang, S. (2020). News Sentiment in the Cryptocurrency Market: An Empirical Comparison with Forex. *International Review of Financial Analysis*, *69*, 101462. DOI: 10.1016/j.irfa.2020.101462

Sahoo, P. K. (2021). COVID-19 Pandemic and Cryptocurrency Markets: An Empirical Analysis from a Linear and Nonlinear Causal Relationship. *Studies in Economics and Finance*, *38*(2), 454–468. DOI: 10.1108/SEF-09-2020-0385

Scharnowski, S. (2021). Understanding Bitcoin Liquidity. *Finance Research Letters*, *38*, 101477. DOI: 10.1016/j.frl.2020.101477

Schellinger, B. (2020). Optimization of Special Cryptocurrency Portfolios. *The Journal of Risk Finance*, *21*(2), 127–157. DOI: 10.1108/JRF-11-2019-0221

Sebastião, H., & Godinho, P. (2020). Bitcoin Futures: An Effective Tool for Hedging Cryptocurrencies. *Finance Research Letters*, *33*, 101230. DOI: 10.1016/j.frl.2019.07.003

Sensoy, A., Silva, T. C., Corbet, S., & Tabak, B. M. (2021). High-Frequency Return and Volatility Spillovers among Cryptocurrencies. *Applied Economics*, *53*(37), 4310–4328. DOI: 10.1080/00036846.2021.1899119

Shi, Y., Tiwari, A. K., Gozgor, G., & Lu, Z. (2020). Correlations among Cryptocurrencies: Evidence from Multivariate Factor Stochastic Volatility Model. *Research in International Business and Finance*, *53*, 101231. DOI: 10.1016/j.ribaf.2020.101231

Silahli, B., Dingec, K. D., Cifter, A., & Aydin, N. (2021). Portfolio Value-at-Risk with Two-SidedWeibull Distribution: Evidence from Cryptocurrency Markets. *Finance Research Letters*, *38*, 101425. DOI: 10.1016/j.frl.2019.101425

Sun, X., Liu, M., & Sima, Z. (2020). A Novel Cryptocurrency Price Trend Forecasting Model Based on LightGBM. *Finance Research Letters*, *32*, 101084. DOI: 10.1016/j.frl.2018.12.032

Tavares, Ricardo de Souza, João Frois Caldeira, and Gerson de Souza Raimundo Júnior. 2020. It's All in the Timing Again: Simple Active Portfolio Strategies That Outperform Naïve Diversification in the Cryptocurrency Market. Applied Economics Letters 29: 118–22.

Thampanya, N., Nasir, M. A., & Toan, L. D. H. (2020). Asymmetric Correlation and Hedging Effectiveness of Gold & Cryptocurrencies: From Pre-Industrial to the 4th Industrial Revolution. *Technological Forecasting and Social Change*, *159*, 120195. DOI: 10.1016/j.techfore.2020.120195 PMID: 32834136

Trucíos, C., Tiwari, A. K., & Alqahtani, F. (2020). Value-at-Risk and Expected Shortfall in Cryptocurrencies' Portfolio: A Vine Copula–Based Approach. *Applied Economics*, *52*(24), 2580–2593. DOI: 10.1080/00036846.2019.1693023

Uddin, M. A., Ali, M. H., & Masih, M. (2020). Bitcoin—A Hype or Digital Gold? Global Evidence. *Australian Economic Papers*, *59*(3), 215–231. DOI: 10.1111/1467-8454.12178

Umar, M., Chi, W. S., Syed, K. A. R., & Xue, F. S. (2021). Bitcoin: A Safe Haven Asset and a Winner amid Political and Economic Uncertainties in the US? *Technological Forecasting and Social Change*, *167*, 120680. DOI: 10.1016/j.techfore.2021.120680

Umar, Z., & Gubareva, M. (2020). A Time–Frequency Analysis of the Impact of the Covid-19 Induced Panic on the Volatility of Currency and Cryptocurrency Markets. *Journal of Behavioral and Experimental Finance*, *28*, 100404. DOI: 10.1016/j.jbef.2020.100404 PMID: 32983899

Umar, Z., Jareño, F., & González, M. O. (2021). The Impact of COVID-19-Related Media Coverage on the Return and Volatility Connectedness of Cryptocurrencies and Fiat Currencies. *Technological Forecasting and Social Change*, *172*, 121025. DOI: 10.1016/j.techfore.2021.121025 PMID: 34658451

Urom, C., Abid, I., Guesmi, K., & Chevallier, J. (2020). Quantile Spillovers and Dependence between Bitcoin, Equities and Strategic Commodities. *Economic Modelling*, *93*, 230–258. DOI: 10.1016/j.econmod.2020.07.012

Van Eck, N. J., & Waltman, L. (2017). Citation-based clustering of publications using CitNetExplorer and VOSviewer. [PubMed]. *Scientometrics*, *111*(2), 1053–1070. DOI: 10.1007/s11192-017-2300-7 PMID: 28490825

Vo, Au, Thomas A. Chapman, and Yen Sheng Lee. 2021. Examining Bitcoin and Economic Determinants: An Evolutionary Perspective. Journal of Computer Information Systems 62: 572–86.

Wang, G. J., Ma, X., & Wu, H. (2020). Are Stablecoins Truly Diversifiers, Hedges, or Safe Havens against Traditional Cryptocurrencies as Their Name Suggests? *Research in International Business and Finance*, *54*, 101225. DOI: 10.1016/j.ribaf.2020.101225

Wang, G. J., Xie, C., Wen, D., & Zhao, L. (2019). When Bitcoin Meets Economic Policy Uncertainty (EPU): Measuring Risk Spillover Effect from EPU to Bitcoin. *Finance Research Letters*, *31*, 489–497. DOI: 10.1016/j.frl.2018.12.028

Wang, J., Ma, F., Bouri, E., & Guo, Y. (2022). Which Factors Drive Bitcoin Volatility: Macroeconomic, Technical, or Both? *Journal of Forecasting*, •••, 1–19.

Wang, J., & Ngene, G. M. (2020). Does Bitcoin Still Own the Dominant Power? An Intraday Analysis. *International Review of Financial Analysis*, *71*, 101551. DOI: 10.1016/j.irfa.2020.101551

Wang, P., Li, X., Shen, D., & Zhang, W. (2020). How Does Economic Policy Uncertainty Affect the Bitcoin Market? *Research in International Business and Finance*, *53*, 101234. DOI: 10.1016/j.ribaf.2020.101234

Wang, P., Zhang, H., Yang, C., & Guo, Y. (2021). Time and Frequency Dynamics of Connectedness and Hedging Performance in Global Stock Markets: Bitcoin versus Conventional Hedges. *Research in International Business and Finance*, *58*, 101479. DOI: 10.1016/j.ribaf.2021.101479

Wu, W., Tiwari, A. K., Gozgor, G., & Huang, L. (2021). Does Economic Policy Uncertainty Affect Cryptocurrency Markets? Evidence from Twitter-Based Uncertainty Measures. *Research in International Business and Finance*, *58*, 101478. DOI: 10.1016/j.ribaf.2021.101478

Xu, Q., Zhang, Y., & Zhang, Z. (2021). Tail-Risk Spillovers in Cryptocurrency Markets. *Finance Research Letters*, *38*, 101453. DOI: 10.1016/j.frl.2020.101453

Yang, B., Sun, Y., & Wang, S. (2020). A Novel Two-Stage Approach for Cryptocurrency Analysis. *International Review of Financial Analysis*, *72*, 101567. DOI: 10.1016/j.irfa.2020.101567

Yang, L., & Hamori, S. (2021). The Role of the Carbon Market in Relation to the Cryptocurrency Market: Only Diversification or More? *International Review of Financial Analysis*, *77*, 101864. DOI: 10.1016/j.irfa.2021.101864

Yen, K. C., & Hui, P. C. (2021). Economic Policy Uncertainty and Cryptocurrency Volatility. *Finance Research Letters*, *38*, 101428. DOI: 10.1016/j.frl.2020.101428

Yi, S., Xu, Z., & Gang, J. W. (2018). Volatility Connectedness in the Cryptocurrency Market: Is Bitcoin a Dominant Cryptocurrency? *International Review of Financial Analysis*, *60*, 98–114. DOI: 10.1016/j.irfa.2018.08.012

Yue, Y., Li, X., Zhang, D., & Wang, S. (2021). How Cryptocurrency Affects Economy? A Network Analysis Using Bibliometric Methods. *International Review of Financial Analysis*, *77*, 101869. DOI: 10.1016/j.irfa.2021.101869

Zeng, T., Yang, M., & Shen, Y. (2020). Fancy Bitcoin and Conventional Financial Assets: Measuring Market Integration Based on Connectedness Networks. *Economic Modelling*, *90*, 209–220. DOI: 10.1016/j.econmod.2020.05.003

Zhang, S., & Gregoriou, A. (2021). Cryptocurrencies in Portfolios: Return–Liquidity Trade-off around China Forbidding Initial Coin Offerings. *Applied Economics Letters*, *28*(12), 1–5. DOI: 10.1080/13504851.2020.1796908

Zhang, W., & Li, Y. (2020). Is Idiosyncratic Volatility Priced in Cryptocurrency Markets? *Research in International Business and Finance*, *54*, 101252. DOI: 10.1016/j.ribaf.2020.101252

Chapter 11

Featuring Global Opacity of Cryptocurrency Regulations:

Pioneer of Legal Genesis and Futuristic Approach

Shirisha Deshpande
https://orcid.org/0000-0002-7218-9303
Chaitanya Bharathi Institute of Technology, Hyderabad, India

Maajid Mohi Ud Din Malik
https://orcid.org/0000-0003-1743-1520
Dr. D.Y. Patil Vidyapeeth University, India

Janmejay Vijaykumar Shukla
https://orcid.org/0000-0001-8042-699X
Ramdeobaba University, Nagpur, India

Bhupinder Singh
https://orcid.org/0009-0006-4779-2553
Sharda University, India

Virendra Disawal
Central Institute of Business Management Research and Development, Nagpur, India

Saurabh Chandra
https://orcid.org/0000-0003-4172-9968
Bennett University, India

ABSTRACT

The advent of cryptocurrency has transformed the global financial landscape, offering an alternative to traditional financial systems. Bitcoin, the first decentralized cryptocurrency, emerged in 2009, followed by a proliferation of various digital currencies. These developments have posed significant challenges to governments and regulatory bodies worldwide. The opaque nature of cryptocurrency regulation, combined with the decentralized structure of these assets, has led to a complex and often inconsistent regulatory environment. Given the growing importance of cryptocurrencies there is a clear need for cohesive and efficient regulatory con-

DOI: 10.4018/979-8-3693-5986-0.ch011

siderations. This chapter focuses on the asserts the lack of true transparency in existing regulations, which is caused by divergent practices between jurisdictions and incompatible legal wordings as well as rapidly developing technology. This also raise concerns that the lack of a clear regulatory stance might generate more market turbulence, slow investment and foster illegal capital flow.

1. INTRODUCTION

Bitcoin and the infinite altcoins have led the rise of digital currencies, a force that will transform how value is created, stored and exchanged across borders. Nevertheless, the worldwide gray areas related to regulatory pioneering efforts still make it difficult for integration of these technology in common financial systems. However, the regulatory picture is very uneven with some countries looking to prohibit their use altogether and others are fully embracing digital assets. This inconsistency creates a patchwork of regulatory environments that are tough to navigate for investors, developers and the often rapidly moving technologies being developed. A significant reason for the ambiguous nature of regulation is because cryptocurrencies are essentially incorporeal.

These digital currencies work in power with the forces of decentralization often existing anonymously, operating outside control established by central authorities rendering difficult to apply conventional regulatory methodologies. Accordingly, on the one hand regulators face a challenge to enable innovation while ensuring risks linked with fraud, money laundering and market manipulation are controlled. As such, it has been a fine line to walk and ultimately an anarchic patchwork of legislative reactions which have emerged from tight controls in some regions through to widespread acceptance elsewhere. The outcome is a fragmented global regulatory patchwork that provides uncertainty to all stakeholders and makes it difficult for cryptocurrencies to fulfil their potential as drivers of economic growth and financial inclusion.

A forward-looking model for regulatory approaches to cryptocurrency will require collaboration from governments, industry participants and international organizations. As the interplay of regulatory standards among jurisdictions and across borders are intervening, so shall it continue to demand international regulation harmonization in transactions across regional boundaries in order to further mitigate gruelling affect associated risks. The new approach also requires the use of technology such as blockchain analytics and artificial intelligence to improve regulatory oversight and enforcement capacity. In addition, the construction of a regulatory framework based on dialogue and cooperation with cryptocurrency group is required. Adhering to these principles will allow policymakers to negotiate the nuances of cryptocurrency regulation, providing an enabling environment that can lead us towards facilitating real financial inclusion and a more resilient global financial system. Increasingly, it will be this more nuanced and evolving regulatory approach by various authorities across the globe which determines a path for cryptocurrencies to continue serving as an agent of purposeful economic change.

1.1 Significance of the Chapter

The significance of this chapter comes in its comprehensive examination of the opaque nature of global cryptocurrency regulations. With identifying pioneering legal frameworks and proposing future regulatory approaches, this research aims to contribute to the development of more coherent and transparent global regulations. This is crucial for fostering a stable and secure environment for the growth of the cryptocurrency industry, which is increasingly becoming integral to the global financial system. While there are obstacles, the cryptocurrency industry with its legal genesis and rapid expansions of existing dynamics that subject intend to revaluation inevitably challenges standing paradigms at a distance. The emergence of smart contracts, decentralized finance (DeFi) and NFTs necessitates a particular legal framework that takes into account the nuances in digital assets. These technologies pose challenges to traditional ideas of ownership, value and contract enforceability which force regulators into a new paradigm that should be forward-thinking. A coherent and flexible structure must be built to fully realize the potential of cryptocurrencies, but also with an assurance that they are protected from malicious actors who mean no good for consumers or integrity in markets.

2. EVOLUTION OF CRYPTOCURRENCY

The cryptocurrency space started evolving when Bitcoin was introduced in 2009 by another unknown entity calling itself Satoshi Nakamoto (Griffith & Clancey-Shang, 2023). This was the beginning of a new kind of money, decentralized digital currency that built by blockchain technology to enable secure peer-to-peer transactions with no central authority needed (Biju & Thomas, 2023). Digital currencies were not unheard of previously cryptographer David Chaum proposed digital cash systems in the 1980s and 1990s but Bitcoin applied these ideas into a useful, workable currency. The years following Bitcoin's introduction saw a rapid proliferation of digital currencies. Litecoin (2011): Litecoin would become the 2nd major altcoin in existence, making itself faster than Bitcoin by design. Next up, in 2012 we have Ripple which was created to solve the problem of cross-border money transfers followed by Ethereum being announced and released in 2015 bringing smart contracts and dApps (decentralized applications) into the blockchain ecosystem (Uzougbo, Ikegwu, & Adewusi, 2024). In 2017 this exploded, and the market was flooded with Initial Coin Offerings (ICOs) which created new cryptocurrencies left and right until more than $100bn were reached in total capitalization. Nevertheless, the market of cryptocurrencies is not without its problems. However, the dramatic increase in value was followed by serious corrections — such as that of early 2018 which wiped out more than 80% off its market value (Uzougbo, Ikegwu, & Adewusi, 2024). It is this volatility that has brought greater regulatory oversight from governments across the globe, with a view to protecting investors and prevent cryptocurrency nefarious activities (Al-Tawil, 2023).

2.1 Global Overview of Cryptocurrency Regulations

The world experienced a new found craze for cryptocurrencies and that was when governments started to get very involved in understanding how they could regulate this emerging asset class. The world of regulations are well diverse and you have a different approach for cryptocurrencies. Many countries have taken the step of banning cryptocurrency trading and ICOs altogether, with some like China expressing fears over financial stability as well as fraud (Bonaparte & Bernile, 2023). On the other hand, superpowers like America and European Union member-states have embraced a more balanced standpoint that can provide a space-friendly approach for cryptocurrencies within their present financial systems while still imposing safeguards to protect buyers and combat money laundering (Khan, Ullah, & Atiq, 2024). Regulatory bodies in the U.S such as Securities and Exchange Commission (SEC) accounts for categorizing cryptocurrencies as well making sure that each of them management what needs to be managed (Khan, Ullah, & Atiq, 2024). One of the SEC's primary concerns regarding cryptocurrencies has been whether or not a few select cryptos are, in fact (under existing law), securities and should be subject to regulation as such. For its part, the CFTC has clearly staked out territory in the nascent and continually developing field of dealing with cryptocurrencies that have disrupted so much already, underlining it as an area appropriate for regulatory oversights (Ba & Şen, 2024). The European Union, for example, has begun the process to regulate cryptocurrencies holistically with its proposed Markets in Crypto-Assets (MiCA) regulation that is intended to address a number of matters related to consumer protection and market integrity as well-as financial stability (Chohan, 2023). The goal of this initiative echoes a common understanding among members about the importance to balance fostering innovation with also protecting investors through convergent regulations across member states.

2.2 Legal Challenges and Controversies

Along with the increase of cryptocurrencies rose a number legal issues and conflicts around it (Zhang, et al., 2023). A key issue is how cryptocurrencies will be classified. Confusion & Inconsistency: driftnet.com Note how different jurisdictions provide an inconsistent definition (Wiwoho, et al., 2024). As an example, certain countries can classify cryptocurrencies as a currency while others see them such in the light of commodities or securities and based on that they are taxed and regulated accordingly. Fraud and market manipulation is another big concern. The appeal of cryptocurrencies to criminals is tied largely to their anonymity and decentralization, which has in turn caused a surge in scams, hacks, and fraud cases. Incidents like the failure in 2014 of Mt. Gox, an exchange through which hundreds of millions of dollars' worth of Bitcoin went missing have drawn attention to potential safety issues for investors that can arise if regulators are not able to directly oversee and regulate this marketplace system and therefore allow it to operate with some degree relative independence from other market support interventions such as stable government regulation or disputes resolution provisions (Najed et al., 2023).

On the other hand, there have been significant debates and legal-inquiry with regard to environment effects of cryptocurrencies mining. Bitcoin mining in particular has come under fire for its heavy energy usage and carbon emissions, leading some jurisdictions to think about regulating or even outlawing the practice domestically (Su, 2023). It has led to doubts over the viability of cryptocurrencies in a world that is growing more environmentally friendly, causing long-time concerns for their sustainability and longevity.

2.3 Case Studies: Pioneer Nations in Cryptocurrency Regulation

2.3.1 United States

One of the earliest authorities to regulate cryptocurrencies, the United States oversees its blockchain sector with a disjointed set of state and federal rules (Putri, Amiludin, et al., 2023). In the USA, SEC has taken a constructive approach around cryptocurrencies by trying to figure out how they would fall into classifications as well help enforce regulation to protect investors. The SEC filed legal actions against many popular cryptocurrency industry players this year, setting a strong precedent about the need to operate in compliance with securities laws (Benson, et al., 2024). What is even more important, however, the Biden administration urged that there needs to be some comprehensive regulatory framework addressing both positive and negative aspects of cryptocurrencies because it finally woke up for what an impactful part they play on today's financial stage (Dhali, et al., 2023).

2.3.2 European Union

The guiding principles for something like MiCA is to make sure that things are harmonised across EU said the European Union. This effort intends to bring about legal clarity on the use of cryptocurrencies, protect consumers better and promote competition in this domain. By creating a harmonized space for regulation, the EU positions its regulatory environment as more nuanced than that in other regions with which it competes (i. Meanwhile, the EU has been leading conversations around green crypto-options that have an environmentally friendly impact on this emerging area of finance (van der Linden & Shirazi, 2023).

2.3.3 Japan

Japan is one of the early adopters in adopting cryptocurrencies as a legal payment method since 2017. The Financial Services Agency (FSA) has established a registration process for cryptocurrency exchanges, which have been instructed to follow security and operational regulations (Tauda, et al., 2023). This regulatory regime has contributed to greater consumer confidence as well now risk management mitigation on cryptodrading. Nevertheless, Japan has not been immune from issues as well with incidences of high profile hacks and breaches so the battle to improve regulation in addition safeguard investors continues

2.3.4 Singapore

On the global level, Singapore has taken advantage of establishing itself as a top innovator in cryptocurrencies and Blockchain. The Monetary Authority of Singapore (MAS) has set out a regulatory framework for the local fintech industry to prevent excessive risk-taking and safeguards consumer protection, as well ensure stability in their country financial systems. First, the Payment Services Act (PSA) came into effect in 2020 where it introduced a licensing for cryptocurrency exchanges and services thus creating an opportunity to have more transparency and security in digital asset transactions (Lindsay, 2023). Its proactive regulatory approach has drawn many cryptocurrency startups and established companies to establish in Singapore, solidifying it as one of the top places for cryptocurrencies worldwide. The cryptocurrency path has been characterized by rapid expansion and regulatory issues coupled with future arguments. The US, the European Union, Japan and Singapore will play a crucial role in defining how cryptocurrencies are integrated into financial systems and society as national regulatory frameworks evolve for this rapidly maturing new asset class (Ordekian, et al., 2023).

3. THEORETICAL FRAMEWORK

A theoretical approach to the understanding of cryptocurrency regulation requires an examination across different dimensions, and such includes Where do they come from legally? How global regulatory frameworks are shrouded in obscurity as far as these digital assets arc concerned / Comparative analysis with various countries approaches Cryptocurrency adoption/Groundbreaking being a cornerstone. The framework is necessary in order to understand the nuances of digital currency regulation and its potential consequences for consumer security, financial stability, as well other critical risks (Olabanji et al., 2024).

3.1 Legal Genesis: The Birth of Cryptocurrency Regulations

The legal foundation for cryptocurrency regulations began with the launch of Bitcoin in 2009, a borderless digital currency that operated without oversight from banks or financial institutions. The innovation was a great challenge for the traditional regulatory frameworks that were primarily created to regulate centralized financial systems (Goodell, et al., 2023). As cryptocurrencies gained in popularity, governances started catching up to protect society at large from this new type of financial asset. At first regulatory responses were far ranging in both scope and location. Certain parts of the world embraced cryptocurrencies while others simply banned them (Klein, et al., 2024). In 2017, Japan the first country to regard Bitcoin as a legal form of payment and from then on set up regulatory rules that made trading with cryptocurrencies subject to registration at the Financial Services Agency (FSA) while cryptocurrency exchanges must comply anti-money laundering regulations. On the opposite end, countries such as China outright banned cryptocurrency trading and Initial Coin Offerings (ICOs), which were justified by claims to protect financial stability and intended fraud prevention (Kellerman & Seddon, 2024). The legislative beginnings of cryptocurrency regulations highlight the struggle between harnessing cryptocurrencies' that may promote innovative avenue with those concerned about consumer safety and financial security. Over time, regulators developed more nuanced frameworks factoring in the decentralization and anonymity features of cryptocurrencies. These changes have given rise to a number of regulators, including tax agencies, securities classifiers and consumer protection (Kayani & Hasan, 2024).

3.2 Opacity in Global Regulatory Frameworks

While there have been advancements in the formation of regulatory structures, a huge degree uncertainty still existent within global cryptocurrency regulation (Guh-Siesel, 2023). The complexity is a product of many elements such as non-uniformity across jurisdictions, rapidly changing tech landscape and the asset type itself. Because of this, different countries have created different definitions and classifications for exchanges like Mt. Gox leading to confusion about what it actually is on a regulatory level. For instance, the Howey Test is mainly utilized in evaluating whether a digital currency meets one of the four types that classify it as security on United States Soil but you also have EU adopting their own set procedures like with Markets in Crypto-Assets (MiCA) bill which seek to provide an extensive legal framework for all crypto assets (Guh-Siesel, 2023). This uniformity is lacking which makes compliance difficult for cross border businesses and allows the same to be used as an opportunity for regulatory arbitrage whereby firms may choose jurisdictions where regulations are lax. In addition, the high pace of development in cryptocurrency technologies often moves faster than regulatory reaction responses. Technological developments are throwing up new challenges, such as DeFi or NFTs (non-fungible tokens), whose regulatory framework still needs to be framed (Murugappan, et al., 2023). As a result, regulators have to deal with an uncertain and nebulous landscape that can make it more difficult for them to provide oversight or protect consumers (Johnson, 2023).

3.3 Comparative Analysis of Regulatory Approaches

This comparative analysis underscores just how varied the activities of different states have been when grappling with cryptocurrencies. The analysis of this report illustrates what comprises the strengths and weaknesses within popular regulatory frameworks, offering insights into how policymakers can craft a balanced framework that promotes innovation while ensuring risks (Poynton, 2023). Although, in the US there is a bit of overlap from different organizations (SEC/CFTC/Fincen) and it seems to be fragmented.

The focus for the SEC has been to classify cryptocurrencies immediately as securities and then subject projects issuing tokens, including cryptocurrency exchanges, will have more stringent disclosure requirements (Poynton, 2023). Critics have said this approach is stifling innovation, as new startups could get bogged down in the murky waters of regulatory uncertainty (Lim, 2024). On the other hand, the European Union plans to adopt MiCA regulation which provides more integrated rules based on accepting some specific features of cryptocurrencies and encouraging innovation. MiCA will clarify definitions and regulatory guidelines to create a single market for such services, providing equality of access for all European citizens while enhancing consumer protection. Opponents, however, caution that regulation of any kind could ultimately stifle the industry (Putri, et al., 2023).

Japan approach to regulation Reactive, proactive In Japan A more pro-active regulatorial stance has been adopted with the FSA engaging industry stakeholders in framing a legislation which is balanced between innovation and consumer protection. Such inclusion has led to a lively crypto industry in Japan, although one that still grapples with security issues after some high-profile exchange breaches (Frediani, 2024). The island city-state, which has become a hotbed for cryptocurrency innovation on account of its progressive regulatory regime (Cioroianu, et al., 2023). To provide greater regulatory clarity and certainty for businesses operating in the payment services sector, the Payment Services Act came into force here last month with a licensing regime for cryptocurrency exchanges that is overseen by MAS. This legal certainty has already enticed a host of startups and businesses from around the world to Singapore, effectively making it one of biggest hubs for cryptocurrency within Asia Pacific (Daye & Verret, 2023).

3.4 Concept of Legal Pioneering in Cryptocurrency

Legal Pioneering In Cryptocurrency Regulation The idea of being legal pioneer in cryptocurrency regulation concerns the jurisdiction that put a stake on creating such legislative appliances which are done and resolve an issue brought out by using digital currencies. Many of these are pioneering efforts that can be flexible and innovative in terms of regulation, working with industry stakeholders or adjusting to an evolving cryptocurrency technology market (Ahsan, et al., 2023).

However, trailblazers such as Singapore and Japan have proven that a proactive regulatory environment can drive innovation while continuing to protect consumers in these emerging industries. These are examples of how the industry has had positive outcomes by working directly with regulators in these jurisdictions to make them cryptocurrency friendly environments. In addition, as a legal pioneer we not only help to develop the rules but help set out best practices and standards that can be followed by other states. As nations watch legal pioneers succeed and falter, they can look for learnings that will strengthen their own regulatory approaches. This culture of knowledge sharing and cooperation goes a long way to lift the veil on global regulatory regimes, pushing for convergence in cryptocurrency regulation (Mateen, 2023).

The theoretical basis of cryptocurrency regulation is built on these four pillars: the regulatory history and its legal grounding worldwide; gaps in global regimes with focus on comparative approaches leading to duplications; interpretation through hypothetical scenario, using comparison again as a common denominator (for instance examining different monetary authorities' interpretations), some sort of "legal case law" or precedents sometimes even economic integration where pertinent. With the ever-changing cryptocurrency landscape, these perspectives will have to be factored in as regulators chart out optimal practices that ring-fences between innovation and protect against consumer & financial threats. Facilitating dialogue between jurisdictions and adopting flexible regulatory frameworks can help stakeholders better navigate the unique landscape of cryptocurrency regulation, supporting responsible innovation whilst ensuring that this groundbreaking technology is built to last.

4. GLOBAL OPACITY IN CRYPTOCURRENCY REGULATIONS

Carey Lening, Chief Operating Officer at VerifyInvestor.com The global opaqueness of regulations around cryptocurrencies is a major headache for anyone who has any kind of business with cryptos investors, businesses and regulators. This part explains the notion of opacity in legal frameworks, reasons for regulatory uncertainty and gives case studies while displaying what that ambiguity is doing not only within respective regions but across decentralized cryptocurrency markets. When it comes to legality the term opacity represents no clear, transparent and consistent regulations in a certain area. Cryptocurrencies in the case of opacity, things such as vague legal definitions being forced into square holes by round peg regulators across jurisdictions and a total vacuum on clear guidance. This ambiguity has created uncertainty for market participants about what they need to do legally, and the enforcement of their rights leaving cryptocurrency markets susceptible to stalling in growth or stability. The sources of this legal opacity are varied: technological developments running ahead too fast for regulatory response, the complexity of cryptocurrency environments and differing national interests. Since cryptocurrencies are decentralized, financial regulators generally find it challenging to apply traditional financial regulations on this new asset class. Therefore, absence of well-defined cohesive regulations can be a breeding ground for illegitimate activities and it also tends to scare the investors off while underpinning further innovation.

4.1 Factors Contributing to Regulatory Opacity

Crypto regulations are opaque for several reasons globally, due to the:

Diverse Regulatory Openings: Some countries have adopted an all-encompassing ban towards cryptocurrencies, whereas others are taking a positively inclined approach. This fragmented approach results in a bizarre tangle of laws that are difficult for enterprises to work with, particularly those operating across state lines.

Fast Pace of Technological Developments: The rate at which new services emerge within the cryptocurrency ecosystem can exceed how quickly regulators are able to adapt. DeFi and NFT introduce new technologies, which are inherently complex for existing regulatory frameworks to fully capture.

Lack of Legal Definitions: Certain terms associated with cryptocurrencies are not clearly defined under some jurisdictions, which confuses both cryptocurrency exchanges and buyers. This ambiguity is frustrating the use of relevant laws and leads to a lack of trust among members in business done there.

Political and Economic Reasons: Differences of national interest or economic reasons can determine the approach to regulatory frameworks. Regulators might be wary of laying down tough rules that could impede innovation or force companies to go overseas for more friendly regimes, hence there may also be a reluctance among governments in drawing clear lines (Burgess, 2024).

No International Collaboration: The overall missing link of a global standard and guideline for cryptocurrencies makes opacity even worse. Countries often put their regulatory interests first, independent from the global context which results in diverging disciplines and practices.

4.2 Case Studies: Examples of Regulatory Opacity

4.2.1 China's Ambiguous Stance

This fear is exemplified in how China approached to cryptocurrency regulation — but never says why. The Chinese government originally took a more laissez-faire approach to cryptocurrencies whose development consequently burgeoned unimpeded. But this became the exact opposite in 2017, when it imposed drastic restrictions against Initial Coin Offerings (ICOs) and cryptocurrency exchanges which were basically tantamount to a ban. That the reasoning behind these regulations has not been made clear to either investors or businesses, has added further confusion. Although the government argues that financial stability and fraud are reasons for such move speaking on conditions of anonymity many fear policy uncertainty will prevail following sudden moves. The lack of clarity around this has caused many cryptocurrency companies to up and leave for more supportive jurisdictions, taking innovation and investment out of China. Additionally, the Chinese government has more recently stepped up efforts to banish cryptocurrency mining from its territories which clearly shows that this isn't a clear one for them. Although the government has been worrying about mining's environmental effects, but this absence of a consistent approach gives miners and others no certainty to run cryptocurrency operations in nation (Wronka, 2024).

4.2.2 India's Uncertain Legal Landscape

Indias crypto regulatory framework is characterized by uncertain and opaque proscriptions. The Reserve Bank of India (RBI) in 2018 imposed a ban on crypto-currency transactions, citing risks to financial stability and consumers. But in 2020, the Supreme Court had reversed this ban after which it sparked a renewed interest in cryptocurrencies. Notwithstanding this legal win, the Indian government has not put in place a regulatory framework for cryptocurrencies. There are proposed bills in the legislature but conflicting views among policymakers have left this legal fight to linger on. This has created a muddled web of legal regulation, posing assorted problems for businesses and investors to overcome before genuinely entering the cryptocurrency space. India is developing some of its thought leadership skills, not least because of the darkness that surrounds India's murky regulatory environment as it relates to innovation and investment. This uncertainty around the legality of cryptocurrencies has thwarted several Indian startups in these domains to not only raise funds but also scale their operations. This highlights why it need clear and consistent rules to allow for a vibrant cryptocurrency market.

4.3 Impacts of Opacity on Global Cryptocurrency Markets

The lack of clarity surrounding cryptocurrency regulations affects the global market and all involved in this complex ecosystem, such as the:

Investor confidence: If the regulations remain uncertain everywhere around even, it can erode investor confidence and imply less participation in this market. If investors are not sure about the legal standing of their investments, they might be reticent to dedicate a part of dollar savings into cryptocurrencies which could slow down growth in this market. Market Volatility: the amount of opacity that regulators have about crypto can create new sources market volatility. Regulations Part 3: Sharp Price Volatility Abnormal pricing behavior can follow sudden announcements or changes in regulations as people either panic buy or sell. However, this volatility understandably has a tendency to scare off institutional investors that rely on more consistent and predictable conditions in order to succeed.

Regulatory Arbitrage: In areas of lack harmonization in regulations, regulatory arbitrage is possible whereby businesses may choose to domiciliate where the laws are lighter. It will stimulate the regionalisation of cryptocurrency operations which may reduce regulatory efficiency. Inhibited Innovation: Cryptocurrency without clear regulations is innovation in shackles. So if you do go about that then startups will not be willing to spend money on a new technology or business model, where they don't know how the underlying regulations might eventually come back and bite them. This can in turn hinder the progress of evolving new solutions and diminish returns deriving from what cryptocurrencies may be able to provide.

When you shuffle feet and mumble in regulatory frameworks, all it does to create is a gray area wherein rampant illicit activities (money laundering) strive on. Similarly, in the absence of robust regulatory frameworks and responsible regulation oversight bodies from national governments around the globe, malicious parties can leverage on said vacuum to commit offences which only bring a further dent to confidence within cryptocurrency as an emerging asset class. To conclude, transparency-related barriers are a global issue in the area of regulation-compliance for cryptocurrency stakeholders. Yet when one dissects the reasons behind this opaqueness and explores examples across countries, it is evident that there is an immediate requirement for transparent unambiguous harmonised regulations. With overcoming these hurdles, confidence in investors and market stability will be boosted for the whole industry leading to further development of ecosystems all around. Even as the landscape changes, regulators and industry stakeholders from all over the world will need to work together on this issue in order to share a unified approach that can set bitcoin and other cryptocurrencies for success as they continue assimilating into our financial system (Falk & Hammer, 2023).

5. PIONEERS OF LEGAL GENESIS: IDENTIFYING PIONEERS IN CRYPTOCURRENCY REGULATION

The rise of cryptocurrency has called for guidelines to cover much needed regulatory framework to regulate various risks that coin type poses. This part would look into the forerunners of legal genesis in crypto regulation and questions how early regulatory frameworks has affected or can shape the global standards. The work of these pioneering nations has been instrumental in developing digital asset laws worldwide. In this setting, Japan is the most outstanding example of readiness for dynamic regulations oriented at forming a structure that would be able to cope with regulatory difficulties connected with cryptocurrencies among any others including The U. S, and E.U.

In 2017 Japan recognized legal cryptocurrencies. Last year, the Financial Services Agency introduced a licensing system for cryptocurrency exchanges which imposed stringent anti fraud measures including capital requirement, segregation of customer accounts and verification process. Businesses also benefited from the certainty of this regulatory framework and reinforced confidence among consumers in our market (Khatana et al., 2023). The US has been establishing a framework for regulating cryptocurrencies in its traditional financial sector. The arrival of the SEC and CFTC has spawned a variety of rulings/guidance to develop definitions around different types/categories/kinds (whatever you want to call it) that aims at placing digital assets in one class or another for regulatory purposes.

A recent bipartisan bill in Congress strives to enshrine federal oversight of cryptocurrency within the industrywide realm and presents an example of a well-co-ordinated regulatory effort. The European Union is taking the lead in cryptocurrency regulation with its proposed Markets in Crypto-Assets (MiCA) regulation. The initiative is designed to establish a unified regulatory structure crafted around consumer protection, market integrity and financial stability – an example for other jurisdictions to follow.

5.1 Impact of Early Regulatory Frameworks

The regulatory frameworks implemented first by these trailblazer countries have shaped the cryptocurrency landscape significantly. These regulations have also set a standard in the industry by making it simple for all participants to know exactly what is required while maintaining consumer protection. This has caused several cryptocurrency exchanges in Japan to be scrutinized more heavily with some being forced to improve their security and operational practices as they go through the FSA licensing process. That said, this proactive regulator attitude has helped Japan keep its reputation as a global center for digital asset trading and engineering. The SEC in the United States has taken measures to bring some sense of settlement as it tries to classify cryptocurrencies, aiming at providing clarity for investors and businesses. The SEC has helped build a model which, by clarifying what digital assets are regulated as securities and how they will be treated in this regard going forward, stresses compliance with the law while deterring fraud.

This kind of regulatory clarity has led to institutional interest in the market, thereby signalling that cryptocurrency is on its way towards greater mainstream acceptance. The MiCA regulation of the European Union is ready to be as influential. MiCA wants to reduce such regulatory ambiguity and make the crypto industry operate in a clear environment across all EU member states by harmonizing rules for cryptocurrencies. The move is seen to attract investment and innovation while also placing the EU at par with other tech-savvy nations that are taking a lead in regulating cryptocurrency across the globe.

5.2 Lessons from Pioneer Countries

Pioneer countries, and their unique experiences set a precedent for other prospective regulatory bodies to hone-in on what works best in this regard. Without clear definitions and guidance, a regulatory environment cannot flourish. Lack of clarity with respect to legal definitions could keep the cryptocurrency market in limbo. Early adopting countries have shown that well-defined regulatory landscapes can improve investor certainty and support participation.

Sector-wise Approach: Implementation of the proposed Act is sector-specific, and therefore a collaborative approach with industry stakeholders will be necessary for an efficient regulatory framework. Through partnership with cryptocurrency companies, regulators can learn about the challenges and advantages that come hand in hand when dealing with digital assets. This collaboration could well result in better regulation that meets the twin goals of innovation and consumer protection.

Flexibility and Adaptability: The cryptocurrency market is in constant change, so any regulations passed must be flexible. Front-line countries have demonstrated the need for regulatory flexibility as technology changes and new trends emerge. This elasticity enables regulators to efficiently react to new threats and create space for innovation (Olorundare et al., 2023).

Protection of the consumer meaning keeping the rights of consumers in mind as one would be setting up with a regulating framework. The experiences of early adopting nations shed light on why it is necessary to have a framework in place that protects investors from fraud and safeguards against market manipulation. Regulators must start to protect the average doing so will increase trust in cryptocurrencies, and make them more sustainable into the future.

6. CONCLUSION

The primordial from legal genesis and futuristic approach as with this strengthening and development of the cryptocurrency marketplace, so does its apparent requirement for well-defined regulatory frameworks to guide it effectively. In doing so, this finding underscores the importance of navigating regulatory opacity and learning from frontrunners while considering best practices to orient global coordinates for resources regarding how cryptocurrencies can be governed. In short, the research indicates that regulatory opacity continues to be an obstacle for participants across cryptocurrency stakeholder groups. Uncertainty exists all over the globe due to ambiguous definitions in law, divergent regulatory systems from one place to another and technology has moved faster than any regulation on earth. In addition, such lack of transparency impairs investor confidence and makes it very difficult for businesses to function through legitimate market practices. These results highlight the need for regulators to take a forward-looking, coordinated approach in order to create clear and flexible standards that are able to evolve with cryptocurrencies. Japan, the United States and several countries in Europe are pioneers of sort as they have begun establishing regulatory frameworks for innovation that take into account consumer protections. Key themes stand out from their experiences that shed light on the importance of clarity, stakeholder engagement and flexibility in regulatory design. These countries, which are still in the process of fine-tuning how they regulate crypto-assets becoming robust sandboxes for other administrations experiencing similar questions. The enterprises RefToken will be routing traffic to, abiding by the token holder interfaced regulations and these are lessons in inclusivity which only lends towards how robust (and yet adaptive) any set of regulation needs to adapt for changes that seen with an emerging industry such as digital assets. In addition, these pioneer countries have a global impact on how regulation of cryptocurrency is carried out and its standardization. With working together like-minded countries can help to influence the eventual regulation of virtual assets as some international bodies, including FATF develop guidance in this sector. Establishing consistent standards will be essential to respond facilities cross-border problems and ensure that cryptocurrencies continue to deliver the benefits, while managing its risks.

It also underscores the need for an ongoing discussion among regulators, industry participants and other stakeholders. Given the potential for money laundering and tax evasion using cryptocurrencies, regulatory intelligence sharing with other jurisdictions will be necessary to establish a common framework that allows these instruments of financial transfer while simultaneously addressing consumer protection concerns. Such cooperation will be necessary in order to deal with the diffusion problems of cryptocurrencies and make sure that all legislation is properly adapted as new technologies develop. The future of cryptocurrencies will ultimately hinge on the ability for government and regulatory bodies to adopt a culture based around clarification, flexibility, and cooperation. In the changing global scenario, setting up regulatory frameworks will be crucial to creating an ecosystem for safe and sustainable cryptocurrency adoption. Building on lessons from early adopters, and striving for global regulatory harmonization provides a pathway through legal uncertainty to deliver the full benefits of cryptocurrencies in finance. Cryptocurrency regulation is constantly evolving and represents a combination of challenge, yet an opportunity for us all to be part of shaping the future landscape in terms setting standards around these new assets.

REFERENCES

Ahsan, Z. B., Gupta, A., & Kar, A. K. (2023). The Effect of Countries' Independent Regulation on Cryptocurrency Markets. [JGIM]. *Journal of Global Information Management, 31*(1), 1–32. DOI: 10.4018/JGIM.323567

Al-Tawil, T. N. E. (2023). Anti-money laundering regulation of cryptocurrency: UAE and global approaches. *Journal of Money Laundering Control, 26*(6), 1150–1164. DOI: 10.1108/JMLC-07-2022-0109

Ba, H. L., & Şen, Ö. F. (2024). Explaining variation in national cryptocurrency regulation: Implications for the global political economy. *Review of International Political Economy, 31*(5), 1–24. DOI: 10.1080/09692290.2024.2325403

Benson, V., Adamyk, B., Chinnaswamy, A., & Adamyk, O. (2024). Harmonising cryptocurrency regulation in Europe: Opportunities for preventing illicit transactions. *European Journal of Law and Economics, 57*(1), 37–61. DOI: 10.1007/s10657-024-09797-w

Biju, A. V. N., & Thomas, A. S. (2023). Uncertainties and ambivalence in the crypto market: An urgent need for a regional crypto regulation. *SN Business & Economics, 3*(8), 136. DOI: 10.1007/s43546-023-00519-z

Bonaparte, Y., & Bernile, G. (2023). A new "Wall Street Darling?" effects of regulation sentiment in cryptocurrency markets. *Finance Research Letters, 52*, 103376. DOI: 10.1016/j.frl.2022.103376

Burgess, T. (2024). A Multi-Jurisdictional Perspective: To What Extent can Cryptocurrency be Regulated? And if so, Who Should Regulate Cryptocurrency?. *Journal of Economic Criminology*, 100086.

Chohan, U. W. (2023). Regulatory and legal issues in cryptocurrencies. In *Cryptocurrency concepts, technology, and applications* (pp. 141–157). Auerbach Publications. DOI: 10.1201/9781003315049-8

Cioroianu, I., Corbet, S., Larkin, C. J., & Oxley, L. (2023). *Developing central bank digital currencies: a reality check during cryptocurrency euphoria*. Economics and Business Letters.

Daye, M., & Verret, J. W. (2023). A Mosaic Approach for Challenging SEC Crypto Regulation: The Major Questions Doctrine and Staff Accounting Bulletin 121. *Wm. & Mary Bus. L. Rev., 15*, 553.

Dhali, M., Hassan, S., Mehar, S. M., Shahzad, K., & Zaman, F. (2023). Cryptocurrency in the Darknet: Sustainability of the current national legislation. *International Journal of Law and Management*, *65*(3), 261–282. DOI: 10.1108/IJLMA-09-2022-0206

Falk, B. H., & Hammer, S. (2023). A Comprehensive Approach to Crypto Regulation. *U. Pa. J. Bus. L.*, *25*, 415.

Frediani, M. E. A. (2024). Crafting the Future of Finance: A Comparative Analysis of Cryptocurrency Regulation in the Global Economy. *Journal of Financial Risk Management*, *13*(1), 193–206. DOI: 10.4236/jfrm.2024.131010

Goodell, J. W., Paltrinieri, A., & Piserà, S. (2023). Comparing search-engine intensity and regulatory attention impacts on cryptocurrencies: Uncovering important heterogeneities. *Review of Corporate Finance*, *3*(4), 571–595. DOI: 10.1561/114.00000051

Griffith, T., & Clancey-Shang, D. (2023). Cryptocurrency regulation and market quality. *Journal of International Financial Markets, Institutions and Money*, *84*, 101744. DOI: 10.1016/j.intfin.2023.101744

Guh-Siesel, A. (2023). Cryptocurrency regulation. In *Harvard Model Congress*.

Ivory Johnson, C. F. P. (2023). What's in Store for Crypto Regulations? *Journal of Financial Planning*, *36*(3), 46–50.

Kayani, U., & Hasan, F. (2024). Unveiling Cryptocurrency Impact on Financial Markets and Traditional Banking Systems: Lessons for Sustainable Blockchain and Interdisciplinary Collaborations. *Journal of Risk and Financial Management*, *17*(2), 58. DOI: 10.3390/jrfm17020058

Kellerman, M., & Seddon, J. (2024). Into the ether or the state? Legibility theory and the cryptocurrency markets. *Business and Politics*, *26*(3), 1–24. DOI: 10.1017/bap.2023.38

Khan, R. U., Ullah, K., & Atiq, M. (2024). Regulatory constraints, responsibilities and consultation (CRC) for legal institutionalization of cryptocurrencies in Pakistan. *Qualitative Research in Financial Markets*, *16*(4), 680–708. DOI: 10.1108/QRFM-03-2023-0053

Khan, R. U., Ullah, K., & Atiq, M. (2024). Regulatory constraints, responsibilities and consultation (CRC) for legal institutionalization of cryptocurrencies in Pakistan. *Qualitative Research in Financial Markets*, *16*(4), 680–708. DOI: 10.1108/QRFM-03-2023-0053

Khatana, S. S., Mahecha, M., & Beniwal, S. (2023, June). An analytical study of regulatory journey of cryptocurrency in India. In *AIP Conference Proceedings* (Vol. 2782, No. 1). AIP Publishing. DOI: 10.1063/5.0154633

Klein, G., Assadi, D., & Zwilling, M. (2024). Fighting Fire with Fire: Combating Criminal Abuse of Cryptocurrency with a P2P Mindset. *Information Systems Frontiers*, •••, 1–27.

Lim, J. W. (2024). A facilitative model for cryptocurrency regulation in Singapore. In *Handbook of Digital Currency* (pp. 341–361). Academic Press. DOI: 10.1016/B978-0-323-98973-2.00023-X

Lindsay, M. G. (2023). International Rise Of Cryptocurrency: A Comparative Review Of The United States, Mexico, Singapore, And Switzerland's Anti-Money Laundering (AML) Regulation. *South Carolina Journal of International Law and Business*, *19*(2), 8.

Mateen, M. (2023). *Regulation in the Cryptocurrency Industry* (Doctoral dissertation, University of Missouri--Kansas City).

Murugappan, M., Nair, R., & Krishnan, S. (2023). Global market perceptions of cryptocurrency and the use of cryptocurrency by consumers: A pilot study. *Journal ofTheoretical andApplied Electronic Commerce Research*, *18*(4), 1955–1970. DOI: 10.3390/jtaer18040098

Najed, A., Al-Malahmeh, H., Al-Amawi, A., Almashaqbeh, M., Alsaaideh, M., & Abdalmajeed, A. A. (2023, March). Impact of Cryptocurrency Regulations and Fintech on the Growth of Innovations. In *2023 International Conference on Business Analytics for Technology and Security (ICBATS)* (pp. 1-5). IEEE. DOI: 10.1109/ICBATS57792.2023.10111475

Olabanji, S. O., Oladoyinbo, T. O., Asonze, C. U., Adigwe, C. S., Okunleye, O. J., & Olaniyi, O. O. (2024). Leveraging fintech compliance to mitigate cryptocurrency volatility for secure us employee retirement benefits: Bitcoin ETF case study. *Available atSSRN* 4739190.

Olorundare, J. K., Fagboyo, R. J., Onyijen, O. H., Oni, M., & Adebunmi, A. A. (2023). Economic Prospect of Cryptocurrency: Nigeria as a Case Study. *Journal homepage:*www. ijrpr. com*ISSN*, *2582*, 7421.

Ordekian, M., Becker, I., & Vasek, M. (2023, May). Shaping Cryptocurrency Gatekeepers with a Regulatory "Trial and Error". In *International Conference on Financial Cryptography and Data Security* (pp. 113-132). Cham: Springer Nature Switzerland. DOI: 10.2139/ssrn.4398362

Podder, B. (2023). Cryptocurrency and central bank digital currency: An insight from the regulatory perspective. *International Journal of Financial Studies. Economics and Management*, *2*(3), 25–35.

Poynton, A. (2023). US cryptocurrency regulation: A slowly evolving state of affairs. *Notre Dame J. on Emerging Tech.*, *4*, 93.

Poynton, A. (2023). US cryptocurrency regulation: A slowly evolving state of affairs. *Notre Dame J. on Emerging Tech.*, *4*, 93.

Putri, C. P., Putra, A. T. E., & Aminuddin, M. (2023, December). The Urgency of Appropriate Legal Regulations on Financial and Tax Aspects in Cryptocurrency Transactions in Indonesia. In *International Conference on "Changing of Law: Business Law, Local Wisdom and Tourism Industry"(ICCLB 2023)* (pp. 305-316). Atlantis Press. DOI: 10.2991/978-2-38476-180-7_34

Putri, T., Amiludin, A., Ahmad, D. N., & Hidayatulloh, H. (2023). Inadequate Cryptocurrency and Money Laundering Regulations in Indonesia (Comparative Law of US and Germany). *Yustisia*, *12*(2), 129–152. DOI: 10.20961/yustisia.v12i2.71835

Su, J. (2023). Redirecting the herd: Informing cryptocurrency regulations through the lens of behavioral science. *Hastings Sci. & Tech. LJ*, *14*, 123.

Tauda, G. A., Omara, A., & Arnone, G. (2023). Cryptocurrency: Highlighting the Approach, Regulations, and Protection in Indonesia and European Union. *Bestuur*, *11*(1), 1–25. DOI: 10.20961/bestuur.v11i1.67125

Uzougbo, N. S., Ikegwu, C. G., & Adewusi, A. O. (2024). International enforcement of cryptocurrency laws: jurisdictional challenges and collaborative solutions. *Magna Scientia Advanced Research and Reviews, 11*(1), 068-083.

Uzougbo, N. S., Ikegwu, C. G., & Adewusi, A. O.Ngozi Samuel UzougboChinonso Gladys IkegwuAdefolake Olachi Adewusi. (2024). Enhancing consumer protection in cryptocurrency transactions: Legal strategies and policy recommendations. *International Journal of Science and Research Archive*, *12*(01), 520–532. DOI: 10.30574/ijsra.2024.12.1.0801

van der Linden, T., & Shirazi, T. (2023). Markets in crypto-assets regulation: Does it provide legal certainty and increase adoption of crypto-assets? *Financial Innovation*, *9*(1), 22. DOI: 10.1186/s40854-022-00432-8 PMID: 36643685

Wiwoho, J., Trinugroho, I., Kharisma, D. B., & Suwadi, P. (2024). Islamic crypto assets and regulatory framework: Evidence from Indonesia and global approaches. *International Journal of Law and Management*, *66*(2), 155–171. DOI: 10.1108/IJLMA-03-2023-0051

Wronka, C. (2024). Crypto-asset activities and markets in the European Union: Issues, challenges and considerations for regulation, supervision and oversight. *Journal of Banking Regulation*, *25*(1), 84–93. DOI: 10.1057/s41261-023-00217-8

Zhang, P., Xu, K., & Qi, J. (2023). The impact of regulation on cryptocurrency market volatility in the context of the COVID-19 pandemic—Evidence from China. *Economic Analysis and Policy*, *80*, 222–246. DOI: 10.1016/j.eap.2023.08.015

Chapter 12
Social Impact of Cryptocurrencies

Jacek Klich
Krakow University of Economics, Poland

ABSTRACT

Cryptocurrencies have changed the financial industry and have the potential to make a considerable social impact. Since cryptocurrencies are a new phenomenon in the financial market, research on the social impact of cryptocurrencies remains in the initial stage. This chapter aims to present the current research stage on the social impact of cryptocurrencies. The findings from the review of the literature are structured to positive (financial inclusion, provision of access to credit, remittances, empowerment of individuals and communities, and philanthropic initiatives) and negative (high risk, illicit activities, and environmental harm). The chapter shows most of the findings are inconsistent and the conclusions vary. It is argued in the chapter that the negative impact of cryptocurrencies on the social fabric prevails due to the very meaning (nature) of cryptocurrencies.

INTRODUCTION

Cryptocurrencies are emerging entities. They represent a considerable and growing part of the global financial market. As of March 2024, there were more than 9,000 crypto projects in existence[1]. As of July 23, 2024, the top 10 cryptocurrencies (according to their market capitalisation) were: Bitcoin (BTC) with a market capitalisation of $1.3 trillion, Ethereum (ETH) ($421.0 billion), Tether (USDT) ($114.3 billion), Binance Coin (BNB) ($85.3 billion), Solana (SOL) ($81.2 billion), U.S. Dollar Coin (USDC) ($34.1 billion), Ripple (XRP) ($33.3 billion), Dogecoin (DOGE) ($19.3 billion), Toncoin (TON) ($17.4 billion), and Cardano (ADA) ($15.1

DOI: 10.4018/979-8-3693-5986-0.ch012

billion) (Adams & Dammeyer, 2024). Year-over-year returns of these ten cryptocurrencies were (appropriately): 128%, 88%, 0%, 145%, 638%, 0%, -15%, 74%, 394%, and 36% (Adams & Dammeyer, 2024). These numbers illustrate on the one hand the considerable scope of the cryptocurrency phenomenon (the compound market capitalisation of ten leading cryptocurrencies on July 23, 2024, totalled $2.121 trillion), and on the other above average level of risk (mirrored by diversified levels of year-over-year return).

Cryptocurrencies impact the financial markets but also possess considerable social consequences. All these outcomes are only partially researched (and understood) because the research on cryptocurrencies remains in the initial stage in general and in particular concerning the social sphere.

The goal of this chapter is to contribute to filling this research gap by presenting the current stage of research on the social impact of cryptocurrencies and identifying the main ways they influence societies. The impact of cryptocurrencies on social life is multifaceted, offering opportunities and challenges. An example of a typology of the social consequences of cryptocurrencies could be ChatGPT's response (on July 12, 2024) to the question of cryptocurrencies and social fabric. AI pointed et the following: *Economic Empowerment and Inclusion* (composed of Financial Inclusion, and Decentralized Finance), *Trust and Transparency* (Trust in Institutions, Transparency and Accountability), *Privacy and Security*, *Social and Cultural Impact* (related to Community and Governance, and Cultural Shifts), *Ethical and Legal Challenges* (Regulations and Ethical Concerns), and *Political and Social Movements* (Political Activism and Social Equity).

The Artificial intelligence typology could be a point of departure (there are references to some of the above categories) because it covers key dimensions of social impact, but the chapter is structured in a much simpler way. The findings from the literature review are presented according to a simple dual typology of the positive and negative social impacts of cryptocurrencies. Then there is a section on some limitations of research on the social implications of cryptocurrencies followed by conclusions.

THE POSITIVE INFLUENCE OF CRYPTOCURRENCIES

In the group of publications presenting mainly positive social influences of cryptocurrencies, one may identify the following categories: financial inclusion, provision of access to financial services, remittances, empowerment of individuals to take control of their financial well-being, and philanthropic initiatives.

Financial Inclusion

Financial inclusion is understood as a process ensuring the ease of access, availability, and use of the financial system for all members of an economy[2] and as such is a desirable social phenomenon crucial for economic growth (Elouaourti & Ibourk, 2024). The scope of financial exclusion is big because in 2023 according to data from the World Bank, there was an estimated 1.4 billion unbanked people worldwide (England, 2023). In the literature cryptocurrencies often are perceived as promoting or – in some cases - enabling financial inclusion.

The promotion of financial inclusion is important, especially for emerging markets (Setyawan et al., 2024). However, it should be acknowledged that financial inclusion is a challenge also for wealthy societies, the US being a good example (Carmona, 2022). One may distinguish between several forms of financial inclusion starting from lowering entry barriers, and then through cross-border transactions, and easier access to credit, to empowering the unbanked (Patel, 2023). The common denominator of financial inclusion is reducing transaction costs. Cryptocurrencies can reduce the cost of financial transactions, making them more affordable for low-income individuals and small businesses (Patel, 2023). It is known, however, that all digital currencies play a similar, if not identical, role (Ozili, 2023). One then may ask which financial tool is more effective in promoting financial inclusion: cryptocurrency or digital currency. The answer remains open.

Provision of Access To Financial Services

The provision of access to financial services identified a positive outcome of using cryptocurrencies (Rodima-Taylor & Grimes, 2018) can be seen as a component and/or tool of financial inclusion. Cryptocurrencies offer an alternative for people who lack access to traditional banking services due to financial or geographical constraints, the latter applying particularly to developing countries. It must be stressed, however, that problems with access to traditional banking services can be observed also in highly developed countries. A good illustration of this could be President Joe Biden's Executive Order (EO) on Ensuring Responsible Development of Digital Assets. It requires government agencies to develop frameworks and policy recommendations that advance six priorities in this respect, one of which is financial inclusion (Carmona, 2022).

It must be acknowledged that as of the time of writing, there is no sufficient proof of such positive benefit of cryptocurrencies at least in the US. In the report issued on September 16, 2022, by the U.S. Department of the Treasury titled: "Crypto-Assets: Implications for Consumers, Investors, and Businesses" one may read that "...the potential financial inclusion benefits of crypto-assets largely have yet to materialize" (U.S. Department of the Treasury, 2022, p.2). At the same time, the report mentions certain risks for some populations because of digital assets.

As far as other countries are concerned, Argentinian experiences with social currency, MonedaPAR, deserve some attention not only to illustrate improved access to financial services but also to show how cryptocurrency may assist in countervailing the economic crisis.

MonedaPAR as a medium of exchange introduced in Argentina in May 2017 is based on the idea of mutual credit and promotes monetary circulation over hoarding and speculation. For more than a year, it has been adopted by some communities grouped into nodes, which operate with it as a social currency in search of mitigating the crisis that the country has been suffering since 2016 (Orzi et al., 2021). MonedaPAR can be seen as a peculiar case of fixed-value (i.e. commensurable) unconvertible associative money. It exhibits both mutual credit and monetary emission technical features. Implementing MonedaPAR was a challenge partly due to the highly decentralized way of proceeding. As of October 2019, MonedaPAR had five nodes running and regularly using the system. The evolution of registered and active accounts account (the latter being this which has done at least one transaction since its creation) showed that the number of active accounts exceeded the level of 500 late, in December 2018, so did the the level of monthly mean transaction value per active account in the whole PAR monetary system (Orzi et al., 2021, p. 20 and p.23). The limitation of Orzi's et al. (2021) study is the low number of open and semi-structured interviews (over 20), carried out in just one province (Buenos Aires Province). The Argentinian case shows that the recent development of cryptocurrencies raises several questions regarding the issues of trust, governance and decentralization when dealing with social currencies.

Providing Access To Credit

In many parts of the world, traditional banking systems are inadequate or nonexistent, leaving people without access to essential financial services like loans, savings accounts, and insurance. Here cryptocurrencies can help. Among the competitive advantages of credits in cryptocurrencies, one may find fast and cost-efficient transactions, global accessibility, security and anonymity, investment opportunities (through integrated credits applications clients have the opportunity to invest in the crypto market directly), and lower financial barriers (Credits, 2023).

One should mention that cryptocurrency has revolutionized the institution of money to the extent that confuses most commodity and credit theorists. Some maintain that neither current theory can accommodate cryptocurrency (Passinsky, 2024). In other words, current cryptocurrency credit transactions operate without an understood and agreed theoretical base.

Cryptocurrencies can provide credit services through decentralized applications (DApps) that operate on blockchain networks. For example, in the USA DApps like AAVE, Compound, and MakerDAO allow users to earn interest on their cryptocurrency holdings or borrow against them without needing a traditional bank account. As a result, people can borrow money using their cryptocurrency as collateral without worrying about meeting traditional banking requirements (Patel, 2023). Unfortunately, there is no easily available data on the size of the cryptocurrency credit market.

Remittances

Another positive outcome of cryptocurrencies is remittances which play an important role in poverty alleviation. For sizable populations in low- and middle-income countries (LMICs), remittances from abroad form a significant portion of their income. After a period of strong growth during 2021-2022, officially recorded remittance flows to LMICs moderated in 2023, reaching an estimated $656 billion (World Bank, 2024).

In 2023, remittance flows increased most to Latin America and the Caribbean (7.7%, reaching $156 billion), followed by South Asia (5.2%, reaching $186 billion), and East Asia and Pacific (4.8%, excluding China, to $85 billion). Sub-Saharan Africa saw a slight decline of 0.3% (to $54 billion) while the Middle East and North Africa experienced a nearly 15% drop (to $55 billion). Also, Europe and Central Asia saw a 10.3% fall (to $71 billion) (World Bank, 2024).

Remittances are essential drivers of economic and human development in developing countries and such a statement is common knowledge shared both by international global players (like for example the World Bank) and by the academic community. In some LMICs, remittances account for as much as 10 to 15% of their annual GDP (Kulkarni et al., 2019, p.1). Remittances are crucial for Pacific Island economies like Palau, Samoa, Tonga, and Vanuatu. Tonga was the most dependent globally, with remittances amounting to 41% as a share of GDP (World Bank, 2024). It must be remembered that third parties (banks, money transfer operators like for example Western Union, Money Gram or WorldRemit, post offices, etc.) charge hefty fees to facilitate such transfers - from 5% to 10% of the total funds per transaction (Kulkarni et al., 2019, p.1). Consequently, the use of cryptocurrencies and blockchain technologies is an alternative to standard money transfers.

As shown by Reeves (2017) methodologies used to transfer remittances to Sub-Saharan Africa lead to even greater surcharges than 5-10%. In 2006 fees were greater than 13%. He showed that if Sub-Saharan African citizens began to utilize cryptocurrencies instead of standard transfer companies like Western Union and MoneyGram, transfer fees could be reduced to as little as (.025%) (Reeves, 2017).

Such findings are corroborated by other studies (Kulkarni et al., 2019; Soufaih, 2020; Fahlander, 2022).

As acknowledged by the World Bank, sending remittances remains costly. In the fourth quarter of 2023, the global average cost of sending $200 was 6.4% of the amount being sent, slightly up from 6.2% a year earlier and well above the UN Sustainable Development Goals target of 3%. It is unacceptable that Sub-Saharan African countries belonging to poor and very poor countries still pay the highest fees. In 2023 sending $200 to the region cost an average of 7.9%, (as compared to an average of 6.4%) almost unchanged from a year before. One may maintain that nothing has changed since Reeves' (2017) findings.

Digital remittances had a lower cost of 5%, compared with 7% for non-digital methods, highlighting the benefits of technological advancements in reducing the financial burden on migrants (World Bank, 2024). This means that cryptocurrencies can help.

Bridging the Wealth Gap

Close to poverty alleviation is cryptocurrencies' ability to bridge the wealth gap indicated by some authors (Cadet, 2023). The problem is, that there is no empirical evidence supporting this. On the contrary, one may argue that cryptocurrencies lead to higher income inequality. This issue is developed in the Discussion.

Empowerment of Individuals

Presenting a list of social benefits resulting from the use of cryptocurrencies, it is worth noting the empowerment of individuals and communities to take control of their financial well-being. This refers not only to emerging economies and developing countries since positive outcomes of local cryptocurrencies have been noticed also in developed countries such as Austria (Janisch & Stapleton, 2021).

Philanthropic Initiatives

The potential of cryptocurrencies was relatively quickly acknowledged by the nonprofit sector in general, especially concerning philanthropic initiatives. As diagnosed in the literature, the traditional philanthropy environment has encountered problems with openness, accountability, and middlemen that obstruct the effective flow of funds. The existing challenges are fraudulent activities, lack of transparency, high administrative costs, inadequate governance, donor misinformation, duplication of efforts, geographic challenges, fundraising practices, public perception, political issues, and regulatory obstacles (Ahmed et al., 2024, p.2). All of these appear to have corroded public trust (Novak, 2024).

It is believed (and expected) that cryptocurrencies may help to address some of these weaknesses and challenges. The main goal of non-profit organizations is to augment and diversify their sources of donations (Keshvari Fard et al., 2024) thus cryptocurrencies may help. Crypto donations are also quick and convenient for donors, reducing checkout time. With cryptocurrencies, donors can also donate anonymously (Bose, 2023). Donors also may take advantage of the blockchain and algorithmic surveillance reflecting their interests. The latter is done by attaching automated conditions to charitable donations facilitated by programmable "crypto-giving" platforms (Howson, 2021). Blockchain technology brings transparency to the charity ecosystem through distributed ledger technology, smart contracts, and cryptography. The entire ledger copy is shared with all nodes in the blockchain (Swati et al., 2022). In many countries, cryptocurrency donations to registered nonprofits are considered tax-deductible and donors won't have to pay capital gain taxes (Bose, 2023).

As in other cases, also regarding charity initiatives, it is difficult to assess the value of cryptocurrencies used in transactions. Estimations vary from $ 500 million in 2021 in the United States[3] (PwC, 2024) to over $2 billion in January 2024 (Duffy & Wilson, 2024). There is fragmented and incomplete information about the size of donations in cryptocurrencies. In 2021 media reported that Ethereum's founder, Vitalik Buterin, donated 50,7 trillion Shiba Inu (over $1.1 billion) to India's COVID-Crypto Relief Fund (NDTV, 2021). This donation represented more than 5% of the total Shiba Inu coins in circulation and caused a 50% drop in Shiba Inu prices.

Several respectable charities for example UNICEF and the Rainforest Foundation have started to accept crypto donations (PwC, 2024). UNICEF, however, was not the first one. *Save the Children* decided to accept donations in Bitcoin in response to Typhoon Haiyan in the Philippines in 2013. In 2014 the *American Red Cross* started accepting Bitcoin in a partnership with *BitPay* - a crypto payment service provider. Also in 2014, *the BitGive Foundation* became the first crypto non-profit organization, recognized as a charitable organization by the US government. It was in 2019 when UNICEF began accepting cryptocurrency with the launch of UNICEF CryptoFund, building on its past blockchain projects (Keshvari Fard et al., 2024). The appearance of cryptocurrencies on the market of charitable organizations gave rise to the creation of third-party platforms like Fundraiseup (launched in 2017), The Giving Block (launched in 2018), and Engiven (2018) all facilitating crypto donations for charities (charging a moderate processing fee). According to the latest report by Duffy & Wilson (2024), as of January 2024, the majority of the top US charities (56% of the top 100) accept cryptocurrency donations. Over two-thirds

(67,8%) of these top crypto-enabled nonprofits aren't just accepting crypto, but are actively fundraising for it (Duffy & Wilson, 2024).

Foreign aid directed to the victims of armed aggression can be treated as a special kind of philanthropy. Keshvari Fard et al. (2024) focus on the *Aid for Ukraine* project, the largest crypto crowdfunding initiative in terms of both the number of donations and contributors, with over 114,000 valid and successful donation transactions from more than 90,000 distinct donor addresses in 227 cryptocurrencies across 13 blockchains by the end of 2022 (Keshvari Fard et al., 2024). The *Aid for Ukraine* was launched on February 26th 2022, just two days after the Russian invasion of Ukraine. The *Aid for Ukraine* project can be perceived as a textbook-like positive example of philanthropic usage of cryptocurrencies.

Despite the potential and promising trend toward crypto philanthropy, there have been very few studies about understanding donors' behaviour and preferences when donating in cryptocurrencies (Keshvari Fard et al., 2024).

Cryptocurrencies and Geopolitical Crises

Cryptocurrencies can be useful during various geopolitical crises. Alexakis et al. (2024) have researched 93 events associated with potential limitations of fiat currency circulation in the context of trading with the use of cryptocurrencies. They considered five cryptocurrencies: Bitcoin, Ethereum, Ripple, Dash, and Tether. They find that trading in cryptocurrencies increases with events of geopolitical tensions. This increase can be motivated by different explanations (e.g., protecting savings as the domestic currency devaluates, making payments as the domestic financial system is no longer available, and avoiding sanctions) which are difficult to disentangle. In such a context cryptocurrencies can be assessed as playing a positive social role. As could be expected, Alexakis et al. (2024) found a strong increase in the outflow from Ukrainian Hrvynia to cryptocurrencies since the beginning of the Russian-Ukrainian military conflict but only on centralized exchanges (decentralized exchanges were not analysed). The authors also show that the EU sanctions established in 2022 on Russia resulted in a slowdown in cryptocurrency trading when crypto-related services (wallet, account or custody services) are explicitly included in EU financial sanctions packages. At the start of the Russian invasion, Ukraine raised over $56 million in total value within the first month (Pinkerton, 2024).

All in all, one may conclude that although there is a lack of complete and reliable data, it can be considered that in the identified above fields cryptocurrencies play a significant positive role. However, as with nearly any other social phenomenon, cryptocurrencies have also the other, negative, side.

NEGATIVE CONSEQUENCES OF CRYPTOCURRENCIES

The above-mentioned and other positive social outcomes of cryptocurrencies notwithstanding, one must also acknowledge some negative social consequences of cryptocurrencies Among the mainstream analysis, one may indicate high risk, vulnerability to illicit activities, environmental harm, and other relatively negative social consequences.

High Risk

Cryptocurrencies are perceived as inclined towards speculative usage due to the inherent high risk of financial loss and the potential for substantial gains during transaction completion. Two anecdotal pieces of evidence of the high volatility of cryptocurrencies and the risk the latter could be Bitcoin and Dogecoin. Bitcoin's value dropped by more than 70%, from its all-time high of $68,789 in November 2021 to around $16,000 by December 2022. On March 5, 2024, Bitcoin reclaimed its previous all-time high of $69,000, marking a remarkable recovery of over 300% from the "crypto winter" of 2022. (Pinkerton, 2024). An illustrative example of a spectacular gain could be the value of Dogecoin which rallied more than 11,000% within one month (April 2021) (NDTV, 2021). It should be also mentioned here that the first sentence about Bitcoin in US mainstream media reported a 900% return when the price reached $8.60 in 2011 (Walker, 2024, p.1).

The high risks of investing in cryptocurrencies are not only broadly acknowledged in the literature but it is also identified by official governmental bodies. A good example of the latter is the US Department of the Treasury which monitors the financial market. In its report on crypto-assets in the section on negative consequences of crypto-assets for investors, one may find the following phrase: "While the data for populations vulnerable to disparate impacts remains limited, available evidence suggests that crypto-asset products may present heightened risks to these groups…" (U.S. Department of the Treasury, 2022, p.2). The report identifies three kinds of risk related to cryptocurrencies: *Conduct Risks* (composed of Fraud, Theft, and Mismanagement, Information Asymmetry: Lack of Transparency), *Operational Risks* (connected with Decentralized Governance, Security and Scalability Tradeoffs and De-anonymization, Peer-to-Peer Verification, Mining Pools, and Validation Incentives), and *Risks in Crypto-asset Intermediation* (composed of Resources and Capabilities Risks, Custody Risks). The report refers not only to investors but also to third parties assessing that the risks associated with centralized crypto-asset platforms (CEXs) are significant. The problem is, that CEXs are not in compliance with U.S. laws and regulations, or that may not be regulated (U.S. Department of the Treasury, 2022, p. 9).

Risks may also arise from crypto exchanges. A good example is the rapid rise and subsequent collapse of the crypto exchange FTX led by Sam Bankman-Fried in 2022. Sam Bankman-Fried was arrested and indicted by the U.S. District Court on multiple criminal charges, including money laundering, wire fraud, campaign finance violations and securities fraud. In November 2023, he was convicted of seven federal counts of fraud and conspiracy. On March 28, 2024, he was sentenced to 25 years in federal prison and ordered to forfeit $11.02 billion (Pinkerton, 2024).

Certain risk originates from the internal mechanisms and processes of cryptocurrencies. This refers first of all to Bitcoin keys i.e. the private credentials stored in a wallet. Similar to a safe deposit box, access to the value within a wallet requires a private, alphanumeric key. If a party loses their key, the Bitcoin becomes inaccessible and effectively worthless. Approximately 20% of Bitcoins have been lost due to misplaced private keys (Pinkerton, 2024). There are public keys (the technology used to encrypt and decrypt transactions. It is "one way," allowing transactions to be unlocked but not reversed. This key enables the blockchain to be uninterrupted) and private keys (the passcode that transacting parties initiate so that the transaction is unique to themselves). To spend Bitcoin, one must know their private key and digitally sign the transaction. The party's signature is verified by the public key without revealing the private key. If a private key is exposed in a security breach, the Bitcoin associated with it can be stolen. In 2022, cryptocurrency investors suffered a record loss of $3.8 billion to hackers (Pinkerton, 2024).

The fundamental issue of using cryptocurrencies as an investment or/and a payment method – besides the mechanism of high instability and volatility of the cryptocurrencies - remains the investor/client's motivation and incentives. These two areas are only partially researched thus there are dozens of unanswered questions.

The very nature of the cryptocurrency market is concisely reflected by Grobys & Junttila (2021) who name the demand in the cryptocurrency market "lottery-like demand". Other authors refer to "the volatile and 24/7 nature of the cryptocurrency market" (Johnson et al., 2023). Research indicates that high volatility and a lack of ease of use are the most common difficulties reported by users (Campino & Yang, 2024). This corroborates that cryptocurrency users are aware of the risks associated with cryptocurrency transactions and accept them. The findings confirm also that cryptocurrency users value the anonymity these transactions offer (Campino & Yang, 2024).

The mechanisms of the cryptocurrency market are intensively researched and one may notice dozens of respective publications. For example[4], Zhang et al. (2023) propose a novel two-stage Variational Mode Decomposition-based multi-scale regression to analyze various cryptocurrency attributes using the Bitcoin case to test it. Empirical results show that out of three modes: low, medium, and high-frequency mode, only the latter represents some speculation (Zhang et al., 2023). Ahmed et al.(2024) propose empowering the existing centralized charity works with the electronic know-your-customer (eKYC) authentication approach and cryptographic HASH. Campino & Yang (2024) offer an innovative approach to analyzing interviews and qualitative questionnaires that can be applied in other research fields. Grobys & Junttila (2021) suggest a new econometric test accounting for unknown dependency structures modifying MAX measure and employing a weekly forecast horizon and daily log returns from the previous week to calculate the metric for their portfolio sorts.

The analysis of the sentiment value – where social media plays an important role - shows a high correlation between the impact of sentiment on the value of cryptocurrencies (Milka, 2021). The limitation of Milka's analysis is that only two cryptocurrencies were researched: Bitcoin in the period 01.01.2016 – 01.06.2021 and Ethereum in the period 01.11.2018 – 01.06.2021, and that only one social media platform (Twitter) was searched.

Research on herding behaviours in the formation of investor sentiment revealed that empirical results (covering the period January 1, 2018, to January 1, 2021) suggest a strong impact of herding behaviour on the formation of sentiment toward highly volatile assets especially concerning cryptocurrencies when the bubble occurred (Nicolas, 2022).

The significant impact that the social media activity of influential individuals can have on cryptocurrencies is documented by Ante (2023) who analysed a sample of 47 cryptocurrency-related Twitter events Elon Musk was involved in. Ante identifies significant positive abnormal returns and trading volume of Bitcoin and Dogecoin following such events. Nicolas (2022) indicates that even a single individual can initiate bubble-like behaviour in the cryptocurrency market.

Also, Horky et al. (2023) reveal Twitter's significance as a primary source of information on the Non-Fungible Token (NFT) market for a broad audience. This refers also - toutes proportions gardées – to Vitalik Buterin's donation to India's COVID-Crypto Relief Fund and a 50% drop in Shiba Inu prices (NDTV, 2021).

Although cryptocurrency users, their profiles and their preferences are the subject of scientific inquiry, the number of related publications remains moderate.

Most cryptocurrency users prefer to invest in cryptocurrencies often choosing coins based on their popularity rather than other intrinsic features. E-commerce payments are the most attractive activity, followed by international transactions when using cryptocurrencies as a payment method (Campino & Yang, 2024).

When motivations and behaviours of cryptocurrency investors are concerned, one should mention Grobys & Junttila's (2021) study. They suggest that parallel to stock markets, similar behavioural mechanisms of underlying investor behaviour are present also in new virtual currency markets.

Some similarities to stock markets can be also identified in Wu & Katz's (2023) findings. They examined how mutual fund managers' performance incentives generated speculative demand during the 2020-2022 cryptocurrency boom and bust. It occurred that managers with strong relative performance incentives began investing in crypto after their competitors began investing in it, while managers with personal wealth invested in the funds they manage, who had strong direct performance incentives, responded much less to their competitors' investment decisions (Wu & Katz, 2023).

Also Johnson et al. (2023) contribute to these similarities showing that the cryptocurrency market allows traders to engage in speculative trading patterns closely resembling gambling. Consequently, investing in cryptocurrencies may be investigated from a public health perspective. They review the literature on cryptocurrency trading and its link to problematic gambling and other mental health outcomes such as depression and anxiety. Their scoping review (based on PubMed, Scopus, Embase, and Google Scholar) revealed associations between problem gambling symptoms and cryptocurrency trading engagement and intensity. Their findings suggested overlap with high-risk stock traders, with similarities in gambling behaviours, demographics, and personality traits. The limitation of this study is the fact that only 8 papers were included after eligibility screening.

A valuable contribution to research on cryptocurrency investors' motivations and behaviours is Kumar Sharma's et al. (2024) study on the influence of subjective norms such as domain knowledge, impulsive investment tendencies, and self-control on decisions related to speculative investments. Utilising structural equation modelling with a dataset of 367 responses in India, the research reveals that subjective norms and domain knowledge play a significant role in influencing impulsive investment and self-control. Additionally, impulsive investment exhibits significant associations with decisions involving speculative investments. This insight underscores the complexity wherein individuals, despite exercising self-control, may still engage in speculative decisions that lead to adverse consequences (Kumar Sharma et al., 2024).

Vulnerability to Illicit Practices

As in other spheres of cryptocurrency functioning, there is a shortfall of consistent studies that assess, from a quantitative perspective, how relevant illicit practices are within the cryptocurrency financial ecosystem (Gonzálvez-Gallego & Pérez-Cárceles, 2021). A wide scope of anonymity (transactions in cryptocurrencies occur within Blockchain networks, which means that they are publicly validated while keeping users' identities anonymous), makes cryptocurrencies vulnerable to illicit activities. Real-time operations, without any lag linked to the traditional banking system, encourage the use of cryptocurrencies to avoid current anti-corruption and anti-money laundering control. The positive correlation between cryptocurrencies and money laundering is documented in the literature (Carlisle, 2023) as well as governmental actions aimed at countervailing these negative processes (Rodrigues & Kurtz, 2019). Research into the use of cryptocurrencies for illicit or criminal purposes highlights its suitability also for other than corruption and money-laundering purposes such as trade in illicit goods and services (for example drugs and controlled substances, explosives and weapons, ivory and wildlife trafficking, antiquities, and child sexual abuse material), and terrorism financing (Silfversten et al., 2020, p.4). Kethineni & Cao (2020) add to this list the theft of cryptocurrencies to kidnapping for ransom and tax evasion. Close to tax evasion is the negative effect of cryptocurrency usage on tax revenue collections. Goel & Mazhar (2024) showed that greater cryptocurrency use undermines tax collections, and this result generally holds across overall tax collections, Value-Added Tax revenues and Goods and Services Tax revenues.

RAND analysis of the literature on illicit or criminal use of cryptocurrencies based on an initial 1,599 sources, of which 119 sources were selected for in-depth data extraction revealed that most publications were on *Money laundering* (34%), followed by *Payment (e.g. on dark web markets) for illegal goods or services* (28%), then *Terrorist financing* (18%), *Ransomware* (13%), *Tax evasion, fraud, Ponzi schemes* (8%), and *Cybercrime/illicit purposes, non-specific* (8%) (Silfversten et al., 2020, p. 5). Although Silfversten's et al. (2020) research has not identified any credible evidence pointing to large-scale use of Zcash (cryptocurrency launched in 2016) for money laundering, terrorism financing or the trade in illicit goods and services, one should keep in mind the relatively small share of Zcash in the cryptocurrency market.

Quantitative analyses of illicit cryptocurrency usage are rare thus it is worth quoting some of the findings by Foley et al. (2019). They estimated that 46% of the Bitcoin transactions are related to illicit purposes and approximately one-quarter of Bitcoin users are involved in illegal activity. The illegal share of Bitcoin activity declines with mainstream interest in Bitcoin and with the emergence of more opaque cryptocurrencies. Their findings suggest that cryptocurrencies are transforming the black markets by enabling "black e-commerce" (Foley et al., 2019).

Environmental Harm

Cryptocurrencies impact the environment in many ways. Wendl et al. (2023) identified seven aspects that affect the environmental impact of cryptocurrencies: resources, energy consumption (high energy consumption is connected with blockchain technologies cryptocurrencies are based upon, for example, Kshetri, 2024), carbon footprint, environmental-related social and economic aspects, policy regulation and subsidization, and electronic waste. They notice that the proposed policy regulation in literature is strongly focusing on miners (for example, Sargisyan, 2023) and researchers and policymakers are advised to focus more on investors and third-party services such as regulated exchanges.

Wendl et al. (2023) conclude that Proof of Work (PoW) cryptocurrencies, especially Bitcoin, are historically associated with an ever-increasing environmental impact. The process requires a massive amount of computing power, as miners use complex algorithms and energy-intensive hardware and software to confirm transactions. For Bitcoin miners increasing computer power means obtaining increasingly specialized hardware equipment with higher computing power. Miners initially used central processing units (CPUs) to find PoWs, which were replaced by graphic processing units (GPUs), and then after 2013, application-specific integrated circuits (ASICs) entered the mining sector as standard hardware. What is important in the context of environmental harm is that ASICs are so specialized that they only fit one mining algorithm. Bitcoin ASIC-based mining devices cannot be used to mine any alternative digital currency. This hyper-specialization of devices also implies that miners rapidly cycle through vast amounts of increasingly powerful mining devices which has a negative environmental impact (e-waste) (de Vries & Stoll, 2021).

On the contrary to PoW, Wendel et al. (2023) address Proof of Stake (PoS) as a sustainable alternative that poses a solution to the environmental issues related to PoW. PoS requires significantly less energy and computing power than the PoW approach, largely due to its limitation of participants. PoS means that the miner must provide a minimum deposit, or stake, to confirm the transaction. The increasing environmental impact of cryptocurrencies is confirmed by other studies on cryptocurrency mining (Sargisyan, 2023; Goodkin et al., 2020).

Electricity Consumption

As of August 2022, published estimates of the total global electricity usage for crypto-assets are between 120 TWh and 240 TWh per year, a range that exceeds the total annual electricity usage of many individual countries, such as Argentina. This is equivalent to 0.4% to 0.9% of annual global electricity usage (Office of Science and Technology Policy, 2022, p. 5).

Bitcoin is the most popular and at the same time the most energy-intensive cryptocurrency. Bitcoin's global electricity consumption of 173.42 TWh from 2020 to 2021 exceeds that of some countries for example, that amount of power exceeds the combined electricity consumption of Argentina and the Philippines (Prat, 2023).

As indicated in the White House report on climate and energy implications of crypto-assets in the US published in September 2022, Bitcoin requires more energy than all other cryptocurrencies combined. It accounted for 60% to 77% of total global crypto-asset electricity use as of 2022. The second highest user was the Ethereum network, accounting for 20% to 39% (Office of Science and Technology Policy,

2022, p.14). It is estimated that a Bitcoin transaction requires 1,449 kWh to finish, roughly the same amount of energy that the average US household consumes in 50 days (Ulaşan, 2022, p.9).

To make the situation worse, researchers estimated that 62% of the electricity used for Bitcoin mining globally in 2022 came from fossil fuels, with coal-generated power being the largest single source (Prat, 2023). Fossil fuels cause other environmental harms like air pollution from fossil fuel burning, water withdrawals and thermal water pollution from power plant cooling, other water pollution, solid waste from fossil fuel combustion, land degradation from exploration and mining, and life cycle impacts of fuel cycles and power plant construction.

High demand for electricity from Bitcoin miners may lead to criminal behaviours. A good example could be Iran, an important Bitcoin player. The annual energy consumption of Bitcoin miners in Iran amounts to 20 TWh, while Bitcoin miners globally consume around 117 TWh annually (as of May 2021). Within Iran, it has been suggested that more than 86% of the electricity used to power Bitcoin mining is obtained illegally (de Vries & Stoll, 2021).

Air Pollution

Studies on carbon dioxide (CO_2) emissions in the processes of mining, storing and circulating cryptocurrencies have charted a wide range of results as shown by de Vries & Stoll (2021) mainly due to the lack of reliable data.

According to available estimates, global electricity generation for the crypto-assets with the largest market capitalizations resulted in a combined 140 ± 30 million metric tons (Mt) of carbon dioxide ($CO_{2)}$ per year, or about 0.3% of global annual greenhouse gas (GHG) emissions (Office of Science and Technology Policy, 2022, p. 6).

Current estimates of CO_2 emissions from crypto-asset mining in 2022 are 110 to 170 (or 140 ± 30) million Mt globally, and about 25 to 50 million Mt in the United States (Office of Science and Technology Policy, 2022, p. 21).

Due to its high share in the cryptocurrency market and high energy consumption, Bitcoin is the leading cryptocurrency regarding greenhouse emissions. According to the Cambridge Bitcoin Electricity Consumption Index (CBECI), which provides estimates on the greenhouse gas emissions related to Bitcoin, crypto mining is responsible for 0.1% of global greenhouse gas emissions (Pinkerton, 2024). It is estimated that Bitcoin mining processes produced 85.89 million Mt of carbon dioxide equivalent, from 2020 to 2021. This figure is comparable to 9,665 gallons of gasoline consumed by passenger vehicles, or 96,210 pounds of coal burned in one year, according to the U.S. Environmental Protection Agency's Greenhouse Gas Equivalencies (Prat, 2023).

Bitcoin emissions have increased rapidly from a range of 2 to 16 million Mt CO_2 per year in 2017 to 100 ± 20 million Mt CO_2 per year from May 30 to June 16, 2022, an increase of approximately 10 times in five years (Office of Science and Technology Policy, 2022, p.21).

The harm of cryptocurrency mining to the environment is considerable (Sargisyan, 2023). A quantitative analysis of the carbon footprint of Bitcoin mining by Xiao et al. (2023) gives us an inspiring picture which can be interpreted as a warning. Employing a top-down measurement approach, the authors assess the carbon footprint of Bitcoin mining in China from 2017 to 2021. The findings reveal that mining activities during this period contributed to a total of 77.84 million tons of carbon dioxide emissions in China. By utilizing data at the provincial level, they find that the seasonal migration of Bitcoin mining pools will lead to regional power demand shocks in China. Equally worrying are the projections for future carbon emissions from Bitcoin mining in China: cumulative carbon dioxide emissions of 76.40 million tons and 722.18 million tons by 2030 and 2060 respectively, in the absence of any policy interventions (Xiao et al., 2023).

Similar research on energy use patterns for mining four prominent cryptocurrencies: Bitcoin, Ethereum, Litecoin, and Monero was done by Goodkin et al. (2020). They estimate the per coin economic damages of air pollution emissions and associated human mortality and climate impacts of mining these cryptocurrencies in the US and China. Results indicate that in 2018, each $1 of Bitcoin value created was responsible for $0.49 in health and climate damages in the US and $0.37 in China. The similar value in China relative to the US occurs despite the extremely large disparity between the value of a statistical life estimate for the US relative to that of China.

Water Demand

Many crypto-asset mining facilities must use air cooling (which is connected to heat and noise) or liquid cooling (use of water) to keep computers within acceptable temperature ranges. In standard computer data centres, a single, typical 10 kW rack of servers will require around 63,000 gallons of potable water per year for air cooling — an amount comparable to the average indoor water use of an individual U.S. household each year (Office of Science and Technology Policy, 2022, p. 25).

Electronic Waste

E-waste represents a growing threat to our environment, from toxic chemicals and heavy metals leaching into soils to air and water pollution caused by improper recycling. Assessing e-waste with accurate estimates is difficult due to a lack of high-quality data thus only more or less rough estimates are available. De Vries & Stoll (2021) offer a methodology to estimate Bitcoin's e-waste and find that it adds up to 30.7 metric kilotons annually (as of May 2021), the volume comparable to the amount of small IT and telecommunication equipment waste produced by a country like the Netherlands. On average Bitcoin generates 272 g of e-waste per transaction processed on the blockchain (de Vries & Stoll, 2021).

Relatively Negative Social Consequences

Some of the positive social consequences of cryptocurrency' usage indicated in the previous section can be relativized.

In El Salvador, in the rural coastal community of El Zonte, Bitcoin has been pioneered as a tool for everyday transactions and social programs targeting the town's majority poor population. Some opportunities for small-scale aid and the business sector notwithstanding, Patel (2024) undermines these benefits pointing at uneven and neocolonial impacts of cryptocurrency on local people, land and resources, and power. White crypto tourists from rich countries have bought up land and patronized exclusive hotels and resorts. Patel maintains that cryptocurrency facilitates novel forms of territorial, resource, and political control. Pinkerton (2024) adds to the above that El Salvador lost an estimated $40 million of its investment. In March 2024 the country moved about $400 million into a cold wallet and placed it into an in-country physical vault. This reflected a doubling of the country's known account and includes assets acquired through the government's new Freedom passport (Pinkerton, 2024).

Another example illustrating the relative character of cryptocurrencies could be the Russian-Ukrainian war. Ukraine posted two crypto wallets at the beginning of the Russian invasion to raise funds, attracting more than $56 million within the first month (Pinkerton, 2024). Since Ukraine was invaded and is a victim, cryptocurrencies in this context play a positive, supportive role. The problem is, however, that cryptocurrencies are also used by the attacker and the fact that Russia has raised only about 1/10th of the Ukrainian amount (Pinkerton, 2024) remains a weak consolation.

Even more ambiguous is the Iranian case. Iran has found Bitcoin to be an effective method to bypass U.S. financial sanctions on the country since the government requires all mined Bitcoin to be sent to the Iranian central bank. Such regulations lead to the proliferation of illegal crypto-mining activities which in turn created significant electrical outages (Pinkerton, 2024).

Highly controversial is also the role of cryptocurrencies role in the war between Israel and Hamas. As estimated by the Financial Crimes Enforcement Network (FinCEN), the U.S. Treasury arm that combats terrorism financing, a combined

$165 million in crypto transactions, consisting of 200 wallets linked to Hamas, are believed to be tied to the October 7, 2023 surprise attack on Israel. (Pinkerton, 2024).

It is interesting to note that some authors perceive cryptocurrencies as a component of cryptoanarchism (Chohan, 2017) understood as a phenomenon advocating for individual freedom and autonomy in the digital realm through the use of encryption, anonymity, and decentralisation (Zhuk, 2024). Assuming that anarchism is rather a destructive social concept, one may consider cryptocurrencies negative.

These four examples show the relative value of cryptocurrency's usage in solving geopolitical tensions and conflicts and invite reflection on other somewhat ambiguous social consequences of cryptocurrencies as well as more general observations. These are presented in the section *Discussion* below.

DISCUSSION

This section - preceded by a remark about a slightly mysterious origin of Bitcoin - is devoted to some limitations in research on cryptocurrencies in general and on the social consequences of cryptocurrencies in particular. In the end, cryptocurrencies are presented as a social threat.

Peculiarity of the Origin of Bitcoin

As broadly acknowledged in the literature, in 2008, Satoshi Nakamoto developed the first cryptocurrency, Bitcoin, to challenge mainstream financial markets (Breidbach & Tana, 2020). In January 2009 the Bitcoin source code was publicly available and this can be seen as the beginning of cryptocurrencies. It must be mentioned, however, that the true identity of Satoshi Nakamoto remains unknown. Some authors consider it fictitious (Wątorek et al., 2021), while others treat it as real (Tarasiewicz & Newman 2015; Keshvari Fard et al., 2024; Zhang et al., 2023; Milka, 2021). Consequently, we do not know who (a person? a group of people? or an organization?) stood behind Bitcoin. Assuming that the launching of Bitcoin was a success, one may wonder why we do not know the real author(s) of this success. Continuing and expanding this issue one may say that for the average citizen, everything related to cryptocurrency transactions is touched by a mist of mystery which is reflected in some findings as a lack of transparency (Chen et al., 2022). This limited knowledge about cryptocurrencies can be also traced among respondents in empirical research on cryptocurrencies (Al-Omoush et al., 2024). This, in turn, may explain why many researchers, authors, and politicians recommend various forms of education regarding cryptocurrencies (Pinkerton, 2024; US Department of the Treasury, 2022; Chimienti et al., 2019).

All in all, social science research on cryptocurrencies, as an *in statu nascendi* phenomenon, faces certain practical limitations and obstacles.

Limitations of Research On Cryptocurrencies In Social Sciences

This section does not provide an exhaustive overview of the literature but identifies two selected (subjectively chosen) limitations influencing (if not shaping) the research on the social impacts of cryptocurrencies followed by examples of methodological weaknesses.

The first limitation arises from the very nature of cryptocurrencies, i.e. their decentralised, personalized, and anonymized character originating from blockchain technologies. This, in turn, implies complicated (if only possible) access to information about cryptocurrency markets, investors and users as well as tough and restricted public access to cryptocurrency transactions. One of the outcomes of this is limited knowledge of cryptocurrency markets. In the vast majority of publications cited above one can find paragraphs on information gaps or lack of high-quality and reliable data. Raw information and low data availability and quality are identified by the European Central Bank as the main limitations (Chimienti et al., 2019). Consequently, cryptocurrencies cannot be effectively managed – one can manage only what is measurable. The issue of managing cryptocurrencies is widely discussed in the literature (Campbell-Verduyn, 2018) and there are many books on various technical aspects of managing cryptocurrencies including personal information. Controlling, one of the four fundamental managerial functions, concerning cryptocurrencies is probably the most challenging due to the decentralised character of the creation and circulation of cryptocurrencies. Some authors maintain, that there is no effective control over players along the crypto-asset value chain which in a borderless environment often hinders access to reliable information (Chimienti et al., 2019). All the above may to some extent explain our still limited knowledge about the way the market of cryptocurrencies works (especially in the context of blockchain technologies, see for example, Sharma et al., 2020; Habek et al., 2022). Also, the cryptocurrency market including its structure is considered as only partially researched (see for example Wątorek et al., 2021).

One more obstacle in researching the social consequences of cryptocurrencies tightly connected to the nature of the cryptocurrencies, is the social perception of finances in general, but incomes, and investment decisions in particular, In many cultures individual incomes and finances are considered personal and sensitive and are protected by law and social norms.

This may to some extent explain why access to cryptocurrency owners/users is difficult which results in a comparatively small size of research samples in questionnaire research on cryptocurrencies. Examples are 251 (Albayati et al., 2020), 295 (Chen et al., 2022), 386 (Al-Omoush et al., 2024), 216 (Lavan et al., 2024), or 367 (Kumar Sharma et al., 2024), One may share the opinion presented by Breidbach & Tana (2021) that actors and mechanisms shaping cryptocurrency markets remain an emerging area of inquiry with limited contributions available. One exception is a report by Checkout.com (2022) based on a panel of 3,000 mostly platform-based online business-to-consumers marketplaces, fintech and e-commerce businesses across 10 countries: Australia, France, Germany, Hong Kong, Italy, Kingdom of Saudi Arabia, Singapore, UK, UAE, and USA) and telephone interviews with nearly 30,000 consumers across 11 countries. One should notice, however, that telephone interviews are not as good as questionnaires.

The limitations regarding the size of research samples are traceable even in publications labelled as in-depth ones. For example, Breidbach & Tana (2021) investigated the roles, actions and resources of individuals collectively shaping cryptocurrency markets and the impact that their micro-level actions have on macro-level market outcomes. Their empirical research is based, however, only on 14 cryptocurrency events (Bitcoin conferences, in Melbourne, Australia held between May and December 2017, with event sizes ranging from 31 to 175 participants), and 31 unstructured ethnographic interviews on site (Breidbach & Tana, 2021).

The second limitation originates from the very nature of social sciences, especially methodologies used in various social sciences disciplines. Cryptocurrencies are difficult to research in general but for social scientists in particular. This is because of the comparatively short history (record) of cryptocurrencies. It impacts both the research methodology and – which is even more important - interpretations of the findings from empirical research on the social consequences of cryptocurrencies One should remember that social sciences require longer time perspectives for inquiries and time intervals for sound empirical research and testing than pure science disciplines. Sixteen years of cryptocurrency existence seems to be not enough for in-depth research and for formulating well-grounded conclusions.

A separate problem in researching on social consequences of cryptocurrencies is a lack of a sound and widely used methodology. One may also find certain weaknesses in the methodology used in research on the social implications of cryptocurrencies. Here the structure of the research samples (especially by sex and age) raises certain concerns. A good example of this could be the sample in Albayati et al. (2020) study composed of 72% of males and 28% of females, where 81% were respondents between 25-44 years of age. This kind of bias toward young people is present (and acknowledged) in other studies (Keshvari Fard et al., 2024; Checkout.com, 2022; Duffy, Wilson, 2024). A question which should be asked here is; what if the structure of the samples is not biased but correctly reflects the structure of actual cryptocurrency holders, because men and young people dominate in cryptocurrency market in real life? Maybe young males dominate in the cryptocurrency markets? If it is so, we touch on the problem of social equity and social coherence. Assuming that cryptocurrency investment brings a higher net profit than in the official financial sector and that investors in cryptocurrency belong to the well-off, above-average groups, one may hypothesize that cryptocurrency not only preserves the existing income inequalities but leads to a widening of income disparities in society. This hypothesis could be supported by such phenomena as volatility and risk, lack of regulation, technological barriers, and wealth concentration. The highly volatile nature of cryptocurrencies can lead to significant financial losses, particularly for individuals without the means to absorb such losses, so this feature promotes well-offs. The relatively unregulated market can be prone to scams, fraud, and manipulation, disproportionately affecting less experienced investors, and again less informed and more vulnerable groups may lose. Effective use of cryptocurrencies requires a certain level of digital literacy, which may be lacking in economically disadvantaged communities. Reliable internet access and technology are prerequisites, which may not be available to everyone. Individuals who invested early in major cryptocurrencies like Bitcoin and Ethereum have seen substantial gains, potentially widening the wealth gap and increasing institutional investment in cryptocurrencies could centralize wealth among already wealthy entities. All these are a guess. Unfortunately, there still is no empirical verification of the hypothesis formulated above.

The digital literacy mentioned above leads to a broader issue which is the level of knowledge of cryptocurrencies. Studies are acknowledging a limited amount of knowledge of cryptocurrencies among respondents.

International research on a big sample (nearly 30 000 consumers) showed that 65% of respondents have never held any form of digital asset and 42% of respondents say they do not know how to buy a digital asset (Checkout.com, 2022, p.4). If questions about digital assets are addressed to average citizens who do not own or invest in cryptocurrencies, their limited knowledge about digital assets is not particularly surprising since also findings by Checkout.com showed the scope of respondents' ignorance in distinguishing between a non-pegged crypto-currency (such as Bitcoin) and stablecoins which are pegged to and backed by another asset, currency or commodity (such as USDC) or have stability in-built through mechanisms such as algorithms (Checkout.com, 2022, p. 7). The lack of proper knowledge by the general population is one thing, but investors' knowledge gap is quite another. Though investing in cryptocurrency is on the rise, the full financial implications of investing in cryptocurrency are not yet widely understood—even among those who have invested. According to Fidelity Charitable research, more than one-in-three cryptocurrency investors (38 percent) are not aware that selling digital assets is a taxable event. Similarly, there is significant confusion about donating these assets to charity—a tax-savvy strategy that can potentially minimize the investor's tax burden. More than half (55 per cent) are not sure that digital assets can be donated to charity (Fidelity Charitable, 2021).

A piece of indirect evidence of a knowledge gap regarding cryptocurrencies could be one of the recommendations of the US Department of the Treasury which says: "Recommendation 3: U.S. authorities should work individually and through the Financial Literacy and Education Commission (FLEC), as appropriate, to ensure that U.S. consumers, investors, and businesses have access to trustworthy information on crypto-assets" (US Department of the Treasury, 2022, p.3). One may conclude that limited knowledge is recognized both by researchers and politicians.

This situation is an incentive for authors of dozens of books presenting the basics of cryptocurrencies and addressing a wide audience (for example Danial, 2023; Reichental, 2023).

There are several gaps in research on cryptocurrencies. Although exploring the drivers of 'individuals' adoption of Information Technology (IT) is well-documented in the literature, little is known about the driving forces of entering the cryptocurrency market by individual people. This can be partially explained by the confidentiality rooted in and connected with financial transactions. In this context, an interesting project is reported by Al-Omoush et al. (2024) who explored the determinants that impact the intention to continue using cryptocurrencies. A questionnaire among 386 participants in Jordan revealed that perceived value, optimism, and cryptocurrency addiction were significant determinants of continued cryptocurrency usage intention. Worth noticing is that in this research optimism and perceptions of cryptocurrency were increased by financial literacy which supports the statement that the cryptocurrency market favours and rewards financial knowledge and risk-taking (not especially in that order.

Staying with methodological issues it is worth referring to Silfversten et al. (2020) proposition of avenues for future research on using cryptocurrencies for illicit purposes which can be extended (and adjusted where necessary) to general inquiry on on cryptocurrencies. They propose:

- Improvements to mechanisms for data gathering and more accurate estimates of the extent of the use of cryptocurrencies
- Transparency in methodological approaches
- A stronger theoretical basis for research on cybercrime
- A more sophisticated understanding of the suitability of privacy coins for conducting illicit and criminal activities (Silfversten et al., 2020, p.IX). The

first two recommendations fully apply to general research on the social implications of cryptocurrencies

Concluding the methodological part of this section one should mention a lack of comparative studies. This gap could be diminished for example by replicating studies by Breidbach & Tana (2021), Chen et al. (2022) or Campino & Yang (2024) in other countries.

To sum up: research on cryptocurrencies remains in its initial stage in general, and on the social consequences of cryptocurrencies in particular. Considerable limitations here are the nature of cryptocurrencies and the academic profile of social sciences.

Having accepted the findings from current research on the social consequences of cryptocurrencies as mainly inconclusive concerning a balance of the positive versus negative outcomes of cryptocurrencies, at the end of this section one may present arguments supporting the hypothesis that cryptocurrencies can be interpreted primarily as a threat to societies.

Cryptocurrencies as a Social Threat

One may maintain that the vast majority of negative social consequences of cryptocurrencies arise from the very nature of cryptocurrencies. One may mention three characteristic traits.

First is anonymity granted by blockchain technologies which are the cornerstone of cryptocurrencies. Anonymity provides opportunities for criminals to hide behind presumed privacy and anonymity (Kethineni & Cao, 2020).

The second is the decentralised nature of cryptocurrencies which - when connected to anonymity -makes it impossible for the state to monitor and control the cryptocurrency markets. Consequently, all recommendations concerning the need for regulation (or even suggestions of such) (Burgess, 2024; Gonzálvez-Gallego & Pérez-Cárceles, 2021; Kethineni & Cao, 2020; Albayati et al., 2020; Checkout.com, 2022; Campino & Yang, 2024; Girasa, 2022; Xiao et al., 2023) can be interpreted as wishful thinking.

The third is the cross-border nature of cryptocurrency transactions. Even if cryptocurrencies were regulated in one state, the execution of the law provisions in countries with no such regulations has been time-consuming and costly (if possible) (Kethineni & Cao, 2020).

One may also prove that the vast majority of negative social consequences presented in the previous section can be linked to these three traits. Consequently one may maintain that cryptocurrency ipso facto is a social threat.

CONCLUSION

To conclude one may point et the following main messages presented in this chapter:

- Research on the social implications of cryptocurrencies remains in its initial stage *(in statu nascendi)*, especially concerning empirical studies
- Publicly available findings often are inconsistent and are based on small research samples
- There is no empirical evidence of the superiority of either negative or positive social effects of cryptocurrencies
- Publications available often show deficiencies in methodological correctness and due diligence
- There is reasonable ground to maintain that cryptocurrencies are conducive to widening the existing income inequalities
- Cryptocurrencies work first of all for young, well-off, and educated males which can be seen as a potential threat to social cohesion

REFERENCES

Adams, M., & Dammeyer, L. (2024, July 23).Top 10 Cryptocurrencies of July 23, 2024. *Forbes Advisor*, https://www.forbes.com/advisor/investing/cryptocurrency/top-10-cryptocurrencies

Ahmed, I., Fumimoto, K., Nakano, T., & Tran, T. H. (2024). Blockchain-Empowered Decentralized Philanthropic Charity for Social Good. *Sustainability (Basel)*, *16*(1), 210. DOI: 10.3390/su16010210

Al-Omoush, K. S., Gomez-Olmedo, A. M., & Gómez Funes, A. (2024). Why do people choose to continue using cryptocurrencies? *Technological Forecasting and Social Change*, *200*, 123151. DOI: 10.1016/j.techfore.2023.123151

Albayati, H., Kim, S. K., & Rho, J. J. (2020). Accepting financial transactions using blockchain technology and cryptocurrency: A customer perspective approach. *Technology in Society*, *62*, 101320. DOI: 10.1016/j.techsoc.2020.101320

Alexakis, C., Anselmi, G. & Petrella, G. (2024). Flight to cryptos: Evidence on the use of cryptocurrencies in times of geopolitical tensions. *International Review of Economics & Finance, 89, A*, 498-523, https://doi.org/.DOI: 10.1016/j.iref.2023.07.054

Ante, L. (2023). How Elon Musk's Twitter activity moves cryptocurrency markets. *Technological Forecasting and Social Change*, *186*, 122112. DOI: 10.1016/j.techfore.2022.122112

Bose, C. (2023, December 21). *Donorbox and The Giving Block: Accept Crypto and Stock Donations with a Seamless Integration*. https://donorbox.org/nonprofit-blog/donorbox-the-giving-block-integration

Breidbach, C. F., & Tana, S. (2021). Betting on Bitcoin: How social collectives shape cryptocurrency markets. *Journal of Business Research*, *122*, 311–320. DOI: 10.1016/j.jbusres.2020.09.017

Burgess, T. (2024). A Multi-Jurisdictional Perspective: To What Extent can Cryptocurrency be Regulated? And if so, Who Should Regulate Cryptocurrency? *Journal of Economic Criminology*, *100086*, 100086. Advance online publication. DOI: 10.1016/j.jeconc.2024.100086

Cadet, F. T. (2023). Cryptocurrency Brings New Meaning to Purchase Power and Bridges the Wealth Gap: A Closer Look at Bitcoin. In Taghipour, A. (Ed.), *Blockchain Applications in Cryptocurrency for Technological Evolution* (pp. 108–117). IGI Global.

Campbell-Verduyn, M. (Ed.). (2018). *Bitcoin and Beyond. Cryptocurrencies, Blockchains, and Global Governance*. Routledge.

Campino, J., & Yang, S. (2024). Decoding the cryptocurrency user: An analysis of demographics and sentiments. *Heliyon, 10*(5), e26671. DOI: 10.1016/j.heliyon.2024.e26671 PMID: 38434267

Carlisle, D. (2023). *The Crypto Launderers: Crime and Cryptocurrencies from the Dark Web to DeFi and Beyond*. Willey.

Carmona, T. (2022, October 26). *Debunking the narratives about cryptocurrency and financial inclusion*. Policy Commons. https://policycommons.net/artifacts/4140537/debunking-the-narratives-about-cryptocurrency-and-financial-inclusion/4949197

Checkout.com. (2022). *Demystifying Crypto. Shedding light on the adoption of digital currencies for payments in 2022*. https://assets.website-files.com/64db80a5e88c6b1723ff760b/654534f5526a1b2080a83a0d_Demystifying_Crypto_Report.pdf

Chen, X., Miraz, M. H., Habib, M., Gazi, A. I., & Hossain, A. I. (2022). Factors affecting cryptocurrency adoption in digital business transactions: The mediating role of customer satisfaction. *Technology in Society*, *70*, 102059. DOI: 10.1016/j.techsoc.2022.102059

Chimienti, M. T., Kochanska, U., & Pinna, A. (2019). Understanding the crypto-asset phenomenon, its risks and measurement issues. *ECB Economic Bulletin, 5*, European Central Bank. https://www.ecb.europa.eu/press/economic-bulletin/articles/2019/html/ecb.ebart201905_03~c83aeaa44c.en.html

Chohan, U. W. (2017, November 27). *Cryptoanarchism and Cryptocurrencies*. http://dx.doi.org/DOI: 10.2139/ssrn.3079241

Credits (2023, October 31). *Cryptocurrency in the Credits' App: A Financial Future Service*. https://credits.com/en/news/671-cryptocurrency-in-the-credits-app-a-financial-future-service.html

Danial, K. (2023). *Cryptocurrency Investing for Dummies*. For Dummies.

de Vries, A., & Stoll, C. (2021). Bitcoin's growing e-waste problem. *Resources, Conservation and Recycling*, *175*, 105901. DOI: 10.1016/j.resconrec.2021.105901

Duffy, P., & Wilson, A. (2024). *2024 Annual Report. Crypto Philanthropy Data, Trends & Predictions. Annual Industry Report on the State of Crypto Philanthropy*. https://thegivingblock.com/annual-report

Elouaourti, Z., & Ibourk, A. (2024). Financial Technologies for All MENA citizens: Tackling barriers and promoting inclusion. *Regional Science Policy & Practice*, *16*(6), 100019. DOI: 10.1016/j.rspp.2024.100019

England, J. (2023, April 24). Crypto regulations and building financial inclusion. *FinTech Magazine*. https://fintechmagazine.com/articles/crypto-regulations-and-building-financial-inclusion

Fahlander, F. (2022, June 3). *Cryptocurrencies, Remittances and Exchange Rates: A quantitative study on the rapid growth of crypto adoption in developing countries*. https://www.diva-portal.org/smash/get/diva2:1683128/FULLTEXT01.pdf

Fidelity Charitable. (2021, October 28). *Cryptocurrency and philanthropy*. https://www.fidelitycharitable.org/insights/cryptocurrency-and-philanthropy.html

Flick, C. (2022). A critical professional ethical analysis of Non-Fungible Tokens (NFTs). *Journal of Responsible Technology*, *12*, 100054. DOI: 10.1016/j.jrt.2022.100054

Foley, S., Karlsen, J. R., & Putniņš, T. J. (2019). Sex, Drugs, and Bitcoin: How Much Illegal Activity Is Financed through Cryptocurrencies? *Review of Financial Studies*, *32*(5), 1798–1853. DOI: 10.1093/rfs/hhz015

Girasa, R. (2022). *Regulation of Cryptocurrencies and Blockchain Technologies: National and International Perspectives*. Palgrave Macmillan.

Goel, R. K., & Mazhar, U. (2024). Cryptocurrency use and tax collections: Direct and indirect channels of influence. *Journal of Financial Stability*, *72*, 101251. DOI: 10.1016/j.jfs.2024.101251

Gonzálvez-Gallego, N., & Pérez-Cárceles, M. C. (2021). Cryptocurrencies and illicit practices: The role of governance. *Economic Analysis and Policy*, *72*, 203–212. DOI: 10.1016/j.eap.2021.08.003

Goodkin, A. L., Jones, B. A., & Berrens, R. P. (2020). Cryptodamages: Monetary value estimates of the air pollution and human health impacts of cryptocurrency mining. *Energy Research & Social Science*, *101281*, 101281. Advance online publication. DOI: 10.1016/j.erss.2019.101281

Grobys, K., & Junttila, J. (2021). Speculation and lottery-like demand in cryptocurrency markets. *Journal of International Financial Markets, Institutions and Money*, *71*, 101289. DOI: 10.1016/j.intfin.2021.101289

Habek, G. C., Toçoğlu, M. A., & Onan, A. (2022). Bi-Directional CNN-RNN Architecture with Group-Wise Enhancement and Attention Mechanisms for Cryptocurrency Sentiment Analysis. *Applied Artificial Intelligence*, *36*(1), 2145641. Advance online publication. DOI: 10.1080/08839514.2022.2145641

Horky, F., Dubbick, L., Rhein, F., & Fidrmuc, J. (2023). Don't miss out on NFTs?! A sentiment-based analysis of the early NFT market. *International Review of Economics & Finance*, *88*, 799–814. DOI: 10.1016/j.iref.2023.07.016

Howson, P. (2021). Crypto-giving and surveillance philanthropy: Exploring the trade-offs in blockchain innovation for nonprofits. *Nonprofit Management & Leadership*, *31*(4), 805–820. DOI: 10.1002/nml.21452

Janisch, F., & Stapleton, L. (2021). Digital Currencies and Community Empowerment in Austria: Gesell's Concept of Effective Demand as a Basis for Local Digital Currencies. *IFAC-PapersOnLine*, *54*(13), 698–703. DOI: 10.1016/j.ifacol.2021.10.533

Johnson, B., Leung, J., Co, S., Sun, T., Saunders, J. B., Lim, C. C. W., & Chan, G. C. K. (2023). Cryptocurrency trading and its associations with gambling and mental health: A scoping review. *Addictive Behaviors*, *136*, 107504. DOI: 10.1016/j.addbeh.2022.107504 PMID: 36174424

Keshvari Fard, M., Liu, J., & Petropoulos, F. (2024, March 5). Decoding Digital Philanthropy Analyzing Donors Choices in Cryptocurrency Donations. http://dx.doi.org/DOI: 10.2139/ssrn.4748710

Kethineni, S., & Cao, Y. (2020). The Rise in Popularity of Cryptocurrency and Associated Criminal Activity. *International Criminal Justice Review*, *30*(3), 325–344. DOI: 10.1177/1057567719827051

Kim, K., & Kauffman, R. J. (2024). On the Effects of Information Asymmetry in Digital Currency Trading. *Electronic Commerce Research and Applications*, *64*, 101366. DOI: 10.1016/j.elerap.2024.101366

Kshetri, N. (2024). Editorial: Economic, social and political impacts of blockchain. *Telecommunications Policy*, *48*(3), 102718. DOI: 10.1016/j.telpol.2024.102718

Kulkarni, R., Schintler, L., Koizumi, N., Olds, J. L., & Stough, R. (2019). *Cryptocurrency, Stablecoins and Blockchain: Exploring digital money solutions for remittances and inclusive economies.* 66th Annual North American Meetings of the Regional Science Association International (13–16 Nov, 2019). Pittsburgh, *PA, USA*. https://papers.ssrn.com/sol3/Papers.cfm?abstract_id=3511139

Kumar Sharma, R., Khan, S., Singh, R., & Birari, A. (2024). Speculative investment decisions in cryptocurrency: A structural equation modelling approach. *Journal of Decision Systems*, •••, 1–22. DOI: 10.1080/12460125.2024.2341194

Lavan, T., Martin, B. A. S., Lim, W. M., & Hollebeek, L. D. (2024). Social isolation and risk-taking behavior: The case of COVID-19 and cryptocurrency. *Journal of Retailing and Consumer Services*, *81*, 103951. DOI: 10.1016/j.jretconser.2024.103951

Milka, P. (2021). Speculation in the cryptocurrency market. *The Review of Economics. Finance & Investments*, *1*(1), 24–33. DOI: 10.53752/refi.2020.1.12

NDTV. (2021, May 14). *Why A $1 Billion Donation To India Covid Relief Shocked Memecoin Traders*. https://www.ndtv.com/india-news/a-1-billion-crypto-donation-to-india-covid-relief-in-memecoins-explained-2441443

Nicolas, M. L. D. (2022). Estimating a model of herding behavior on social networks. *Physica A*, *604*, 127884. DOI: 10.1016/j.physa.2022.127884

Novak, M. (2024). Crypto altruism: Applying blockchain to charitable and humanitarian activities. *Chinese Public Administration Review*, *15*(1), 11–23. DOI: 10.1177/15396754231175173

Office of Science and Technology Policy. (2022). *Climate and Energy Implications of Crypto-Assets in the United States*. White House Office of Science and Technology Policy. Washington, D.C. https://www.whitehouse.gov/wp-content/uploads/2022/09/09-2022-Crypto-Assets-and-Climate-Report.pdf

Orzi, R., Porcherot, R., & Valdecantos, S. (2021). Cryptocurrencies for Social Change: The Experience of MonedaPAR in Argentina. *International Journal of Community Currency Research*, *25*(1), 16–33. DOI: 10.15133/j.ijccr.2021.002

Ozili, P. K. (2023). Determinants of interest in eNaira and financial inclusion information in Nigeria: Role of FinTech, cryptocurrency and central bank digital currency. *Digital Transformation and Society.*, *2*(2), 202–214. DOI: 10.1108/DTS-08-2022-0040

Passinsky, A. (2024). Cryptocurrency: Commodity or Credit? In Sandberg, A., & Warenski, I. (Eds.), *The Philosophy of Money and Finance* (pp. 32–53). Academic., DOI: 10.1093/oso/9780192898807.003.0003

Patel, E. (2023, May 13). How can cryptocurrencies play a role in promoting financial inclusion? *The Economic Times*. https://economictimes.indiatimes.com/markets/cryptocurrency/how-can-cryptocurrencies-play-a-role-in-promoting-financial-inclusion/articleshow/100205450.cms?from=mdr

Patel, R. (2024). Economic freedom or crypto-colonialism? Materialities of Bitcoin adoption in El Salvador. *Geoforum, 151*, 103980. DOI: 10.1016/j.geoforum.2024.103980

Pinkerton, J. (2024, July 24). The History of Bitcoin. *USNews,* https://money.usnews.com/investing/articles/the-history-of-bitcoin

Prat, M. K. (2023, November 30). The environmental impact of bitcoin mining explained. *TechTarget,* https://www.techtarget.com/sustainability/feature/The-environmental-impact-of-bitcoin-mining-explained

PwC. (2024). *Crypto Contributions. Redefining Charitable Giving in the Digital Age.* https://www.pwc.ch/en/insights/fs/crypto-contributions.html

Reeves, M. (2017). Cryptocurrency-Remittance Transfers Futuristic Technologies & Poverty Alleviation. *Economics Student Theses and Capstone Projects, 56*. https://creativematter.skidmore.edu/econ_studt_schol/56

Reichental, J. (2023). *Cryptocurrency QuickStart Guide: The Simplified Beginner's Guide to Digital Currencies, Bitcoin, and the Future of Decentralized Finance.* ClydeBank Media LLC.

Rodima-Taylor, D., & Grimes, W. W. (2018). Cryptocurrencies and digital payment rails in networked global governance: perspectives on inclusion and innovation. In Campbell-Verduyn, M. (Ed.), *Bitcoin and Beyond. Cryptocurrencies, Blockchains, and Global Governance* (pp. 109–132). Routledge.

Rodrigues, G., & Kurtz, L. (2019). *Cryptocurrencies and anti-money laundering regulation in the G20.* Institute for Research on Internet and Society. Belo Horizonte. http://bit.ly/32Fw4xD

Sargisyan, A. G. (2023). The Harm of Cryptocurrency Mining to the Environment: How Serious is It. In Popkova, E. G., & Sergi, B. S. (Eds.), *Current Problems of the Global Environmental Economy Under the Conditions of Climate Change and the Perspectives of Sustainable Development. Advances in Global Change Research, 73* (pp. 13–21). Springer., DOI: 10.1007/978-3-031-19979-0_2

Sarma, M. (2008). Index of financial inclusion. *Working Paper No.215.* Indian Council for Research on International Economic Relations. New Delhi.

Setyawan, A. A., Winotoatmojo, H. P., & Puspa Ananda, N. K. (2024). Cryptocurrency and Financial Inclusion: Bridging the Gap in Emerging Countries. *Dinasti international journal of economics. Finance & accounting*, *5*(2), 510–516. DOI: 10.38035/dijefa.v5i2.2554

Sharma, D. K., Pant, S., Sharma, M., & Brahmachari, S. (2020). Cryptocurrency Mechanisms for Blockchains: Models, Characteristics, Challenges, and Applications. In Krishnan, S., Balas, V. E., Golden Julie, E., Robinson, Y. H., Balaji, S., & Kumar, R. (Eds.), *Handbook of Research on Blockchain Technology* (pp. 323–348). Academic Press. DOI: 10.1016/B978-0-12-819816-2.00013-7

Silfversten, E., Favaro, M., Slapakova, L., Ishikawa, S., Liu, J., & Salas, A. (2020). *Exploring the use of Zcash cryptocurrency for illicit or criminal purposes*. RAND Europe. https://www.rand.org/content/dam/rand/pubs/research_reports/RR4400/RR4418/RAND_RR4418.pdf

Soufaih, A. (2020). *Revolutionizing International Remittance Payments Using Cryptocurrency and Blockchain-based Technology Cryptocurrency and Blockchain-based Technology*. https://repository.upenn.edu/server/api/core/bitstreams/f4a63a05-8edf-4113-a9c2-e84797629a48/content

Swati, J., Nitin, P., Saurabh, P., Parikshit, D., Gitesh, P., & Rahul, S. (2022). Blockchain based Trusted Secure Philanthropy Platform: Crypto-GoCharity. *6th International Conference on Computing, Communication, Control and Automation (ICCUBEA)*. Pune, India. DOI: 10.1109/ICCUBEA54992.2022.10011026

Ulaşan, F. (2022). The Environmental Effects of Cryptocurrency Mining in the World. *Journal of Sustainable Economics and Management Studies*, *3*(1), 1–20.

U.S. Department of the Treasury. (2022). *Crypto-Assets: Implications for Consumers, Investors, and Businesses*. U.S. Department of the Treasury. https://home.treasury.gov/system/files/136/CryptoAsset_EO5.pdf

Walker, C. B. (2024). Going mainstream: Cryptocurrency narratives in newspapers. *International Review of Financial Analysis*, *94*, 103305. DOI: 10.1016/j.irfa.2024.103305

Wątorek, M., Drożdż, S., Kwapień, J., Minati, L., Oświęcimka, P., & Stanuszek, M. (2021). Multiscale characteristics of the emerging global cryptocurrency market. *Physics Reports*, *901*, 1–82. DOI: 10.1016/j.physrep.2020.10.005

Wendl, M., Doan, M. D., & Sassen, R. (2023). The environmental impact of cryptocurrencies using proof of work and proof of stake consensus algorithms: A systematic review. *Journal of Environmental Management*, *326*, 116530. DOI: 10.1016/j.jenvman.2022.116530 PMID: 36372031

World Bank. (2024, June 26). *Remittances Slowed in 2023, Expected to Grow Faster in 2024*. https://www.worldbank.org/en/news/press-release/2024/06/26/remittances-slowed-in-2023-expected-to-grow-faster-in-2024

Wu, A. A., & Katz, J. (2023). *Competition and Speculation in Cryptocurrencies*. https://www.hbs.edu/ris/Publication%20Files/competition_speculation_78d8a8a7-4a79-4fc4-af7a-7c2a361fc80a.pdf

Xiao, Z., Cui, S., Xiang, L., Liu, P. J., & He Zhang, H. (2023). The environmental cost of cryptocurrency: Assessing carbon emissions from bitcoin mining in China. *Journal of Digital Economy*, *2*, 119–136. DOI: 10.1016/j.jdec.2023.11.001

Zhang, D., Sun, Y., Duan, H., Hong, Y., & Wang, S. (2023). Speculation or currency? Multi-scale analysis of cryptocurrencies -The case of Bitcoin. *International Review of Financial Analysis*, *88*, 102700. DOI: 10.1016/j.irfa.2023.102700

Zhuk, A. (2024). Crypto-anarchy: a paradigm shift for society and the legal system. *Journal of Computer Virology and Hacking Techniques*, https://doi.org/.DOI: 10.1007/s11416-024-00525-1

ENDNOTES

1. Estimated numbers of cryptocurrencies vary. For example according to Keshvari Fard et al. (2024) "…by 2023 more than 20,000 cryptocurrencies have been developed over hundreds of different blockchain networks" (Keshvari Fard et al., 2024, p.2).

2. This definition resembles this of Sarma (2008) but differs because Sarma's covers only formal financial system.

3. This seems to be an underestimation since Fidelity Charitable alone received in 2021 $158 million of donations in cryptocurrency assets to their donor-advised funds (Fidelity Charitable, 2021).

4. This paragraph does not contain findings from an organized review of the literature but offers only few examples.

Chapter 13
Unveiling the Illegal Uses of Cryptocurrencies in Dark Web and Advanced AI and Machine Learning Techniques in Cryptocurrency Forensics

Ramy El-Kady
https://orcid.org/0000-0003-2208-7576
Police Academy, Egypt

ABSTRACT

The chapter delves into the digital forensics of cryptocurrencies, focusing on the role of blockchain, computers, and mobile phones in gathering evidence. It underscores the pressing need for immediate and extensive research in digital cryptocurrency forensics, especially for significant cryptocurrencies increasingly attracting legitimate and malicious users. The chapter also highlights a critical gap in research on host-based cryptocurrency forensics, particularly mobile-based forensics. Most studies on host-based forensics concentrate on outdated operating systems or platforms, highlighting the necessity for more current versions, and the urgency of updating your methods in host-based forensics is apparent. Cryptocurrency forensics primarily involves the analysis of publicly accessible blockchains using clustering heuristics and machine learning-based analysis to identify anonymous entities or provide investigation guidance. Security and vulnerability assessment studies are crucial in examining forensic methods for cryptocurrencies, offering insights into potential exploits.

DOI: 10.4018/979-8-3693-5986-0.ch013

INTRODUCTION

In the face of the escalating use of modern technology and the exploitation of the Internet by criminal groups and terrorist organizations to achieve their criminal purposes and given the rising rates of cybercrimes such as identity theft, online fraud, and data breaches, there is a significant need to highlight the forensic science of digital evidence (El-Kady, 2025). It is one of the most critical tools of criminal justice and law enforcement agencies in the battle against cybercrime, and it is pivotal in reducing its prevalence. Your work in digital evidence is crucial in this fight (El-Kady, 2023).

In this context, Digital forensics could be defined as "a specialized field within forensic science that deals explicitly with identifying, acquiring, processing, analyzing, and reporting electronically stored data" (El-Kady, 2025) Electronic evidence is not just a part but often the crux of nearly all illegal acts, and the assistance of digital forensics is vital for law enforcement investigations (El-Kady, 2023).

As digital evidence continues to evolve in its dynamic and delicate nature, the importance of digital forensics is rising. This evidence necessitates law enforcement agencies to implement stringent safety, health, and reliability measures to ensure its admissibility and authenticity in criminal courts (El-Kady, 2024). The ever-changing landscape of digital evidence underscores the need for law enforcement professionals to stay current with technological advancements, a crucial aspect of their ongoing efforts to combat cybercrime. Your continuous learning and adaptation to these advancements, combined with your expertise in digital forensics, are critical to our success (El-Kady, 2025).

Successive technological developments have contributed to the emergence of cryptocurrencies, which have gained global recognition in various legal fields. At the same time, these new currencies have not been spared from being used by criminal groups and terrorist organizations to commit many criminal activities, especially in the vicinity of the dark web, exploiting the characteristics of these currencies and this dark network that contributes to the anonymity of the personalities of the perpetrators and make it difficult for law enforcement agencies to pursue them.

With these successive developments, law enforcement authorities face numerous challenges in combating online criminal activities. The most significant problem is proving these crimes through digital evidence. This study underscores the urgency and importance of addressing the role of digital forensics in this context (El-Kady, 2025).

The study aims to shed light on the digital forensics of cryptocurrencies and the dark web by reviewing the role of the elements and tools involved in their formation, such as blockchain, computers, and mobile phones, and learning evidence. It will focus on its methods and review the extent to which artificial intelligence (AI) and machine learning (ML) can be relied upon in forensics on the dark web (El-Kady, 2024).

LITERATURE REVIEW

New studies are focusing on the illicit uses of cryptocurrencies on the Dark Web. They demonstrated that cryptocurrencies are frequently used for illicit activities on the Dark Web due to their pseudonymous nature, which complicates transaction tracking and monitoring. However, advanced AI and ML techniques are being developed to enhance cryptocurrency forensics and combat these illicit uses (EL-Kady, 2025).

Some scholars have demonstrated that a substantial portion of cryptocurrency transactions on the Dark Web are utilized for illicit purposes. For instance, over 80% of Bitcoin addresses on the Dark Web have been linked to malicious activities, with transactions totaling approximately $180 million. They highlighted the extensive use of cryptocurrencies for illicit activities on the Dark Web, utilizing a framework called MFScope. The researchers collected data from over 27 million dark webpages, identifying that more than 80% of Bitcoin addresses were used with malicious intent. They revealed that these addresses were involved in transactions worth approximately $180 million, often linked to popular cryptocurrency services for laundering purposes (Lee et al., 2019).

On the other hand, others demonstrated that Criminals often utilize coin-mixing services to obscure financial transactions, thereby making it difficult to trace the flow of money. They present a framework for collecting data from Tor hidden services, with a focus on Bitcoin addresses linked to criminal activities. The study aims to understand the interrelationships between illicit activities and the lifecycle of ".onion" domains, providing case studies for profiling dark vendors and identifying mixed Bitcoin addresses (Kim et al., 2024).

Some researchers have proven that Cryptocurrencies are the primary medium for transactions in darknet marketplaces, where they are used for both legal and illicit activities. This research focuses on the AlphaBay marketplace, utilizing blockchain analysis to track both legitimate and illicit cryptocurrency transactions. They found that 90% of transactions were identifiable and often involved illegal activities or attempts to obfuscate other transactions. This work underscores the potential for criminologists to contribute to understanding the patterns and contexts of these transactions (Dearden & Tucker, 2023).

On the other hand, several studies indicate that advanced AI and ML methods are essential in cryptocurrency forensics. These techniques effectively identify fraudulent transactions with high accuracy, improving the efficiency and precision of cyber forensic investigations. The emergence of cryptocurrencies has led to notable progress in financial technology, although it has also given rise to a surge in fraudulent activity. Cryptocurrency forensics is being enhanced through the application of advanced AI and ML methods. The goal is to identify and prevent fraudulent transactions and cyber risks successfully.

Advanced AI and ML algorithms are crucial in Bitcoin forensics, as they effectively identify fraudulent transactions and enhance cyber forensic investigations. These technologies enhance the precision of fraud detection and the efficiency of forensic investigations, resulting in faster responses to cyberattacks and reduced risk exposure for enterprises. Machine learning (ML) techniques, such as Logistic Regression, Random Forest Classifier, and XGB Classifier, have demonstrated a remarkable ability to identify fraudulent cryptocurrency transactions accurately. Among these options, the XGB Classifier exhibits superior accuracy compared to the others (Kumar & Sharma, 2023).

AI and ML are highly effective technologies for enhancing cyber forensic investigations. They enhance the effectiveness and accuracy of identifying and categorizing threats, leading to faster analytical processes and improved detection capabilities (Fakiha, 2023). Additional research indicates that AI and ML can enhance the efficiency of cyber forensic investigations by automating various processes, boosting the detection and response to threats, and enhancing the analysis and recognition of patterns in data.

Incorporating AI and ML into cyber forensic investigations has demonstrated considerable potential in improving the effectiveness and precision of these procedures. This synthesis examines how AI and ML technologies enhance cyber forensic investigations by automating processes, enhancing threat detection, and providing robust analytical capabilities (Izadiyan et al., 2025).

AI and ML are revolutionizing cyber forensic investigations by automating the identification and analysis of threats, thereby minimizing the need for human intervention and enhancing the precision of detecting malware and anomalies. These technologies provide more effective and proactive reactions to cyber threats. However, continuous study and improvement are necessary to address challenges and fulfill their potential (Lawlor, 2021).

Some studies have shown that AI and ML greatly enhance the effectiveness and accuracy of identifying and categorizing risks in cyber forensic investigations, allowing quicker responses to cyber threats (Fakiha, 2023; Benkerroum & Chougdali, 2023; Dunsin et al., 2023).

Additional research suggests that utilizing ML algorithms to automate manual forensic activities reduces the time and effort required for investigations, resulting in a more streamlined and effective process (Benkerroum & Chougdali, 2023; G. S. et al., 2023).

Additional research has confirmed that machine learning (ML) techniques, such as Random Forest and Gradient Boosted Trees, have demonstrated a notable level of precision in identifying malware (Viroonluecha & Kaewkiriya, 2018). Consequently, this has enhanced the dependability of forensic investigations (Benkerroum & Chougdali, 2023; Patil et al., 2021).

Additional research has demonstrated that ML approaches enable cybersecurity systems to acquire knowledge from patterns and adapt to emerging threats, facilitating proactive prevention and prompt responses to hostile activity (Gupta et al., 2021; Swaminathan et al., 2022; Suryawanshi et al., 2023).

A recent study has found that advanced machine learning (ML) models, such as Siamese Neural Networks, can significantly enhance the accuracy of anomaly detection in industrial cyber-physical systems. This improvement reduces false alarm rates and enhances security overall (Zhou et al., 2021). Other research indicates that, although there are advantages, the use of AI and ML in cyber forensics encounters obstacles such as the need for high-quality training data, potential algorithmic biases, and the ever-changing characteristics of cyber threats (Dunsin et al., 2023; G. S et al., 2023).

On the other hand, recent studies have shown that cryptocurrencies are widely used for illicit activities on the Dark Web; however, advancements in AI and ML are enhancing the ability to detect and track these activities. Techniques such as graph-based detection, ML models, and NLP-driven approaches are proving effective in enhancing cryptocurrency forensics, offering law enforcement agencies powerful tools to combat cryptocurrency-enabled crimes.

They demonstrated techniques such as Hyperedge Classification and frameworks like CENSor, which utilize graph data to detect illegal Bitcoin operations with high precision, achieving an F1-score of 0.867. They introduced a novel approach using Hyperedge Classification to detect illegal Bitcoin transactions. The CENSor framework, based on a cluster-based Hyperedge-Node Switching technique, significantly improves detection capabilities, achieving an F1-score of 0.867. This method underscores the significance of graph data in refining the precision of cryptocurrency forensics (Lee et al., 2024).

Additionally, Approaches like VTAC leverage ML to detect illegal transactions with high accuracy, utilizing models such as XGBoost to achieve a 97.5% accuracy rate. They present the VTAC approach, which utilizes ML to detect illegal transactions on the blockchain with an accuracy rate of 97.5%. This method combines ML algorithms with a pre-training process to effectively analyze and identify illicit transactions, outperforming existing methods (Venčkauskas et al., 2025).

In addition to advanced NLP models, such as TextCNN, some researchers are utilized for rapid mnemonic identification, which is crucial for accessing cryptocurrency wallets, achieving near-perfect accuracy, and significantly improving processing speed (Kao, 2025). Meanwhile, others examine the application of blockchain analysis, AI, and ML in combating crimes enabled by cryptocurrencies. It emphasizes a multi-layered approach that combines technological innovations with regulatory efforts to detect and prevent illicit activities, using case studies such as the shutdown of the Silk Road to illustrate its effectiveness (Chitsungo, 2024).

In the same context, others showed that combining mutual information with self-supervised learning enhances the detection of illicit cryptocurrency transactions, addressing issues such as sample imbalance and unlabeled data. They combine mutual information and self-supervised learning to improve the detection of illegal cryptocurrency transactions. By addressing sample imbalance and utilizing a novel loss function, the study enhances the performance of illegal behavior detection in cryptocurrency networks (Zhao et al., 2023).

In Conclusion, the studies reviewed highlight the dual role of cryptocurrencies as both a tool for illicit activities on the Dark Web and a focus for advanced forensic techniques. While cryptocurrencies facilitate anonymity and ease of illegal transactions, innovative AI and ML methods are proving effective in detecting and preventing these activities. A combination of technological advancements and regulatory frameworks is essential for addressing the challenges posed by cryptocurrency-related crimes.

METHODOLOGY

The descriptive-analytical method is the most suitable research approach for examining social and legal phenomena. It is defined as: "studying the phenomenon as it exists in reality, describing it closely and expressing it qualitatively or quantitatively to reach conclusions that contribute to understanding and developing this reality" (Obeidat et al., 1996). Additionally, the research subject's transnational character imposes on the researcher the use of a comparative approach, referring to facts and incidents related to cryptocurrencies and dark web forensics, with a focus on their methods.

The descriptive-analytical method is the most suitable research approach for studying dark web crimes, as it involves closely describing and analyzing the phenomenon, using a comparative approach to examine facts and incidents. The research tools that the researcher will use as scientific sources in preparing this research include the Arab and foreign legal literature related to the subject of research in the field of criminal law, as well as relevant specialized literature, such as books, papers, and university dissertations. Alternatively, a master's degree or articles published in scientific journals on the topic, in addition to news published in various media outlets and on the Internet.

RESULTS

The development of cryptocurrency forensics can be summarized as the most extensively studied cryptocurrency, Bitcoin, introduced by Nakamoto in 2008 (Nakamoto, 2008), which has been the primary focus of forensic platforms. However, research on other cryptocurrencies, such as Ether, Monero, and Verge, is lacking. An initial study on Blockchain-based cryptocurrency forensics was conducted in 2011. According to the FBI, this research emerged as criminal actors began to show interest in cryptocurrencies around two years after the introduction of Bitcoin in 2008 (Reid & Harrigan, 2013). The initial investigation into Bitcoin forensics was conducted in 2014, with separate studies focusing on mobile-based (Montanez, 2014) and computer-based approaches. These studies, presented as master's theses, demonstrate academic curiosity in this field (Doran, 2014).

Research in digital cryptocurrency forensics experienced a hiatus of approximately 3-4 years before resuming around 2017-2018. This resurgence coincided with the growing popularity of cryptocurrency among the public and criminal individuals. Research on cryptocurrencies conducted on mobile devices is scarce, with a significant focus on the security and privacy of cryptocurrency wallet applications. This suggests a need for more excellent studies on forensic analysis of mobile platforms to uncover digital evidence (Dudani et al., 2023).

Regarding computer-based cryptocurrency studies, research using Windows-based systems is the most prevalent, followed by research using Linux and macOS operating systems. Research might be undertaken to analyze Bitcoin artifacts on Mac OS platforms. Windows 7 is the most extensively studied computer platform for Bitcoin artifacts, so this area lacks research on Windows 10 and 11 computers.

Most studies on cryptocurrency forensics focus on analyzing the publicly accessible blockchain. This involves utilizing clustering heuristics and machine learning (ML)- based analysis to extract valuable insights. The goal is to either identify anonymous entities or provide guidance for investigations. Some scholars developed an Elliptic Dataset as a significant resource for researching the application of ML and graph-based methods in Bitcoin forensics based on Blockchain technology (Weber et al., 2019).

DISCUSSION

In this study, we will examine the illicit uses of cryptocurrencies on the Dark Web and how criminals utilize them to conceal their financial activities. After that, we will focus on emerging technologies, such as AI, ML, and Blockchain, that assist in tracking its illegal paths and present digital evidence to prove it.

Illegal Uses of Cryptocurrencies on the Dark Web

In this section, we will examine the Dark Web and cryptocurrencies, their unique characteristics, and how criminals utilize them as a principal payment tool in illicit transactions. Moreover, how can it be used as a digital forensic tool to prove illegal activities?

The Dark Web as a Hidden Part of the Internet

The dark web is a hidden part of the Internet, divided into three main sections: the Surface Network, which contains only 0.03% of the information accessible through traditional search engines; the Deep Network, which includes academic databases, government records, corporate and commercial bank databases, email content, and TV broadcast services; and the Dark Web, which is not commonly accessed and is a breeding ground for illegal criminal activities, as not everything on the Internet can be accessed by users.

The concept of Black Networks, also known as the Dark Web, has emerged, and much of its content is confidential. They provide privacy to their users, shielding them from censorship (El-Kady, 2024), and offer relevant services. Information is exchanged confidentially among its members, and no user outside the network can view its content or search for it in traditional ways.

Unlike the clear web, also called the "Surface Web," which refers to information that is publicly available and indexed by conventional search engines, the dark web consists of encrypted hidden networks that allow the owner and users of the site to keep their identity anonymous while being relatively difficult to track (Guccione, 2019), which makes it the preferred network for all criminals, as it provides a safe environment for their illegal activities (El-Kady, 2024).

In summary, the dark web can be defined as a part of the Internet that allows the issuance of websites and the dissemination of information without revealing the identity or location of the publisher. It also requires software, settings, and special authorization to access it. It is a part of the web that is not indexed by search engines and can be accessed on the dark web through certain services, such as Tor (Biddle et al., 2003).

It is a compilation of interconnected networks and advanced technologies for exchanging and disseminating digital content. The dark web is not an independent network, but rather a means of accessing unindexed resources on the existing physical network using specialized technologies (Dudani et al., 2023).

According to some estimates, the global internet has a daily user base of 5.07 billion individuals. Although the darknet's daily user base represents a mere 0.04% of the total daily Internet users, it nonetheless encompasses approximately 2.5 million users every day (Gannon et al., 2023).

The Internet was typically born in the second half of the 1990s, but it was not until 2004 that it became a core part of daily routine activities. By 2018, 90% of households in North America and European countries had internet access (Martin, 2021). Technological advancements facilitated the Internet's global expansion, enabling households to access the necessary hardware and software for data transfer and storage.

The Internet has transformed from a publishing medium to a participatory medium, enabling users to communicate, interact, and create user-generated content within virtual communities. Some of these communities have become household names, serving billions of users worldwide. However, hundreds of thousands of smaller virtual communities exist outside the mainstream, focusing on personal characteristics, experiences, religious beliefs, political opinions, and other shared interests (Gannon et al., 2023).

The global use of the Internet has led to a need for anonymous online interactions, particularly for military personnel, journalists, and political and religious minorities living under autocratic regimes. In the 1990s, the US Navy developed prototypes for The Onion Router (TOR) to provide this anonymity.

TOR became publicly available in 2002, providing thousands of servers to obscure user identities. It encrypts online traffic by rerouting the IP address through randomly chosen servers, making it nearly impossible to trace it back to its original address. TOR quickly gained popularity in 2008 with the release of its browser version, making it easily accessible to the broader public (El-Kady, 2024).

The TOR browser functions as an Internet browser, enabling users to access the Web while ensuring anonymity. It also accommodates darknet or onion sites, websites, forums, and other online archives not indexed by publicly recognized search engines. These darknet sites, known as “hidden services” or HSes, are home to a broad array of criminal marketplaces, such as Silk Road and Alphabay, which mirror the workings of legal marketplaces on the Clearnet (Gannon et al., 2023).

Cryptocurrency as a New Tool of Payment in the Virtual World

Cryptocurrencies are defined as a virtual digital currency that has no tangible physical entity or physical existence, is produced by computer programs, and is not subject to control or control by a central bank or any official international administration, nor does it carry a serial number, it is used via the Internet In buying and selling transactions or converting them into other currencies, and receiving voluntary acceptance from those dealing in them (Al-Bahouth, 2017). Following the inception of Bitcoin, numerous other cryptocurrencies have emerged. The most prominent cryptocurrencies are Ripple, which appeared in 2012; Litecoin and Monroe, which appeared in 2014; the Chinese currency NEO, which the Chinese government launched in the same year to support the Chinese economy; Ethereum, which appeared in 2015; Bitcoin Volt, which appeared in 2019; and Facebook's Libra currency (Diem), which is expected to be launched soon (Nour, 2022).

The emergence of cryptocurrencies as a result of the continuous technological development in our world is due to the tendency of most institutions, authorities, and countries to digitize their various systems and transform them into a digital economy and a system of financial inclusion, where the need to develop new tools that bear the digital character for dealing within this world has emerged, and cryptocurrencies and blockchain have been one of the tools of financial dealing on the Internet, which includes millions of financial transactions. The names of these currencies have proliferated since they emerged as encrypted digital currencies, commonly referred to as “Cryptocurrencies.”

Scholars note that the emergence of cryptocurrency began in 2008; the virtual currency landscape underwent a significant transformation with the introduction of Bitcoin by Satoshi Nakamoto, the pseudonymous creator (Nakamoto, 2008). Bitcoin is built upon blockchain, a decentralized record-keeping technology (Casino et al., 2019). Nakamoto asserts that implementing a decentralized electronic cash system will eliminate the need for transactions to pass through financial institutions, thereby resolving the inherent issue of double-spending, which is both illicit and erodes confidence in any currency, ultimately leading to inflation. Following Nakamoto's findings, the network utilizes hashing to timestamp transactions and create an unalterable chain of hash-based proof-of-work, thereby establishing an immutable record.

This creates a ledger that undergoes peer review and is immune to alteration by a single user, rendering it more dependable than a centralized system where the sole verification point is the engaged agency. Following the development of Bitcoin, several other cryptocurrencies, including Litecoin, Dash, Ethereum, Monero, Dogecoin, and others, were introduced. These cryptocurrencies were built using various hashing algorithms and anonymization approaches (Dudani et al., 2023).

Anonymity as an Advantage Element of Cryptocurrencies

In March 2013, Dark Coin, now known as Dash, was developed to address the issue of absolute anonymity in cryptocurrencies. It achieved this by implementing Dark Send, which prevents tracing transactions to their source or destination addresses. Some scholars state that when Dark Send is activated, it automatically divides a payment request into smaller amounts. These smaller amounts are then pooled with other divided transactions to create a pool of more significant transactions (Duffield & Hagan, 2014).

After this, a controller node is created for each pool. After completing this process, the input transactions are rearranged to provide nearly identical outputs, a process known as mixing. Blind signatures ensure that the output of a pool is exclusively accessible to the pool participants while preventing any disclosure to the controller node. After all users have confirmed the accuracy of their input and output amounts, transactions are digitally signed and then distributed to the network. The blockchain stores all transaction data but does not allow viewers to establish a direct link between a sender and a receiver.

Mixing services enhance anonymity and provide challenges for investigators attempting to decipher transactions. Cryptocurrencies themselves do not pose a threat; however, the utilization of cryptocurrencies and methodologies that serve the interests of criminals necessitates the field of cryptocurrency forensics, which will be explored in the next section (Dudani et al., 2023).

Cryptocurrencies as a Primary Payment Tool in the Dark Web

Numerous Scholars note that several indicators suggest a close relationship between cryptocurrencies and dark web markets. According to INTERPOL, it regularly receives a significant volume of cases relating to cryptocurrencies, which perplexes the international law enforcement community. The Onion Scan Report reveals that Darknet markets, such as Silk Road, AlphaBay, and Hansa, generated around $3,000,000 from September 2015 to December 2016 (Tziakouris, 2018).

According to a joint source for the FBI (2012), a cybercriminal selling a ZeuS botnet Trojan was reported to exclusively accept payments using Bitcoin, Liberty Reserve, or WebMoney. The source of this information was the Federal Bureau of Investigation (FBI) in 2012 (FBI, 2012). Another open-source report cited the utilization of Bitcoin on Silk Road (Montanez, 2014), which was likened to the Darknet equivalents of Amazon or eBay, facilitating the illicit trade of diverse items. Some scholars examine the involvement of the Dark Web and Cryptocurrencies in cybercrime, including a thorough analysis of the trustworthiness of these digital assets. They also emphasize the importance of investor awareness (Taleby et al., 2021).

In contrast, others utilize Clear Net as a source of intelligence to analyze the transition to using Bitcoin and Monero for the illicit drug trade in Dark Net markets. According to their analysis, the news about Bitcoin traceability in 2015 had the opposite effect, promoting the use of Bitcoin for illegal drug trafficking on dark markets (Bahamazava & Nanda, 2022). However, the 2017 privacy update of

Monero led to a shift in preference from Bitcoin to Monero for the same purpose (Dudani et al., 2023).

INTERPOL has identified another application of Bitcoin, which involves transferring funds to regions subject to financial monitoring or embargo (Tziakouris, 2018). This practice likely supports illicit activity in those locations. Bitcoin has the potential to serve as a significant means of financing for various groups, both lawful and unlawful, which presents a risk to a nation's security. This evaluation was based on the FBI Intelligence Evaluation Report (FBI, 2012), which also noted that the internet hacktivist group LulzSec received more than $18,000 in Bitcoins from anonymous followers and supporters who made donations.

INTERPOL is concerned about money laundering through Initial Coin Offering (ICOs) or cryptocurrency exchanges. This is evident from cases such as the Bitcoin exchange OKCoin, which laundered hundreds of thousands of US dollars, and the case of BitInstant, which laundered approximately $1,000,000 for Silk Road market customers (Tziakouris, 2018). Regarding money laundering using Bitcoins, the FBI encountered a case where virtual game currency was used to acquire in-game virtual products sold to other players in exchange for "clean money." According to a separate tip to the FBI, an individual engaged in money laundering activities outside the United States (FBI, 2012). This person utilized fraudulent accounts on the WebMoney platform to assist cybercriminals who generated profits through carding operations. In June 2010, unidentified individuals created 3,000 online membership accounts using 16,000 bank accounts at a US banking institution. The purpose of these accounts was to deceive victims into providing payments for non-existent auction items (Dudani et al., 2023).

In 2012, the FBI received numerous reports regarding the use of Bitcoin in illicit transactions. However, as early as 2011, the theft of Bitcoins also became a concern. Researchers from a computer security firm discovered a malware called "Infostelar. Coinbit" specifically designed to steal bitcoins from compromised users' Bitcoin wallets and transfer them to a server in Poland. Subsequently, the FBI received numerous reports regarding the misappropriation of Bitcoins from unencrypted wallets, trading platforms, game sites, and similar sources (FBI, 2012).

In 2021, some scholars conducted a case study on the Coincheck hacking incident, which entailed the illicit acquisition of $530 million of cryptocurrencies. The study effectively demonstrates the process of laundering Bitcoin. The Binance Blockchain suffered a $570 million hack on October 7, 2022, due to flaws in cross-chain bridges. Chainalysis5 projects a total cryptocurrency loss of $2 billion in 2022, resulting from 13 cross-chain bridge assaults (Tsuchiya & Hiramoto, 2021).

Below are several further unauthorized applications of cryptocurrencies identified by INTERPOL: Cryptojacking, specifically through the use of Jenkins-Miner, has accumulated almost $3,000,000 worth of Monero, Crypto-stealing Trojans, like CryptoShuffler, pilfer funds by explicitly targeting the data stored in volatile memory or the clipboard, Non-standard Bitcoin transactions have the potential to include encoded data chunks that can be used to distribute illegal content, such as child exploitation material.

The primary obstacle for law enforcement is the difficulty of removing such content due to the immutable nature of the blockchain. ICO exit scams involve criminals deceiving victims by soliciting funds for non-existent coins and subsequently vanishing, thereby defrauding the victims (Tziakouris, 2018). The issue of law enforcement dealing with nation-state attacks financed through cryptocurrencies is another challenge (Dudani et al., 2023).

The issues mentioned above are not exclusive; advancements in cryptocurrencies are giving rise to increasingly intricate predicaments for law enforcement. Every cryptocurrency has its unique challenges that arise from the underlying technology. Litecoin, Monero, Dogecoin, and Dash have gained significant popularity as digital currencies. Darkcoin, also known as Dash, achieves true anonymity using DarkSend (Duffield & Hagan, 2014), which utilizes mixing techniques and blind signatures. This ensures that transactions cannot be linked to specific users, as the public ledger contains no information about the individuals involved.

Due to advancements in cryptocurrency, criminals are attempting to outsmart the legal system, prompting law enforcement agencies to prioritize the field of Bitcoin forensics. Forensics plays a crucial role in uncovering evidence from digital devices, blockchains, and other sources that may contain artifacts related to cryptocurrencies. Advancements in Bitcoin forensics will also deter future cryptocurrency-related offenses, thereby diminishing criminal interest in cryptocurrency (Dudani et al., 2023).

USING CRYPTOCURRENCIES IN CRIMINAL DIGITAL FORENSICS

Scholars believe that these cryptocurrencies could be beneficial in the criminal justice system as a tool for digital forensics. Cryptocurrency forensics, also known as Bitcoin forensics, is a field of study that establishes the connection between the flow of virtual currency and the transactions or actors responsible for initiating that flow. This is particularly relevant as most unlawful activities involve using Bitcoin as a form of payment. The intricate nature of Bitcoin forensics involves meticulously tracking and understanding the movement of funds, identifying the addresses involved in transactions, establishing intricate links between various cryptocurrency wallets, and unveiling complex patterns and linkages within the Blockchain (Joshi, 2023).

Some scholars have emphasized the necessity of cryptocurrency forensics (Dudani et al., 2023); due to the FBI's 2012 Intelligence Assessment Report, there is moderate confidence that Bitcoin will be a profitable payment method for cybercriminals. This conclusion is based on the observed fluctuations in the Bitcoin exchange rate in 2011 and the limited information available regarding the acceptance of Bitcoin. Based on available data from criminal investigations concerning the usage of e-Gold and WebMoney, the FBI has identified a potential future risk of Bitcoin being used for money laundering. The paper also addresses the problem of attackers utilizing malware and hacking techniques to steal Bitcoins, as well as the creation of Bitcoins through botnets (FBI, 2012).

Advancements in cryptocurrency forensics are underscored by real-world events, such as the FTX scandal, one of the most significant financial frauds since the Enron collapse. This case, involving cryptocurrencies, demonstrates the need for robust forensic techniques. Cryptocurrency forensics, a multidisciplinary field encompassing digital forensics and forensic accounting, is crucial in investigations involving various stakeholders (Dudani et al., 2023).

Cryptocurrency forensics is not just an investigative technique; it is a powerful tool that empowers law enforcement agencies and financial investigators to safeguard individuals from the perils of the digital world. It effectively identifies culprits and determines the whereabouts of assets, providing a robust sense of security. Tracing cryptocurrency is not just a standard practice; it is a vital tool in investigating and recovering individuals who have fallen victim to online fraud, theft, hacking, and extortion operations, offering them a shield of protection in the digital world.

Emerging Technologies That are Used to Detect Illegal Activities on the Dark Web

In this section, we will explore emerging technologies used to detect illegal activities on the Dark Web, including AI, machine learning (ML), and Blockchain, and focus on the primary challenges that face their application.

Blockchain as a Means for Digital Forensics

Scholars emphasize the nexus between blockchain and cryptocurrency, as described by Nakamoto. According to Nakamoto, a cryptocurrency, such as Bitcoin, is an electronic coin that is a sequence of digital signatures, including a hash of previous transactions and the recipient's public key (Nakamoto, 2008). This allows for the verification of the coin's ownership history. However, the recipient cannot determine whether the coin has been double-spent. A proposed solution to address this problem and maintain Bitcoin's decentralized nature involves implementing a timestamp server. This server would broadcast the hash of a block to the network for verification purposes (Dudani et al., 2023).

Blockchain, a decentralized database structured as a sequence of ordered blocks, is a critical component of cryptocurrency forensics. Cryptocurrency transactions are recorded in blocks on the blockchain, which serves as a transparent ledger and a significant repository of forensic evidence and other network-related artifacts. Its immutable nature and miners' role in maintaining a verifiable record of all transactions have significantly disrupted traditional banking and corporate systems. This technology enables decentralized currencies to operate with a level of trust comparable to that of a reputable financial institution (Casino et al., 2019).

Cryptocurrencies like Bitcoin and other virtual currencies do not offer perfect anonymity. Transactions are recorded on digital blockchain ledgers powered by innovative blockchain technology, which reveal users through their Bitcoin address without disclosing personal information. Law enforcement agencies, regulators, and financial investigators have developed techniques to penetrate this anonymity, using blockchain intelligence tools and investigative methods to uncover identities in cryptocurrency transactions.

Transferring cryptocurrencies involves an individual installing a digital wallet, acquiring a collection of coins through third-party trade or donation, and initiating a request to transfer a specific amount of cryptocurrency to another user. The transaction's information is gathered into a block, sent to the user network for verification, and then added to the blockchain. The recipient's wallet receives the transferred coins after the new block is added to the blockchain. Coins, in a technical sense, lack physical existence and cannot be physically moved. They function as a type of digital currency that relies on the trust of its users.

According to the FBI's 2012 assessment, several deficiencies in intelligence were identified regarding specific criminal activities. These included insufficient information on individuals or groups attempting to evade compliance with the United States Bank Secrecy Act (BSA) regulations, as well as other criminal organizations and Bitcoin services facilitating illicit activities. These gaps in intelligence present numerous obstacles for law enforcement agencies (FBI, 2012).

Digital forensics play a crucial role in addressing these inquiries. By analyzing computers, hard drives, mobile devices, and other relevant sources, crucial details about the methods employed in illicit activities that Bitcoin finances can be uncovered. Forensic accounting professionals require specific information, including wallet IDs, public-private vital combinations, and transaction data, to track money flow (Dudani et al., 2023).

Digital forensics plays a crucial role in extracting and evaluating this information. If an investigator has identified a suspect and has access to the suspect's devices, they would use host-based forensics methods. This involves examining the suspect's mobile devices, computers, and memory to gather evidence, such as application data, wallet information, public and private keys, and other relevant artifacts related to cryptocurrency. This evidence can potentially aid in further investigation of the blockchain for additional proof.

Alternatively, if a specific suspect has not been identified, detectives rely on publicly accessible blockchains and potentially valuable network artifacts. These artifacts may help identify suspects whose devices may be thoroughly examined for more evidence. This analysis will discuss the current research on extracting and analyzing Bitcoin artifacts from various sources, such as mobile devices, computers, memory, blockchains, and network-based platforms (Dudani et al., 2023).

Methods of Cryptocurrency Forensics Investigations

Cryptocurrency forensics aims to identify the responsible party and locate their funds through various analytical and investigative methods. Blockchain intelligence technologies collect and analyze ownership attribution data for businesses, enabling the identification of criminals and investigation topics by de-anonymizing blockchain addresses. Transaction mapping converts transactional data into visual maps and flowcharts, tracing financial transfers to their ultimate endpoints.

Cluster analysis identifies groups of cryptocurrency addresses under the control of a single individual or institution, thereby broadening the scope of the investigation. Subpoena targets are focused on commercial cryptocurrency exchanges, decentralized finance organizations, and virtual asset service providers that adhere to Know Your Customer (KYC) and Anti-Money Laundering (AML) standards. Total transactions indicate the potential scale of a fraudulent scheme and the number of individuals affected. Law enforcement agencies prioritize complaints involving crime syndicates that cause harm to many individuals, while class action cases may be more suitable for larger schemes.

Forensic Analysis of Mobile Devices

Mobile devices play a crucial role in cryptocurrency forensics because they are widely used for mobile wallets and cryptocurrency applications. These mobile-based cryptocurrency exchange applications generate nearly $40 billion in annual revenue for the top 7 platforms. Some scholars conducted studies in which the most widely used cryptocurrency wallets for Bitcoin, Darkcoin, and Litecoin were downloaded and used on iOS and Android devices. The wallets were utilized in their simplest form, with only essential user functions (Montanez, 2014).

The experiment utilized an Apple iPhone 4 running iOS 7.1.1, a Samsung Galaxy S4 running Android 4.4.2, and two virtual Samsung Galaxy S4 smartphones running Android 4.4.2. Information was obtained from each device using Cellebrite UFED, Cellebrite Physical Analyzer, and iFunBox for iOS, following specific device or wallet occurrences (Dudani et al., 2023).

To investigate cryptocurrency transactions, digital forensic examiners must focus on identifying databases that store information, such as the names of cryptocurrency wallets, the public-private keys of the sender and receiver, the user IDs of the sender and receiver, and the files related to the timestamps of the transactions. The ability to retrieve these artifacts significantly relies heavily on the security and privacy measures implemented by the operating system and the wallet application being examined. Additionally, when considering host-based forensics for cryptocurrency, both computer and memory forensics hold equal significance alongside mobile forensics (Dudani et al., 2023).

The concept of machine learning (ML) is becoming increasingly prevalent and is also being applied in Bitcoin forensics. In 2018, some scholars introduced a new method based on supervised ML to decrease anonymity on the Bitcoin Blockchain (Harlev et al., 2018). The training data set from Chainalysis comprised almost 200 million transactions involving 434 identified businesses. Using their classifier, they could categorize an entity into one of ten distinct categories. By implementing Gradient Boosting, they attained an F1 score of 0.75.

Some scholars presented the Elliptic Data Set, which includes more than 200,000 Bitcoin transactions, 234,000 directed payment flows, and 166 node characteristics. Using different machine learning (ML) algorithms, they then analyzed the outcomes of a binary classification task aimed at distinguishing between illegal and legitimate transactions (Dudani et al., 2023).

Additionally, they offer Chronograph, a visualization prototype designed to help analysts examine and comprehend Bitcoin transactions. The Elliptic Data Set has made a significant impact on blockchain forensics. Researchers have widely utilized this publicly accessible dataset to gain insights into and potentially uncover participants' identities in the Bitcoin blockchain (Weber et al., 2019).

USING AI AND ML IN DIGITAL FORENSICS

Digital forensics investigators can utilize web crawling and data mining techniques to uncover hidden services and gather evidence of illicit behavior. The dark web is an unindexed section that requires access to specific software known for facilitating illicit activities like gun sales, drug trafficking, and cybercrimes. This software is also customized to allow users to access the dark web by directing their internet traffic through a global network of volunteer-operated computer nodes.

The dark web was initially created for lawful reasons, such as safeguarding the anonymity of internet users in nations with authoritarian regimes and providing secure communication for activists, journalists, and law enforcement personnel. However, it has been exploited by criminals and other malicious individuals for illicit activities, just as many other technologies have been. Investigating illegal activity on the dark web is challenging due to the anonymity of its users and the encryption technologies used. Some scholars believe that AI and ML can aid digital forensics investigators by automating data analysis and identifying patterns of illicit behavior (Sukumar, 2023).

Cryptocurrency transactions can be traced due to the inherent anonymity of cryptocurrency like Bitcoin, which is commonly used for illicit operations on the dark web. Every cryptocurrency transaction is recorded on a public ledger known as the blockchain. Digital forensics investigators can track the flow of illicit funds and identify individuals involved in criminal behavior by examining the blockchain. Advanced data analysis methods can identify activity patterns and link transactions to specific individuals or organizations. Clustering analysis is a technique used to track the flow of funds on the blockchain. Chain analysis is another method employed to track the flow of funds within the blockchain by monitoring fund transfers between different addresses.

Examining conversation records reveals that criminals frequently use dark web chatrooms to coordinate and strategize illicit activities. AI and ML are especially beneficial in this context. Detectives can quickly pinpoint conversations likely linked to illegal behavior by analyzing chat logs and focusing on those chats. This can optimize the investigation process and decrease the time and resources needed to review extensive conversation log data.

Data encryption involves using AI algorithms to evaluate patterns in encrypted data to determine the encryption mechanism employed. Natural Language Processing (NLP) can help understand the context of messages and communications on the dark web. Machine learning algorithms can examine extensive datasets of encrypted data to detect trends and develop future models for decrypting similar material. Predictive analytics can anticipate user behavior on the dark web to discover potential dangers and flaws in the system. For example, ML can forecast prime numbers used in the critical generation procedure for RSA encryption.

AI and ML are enhancing digital forensics by automating the preliminary analysis of digital evidence, including the recognition of file types, timestamps, and metadata. This accelerates the investigation process, enabling investigators to focus on more complex tasks. AI and ML can also help investigators by automatically organizing and ranking data to uncover significant evidence, simplifying the process of finding crucial information.

AI and ML systems can analyze distinctive malware codes associated with particular strains. By recognizing these patterns, investigators can promptly detect malware infections and take steps to eliminate them before they result in substantial harm. Automating data analysis and identifying patterns of criminal activity enables detectives to streamline the investigation process, allowing them to focus on more complex tasks. The future of digital forensics appears promising as technology advances, enhancing the effectiveness of combating cybercrime (Sukumar, 2023).

STANDARD ML ALGORITHMS USED IN CYBER FORENSIC INVESTIGATIONS

Several studies indicate that machine learning (ML) techniques commonly employed in cyber forensic investigations include Random Forests, neural networks (including deep learning and recurrent neural networks), and Logistic Regression. ML algorithms are now essential in cyber forensic investigations, as they offer automated, efficient, and precise techniques for identifying and examining cyber risks. This synthesis examines the prevalent machine learning (ML) methods in cyber forensic investigations, drawing lessons from numerous research articles.

Several studies have found that the Random Forest and Gradient Boosted Trees algorithms are effective in detecting malware. These algorithms consistently achieve high levels of accuracy, as demonstrated in various research papers (Benkerroum & Chougdali, 2023; Swaminathan et al., 2022).

In addition, Support Vector Machine algorithms (SVM) are commonly employed in cyber forensics to perform binary classification tasks. They accurately detect cyber risks (Benkerroum & Chougdali, 2023; Buczak & Guven, 2016). K-Nearest Neighbors algorithms (KNN) are a method valued for their simplicity and efficiency in forecasting cyberattacks and analyzing forensic evidence (Benkerroum & Chougdali, 2023; Swaminathan et al., 2022).

Additionally, the Naive Bayes method is utilized due to its high efficiency in processing extensive datasets and its ability to accurately classify cyber threats (Benkerroum & Chougdali, 2023; Buczak & Guven, 2016). Logistic Regression, although frequently employed, tends to exhibit inferior performance in cyber forensic tasks when compared to other algorithms, such as Random Forests and gradient-boosted trees (Benkerroum & Chougdali, 2023; Swaminathan et al., 2022).

Other studies see that Deep learning models, including Deep Neural Networks (DNN), Long Short-Term Memory (LSTM), and Gated Recurrent Units (GRU), are increasingly used for their ability to handle complex and high-dimensional data, providing superior performance in intrusion detection and anomaly detection (Vinayakumar et al., 2019; Li et al., 2021).

Some experts recognize that Decision Trees are utilized for their interpretability and efficacy in categorizing cyber risks, frequently functioning as a benchmark for more intricate models (Benkerroum & Chougdali, 2023; Buczak & Guven, 2016). Some scholars argue that combining AI with machine learning (ML) algorithms enhances the effectiveness and accuracy of cyber forensic investigations. This integration allows for automated detection and classification of threats (Fakiha, 2023).

To summarize, cyber forensic investigations employ various ML methods, each with its advantages and disadvantages. Random Forests and Gradient-Boosted Trees are renowned for their exceptional accuracy in detecting viruses. Support Vector Machines, K-Nearest Neighbors, and Naive Bayes are frequently employed due to their resilience and effectiveness (Russo & Lax, 2022). Deep learning models, such as DNN, LSTM, and GRU, are gaining popularity due to their ability to process complex data effectively. AI integration boosts algorithms' capabilities, increasing the efficiency and precision of cyber forensic investigations.

CHALLENGES IN IMPLEMENTING ML FOR ANOMALY-BASED INTRUSION DETECTION

Some research indicates that several significant challenges arise when implementing ML for anomaly-based intrusion detection. These challenges include effectively managing various network structures, adapting to emerging technologies, handling imbalanced data sets, keeping attack definitions up to date, achieving real-time detection, and overcoming issues of low accuracy and performance.

Deploying machine learning (ML) in anomaly-based intrusion detection systems (IDSs) poses numerous obstacles. The problems arise due to the ever-changing nature of network settings, the intricate nature of data, and the requirement for immediate processing. This synthesis focuses on the primary obstacles found in several study publications.

Many experts observe that ML models often encounter difficulties with class imbalance, resulting in an inadequate number of training instances for each potential class. This imbalance typically results in erroneous identification of specific intrusions (Chkirbene et al., 2020; Abdelmoumin et al., 2021). In addition, the abundance and variety of data produced by contemporary networks, including IoT and IIoT, complicate the training procedure and impact the efficiency of ML models (Agrawal et al., 2021; Gyamfi & Jurcut, 2023).

Several experts recognize that real-time detection is essential yet complex, requiring constant updates and addressing ever-changing cyberattacks (Gyamfi & Jurcut, 2023; Alrawashdeh & Purdy, 2016). Implementing effective ML-based intrusion detection systems (IDSs) is challenging due to resource constraints, such as limited memory, computational power, and energy supply, in IoT devices (Gyamfi & Jurcut, 2023; Sommer & Paxson, 2010).

Others note that anomaly-based intrusion detection systems (IDSs) often exhibit elevated rates of false positives, which can lead to a security system overload and diminished efficacy (Abdelmoumin et al., 2021; Sommer & Paxson, 2010). The disparity between the training and testing data exacerbates this problem, leading to imprecise predictions and an increased number of false alarms (Abdelmoumin et al., 2021).

Some scientists observe that the extensive and ever-changing datasets needed to train ML models result in a substantial computational burden, especially in situations with limited resources. Parallel processing designs and optimization approaches are crucial for managing computational workloads and enhancing the effectiveness of machine learning (ML)- based intrusion detection systems (IDSs) (Joshi & Korah, 2022).

Other experts argue that Centralized ML techniques pose a privacy and security risk, as they require data storage and transmission to a single server. Federated Learning (FL) offers a method for maintaining privacy by training models on local devices and exchanging parameters. However, this approach is also tricky (Agrawal et al., 2021).

Several experts argue that traditional ML models, such as KNN and SVM, heavily rely on manual feature engineering and may not deliver satisfactory performance in the era of big data (Su et al., 2020). Although more precise, deep learning models are intricate and demand substantial computational resources, rendering them less appropriate for real-time applications in resource-limited contexts (Su et al., 2020; Alrawashdeh & Purdy, 2016).

In summary, implementing ML for anomaly-based intrusion detection presents significant challenges, including imbalanced data, the requirement for real-time processing, a high frequency of false positives, difficulties in scaling, concerns over privacy, and the complexity of models. Advanced ML techniques, optimization strategies, and innovative methods, such as federated learning, are crucial for addressing these challenges. These approaches aim to enhance the effectiveness and efficiency of intrusion detection systems in diverse and ever-evolving network environments.

LEGAL AND ETHICAL CHALLENGES

Emerging technologies, such as artificial intelligence (AI), machine learning (ML), and blockchain, present both opportunities and challenges in digital forensics and the detection of illicit activities on the dark web. While these technologies can enhance the detection and prevention of cybercrimes, they also introduce significant legal and ethical challenges.

Scholars showed that the use of AI and ML in cybercrime investigations raises concerns about privacy and data protection. These technologies often require access to large datasets, which may include sensitive personal information, potentially leading to privacy violations (Gautam & Renu, 2024; Stoyanova et al., 2020).

On the other hand, others focused on the lack of standardized legal frameworks for blockchain and AI technologies, which complicates their use in digital forensics. This includes challenges in cross-border investigations due to varying international laws and regulations (Agarwal et al., 2023; Chitsungo, 2024; Stoyanova et al., 2020). Additionally, AI systems can inadvertently introduce bias, which can affect the fairness of investigations. Ensuring that AI models are unbiased and transparent is crucial to maintaining legal integrity (Gautam & Renu, 2024).

Otherwise, the dark web's inherent anonymity, combined with the use of encryption technologies, makes it difficult to trace illegal activities. This presents a significant challenge for law enforcement agencies trying to gather admissible evidence (Nazah et al., 2020; Raman et al., 2023). In the same context, maintaining the integrity of digital evidence is critical. The volatile nature of digital data and the use of decentralized systems, such as blockchain, can complicate the chain of custody, potentially impacting the admissibility of evidence in court (Stoyanova et al., 2020).

In Conclusion, the previous studies ensured that the Legal and Ethical Challenges are a crucial issue for using the emerging technologies in digital forensics in the dark web, While AI, ML, and blockchain offer powerful tools for enhancing digital forensics and combating illegal activities on the dark web, they also pose significant legal challenges. These include privacy concerns, regulatory inconsistencies, potential biases, and difficulties in maintaining evidence integrity. Addressing these challenges requires developing adaptive legal frameworks and ensuring ethical use of these technologies.

THE ROLE OF THE EU AI ACT IN REGULATING THE USE OF EMERGING TECHNOLOGIES TO DETECT ILLEGAL ACTIVITIES

Academics consider the EU AI Act to be a comprehensive legislative proposal designed to regulate artificial intelligence technologies within the European Union, with a focus on ensuring the ethical and safe development and deployment of AI. It addresses the legal and ethical challenges associated with emerging technologies, such as AI, machine learning, and blockchain, particularly in the detection of illegal activities.

They explained that the AI Act categorizes AI systems into four risk levels: unacceptable, high, low, and minimal risk. Unacceptable risks, which contravene EU values, are prohibited under Article 5. These include AI systems that utilize subliminal techniques, exploit vulnerabilities, employ social scoring, and employ real-time biometric identification systems (Neuwirth, 2023; Stuurman & Lachaud, 2022).

Otherwise, others explained that the Act emphasizes the protection of fundamental rights and the ethical use of AI, aiming to set global standards for responsible AI. It seeks to balance innovation with ethical oversight, ensuring AI systems are human-centric, ethical, and transparent (Helberger & Diakopoulos, 2022; Dokumacı, 2024).

On the other hand, others showed that the Act introduces a framework for AI liability, addressing the unpredictability and complexity of AI systems. It aims to ensure accountability and transparency, particularly in high-risk applications like financial services, where AI-driven activities could impact market stability (Outeda, 2024; Montagnani et al., 2024).

Meanwhile, some considered that A European Artificial Intelligence Office and Board should be established to oversee the implementation of the Act, promoting collaborative governance across the EU. This structure aims to ensure effective regulation and compliance with the Act's provisions (Outeda, 2024).

Otherwise, others have shown that the Act underscores the importance of explainable AI (XAI), particularly in sectors where accountability and fairness are critical. It aims to integrate XAI into EU law, addressing challenges in standard-setting and enforcement (Pavlidis, 2024).

In conclusion, scholars consider the EU AI Act to provide a structured approach to managing the legal and ethical challenges posed by AI technologies. By categorizing AI risks, emphasizing the ethical use of AI, and establishing governance mechanisms, the Act aims to foster trust and accountability in AI systems while promoting innovation within a regulated framework.

CONCLUSION

Due to its distinctive characteristics and appeal to a wide range of consumers, indications suggest that Bitcoin will progressively integrate into global financial institutions. Consequently, the utilization of cryptocurrency by wrongdoers is increasing due to the currency's uncontrolled and anonymous characteristics, propelling us towards a future dominated by cybercrime driven by cryptocurrency. The existing technological capabilities of law enforcement agencies and researchers worldwide may be inadequate, underscoring the need for advancements in digital forensics, particularly in the context of Bitcoin artifacts. Furthermore, it requires unrestricted dissemination of information concerning cryptocurrency investigations across international agencies, which can then be shared with local law enforcement organizations.

The studies identified the need to address several areas of digital cryptocurrency forensics, in which gaps can be filled by developing advanced solutions for cryptocurrency forensics. Further investigation is required in digital forensics regarding significant cryptocurrencies, such as Monero, Ethereum, Verge, Dogecoin, and others. This is necessary because these currencies are becoming increasingly popular among both legitimate users and evil individuals. The survey highlighted another research gap: the limited amount of substantial research on host-based cryptocurrency forensics, particularly in mobile-based cryptocurrency forensics.

Host-based forensics is crucial in identifying initial evidence to guide blockchain forensics investigations, which track money flows. The majority of research conducted on host-based forensics focuses on outdated operating systems or platforms, underscoring the need for studies on more current versions. When examining forensic methods for cryptocurrencies, it is crucial to consider security and vulnerability assessment studies.

These studies can provide valuable insights into potential exploits or attacks that are useful for forensic investigations. To summarize, research in Blockchain-based forensics is advancing organically alongside technological advancements. However, there is a need for focused attention on host-based forensics for cryptocurrency.

REFERENCES

Abdelmoumin, G., Rawat, D., & Rahman, A. (2021). On the Performance of Machine Learning Models for Anomaly-Based Intelligent Intrusion Detection Systems for the Internet of Things. *IEEE Internet of Things Journal*, *9*(6), 4280–4290. DOI: 10.1109/JIOT.2021.3103829

Agarwal, U., Rishiwal, V., Tanwar, S., & Yadav, M. (2023). Blockchain and crypto forensics: Investigating crypto frauds. *International Journal of Network Management*, *34*(2), e2255. Advance online publication. DOI: 10.1002/nem.2255

Agrawal, S., Sarkar, S., Aouedi, O., Yenduri, G., Piamrat, K., Bhattacharya, S., Maddikunta, P., & Gadekallu, T. (2021). Federated Learning for Intrusion Detection System: Concepts, Challenges and Future Directions. *Computer Communications*, *195*, 346–361. DOI: 10.1016/j.comcom.2022.09.012

Al-bahouth, A. B. S. B. A. (2017). *Virtual Money: Its concept, types, and economic effects. Scientific Journal of Economics and Trade*. Faculty of Commerce, Ain Shams University.

Alrawashdeh, K., & Purdy, C. (2016). Toward an Online Anomaly Intrusion Detection System Based on Deep Learning. *2016 15th IEEE International Conference on Machine Learning and Applications (ICMLA)*, 195-200. DOI: 10.1109/ICMLA.2016.0040

Bahamazava, K., & Nanda, R. (2022). The Shift in DarkNet Illegal Drug Trade Preferences toward Cryptocurrency: The Question of Traceability and Deterrence. *Forensic Science International Digital Investigation*, *40*, 301377. DOI: 10.1016/j.fsidi.2022.301377

Benkerroum, S., & Chougdali, K. (2023). Enhancing Forensic Analysis Using a Machine Learning-based Approach. *2023 6th International Conference on Advanced Communication Technologies and Networking (CommNet)*, pp. 1-6. DOI: 10.1109/CommNet60167.2023.10365260

Biddle, P., England, P., Peinado, M., & Willman, B. (2003). The darknet and the future of content protection. In *Digital Rights Management: ACM CCS-9 Workshop, DRM 2002, Washington, DC, USA, November 18, 2002. Revised Papers* (pp. 155-176). Springer Berlin Heidelberg.

Buczak, A., & Guven, E. (2016). A Survey of Data Mining and Machine Learning Methods for Cyber Security Intrusion Detection. *IEEE Communications Surveys and Tutorials*, *18*(2), 1153–1176. DOI: 10.1109/COMST.2015.2494502

Casino, F., Dasaklis, T. K., & Patsakis, C. (2019). A systematic literature review of blockchain-based applications: Current status, classification, and open issues. *Telematics and Informatics*, *36*, 55–81. DOI: 10.1016/j.tele.2018.11.006

Chitsungo, C. (2024). *Harnessing Digital Strategies to Combat Cryptocurrency-Enabled Crimes: Addressing Money Laundering, Illicit Trade, and Cyber Threats*. American Journal of International Relations., DOI: 10.47672/ajir.2523

Chkirbene, Z., Erbad, A., Hamila, R., Gouissem, A., Mohamed, A., & Hamdi, M. (2020). Machine Learning Based Cloud Computing Anomalies Detection. *IEEE Network*, *34*(6), 178–183. DOI: 10.1109/MNET.011.2000097

Dearden, T., & Tucker, S. (2023). Follow the Money: Analyzing Darknet Activity Using Cryptocurrency and the Bitcoin Blockchain. *Journal of Contemporary Criminal Justice*, *39*(2), 257–275. DOI: 10.1177/10439862231157521

Dokumacı, M. (2024). Legal Frameworks for AI Regulations. *Human-Computer Interaction*, *8*(1), 133. Advance online publication. DOI: 10.62802/ytst2927

Doran, M. D. (2014). *A forensic look at bitcoin cryptocurrency* (Master's thesis, Utica College).

Dudani, S., Baggili, I., Raymond, D., & Marchany, R. (2023). The current state of cryptocurrency forensics. *Forensic Science International Digital Investigation*, *46*, 301576. DOI: 10.1016/j.fsidi.2023.301576

Duffield, E., & Hagan, K. (2014). Darkcoin: Peertopeer cryptocurrency with anonymous blockchain transactions and an improved proof of work system. *bitpaper.Info*.

Dunsin, D., Ghanem, M., Ouazzane, K., & Vassilev, V. 2023. A Comprehensive Analysis of the Role of Artificial Intelligence and Machine Learning in Modern Digital Forensics and Incident Response. *ArXiv*, abs/2309.07064. /arXiv.2309.07064. DOI: 10.2139/ssrn.4554035

El-Kady, R. (2023). Handling E-evidence in Egyptian and Comparative Legislation: A Comparative Analytical Study. *Arab Journal of Forensic Sciences & Forensic Medicine*, *6*(1), 37–68. DOI: 10.26735/WGZY6322

El-Kady, R. (2024). *Challenges of Criminal Liability for Artificial Intelligence Systems*. IGI Global Scientific Publishing., DOI: 10.4018/979-8-3693-7205-0.ch001

El-Kady, R. (2024). *Leveraging AI and Machine Learning for Digital Forensics*. Advances in Computational Intelligence and Robotics Book Series., DOI: 10.4018/979-8-3373-1657-4.ch011

El-Kady, R. (2024). *Leveraging Artificial Intelligence to Combat Illicit Activities on the Dark Web: A Descriptive Analytical Study*. IGI Global Scientific Publishing., DOI: 10.4018/979-8-3693-9591-2.ch013

El-Kady, R. (2024). Artificial Intelligence and Criminal Law. In *Artificial Intelligence Approaches to Sustainable Accounting* (pp. 34–52). IGI Global. DOI: 10.4018/979-8-3693-0847-9.ch003

El-Kady, R. (2025). Artificial Intelligence from the Criminal Law Perspective. *AISI 2024. LNDECT, 233*, 162–173. Advance online publication. DOI: 10.1007/978-3-031-77299-3_16

El-Kady, R. (2025). Leveraging Artificial Intelligence for Enhanced Detection and Mitigation of Illicit Activities on the Dark Web (A. E. Hassanien, . . ., Eds.). AISI., , LNDECT 238.DOI: 10.1007/978-3-031-81308-5_8

El-Kady, R. M. (2024). Investigating Forensic Evidence in Metaverse: A Comparative Analytical Study. In *Forecasting Cyber Crimes in the Age of the Metaverse* (pp. 227-258). IGI Global.

Fakiha, B. (2023). Enhancing Cyber Forensics with AI and Machine Learning: A Study on Automated Threat Analysis and Classification. *International Journal of Safety and Security Engineering, 13*(4), 701–707. Advance online publication. DOI: 10.18280/ijsse.130412

FBI, D., (2012). Bitcoin virtual currency: Unique features present distinct challenges for deterring illicit activity. *Intelligence Assessment.*

Gannon, C., Blokland, A. A., Huikuri, S., Babchishin, K. M., & Lehmann, R. J. (2023). Child sexual abuse material on the darknet. *Forensische Psychiatrie, Psychologie, Kriminologie, 17*(4), 353–365. DOI: 10.1007/s11757-023-00790-8

Gautam, Y. & Renau. (2024). Integrating Artificial Intelligence into Cybercrime Investigation: Challenges and Future Directions. International Journal For Multidisciplinary Research. DOI: 10.36948/ijfmr.2024.v06i05.28909

Guccione, D. (2019). *What is the dark web? How to access it and what you'll find, The state of cybersecurity*. CSO Online.

Gupta, A., Gupta, R., & Sankaran, A. (2021). *Machine Learning Forensics*., DOI: 10.4018/978-1-7998-4900-1.ch003

Gyamfi, E., & Jurcut, A. (2023). Novel Online Network Intrusion Detection System for Industrial IoT Based on OI-SVDD and AS-ELM. *IEEE Internet of Things Journal, 10*(5), 3827–3839. DOI: 10.1109/JIOT.2022.3172393

Helberger, N., & Diakopoulos, N. (2022). The European AI Act and How It Matters for Research into AI in Media and Journalism. *Digital Journalism (Abingdon, England), 11*(9), 1751–1760. DOI: 10.1080/21670811.2022.2082505

Izadiyan, Z., Misran, M., Kalantari, K., Webster, T., Kia, P., Rasouli, E., & Shameli, K. (2025). Advancements in Liposomal Nanomedicines: Innovative Formulations, Therapeutic Applications, and Future Directions in Precision Medicine. *International Journal of Nanomedicine*, *20*, 1213–1262. DOI: 10.2147/IJN.S488961 PMID: 39911259

Joshi, C. (2023). Cryptocurrency Forensics: The Ultimate Guide to 6 Important Aspects. Indiaforensic. https://indiaforensic.com/cryptocurrency-forensics/

Joshi, V., & Korah, J. (2022). Formulating Parallel Supervised Machine Learning Designs for Anomaly-Based Network Intrusion Detection in Resource-Constrained Use Cases. *2022 IEEE 19th International Conference on Mobile Ad Hoc and Smart Systems (MASS)*, 748-753. DOI: 10.1109/MASS56207.2022.00117

Kao, H. (2025). Accelerating Multilingual Cryptocurrency Forensics: An NLP-Driven Approach for Efficient Mnemonic Identification. *IEEE Access : Practical Innovations, Open Solutions*, *13*, 10513–10526. DOI: 10.1109/ACCESS.2025.3528829

Kim, D., Park, Y., & Kim, S. (2024). A Measurement Study on Tor Hidden Services via Keyword-Based Dark Web Collection Framework. *IEEE Access : Practical Innovations, Open Solutions*, *12*, 136936–136945. DOI: 10.1109/ACCESS.2024.3465629

Kumar, A., & Sharma, I. (2023). Preserving Security of Crypto Transactions with Machine Learning Methodologies. *2023 International Conference on Sustainable Computing and Smart Systems (ICSCSS)*, pp. 129-134. DOI: 10.1109/ICSCSS57650.2023.10169192

Lawlor, B. (2021). Artificial Intelligence and Machine Learning. *Chemistry International*, *43*(1), 8–13. Advance online publication. DOI: 10.1515/ci-2021-0103

Lee, S., Kim, J., Seo, M., Na, S., Shin, S., & Kim, J. (2024). CENSor: Detecting Illicit Bitcoin Operation via GCN-Based Hyperedge Classification. *IEEE Access : Practical Innovations, Open Solutions*, *12*, 152330–152346. DOI: 10.1109/ACCESS.2024.3466650

Lee, S., Yoon, C., Kang, H., Kim, Y., Kim, Y., Han, D., Son, S., & Shin, S. (2019). Cybercriminal Minds: An investigative study of cryptocurrency abuses in the Dark Web. *Proceedings 2019 Network and Distributed System Security Symposium*. DOI: 10.14722/ndss.2019.23055

Li, Z., Rios, A., & Trajković, L. (2021). Machine Learning for Detecting Anomalies and Intrusions in Communication Networks. *IEEE Journal on Selected Areas in Communications, 39*(7), 2254–2264. DOI: 10.1109/JSAC.2021.3078497

Martin, M. (2021). *Computer and Internet use in the United States: 2018*. American Community Survey Reports.

Montagnani, M., Najjar, M., & Davola, A. (2024). The EU Regulatory approach(es) to AI liability, and its Application to the financial services market. *Computer Law & Security Review, 53*, 105984. DOI: 10.1016/j.clsr.2024.105984

Montanez, A. (2014). *Investigation of cryptocurrency wallets on iOS and Android mobile devices for potential forensic artifacts. Department Forensic Science*. Marshall University.

Nakamoto, S., & Bitcoin, A. (2008). A peer-to-peer electronic cash system. *Bitcoin.–URL:*https://bitcoin. org/bitcoin. pdf, *4*(2), p.15.

Nazah, S., Huda, S., Abawajy, J., & Hassan, M. (2020). Evolution of Dark Web Threat Analysis and Detection: A Systematic Approach. *IEEE Access : Practical Innovations, Open Solutions, 8*, 171796–171819. DOI: 10.1109/ACCESS.2020.3024198

Neuwirth, R. (2023). Prohibited artificial intelligence practices in the proposed EU artificial intelligence act (AIA). *Computer Law & Security Review, 48*, 105798. DOI: 10.1016/j.clsr.2023.105798

Nour, K. (2022). Criminal confrontation of cryptocurrency use in the financing of terrorism. *Jolets*. 16;2(2):79-152. Available from: https://jolets.org/ojs/index.php/jolets/article/view/12

Obeidat, T. (1996). *Methods and Techniques of Scientific Research*. Dar Sana'a for Publishing. (In Arabic)

Outeda, C. (2024). The EU's AI act: A framework for collaborative governance. *Internet of Things : Engineering Cyber Physical Human Systems, 27*, 101291. DOI: 10.1016/j.iot.2024.101291

Patil, S., Vijayakumar, V., Walimbe, D., Gulechha, S., Shenoy, S., Raina, A., & Kotecha, K. (2021). Improving the Robustness of AI-Based Malware Detection Using Adversarial Machine Learning. *Algorithms, 14*(10), 297. DOI: 10.3390/a14100297

Pavlidis, G. (2024). Unlocking the black box: Analysing the EU artificial intelligence act's framework for explainability in AI. *Law, Innovation and Technology, 16*(1), 293–308. DOI: 10.1080/17579961.2024.2313795

Raman, R., Nair, V., Nedungadi, P., Ray, I., & Achuthan, K. (2023). Darkweb research: Past, present, and future trends and mapping to sustainable development goals. *Heliyon*, *9*(11), e22269. Advance online publication. DOI: 10.1016/j.heliyon.2023.e22269 PMID: 38058627

Reid, F., & Harrigan, M. (2013). *An analysis of anonymity in the Bitcoin system*. Springer. DOI: 10.1007/978-1-4614-4139-7_10

Russo, A., & Lax, G. (2022). Using Artificial Intelligence for Space Challenges: A Survey. *Applied Sciences (Basel, Switzerland)*, *12*(10), 5106. DOI: 10.3390/app12105106

Sommer, R., & Paxson, V. (2010). Outside the Closed World: On Using Machine Learning for Network Intrusion Detection. *2010 IEEE Symposium on Security and Privacy*, 305-316. DOI: 10.1109/SP.2010.25

Stoyanova, M., Nikoloudakis, Y., Panagiotakis, S., Pallis, E., & Markakis, E. (2020). A Survey on the Internet of Things (IoT) Forensics: Challenges, Approaches, and Open Issues. *IEEE Communications Surveys and Tutorials*, *22*(2), 1191–1221. DOI: 10.1109/COMST.2019.2962586

Stuurman, K., & Lachaud, E. (2022). Regulating AI. A label to complete the proposed Act on Artificial Intelligence. *Computer Law & Security Review*, *44*, 105657. DOI: 10.1016/j.clsr.2022.105657

Su, T., Sun, H., Zhu, J., Wang, S., & Li, Y. (2020). BAT: Deep Learning Methods on Network Intrusion Detection Using NSL-KDD Dataset. *IEEE Access : Practical Innovations, Open Solutions*, *8*, 29575–29585. DOI: 10.1109/ACCESS.2020.2972627

Sukumar, S. (2023). Digital Forensics in The Dark. https://www.linkedin.com/pulse/digital-forensics-dark-sandhya-sukumar/

Suryawanshi, S., Katkar, T., Ghute, Y., Kawase, P., & Sharma, P. (2023). Detection of Cyber Attacks and Network Attacks Using Machine Learning Algorithms. *Proceeding International Conference on Science and Engineering*. DOI: 10.52783/cienceng.v11i1.120

Swaminathan, A., & Ramakrishnan, B., M, K., & R, S., (2022). Prediction of Cyberattacks and Criminality Using Machine Learning Algorithms. *2022 International Conference on Innovation and Intelligence for Informatics, Computing, and Technologies (3ICT)*, pp. 547-552. DOI: 10.1109/3ICT56508.2022.9990652

Taleby Ahvanooey, M., Zhu, M. X., Mazurczyk, W., Kilger, M., & Choo, K. K. R. (2021, December). Do dark web and cryptocurrencies empower cybercriminals? In *International Conference on Digital Forensics and Cyber Crime* (pp. 277-293). Cham: Springer International Publishing.

Tsuchiya, Y., & Hiramoto, N. (2021). How cryptocurrency is laundered: Case study of Coincheck hacking incident. *Forensic Science International. Reports*, *4*, 100241. DOI: 10.1016/j.fsir.2021.100241

Tziakouris, G. (2018). Cryptocurrencies—A forensic challenge or opportunity for law enforcement? An Interpol perspective. *IEEE Security and Privacy*, *16*(4), 92–94. DOI: 10.1109/MSP.2018.3111243

Venčkauskas, A., Grigaliūnas, Š., Pocius, L., Brūzgienė, R., & Romānovs, A. (2025). Machine Learning in Money Laundering Detection Over Blockchain Technology. *IEEE Access : Practical Innovations, Open Solutions*, *13*, 7555–7573. DOI: 10.1109/ACCESS.2024.3452003

Vinayakumar, R., Alazab, M., Soman, K., Poornachandran, P., Al-Nemrat, A., & Venkatraman, S. (2019). Deep Learning Approach for Intelligent Intrusion Detection System. *IEEE Access : Practical Innovations, Open Solutions*, *7*, 41525–41550. DOI: 10.1109/ACCESS.2019.2895334

Viroonluecha, P., & Kaewkiriya, T. (2018). Salary Predictor System for Thailand Labour Workforce using Deep Learning. DOI: 10.1109/ISCIT.2018.8587998

Weber, M., Domeniconi, G., Chen, J., Weidele, D. K. I., Bellei, C., Robinson, T., & Leiserson, C. E. 2019. Anti-money laundering in bitcoin: Experimenting with graph convolutional networks for financial forensics. *arXiv preprint arXiv:1908.02591.*

Zhao, K., Dong, G., & Bian, D. (2023). Detection of Illegal Transactions of Cryptocurrency Based on Mutual Information. *Electronics (Basel)*, *12*(7), 1542. Advance online publication. DOI: 10.3390/electronics12071542

Zhou, X., Liang, W., Shimizu, S., Ma, J., & Jin, Q. (2021). Siamese Neural Network Based Few-Shot Learning for Anomaly Detection in Industrial Cyber-Physical Systems. *IEEE Transactions on Industrial Informatics*, *17*(8), 5790–5798. DOI: 10.1109/TII.2020.3047675

Chapter 14
BinancePy:
Python Powered Crypto Trading

T. Kavitha
https://orcid.org/0000-0001-6559-0302
Visveswaraya Technological University, India & New Horizon College of Engineering, Bengaluru, India

Bhimaraya Patil
https://orcid.org/0000-0002-3331-9195
Department of Computer Science & Engineering, New Horizon College of Engineering, Bengaluru, India

M. Nagalingayya
https://orcid.org/0009-0000-3086-3526
Sharnbasva University, India

ABSTRACT

This paper describes the creation and implementation of a cryptocurrency trading bot that uses the Binance API and the Relative Strength Index(RSI) indicator. The trading bot is intended to automate the process of purchasing and selling digital assets on the Binance exchange, capitalizing on market inefficiencies while reducing the need for ongoing manual involvement. The RSI indicator, a momentum oscillator that measures the pace and change of price movements, is used to determine if the market is overbought or oversold. By combining the RSI indicator with the Binance API, the bot may execute trades based on predetermined RSI criteria, allowing for more timely and strategic trading choices. The system architecture includes modules for data retrieval, signal creation, trade execution, and performance monitoring. Initial backtesting findings show that the bot may efficiently produce lucrative trades in certain market situations.

DOI: 10.4018/979-8-3693-5986-0.ch014

I. INTRODUCTION

In recent years, the cryptocurrency market has expanded ex- potentially, drawing a diverse variety of investors and traders. As popularity grows, so does interest in automated trading systems that can profit from market changes. One such method is based on the Relative Strength Index (RSI), a common technical indicator used by traders to identify overbought or oversold levels in an asset's price. This project investigates the creation and implementation of a crypto trading bot using the Binance API, a popular cryptocurrency exchange platform, and the RSI approach. The major goal of this bot is to execute trades autonomously based on RSI indicator indications to improve trading performance and maximize profits. This bot uses complex algorithmic trading techniques and real-time market data from the Binance API to discover prospective buying or selling opportunities in the cryptocurrency market (H. Chen et al, 2022). The Binance API is the project's foundation, allowing users to access real-time market data, make orders, and manage their accounts within the Binance cryptocurrency exchange. With its powerful and well-documented interface, the Binance API allows developers to effortlessly connect their trading methods and algorithms with the exchange platform. Users may use the API to get up-to-date information on asset prices, order book depth, transaction history, and other topics, helping them to make educated decisions and execute trades quickly (Y. Li et al., 2023). The Binance API is the project's foundation, allowing users to access real-time market data, make orders, and manage their accounts within the Binance cryptocurrency exchange. With its powerful and well-documented interface, the Binance API allows developers to effortlessly connect their trading methods and algorithms with the exchange platform. Users may use the API to get up-to-date information on asset prices, order book depth, transaction history, and other topics, helping them to make educated decisions and execute trades quickly. The bot seeks to reduce emotional biases and improve consistency in trading decisions by automating trade execution based on predetermined parameters, such as RSI thresholds. This project will explore the theoretical underpinnings of the RSI approach and give a summary of its uses in bitcoin trading. It will also go into detail regarding the trading bot's technical architecture and implementation, including important features, data flow, and integration with the Binance API (Y. Zhao et al, 2021). In addition, the project will include performance data and empirical findings from live trading tests and back testing carried out with the bot. Important insights into the practicality and potential drawbacks of automated RSI-based trading systems will be obtained by examining the efficacy of the RSI strategy in various market conditions and its influence on trading outcomes. This project's overall goal is to offer a thorough understanding of the conception, application, and performance of a cryptocurrency trading bot that makes use of the RSI strategy through the Binance API, illuminating the strategy's usefulness as an algorithmic trading tool in the ever-changing world of cryptocurrency markets.

II. COMPARISON OF EXISTING TRADING BOTS

A review of the literature in cryptocurrency trading bots demonstrates the wide variety of methods, tactics, and plat- forms that developers and traders employ. Several scholarly investigations and writings have examined the efficiency, performance, and difficulties related to automated trading systems in the bitcoin industry (Y. Wang, et al, 2022). The creation of certain trading algorithms and tactics, such as those based on technical indicators like Bollinger Bands, Moving Averages, and Relative Strength Index (RSI), is the subject of some research. Others look at how artificial intelligence and machine learning approaches (S Pavithra et al 2023) might improve trading bot performance and flexibility in response to changing market conditions. Furthermore, the literature in this field frequently assesses the security (T.Kavitha & D.Sridharan 2013), and dependability of cryptocurrency trading platforms and exchanges in addition to the regulatory environment that governs algorithmic trading in the cryptocurrency market (X. Zhang et al, 2020). Researchers can improve algorithmic trading techniques and technologies in the digital asset market by combining the results of these studies to provide important insights into the development, application, and assessment of bitcoin trading bots.

A. ZenBot

Zenbot is an open-source cryptocurrency trading bot that supports multiple exchanges and trading strategies. It offers customizable trading strategies and back testing capabilities. Supports multiple exchanges - Customizable trading strategies (B. Bunz et al, 2020)

- Backtesting capabilities
- Supports multiple exchanges
- Open- source and free to use
- Flexible and customizable strategies (M. Li et al, 2023)

B. 3Commas

3Commas is a cloud-based cryptocurrency trading platform that offers automated trading bots, smart trading terminals, and portfolio management tools. It supports multiple exchanges (K. Zhao et al, 2021) and provides a user-friendly interface. Automated trading bots

- Smart trading terminals
- Portfolio management tools
- Multiple exchange support
- User-friendly interface
- Diverse range of trading tools

C. HaasOnline

HaasOnline is a cryptocurrency trading platform that offers a range of automated trading bots, including HaasBot. HaasBot supports advanced trading strategies, backtesting, and custom indicators.

- HaasBot with advanced trading strategies
- Back- testing capabilities
- Custom indicators support

D. GunBot

Gunbot is a popular cryptocurrency trading bot that supports automated trading on multiple exchanges. It offers a wide range of customizable trading strategies and provides real- time trading data. Automated trading on multiple exchanges

– Customizable trading strategies
    - Real-time trading data
    - Wide range of customizable strategies
    - Real-time trading data for quick decision-making

E. Cryptohopper

Cryptohopper is a cloud-based cryptocurrency trading bot that offers automated trading, arbitrage, and market-making strategies. It supports multiple exchanges and provides a user- friendly interface (Dual Finances 2023 & M. Yao et al, 2023).

- Automated trading
- Arbitrage and market- making strategies
- User-friendly interface
- Easy setup and configuration
- Diverse range of trading strategies
- Multi-exchange support for portfolio diversification (J. Bonneau et al, 2015)

Figure 1. Flowchart for the working of the trading bot

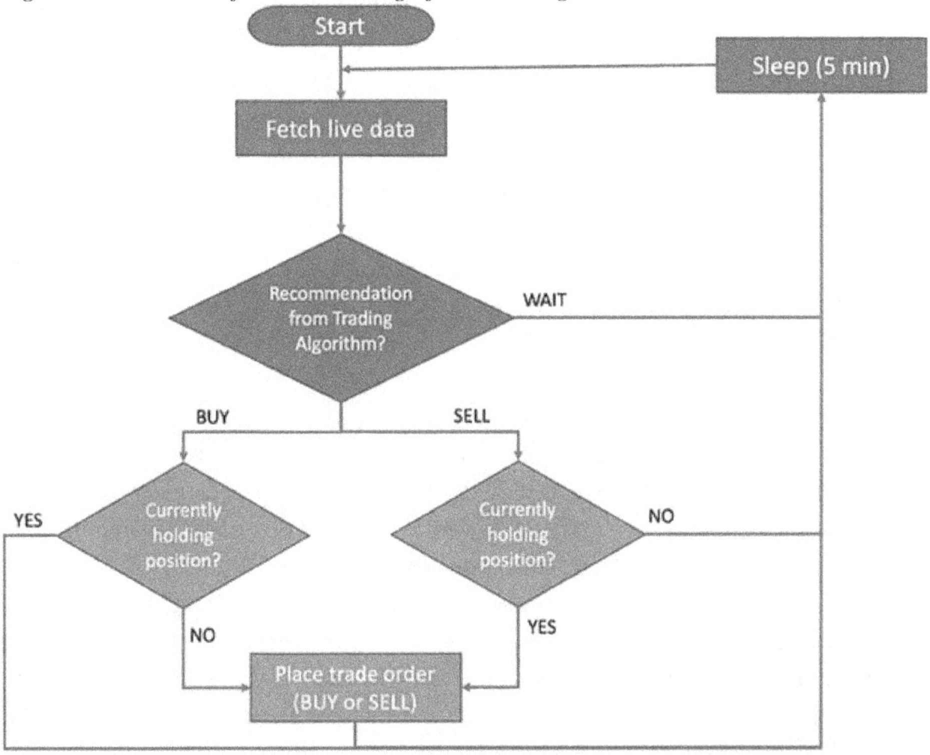

III. METHODOLOGY

Application and Analysis of Some Basic Candlestick Patterns Single Patterns: Doji Candle Marubozu Candle Multiple Patterns: Engulfing Pattern Morning/Evening Star Pattern Applying a Few Favorite Python Trading Indicators and Strategies Relative Strength Index (RSI) Indicator Moving Average Strategies Moving Average Convergence Divergence (MACD) Bollinger Bands Indicator (Y. Li, & L. Zhang, 2023)

Creating a Trading Bot: A Three-Step Guide

A. Link to an Exchange to Get Live Data: Connect to an exchange to receive real-time market data.
B. Apply a Trading Algorithm to the Data: Implement an algorithm to analyze the data and generate trading signals.
C. Perform the Trade: Execute trades based on the algorithm's signals.

There are two situations where we must communicate with the exchange. Obtaining the data and applying the trading algorithm to it comes first. The second step is to execute purchase and sell orders to exchange the assets. For these interactions, we use two separate packages in this case. The data is retrieved from the exchange using the CCXT program. This data is then used to execute the trading algorithm. We use the APIs offered by an exchange (Binance) that we have an account with when placing a trade order. If you have an account with any other exchange that offers public APIs for ordering as well as data retrieval, those can also be easily incorporated into the process. (Y. Wang, & X. Li, 2023)

STEP 1: Fetch live data.

The Crypto Currency exchange Trading Library, or CCXT for short, is a global payment processing library that facilitates trading with cryptocurrency exchanges. To obtain the cryptocurrency price data, we will be using this library in conjunction with the Binance exchange. This can also be done with any other exchange or API(A. Kumar et al, 2023). The exchange classes or available crypto exchanges are gathered in the CCXT library. For a certain cryptocurrency exchange, each class implements the public and private API. Each exchange inherits a common set of methods from the main Exchange class. An instance of the matching exchange class must be created to access a specific exchange from the CCXT library. Regular updates are made to support exchanges, and new exchanges are introduced on a regular basis.

Figure 2. Step 1

```
exchange = ccxt.binance()

# STEP 1: FETCH THE DATA
def fetch_data(ticker):
    global exchange
    bars,ticker_df = None, None

    try:
        bars = exchange.fetch_ohlcv(ticker, timeframe=f'{CANDLE_DURATION_IN_MIN}m', limit=100)
    except:
        print(f"Error in fetching data from the exchange:{ticker}")

    if bars is not None:
        ticker_df = pd.DataFrame(bars[:-1], columns=['at', 'open', 'high', 'low', 'close',
'vol'])
        ticker_df['Date'] = pd.to_datetime(ticker_df['at'], unit='ms')
        ticker_df['symbol'] = ticker

    return ticker_df
```

STEP 2: Apply the trading strategy.

Establish RSI criteria: To determine when an asset is overbought or oversold, set criteria for the RSI indicator. For instance, overbought conditions may be indicated by RSI values above 70, and oversold conditions may be indicated by RSI values below 30. Start Buy/Sell Signals: The RSI indicator starts to produce a sell signal, indicating that the asset's price is probably going to drop, when it goes above the overbought threshold (for example, 70). In contrast, the RSI indicator produces a buy signal, indicating that the asset's price is likely to climb, when it crosses below the oversold threshold (e.g., 30).

Apply Risk Management: To reduce possible losses and efficiently manage position sizes, apply risk management strategies. This could entail establishing position-sizing guidelines based on account size and risk tolerance as well as placing stop-loss orders to restrict losses. (H. Chen et al, 2023)

Figure 3. Crypto currency exchange trading library architecture

```
                             User
+-------------------------------------------------------------+
|                            CCXT                             |
+------------------------------+------------------------------+
|            Public            |           Private            |
+=============================================================+
|                              .                              |
|                    The Unified CCXT API                     |
|                              .                              |
|       loadMarkets            .           fetchBalance       |
|       fetchMarkets           .            createOrder       |
|       fetchCurrencies        .            cancelOrder       |
|       fetchTicker            .             fetchOrder       |
|       fetchTickers           .            fetchOrders       |
|       fetchOrderBook         .        fetchOpenOrders       |
|       fetchOHLCV             .      fetchClosedOrders       |
|       fetchStatus            .          fetchMyTrades       |
|       fetchTrades            .                deposit       |
|                              .               withdraw       |
|                              .                              |
+=============================================================+
|                              .                              |
|                     Custom Exchange API                     |
|         (Derived Classes And Their Implicit Methods)        |
|                              .                              |
|       publicGet...           .          privateGet...       |
|       publicPost...          .         privatePost...       |
|                              .          privatePut...       |
|                              .       privateDelete...       |
|                              .                   sign       |
|                              .                              |
+=============================================================+
|                              .                              |
|                      Base Exchange Class                    |
|                              .                              |
+=============================================================+
```

STEP 3: Execute the trade.

APIs Provided by the Trading Exchange: The trading exchange must have APIs (Application Programming Interfaces) that let users communicate with their trading platform programmatically to conduct deals programmatically. Typically, these APIs include endpoints for managing accounts, making orders, getting market data, and accessing other exchange-provided features.

Account with the Trading Exchange: You need to have an account with the trading exchange to access the trading APIs. To do this, you must create an account on the exchange website or platform and fulfil any identity verification (M. Hassan et al, 2022)

requirements, such KYC (Know Your Customer) checks. API Key and Secret: To access your trading account programmatically, you must generate an API key and secret after creating an account with the trading exchange. With the use of these API credentials, you can safely authenticate your queries to the exchange's API and make sure that only users with permission may access their accounts and make trades. Sufficient Funds in the Trading Account: Make sure you have enough money or assets in your trading account to cover the orders you plan to place before you execute any deals. This could entail adding money to your account or moving assets from other exchanges or wallets. Insufficient money can cause your orders to be declined or only partially filled, which could result in losses or the loss of market opportunities. (X. Zhang et al, 2023)

Figure 4. Step 2

```
# STEP 2: COMPUTE THE TECHNICAL INDICATORS & APPLY THE TRADING STRATEGY
def get_trade_recommendation(ticker_df):

    macd_result, final_result = 'WAIT','WAIT'

    # BUY or SELL based on MACD crossover points and the RSI value at that point
    macd, signal, hist = talib.MACD(ticker_df['close'], fastperiod = 12, slowperiod = 26,
signalperiod = 9)
    last_hist = hist.iloc[-1]
    prev_hist = hist.iloc[-2]
    if not np.isnan(prev_hist) and not np.isnan(last_hist):
        # If hist value has changed from negative to positive or vice versa, it indicates a
crossover
        macd_crossover = (abs(last_hist + prev_hist)) != (abs(last_hist) + abs(prev_hist))
        if macd_crossover:
            macd_result = 'BUY' if last_hist > 0 else 'SELL'

    if macd_result != 'WAIT':
        rsi = talib.RSI(ticker_df['close'], timeperiod = 14)
        last_rsi = rsi.iloc[-1]

        if (last_rsi <= RSI_OVERSOLD):
            final_result = 'BUY'
        elif (last_rsi >= RSI_OVERBOUGHT):
            final_result = 'SELL'

    return final_result
```

IV. RELATIVE STRENGTH INDEX (RSI) INDICATOR

The RSI is a popular technical analysis indicator used by many traders. It is used to analyze the momentum of a stock. It compares the recent gains with the recent losses. It gives an indication of the oversold or overbought condition of a stock.

Mathematically, the RSI can be computed as below. Typically, a window period of 14 is considered to compute the RS value.

RSI = 100 – *100 / (* 1 + RS)

where, RS = Average Gain / Average Loss

Figure 5. Step 3

```
wx_client = Client(api_key=wazirx_config.API_KEY, secret_key=wazirx_config.API_SECRET)

# STEP 3: EXECUTE THE TRADE
def execute_trade(trade_rec_type, trading_ticker):
    global wx_client, HOLDING_QUANTITY
    order_placed = False
    side_value = 'buy' if (trade_rec_type == "BUY") else 'sell'
    try:
        ticker_price_response = wx_client.send("ticker", { "symbol": trading_ticker})
        if (ticker_price_response[0] in [200, 201]):
            current_price = float(ticker_price_response[1]['lastPrice'])
            scrip_quantity = round(INVESTMENT_AMOUNT_DOLLARS/current_price,5) if trade_rec_type
== "BUY" else HOLDING_QUANTITY

            print(f"PLACING ORDER {datetime.now().strftime('%d/%m/%Y %H:%M:%S')}: "
                  f"{trading_ticker}, {side_value}, {current_price}, {scrip_quantity},
{int(time.time() * 1000)} ")
            order_response = wx_client.send("create_order",
                                            {"symbol": trading_ticker, "side": side_value, "type":
"limit",
                                             "price": current_price, "quantity": scrip_quantity,
                                             "recvWindow": 10000, "timestamp": int(time.time() *
1000)})
            print(f'ORDER PLACED. RESPONSE: {order_response}')

            HOLDING_QUANTITY = scrip_quantity if trade_rec_type == "BUY" else HOLDING_QUANTITY
            order_placed = True
    except:
        print(f"\nALERT!!! UNABLE TO COMPLETE THE ORDER.")

    return order_placed
```

Here's what each term represents:

- RSI: Relative Strength Index, a momentum oscillator that measures the speed and change of price movements.
- RS: Relative Strength, calculated as the ratio of Average Gain to Average Loss over a specified period.
- Average Gain: Average gain in price over the specified period (typically 14 periods).
- Average Loss: Average loss in price over the specified period.
- RSI < 30 indicates an oversold condition BUY signal.
- RSI > 70 indicates an overbought condition SELL signal.

V. TRADING STRATEGY

- **BUY:** MACD crossover with BUY signal & RSI in oversold region.

- **SELL:** MACD crossover with SELL signal & RSI in overbought region.
- **WAIT:** Otherwise.

Figure 6. MACD and RSI

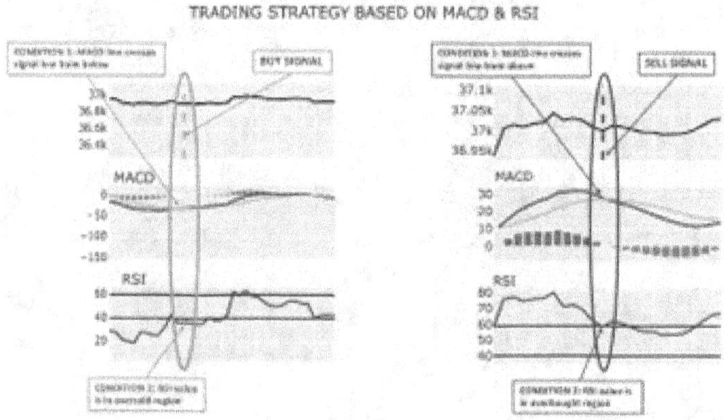

- Implement a robust back testing framework to evaluate trading strategies using historical cryptocurrency price data.
- Utilize popular technical indicators such as Moving Average Convergence Divergence (MACD) and Relative Strength Index (RSI) to generate buy and sell signals.
- Develop automated trading algorithms based on these signals to execute trades on a simulated exchange platform.

Throughout the project, we have achieved the following milestones:

- Data Collection and Preprocessing: We gathered historical price data from cryptocurrency exchanges and prepared it for analysis and back testing.
- Technical Indicator Implementation: Implemented key technical indicators such as MACD and RSI using Python libraries like NumPy and Pandas.
- Strategy Development: Developed trading strategies based on combinations of technical indicators and defined clear buy, sell, and wait conditions.
- Back testing and Performance Evaluation: Created a back- testing framework to simulate the performance of our strategies over historical data, allowing us to analyze profitability, drawdowns, and other metrics.

- Simulation of Automated Trading: Integrated our strategies with simulated trading environments to execute automated trades based on predefined conditions.
- Results Analysis: Evaluated the performance of our strategies using metrics such as cumulative returns, Sharpe ratio, and maximum drawdown, comparing them against a buy-and-hold strategy and benchmark indices.

In conclusion, this project has provided valuable insights into the complexities of cryptocurrency trading and algorithmic strategies. While our simulated results have shown promising returns under historical conditions, it's important to note the inherent risks and uncertainties in real-world trading environments. Further enhancements could include:

- Incorporating additional technical indicators or machine learning models for improved decision-making.
- Implementing risk management techniques such as position sizing and stop-loss orders to mitigate potential losses.
- Integrating real-time data feeds and executing trades on actual cryptocurrency exchanges for live testing.

REFERENCES

Bonneau, J., Miller, A., Clark, J., Narayanan, A., Kroll, J. A., Felten, E. W., & Goldberg, S. (2015). "Multi-signature Crypto wallets: Theory, Implementation, and Applications," in *Proceedings of the 2015 ACM SIGSAC Conference on Computer and Communications Security*, 2015, pp. 243- 256.

Bunz, B., Decker, M., & Sassmannshausen, S. (2020). "Automatic Coin Switching Strategies for Crypto Arbitrage," in *International Conference on Financial Cryptography and Data Security*, Springer, Cham, 2020, pp. 77-97.

Chen, H., Li, J., & Zhang, Y. (2022). Energy Efficiency Analysis of Duino Coin Mining on Embedded Systems. In *Embedded Systems: Research and Practice* (pp. 115–132). Springer.

Chen, H., Li, J., & Zhang, Y. (2023). "Exploration of ASIC-Resistant Mining Algorithms for Duino Coin," arXiv preprint arXiv:2310.16543, 2023.

Dual Finances. (2023). "Tax Implications of Coin Switching for Crypto Investors," Retrieved from https://www.dualfinances.com/tax-implications- of-cryptocurrency-transactions/, 2023.

Kavitha, T., & Sridharan, D. (2013). Optimal resource key management protocol for clustered heterogeneous wireless sensor networks. *Malaysian Journal of Computer Science*, *26*(3), 211–231.

Kumar, A., Sharma, D., & Singh, S. (2023). "Duino Coin Mining Bot Development and Performance Evaluation," in *Proceedings of the International Conference on Information Systems and Data Management*, Springer, Cham, 2023, pp. 12-21.

Li, M., Wang, C., & Zhang, L. (2023). "Decentralized Coin Switching Protocols for Secure and Trustless Arbitrage," arXiv preprint arXiv:2306.17742.

Li, Y., Wang, Y., & Zhang, X. (2023). Duino Coin Mining Pool Performance Analysis and Optimization. *Journal of Parallel and Distributed Computing*, *174*, 11–22.

Li, Y., & Zhang, L. (2023). Cryptocurrency Wallet: A Review. *International Journal of Computer Applications*, *102*, 1–10.

Pavithra, S., Shreyashwini, N. K., Bhavana, H. S., Nikhitha, G., & Kavitha, T. (2023). Hand-drawn electronic component recognition using ORB. *Procedia Computer Science*, *218*, 504–513.

Wang, Y., & Li, X. (2023). Privacy-Preserving Crypto Wallets for Enhanced Transaction Anonymity, arXiv preprint arXiv:2303.12940

Wang, Y., Xu, J., & Chen, B. (2022). "Duino Coin Mining Algorithm Analysis and Improvement," in *International Conference on High Performance Computing and Communications*, Springer, Cham, pp. 146-157.

Wang, Y., Xu, J., & Chen, B. (2022). Security Analysis of Duino Coin Smart Contracts. *International Journal of Software Engineering and Knowledge Engineering*, *32*(10), 1435–1457.

Zhang, X., Li, Y., & Wang, Y. (2022). Duino Coin Mining Hardware Design and Optimization. *Journal of Low Power Electronics and Applications*, *12*(4), 34.

Zhang, X., Li, Y., & Wang, Y. (2023). Economic Analysis of Duino Coin Mining Profitability. *Journal of Financial Technology*, *12*(3), 182–201.

Zhao, K., Huang, C., & Zhang, W. (2021). "Market Data Analysis and Prediction for Optimal Coin Switching," arXiv preprint arXiv:2106.12961, 2021.

Zhao, Y., Sun, J., & Li, X. (2021). "Security Analysis of Duino Coin Mining Protocols," in *Proceedings of the 2021 IEEE International Conference on Blockchain and Cryptocurrency (ICBC)*, IEEE, 2021, pp. 1-7.

Chapter 15
Volume of Transactions and Potential Monetary Base:
Monetary Development in the Era of Virtual Economy

Grigoris Zarotiadis
Aristotle University of Thessaloniki, Greece

Dimitra Giannopoulou
Aristotle University of Thessaloniki, Greece

ABSTRACT

In the first part we present the evolution of the volume of transactions, as a result of the continued intensification of the division of labor, as well as the sectoral and the spatial expansion of capitalist relations (internationalization). The contribution of financialization and the expansion of speculative capital portfolio movements is highlighted, especially in the late period of our days. Next, we proceed with the definition of the "potential monetary base". In the second part, we use the pre-defined terms in order to justify the evolution of money over three main phases - commodity money, tangible and intangible (digital) fiat-money. Moreover, the combined analysis of the two – volume of transactions and potential monetary base – is matched with international economic and political development. Finally, in the forth part, we evaluate the prospects of the new phase of monetary expansion (cryptocurrencies), given the technological possibilities of the virtual economy, and formulate the basic questions of institutional, economic and social nature.

DOI: 10.4018/979-8-3693-5986-0.ch015

1. INTRODUCTION

In a sense, economic history can be reduced to a course of expansion in the volume of transactions. Especially in the era of pre- and bourgeois evolution, the continued intensification of labor division and the resulting deepening of commercialization, along with the spatial expansion of 'generalized commodity production'[1] (post-medieval stage of internationalization) dominated as the main causes for the emergence of exponentially rising and more complex commercial exchanges.

In the late phase of post-modern neoliberal capitalism, the sectoral expansion of private ownership and commercialization even in sectors of traditional, widely recognized public goods, the vertical segmentation of production and the resulting outsourcing, as well as the extremely intensified financialization and especially the expansion of speculative portfolio capital movements have driven the volume of transactions to unprecedented historical levels, to an extent that exceeds multiplicatively the growing real economy.

In the present paper, we intend to explain the evolution of money as an induced historical process that responds to the necessities caused by the above systemic trajectory. Therefore, we need first to define a key term, namely the specific, potential volume of money, determined by the material, technical and institutional limitations of each type of currency.

Following this, in the 3rd part we proceed with a detailed discussion of the three main phases currencies went through till now – (i) commodity money, (ii) tangible and (iii) intangible 'fiat' money. Beside explaining the differences, we reveal the way how this evolution is actually a continuous effort to break the 'natural' limits in money quantity. Moreover, we introduce a combinatory analysis of the (re-) emerging systemic currency crises with the succession of different exchange rate regimes (fixed or floating) next to the historical path of transactions' volume and money types.

Having studied the evolution till the present, we use the introduced analytical tools in order to understand the newly raised meta-, pseudo- or crypto-currencies. The 4th part of the paper considers these new forms of virtual means of exchange as the rise of the next phase in the evolution of money that wants to break the limits of the assets of the banking system itself, given the continuous rise of transactions. Nevertheless, the prospectively possible loss of bourgeois state's main tool for exercising political power – namely the control of money supply – and the fact that the underlying financialization induces deep systemic deficiencies speak for the greatly challenging effects that this development may have. Therefore, the last part in the 4th section of the paper focuses on the probable socioeconomic and political effects and the related challenges.

Finally, we proceed with conceptual conclusions and proposals for alternative policies for dealing with the inescapable challenges of meta-currencies in a feasible, progressive way: towards a new, global financial settlement of democratically, socially legitimized global representations to set up control mechanisms and indirect limitations against financial unaccountability and to coordinate a worldwide expansionary fiscal policy redistributing funding instruments in lagging regions, seeking for social justice and environmental sustainability.

2. INTRODUCING POTENTIAL MONETARY BASE

Monetary literature has come up with the following two basic concepts to describe the availability of money. On the one hand, we have *monetary base*, which is actually the sum of any currency – banknotes and coins – in circulation, as well as that held in reserves at banks and with the central bank. *Money supply* on the other refers to the total amount of money in circulation; this adds to the monetary base all money held by economic agents – physical or legal persons – at bank accounts. There are different measures for money supply depending on the degree of liquidity of the deposits involved.

The meaning and the relationship between the two terms will become more obvious, when we take a closer look in the main types of money that existed over history (check diagram 1). For instance, in the traditional version of 'commodity money', monetary base is simply identical to the money supply. In this first phase of money's evolution, transactions have been facilitated by the use of currencies, where their exchange value was determined by the same exchange value of the material of which the currency was constructed. Being the currencies in circulation or the number of currencies held as deposits by the economic agents and the state (whichever), this was at the same time the monetary base and the money supply.

Things turned out to be different in the second phase with the introduction of tangible 'fiat' ('let it be' in Latin) money, or in other words tangible fictitious money. Along with the appearance of material banknotes and coins that represent however a disproportionately larger exchange value than the costs of their material nature, we have also the emergence of the institutions that have the responsibility of issuing and reserve this new form of money, in other words, the establishment of the modern banking system. As long as this is the case, money existing in physical form (in circulation or held as banks' reserves), representing the monetary base, is less than the money supply (being defined in a 'narrow' or 'broader' sense), for this includes also the different types of deposits of economic agents in the banking system.[2]

The situation changes again as we move to the current era of intangible 'fiat' money. Increasingly, in many markets already almost exclusively, transactions are processed by digital money exchange and the use of coins and banknotes is marginalized. Therefore, monetary base includes respectively all deposits available by demand in bank accounts, because they can be used directly as a means for payment without being necessarily withdrawn. In this case, the monetary base becomes identical to the money supply defined in a narrow sense. The differentiation remains only for the so-called broad-money supply that aggregates also the deposits of non-immediate liquidation.

Figure 1. Monetary base and money supply over the different historical phases of money

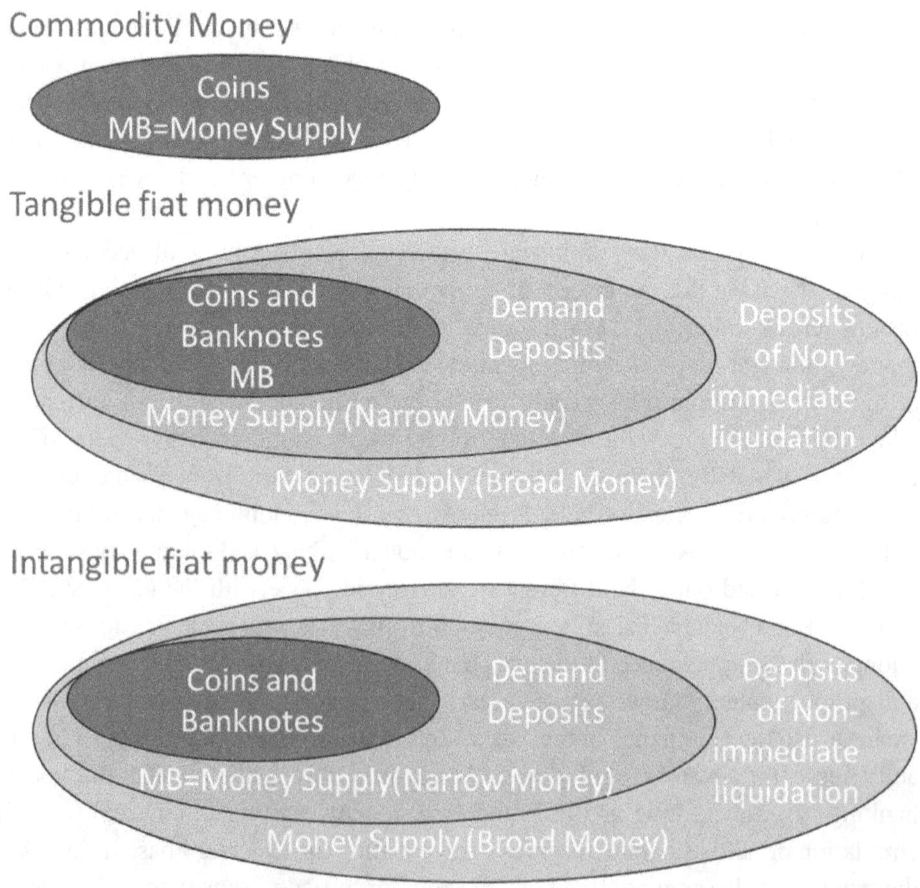

In general, monetary literature deals with the quantity of money in relation to the induced inflationary pressures. Following more or less different approaches, the question is still what the limits of money supply are so that the price level will not accelerate. In terms of a macroeconomic analogy, we could speak for a 'non-accelerating inflation' level of money supply as the equivalent to the non-accelerating inflation rate of unemployment (NAIRU).

Nevertheless, beyond the concepts of monetary base and money supply, there is a restrictive notion of deterministic nature, which we introduce in the present paper: ***potential monetary base*** can be defined as *the 'natural' limit in the quantity of money determined by the type of money itself, i.e. the relevant technical requirements and specificities, as well as systemic socioeconomic and institutional conditions.*

Even if these are less obvious and difficult to quantify, there are certain constraints in as how much a specific type of money can satisfy the increasing volume of transactions. The existence and the significance of this natural limitation becomes obvious when we take a macroscopic, historical approach with respect to the expansion of the volume of transactions and the evolution of money.

In fact, there are two standard justifications for the development of price levels[3]: (i) 'real' inflationary or deflationary pressures resulting out of the relation between the (increasing) needs of the society on the one hand and the supply of economic goods on the other, due to the restraints of natural resources and the particular productivity of labor[4]; (ii) 'monetary' inflation (or deflation) resulting out of money supply expansions (or contractions) that do not correspond to equivalent improvements in the prospective supply of economic goods.

However, as we introduce the concept of potential monetary base, we get an additional way of arguing for the development of the price level: when the expansion of transactions violates the limits of potential monetary base, creation of the necessary extra money becomes impossible or enormously costly. This is in fact like a 'naturally' imposed restrictive monetary policy, holding back the economic growth and leading even to recessionary pressures, which can be removed only through the appropriate evolution of the type of money. In the following section we discuss this approach in detail, drawing on historical data and information.

3. VOLUME OF TRANSACTIONS AND POTENTIAL MONETARY BASE OVER TIME

In terms of economic development, the period following the industrial revolution and the prevalence of bourgeois socioeconomic system unquestionably is an immense transformation in the history of Mankind. The path of GDP in constant 2011 prices in diagram 2 reveals this[5]: from the beginning of the 19th century, economic output experienced for two centuries an exponential rise due to the continued intensification of division of labor and the resulting deepening of commercialization on the one hand and technological expansion on the other. Together with the spatial expansion of 'generalized commodity production' through trade and FDI, these were the main causes for the analogously exponentially rising commercial exchanges all over the world.

Figure 2. Regional GDP (2011 constant prices) based on country- and region-estimations

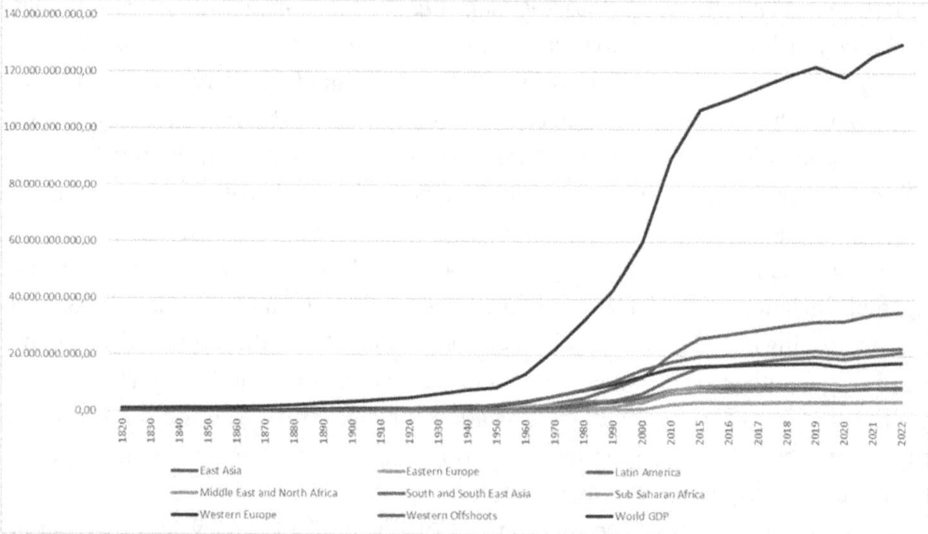

Things changed in the late phase of post-modern neoliberal capitalism. Since the rise of the 21st century global capitalistic development has shown an ongoing slow down. The previous exponential path converted in a gradually lowering rate of growth, which, in our days, clearly moves towards stagnation. Trade volume, that was one of the main reasons for the increase of transactions, remained also stable compared to world GDP. The following diagram depicts this. The share of world exports in goods and services in the last decades stabilized at around 30% of world output (GDP).

Still, transactions kept growing more or less in the same way as in the previous expansionary period. On the one hand, this is because of reasons that have to do with 'real' economic activities: (i) in the era of neoliberalism there is an ongoing sectoral expansion of capitalist relations of ownership and production. Economic goods that have been till now acknowledged as social ones are being (re-) privatized, which introduces commercial transactions in sectors where relevant needs used to be covered in a public, non-commercialized sense; (ii) there was an expansion of outsourcing, or in other words of vertical segmentation (existing along to the horizontal centralization and the creation of oligopolies).

Figure 3. Product and services world exports (current prices, trillions US$) 1988-2021

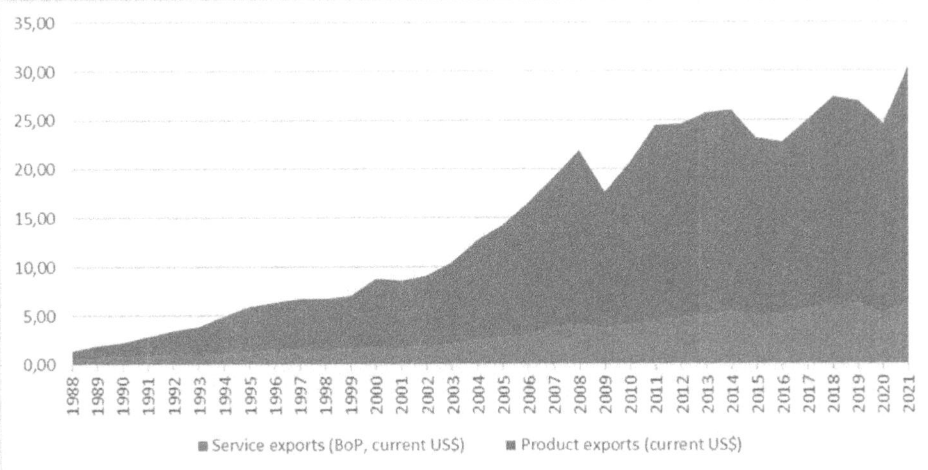

Besides to those 'real' economic transformations, sustaining the upwards trend of transactions volume towards unprecedented historical levels majorly resulted from the exceptional intensification of speculative portfolio capital movements and the induced financialization to an extent that exceeds multiplicatively the 'real' economic activity. The notional value of outstanding 'over the counter' (OTC) derivatives alone became almost 4 times as large as the world GDP, reaching $715 trillion in the first half of 2023, a rise of more than 40% in 7 years (from 2016).[6] As for the transactions with stocks, the value of global equity trading worldwide in 2021 exceeded the 160 trillion US$! Despite a decrease down to more than 129 in 2023, this was still 37% more than the volume of stock markets in 2017, reaching the level of World GDP in the same year.[7]

The theoretical approach presented in the previous section helps us understand why the unparalleled expansion of transactions in the 19th and 20th century provoked the two major transformations in the type of money. The 'natural' limit in the potential monetary base of commodity money, determined by the restrictive abundance of the material used (gold, silver etc.) made it necessary to proceed with the issuing of tangible 'fiat' money. Introducing banknotes and coins that represented an exchange value so much higher than the costs for producing them, was essential in order to serve the growth of commercialized output and the first stages of capitalism's spatial expansion. Before the rise of the previous century, banknotes and coins that represented in a certified way the claim on a specific amount of gold gradually replaced bimetallism (diagram 4).

Figure 4. Fixed and floating exchange rate regimes in relation to the type of money

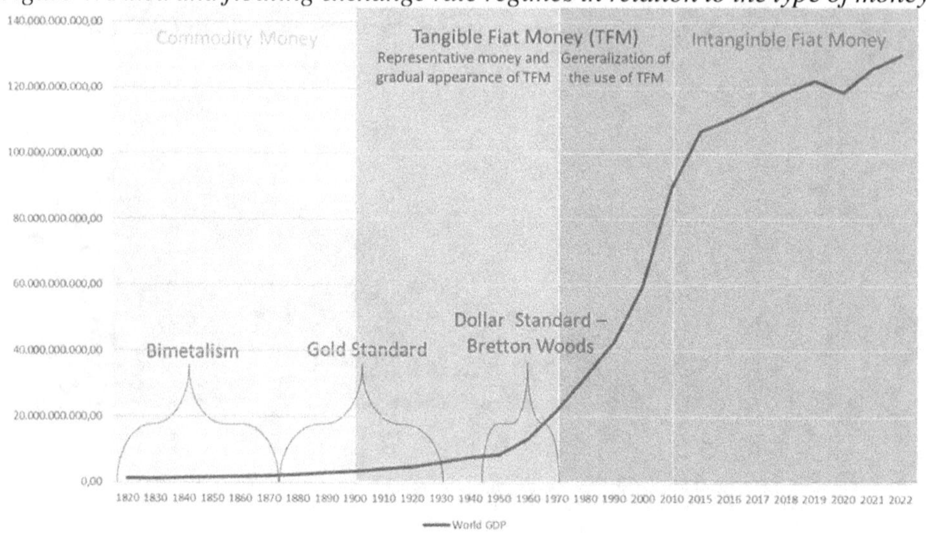

Apparently, given also the intensified internationalization of economic transactions (which on the other hand, as we said, was a main reason for the rise of the new type of money), establishing a certain, constant way of settlement that secured 'fair' proportionality between the different currencies became a necessity. In the absence of effective communication and data processing technology, Gold Standard turned out to be a notably significant tool for global capitalist development. At the end, as the expansion in the volume of transactions was progressing, the evolution of currencies in this new phase completed in the form of (tangible) fiat money. This was generalized especially after the collapse of Dollar Standard: Bretton Woods was in a sense an intermediate regime of fixed exchange rates that settled the even more 'distanced' representation of banknotes, before the generalization of fiat money. The spatial expansion of trade and capital movements kept on rising, nevertheless, as we saw, more and more in terms of speculative activity, rather than transactions that represent actual exchanges of economic goods. In fact, the prevalence of the (still) existing system of floating exchange rates in response to the inability of dollar to respond to its representative nature, opened more potentials for a further intensification of financial speculation and intensified the process of the generalization of fiat money.

Once this process was triggered, the volume of transactions began to grow beyond any limits of real economic activity. The data we provided above on the upsurge of the financial markets prove the actuality of the hypotheses that the total financial capital worldwide exceeds more than twenty times the annually produced wealth in the world (Wilmott, 1998). In such an environment, even fiat money faced 'natural' limitations determined by its relevant production costs (even if those were lower than the previous type of commodity currencies) and especially by the functional difficulties resulting from its tangibility itself. This unveiled the need for a new, even more 'efficient' form of money in the new era of intensified, financialized globalization and led to the evolution of intangible, digital 'fiat' money, which is far more suitable for serving the needs for even more, faster, complex and spatially extended transactions.

The theoretical tools we introduced helped us understand better the (re-) emerging of systemic currency crises with the succession of different exchange rate regimes (fixed or floating), linking it to the historical evolution of the volume of transactions, as well as to important economic and political incidences and the transition between the phases of evolution in the form of money. This is a discussion that can (and will) be done in educational and illuminating details. For the needs of the present paper, we keep the rationalization of money's evolution, and we move in the next part with a justified analysis of the next phase.

4. THE EVOLVING PHASE OF PSEUDO- OR CRYPTOCURRENCIES AND RELEVANT CHALLENGES

As financialization goes beyond any limit related to the actual economic performance, speculative transactions break the relevant records, one after the other. According to the Bank for International Settlements (BIS) trading in foreign exchange markets averaged US$ 7,5 trillion per day in April 2022 (!), where trading in foreign exchange swaps alone came up to US$ 3,8 trillion, followed by spot trading at US$ 2,1 trillion (BIS, 2022).

Obviously, preserving the tangibility of money in such a reality would be absolutely incompatible. Nonetheless, even the intangible type of currency seems to act restrictively for the hyper-growing volume of global transactions. This is because of the fact that, despite its intangibility, also for digital fiat money there is a potential monetary base defined by the very assets of the banking system itself.

The pressure for even more transactions of unthinkable volume, which however is irrelevant to the real economic needs, coincides with rapid technological development in the management and transfer of information and opens the way for the next phase of money evolution overcoming even the limitations of banking sector. Following the achievements in 'digital economy', where socio-economic relationships with a direct or indirect economic impact are being processed in a remote, digital way, contemporary capitalism moves towards 'virtual economy', where digitalization occurs in the production and use of economic goods itself. Having in mind that money is in fact an economic good and indeed a commodity, the emergence of cryptocurrencies is the forerunner of economic virtuality – in the sense that they have a completely digitalized nature, beyond and above any representative association to the real assets of the institutions that (still) reserve the control over standard money supply – while at the same time it serves the new expansion of potential monetary base beyond the limits of the banking system.

In general, digitalization and virtualization have three main consequences of systemic significance:

(i) Strengthen the exponential increase in labor productivity that intensifies the necessity of drastic interventions for reversing the social class inequality, while it induces the socialization of produced goods, even if the oligopolies resist through the artificial preservation of their commercial character
(ii) Contribute to the modification of individual and collective preferences so that inter-industry and inter-regional reallocation of profitability and therefore of investments gets faster and more intense
(iii) Induce social distancing despite the continuous broadening of interpersonal and collective interactions, along to the development of more effective and 'cheaper' external control mechanisms, which, following the approach of Norbert Elias (1939), open a new era in the 'civilizing process', provoking emotional disorders, new forms of (anti-) social behavior, challenging the limits of contemporary bourgeois ethical order (Zarotiadis, 2023)

The appearance of cryptocurrencies, although the forerunner, is by far not the only aspect of the arising virtual economy. Nonetheless, in addition to the above, it has specific, deeper ramifications that affect the very nature of the bourgeois economic and political order. On the one hand, prospectively it opens the possibility of direct democratization and socialization of money supply, as the creation of money (mining in cryptocurrency slang) becomes technologically feasible to be an individual right on the basis of socially determined individual and collective needs. Yet, this has an obvious important prerequisite: it presupposes the emergence of a socially and democratically legitimized process that determines these needs and thereby the quantity of socialized money. Otherwise, the evolution triggered by the emergence of cryptocurrencies could end up in a completely different situation, facilitating the boundless intensification of speculative behavior and an outbreak of financial unaccountability, as well as the complete privatization of state power itself, in the frame of a technocratic, metaversal capitalistic anarchism.

5. CONCLUDING REMARKS, POLICY RECOMMENDATIONS AND PROPOSALS FOR FURTHER RESEARCH

In a course of continuous expansion of the volume and spatial extent of transactions, the mean that enables transactions needs to adapt accordingly so that the limitations of its potential abundance will be overcome. This is in short, the story of money over the socioeconomic development of Mankind. Starting with gold and silver coins, going to the representative and then 'fiat' banknotes, till the digital, intangible currency of our time, potential money supply grew constantly in order to respond to the needs provoked by the division of labor, commercialization, internationalization and lately financialization.

The analytical tools we introduced may also help us understand better the (re-) emerging of systemic currency crises in relation to the succession of different exchange rate regimes, linking it to the historical evolution of the volume of transactions, as well as to important economic and political incidences and the transition between the phases of evolution in the form of money. This is a discussion that can (and will) be done in details.

Following the above theoretical view, we can also explain the appearance of cryptocurrencies in the frame of the evolving digitalization and especially the virtualization of the economy. Also here, the point is to break the last limitation of digital money: despite its intangibility it is still necessary not to exceed overproportionally the very assets of the banking system. Nevertheless, this new phase is different than the previous, as it induces significant changes that affect the socioeconomic system itself: the evolution triggered could facilitate the boundless intensification of speculative behavior, while it challenges the basic source of bourgeois state's economic power.

Putting it together, the new, arising era in the evolution of money brings about two political questions of absolute structural importance. Derivatives and other forms or expression of financial capital are reaching a volume of more than 20 times the world annual GDP, desperately seeking for ways to be materialized. Nervousness gets deeper in global financial markets, increasing the likelihood of a global bank-run, while exacerbating the modern inter-imperialistic antagonisms in the frame of the arising multipolarized world order.

Therefore, the first question is how to prevent an outbreak of a destructive financial crisis, by limiting the prospects of extreme overaccumulation of financial capital, or in other words how to restrain the potential monetary base in the epoch of virtual economy in relation to the real assets of the world economy (rather than those of the banking system).

Second, the social struggle in the next future has to indicate, whether we will democratize and socialize money supply, letting the creation of money to be a right, yet, on the basis of socially determined individual and collective needs, or if we will move to the complete privatization of state power itself, in the frame of a technocratic, metaversal capitalistic anarchism.

A key to the above dilemmas can be the idea to make an opportunity out of the already evolving extreme overaccumulation of financial capital, through a strategy of a controlled, coordinated (corrective) inflation to finance socially and environmentally sustainable development. We can move towards a progressive alternative of a new, global financial settlement: an alliance of democratically, socially legitimized global representations (i) to set up control mechanisms and indirect limitations against financial unaccountability and (ii) to coordinate a worldwide expansionary fiscal policy redistributing funding instruments in lagging regions, seeking for social justice and environmental sustainability. As democratic legitimacy will regain its supremacy against neoliberal technocracy, even financial capital concentrations can receive a new role: funding this globally coordinated expansion, ensuring thereby a socially fair recognition, before facing a violent, yet historically justified correction (Zarotiadis, 2014).

REFERENCES

Bank for International Settlements BIS. (2022). "Triennial Central Bank Survey of foreign exchange and OTC derivatives markets in 2022", https://www.bis.org/statistics/rpfx22_fx.pdf, October 2022

Elias, N. (1939). *Über den Prozeß der Zivilisation [On the process of civilization].*

Marx, K. (1867). *Capital: A Critique of Political Economy* (Vol. 1). Verlag von Otto Meisner.

Wilmott, P. (1998). *Derivatives: the theory and practice of financial engineering.* No Title.

Zarotiadis, G. (2014). Relieving Inflation or Palliative Self-destruction? *Journal of Stock & Forex Trading*, *3*(4), 4. DOI: 10.4172/2168-9458.1000133

Zarotiadis, G. (2023). Guilt Economics: Rediscovering the Civilizing Process. In *Handbook of Research on Socio-Economic Sustainability in the Post-Pandemic Era.* IGI Global., DOI: 10.4018/978-1-7998-9760-6.ch017

ENDNOTES

1 Karl Marx, 1867.

2 The literature has sufficiently outlined the way how commercial banks contribute in that sense to the money supply, or, expressed in another way, how they implicitly create money.

3 Be aware that here we speak for the evolution of the price level and not for the real prices, in other words the relative prices that determine the exchange relationship between commodities. These remain determined by the relationship of the quantity of labor incorporated, directly and indirectly, in the production of one or the other commodity (labor theory of value still holds).

4 It is worth mentioning that the actual productivity of labor is not only defined by the technological achievements, but also by the current socioeconomic and political conditions, e.g. wars etc., locally and internationally.

5 The diagram is based on historical data from Maddison Project Database 2023 for the different regions of the world; see in https://www.rug.nl/ggdc/historicaldevelopment/maddison/releases/maddison-project-database-2023?lang=en.

6 See in the Bank for International Settlements (BIS) OTC derivatives statistics, https://data.bis.org/.

7 See the data published in https://www.statista.com/.

Compilation of References

Abdelmoumin, G., Rawat, D., & Rahman, A. (2021). On the Performance of Machine Learning Models for Anomaly-Based Intelligent Intrusion Detection Systems for the Internet of Things. *IEEE Internet of Things Journal*, *9*(6), 4280–4290. DOI: 10.1109/JIOT.2021.3103829

Adams, M., & Dammeyer, L. (2024, July 23).Top 10 Cryptocurrencies of July 23, 2024. *Forbes Advisor*, https://www.forbes.com/advisor/investing/cryptocurrency/top-10-cryptocurrencies

Adhami, S., Giudici, G., & Martinazzi, S. (2018). Cryptocurrency: A new asset class? *Journal of Corporate Finance*, *50*, 225–241.

Agarwal, U., Rishiwal, V., Tanwar, S., & Yadav, M. (2023). Blockchain and crypto forensics: Investigating crypto frauds. *International Journal of Network Management*, *34*(2), e2255. Advance online publication. DOI: 10.1002/nem.2255

Aggarwal, D. (2019). Do bitcoins follow a random walk model? *Research in Economics*, *73*(1), 15–22. DOI: 10.1016/j.rie.2019.01.002

Agrawal, S., Sarkar, S., Aouedi, O., Yenduri, G., Piamrat, K., Bhattacharya, S., Maddikunta, P., & Gadekallu, T. (2021). Federated Learning for Intrusion Detection System: Concepts, Challenges and Future Directions. *Computer Communications*, *195*, 346–361. DOI: 10.1016/j.comcom.2022.09.012

Agur, I., Ari, A., & Dell'Ariccia, G. (2019). Designing Central Bank Digital Currencies, IMF Working Paper 19/252.

Aharon, D. Y., Demir, E., Chi, K. M. L., & Zaremba, A. (2022). Twitter-Based Uncertainty and Cryptocurrency Returns. *Research in International Business and Finance*, *59*, 101546. DOI: 10.1016/j.ribaf.2021.101546

Ahelegbey, D. F., Giudici, P., & Mojtahedi, F. (2021). Tail Risk Measurement in Crypto-Asset Markets. *International Review of Financial Analysis*, *73*, 101604. DOI: 10.1016/j.irfa.2020.101604

Ahmed, I., Fumimoto, K., Nakano, T., & Tran, T. H. (2024). Blockchain-Empowered Decentralized Philanthropic Charity for Social Good. *Sustainability (Basel)*, *16*(1), 210. DOI: 10.3390/su16010210

Ahmed, W. M. A. (2021). Stock Market Reactions to Upside and Downside Volatility of Bitcoin: A Quantile Analysis. *The North American Journal of Economics and Finance*, *57*, 101379. DOI: 10.1016/j.najef.2021.101379

Ahn, Y., & Kim, D. (2021). Emotional Trading in the Cryptocurrency Market. *Finance Research Letters*, *42*, 101912. DOI: 10.1016/j.frl.2020.101912

Ahsan, Z. B., Gupta, A., & Kar, A. K. (2023). The Effect of Countries' Independent Regulation on Cryptocurrency Markets. [JGIM]. *Journal of Global Information Management*, *31*(1), 1–32. DOI: 10.4018/JGIM.323567

Akhtaruzzaman, M., Sensoy, A., & Corbet, S. (2020). The Influence of Bitcoin on Portfolio Diversification and Design. *Finance Research Letters*, *37*, 101344. DOI: 10.1016/j.frl.2019.101344

Akther, U. (2020). Bitcoin—A hype or digital gold? Global evidence. *Australian Economic Papers*, *59*(3), 215–231. DOI: 10.1111/1467-8454.12178

Akyildirim, E., Aysan, A. F., Cepni, O., & Pinar Ceyhan Darendeli, S. (2021a). Do Investor Sentiments Drive Cryptocurrency Prices? *Economics Letters*, *206*, 109980. DOI: 10.1016/j.econlet.2021.109980

Akyildirim, E., Cepni, O., Corbet, S., & Uddin, G. S. (2021b). Forecasting Mid-Price Movement of Bitcoin Futures Using Machine Learning. *Annals of Operations Research*, *•••*, 1–32. PMID: 34316087

Akyildirim, E., Corbet, S., Lucey, B., Sensoy, A., & Yarovaya, L. (2020). The relationship between implied volatility and cryptocurrency returns. *Finance Research Letters*, *33*, 101212. Advance online publication. DOI: 10.1016/j.frl.2019.06.010

Alahmad, M., Alfouderi, A. D. E. L., Alonaizi, A. H. M. A. D., & Aldhamen, M. (2023). Comparison Study of the Top 5 Leading Cryptocurrencies based on General Consensus Protocol: Bitcoin, Ethereum, Tether, XRP and Bitcoin Cash. *WSEAS Transactions on Computer Research*, *11*, 23–32.

Al-Amri, R., Zakaria, N. H., Habbal, A., & Hassan, S. (2019). Cryptocurrency adoption: Current stage, opportunities, and open challenges. *International Journal of Advanced Computer Research, 9*(44), 293–307. DOI: 10.19101/IJACR.PID43

Al-bahouth, A. B. S. B. A. (2017). *Virtual Money: Its concept, types, and economic effects. Scientific Journal of Economics and Trade*. Faculty of Commerce, Ain Shams University.

Albayati, H., Kim, S. K., & Rho, J. J. (2020). Accepting financial transactions using blockchain technology and cryptocurrency: A customer perspective approach. *Technology in Society, 62*, 101320. DOI: 10.1016/j.techsoc.2020.101320

Albizri, A., & Appelbaum, D. (2021). Trust but Verify: The Oracle Paradox of Blockchain Smart Contracts. *Journal of Information Systems, 35*(2), 1–16. DOI: 10.2308/ISYS-19-024

Alekseenko, A. (2022). Ban of Cryptocurrencies in China and Judicial Practice of Chinese Courts. *China and WTO Review, 8* (June), 361–388. DOI: 10.14330/cwr.2022.8.2.06

Alexakis, C., Anselmi, G. & Petrella, G. (2024). Flight to cryptos: Evidence on the use of cryptocurrencies in times of geopolitical tensions. *International Review of Economics & Finance, 89, A*, 498-523, https://doi.org/.DOI: 10.1016/j.iref.2023.07.054

Alexander, C., Choi, J., Massie, H. R. A., & Sohn, S. (2020). Price Discovery and Microstructure in Ether Spot and Derivative Markets. *International Review of Financial Analysis, 71*, 101506. DOI: 10.1016/j.irfa.2020.101506

Allen, B., & Bryant, S. K. (2019). The market for cryptocurrency: How will it evolve? *Global Economy Journal, 19*(03), 1950019. Advance online publication. DOI: 10.1142/S2194565919500192

Allen, F., Morris, S., & Pastlewaite, A. (1993). Finite Bubbles with short sale constraints and asymmetric information. *Journal of Economic Theory, 61*(2), 206–229. DOI: 10.1006/jeth.1993.1067

Almansour, B. Y., Elkrghli, S., & Almansour, A. Y. (2023). Behavioral finance factors and investment decisions: A mediating role of risk perception. *Cogent Economics & Finance, 11*(2), 2239032. Advance online publication. DOI: 10.1080/23322039.2023.2239032

Almeida, J. (2021). Cryptocurrencies and Financial Markets–Extant Literature and Future Venues. *European Journal of Economics Finance and Administrative Sciences, 109*, 29–40.

Almeida, J., & Gonçalves, T. C. (2022). A Systematic Literature Review of Volatility and Risk Management on Cryptocurrency Investment: A Methodological Point of View. *Risks, 10*(5), 107. DOI: 10.3390/risks10050107

Alomari, A. S. A., & Abdullah, N. L. (2023). Factors influencing the behavioral intention to use Cryptocurrency among Saudi Arabian public university students: Moderating role of financial literacy. *Cogent Business & Management, 10*(1), 2178092. Advance online publication. DOI: 10.1080/23311975.2023.2178092

Al-Omoush, K. S., Gomez-Olmedo, A. M., & Gómez Funes, A. (2024). Why do people choose to continue using cryptocurrencies? *Technological Forecasting and Social Change, 200*, 123151. DOI: 10.1016/j.techfore.2023.123151

Aloui, C., Hamida, H., & Yarovaya, L. (2021). Are Islamic Gold-Backed Cryptocurrencies Different? *Finance Research Letters, 39*, 101615. DOI: 10.1016/j.frl.2020.101615

Alrawashdeh, K., & Purdy, C. (2016). Toward an Online Anomaly Intrusion Detection System Based on Deep Learning. *2016 15th IEEE International Conference on Machine Learning and Applications (ICMLA)*, 195-200. DOI: 10.1109/ICMLA.2016.0040

Al-Tawil, T. N. E. (2023). Anti-money laundering regulation of cryptocurrency: UAE and global approaches. *Journal of Money Laundering Control, 26*(6), 1150–1164. DOI: 10.1108/JMLC-07-2022-0109

Alvares, F., Argente, D., & Van Patten, D. (2023). Are cryptocurrencies currencies? Bitcoin as legal tender in El Salvador, Science, 22 December, 22 Dec 2023, Vol 382, Issue 6677. DOI: DOI: 10.1126/science.add2844

Al-Yahyaee, K. H., Rehman, M. U., Mensi, W., & Idries, M. W. A.-J. (2019). Can Uncertainty Indices Predict Bitcoin Prices? A Revisited Analysis Using Partial and MultivariateWavelet Approaches. *The North American Journal of Economics and Finance, 49*, 47–56. DOI: 10.1016/j.najef.2019.03.019

Alzhrani, F. E., Saeedi, K. A., & Zhao, L. (2022). A Taxonomy for Characterizing Blockchain Systems. *IEEE Access : Practical Innovations, Open Solutions, 10*, 110568–110589. DOI: 10.1109/ACCESS.2022.3214837

Ammous, S. (2018). Can cryptocurrencies fulfil the functions of money? *Quarterly Review of Economics and Finance. The Quarterly Review of Economics and Finance, 70*, 38–51. DOI: 10.1016/j.qref.2018.05.010

Anaza, N. A., Upadhyaya, B., Bennett, D., & Ruvalcaba, C. (2024). Is it FOMO or is it ME? The influence of personality traits on cryptocurrency consumption. *Psychology and Marketing*, *41*(1), 184–202. DOI: 10.1002/mar.21919

Andrada-Félix, J., Fernandez-Perez, A., & Sosvilla-Rivero, S. (2020). Distant or Close Cousins: Connectedness between Cryptocurrencies and Traditional Currencies Volatilities. *Journal of International Financial Markets, Institutions and Money*, *67*, 101219. DOI: 10.1016/j.intfin.2020.101219

Androulaki, E., Barger, A., Bortnikov, V., Cachin, C., Christidis, K., De Caro, A., & Yellick, J. (2018, April). Hyperledger fabric: a distributed operating system for permissioned blockchains. In *Proceedings of the thirteenth EuroSys conference* (pp. 1-15).

Angerer, M., Hoffmann, C. H., Neitzert, F., & Kraus, S. (2020). Objective and Subjective Risks of Investing into Cryptocurrencies. *Finance Research Letters*, *40*, 101737. DOI: 10.1016/j.frl.2020.101737

Anser, M. K., Zaigham, G. H. K., Imran Rasheed, M., Pitafi, A. H., Iqbal, J., & Luqman, A. (2020). Social media usage and individuals' intentions toward adopting Bitcoin: The role of the theory of planned behavior and perceived risk. *International Journal of Communication Systems*, *33*(17), e4590. Advance online publication. DOI: 10.1002/dac.4590

Ante, L. (2023a). How Elon Musk's Twitter activity moves cryptocurrency markets. *Technological Forecasting and Social Change*, *186*, 122112. DOI: 10.1016/j.techfore.2022.122112

Ante, L. (2023b). Non-fungible token (NFT) markets on the Ethereum blockchain: Temporal development, cointegration and interrelations. *Economics of Innovation and New Technology*, *32*(8), 1216–1234. DOI: 10.1080/10438599.2022.2119564

Ante, L., Fiedler, I., & Strehle, E. (2021). The Influence of Stablecoin Issuances on Cryptocurrency Markets. *Finance Research Letters*, *41*, 101867. DOI: 10.1016/j.frl.2020.101867

Apergis, N., Koutmos, D., & Payne, J. E. (2020). Convergence in Cryptocurrency Prices? The Role of Market Microstructure. *Finance Research Letters*, *40*, 101685. DOI: 10.1016/j.frl.2020.101685

Appel, D., & Grabinski, M. (2011). The origin of financial crisis: A wrong definition of value. *Portuguese Journal of Quantitative Methods*, *2*, 33–51.

Aquilina, M., Frost, J., & Schrimpf, A. (2024). Decentralized finance (DeFi): A functional approach. *Journal of Financial Regulation, 10*(1), 1–27. DOI: 10.1093/jfr/fjad013

Arslanian, H., & Fischer, F. (2019). A High-Level Taxonomy of Crypto-assets. In H. Arslanian & F. Fischer, The Future of Finance (pp. 139–156). Springer International Publishing. DOI: 10.1007/978-3-030-14533-0_12

Arslanian, H. (2022). The History of Money. In Arslanian, H. (Ed.), *The Book of Crypto* (pp. 1–43). Springer International Publishing., DOI: 10.1007/978-3-030-97951-5_1

Arslanian, H., & Fisher, F. (2019). *The Future of Finance, The Impact of Fintech, AI, and Crypto on Financial Services*. Palgrave Mac Millan., DOI: 10.1007/978-3-030-14533-0

Asadov, A., Yildirim, R., & Masih, M. (2023). Toward greater stability in stablecoins: Empirical evidence from an analysis of precious metals. *Borsa Istanbul Review, 23*(5), 1152–1172. DOI: 10.1016/j.bir.2023.07.004

Asena Deniz, E., & Teker, D. (2020). Crypto currency applications in financial markets: Factors affecting crypto currency prices. *Pressacademia Procedia, 11*(1), 34–37. DOI: 10.17261/Pressacademia.2020.1235

Attri, S., Gupta, S., & Singh, S. (2025). Risk Forecasting Using Artificial Intelligence and Machine Learning: Evidence From Stock and Cryptocurrency Markets. In *Artificial Intelligence for Financial Risk Management and Analysis* (pp. 187–196). DOI: 10.4018/979-8-3373-1200-2.ch009

Auer, R. & Böhme, R. (2020). The technology of retail central bank digital currency, *BIS Quarterly Review*, March.

Auer, R., & Claessens, S. (2021). Cryptocurrency and the future of monetary policy. *The Journal of Economic Perspectives, 35*(2), 123–146.

Ayedh, A., Echchabi, A., Battour, M., & Omar, M. (2020). Malaysian Muslim investors' behaviour towards the blockchain-based Bitcoin cryptocurrency market. *Journal of Islamic Marketing, 12*(4), 690–704. DOI: 10.1108/JIMA-04-2019-0081

Aysan, A. F., Demir, E., Gozgor, G., & Lau, C. K. M. (2021). Effects of the cryptocurrency market on global economic conditions: Evidence from Bitcoin. *Economic Modelling, 94*, 283–292.

Aysan, A. F., Demirta¸s, H. B., & Saraç, M. (2021). The Ascent of Bitcoin: Bibliometric Analysis of Bitcoin Research. *Journal of Risk and Financial Management, 14*(9), 427. DOI: 10.3390/jrfm14090427

Azhar, T. & Hassan, S. (2022). Current Challenges of Cryptocurrencies faced by governments, *Journal of Research and Reviews in Social Sciences Pakistan*, Vol 5 (1), Benedetti, H., and L. Kostovetsky. 2018. "Digital Tulips? Returns to Investors in Initial Coin Offerings."

B˛edowska-Sójka, B., & Kliber, A. (2021). Is There One Safe-Haven for Various Turbulences? The Evidence from Gold, Bitcoin and Ether. *The North American Journal of Economics and Finance*, *56*, 101390. DOI: 10.1016/j.najef.2021.101390

Babich, V., & Hilary, G. (2018). Distributed ledgers and operations: What operations management researchers should know about blockchain technology. *Manufacturing & Service Operations Management*, *22*(2), 223–240. DOI: 10.1287/msom.2018.0752

Baer, K., de Mooij, R., Hebous, S., & Keen, M. (2023). *Taxing cryptocurrencies, WP/23/143, July 2023*. International Monetary Fund.

Ba, H. L., & Şen, Ö. F. (2024). Explaining variation in national cryptocurrency regulation: Implications for the global political economy. *Review of International Political Economy*, *31*(5), 1–24. DOI: 10.1080/09692290.2024.2325403

Bahamazava, K., & Nanda, R. (2022). The Shift in DarkNet Illegal Drug Trade Preferences toward Cryptocurrency: The Question of Traceability and Deterrence. *Forensic Science International Digital Investigation*, *40*, 301377. DOI: 10.1016/j.fsidi.2022.301377

Bakhtiar, T., Luo, X., & Adelopo, I. (2023). Network effects and store-of-value features in the cryptocurrency market. *Technology in Society*, *74*, 102320. DOI: 10.1016/j.techsoc.2023.102320

Bakry, W., Rashid, A., Al-Mohamad, S., & El-Kanj, N. (2021). Bitcoin and Portfolio Diversification: A Portfolio Optimization Approach. *Journal of Risk and Financial Management*, *14*(7), 1–24. DOI: 10.3390/jrfm14070282

Balli, F., de Bruin, A., Md, I. H. C., & Naeem, M. A. (2020). Connectedness of Cryptocurrencies and Prevailing Uncertainties. *Applied Economics Letters*, *27*(16), 1316–1322. DOI: 10.1080/13504851.2019.1678724

Bamakan, S. M. H., Motavali, A., & Bondarti, A. B. (2020). A survey of blockchain consensus algorithms performance evaluation criteria. *Expert Systems with Applications*, *154*, 113385. DOI: 10.1016/j.eswa.2020.113385

Banerjee, B. (2020). Digital Currencies and Cross-Border Policy Cooperation and Coordination. *G20 Digest, 2*(Special Issue), 23–34. https://ris.org.in/sites/default/files/2021-09/Biswajit Banerjee_2.pdf

Bank for International Settlements BIS. (2022). “Triennial Central Bank Survey of foreign exchange and OTC derivatives markets in 2022”, https://www.bis.org/statistics/rpfx22_fx.pdf, October 2022

Bankrate. (2024). Federal Reserve impact on stocks, crypto, and other investments. https://www.bankrate.com/investing/federal-reserve-impact-on-stocks-crypto-other-investments/

Bao, H., & Rouband, D. (2022). Non-Fungible Token: A Systematic Review and Research Agenda. *Journal of Risk and Financial Management, 15*(5), 215. DOI: 10.3390/jrfm15050215

Bariviera, A. (2017). The inefficiency of Bitcoin revisited: A dynamic approach. *Economics Letters, 161*, 1–4. Advance online publication. DOI: 10.1016/j.econlet.2017.09.013

Bariviera, A. F., & Merediz-Solà, I. (2021). Where Do We Stand in Cryptocurrencies Economic Research? A Survey Based on Hybrid Analysis. *Journal of Economic Surveys, 35*(2), 377–407. DOI: 10.1111/joes.12412

Bartolacci, F., Caputo, A., & Soverchia, M. (2020). Sustainability and Financial Performance of Small and Medium Sized Enterprises: A Bibliometric and Systematic Literature Review. *Business Strategy and the Environment, 29*(3), 1297–1309. DOI: 10.1002/bse.2434

Baur, D. G., & Hoang, L. (2021). The Bitcoin gold correlation puzzle. *Journal of Behavioral and Experimental Finance, 32*, 100561. DOI: 10.1016/j.jbef.2021.100561

Baur, D. G., & Hoang, L. T. (2021). A crypto safe haven against Bitcoin. *Finance Research Letters, 38*, 101431. DOI: 10.1016/j.frl.2020.101431

Baur, D. G., Hong, K. H., & Lee, A. D. (2017). Bitcoin: Medium of exchange or speculative assets? *Journal of International Financial Markets, Institutions and Money*. Advance online publication. DOI: 10.1016/j.intfin.2017.12.004

Bazán-Palomino, W. (2020). How Are Bitcoin Forks Related to Bitcoin? *Finance Research Letters, 40*, 101723. DOI: 10.1016/j.frl.2020.101723

Beaman, C., Barkworth, A., Akande, T. D., Hakak, S., & Khan, M. K. (2021). Ransomware: Recent advances, analysis, challenges and future research directions. *Computers & Security, 111*, 102490. DOI: 10.1016/j.cose.2021.102490 PMID: 34602684

Bedi, P., & Nashier, T. (2020). On the Investment Credentials of Bitcoin: A Cross-Currency Perspective. *Research in International Business and Finance*, *51*, 101087. DOI: 10.1016/j.ribaf.2019.101087

Benkerroum, S., & Chougdali, K. (2023). Enhancing Forensic Analysis Using a Machine Learning-based Approach. *2023 6th International Conference on Advanced Communication Technologies and Networking (CommNet)*, pp. 1-6. DOI: 10.1109/CommNet60167.2023.10365260

Benson, V., Adamyk, B., Chinnaswamy, A., & Adamyk, O. (2024). Harmonising cryptocurrency regulation in Europe: Opportunities for preventing illicit transactions. *European Journal of Law and Economics*, *57*(1), 37–61. DOI: 10.1007/s10657-024-09797-w

Berwick, A. (2023). Hamas Needed a New Way to Get Money From Iran. It Turned to Crypto. *Wall Street Journal*, November 12

Bhaskar, N. D., & Chuen, D. L. K. (2024). Bitcoin Exchanges. In D. B. T.-H. of D. C. (Second E. Lee Kuo Chuen (Ed.), *Handbook of Digital Currency* (pp. 537–551). Elsevier. DOI: 10.1016/B978-0-323-98973-2.00008-3

Bhaskar, N. D., Wanfeng, C., Haili, L., & Chuen, D. L. K. (2024). Bitcoin Mining Technology. In D. B. T.-H. of D. C. (Second E. Lee Kuo Chuen (Ed.), *Handbook of Digital Currency* (pp. 41–64). Elsevier. DOI: 10.1016/B978-0-323-98973-2.00002-2

Bhuiyan, R. A., Husain, A., & Zhang, C. (2021). A Wavelet Approach for Causal Relationship between Bitcoin and Conventional Asset Classes. *Resources Policy*, *71*, 101971. DOI: 10.1016/j.resourpol.2020.101971

Białkowski, J. (2020). Cryptocurrencies in Institutional Investors' Portfolios: Evidence from Industry Stop-Loss Rules. *Economics Letters*, *191*, 108834. DOI: 10.1016/j.econlet.2019.108834

Biddle, P., England, P., Peinado, M., & Willman, B. (2003). The darknet and the future of content protection. In *Digital Rights Management: ACM CCS-9 Workshop, DRM 2002, Washington, DC, USA, November 18, 2002. Revised Papers* (pp. 155-176). Springer Berlin Heidelberg.

Bielinskyi, A. O., Serdyuk, O. A., Semerikov, S. O., & Soloviev, V. N. (2021). *Econophysics of cryptocurrency crashes: a systematic review* (Vol. 3048). DOI: 10.31812/123456789/6974

Biju, A. V. N., & Thomas, A. S. (2023). Uncertainties and ambivalence in the crypto market: An urgent need for a regional crypto regulation. *SN Business & Economics*, *3*(8), 136. DOI: 10.1007/s43546-023-00519-z

Bilotta, N., & Botti, F. (2021). *The (Near) Future of Central Bank Digital Currencies.* Risks and Opportunities for the Global Economy and Society, Peter Lang AG. DOI: 10.3726/b18087

Birkenmaier, J., & Fu, Q. (2018). Household Financial Access and Use of Alternative Financial Services in the U.S.: Two Sides of the Same Coin? *Social Indicators Research, 139*(3), 1169–1185. DOI: 10.1007/s11205-017-1770-6

Biryukov, A., & Tikhomirov, S. (2019, June). Deanonymization and linkability of cryptocurrency transactions based on network analysis. In *2019 IEEE European symposium on security and privacy (EuroS&P)* (pp. 172-184). IEEE. DOI: 10.1109/EuroSP.2019.00022

BISIH. (2024a). The Hong Kong Monetary Authority, Central Bank of Malaysia, Monetary Authority of Singapore, and South African Reserve Bank. 2022. "Project mBridge: Connecting Economies Through CBDC" Bank of International Settlements [online]. Accessed December 1, 2024.https:// www. bis. org/ publ/ othp59. htm

BISIH. (2024b). Reserve Bank of Australia, et al. 2022. "Project Dunbar -International Settlements Using Multi-CBDCs." Bank of International Settlements [online]. Accessed December 1, 2024. https:// www. bis. org/publ/ othp47. htm

BitTime. (2024). The potential impact of Tether (USDT) on the future of cryptocurrencies. https://support.bittime.com/hc/en-us/articles/9379605185295-The-Potential-Impact-of-Tether-USDT-on-the-Future-of-Cryptocurrencies

Bofinger, P. (2018). Digitalisation of money and the future of monetary policy, *Vox – CEPR Policy portal*

Böhme, R., Christin, N., Edelman, B., & Moore, T. (2015). Bitcoin: Economics, technology, and governance. *The Journal of Economic Perspectives, 29*(2), 213–238. DOI: 10.1257/jep.29.2.213

Bolici, F., & Della Rosa, S. (2016). Mt.Gox Is Dead, Long Live Bitcoin! In Torre, T., Braccini, A. M., & Spinelli, R. (Eds.), *Empowering Organizations: Enabling Platforms and Artefacts* (pp. 285–296). Springer International Publishing., DOI: 10.1007/978-3-319-23784-8_22

Bolt, W., & van Oordt, M. R. C. (2020). On the value of virtual currencies. *Journal of Money, Credit and Banking, 52*(4), 841–861. DOI: 10.1111/jmcb.12619

Bonaparte, Y., & Bernile, G. (2023). A new "Wall Street Darling?" effects of regulation sentiment in cryptocurrency markets. *Finance Research Letters, 52*, 103376. DOI: 10.1016/j.frl.2022.103376

Bonneau, J., Miller, A., Clark, J., Narayanan, A., Kroll, J. A., Felten, E. W., & Goldberg, S. (2015). "Multi-signature Crypto wallets: Theory, Implementation, and Applications," in *Proceedings of the 2015 ACM SIGSAC Conference on Computer and Communications Security*, 2015, pp. 243- 256.

Bose, C. (2023, December 21). *Donorbox and The Giving Block: Accept Crypto and Stock Donations with a Seamless Integration.* https://donorbox.org/nonprofit-blog/donorbox-the-giving-block-integration

Bouoiyour, J., & Selmi, R. (2015). Greece withdraws from Euro and runs on Bitcoin; April Fools Prank or Serious Possibility? *Grexit And Bitcoin.* https://mpra.ub.uni-muenchen.de/65317/

Bouri, E., Chi, K. M. L., Lucey, B., & Roubaud, D. (2019). Trading Volume and the Predictability of Return and Volatility in the Cryptocurrency Market. *Finance Research Letters*, *29*, 340–346. DOI: 10.1016/j.frl.2018.08.015

Bouri, E., Gabauer, D., Gupta, R., & Tiwari, A. K. (2021a). Volatility Connectedness of Major Cryptocurrencies: The Role of Investor Happiness. *Journal of Behavioral and Experimental Finance*, *30*, 100463. DOI: 10.1016/j.jbef.2021.100463

Bouri, E., Kristoufek, L., & Azoury, N. (2022). Bitcoin and S&P500: Co-Movements of High-Order Moments in the Time-Frequency Domain. *PLoS One*, *17*(11), e0277924. DOI: 10.1371/journal.pone.0277924 PMID: 36413562

Bouri, E., Lucey, B., & Roubaud, D. (2020a). Cryptocurrencies and the Downside Risk in Equity Investments. *Finance Research Letters*, *33*, 101211. DOI: 10.1016/j.frl.2019.06.009

Bouri, E., Lucey, B., & Roubaud, D. (2020b). The Volatility Surprise of Leading Cryptocurrencies: Transitory and Permanent Linkages. *Finance Research Letters*, *33*, 101188. DOI: 10.1016/j.frl.2019.05.006

Bouri, E., Roubaud, D., & Syed, J. H. S. (2020c). Do Bitcoin and Other Cryptocurrencies Jump Together? *The Quarterly Review of Economics and Finance*, *76*, 396–409. DOI: 10.1016/j.qref.2019.09.003

Bouri, E., Saeed, T., Vo, X. V., & Roubaud, D. (2021b). Quantile Connectedness in the Cryptocurrency Market. *Journal of International Financial Markets, Institutions and Money*, *71*, 101302. DOI: 10.1016/j.intfin.2021.101302

Bouri, E., Syed, J. H. S., & Roubaud, D. (2020d). Cryptocurrencies as Hedges and Safe-Havens for US Equity Sectors. *The Quarterly Review of Economics and Finance*, *75*, 294–307. DOI: 10.1016/j.qref.2019.05.001

Bouri, E., Vo, X. V., & Saeed, T. (2021c). Return Equicorrelation in the Cryptocurrency Market: Analysis and Determinants. *Finance Research Letters*, *38*, 101497. DOI: 10.1016/j.frl.2020.101497

Branch, S., Ward, L., & Allan Wright, A. (2023). The Evolution of SandDollar. *Inter Economics*, *58*(4), 178–184. DOI: 10.2478/ie-2023-0038

Brasse, A., & Hyun, S. (2023). Cryptocurrency Exchanges and the Future of Cryptoassets. In *The Emerald Handbook on Cryptoassets: Investment Opportunities and Challenges* (pp. 341–353). Emerald Publishing Limited. DOI: 10.1108/978-1-80455-320-620221022

Breidbach, C. F., & Tana, S. (2021). Betting on Bitcoin: How social collectives shape cryptocurrency markets. *Journal of Business Research*, *122*, 311–320. DOI: 10.1016/j.jbusres.2020.09.017

Briere, M., Oosterlinck, K., & Szafarz, A. (2015). Virtual currency, tangible return: Portfolio diversification with bitcoin. *Journal of Asset Management*, *16*(6), 365–373. DOI: 10.1057/jam.2015.5

Brody, D., & Bunnell, T. (2019). *Blockchain, cryptocurrencies, and smart contracts: Innovations and legal issues*. Wolters Kluwer Law & Business.

Brunnermeir, M., & Landau, J.-P. (2022). The digital euro: policy implications and perspectives, *Study Requested by the ECON Committee*, European Parliament, January. https://bankenverband.de/files/2022-12/report_digitaler_euro.pdf

Buckley, R. P., Arner, D. W., Zetzsche, D. A., & Didenko, A. N. Romburg, van. L., (2021). Sovereign Digital Currencies: Reshaping the Design of Money and Payments Systems, *Journal of Payments Strategy and Systems*, Volume 15, Number 1, pp.7-22. https://www.ssrn.com/link/UNSW-LEG.html

Buczak, A., & Guven, E. (2016). A Survey of Data Mining and Machine Learning Methods for Cyber Security Intrusion Detection. *IEEE Communications Surveys and Tutorials*, *18*(2), 1153–1176. DOI: 10.1109/COMST.2015.2494502

Bunz, B., Decker, M., & Sassmannshausen, S. (2020). “Automatic Coin Switching Strategies for Crypto Arbitrage,” in *International Conference on Financial Cryptography and Data Security*, Springer, Cham, 2020, pp. 77-97.

Burgess, T. (2024). A Multi-Jurisdictional Perspective: To What Extent can Cryptocurrency be Regulated? And if so, Who Should Regulate Cryptocurrency?. *Journal of Economic Criminology*, 100086.

Burgess, T. (2024). A Multi-Jurisdictional Perspective: To What Extent can Cryptocurrency be Regulated? And if so, Who Should Regulate Cryptocurrency? *Journal of Economic Criminology, 100086*, 100086. Advance online publication. DOI: 10.1016/j.jeconc.2024.100086

Burggraf, T. (2021). Beyond Risk Parity–A Machine Learning-Based Hierarchical Risk Parity Approach on Cryptocurrencies. *Finance Research Letters, 38*, 101523. DOI: 10.1016/j.frl.2020.101523

Burke, Q. J. (2022). The Great Bitcoin Experiment: A Social Analysis of Cryptocurrency in El Salvador. *Senior Scholar Papers*. Paper 567

Burnie, A., & Yilmaz, E. (2019). Social media and bitcoin metrics: Which words matter. *Royal Society Open Science, 6*(10), 191068. DOI: 10.1098/rsos.191068 PMID: 31824713

Burniske, C. (2018). *Cryptoassets: The innovative investor's guide to Bitcoin and beyond*. McGraw-Hill Education.

Buterin, V. (2013). "Ethereum White Paper: A Next Generation Contract & Decentralized Application Platform." http://www.the-blockchain.com/docs/Ethereum _white_paper-a_ next_generation_smart_contract_and_decentralized_application_platform-vitalik-buterin.pdf

Buterin, V. (2013). Ethereum White Paper: A Next-Generation Smart Contract and Decentralized Application Platform.

Buterin, V. (2013). Ethereum: The World Computer. Ethereum White Paper.

Cadet, F. T. (2023). Cryptocurrency Brings New Meaning to Purchase Power and Bridges the Wealth Gap: A Closer Look at Bitcoin. In Taghipour, A. (Ed.), *Blockchain Applications in Cryptocurrency for Technological Evolution* (pp. 108–117). IGI Global.

Cai, J., & Pinto, G. (2024). Altcoins as safe havens for bitcoin investors. *Studies in Economics and Finance, ahead-of-p*(ahead-of-print). DOI: 10.1108/SEF-01-2024-0026

Campbell, D. T. (1960). Variation and selective retention in creative thought as in other knowledge process. *Psychological Review, 67*(6), 380–400. DOI: 10.1037/h0040373 PMID: 13690223

Campbell, D. T. (1969). Variation and selective retention in sociocultural evolution. *General Systems, 14*, 69–85.

Campbell-Verduyn, M. (Ed.). (2018). *Bitcoin and Beyond. Cryptocurrencies, Blockchains, and Global Governance*. Routledge.

Campino, J., & Yang, S. (2024). Decoding the cryptocurrency user: An analysis of demographics and sentiments. *Heliyon*, *10*(5), e26671. DOI: 10.1016/j.heliyon.2024.e26671 PMID: 38434267

Cao, G., & Xie, W. (2021). The Impact of the Shutdown Policy on the Asymmetric Interdependence Structure and Risk Transmission of Cryptocurrency and China's Financial Market. *The North American Journal of Economics and Finance*, *58*, 101514. DOI: 10.1016/j.najef.2021.101514

Cao, L. (2022). Decentralized ai: Edge intelligence and smart blockchain, metaverse, web3, and desci. *IEEE Intelligent Systems*, *37*(3), 6–19. DOI: 10.1109/MIS.2022.3181504

Caputo, A., Marzi, G., Maley, J., & Silic, M. (2019). Ten Years of Conflict Management Research 2007-2017: An Update on Themes, Concepts and Relationships. *International Journal of Conflict Management*, *30*(1), 87–110. DOI: 10.1108/IJCMA-06-2018-0078

Carlisle, D. (2023). *The Crypto Launderers: Crime and Cryptocurrencies from the Dark Web to DeFi and Beyond*. Willey.

Carmona, T. (2022, October 26). *Debunking the narratives about cryptocurrency and financial inclusion*. Policy Commons. https://policycommons.net/artifacts/4140537/debunking-the-narratives-about-cryptocurrency-and-financial-inclusion/4949197

Carroll, G. R., & Khessina, O. M. (2005). 'The ecology of entrepreneurship. In Alvarez, S. A., Agarwal, R., & Sorensen, O. (Eds.), *Handbook of Entrepreneurship Research* (pp. 167–200). Springer. DOI: 10.1007/0-387-23622-8_9

Carroll, R., Conlon, T., Cotter, J., & Salvador, E. (2017). Asset allocation with correlation: A composite trade-off. *European Journal of Operational Research*, *262*(3), 1164–1180. DOI: 10.1016/j.ejor.2017.04.015

Casino, F., Dasaklis, T. K., & Patsakis, C. (2019). A systematic literature review of blockchain-based applications: Current status, classification, and open issues. *Telematics and Informatics*, *36*, 55–81. DOI: 10.1016/j.tele.2018.11.006

Catalini, C., & Gans, J. S. (2016). Some Simple Economics of the Blockchain. National Bureau of Economic Research Working Paper No. 22952.

Chaim, P., & Laurini, M. P. (2019). Is Bitcoin a bubble? *Physica A*, *517*, 222–232. DOI: 10.1016/j.physa.2018.11.031

Chan, Q., Ding, W., Lin, C., & Rossi, A. G. (2020). An inside look into cryptocurrency exchanges. *Available atSSRN* 3759062. http://dx.doi.org/DOI: 10.2139/ssrn.3759062

Charfeddine, L., Benlagha, N., & Maouchi, Y. (2020). Investigating the Dynamic Relationship between Cryptocurrencies and Conventional Assets: Implications for Financial Investors. *Economic Modelling*, *85*, 198–217. DOI: 10.1016/j.econ-mod.2019.05.016

Chaturvedi, V. (2024). *Everything to Know About Bitcoin Pizza Day*. Quartz. https://qz.com/bitcoin-pizza-day-date-origin-history-cryptocurrency-1851481975

Chaum, D. (1985, a). "Security without Identification: Transaction Systems to Make Big Brother Obsolete," *Communications of the ACM* 28, no. 10 (October 1), pp.1030–44, .DOI: 10.1145/4372.4373

Chaum, D. (1985, b). Cryptographic identification, financial transaction, and credential device. July 16. US Patent 4,529,870.

Chaum, D. L. (1988). Blind signature systems. US Patent 4,759,063.

Chaum, David. (1992). Achieving electronic privacy. *Scientific American*, 267(2), 96{101.

Chaum, D. (1983). Blind signatures for untraceable payments. *Advances in Cryptology Proceedings of Crypto*, *82*(3), 199–203.

Chaum, D. (1983). Blind signatures for untraceable payments. *Advances in Cryptology Proceedings of Crypto*, *82*, 199–203.

Chaum, D. (1983). Blind Signatures for Untraceable Payments. In Chaum, D., Rivest, R. L., & Sherman, A. T. (Eds.), *Advances in Cryptology* (pp. 199–203). Springer US., DOI: 10.1007/978-1-4757-0602-4_18

Chaum, D. (1992). Achieving Electronic Privacy. *Scientific American*, *267*(2), 96–101. https://www.jstor.org/stable/24939181. DOI: 10.1038/scientificamerican0892-96

Chaum, D. (2002). The Beginnings of Digital Money (1992). In *The Money Changers* (p. 4). Routledge., https://www.taylorfrancis.com/chapters/edit/10.4324/9781315071992-50/beginnings-digital-money-1992-david-chaum?context=ubx&refId=913eade8-aad5-4dea-8004-7a3979224feb

Checkout.com. (2022). *Demystifying Crypto. Shedding light on the adoption of digital currencies for payments in 2022*. https://assets.website-files.com/64db80a5e88c6b1723ff760b/654534f5526a1b2080a83a0d_Demystifying_Crypto_Report.pdf

Chemkha, R., BenSaïda, A., Ghorbel, A., & Tayachi, T. (2021). Hedge and Safe Haven Properties during COVID-19: Evidence from Bitcoin and Gold. *The Quarterly Review of Economics and Finance*, *82*, 71–85. DOI: 10.1016/j.qref.2021.07.006 PMID: 34898971

Chen, H., Li, J., & Zhang, Y. (2023). "Exploration of ASIC-Resistant Mining Algorithms for Duino Coin," arXiv preprint arXiv:2310.16543, 2023.

Chen, W., Wu, J., Zheng, Z., Chen, C., & Zhou, Y. (2019). Market Manipulation of Bitcoin: Evidence from Mining the Mt. Gox Transaction Network. *IEEE INFOCOM 2019 - IEEE Conference on Computer Communications*, 964–972. DOI: 10.1109/INFOCOM.2019.8737364

Chen, C., & Liu, L. (2022). How effective is China's cryptocurrency trading ban? *Finance Research Letters*, *46*, 102429. DOI: 10.1016/j.frl.2021.102429

Cheng, M., Chong, H.-Y., & Xu, Y. (2023). Blockchain-smart contracts for sustainable project performance: Bibliometric and content analyses. *Environment, Development and Sustainability*, *26*(4), 8159–8182. DOI: 10.1007/s10668-023-03063-w PMID: 37363021

Chen, H., Li, J., & Zhang, Y. (2022). Energy Efficiency Analysis of Duino Coin Mining on Embedded Systems. In *Embedded Systems: Research and Practice* (pp. 115–132). Springer.

Chen, H., & Zhang, Y. (2019). Blockchain-based decentralized cryptocurrency exchanges. *Electronic Commerce Research and Applications*, *35*, 100830.

Chen, J., Lin, D. C., & Han, C. H. (2020, March). Volatility effect on the adoption and valuation of tokenomics. In *Proceedings of the 35th Annual ACM Symposium on Applied Computing* (pp. 294-300). DOI: 10.1145/3341105.3373891

Chen, X., Miraz, M. H., Gazi, M. A. I., Rahaman, M. A., Habib, M. M., & Hossain, A. I. (2022). Factors affecting cryptocurrency adoption in digital business transactions: The mediating role of customer satisfaction. *Technology in Society*, *70*, 102059. Advance online publication. DOI: 10.1016/j.techsoc.2022.102059

Chen, Y. (2021). Empirical analysis of bitcoin price. *Journal of Economics and Finance*, *45*(4), 692–715. DOI: 10.1007/s12197-021-09549-5

Cheraghali, H., Molnár, P., Storsveen, M., & Veliqi, F. (2024). The impact of cryptocurrency-related cyberattacks on return, volatility, and trading volume of cryptocurrencies and traditional financial assets. *International Review of Financial Analysis*, *95*, 103439. DOI: 10.1016/j.irfa.2024.103439

Cheung, A., Roca, E., & Su, J.-J. (2015). Crypto-currency bubbles: An application of the Phillips–Shi–Yu (2013) methodology on Mt. Gox bitcoin prices. *Applied Economics*, *47*(23), 2348–2358. DOI: 10.1080/00036846.2015.1005827

Chimienti, M. T., Kochanska, U., & Pinna, A. (2019). Understanding the crypto-asset phenomenon, its risks and measurement issues. *ECB Economic Bulletin, 5*, European Central Bank. https://www.ecb.europa.eu/press/economic-bulletin/articles/2019/html/ecb.ebart201905_03~c83aeaa44c.en.html

Chitsungo, C. (2024). *Harnessing Digital Strategies to Combat Cryptocurrency-Enabled Crimes: Addressing Money Laundering, Illicit Trade, and Cyber Threats*. American Journal of International Relations., DOI: 10.47672/ajir.2523

Chkirbene, Z., Erbad, A., Hamila, R., Gouissem, A., Mohamed, A., & Hamdi, M. (2020). Machine Learning Based Cloud Computing Anomalies Detection. *IEEE Network*, *34*(6), 178–183. DOI: 10.1109/MNET.011.2000097

Chohan, U. W. (2017, November 27). *Cryptoanarchism and Cryptocurrencies*. http://dx.doi.org/DOI: 10.2139/ssrn.3079241

Chohan, U. W. (2023). Regulatory and legal issues in cryptocurrencies. In *Cryptocurrency concepts, technology, and applications* (pp. 141–157). Auerbach Publications. DOI: 10.1201/9781003315049-8

Choi, T.-M. (2022). Financing Product Development Projects in the Blockchain Era: Initial Coin Offerings Versus Traditional Bank Loans. *IEEE Transactions on Engineering Management*, *69*(6), 3184–3196. DOI: 10.1109/TEM.2020.3032426

Christidis, K., & Devetsikiotis, M. (2016). Blockchains and smart contracts for the internet of things. *IEEE Access : Practical Innovations, Open Solutions*, *4*, 2292–2303. https://ieeexplore.ieee.org/abstract/document/758150. DOI: 10.1109/ACCESS.2016.2566339

Chuen, D. L. K., Guo, L., & Wang, Y. (2017). Cryptocurrency: A new investment opportunity? *Journal of Alternative Investments*, *20*(3), 16–40. DOI: 10.3905/jai.2018.20.3.016

Chu, Y., & Rathbun, N. S. (2025). 'Monetary Sovereignty and Central Bank Digital Currencies: Competing Models for Future Cross-Border Payment Platforms'. *Global Policy*, •••, 1–12. DOI: 10.1111/1758-5899.13495

Ciaian, P., Rajcaniova, M., & Kancs, D. A. (2016). The economics of BitCoin price formation. *Applied Economics*, *48*(19), 1799–1815. DOI: 10.1080/00036846.2015.1109038

Cioroianu, I., Corbet, S., Larkin, C. J., & Oxley, L. (2023). *Developing central bank digital currencies: a reality check during cryptocurrency euphoria*. Economics and Business Letters.

Claeys, G., Demertzis, M., & Efstathiou, K. (2018). Cryptocurrencies and monetary policy. Policy Department A at the request of the Economic and Monetary Affairs Committee, June

Coase, R. H. (1972). Durability and monopoly. *The Journal of Law & Economics, 15*(1), 143–149. DOI: 10.1086/466731

CoinDesk. (2023). Crypto's interest in rates. https://www.coindesk.com/markets/2023/09/13/cryptos-interest-in-rates/

CoinMarketCap. (2024). CoinMarketCap. Retrieved June 20, 2024, from https://coinmarketcap.com/

Cointelegraph. (2024). Impact of Fed interest rates on crypto holders. https://cointelegraph.com/explained/impact-of-fed-interest-rates-on-crypto-holders

Colon, F., Kim, C., Kim, H., & Kim, W. (2021). The Effect of Political and Economic Uncertainty on the Cryptocurrency Market. *Finance Research Letters, 39*, 101621. DOI: 10.1016/j.frl.2020.101621

Cong, L. W., Li, Y., & Wang, N. (2018). Tokenomics: Dynamic adoption and valuation. *Review of Financial Studies, 34*(3), 1105–1155. DOI: 10.1093/rfs/hhaa089

Conlon, T., Corbet, S., & McGee, R. J. (2020). Are Cryptocurrencies a Safe Haven for Equity Markets? An International Perspective from the COVID-19 Pandemic. *Research in International Business and Finance, 54*, 101248. DOI: 10.1016/j.ribaf.2020.101248 PMID: 34170988

Conlon, T., Corbet, S., & McGee, R. J. (2021). Inflation and cryptocurrencies revisited: A time-scale analysis. *Economics Letters, 206*, 109996. DOI: 10.1016/j.econlet.2021.109996

Conrad, C., Custovic, A., & Ghysels, E. (2018). Long-and short-term cryptocurrency volatility components: A GARCH-MIDAS analysis. *Journal of Risk and Financial Management, 11*(2), 23. DOI: 10.3390/jrfm11020023

Conti, M., Kumar, E. S., Lal, C., & Ruj, S. (2018). A survey on security and privacy issues of bitcoin. *IEEE Communications Surveys and Tutorials, 20*(4), 3416–3452.

Corbet, S., Hou, Y. G., Hu, Y., Larkin, C., & Oxley, L. (2020). Any port in a storm: Cryptocurrency safe-havens during the COVID-19 pandemic. *Economics Letters, 194*, 109377. DOI: 10.1016/j.econlet.2020.109377 PMID: 32834235

Corbet, S., Katsiampa, P., & Chi, K. M. L. (2020b). Measuring Quantile Dependence and Testing Directional Predictability between Bitcoin, Altcoins and Traditional Financial Assets. *International Review of Financial Analysis, 71*, 101571. DOI: 10.1016/j.irfa.2020.101571

Corbet, S., Larkin, C., & Lucey, B. (2020c). The Contagion Effects of the COVID-19 Pandemic: Evidence from Gold and Cryptocurrencies. *Finance Research Letters, 35*, 101554. DOI: 10.1016/j.frl.2020.101554 PMID: 38620241

Corbet, S., Lucey, B., Urquhart, A., & Yarovaya, L. (2019). Cryptocurrencies as a financial asset: A systematic analysis. *International Review of Financial Analysis, 62*, 182–199. DOI: 10.1016/j.irfa.2018.09.003

Corbet, S., Lucey, B., & Yarovaya, L. (2019). The future of cryptocurrencies: A research agenda. *Finance Research Letters, 29*, 469–478.

Corbet, S., Lucey, B., & Yarovaya, L. (2021). Bitcoin-Energy Markets Interrelationships—New Evidence. *Resources Policy, 70*, 101916. DOI: 10.1016/j.resourpol.2020.101916

Crane, E. (2021). Ted Cruz says Senate can't regulate crypto without knowing 'what in the hell' it is. *NY Post*, August 10

Credits (2023, October 31). *Cryptocurrency in the Credits' App: A Financial Future Service*. https://credits.com/en/news/671-cryptocurrency-in-the-credits-app-a-financial-future-service.html

Cristofaro, M., Giardino, P. L., Misra, S., Pham, Q. T., & Hiep Phan, H. (2022). Behavior or culture? Investigating the use of cryptocurrencies for electronic commerce across the USA and China. *Management Research Review, 46*(3), 340–368. DOI: 10.1108/MRR-06-2021-0493

Crypto.com. (2021). Macroeconomic factors that impact the crypto market. https://crypto.com/research/macroeconomic-factors-that-impact-crypto-market

Cryptopotato. (2023). Ethereum is more correlated to stocks than Bitcoin: IntoTheBlock. https://cryptopotato.com/ethereum-is-more-correlated-to-stocks-than-bitcoin-intotheblock/

Cryptoslate. (2023). Bitcoin and gold are becoming increasingly correlated in conservative investment strategies. https://cryptoslate.com/bitcoin-and-gold-are-becoming-increasingly-correlated-in-conservative-investment-strategies/

Cunliffe, J. (2023). ''The Digital Pound'', Bank of England, February, https://www.bankofengland.co.uk/speech/2023/february/jon-cunliffe-speech-at-uk-finance-update-on-central-bank-digital-currency

Cusumano, M. A., & Yoffie, D. B. (2019). Competing in the age of ai: Strategy and leadership when algorithms and networks run the world. *Harvard Business Review*.

Dabrowski, M., & Janikowski, L. (2018). Virtual currencies and central banks monetary policy: challenges ahead. *In-depth analysis requested by the ECON committee*, Brussels: European parliament

Dai, W. (2008). Bitcoin Whitepaper. In *List, Cryptography Mailing*. https://www.bitcoin.com/satoshi-archive/emails/wei-dai/1/

Dai, W. (1998). *B-Money*. https://bitcoinstan.io/prehistory/doc/1998_3.pdf

Dale, A. (2015). Walwet and Kukalim. Lydian coin legends, dynastic succession, and the chronology of Mermnad kings. *Kadmos*, *54*(1/2), 151–166. DOI: 10.1515/kadmos-2015-0008

Danial, K. (2023). *Cryptocurrency Investing for Dummies*. For Dummies.

Das, M., Mancini Griffoli, T., Nakamura, F., Otten, J., Soderberg, G., Sole, J., Tan, B. (2023). Implications of Central Bank Digital Currencies for Monetary Policy Transmission, International Monetary Fund, Fintech Note, September.

Dasgupta, S., & Shetty, S. (2018). Blockchain and cybersecurity: Issues and challenges. *IEEE Potentials*, *37*(2), 38–43.

Davis, F. D. (1989). Perceived usefulness, perceived ease of use, and user acceptance of information technology. *Management Information Systems Quarterly*, *13*(3), 319–340. DOI: 10.2307/249008

Daye, M., & Verret, J. W. (2023). A Mosaic Approach for Challenging SEC Crypto Regulation: The Major Questions Doctrine and Staff Accounting Bulletin 121. *Wm. & Mary Bus. L. Rev.*, *15*, 553.

de Andrés, P., Arroyo, D., Correia, R., & Rezola, A. (2022). Challenges of the market for initial coin offerings. *International Review of Financial Analysis*, *79*, 101966. https://doi.org/https://doi.org/10.1016/j.irfa.2021.101966. DOI: 10.1016/j.irfa.2021.101966

De Araujo Consolino, A., & Pedrosa-Garcia, J. A. (2018). *Regulation of cryptocurrencies : evidence from Asia and the Pacific*. https://hdl.handle.net/20.500.12870/1212

De Filippi, P. (2014). Bitcoin: A regulatory nightmare to a libertarian dream.... *Internet Policy Review*, *3*(2), Hal-0102612. DOI: 10.14763/2014.2.286

De Filippi, P. (2018). *Blockchain et cryptomonnaies*. PUF. DOI: 10.3917/puf.filip.2018.01

de Sèze, N. (2023). Central bank digital currencies: A perspective of work across the world. *Revue d'Economie Financiere*, *149*(1), 91–105.

de Vries, A., & Stoll, C. (2021). Bitcoin's growing e-waste problem. *Resources, Conservation and Recycling*, *175*, 105901. DOI: 10.1016/j.resconrec.2021.105901

Dearden, T., & Tucker, S. (2023). Follow the Money: Analyzing Darknet Activity Using Cryptocurrency and the Bitcoin Blockchain. *Journal of Contemporary Criminal Justice*, *39*(2), 257–275. DOI: 10.1177/10439862231157521

del Castillo, M. (2018). *Fidelity Launches Institutional Platform For Bitcoin And Ethereum*. Forbes. https://www.forbes.com/sites/michaeldelcastillo/2018/10/15/fidelity-launches-institutional-platform-for-bitcoin-and-ethereum/

Delfabbro, P., & King, D. (2023). The evolution of young gambling studies: Digital convergence of gaming, gambling and cryptocurrency technologies. *International Gambling Studies*, *23*(3), 491–504. DOI: 10.1080/14459795.2023.2171469

Deloitte. (2020). Global Blockchain Survey 2020. Retrieved from https://www2.deloitte.com/content/dam/Deloitte/cn/Documents/financial-services/deloitte-cn-fs-global-blockchain-survey2020-en-201007.pdf

Demiralay, S., & Bayracı, S. (2020). Should Stock Investors Include Cryptocurrencies in Their Portfolios after All? Evidence from a Conditional Diversification Benefits Measure. *International Journal of Finance & Economics*, *26*(4), 6188–6204. DOI: 10.1002/ijfe.2116

Demiralay, S., & Golitsis, P. (2021). On the Dynamic Equicorrelations in Cryptocurrency Market. *The Quarterly Review of Economics and Finance*, *80*, 524–533. DOI: 10.1016/j.qref.2021.04.002

Demir, E., Bilgin, M. H., Karabulut, G., & Doker, A. C. (2020a). The Relationship between Cryptocurrencies and COVID-19 Pandemic. *Eurasian Economic Review*, *10*(3), 349–360. DOI: 10.1007/s40822-020-00154-1

Demir, E., Simonyan, S., García-Gómez, C. D., & Chi, K. M. L. (2020b). The Asymmetric Effect of Bitcoin on Altcoins: Evidence from the Nonlinear Autoregressive Distributed Lag (NARDL) Model. *Finance Research Letters*, *40*, 101754. DOI: 10.1016/j.frl.2020.101754

Demirgüç-Kunt, A., Klapper, L., Singer, D., & Ansar, S. (2022). *The Global Findex Database 2021*. The World Bank. DOI: 10.1596/978-1-4648-1897-4

Demirgüç-Kunt, A., Klapper, L., Singer, D., Ansar, S., & Hess, J. (2018). *The Global Findex database 2017: Measuring financial inclusion and the fintech revolution*. World Bank Group. DOI: 10.1596/978-1-4648-1259-0

Demir, I. (2018). Blockchain Technology for Social Impact: Opportunities and Challenges Ahead. *Journal of Economic and Social Policy*, *20*(1), 1–18.

Deng, H., Garcia, M. L., & Kaminsky, P. (2018). Blockchain-based platform for industrial iot: A case study. *IEEE Transactions on Industrial Informatics*, *14*(7), 3204–3212.

Dhali, M., Hassan, S., Mehar, S. M., Shahzad, K., & Zaman, F. (2023). Cryptocurrency in the Darknet: Sustainability of the current national legislation. *International Journal of Law and Management*, *65*(3), 261–282. DOI: 10.1108/IJLMA-09-2022-0206

Dickson, P., & Mahwera, D. A. (2022). Financial Institutions Readiness Towards Cryptocurrency Adoption: A Case of Banks in Tanzania. *Journal of Business and Management Review*, *3*(10), 740–753. DOI: 10.47153/jbmr310.4672022

Dimpfl, Thomas, and Dalia Elshiaty. 2021. Volatility Discovery in Cryptocurrency Markets. Journal of Risk Finance. ahead-of-print.

Ding, Ying, Ronald Rousseau, and DietmarWolfram. 2014. Measuring Scholarly Impact. Cham: Springer.

Disli, M., Nagayev, R., Salim, K., Rizkiah, S. K., & Aysan, A. F. (2021). In Search of Safe Haven Assets during COVID-19 Pandemic: An Empirical Analysis of Different Investor Types. *Research in International Business and Finance*, *58*, 101461. DOI: 10.1016/j.ribaf.2021.101461 PMID: 36540341

Dokumacı, M. (2024). Legal Frameworks for AI Regulations. *Human-Computer Interaction*, *8*(1), 133. Advance online publication. DOI: 10.62802/ytst2927

Doran, M. D. (2014). *A forensic look at bitcoin cryptocurrency* (Master's thesis, Utica College).

Dostov, V., & Shust, P. (2014). Cryptocurrencies: An unconventional Challenge to The AML/CFT Regulators? *Journal of Financial Crime*, *21*(3), 249–263. DOI: 10.1108/JFC-06-2013-0043

Dual Finances. (2023). "Tax Implications of Coin Switching for Crypto Investors," Retrieved from https://www.dualfinances.com/tax-implications- of-cryptocurrency-transactions/, 2023.

Ducas, E., & Wilner, A. (2017). The security and financial implications of blockchain technologies: Regulating emerging technologies in Canada. *International Journal (Toronto, Ont.)*, *72*(4), 538–562. DOI: 10.1177/0020702017741909

Dudani, S., Baggili, I., Raymond, D., & Marchany, R. (2023). The current state of cryptocurrency forensics. *Forensic Science International Digital Investigation*, *46*, 301576. DOI: 10.1016/j.fsidi.2023.301576

Duffield, E., & Hagan, K. (2014). Darkcoin: Peertopeer cryptocurrency with anonymous blockchain transactions and an improved proof of work system. *bitpaper.Info.*

Duffy, P., & Wilson, A. (2024). *2024 Annual Report. Crypto Philanthropy Data, Trends & Predictions. Annual Industry Report on the State of Crypto Philanthropy.* https://thegivingblock.com/annual-report

Dunsin, D., Ghanem, M., Ouazzane, K., & Vassilev, V. 2023. A Comprehensive Analysis of the Role of Artificial Intelligence and Machine Learning in Modern Digital Forensics and Incident Response. *ArXiv*, abs/2309.07064. /arXiv.2309.07064. DOI: 10.2139/ssrn.4554035

Dupuis, D., & Gleason, K. (2020). Money laundering with cryptocurrency: Open doors and the regulatory dialectic. *Journal of Financial Crime*, *28*(1), 60–74. DOI: 10.1108/JFC-06-2020-0113

Dwdollar (2010). New exchange (Bitcoin Market). Bitcointalk Forum. https: // bitcointalk.org/index.php?topic=20.msg265#msg265

Dwyer, G. P. (2015). The economics of bitcoin and similar private digital currencies. *Journal of Financial Stability*, *17*, 81–91. DOI: 10.1016/j.jfs.2014.11.006

Easley, D., O'Hara, M., & Basu, S. (2019). From mining to markets: The evolution of bitcoin transaction fees. *Journal of Financial Economics*, *134*(1), 91–109. DOI: 10.1016/j.jfineco.2019.03.004

EBA. (2019). Report with advice for the European Commission on crypto-assets (p. 30). European Banking Authority EBA. https://www.eba.europa.eu/sites/default/files/documents/10180/2545547/67493daa-85a8-4429-aa91-e9a5ed880684/EBA%20Report%20on%20crypto%20assets.pdf

Ebizie, P. I., Nkamnebe, A. D., & Ojiaku, O. C. (2022). Factors Influencing Cryptocurrency Adoption Among Nigerian University Fintech Entrepreneurs: An UTAUT perspective. *British Journal of Marketing Studies*, *10*(3), 25–37. DOI: 10.37745/bjms.2013/vo10.n3pp2537

El Hajj, M., & Farran, I. (2024). The Cryptocurrencies in Emerging Markets: Enhancing Financial Inclusion and Economic Empowerment. *Journal of Risk and Financial Management*, *17*(10), 467. DOI: 10.3390/jrfm17100467

El Ioini, N., & Pahl, C. (2018). *A Review of Distributed Ledger Technologies*., DOI: 10.1007/978-3-030-02671-4_16

Elias, N. (1939). *Über den Prozeß der Zivilisation [On the process of civilization].*

El-Kady, R. (2025). Leveraging Artificial Intelligence for Enhanced Detection and Mitigation of Illicit Activities on the Dark Web (A. E. Hassanien, . . ., Eds.). AISI., , LNDECT 238.DOI: 10.1007/978-3-031-81308-5_8

El-Kady, R. M. (2024). Investigating Forensic Evidence in Metaverse: A Comparative Analytical Study. In *Forecasting Cyber Crimes in the Age of the Metaverse* (pp. 227-258). IGI Global.

El-Kady, R. (2023). Handling E-evidence in Egyptian and Comparative Legislation: A Comparative Analytical Study. *Arab Journal of Forensic Sciences & Forensic Medicine*, *6*(1), 37–68. DOI: 10.26735/WGZY6322

El-Kady, R. (2024). Artificial Intelligence and Criminal Law. In *Artificial Intelligence Approaches to Sustainable Accounting* (pp. 34–52). IGI Global. DOI: 10.4018/979-8-3693-0847-9.ch003

El-Kady, R. (2024). *Challenges of Criminal Liability for Artificial Intelligence Systems*. IGI Global Scientific Publishing., DOI: 10.4018/979-8-3693-7205-0.ch001

El-Kady, R. (2024). *Leveraging AI and Machine Learning for Digital Forensics*. Advances in Computational Intelligence and Robotics Book Series., DOI: 10.4018/979-8-3373-1657-4.ch011

El-Kady, R. (2024). *Leveraging Artificial Intelligence to Combat Illicit Activities on the Dark Web: A Descriptive Analytical Study*. IGI Global Scientific Publishing., DOI: 10.4018/979-8-3693-9591-2.ch013

El-Kady, R. (2025). Artificial Intelligence from the Criminal Law Perspective. *AISI 2024. LNDECT*, *233*, 162–173. Advance online publication. DOI: 10.1007/978-3-031-77299-3_16

Elouaourti, Z., & Ibourk, A. (2024). Financial Technologies for All MENA citizens: Tackling barriers and promoting inclusion. *Regional Science Policy & Practice*, *16*(6), 100019. DOI: 10.1016/j.rspp.2024.100019

Emmert, F. (2023). The regulation of cryptocurrencies in the United States of America. *European Journal of Law Reform, 25*(1-2), 1–2. DOI: 10.5553/EJLR/138723702023025001002

Energy Web Foundation. (2020). Blockchain for Energy Transition.

England, J. (2023, April 24). Crypto regulations and building financial inclusion. *FinTech Magazine*. https://fintechmagazine.com/articles/crypto-regulations-and-building-financial-inclusion

ESMA. (2024). Consultation paper on the draft guidelines on the conditions and criteria for the qualification of crypto-assets as financial instruments (ESMA75-453128700–52; p. 39). European Securities and Market Authority.

Espinoza, J. (2014). Mobile Money: The Battle for Africa. *Wall street journal*, September 3

Euler, T. (2018). *The Token Classification Framework: A multi-dimensional tool for understanding and classifying crypto tokens*. Untitled Inc.

European Commission (2018) Directive (EU) 2018/843 of the European Parliament and of the Council of 30 May 2018 amending Directive (EU) 2015/849 on the prevention of the use of the financial system for the purposes of money laundering or terrorist financing, and amending Directives 2009/138/EC and 2013/36/EU, Official Journal of European Union, L series

European Securities and Markets Authority (ESMA). (2024). Risk article: Crypto assets, market structures, and EU relevance. https://www.esma.europa.eu/sites/default/files/2024-04/ESMA50-524821-3153_risk_article_crypto_assets_market_structures_and_eu_relevance.pdf

European Systemic Risk Board. (2023). Crypto-assets and decentralised finance. ESRB Report.

Fahlander, F. (2022, June 3). *Cryptocurrencies, Remittances and Exchange Rates: A quantitative study on the rapid growth of crypto adoption in developing countries*. https://www.diva-portal.org/smash/get/diva2:1683128/FULLTEXT01.pdf

Fahlenbrach, R., & Frattini, F. (2022). Innovation and regulation in the cryptocurrency market. *Journal of Financial Stability, 60*, 101021.

Fakhfekh, M., Jeribi, A., Ghorbel, A., & Hachicha, N. (2021). Hedging Stock Market Prices with WTI, Gold, VIX and Cryptocurrencies: A Comparison between DCC, ADCC and GO-GARCH Models. *International Journal of Emerging Markets*.

Fakiha, B. (2023). Enhancing Cyber Forensics with AI and Machine Learning: A Study on Automated Threat Analysis and Classification. *International Journal of Safety and Security Engineering*, *13*(4), 701–707. Advance online publication. DOI: 10.18280/ijsse.130412

Falk, B. H., & Hammer, S. (2023). A Comprehensive Approach to Crypto Regulation. *U. Pa. J. Bus. L.*, *25*, 415.

Fang, F., Chung, W., Ventre, C., Basios, M., Kanthan, L., Li, L., & Wu, F. (2021). Ascertaining Price Formation in Cryptocurrency Markets with Machine Learning. *European Journal of Finance*, •••, 1–23.

Fang, T., Su, Z., & Yin, L. (2020). Economic Fundamentals or Investor Perceptions? The Role of Uncertainty in Predicting Long-Term Cryptocurrency Volatility. *International Review of Financial Analysis*, *71*, 101566. DOI: 10.1016/j.irfa.2020.101566

Fast, R. (2021). Cryptocurrencies in hyperinflationary Venezuela. *Risk Governance and Control: Financial Markets and Institutions*, *11*(4), 62–67. DOI: 10.22495/rgcv11i4p5

FATF. (2014). Report: Virtual Currencies Key Definitions and Potential AML/CFT Risks, June. https://www.fatf-gafi.org/content/dam/fatf-gafi/reports/Virtual-currency-key-definitions-and-potential-aml-cft-risks.pdf

FBI, D., (2012). Bitcoin virtual currency: Unique features present distinct challenges for deterring illicit activity. *Intelligence Assessment*.

Feder, A., Gandal, N., Hamrick, J. T., Moore, T., & Vasek, M. (2018). "The Rise and Fall of Cryptocurrencies." In *The Workshop on the Economics of Information Security* (WEIS), chaired by R. Böhme. Innsbruck, Austria: University of Innsbruck.

Feng, W., Wang, Y., & Zhang, Z. (2018). Informed Trading in the Bitcoin Market. *Finance Research Letters*, *26*, 63–70. DOI: 10.1016/j.frl.2017.11.009

Ferreira, A., & Sandner, P. (2021). Eu search for regulatory answers to crypto assets and their place in the financial markets' infrastructure. *Computer Law & Security Review*, *43*(November), 105632. Advance online publication. DOI: 10.1016/j.clsr.2021.105632

Fidelity Charitable. (2021, October 28). *Cryptocurrency and philanthropy*. https://www.fidelitycharitable.org/insights/cryptocurrency-and-philanthropy.html

FINMA. (2018). Guidelines for enquiries regarding the regulatory framework for initial coin offerings (ICOs) (p. 11). Swiss Financial Market Supervisory Authority FINMA. https://www.finma.ch/~/media/finma/dokumente/dokumentencenter/myfinma/1bewilligung/fintech/wegleitung-ico.pdf?sc_lang=en&hash=C9899ACF22747D56C800C6C41A7E28AB

Fishbein, M., Ajzen, I., & Tra, T. (1967). *Theory of reasoned action.*

Fleder, M., & Hosanagar, K. (2009). Blockbuster culture's next rise or fall: The impact of recommender systems on sales diversity. *Management Science, 55*(5), 697–712. DOI: 10.1287/mnsc.1080.0974

Flick, C. (2022). A critical professional ethical analysis of Non-Fungible Tokens (NFTs). *Journal of Responsible Technology, 12*, 100054. DOI: 10.1016/j.jrt.2022.100054

Flori, A. (2019a). Cryptocurrencies in Finance: Review and Applications. *International Journal of Theoretical and Applied Finance*, •••, 22.

Flori, A. (2019b). News and Subjective Beliefs: A Bayesian Approach to Bitcoin Investments. *Research in International Business and Finance, 50*, 336–356. DOI: 10.1016/j.ribaf.2019.05.007

Flow Traders. (2023). Navigating the convergence of crypto and traditional financial markets. https://www.flowtraders.com/media/1kymgo0i/navigating-the-convergence-of-crypto-and-traditional-financial-markets.pdf

Foley, S., Karlsen, J. R., & Putniņš, T. J. (2019). Sex, Drugs, and Bitcoin: How Much Illegal Activity Is Financed through Cryptocurrencies? *Review of Financial Studies, 32*(5), 1798–1853. DOI: 10.1093/rfs/hhz015

Folkinshteyn, D., & Lennon, M. (2017). Braving Bitcoin: A technology acceptance model (TAM) analysis. *Journal of Information Technology Case and Application Research, 18*(4), 220–249. DOI: 10.1080/15228053.2016.1275242

Foroutan, P., & Lahmiri, S. (2024). Connectedness of cryptocurrency markets to crude oil and gold: An analysis of the effect of COVID-19 pandemic. *Financial Innovation, 10*(1), 68. DOI: 10.1186/s40854-023-00596-x

Frediani, M. E. A. (2024). Crafting the Future of Finance: A Comparative Analysis of Cryptocurrency Regulation in the Global Economy. *Journal of Financial Risk Management, 13*(1), 193–206. DOI: 10.4236/jfrm.2024.131010

Furtula, S., & Marković, D. (2010). *Monetarni system Evropske unije.* Kragujevac: Ekonomski fakultet u Kragujevcu

Galang Prasetyo, T., & Kurniasari, F. (2023). *The Influence of Subjective Norms, Financial Literacy, Trust, and Government Regulation on Behavioral Intention to Invest in Crypto Assets. January*, 1–24. DOI: 10.20944/preprints202301.0400.v1

Galvao, A., Mascarenhas, C., Marques, C., Ferreira, J., & Ratten, V. (2019). Triple Helix and Its Evolution: A Systematic Literature Review. *Journal of Science and Technology Policy Management*, *10*(3), 812–833. DOI: 10.1108/JSTPM-10-2018-0103

Gangwal, S. (2016). Analyzing the effect of adding Bitcoin to portfolio. International Journal of Economics and Management Engineering, 3519-3532.

Gannon, C., Blokland, A. A., Huikuri, S., Babchishin, K. M., & Lehmann, R. J. (2023). Child sexual abuse material on the darknet. *Forensische Psychiatrie, Psychologie, Kriminologie*, *17*(4), 353–365. DOI: 10.1007/s11757-023-00790-8

Gans, J. S., & Leigh, A. (2017). Artificial intelligence and healthcare. *Harvard Business Review*, *95*(1), 50–60.

Gao, X., & Nardari, F. (2018). Do commodities add economic value in asset allocation? New evidence from time-varying moments. *Journal of Financial and Quantitative Analysis*, *53*(1), 365–393. DOI: 10.1017/S002210901700103X

García-Corral, F. J., Cordero-García, J. A., de Pablo-Valenciano, J., & Uribe-Toril, J. (2022). A Bibliometric Review of Cryptocurrencies: How Have They Grown? *Financial Innovation*, *8*(1), 1–31. DOI: 10.1186/s40854-021-00306-5 PMID: 35024296

Gautam, Y. & Renau. (2024). Integrating Artificial Intelligence into Cybercrime Investigation: Challenges and Future Directions. International Journal For Multidisciplinary Research. DOI: 10.36948/ijfmr.2024.v06i05.28909

Gefen, D., Karahanna, E., & Straub, D. W. (2003). Trust and TAM in Online Shopping: An Integrated Model. *Management Information Systems Quarterly*, *27*(1), 51–90. DOI: 10.2307/30036519

Gemici, E., & Polat, M. (2020). Causality-in-Mean and Causality-in-Variance among Bitcoin, Litecoin, and Ethereum. *Studies in Economics and Finance*, *38*(4), 861–872. DOI: 10.1108/SEF-07-2020-0251

Ghabri, Y., Guesmi, K., & Zantour, A. (2020). Bitcoin and Liquidity Risk Diversification. *Finance Research Letters*, *40*, 101679. DOI: 10.1016/j.frl.2020.101679

Ghelani, D., & Kian Hua, T. (2022). Conceptual Framework of Web 3.0 and Impact on Marketing, Artificial Intelligence, and Blockchain. *International Journal of Information and Communication Sciences*, *7*(1), 10. DOI: 10.11648/j.ijics.20220701.12

Ghorbel, A., & Jeribi, A. (2021a). Investigating the Relationship between Volatilities of Cryptocurrencies and Other Financial Assets. *Decisions in Economics and Finance*, *44*(2), 817–843. DOI: 10.1007/s10203-020-00312-9

Ghorbel, A., & Jeribi, A. (2021b). Volatility Spillovers and Contagion between Energy Sector and Financial Assets during COVID-19 Crisis Period. *Eurasian Economic Review*, *11*(3), 449–467. DOI: 10.1007/s40822-021-00181-6

Gidea, M., Goldsmith, D., Katz, Y., Roldan, P., & Shmalo, Y. (2020). Topological recognition of critical transitions in time series of cryptocurrencies. *Physica A*, *548*, 123843. DOI: 10.1016/j.physa.2019.123843

Girasa, R. (2022). *Regulation of Cryptocurrencies and Blockchain Technologies: National and International Perspectives*. Palgrave Macmillan.

Giudici, G., Milne, A., & Vinogradov, D. (2020). Cryptocurrencies: Market analysis and perspectives. *Economia e Politica Industriale*, *47*(1), 1–18. DOI: 10.1007/s40812-019-00138-6

Goel, R. K., & Mazhar, U. (2024). Cryptocurrency use and tax collections: Direct and indirect channels of influence. *Journal of Financial Stability*, *72*, 101251. DOI: 10.1016/j.jfs.2024.101251

Goetzmann, W. N. (2016). *Money Changes Everything: How Finance Made Civilization Possible*. Princeton University Press. DOI: 10.1515/9781400881307

Goetzmann, W. N., & Rouwenhorst, K. G. (2005). *The Origins of Value. The Financials Innovations that Created Modern Capital Markets*. Oxford University Press., DOI: 10.1093/oso/9780195175714.001.0001

Gomzin, S. (2022). How Monero Works. In Gomzin, S. (Ed.), *Crypto Basics* (pp. 119–137). Apress., DOI: 10.1007/978-1-4842-8321-9_6

González, M. O., Jareño, F., & Skinner, F. S.González. (2021). Asymmetric Interdependencies between Large Capital Cryptocurrency and Gold Returns during the COVID-19 Pandemic Crisis. *International Review of Financial Analysis*, *76*, 101773. DOI: 10.1016/j.irfa.2021.101773

Gonzálvez-Gallego, N., & Pérez-Cárceles, M. C. (2021). Cryptocurrencies and illicit practices: The role of governance. *Economic Analysis and Policy*, *72*, 203–212. DOI: 10.1016/j.eap.2021.08.003

Goodell, J. W., & Goutte, S. (2021a). Co-Movement of COVID-19 and Bitcoin: Evidence from Wavelet Coherence Analysis. *Finance Research Letters*, *38*, 101625. DOI: 10.1016/j.frl.2020.101625 PMID: 36569647

Goodell, J. W., & Goutte, S. (2021b). Diversifying Equity with Cryptocurrencies during COVID-19. *International Review of Financial Analysis*, *76*, 101781. DOI: 10.1016/j.irfa.2021.101781

Goodell, J. W., Paltrinieri, A., & Piserà, S. (2023). Comparing search-engine intensity and regulatory attention impacts on cryptocurrencies: Uncovering important heterogeneities. *Review of Corporate Finance*, *3*(4), 571–595. DOI: 10.1561/114.00000051

Goodkin, A. L., Jones, B. A., & Berrens, R. P. (2020). Cryptodamages: Monetary value estimates of the air pollution and human health impacts of cryptocurrency mining. *Energy Research & Social Science*, *101281*, 101281. Advance online publication. DOI: 10.1016/j.erss.2019.101281

Gorton, G., & Rouwenhorst, K. (2006). Facts and fantasies about commodity futures. *Financial Analysts Journal*, *62*(2), 47–68. DOI: 10.2469/faj.v62.n2.4083

Gould, A., & Criscoe, J. (2020). *PayPal Launches New Service Enabling Users to Buy, Hold and Sell Cryptocurrency*. Paypal Newsroom. https://newsroom.paypal-corp.com/2020-10-21-PayPal-Launches-New-Service-Enabling-Users-to-Buy-Hold-and-Sell-Cryptocurrency

Gozgor, G., Tiwari, A. K., Demir, E., & Akron, S. (2019). The Relationship between Bitcoin Returns and Trade Policy Uncertainty. *Finance Research Letters*, *29*, 75–82. DOI: 10.1016/j.frl.2019.03.016

Grabinski, M., & Klinkova, G. (2019). Wrong use of averages implies wrong results from many heuristic models. *Applied Mathematics*, *10*(7), 605–618. DOI: 10.4236/am.2019.107043

Grabinski, M., & Klinkova, G. (2020). Scrutinizing distributions proves that IQ is inherited and explains the fat tail. *Applied Mathematics*, *11*(10), 957–984. DOI: 10.4236/am.2020.1110063

Grau, C. (2021). Stochastic valuation of revenue-collecting tokens in cryptoeconomic organizations. SSRN Electronic Journal. https://doi.org/DOI: 10.2139/ssrn.3641234

Grauer, R. R. (1986). Normality, solvency, and portfolio choice. *Journal of Financial and Quantitative Analysis*, *21*(3), 265–278. DOI: 10.2307/2331041

Griffith, T., & Clancey-Shang, D. (2023). Cryptocurrency regulation and market quality. *Journal of International Financial Markets, Institutions and Money*, *84*, 101744. DOI: 10.1016/j.intfin.2023.101744

Grobys, K., & Huynh, T. L. D. (2022). When Tether says "JUMP!" Bitcoin asks "How low?". *Finance Research Letters*, *47*, 102644. DOI: 10.1016/j.frl.2021.102644

Grobys, K., & Junttila, J. (2021). Speculation and lottery-like demand in cryptocurrency markets. *Journal of International Financial Markets, Institutions and Money*, *71*, 101289. DOI: 10.1016/j.intfin.2021.101289

Grobys, K., Junttila, J., Kolari, J. W., & Sapkota, N. (2021). On the Stability of Stablecoins. *Journal of Empirical Finance*, *64*, 207–223. DOI: 10.1016/j.jempfin.2021.09.002

Grobys, K., & Sapkota, N. (2019). Cryptocurrencies and momentum. *Economics Letters*, *6-10*, 6–10. Advance online publication. DOI: 10.1016/j.econlet.2019.03.028

Guadamuz, A., & Marsden, C. (2015). Blockchains and Bitcoin: Regulatory Responses to Cryptocurrencies. *First Monday*, *20*(12). Advance online publication. DOI: 10.5210/fm.v20i12.6198

Guccione, D. (2019). *What is the dark web? How to access it and what you'll find, The state of cybersecurity*. CSO Online.

Guh-Siesel, A. (2023). Cryptocurrency regulation. In *Harvard Model Congress*.

Güler, D. (2023). The Impact of Investor Sentiment on Bitcoin Returns and Conditional Volatilities during the Era of Covid-19. *Journal of Behavioral Finance*, *24*(3), 276–289. DOI: 10.1080/15427560.2021.1975285

Guo, X., Lu, F., & Wei, Y. (2021). Capture the Contagion Network of Bitcoin–Evidence from Pre and Mid COVID-19. *Research in International Business and Finance*, *58*, 101484. DOI: 10.1016/j.ribaf.2021.101484 PMID: 34518717

Gupta, A., Gupta, R., & Sankaran, A. (2021). *Machine Learning Forensics.*, DOI: 10.4018/978-1-7998-4900-1.ch003

Gupta, H., & Chaudhary, R. (2022). An empirical study of volatility in cryptocurrency market. *Journal of Risk and Financial Management*, *15*(11), 513. DOI: 10.3390/jrfm15110513

Gupta, S., & Shrivastava, M. (2022). Herding and loss aversion in stock markets: Mediating role of fear of missing out (FOMO) in retail investors. *International Journal of Emerging Markets*, *17*(7), 1720–1737. DOI: 10.1108/IJOEM-08-2020-0933

Guttmann, R. (2003). *Cybercash: The Coming Era of Electronic Money*. Palgrave Macmillan. DOI: 10.1057/9781403914507

Gyamfi, E., & Jurcut, A. (2023). Novel Online Network Intrusion Detection System for Industrial IoT Based on OI-SVDD and AS-ELM. *IEEE Internet of Things Journal*, *10*(5), 3827–3839. DOI: 10.1109/JIOT.2022.3172393

Habek, G. C., Toçoğlu, M. A., & Onan, A. (2022). Bi-Directional CNN-RNN Architecture with Group-Wise Enhancement and Attention Mechanisms for Cryptocurrency Sentiment Analysis. *Applied Artificial Intelligence*, *36*(1), 2145641. Advance online publication. DOI: 10.1080/08839514.2022.2145641

Hair, J. F., Black, W. C., Babin, B. J., & Anderson, R. E. (2019). Multivariate Data Analysis. In *Mathematics of Computation* (7th ed., Vol. 50, Issue 181). Annabel Ainscow. DOI: 10.2307/2007941

Hairudin, A., Sifat, I. M., Mohamad, A., & Yusof, Y. (2020). Cryptocurrencies: A Survey on Acceptance, Governance and Market Dynamics. *International Journal of Finance & Economics*, *27*(4), 4633–4659. DOI: 10.1002/ijfe.2392

Han, X., Yuan, Y., & Wang, F. Y. (2019, November). A blockchain-based framework for central bank digital currency. In 2019 IEEE International conference on service operations and logistics, and informatics (SOLI) (pp. 263-268). IEEE.

Hannan, M. T., & Freeman, J. (1977, March). The Population Ecology of Organizations. *American Journal of Sociology*, *82*(5), 929–964. DOI: 10.1086/226424

Haq, I. U., Maneengam, A., Chupradit, S., Suksatan, W., & Huo, C. (2021). Economic Policy Uncertainty and Cryptocurrency Market as a Risk Management Avenue: A Systematic Review. *Risks*, *9*(9), 163. DOI: 10.3390/risks9090163

Haque, M. A., & Shoaib, M. (2023). The digital currency in India: Challenges and prospects. BenchCouncil Transactions on Benchmarks. *Standards and Evaluations*, *3*(1), 100107.

Harb, E., Bassil, C., Kassamany, T., & Baz, R. (2022). Volatility Interdependence Between Cryptocurrencies, Equity, and Bond Markets. *Computational Economics*. Advance online publication. DOI: 10.1007/s10614-022-10318-7 PMID: 36187467

Härdle, W. K., Harvey, C. R., & Reule, R. C. (2020). Understanding cryptocurrencies. *Journal of Financial Econometrics*, *18*(2), 181–208.

Härdle, W. K., Harvey, C. R., & Reule, R. C. G. (2020). Understanding Cryptocurrencies. *Journal of Financial Econometrics*, *1*(19), 1–28. DOI: 10.1093/jjfinec/nbz033

Haribedel, B., & Perez-Saiz, H. (2023, September). Assessing Macrofinancial Risks from Crypto Assets. *IMF Working Paper*, *29*(214), 1. Advance online publication. DOI: 10.5089/9798400255083.001

Harvey, C. R., Abou Zeid, T., Draaisma, T., Luk, M., Neville, H., Rzym, A., & Van Hemert, O. (2022). An investor's guide to crypto. Available at *SSRN* 4124576.

Hashemi Joo, M., Nishikawa, Y., & Dandapani, K. (2019). Cryptocurrency, a Successful Application of Blockchain Technology. *Managerial Finance*, *46*(6), 715–733. DOI: 10.1108/MF-09-2018-0451

Hassan, M. K., Hasan, M. B., & Rashid, M. M. (2021). Using Precious Metals to Hedge Cryptocurrency Policy and Price Uncertainty. *Economics Letters*, *206*, 109977. DOI: 10.1016/j.econlet.2021.109977

Hattori, T., & Ishida, R. (2021). Did the Introduction of Bitcoin Futures Crash the Bitcoin Market at the End of 2017? *The North American Journal of Economics and Finance*, *56*, 101322. DOI: 10.1016/j.najef.2020.101322

Hayashi, F. & Toh Y. L. (2022). Assessing the Case for Retail CBDCs: Central Banks' Considerations, *kcFED Payments System Research Breiefing*, Federal Reserve Bank of Kansas City, May 26.

Hayek, M., Kondor, D., & Vayanos, D. (2018). Liquidity in the time of covid-19: A preliminary report. *Journal of Financial Economics*, *21*(3), 1–35.

Hayes, A. S. (2017). Cryptocurrency value formation: An empirical study leading to a cost of production model for valuing bitcoin. *Telematics and Informatics*, *34*(7), 1308–1321. DOI: 10.1016/j.tele.2016.05.005

Haynes, N. (2021). "A Primer on BOJ's Central Bank Digital Currency." *Jamaica Observer*, March 31

Hazar, H. B. (2020). Anonymity in cryptocurrencies. In *Eurasian Economic Perspectives: Proceedings of the 26th and 27th Eurasia Business and Economics Society Conferences* (pp. 171-178). Springer International Publishing.

Hebous, S., & Vernon-Lin, N. (2024). *Carbon Emissions from AI and Crypto Are Surging and Tax Policy Can Help*. International Monetary Fund. https://www.imf.org/en/Blogs/Articles/2024/08/15/carbon-emissions-from-ai-and-crypto-are-surging-and-tax-policy-can-help

He, C., Li, Y., Wang, T., & Shah, S. A. (2024). Is cryptocurrency a hedging tool during economic policy uncertainty? An empirical investigation. *Humanities & Social Sciences Communications*, *11*(1), 1–10. DOI: 10.1057/s41599-023-02532-x

Helberger, N., & Diakopoulos, N. (2022). The European AI Act and How It Matters for Research into AI in Media and Journalism. *Digital Journalism (Abingdon, England)*, *11*(9), 1751–1760. DOI: 10.1080/21670811.2022.2082505

Heo, K., & Yi, S. (2023). (De) centralization in the governance of blockchain systems: Cryptocurrency cases. *Journal of Organization Design*, *12*(3), 59–82. DOI: 10.1007/s41469-023-00138-w

Hérodote. (1970). *Histoire, 1, 94*. Les Belles Lettres.

Herrera Anchustegui, I., & Hunter, T. (2018). Oil as Currency: Venezuela's Petro, a New 'Oil Pattern'? (2018). http://dx.doi.org/DOI: 10.2139/ssrn.3291272

Hewa, T., Gür, G., Kalla, A., Ylianttila, M., Bracken, A., & Liyanage, M. (2020). The role of blockchain in 6G: Challenges, opportunities and research directions. *2020 2nd 6G Wireless Summit (6G SUMMIT)*, 1-5.

Hill, M. (2024). Islamic State Is Increasingly Using Crypto to Fund Africa Militant Goals. *Bloomberg*, March 11

Hillier, D., Draper, P., & Faff, R. (2006). Do precious metals shine? An investment perspective. *Financial Analysts Journal*, *62*(2), 98–106. DOI: 10.2469/faj.v62.n2.4085

Hoang, L. T., & Baur, D. G. (2021). How Stable Are Stablecoins? *European Journal of Finance*, •••, 1–17.

Holub, M., & Johnson, J. (2019). The Impact of the Bitcoin Bubble of 2017 on Bitcoin's P2P Market. *Finance Research Letters*, *29*, 357–362. DOI: 10.1016/j.frl.2018.09.001

Hong, K. (2016). Bitcoin as an alternative investment vehicle. *Information Technology and Management*, *18*(4), 265–275. DOI: 10.1007/s10799-016-0264-6

Horky, F., Dubbick, L., Rhein, F., & Fidrmuc, J. (2023). Don't miss out on NFTs?! A sentiment-based analysis of the early NFT market. *International Review of Economics & Finance*, *88*, 799–814. DOI: 10.1016/j.iref.2023.07.016

Horton-Eddison, M., Shortis, P., Aldridge, J., & Caudevilla, F. (2021). Drug cryptomarkets in the 2020s: Policy, enforcement, harm, and resilience. *Global Drug Policy Observatory*. https://orca.cardiff.ac.uk/id/eprint/167557/1/Drug-Crypto-Markets_FINAL_June_2021.pdf

Hossain, M. S. (2021). What do we know about cryptocurrency? Past, present, future. *China Finance Review International*, *11*(4), 552–572. DOI: 10.1108/CFRI-03-2020-0026

Houy, S., Schmid, P., & Bartel, A. (2023). Security aspects of cryptocurrency wallets—A systematic literature review. *ACM Computing Surveys*, *56*(1), 1–31. DOI: 10.1145/3596906

Howson, P. (2021). Crypto-giving and surveillance philanthropy: Exploring the trade-offs in blockchain innovation for nonprofits. *Nonprofit Management & Leadership, 31*(4), 805–820. DOI: 10.1002/nml.21452

Hsinchun, C., Roger, C., & Veda, S. (2012). Business intelligence and analytics: From big data to big impact. *Management Information Systems Quarterly, 36*(4), 1171–1172.

Hsu, S. H., Sheu, C., & Yoon, J. (2021). Risk Spillovers between Cryptocurrencies and Traditional Currencies and Gold under Different Global Economic Conditions. *The North American Journal of Economics and Finance, 57*, 101443. DOI: 10.1016/j.najef.2021.101443

Huang, X., Lin, J., & Wang, P. (2022). Are institutional investors marching into the crypto market? *Economics Letters, 220*, 110856. DOI: 10.1016/j.econlet.2022.110856

Hughes, E. (1993). "A Cypherpunk's Manifesto," Activism.net, March 1993, https://www.activism.net/cypherpunk/manifesto.html

Hughes, E. (1993). *A Cypherpunk's Manifesto*. Archived from the original on March 24, 2021. Retrieved January 20, 2025, from https://nakamotoinstitute.org/library/cypherpunk-manifesto/

Hughes, A., Park, A., Kietzmann, J., & Archer-Brown, C. (2019). Beyond Bitcoin: What blockchain and distributed ledger technologies mean for firms. *Business Horizons, 62*(3), 1–9. DOI: 10.1016/j.bushor.2019.01.002

Huynh, A. N. Q., Duong, D., Burggraf, T., Hien, T. T. L., & Bui, N. H. (2021). Energy Consumption and Bitcoin Market. *Asia-Pacific Financial Markets, 29*(1), 79–93. DOI: 10.1007/s10690-021-09338-4

Huynh, T. L. D. (2021). Does Bitcoin React to Trump's Tweets? *Journal of Behavioral and Experimental Finance, 31*, 100546. DOI: 10.1016/j.jbef.2021.100546

Huynh, T. L. D., Hille, E., & Nasir, M. A. (2020a). Diversification in the Age of the 4th Industrial Revolution: The Role of Artificial Intelligence, Green Bonds and Cryptocurrencies. *Technological Forecasting and Social Change, 159*, 120188. DOI: 10.1016/j.techfore.2020.120188

Huynh, T. L. D., Nasir, M. A., Vo, X. V., & Nguyen, T. T. (2020b). 'Small Things Matter Most': The Spillover Effects in the Cryptocurrency Market and Gold as a Silver Bullet. *The North American Journal of Economics and Finance, 54*, 101277. DOI: 10.1016/j.najef.2020.101277

IBM. (2019). IBM Blockchain Platform Overview.

Idelberger, F., Governatori, G., Riveret, R., & Sartor, G. (2016). Evaluation of Logic-Based Smart Contracts for Blockchain Systems, *RuleML2016*, Stony Brook, NY

Iqbal, N., Fareed, Z., Wan, G., & Shahzad, F. (2021). Asymmetric Nexus between COVID-19 Outbreak in the World and Cryptocurrency Market. *International Review of Financial Analysis*, *73*, 101613. DOI: 10.1016/j.irfa.2020.101613 PMID: 38620823

Ismail, L., & Materwala, H. (2019). A Review of Blockchain Architecture and Consensus Protocols: Use Cases, Challenges, and Solutions. *Symmetry*, *2019*(11), 1198. DOI: 10.3390/sym11101198

Ivory Johnson, C. F. P. (2023). What's in Store for Crypto Regulations? *Journal of Financial Planning*, *36*(3), 46–50.

Izadiyan, Z., Misran, M., Kalantari, K., Webster, T., Kia, P., Rasouli, E., & Shameli, K. (2025). Advancements in Liposomal Nanomedicines: Innovative Formulations, Therapeutic Applications, and Future Directions in Precision Medicine. *International Journal of Nanomedicine*, *20*, 1213–1262. DOI: 10.2147/IJN.S488961 PMID: 39911259

Jajodia, S., & Krotov, V. (2019). *Blockchain and healthcare: The coming disruption*. CRC Press.

Jalal, R. N. U. D., Alon, I., & Paltrinieri, A. (2021). A Bibliometric Review of Cryptocurrencies as a Financial Asset. *Technology Analysis and Strategic Management*, •••, 1–16.

Jalan, A., Matkovskyy, R., & Urquhart, A. (2021). What Effect Did the Introduction of Bitcoin Futures Have on the Bitcoin Spot Market? *European Journal of Finance*, *27*(13), 1251–1281. DOI: 10.1080/1351847X.2020.1869992

Janisch, F., & Stapleton, L. (2021). Digital Currencies and Community Empowerment in Austria: Gesell's Concept of Effective Demand as a Basis for Local Digital Currencies. *IFAC-PapersOnLine*, *54*(13), 698–703. DOI: 10.1016/j.ifacol.2021.10.533

Jareño, F., González, M. O., López, R., & Ramos, A. R. (2021). Cryptocurrencies and Oil Price Shocks: A NARDL Analysis in the COVID-19 Pandemic. *Resources Policy*, *74*, 102281. DOI: 10.1016/j.resourpol.2021.102281 PMID: 34658484

Jareño, F., González, M. O., Tolentino, M., & Sierra, K. (2020). Bitcoin and Gold Price Returns: A Quantile Regression and NARDL Analysis. *Resources Policy*, *67*, 101666. DOI: 10.1016/j.resourpol.2020.101666

Jegerson, D., Khan, M., & Mertzanis, C. (2023). Adoption of cryptocurrencies for remittances in the UAE: The mediation effect of consumer innovation. *European Journal of Innovation Management. Sdg, 10*. Advance online publication. DOI: 10.1108/EJIM-09-2022-0538

Jeribi, A., & Ghorbel, A. (2021). Forecasting Developed and BRICS Stock Markets with Cryptocurrencies and Gold: Generalized Orthogonal Generalized Autoregressive Conditional Heteroskedasticity and Generalized Autoregressive Score Analysis. *International Journal of Emerging Markets*.

Jia, A., Fan, M., Xu, X., Cui, D., Wei, W., Yang, Z., Ye, K., & Liu, T. (2021). *From Innovations to Prospects: What Is Hidden Behind Cryptocurrencies?* DOI: 10.1145/3379597.3387439

Jiang, L., & Zhang, X. (2021). Cryptocurrency as an Investment Tool: A Critical Review. *Frontiers in Blockchain*, *4*, 31.

Jiang, S., Li, X., & Wang, S. (2021). Exploring Evolution Trends in Cryptocurrency Study: From Underlying Technology to Economic Applications. *Finance Research Letters*, *38*, 101532. DOI: 10.1016/j.frl.2020.101532

Jiang, S., Li, Y., Lu, Q., Wang, S., & Wei, Y. (2022). Volatility communicator or receiver? Investigating volatility spillover mechanisms among Bitcoin and other financial markets. *Research in International Business and Finance*, *59*, 101543. DOI: 10.1016/j.ribaf.2021.101543

Jiang, Y., Lie, J., Wang, J., & Mu, J. (2021a). Revisiting the Roles of Cryptocurrencies in Stock Markets: A Quantile Coherency Perspective. *Economic Modelling*, *95*, 21–34. DOI: 10.1016/j.econmod.2020.12.002

Jiang, Y., Wu, L., Tian, G., & Nie, H. (2021). Do cryptocurrencies hedge against EPU and the equity market volatility during COVID-19? – New evidence from quantile coherency analysis. *Journal of International Financial Markets, Institutions and Money*, *72*, 101324. DOI: 10.1016/j.intfin.2021.101324

Jin, X., Zhu, K., Yang, X., & Wang, S. (2021). Estimating the Reaction of Bitcoin Prices to the Uncertainty of Fiat Currency. *Research in International Business and Finance*, *58*, 101451. DOI: 10.1016/j.ribaf.2021.101451

Ji, Q., Bouri, E., Chi, K. M. L., & Roubaud, D. (2019a). Dynamic Connectedness and Integration in Cryptocurrency Markets. *International Review of Financial Analysis*, *63*, 257–272. DOI: 10.1016/j.irfa.2018.12.002

Ji, Q., Bouri, E., Roubaud, D., & Kristoufek, L. (2019b). Information Interdependence among Energy, Cryptocurrency and Major Commodity Markets. *Energy Economics*, *81*, 1042–1055. DOI: 10.1016/j.eneco.2019.06.005

Jobes, M. (2019). *Fintech: Financial technology beginner guide cherrytree style*. Independently published.

Johnson, S., Robinson, P., & Brainard, J. (2019). Sidechains and interoperability. *arXiv preprint arXiv:1903.04077*.

Johnson, B., Leung, J., Co, S., Sun, T., Saunders, J. B., Lim, C. C. W., & Chan, G. C. K. (2023). Cryptocurrency trading and its associations with gambling and mental health: A scoping review. *Addictive Behaviors*, *136*, 107504. DOI: 10.1016/j.addbeh.2022.107504 PMID: 36174424

Jonker, N. (2019). What drives the adoption of crypto-payments by online retailers? *Electronic Commerce Research and Applications*, *35*, 100848. DOI: 10.1016/j.elerap.2019.100848

Joshi, C. (2023). Cryptocurrency Forensics: The Ultimate Guide to 6 Important Aspects. Indiaforensic. https://indiaforensic.com/cryptocurrency-forensics/

Joshi, V., & Korah, J. (2022). Formulating Parallel Supervised Machine Learning Designs for Anomaly-Based Network Intrusion Detection in Resource-Constrained Use Cases. *2022 IEEE 19th International Conference on Mobile Ad Hoc and Smart Systems (MASS)*, 748-753. DOI: 10.1109/MASS56207.2022.00117

Judmayer, A., Stifter, N., Schindler, P., & Weippl, E. (2017). Blocks and chains: Introduction to Bitcoin, cryptocurrencies, and their consensus mechanisms. *Synthesis Lectures on Information Security, Privacy, and Trust*, *9*(1), 1–123. DOI: 10.1007/978-3-031-02352-1

Kaal, W. A., Evans, S. R., & Howe, H. A. (2021). Digital Asset Valuation. *Rich. JL & Tech.*, *28*, 657.

Kajtazi, A., & Moro, A. (2019). The Role of Bitcoin in Well Diversified Portfolios: A comparative Global Study. *International Review of Financial Analysis*, *61*, 143–157. DOI: 10.1016/j.irfa.2018.10.003

Kala, D., Chaubey, D. S., & Al-Adwan, A. S. (2023). Cryptocurrency investment behaviour of young Indians: Mediating role of fear of missing out. *Global Knowledge, Memory and Communication*, (February). Advance online publication. DOI: 10.1108/GKMC-07-2023-0237

Kaloudis, G. (2022). The Collapse of UST and LUNA Was Devastating, but There Is Still Hope for Crypto. *coindesk.com*, May 15

Kang, S. H., McIver, R. P., & Hernandez, J. A. (2019). Co-movements between Bitcoin and Gold: A wavelet coherence analysis. *Physica A*, *536*, 120888. DOI: 10.1016/j.physa.2019.04.124

Kao, H. (2025). Accelerating Multilingual Cryptocurrency Forensics: An NLP-Driven Approach for Efficient Mnemonic Identification. *IEEE Access : Practical Innovations, Open Solutions*, *13*, 10513–10526. DOI: 10.1109/ACCESS.2025.3528829

Katsiampa, P. (2019). An empirical investigation of volatility dynamics in the cryptocurrency market. *Research in International Business and Finance*, *50*, 322–335. DOI: 10.1016/j.ribaf.2019.06.004

Katsiampa, P., Corbet, S., & Lucey, B. (2019). High Frequency Volatility Co-Movements in Cryptocurrency Markets. *Journal of International Financial Markets, Institutions and Money*, *62*, 35–52. DOI: 10.1016/j.intfin.2019.05.003

Kaur, G., Habibi Lashkari, A., Sharafaldin, I., & Habibi Lashkari, Z. (2023). Introduction to Smart Contracts and DeFi. In Kaur, G., Habibi Lashkari, A., Sharafaldin, I., & Habibi Lashkari, Z. (Eds.), *Understanding Cybersecurity Management in Decentralized Finance. Financial Innovation and Technology* (pp. 29–56). Springer International Publishing., DOI: 10.1007/978-3-031-23340-1_2

Kavaloski, M. (2024). A Global Crypto Code of Conduct: Crafting and Internationally Centralized Regulatory Body for a Decentralized Asset. *Vand. J. Transnat'l L.*, *57*, 301.

Kavitha, T., & Sridharan, D. (2013). Optimal resource key management protocol for clustered heterogeneous wireless sensor networks. *Malaysian Journal of Computer Science*, *26*(3), 211–231.

Kavuri, A. S., & Milne, A. (2021). Trading and regulation of cryptocurrencies, stablecoins and other. In *K* (pp. 147–162). Thomas Liaw, The Routledge Handbook of FinTech.

Kayani, U., & Hasan, F. (2024). Unveiling Cryptocurrency Impact on Financial Markets and Traditional Banking Systems: Lessons for Sustainable Blockchain and Interdisciplinary Collaborations. *Journal of Risk and Financial Management*, *17*(2), 58. DOI: 10.3390/jrfm17020058

Kechagias, E. P., Gayialis, S. P., Papadopoulos, G. A., & Papoutsis, G. (2023). An ethereum-based distributed application for enhancing food supply chain traceability. *Foods*, *12*(6), 1220. DOI: 10.3390/foods12061220 PMID: 36981145

Kellerman, M., & Seddon, J. (2024). Into the ether or the state? Legibility theory and the cryptocurrency markets. *Business and Politics*, *26*(3), 1–24. DOI: 10.1017/bap.2023.38

Keshvari Fard, M., Liu, J., & Petropoulos, F. (2024, March 5). Decoding Digital Philanthropy Analyzing Donors Choices in Cryptocurrency Donations. http://dx.doi.org/DOI: 10.2139/ssrn.4748710

Kethineni, S., & Cao, Y. (2020). The Rise in Popularity of Cryptocurrency and Associated Criminal Activity. *International Criminal Justice Review*, *30*(3), 325–344. DOI: 10.1177/1057567719827051

Kethineni, S., Cao, Y., & Dodge, C. (2017). Use of Bitcoin in Darknet Markets: Examining Facilitative Factors on BitcoinRelated Crimes. *American Journal of Criminal Justice*, *43*(2), 141–157. DOI: 10.1007/s12103-017-9394-6

Khaniki, M. A. L., & Manthouri, M. (2024). Enhancing Price Prediction in Cryptocurrency Using Transformer Neural Network and Technical Indicators. *ArXiv Preprint ArXiv:2403.03606*.

Khan, M. Z., Ali, Y., Sultan, H. B., Hasan, M., & Baloch, S. (2020). Future of currency: A comparison between traditional, digital fiat and cryptocurrency exchange mediums. *International Journal of Blockchains and Cryptocurrencies*, *1*(2), 206–224. DOI: 10.1504/IJBC.2020.109003

Khan, R. U., Ullah, K., & Atiq, M. (2024). Regulatory constraints, responsibilities and consultation (CRC) for legal institutionalization of cryptocurrencies in Pakistan. *Qualitative Research in Financial Markets*, *16*(4), 680–708. DOI: 10.1108/QRFM-03-2023-0053

Khatana, S. S., Mahecha, M., & Beniwal, S. (2023, June). An analytical study of regulatory journey of cryptocurrency in India. In *AIP Conference Proceedings* (Vol. 2782, No. 1). AIP Publishing. DOI: 10.1063/5.0154633

Khelifa, S. B., Guesmi, K., & Urom, C. (2021). Exploring the relationship between cryptocurrencies and hedge funds during COVID-19 crisis. *International Review of Financial Analysis*, *76*, 101777. DOI: 10.1016/j.irfa.2021.101777 PMID: 36569817

Kiff, J., Alwazir, J., Davidovic, S., Farias, A., Khan, A., Khiaonarong, T., Malaika, M., Monroe, H., Sugimoto, N., Tourpe, H., & Zhou, P. (2020). A Survey of Research on Retail Central Bank Digital Currency, IMF Working Paper, June. file:///C:/Users/jeanm/Downloads/wpiea2020104-print-pdf.pdf

Kifokeris, D., Dounas, T., Tezel, A., & Moon, S. (2023). What is the potential value of tokens and token engineering for the architecture, engineering, and construction industry? A positional paper.

Kim, D., Park, Y., & Kim, S. (2024). A Measurement Study on Tor Hidden Services via Keyword-Based Dark Web Collection Framework. *IEEE Access : Practical Innovations, Open Solutions*, *12*, 136936–136945. DOI: 10.1109/ACCESS.2024.3465629

Kim, J. H. (2022). Analyzing diversification benefits of cryptocurrencies through backfill simulation. *Finance Research Letters*, *50*, 103238. DOI: 10.1016/j.frl.2022.103238

Kim, K., & Kauffman, R. J. (2024). On the Effects of Information Asymmetry in Digital Currency Trading. *Electronic Commerce Research and Applications*, *64*, 101366. DOI: 10.1016/j.elerap.2024.101366

Kim, M. J., Canh, N. P., & Park, S. Y. (2021). Causal Relationship among Cryptocurrencies: A Conditional Quantile Approach. *Finance Research Letters*, *42*, 1–8. DOI: 10.1016/j.frl.2020.101879

Kinkyo, T. (2020). Hedging Capabilities of Bitcoin for Asian Currencies. *International Journal of Finance & Economics*, *27*(2), 1769–1784. DOI: 10.1002/ijfe.2241

Kitco News. (2013). "2013: Year of the Bitcoin". Forbes, https://www.forbes.com/sites/ kitconews/2013/12/10/2013-year-of-the-bitcoin/#2f0b622e303c

Klein, G., Assadi, D., & Zwilling, M. (2024). Fighting Fire with Fire: Combating Criminal Abuse of Cryptocurrency with a P2P Mindset. *Information Systems Frontiers*, •••, 1–27.

Klein, T., Pham Thu, H., & Walther, T. (2018). Bitcoin is not the New Gold – A comparison of volatility, correlation, and portfolio performance. *International Review of Financial Analysis*, *59*, 105–116. DOI: 10.1016/j.irfa.2018.07.010

Klinkova, G., & Grabinski, M. (2017). Due to Instability Gambling is the best Model for most Financial Products. *Archives of Business Research*, *5*(3), 255–261. DOI: 10.14738/abr.53.3029

Koki, C., Leonardos, S., & Piliouras, G. (2022). Exploring the predictability of cryptocurrencies via Bayesian hidden Markov models. *Research in International Business and Finance*, *59*, 101554. DOI: 10.1016/j.ribaf.2021.101554

Kolm, P., Tütüncü, R., & Fabozzi, F. (2014). 60 Years of portfolio optimization: Practical challenges and current trends. *European Journal of Operational Research*, *234*(2), 356–371. DOI: 10.1016/j.ejor.2013.10.060

Komalavalli, C., Saxena, D., & Laroiya, C. (2020). Overview of Blockchain Technology Concepts. In S. Krishnan, V. E. Balas, E. G. Julie, Y. H. Robinson, S. Balaji, & R. B. T.-H. of R. on B. T. Kumar (Eds.), *Handbook of Research on Blockchain Technology* (pp. 349–371). Elsevier. DOI: 10.1016/B978-0-12-819816-2.00014-9

Koo, E., & Kim, G. (2024). Centralized decomposition approach in LSTM for Bitcoin price prediction. *Expert Systems with Applications*, *237*, 121401. DOI: 10.1016/j.eswa.2023.121401

Kosba, A., Miller, A., Shi, E., Wen, Z., & Papamanthou, C. (2016). Hawk: The blockchain model of cryptography and privacy-preserving smart contracts. In *Proceedings of the 2016 ACM SIGSAC Conference on Computer and Communications Security* (pp. 839-851). ACM. DOI: 10.1109/SP.2016.55

Kostoula, T. (2023). Valuation of cryptoassets in EU insolvency: Challenges and prospects. *INSOL International Insolvency Review*, *32*(1), 8–40. DOI: 10.1002/iir.1490

KPMG. (2022). *Crypto: rise in institutional interest - Rapid loss of value is not isolated.* KPMG. https://kpmg.com/xx/en/home/insights/2022/12/crypto-rise-in-institutional-interest.html

Kräussl, R., & Tugnetti, A. (2024). Non-Fungible Tokens (NFTs): A Review of Pricing Determinants, Applications and Opportunities. *Journal of Economic Surveys*, *38*(2), 555–574. DOI: 10.1111/joes.12597

Krishnan, S., Balas, V., Julie, E. G., Harold, R. Y., Balaji, S., & Kumar, R. (2020). *Handbook Of Research On Blockchain Technology*. Elsevier.

Kshetri, N. (2018). Blockchain's roles in meeting key supply chain management objectives. *International Journal of Information Management*, *39*, 80–89. DOI: 10.1016/j.ijinfomgt.2017.12.005

Kshetri, N. (2024). Editorial: Economic, social and political impacts of blockchain. *Telecommunications Policy*, *48*(3), 102718. DOI: 10.1016/j.telpol.2024.102718

Kulkarni, R., Schintler, L., Koizumi, N., Olds, J. L., & Stough, R. (2019). *Cryptocurrency, Stablecoins and Blockchain: Exploring digital money solutions for remittances and inclusive economies.* 66th Annual North American Meetings of the Regional Science Association International (13–16 Nov, 2019). Pittsburgh, *PA, USA*. https://papers.ssrn.com/sol3/Papers.cfm?abstract_id=3511139

Kumah, S. P., & Mensah, J. O. (2020). Are cryptocurrencies connected to gold? A wavelet-based quantile-in-quantile approach. *International Journal of Finance & Economics*, *27*(3), 3640–3659. DOI: 10.1002/ijfe.2342

Kumah, S. P., & Odei-Mensah, J. (2021). Are Cryptocurrencies and African stock markets integrated? *The Quarterly Review of Economics and Finance*, *81*, 330–341. DOI: 10.1016/j.qref.2021.06.022

Kumar, A., Iqbal, N., Mitra, S. K., Kristoufek, L., & Bouri, E. (2022). Connectedness among major cryptocurrencies in standard times and during the COVID-19 outbreak. *Journal of International Financial Markets, Institutions and Money*, *77*, 101523. DOI: 10.1016/j.intfin.2022.101523

Kumar, A., Sharma, D., & Singh, S. (2023). "Duino Coin Mining Bot Development and Performance Evaluation," in *Proceedings of the International Conference on Information Systems and Data Management*, Springer, Cham, 2023, pp. 12-21.

Kumar, A., & Sharma, I. (2023). Preserving Security of Crypto Transactions with Machine Learning Methodologies. *2023 International Conference on Sustainable Computing and Smart Systems (ICSCSS)*, pp. 129-134. DOI: 10.1109/ICSCSS57650.2023.10169192

Kumari, V., Bala, P. K., & Chakraborty, S. (2023). An Empirical Study of User Adoption of Cryptocurrency Using Blockchain Technology: Analysing Role of Success Factors like Technology Awareness and Financial Literacy. *Journal of Theoretical and Applied Electronic Commerce Research*, *18*(3), 1580–1600. DOI: 10.3390/jtaer18030080

Kumar, R., Jangir, S., Kumar, V., & Kaushal, R. (2020). Staking in Proof-of-Stake Blockchain. In *2020 International Conference on Computer Science, Engineering and Applications (ICCSEA)* (pp. 1-6). IEEE.

Kutler, J. (1995). "Digicash to test live Internet cash system with Mo. bank". *American Banker*, vol. 160, no. 204, 23 October, pp. 1

Kwon, J. H. (2020). Tail behavior of Bitcoin, the dollar, gold and the stock market index. *Journal of International Financial Markets, Institutions and Money*, *67*, 101202. DOI: 10.1016/j.intfin.2020.101202

Kyriazis, N., Papadamou, S., & Corbet, S. (2020). A Systematic Review of the Bubble Dynamics of Cryptocurrency Prices. *Research in International Business and Finance*, *54*, 101254. DOI: 10.1016/j.ribaf.2020.101254

Kyriazis, N., Papadamou, S., Tzeremes, P., & Corbet, S. (2022). The differential influence of social media sentiment on cryptocurrency returns and volatility during COVID-19. *The Quarterly Review of Economics and Finance*, *xxxx*, 1–11. DOI: 10.1016/j.qref.2022.09.004 PMID: 36281469

Laboure, M., & Deffrennes, N. (2022). *Democratizing Finance: The Radical Promise of Fintech*. Harvard University Press.

Labs, C. T. O. (2024). Bitcoin's future: US Treasury refinancing and the crypto market. https://www.ctol.digital/news/bitcoins-future-us-treasury-refinancing-crypto-market

Lagarde, C., & Panetta, F. (2022). "Key Objectives of the Digital Euro". *The ECB blog*, juillet, https://www.ecb.europa.eu/press/blog/date/2022/html/ecb.blog220713~34e21c3240.fr.html

Lahajnar, S., & Rozanec, A. (2020). The correlation strength of the most important cryptocurrencies in the bull and bear market. *Investment Management and Financial Innovations*, *17*(3), 67–81. DOI: 10.21511/imfi.17(3).2020.06

Lahiani, A., jeribi, A., & Jlassi, N. B. (2021). Nonlinear Tail Dependence in Cryptocurrency-Stock Market Returns: The Role of Bitcoin Futures. *Research in International Business and Finance*, *56*, 101351. DOI: 10.1016/j.ribaf.2020.101351

Lam, D., & Mizerski, D. (2005). The effects of locus of control on word-of-mouth communication. *Journal of Marketing Communications*, *11*(3), 215–228. DOI: 10.1080/1352726042000333180

Lamothe-López, P., Lamothe-Fernández, P., & Rodríguez-Valencia, L. (2024). Cryptocurrencies - Financial Technologies of the Future. In P. Lamothe-López, P. Lamothe-Fernández, & L. Rodríguez-Valencia, The Inclusion of Bitcoin and Other Cryptocurrencies in Investors' Portfolios. doi:DOI: DOI: 10.5772/intechopen.1003990

Lansky, J. (2016). Analysis of Cryptocurrencies Price Development. *Acta Informatica Pragensia*, *5*(2), 118–137. DOI: 10.18267/j.aip.89

Lansky, J. (2020). Cryptocurrency Survival Analysis. *The Journal of Alternative Investment Analysis*, (Winter), 55–63.

Lavan, T., Martin, B. A. S., Lim, W. M., & Hollebeek, L. D. (2024). Social isolation and risk-taking behavior: The case of COVID-19 and cryptocurrency. *Journal of Retailing and Consumer Services*, *81*, 103951. DOI: 10.1016/j.jretconser.2024.103951

Law, L., Sabett, S., & Solinas, J. (1997). How to make mint: The cryptography of anonymous electronic cash. *The American University Law Review*, *46*(4), 1131–1162. https://heinonline.org/HOL/P?h=hein.journals/aulr46&i=1145

Lawlor, B. (2021). Artificial Intelligence and Machine Learning. *Chemistry International*, *43*(1), 8–13. Advance online publication. DOI: 10.1515/ci-2021-0103

Lee, S. C. (2022). Magical capitalism, gambler subjects: South Korea's bitcoin investment frenzy. *Cultural Studies, 36*(1), 96–119. DOI: 10.1080/09502386.2020.1788620

Lee, S., Kim, J., Seo, M., Na, S., Shin, S., & Kim, J. (2024). CENSor: Detecting Illicit Bitcoin Operation via GCN-Based Hyperedge Classification. *IEEE Access : Practical Innovations, Open Solutions, 12*, 152330–152346. DOI: 10.1109/ACCESS.2024.3466650

Lee, S., Lee, J., & Lee, Y. (2023). Dissecting the Terra-LUNA crash: Evidence from the spillover effect and information flow. *Finance Research Letters, 53*, 103590. DOI: 10.1016/j.frl.2022.103590

Lee, S., Yoon, C., Kang, H., Kim, Y., Kim, Y., Han, D., Son, S., & Shin, S. (2019). Cybercriminal Minds: An investigative study of cryptocurrency abuses in the Dark Web. *Proceedings 2019 Network and Distributed System Security Symposium*. DOI: 10.14722/ndss.2019.23055

Lehdonvirta, V., & Castronova, E. (2014). *Virtual economies: Design and analysis*. MIT Press. DOI: 10.7551/mitpress/9525.001.0001

Levi, M., & Reuter, P. (2011). Money Laundering. In Tonry, M. (Ed.), *The Oxford handbook of crime and public policy* (pp. 289–375). Oxford University Press.

Levy, H., & Levy, M. (2014). The benefits of differential variance-based constraints in portfolio optimization. *European Journal of Operational Research, 234*(2), 372–381. DOI: 10.1016/j.ejor.2013.04.019

Li, J., & Mann, W. (2018). Initial coin offering and platform building. SSRN *Electronic Journal*, 1-56.

Li, M., Wang, C., & Zhang, L. (2023). "Decentralized Coin Switching Protocols for Secure and Trustless Arbitrage," arXiv preprint arXiv:2306.17742.

Li, X., Wu, X., Pei, X., & Yao, Z. (2019, March). Tokenization: Open asset protocol on blockchain. In 2019 IEEE 2nd International Conference on Information and Computer Technologies (ICICT) (pp. 204-209). IEEE.

Liang, X., Yang, Y., & Wang, J. 2016. Internet Finance: A Systematic Literature Review and Bibliometric Analysis. Proceedings of the International Conference on Electronic Business (ICEB) 38. Available online: https://aisel.aisnet.org/iceb2016/38 (accessed on 14 November 2022).

Liao, M. (2021). A survey of blockchain technology applied to digital asset trading. *Journal of Business Research, 136*, 509–516.

Li, C., Zhang, Y., & Xu, Y. (2022). Factors Influencing the Adoption of Blockchain in the Construction Industry: A Hybrid Approach Using PLS-SEM and fsQCA. *Buildings (Basel, Switzerland)*, *12*(9), 1349. Advance online publication. DOI: 10.3390/buildings12091349

Li, J., Li, N., Peng, J., Cui, H., & Wu, Z. (2019). Energy consumption of cryptocurrency mining: A study of electricity consumption in mining cryptocurrencies. *Energy*, *168*, 160–168. DOI: 10.1016/j.energy.2018.11.046

Lim, J. W. (2024). A facilitative model for cryptocurrency regulation in Singapore. In *Handbook of Digital Currency* (pp. 341–361). Academic Press. DOI: 10.1016/B978-0-323-98973-2.00023-X

Lindsay, M. G. (2023). International Rise Of Cryptocurrency: A Comparative Review Of The United States, Mexico, Singapore, And Switzerland's Anti-Money Laundering (AML) Regulation. *South Carolina Journal of International Law and Business*, *19*(2), 8.

Linnenluecke, M. K., Marrone, M., & Singh, A. K. (2020). Conducting Systematic Literature Reviews and Bibliometric Analyses. *Australian Journal of Management*, *45*(2), 175–194. DOI: 10.1177/0312896219877678

Lin, Z. Y. (2021). Investor Attention and Cryptocurrency Performance. *Finance Research Letters*, *40*, 101702. DOI: 10.1016/j.frl.2020.101702

Li, R., Li, S., Yuan, D., & Zhu, H. (2021). Investor Attention and Cryptocurrency: Evidence from Wavelet-Based Quantile Granger Causality Analysis. *Research in International Business and Finance*, *56*, 101389. DOI: 10.1016/j.ribaf.2021.101389

Lisdorf, A. (2023). Virtual Currency. In Lisdorf, A. (Ed.), *Still Searching for Satoshi. Unveiling the Blockchain Revolution*. Apress., DOI: 10.1007/978-1-4842-9639-4_1

Liu, F., & Conlon, J. (2018). The simplest rational greater-fool bubble model. *Journal of Economic Theory*, *175*, 38–59. DOI: 10.1016/j.jet.2018.01.001

Liu, J., & Serletis, A. (2019). Volatility in the cryptocurrency market. *Open Economies Review*, *30*(4), 779–811. DOI: 10.1007/s11079-019-09547-5

Liu, R., Wan, S., Zhang, Z., & Zhao, X. (2020). Is the Introduction of Futures Responsible for the Crash of Bitcoin? *Finance Research Letters*, *34*, 101259. DOI: 10.1016/j.frl.2019.08.007

Liu, W. (2019). Portfolio diversification across cryptocurrencies. *Finance Research Letters*, *29*, 200–205. DOI: 10.1016/j.frl.2018.07.010

Liu, W., Du, Y., & Deng, X. (2019). An adaptive machine learning-based dynamic prediction model for stock price trend forecasting. *Expert Systems with Applications*, *128*, 1–12.

Liu, W., Semeyutin, A., Chi, K. M. L., & Gozgor, G. (2020). Forecasting Value-at-Risk of Cryptocurrencies with RiskMetrics Type Models. *Research in International Business and Finance*, *54*, 101259. DOI: 10.1016/j.ribaf.2020.101259

Li, X., & Wang, C. A. (2017). The technology and economic determinants of cryptocurrency exchange rates: The case of Bitcoin. *Decision Support Systems*, *95*, 49–60. DOI: 10.1016/j.dss.2016.12.001

Li, X., & Whinston, A. B. (2020). Analyzing cryptocurrencies. *Information Systems Frontiers*, *22*(1), 17–22. DOI: 10.1007/s10796-019-09966-2

Li, Y., Wang, Y., & Zhang, X. (2023). Duino Coin Mining Pool Performance Analysis and Optimization. *Journal of Parallel and Distributed Computing*, *174*, 11–22.

Li, Y., & Zhang, L. (2023). Cryptocurrency Wallet: A Review. *International Journal of Computer Applications*, *102*, 1–10.

Li, Z., Rios, A., & Trajković, L. (2021). Machine Learning for Detecting Anomalies and Intrusions in Communication Networks. *IEEE Journal on Selected Areas in Communications*, *39*(7), 2254–2264. DOI: 10.1109/JSAC.2021.3078497

Li, Z.-Z., Tao, R., Su, C.-W., & Lobonţ, O.-R. (2019). Does Bitcoin bubble burst? *Quality & Quantity*, *53*(1), 91–105. DOI: 10.1007/s11135-018-0728-3

Lo, Y. C., & Medda, F. (2021). Uniswap and the Emergence of the Decentralized Exchange. *Journal of financial market infrastructures, 10*(2), 1-25.

López-Cabarcos, M. Á., Pérez-Pico, A. M., Piñeiro-Chousa, J., & Ševi'c, A. (2021). Bitcoin Volatility, Stock Market and Investor Sentiment. Are They Connected? *Finance Research Letters*, *38*, 101399. DOI: 10.1016/j.frl.2019.101399

Luchkin, A. G., Lukasheva, O. L., Novikova, N. E., Melnikov, V. A., Zyatkova, A. V., & Yarotskaya, E. V. (2020). Cryptocurrencies in the Global Financial System: Problems and Ways to Overcome them, *Advances in Economics, Business and Management Research, volume 148,* Proceedings of the Russian Conference on Digital Economy and Knowledge Management (RuDEcK 2020)

Lund, B. (2022). The Cryptocurrency "Pump-and-Dump." In *Handbook of Research on Cyber Law, Data Protection, and Privacy* (pp. 202–211). IGI Global. DOI: 10.4018/978-1-7998-8641-9.ch012

Luo, M., & Yu, S. (2024). Financial reporting for cryptocurrency. *Review of Accounting Studies*, *29*(2), 1707–1740. DOI: 10.1007/s11142-022-09741-w

Lusardi, A. (2019). Financial literacy and the need for financial education: Evidence and implications. *Swiss Journal of Economics and Statistics*, *155*(1), 1–8. DOI: 10.1186/s41937-019-0027-5

Lyons, R. K., & Viswanath-Natraj, G. (2023). What keeps stablecoins stable? *Journal of International Money and Finance*, *131*, 102777. DOI: 10.1016/j.jimonfin.2022.102777

Mahdavieh, R. (2022, June). State Adoption of Cryptocurrency: A Case Study Analysis of Iran, Russia, and Venezuela. *American Journal of Undergraduate Research*, *19*(1), 13–22. DOI: 10.33697/ajur.2022.055

Maier, M. (2023). *Web3 and Token Engineering. in 6G and Onward to Next G: The Road to the Multiverse*. IEEE., DOI: 10.1002/9781119898566

Maitra, D., Ur Rehman, M., Ranjan Dash, S., & Hoon Kang, S. (2022). Do cryptocurrencies provide better hedging? Evidence from major equity markets during COVID-19 pandemic. *The North American Journal of Economics and Finance*, *62*, 101776. DOI: 10.1016/j.najef.2022.101776

Majdoub, J., Ben Sassi, S., & Bejaoui, A. (2021). Can Fiat Currencies Really Hedge Bitcoin? Evidence from Dynamic Short-Term Perspective. *Decisions in Economics and Finance*, *44*(2), 789–816. DOI: 10.1007/s10203-020-00314-7

Makhdoom, I., Abolhasan, M., Abbas, H., & Ni, W. (2019). Blockchain's adoption in IoT: The challenges, and a way forward. *Journal of Network and Computer Applications*, *125*, 251–279. DOI: 10.1016/j.jnca.2018.10.019

Makridis, C. A., Fröwis, M., Sridhar, K., & Böhme, R. (2023). The rise of decentralized cryptocurrency exchanges: Evaluating the role of airdrops and governance tokens. *Journal of Corporate Finance*, *79*, 102358. DOI: 10.1016/j.jcorpfin.2023.102358

Malhotra, A., & Maloo, M. (2014). Bitcoin is it a Bubble? Evidence from Unit Root Tests. SSRN *Electronic Journal*. DOI: 10.2139/ssrn.2476378

Mankiw, G. (2015). *Macroeconomics* (9th edition), New York, NY: MacMillan education

Manzoor, A., Jan, A., Shafi, M., Ashraf Parry, M., & Mir, T. (2023). Role of perceived COVID-19 disruption, personality traits and risk perception in determining the investment behavior of retail investors: a hybrid regression-neural network approach. *Journal of Economic and Administrative Sciences*. DOI: 10.1108/JEAS-01-2023-0026

Maouchi, Y., Charfeddine, L., & El Montasser, G. (2022). Understanding digital bubbles amidst the COVID-19 pandemic: Evidence from DeFi and NFTs. *Finance Research Letters*, *47*, 102584. Advance online publication. DOI: 10.1016/j.frl.2021.102584 PMID: 36406743

Mariana, C. D., Ekaputra, I. A., & Husodo, Z. A. (2021). Are Bitcoin and Ethereum Safe-Havens for Stocks during the COVID-19 Pandemic? *Finance Research Letters*, *38*, 101798. DOI: 10.1016/j.frl.2020.101798 PMID: 33100925

Markets.com. (2024). Tether's impact on the cryptocurrency market. https://www.markets.com/education-centre/tether-on-cryptocurrency-market/

Markowitz, H. (1952). Portfolio Selection. *The Journal of Finance*, *7*(1), 77–91.

Markowitz, H. (2014). Mean–variance approximations to expected utility. *European Journal of Operational Research*, *234*(2), 346–355. DOI: 10.1016/j.ejor.2012.08.023

Marthinsen, J. E., & Gordon, S. R. (2022a). Hyperinflation, Optimal Currency Scopes, and a Cryptocurrency Alternative to Dollarization. *The Quarterly Review of Economics and Finance*, *85*, 161–173. DOI: 10.1016/j.qref.2020.12.007

Marthinsen, J. E., & Gordon, S. R. (2022b). The price and cost of bitcoin. *The Quarterly Review of Economics and Finance*, *85*, 280–288. DOI: 10.1016/j.qref.2022.04.003

Martin, M. (2021). *Computer and Internet use in the United States: 2018*. American Community Survey Reports.

Marx, K. (1867). *Capital: A Critique of Political Economy* (Vol. 1). Verlag von Otto Meisner.

Mason, E. (2021). *Bitcoin About-Face: JPMorgan Opens Crypto Trading To All Clients*. Forbes. https://www.forbes.com/sites/emilymason/2021/07/22/bitcoin-about-face-jpmorgan-opens-crypto-trading-to-all-clients/

Mateen, M. (2023). *Regulation in the Cryptocurrency Industry* (Doctoral dissertation, University of Missouri--Kansas City).

Matkovskyy, R., Jalan, A., Dowling, M., & Bouraoui, T. (2021). From Bottom Ten to Top Ten: The Role of Cryptocurrencies in Enhancing Portfolio Return of Poorly Performing Stocks. *Finance Research Letters*, *38*, 101405. DOI: 10.1016/j.frl.2019.101405

Ma, Y., Ahmad, F., Liu, M., & Wang, Z. (2020). Portfolio Optimization in the Era of Digital Financialization Using Cryptocurrencies. *Technological Forecasting and Social Change*, *161*, 120265. DOI: 10.1016/j.techfore.2020.120265 PMID: 32863444

Mazur, M., & Polyzos, E. (2024). Non-fungible tokens (NFTs). In *The Elgar Companion to Decentralized Finance, Digital Assets, and Blockchain Technologies* (pp. 280-297). Edward Elgar Publishing.

Mazur, M., & Polyzos, E. (2024). Non-fungible tokens (NFTs). In *The Elgar Companion to Decentralized Finance, Digital Assets, and Blockchain Technologies.* Edward Elgar Publishing., DOI: 10.4337/9781035307760.00019

McCaffrey, M. (2019). The macro problem of microtransactions: The self-regulatory challenges of video game loot boxes. *Business Horizons, 62*(4), 483–495. DOI: 10.1016/j.bushor.2019.03.001

McSweeney, M. (2024). *Bitcoin's 'genesis' block of transaction was created 15 years ago.* Blockworks.Co. https://blockworks.co/news/bitcoin-genesis-block-fifteeth-birthday

Mensi, W., Al-Yahyaee, K. H., Idries, M. W. A.-J., Vo, X. V., & Kang, S. H. (2020a). Dynamic Volatility Transmission and Portfolio Management across Major Cryptocurrencies: Evidence from Hourly Data. *The North American Journal of Economics and Finance, 54*, 101285. DOI: 10.1016/j.najef.2020.101285

Mensi, W., Rehman, M. U., Maitra, D., Al-Yahyaee, K. H., & Sensoy, A. (2020b). Does Bitcoin Co-Move and Share Risk with Sukuk and World and Regional Islamic Stock Markets? Evidence Using a Time-Frequency Approach. *Research in International Business and Finance, 53*, 101230. DOI: 10.1016/j.ribaf.2020.101230

Mensi, W., Sensoy, A., Aslan, A., & Kang, S. H. (2019). High-Frequency Asymmetric Volatility Connectedness between Bitcoin and Major Precious Metals Markets. *The North American Journal of Economics and Finance, 50*, 101031. DOI: 10.1016/j.najef.2019.101031

Metcalfe, W. (2020). Ethereum, Smart Contracts, DApps. In *Blockchain and Crypt Currency* (pp. 77–93). DOI: 10.1007/978-981-15-3376-1_5

Meynkhard, A. (2019). Fair market value of bitcoin: Halving effect. *Investment Management and Financial Innovations, 16*(4), 72–85. DOI: 10.21511/imfi.16(4).2019.07

Mik, E. (2021). Decentralized Finance: The future of finance or just another hype? *Financial Innovation, 7*(1), 8.

Mikhaylov, A. (2020). Cryptocurrency market analysis from the open innovation perspective. *Journal of Open Innovation, 6*(4), 1–19. DOI: 10.3390/joitmc6040197

Milian, E. Z., Spinola, M. M., & Carvalho, M. M. (2019). Fintechs: A Literature Review and Research Agenda. *Electronic Commerce Research and Applications*, *34*, 100833. DOI: 10.1016/j.elerap.2019.100833

Milka, P. (2021). Speculation in the cryptocurrency market. *The Review of Economics Finance & Investments*, *1*(1), 24–33. DOI: 10.53752/refi.2020.1.12

Milunovich, G. (2018). Cryptocurrencies, Mainstream Asset Classes and Risk Factors: A Study of Connectedness. *The Australian Economic Review*, *51*(4), 551–563. DOI: 10.1111/1467-8462.12303

Mironeanu, A., Irimia, B., Săndulescu, V., & Teodoroiu, C. (2021). The impact of Tesla's bitcoin investment and its plans to accept it as payment method on the evolution of bitcoin. *Proceedings of the International Conference on Business Excellence, 15*(1), 58–74. DOI: 10.2478/picbe-2021-0007

Mitchell, M. (2009). *Complexity: A guided tour*. Oxford university press. DOI: 10.1093/oso/9780195124415.001.0001

Moghadam, S., Reza, M., Safari, H., & Yousefi, N. (2021). Clustering Quality Management Models and Methods: Systematic Literature Review and Text-Mining Analysis Approach. *Total Quality Management & Business Excellence*, *32*(3-4), 241–264. DOI: 10.1080/14783363.2018.1540927

Mokni, K. (2021). When, Where, and How Economic Policy Uncertainty Predicts Bitcoin Returns and Volatility? A Quantiles-Based Analysis. *The Quarterly Review of Economics and Finance*, *80*, 65–73. DOI: 10.1016/j.qref.2021.01.017

Montagnani, M., Najjar, M., & Davola, A. (2024). The EU Regulatory approach(es) to AI liability, and its Application to the financial services market. *Computer Law & Security Review*, *53*, 105984. DOI: 10.1016/j.clsr.2024.105984

Montanez, A. (2014). *Investigation of cryptocurrency wallets on iOS and Android mobile devices for potential forensic artifacts. Department Forensic Science*. Marshall University.

Moratis, G. (2021). Quantifying the Spillover Effect in the Cryptocurrency Market. *Finance Research Letters*, *38*, 101534. DOI: 10.1016/j.frl.2020.101534

Morozova, T., Akhmadeev, R., Lehoux, L., Yumashev, A. V., Meshkova, G. V., & Lukiyanova, M. (2020). Crypto asset assessment models in financial reporting content typologies. *Entrepreneurship and Sustainability Issues*, *7*(3), 2196–2212. DOI: 10.9770/jesi.2020.7.3(49)

Morris, D. Z. (2018). *The blockchain: A guide for legal and business professionals*. Thomson Reuters.

Morton, D. T. (2020). The future of cryptocurrency: An unregulated instrument in an increasingly regulated global economy. *Loy. U. Chi. Int'l L. Rev.*, *16*, 129.

Motsi-Omoijiade, I. D. (2018). Financial intermediation in cryptocurrency markets–regulation, gaps and bridges. In *Handbook of Blockchain, Digital Finance, and Inclusion, Volume 1* (pp. 207-223). Academic Press. https://doi.org/DOI: 10.1016/B978-0-12-810441-5.00009-9

Mundell, R. A. (1961). A Theory of Optimum Currency Areas. *The American Economic Review*, *51*(4), 657–665.

Murugappan, M., Nair, R., & Krishnan, S. (2023). Global market perceptions of cryptocurrency and the use of cryptocurrency by consumers: A pilot study. *Journal of Theoretical and Applied Electronic Commerce Research*, *18*(4), 1955–1970. DOI: 10.3390/jtaer18040098

Mutambik, I., Almuqrin, A., Zhang, J. Z., & Alharbi, Z. H. (2024). Trust in Cryptocurrency Payments. *Journal of Organizational and End User Computing*, *36*(1), 1–36. DOI: 10.4018/JOEUC.353910

Nadarajah, S., & Chu, J. (2017). On the inefficiency of Bitcoin. *Economics Letters*, *150*, 6–9. DOI: 10.1016/j.econlet.2016.10.033

Nadini, M., Alessandretti, L., Di Giacinto, F., Martino, M., Aiello, L. M., & Baronchelli, A. (2021). Mapping the NFT revolution: Market trends, trade networks, and visual features. *Scientific Reports*, *11*(1), 1–11. DOI: 10.1038/s41598-021-00053-8 PMID: 34686678

Naeem, M. A., Farid, S., Balli, F., & Syed, J. H. S. (2021a). Hedging the Downside Risk of Commodities through Cryptocurrencies. *Applied Economics Letters*, *28*(2), 153–160. DOI: 10.1080/13504851.2020.1739609

Naeem, M. A., Qureshi, S., Rehman, M. U., & Balli, F. (2021b). COVID-19 and Cryptocurrency Market: Evidence from Quantile Connectedness. *Applied Economics*, *54*(3), 280–306. DOI: 10.1080/00036846.2021.1950908

Naeem, M., Bouri, E., Boako, G., & Roubaud, D. (2020). Tail Dependence in the Return-Volume of Leading Cryptocurrencies. *Finance Research Letters*, *36*, 101326. DOI: 10.1016/j.frl.2019.101326

Najed, A., Al-Malahmeh, H., Al-Amawi, A., Almashaqbeh, M., Alsaaideh, M., & Abdalmajeed, A. A. (2023, March). Impact of Cryptocurrency Regulations and Fintech on the Growth of Innovations. In *2023 International Conference on Business Analytics for Technology and Security (ICBATS)* (pp. 1-5). IEEE. DOI: 10.1109/ICBATS57792.2023.10111475

Nakamoto, S. (2008). "Bitcoin: A Peer-to-Peer Electronic Cash System". *White Paper*. https://bitcoin.org/bitcoin.pdf

Nakamoto, S. (2008). Bitcoin: A peer-to-peer electronic cash system, available at: https://bitcoin.org/bitcoin.pdf, retrieved August 10, 2024

Nakamoto, S. (2008). Bitcoin: A peer-to-peer electronic cash system.

Nakamoto, S. (2008). *Bitcoin: A peer-to-peer electronic cash system*. Bitcoin: A Peer-to-Peer Electronic Cash System. https://bitcoin.org/bitcoin.pdf

Nakamoto, S. (2008). *Bitcoin: A peer-to-peer electronic cash system*. https://bitcoin .org/bitcoin.pdf

Nakamoto, S. 2008. Bitcoin: A Peer-to-Peer Electronic Cash System. Available online: https://bitcoin.org/en/bitcoin-paper (accessed on 10 October 2022).

Nakamoto, S. Bitcoin: A peer-to-peer ElectronicCash system, 2009, Available online: https://bitcoin.org/bitcoin.pdf

Nakamoto, S., & Bitcoin, A. (2008). A peer-to-peer electronic cash system. *Bitcoin.–URL:*https://bitcoin. org/bitcoin. pdf, *4*(2), p.15.

Nakamoto, S. (2008). *Bitcoin: A Peer-to-Peer Electronic Cash System*. 1–9. DOI: 10.2139/ssrn.3977007

Nakamoto, S. (2008). *Bitcoin: A peer-to-peer electronic cash system*. Decentralized Business Review.

Nani, A. (2022). The doge worth 88 billion dollars: A case study of Dogecoin. *Convergence (London)*, *28*(6), 1719–1736. DOI: 10.1177/13548565211070417

Narayanan, A., Bonneau, J., Felten, E., Miller, A., & Goldfeder, S. (2016). *Bitcoin and cryptocurrency technologies*.

Narayanan, A., Bonneau, J., Felten, E., Miller, A., & Goldfeder, S. (2016). *Bitcoin and cryptocurrency technologies*. Princeton university press.

Narayanan, A., Bonneau, J., Felten, E., Miller, A., & Goldfeder, S. (2016). *Bitcoin and Cryptocurrency Technologies: A Comprehensive Introduction*. Princeton University Press.

Narayanan, A., & Clark, J. (2017). Bitcoin's academic pedigree. *Communications of the ACM*, *60*(12), 36–45. DOI: 10.1145/3132259

Nasdaq. (2023). The Tether price connection: USDT's impact on the crypto market. https://www.nasdaq.com/articles/the-tether-price-connection%3A-usdts-impact-on-the-crypto-market

Nazah, S., Huda, S., Abawajy, J., & Hassan, M. (2020). Evolution of Dark Web Threat Analysis and Detection: A Systematic Approach. *IEEE Access : Practical Innovations, Open Solutions*, *8*, 171796–171819. DOI: 10.1109/ACCESS.2020.3024198

NDTV. (2021, May 14). *Why A $1 Billion Donation To India Covid Relief Shocked Memecoin Traders.* https://www.ndtv.com/india-news/a-1-billion-crypto-donation-to-india-covid-relief-in-memecoins-explained-2441443

Neuwirth, R. (2023). Prohibited artificial intelligence practices in the proposed EU artificial intelligence act (AIA). *Computer Law & Security Review*, *48*, 105798. DOI: 10.1016/j.clsr.2023.105798

NewLibertyStandard. (2009). 2009 Exchange Rate. New Liberty Standard. http://newlibertystandard.wetpaint.com/page/2009+

Nguyen, K. Q. (2022). The correlation between the stock market and Bitcoin during COVID-19 and other uncertainty periods. *Finance Research Letters*, *46*, 102284. DOI: 10.1016/j.frl.2021.102284 PMID: 35431674

Nguyen, L. H., Chevapatrakul, T., & Yao, K. (2020). Investigating Tail-Risk Dependence in the Cryptocurrency Markets: A LASSO Quantile Regression Approach. *Journal of Empirical Finance*, *58*, 333–355. DOI: 10.1016/j.jempfin.2020.06.006

Nguyen, T. V. H., Nguyen, B. T., Nguyen, K. S., & Pham, H. (2019). Asymmetric Monetary Policy Effects on Cryptocurrency Markets. *Research in International Business and Finance*, *48*, 335–339. DOI: 10.1016/j.ribaf.2019.01.011

Nicolas, M. L. D. (2022). Estimating a model of herding behavior on social networks. *Physica A*, *604*, 127884. DOI: 10.1016/j.physa.2022.127884

Noll, F. (2024). Observations from the Retail CBDCs of the Caribbean, *kcFED Payments System Research Breiefing,* Federal Reserve Bank of Kansas City, April 10.

Nour, K. (2022). Criminal confrontation of cryptocurrency use in the financing of terrorism. *Jolets.* 16;2(2):79-152. Available from: https://jolets.org/ojs/index.php/jolets/article/view/12

Novak, M. (2019). Crypto-friendliness: Understanding blockchain public policy. *Journal of Entrepreneurship and Public Policy*, *9*(2), 165–184. DOI: 10.1108/JEPP-03-2019-0014

Novak, M. (2024). Crypto altruism: Applying blockchain to charitable and humanitarian activities. *Chinese Public Administration Review*, *15*(1), 11–23. DOI: 10.1177/15396754231175173

Nurbarani, B. S., & Soepriyanto, G. (2022). Determinants of Investment Decision in Cryptocurrency: Evidence from Indonesian Investors. *Universal Journal of Accounting and Finance*, *10*(1), 254–266. DOI: 10.13189/ujaf.2022.100126

O'Dwyer, K. J., & Malone, D. (2014). Bitcoin mining and its energy footprint. *25th IET Irish Signals and Systems Conference and China-Ireland International Conference on Information and Communications Technologies (ISSC/CIICT 2014)*. 26-27 June 2014, Limerick, Ireland.

O'Kane, P., Sezer, S., & Carlin, D. (2018). Evolution of ransomware. *IET Networks*, *7*(5), 321–327. DOI: 10.1049/iet-net.2017.0207

O'Reilly, T. (2019). *WTF?: What's the future and why it's up to us*. HarperCollins.

Obeidat, T. (1996). *Methods and Techniques of Scientific Research*. Dar Sana'a for Publishing. (In Arabic)

OECD. (2009). *Money laundering awareness handbook for tax examiners and tax auditors*. OECD.

Office of Science and Technology Policy. (2022). *Climate and Energy Implications of Crypto-Assets in the United States*. White House Office of Science and Technology Policy. Washington, D.C. https://www.whitehouse.gov/wp-content/uploads/2022/09/09-2022-Crypto-Assets-and-Climate-Report.pdf

Okorie, D. I., & Lin, B. (2020). Crude Oil Price and Cryptocurrencies: Evidence of Volatility Connectedness and Hedging Strategy. *Energy Economics*, *87*, 104703. DOI: 10.1016/j.eneco.2020.104703

Olabanji, S. O., Oladoyinbo, T. O., Asonze, C. U., Adigwe, C. S., Okunleye, O. J., & Olaniyi, O. O. (2024). Leveraging fintech compliance to mitigate cryptocurrency volatility for secure us employee retirement benefits: Bitcoin ETF case study. *Available atSSRN* 4739190.

Oliveira, L., Zavolokina, L., Bauer, I., & Schwabe, G. (2018, December). To token or not to token: Tools for understanding blockchain tokens. ICIS.

Oliveira, M. T., Reis, L. H. A., Medeiros, D. S. V., Carrano, R. C., Olabarriaga, S. D., & Mattos, D. M. F. (2020). Blockchain reputation-based consensus: A scalable and resilient mechanism for distributed mistrusting applications. *Computer Networks*, *179*, 107367. DOI: 10.1016/j.comnet.2020.107367

Olorundare, J. K., Fagboyo, R. J., Onyijen, O. H., Oni, M., & Adebunmi, A. A. (2023). Economic Prospect of Cryptocurrency: Nigeria as a Case Study. *Journal homepage:*www. ijrpr. com*ISSN, 2582*, 7421.

Oman, Z. U., & Suryanarayana, K. A Study on Latest Trends and Growth of Crypto Currencies and Its Regulatory Aspect in India. https://doi:DOI: 10.14445/23939125/IJEMS-V9I12P103

Omane-Adjepong, M., & Alagidede, I. P. (2020). Dynamic Linkages and Economic Role of Leading Cryptocurrencies in an Emerging Market. In *Asia-Pacific Financial Markets* (Vol. 27). Springer. DOI: 10.1007/s10690-020-09306-4

Ordekian, M., Becker, I., & Vasek, M. (2023, May). Shaping Cryptocurrency Gatekeepers with a Regulatory "Trial and Error". In *International Conference on Financial Cryptography and Data Security* (pp. 113-132). Cham: Springer Nature Switzerland. DOI: 10.2139/ssrn.4398362

Orzi, R., Porcherot, R., & Valdecantos, S. (2021). Cryptocurrencies for Social Change: The Experience of MonedaPAR in Argentina. *International Journal of Community Currency Research*, *25*(1), 16–33. DOI: 10.15133/j.ijccr.2021.002

Osakwe, C. N. (2024). *An integrative model for understanding cryptocurrency investment-related behaviours : A comparison between millennials and pre-millennials. November 2022*, 1–19. DOI: 10.1002/ijfe.3031

Osborne, C. (2018). Trump bans Venezuela's cryptocurrency Petro in the US. *ZDNet*, March 20

Osterland, T., & Rose, T. (2020). Model checking smart contracts for Ethereum. *Pervasive and Mobile Computing*, *63*, 101129. DOI: 10.1016/j.pmcj.2020.101129

Outeda, C. (2024). The EU's AI act: A framework for collaborative governance. *Internet of Things : Engineering Cyber Physical Human Systems*, *27*, 101291. DOI: 10.1016/j.iot.2024.101291

Oza, V. J., Nikte, A., Bhanushali, V., & Rote, U. (2024). Smart Contracts and Tokenization: Revolutionizing Real Estate Transactions with Blockchain Technology. *2024 International Conference on Inventive Computation Technologies (ICICT)*, 1598–1604. DOI: 10.1109/ICICT60155.2024.10544886

Özdemir, O. (2022). Cue the volatility spillover in the cryptocurrency markets during the COVID-19 pandemic: Evidence from DCC-GARCH and wavelet analysis. *Financial Innovation*, *8*(1), 12. DOI: 10.1186/s40854-021-00319-0 PMID: 35132369

Ozili, P. K. (2023). Determinants of interest in eNaira and financial inclusion information in Nigeria: Role of FinTech, cryptocurrency and central bank digital currency. *Digital Transformation and Society.*, *2*(2), 202–214. DOI: 10.1108/DTS-08-2022-0040

Packin, N. G. (2024). The Nexus of Gaming and NFTs: A Deep Dive Into the Future of Digital Interaction. *The Cambridge Handbook on Law and Policy for NFTs (Nizan Geslevich Packin, Ed.), Forthcoming*. https://ssrn.com/abstract=4787912

Papadamou, S., Kyriazis, N. A., & Tzeremes, P. G. (2021). Non-Linear Causal Linkages of EPU and Gold with Major Cryptocurrencies during Bull and Bear Markets. *The North American Journal of Economics and Finance*, *56*, 101343. DOI: 10.1016/j.najef.2020.101343

Parampathu, J. (2024). From securities to currencies: The regulatory consequences of adopting cryptocurrencies as legal tender. *Transnational Legal Theory*, *15*(2), 288–339. DOI: 10.1080/20414005.2024.2366140

Passinsky, A. (2024). Cryptocurrency: Commodity or Credit? In Sandberg, A., & Warenski, I. (Eds.), *The Philosophy of Money and Finance* (pp. 32–53). Academic., DOI: 10.1093/oso/9780192898807.003.0003

Patel, E. (2023, May 13). How can cryptocurrencies play a role in promoting financial inclusion? *The Economic Times*.https://economictimes.indiatimes.com/markets/cryptocurrency/how-can-cryptocurrencies-play-a-role-in-promoting-financial-inclusion/articleshow/100205450.cms?from=mdr

Patel, R. (2024). Economic freedom or crypto-colonialism? Materialities of Bitcoin adoption in El Salvador. *Geoforum*, *151*, 103980. DOI: 10.1016/j.geoforum.2024.103980

Patil, S., Vijayakumar, V., Walimbe, D., Gulechha, S., Shenoy, S., Raina, A., & Kotecha, K. (2021). Improving the Robustness of AI-Based Malware Detection Using Adversarial Machine Learning. *Algorithms*, *14*(10), 297. DOI: 10.3390/a14100297

Patra, G. R., & Mohanty, M. N. (2023). Price prediction of cryptocurrency using a multi-layer gated recurrent unit network with multi features. *Computational Economics*, *62*(4), 1525–1544. DOI: 10.1007/s10614-022-10310-1

Patras, W., Rasool, A., & Idrees, M. (2023). Assessment of Investors' Investment Behaviour: Mediating Effect of Risk Tolerance: a Case of Pakistan Stock Exchange. *Journal of Social Research Development*, *4*(2), 305–315. DOI: 10.53664/JSRD/04-02-2023-07-305-315

Paul, A. K., Qu, X., & Wen, Z. (2021). Blockchain–a promising solution to internet of things: A comprehensive analysis, opportunities, challenges and future research issues. *Peer-to-Peer Networking and Applications*, *14*(5), 2926–2951. DOI: 10.1007/s12083-021-01151-0

Paul, P., Aithal, P. S., Saavedra, R., & Ghosh, S. (2021). Blockchain technology and its types—A short review. [IJASE]. *International Journal of Applied Science and Engineering*, *9*(2), 189–200. DOI: 10.30954/2322-0465.2.2021.7

Pavithra, S., Shreyashwini, N. K., Bhavana, H. S., Nikhitha, G., & Kavitha, T. (2023). Hand-drawn electronic component recognition using ORB. *Procedia Computer Science*, *218*, 504–513.

Pavlidis, G. (2024). Unlocking the black box: Analysing the EU artificial intelligence act's framework for explainability in AI. *Law, Innovation and Technology*, *16*(1), 293–308. DOI: 10.1080/17579961.2024.2313795

PBoC (People's Bank of China). (2021). ''Progress of Research & Development of e-CNY in China''. July. http://www.pbc.gov.cn/en/3688110/3688172/4157443/4293696/2021071614584691871.pdf

PBoC. (2022). ''Pressing Ahead with the Pilot Program of e-CNY R&D''. October, http://www.pbc.gov.cn/en/3688006/4671762/4688130/index.html

Pham, Q. T., Phan, H. H., Cristofaro, M., Misra, S., & Giardino, P. L. (2021). Examining the Intention to Invest in Cryptocurrencies. *International Journal of Applied Behavioral Economics*, *10*(3), 59–79. DOI: 10.4018/IJABE.2021070104

Phemex. (2022). How interest rates affect cryptocurrency. https://phemex.com/blogs/how-interest-rates-affect-cryptocurrency

Philippas, D., Philippas, N., Tziogkidis, P., & Rjiba, H. (2020). Signal-Herding in Cryptocurrencies. *Journal of International Financial Markets, Institutions and Money*, *65*, 101191. DOI: 10.1016/j.intfin.2020.101191

Phiri, A., & Anyikwa, I. (2024). A multiscale analysis of returns and volatility spillovers in cryptocurrency markets: A post-COVID perspective. *The Investment Analysts Journal*, •••, 1–21.

Pho, K. H., Ly, S., Lu, R., Van Hoang, T. H., & Wong, W. K. (2021). Is Bitcoin a Better Portfolio Diversifier than Gold? A Copula and Sectoral Analysis for China. *International Review of Financial Analysis*, *74*, 101674. DOI: 10.1016/j.irfa.2021.101674

Pidun, U., Rubner, H., Krühler, M., Untiedt, R., & Nippa, M.Boston Consulting Group. (2011). Corporate portfolio management: Theory and practice. *The Bank of America Journal of Applied Corporate Finance*, *23*(1), 63–76. DOI: 10.1111/j.1745-6622.2011.00315.x

Piguet Galland. (2024). Rate hikes vs crypto hype. https://www.piguetgalland.ch/en/news/rate-hikes-vs-crypto-hype

Pilatin, A., & Dilek, Ö. (2023). Investor intention, investor behavior and crypto assets in the framework of decomposed theory of planned behavior. *Current Psychology, Cc*. DOI: 10.1007/s12144-023-04307-8

Pilkington, M. (2016). *Blockchain Technology: Principles and Applications.* Research Handbook on Digital Transformations.

Pinjarkar, L., Agrawal, P., Gupta, G. K., Kaur, G., Sheikh, F., & Perwez, S. (2024, September). Blockchain security in cryptocurrency: Challenges, solutions, and future prospects. In *AIP Conference Proceedings* (Vol. 3242, No. 1). AIP Publishing.

Pinkerton, J. (2024, July 24). The History of Bitcoin. *USNews,* https://money.usnews.com/investing/articles/the-history-of-bitcoin

Platanakis, E., Sutcliffe, C., & Urquhart, A. (2018). Optimal vs naïve diversification in cryptocurrencies. *Economics Letters*, *171*, 93–96. DOI: 10.1016/j.econlet.2018.07.020

Platanakis, E., & Urquhart, A. (2019). Portfolio Management with Cryptocurrencies: The Role of Estimation Risk. *Economics Letters*, *177*, 76–80. DOI: 10.1016/j.econlet.2019.01.019

Platanakis, E., & Urquhart, A. (2020). Should investors include Bitcoin in their portfolios? A portfolio theory approach. *The British Accounting Review*, *52*(4), 100837. Advance online publication. DOI: 10.1016/j.bar.2019.100837

Podder, B. (2023). Cryptocurrency and central bank digital currency: An insight from the regulatory perspective. *International Journal of Financial Studies. Economics and Management*, *2*(3), 25–35.

Pointcheval, D., & Stern, J. (1996). *Provably secure blind signature schemes* (K. Kim & T. Matsumoto, Eds.; pp. 252–265). Springer Berlin Heidelberg. DOI: 10.1007/BFb0034852

Polat, O., & Günay, E. K. (2021). Cryptocurrency Connectedness Nexus the COVID-19 Pandemic: Evidence from Time-Frequency Domains. *Studies in Economics and Finance*, *38*(5), 946–963. DOI: 10.1108/SEF-01-2021-0011

Ponciano, J. (2021). *Goldman Sachs To Launch Crypto Trading Operation This Month After Bitcoin's Big Surge*. Forbes. https://www.forbes.com/sites/jonathanponciano/2021/03/01/goldman-sachs-to-launch-crypto-trading-operation-this-month-after-bitcoins-big-surge/

Poongodi, M., Nguyen, T. N., Hamdi, M., & Cengiz, K. (2021). Global cryptocurrency trend predictionusing social media. *Information Processing & Management*, *58*(6), 102708. DOI: 10.1016/j.ipm.2021.102708

Poynton, A. (2023). US cryptocurrency regulation: A slowly evolving state of affairs. *Notre Dame J. on Emerging Tech.*, *4*, 93.

Prat, M. K. (2023, November 30). The environmental impact of bitcoin mining explained. *TechTarget,* https://www.techtarget.com/sustainability/feature/The-environmental-impact-of-bitcoin-mining-explained

Prime, E. L., & Solomon, D. H. (2010). Australias Plastic Banknotes: Fighting Counterfeit Currency. *Angewandte Chemie International Edition*, *49*(22), 2–13. DOI: 10.1002/anie.200904538 PMID: 20358564

Przybylski, A. K., Murayama, K., Dehaan, C. R., & Gladwell, V. (2013). Motivational, emotional, and behavioral correlates of fear of missing out. *Computers in Human Behavior*, *29*(4), 1841–1848. DOI: 10.1016/j.chb.2013.02.014

Putra, I. G. N. A. P., & Darma, G. S. (2019). Is Bitcoin Accepted in Indonesia? *International Journal of Innovative Science and Research Technology, 4*(2), 424–430. www.ijisrt.com424

Putri, C. P., Putra, A. T. E., & Aminuddin, M. (2023, December). The Urgency of Appropriate Legal Regulations on Financial and Tax Aspects in Cryptocurrency Transactions in Indonesia. In *International Conference on "Changing of Law: Business Law, Local Wisdom and Tourism Industry"(ICCLB 2023)* (pp. 305-316). Atlantis Press. DOI: 10.2991/978-2-38476-180-7_34

Putri, T., Amiludin, A., Ahmad, D. N., & Hidayatulloh, H. (2023). Inadequate Cryptocurrency and Money Laundering Regulations in Indonesia (Comparative Law of US and Germany). *Yustisia*, *12*(2), 129–152. DOI: 10.20961/yustisia.v12i2.71835

PwC. (2024). *Crypto Contributions. Redefining Charitable Giving in the Digital Age*. https://www.pwc.ch/en/insights/fs/crypto-contributions.html

Qiao, X., Zhu, H., & Hau, L. (2020). Time-Frequency Co-Movement of Cryptocurrency Return and Volatility: Evidence fromWavelet Coherence Analysis. *International Review of Financial Analysis*, *71*, 101541. DOI: 10.1016/j.irfa.2020.101541

Qiu, Y., Wang, Y., & Xie, T. (2021). Forecasting Bitcoin Realized Volatility by Measuring the Spillover Effect among Cryptocurrencies. *Economics Letters*, *208*, 110092. DOI: 10.1016/j.econlet.2021.110092

Quang, N., Binh, T. H. L., & Phuc, C. N. (2020). Influences of Uncertainty on the Returns and Liquidity of Cryptocurrencies: Evidence from a Portfolio Approach. *International Journal of Finance & Economics*, *27*(2), 2497–2513. DOI: 10.1002/ijfe.2283

Raheem, I. D. (2021). COVID-19 Pandemic and the Safe Haven Property of Bitcoin. *The Quarterly Review of Economics and Finance*, *81*, 370–375. DOI: 10.1016/j.qref.2021.06.004

Raman, R., Nair, V., Nedungadi, P., Ray, I., & Achuthan, K. (2023). Darkweb research: Past, present, and future trends and mapping to sustainable development goals. *Heliyon*, *9*(11), e22269. Advance online publication. DOI: 10.1016/j.heliyon.2023.e22269 PMID: 38058627

Rancic, M., & Stankovic, J. (2019). "The Use of Cryptocurrencies in Trade Finance." Facta Universitatis, Series. *Economics and Organization*, *16*(2), 151–166.

RBI (Reserve Bank of India). (2022), *Concept Note on CBDC*, October, https://rbi.org.in/Scripts/PublicationReportDetails.aspx?UrlPage=&ID=1218

Redish, A. (1993, November). Anchors Aweigh: The Transition from Commodity Money to Fiat Money in Western Economies. *The Canadian Journal of Economics. Revue Canadienne d'Economique*, *26*(4), 777–795. http://links.jstor.org/sici?sici=0008-4085%28199311%2926%3A4%3C777%3AAATTFC%3E2.0.CO%3B2-Q. DOI: 10.2307/135820

Reeves, M. (2017). Cryptocurrency-Remittance Transfers Futuristic Technologies & Poverty Alleviation. *Economics Student Theses and Capstone Projects, 56*. https://creativematter.skidmore.edu/econ_studt_schol/56

Rehman, W., Zainab, H., Imran, J., & Bawany, N. Z. (2021). NFTs: Applications and Challenges. In *22nd International Arab Conference on Information Technology (ACIT)* (pp. 1-7). IEEE. DOI: 10.1109/ACIT53391.2021.9677260

Reichental, J. (2023). *Cryptocurrency QuickStart Guide: The Simplified Beginner's Guide to Digital Currencies, Bitcoin, and the Future of Decentralized Finance.* ClydeBank Media LLC.

Reid, F., & Harrigan, M. (2013). *An analysis of anonymity in the Bitcoin system.* Springer. DOI: 10.1007/978-1-4614-4139-7_10

Reiff, N. (2019). *Investing in blockchain: Cryptocurrency, fintech, and beyond.* Skyhorse Publishing.

Renduchintala, T., Alfauri, H., Yang, Z., Di Pietro, R., & Jain, R. (2022). A Survey of Blockchain Applications in the FinTech Sector. *Journal of Open Innovation*, *8*(4), 185. DOI: 10.3390/joitmc8040185

Reshef Kera, D. (2020). Sandboxes and Testnets as "Trading Zones" for Blockchain Governance. In Prieto, J., Pinto, A., Das, A. K., & Ferretti, S. (Eds.), *Blockchain and Applications* (pp. 3–12). Springer International Publishing., DOI: 10.1007/978-3-030-52535-4_1

Reuter, P., & Turman, E. M. (2004). *Chasing dirty money*. Institute for International Economics.

Rialti, R., Marzi, G., Ciappei, C., & Busso, D. (2019). Big Data and Dynamic Capabilities: A Bibliometric Analysis and Systematic Literature Review. *Management Decision*, *57*(8), 2052–2068. DOI: 10.1108/MD-07-2018-0821

Riley, J. (2021). The current status of cryptocurrency regulation in China and its effect around the world. *China and WTO Review*, *7*(1), 135–152. DOI: 10.14330/cwr.2021.7.1.06

Rocchi, J.-M. (2022). Crisp Set vs Fuzzy Set Qualitative Comparative Analysis, Technical Differences, and Much More in Said Broumi (Ed.). Handbook of Research on Advances and Applications of Fuzzy Sets and Logic, IGI Global. pp.1-28

Rochet, J., & Villeneuve, S. (2005). Corporate portfolio management. *Annals of Finance*, *1*(3), 225–243. DOI: 10.1007/s10436-005-0018-7

Rodrigues, G., & Kurtz, L. (2019). *Cryptocurrencies and anti-money laundering regulation in the G20*. Institute for Research on Internet and Society. Belo Horizonte. http://bit.ly/32Fw4xD

Rodríguez-Valencia, L., Lamothe-Fernández, P., & Alaminos, D. (2023). The market value of SMEs: A comparative study between private and listed firms in alternative stock markets. *Annals of Finance*, *19*(1), 95–117. DOI: 10.1007/s10436-022-00420-z

Rognone, L., Hyde, S., & Sarah Zhang, S. (2020). News Sentiment in the Cryptocurrency Market: An Empirical Comparison with Forex. *International Review of Financial Analysis*, *69*, 101462. DOI: 10.1016/j.irfa.2020.101462

Rolle, J. (2022). "The Bahamas' Experience with the Sand Dollar". *Remarks at the Digital Euro Conference*. CBOB, November 7 https://www.centralbankbahamas.com/news/general-news/the-bahamas-experience-with-the-sand-dollar-remarks-by-governor-john-rolle

Roosenboom, P., van der Kolk, T., & de Jong, A. (2020). What determines success in initial coin offerings? *Venture Capital*, *22*(2), 161–183. DOI: 10.1080/13691066.2020.1741127

Rosales, A. (2019). Radical rentierism: Gold mining, cryptocurrency and commodity collateralization in Venezuela. *Review of International Political Economy*, *26*(6), 1311–1332. Advance online publication. DOI: 10.1080/09692290.2019.1625422

Rotta, T. N., & Paraná, E. (2022). Bitcoin as a digital commodity. *New Political Economy*, *27*(6), 1046–1061. DOI: 10.1080/13563467.2022.2054966

Ruimy, M., & Rocchi, J.-M. (2017). La monnaie à l'ère de la digitalization in Jean-Michel Rocchi (Ed.), MBA Finance, Eyrolles. (pp.817-852).

Russo, A., & Lax, G. (2022). Using Artificial Intelligence for Space Challenges: A Survey. *Applied Sciences (Basel, Switzerland)*, *12*(10), 5106. DOI: 10.3390/app12105106

Saengchote, K. (2023). Decentralized lending and its users: Insights from Compound. *Journal of International Financial Markets, Institutions and Money*, *87*, 101807. DOI: 10.1016/j.intfin.2023.101807

Sahoo, P. K. (2021). COVID-19 Pandemic and Cryptocurrency Markets: An Empirical Analysis from a Linear and Nonlinear Causal Relationship. *Studies in Economics and Finance*, *38*(2), 454–468. DOI: 10.1108/SEF-09-2020-0385

Said, A. (2019). The Economic Impact of Digital Fiat Currency (DFC): Opportunities and Challenges, 2nd Europe - Middle East - North African Regional Conference of the International Telecommunications Society (ITS): "Leveraging Technologies For Growth", Aswan, Egypt, 18th-21st February, 2019, International Telecommunications Society (ITS), Calgary. https://hdl.handle.net/10419/201744

Salehi, A., & Rafsanjani, M. K. (2024). Risk analysis of blockchain technology in financial markets. Physica A: Statistical Mechanics and its Applications. https://www.sciencedirect.com/science/article/pii/S0378437124004126

Salman, M. (2020). *The impact of heuristic availability bias on investment decision-making: Moderated mediation model. September*, 1–12. DOI: 10.1002/bsd2.148

Sambana, B. (2021). Blockchain Technology: Bitcoins, Cryptocurrency and Applications. *ArXiv Preprint ArXiv:2107.07964*. http://arxiv.org/abs/2107.07964

Sanka, A. I., & Cheung, R. C. (2021). A systematic review of blockchain scalability: Issues, solutions, analysis and future research. *Journal of Network and Computer Applications, 195*, 103232. DOI: 10.1016/j.jnca.2021.103232

Sargisyan, A. G. (2023). The Harm of Cryptocurrency Mining to the Environment: How Serious is It. In Popkova, E. G., & Sergi, B. S. (Eds.), *Current Problems of the Global Environmental Economy Under the Conditions of Climate Change and the Perspectives of Sustainable Development. Advances in Global Change Research, 73* (pp. 13–21). Springer., DOI: 10.1007/978-3-031-19979-0_2

Sarkodie, S. A., Ahmed, M. Y., & Owusu, P. A. (2022). COVID-19 pandemic improves market signals of cryptocurrencies–evidence from Bitcoin, Bitcoin Cash, Ethereum, and Litecoin. *Finance Research Letters, 44*, 102049. DOI: 10.1016/j.frl.2021.102049 PMID: 35475023

Sarma, M. (2008). Index of financial inclusion. *Working Paper No.215*. Indian Council for Research on International Economic Relations. New Delhi.

Sarmah, S. S. (2018). Understanding blockchain technology. *Computing in Science & Engineering, 8*(2), 23–29. DOI: 10.5923/j.computer.20180802.02

Sas, C., & Khairuddin, I. E. (2019). Risks and Opportunities in the Cryptocurrency Market. Ovidius University Annals. *Economic Sciences Series, 19*(2), 879–883. DOI: 10.1145/2838739.2838821

Schaar, L., & Kampakis, S. (2022). Non-fungible tokens as an alternative investment: Evidence from cryptopunks. *The Journal of The British Blockchain Association*.

Schär, F. (2021). Decentralized Finance: On Blockchain- and Smart Contract-based Financial Markets. *Review - Federal Reserve Bank of St. Louis, 103*(3), 115–136.

Scharfman, J. (2022). Additional Crypto Operations and Compliance Topics. In Scharfman, J. (Ed.), *Cryptocurrency Compliance and Operations* (pp. 205–221). Springer International Publishing., DOI: 10.1007/978-3-030-88000-2_11

Scharfman, J. (2024). Decentralized Finance (DeFi) Fraud and Hacks: Part 3. In Scharfman, J. (Ed.), *The Cryptocurrency and Digital Asset Fraud Casebook* (Vol. II, pp. 159–191). Springer Nature Switzerland., DOI: 10.1007/978-3-031-60836-0_6

Scharnowski, S. (2021). Understanding Bitcoin Liquidity. *Finance Research Letters*, *38*, 101477. DOI: 10.1016/j.frl.2020.101477

Schellinger, B. (2020). Optimization of Special Cryptocurrency Portfolios. *The Journal of Risk Finance*, *21*(2), 127–157. DOI: 10.1108/JRF-11-2019-0221

Schneider, F. (1990). Implementing Fault-Tolerant Services Using the State Machine Approach: A Tutorial. *ACM Computing Surveys*, *22*(4), 299–319. DOI: 10.1145/98163.98167

Schwiderowski, J., Pedersen, A. B., & Beck, R. (2024). Crypto tokens and token systems. *Information Systems Frontiers*, *26*(1), 319–332. DOI: 10.1007/s10796-023-10382-w

Sebastião, H., & Godinho, P. (2020). Bitcoin Futures: An Effective Tool for Hedging Cryptocurrencies. *Finance Research Letters*, *33*, 101230. DOI: 10.1016/j.frl.2019.07.003

Selgin, G. (2015). Synthetic commodity money. *Journal of Financial Stability*, *17*, 92–99. DOI: 10.1016/j.jfs.2014.07.002

Sensoy, A., Silva, T. C., Corbet, S., & Tabak, B. M. (2021). High-Frequency Return and Volatility Spillovers among Cryptocurrencies. *Applied Economics*, *53*(37), 4310–4328. DOI: 10.1080/00036846.2021.1899119

Serena, L., Ferretti, S., & D'Angelo, G. (2022). Cryptocurrencies activity as a complex network: Analysis of transactions graphs. *Peer-to-Peer Networking and Applications*, *15*(2), 839–853. DOI: 10.1007/s12083-021-01220-4

Setyawan, A. A., Winotoatmojo, H. P., & Ananda, N. K. (2024). Cryptocurrency and Financial Inclusion: Bridging the Gap in Emerging Countries. *Dinasti International Journal of Economics. Finance & Accounting*, *5*, 510–516.

Setyawan, A. A., Winotoatmojo, H. P., & Puspa Ananda, N. K. (2024). Cryptocurrency and Financial Inclusion: Bridging the Gap in Emerging Countries. *Dinasti international journal of economics. Finance & accounting*, *5*(2), 510–516. DOI: 10.38035/dijefa.v5i2.2554

Sgroi, D., Proto, E., & Oswald, A. J. (2019). Artificial intelligence and life satisfaction. *Proceedings of the National Academy of Sciences of the United States of America*, *116*(20), 9788–9795.

Shah, A. S., Karabulut, M. A., Akhter, A. S., Mustari, N., Pathan, A. S. K., Rabie, K. M., & Shongwe, T. (2023). On the vital aspects and characteristics of cryptocurrency—A survey. *IEEE Access : Practical Innovations, Open Solutions*, *11*, 9451–9468. DOI: 10.1109/ACCESS.2023.3240103

Shahzad, F., Xiu, G., Wang, J., & Shahbaz, M. (2018). An Empirical Investigation on the Adoption of Cryptocurrencies Among the People of Mainland China. *Technology in Society*, *55*, 33–40. DOI: 10.1016/j.techsoc.2018.05.006

Shanaev, S., Sharma, S., Shuraeva, A., & Ghimire, B. (2020). The marginal cost of mining, Metcalfe's law and cryptocurrency value formation: Causal inferences from the instrumental variable approach. SSRN Electronic Journal. https://doi.org/ DOI: 10.2139/ssrn.3432431

Sharma, D. K., Pant, S., Sharma, M., & Brahmachari, S. (2020). Cryptocurrency Mechanisms for Blockchains: Models, Characteristics, Challenges, and Applications. In Krishnan, S., Balas, V. E., Golden Julie, E., Robinson, Y. H., Balaji, S., & Kumar, R. (Eds.), *Handbook of Research on Blockchain Technology* (pp. 323–348). Academic Press. DOI: 10.1016/B978-0-12-819816-2.00013-7

Sharma, R. K., Khan, S., Singh, R., & Birari, A. (2024). Speculative investment decisions in cryptocurrency: A structural equation modelling approach. *Journal of Decision Systems*, •••, 1–22. DOI: 10.1080/12460125.2024.2410030

Shen, M. (2024). *MicroStrategy Owns About 1% of All Bitcoin With Latest Purchase*. Bloomberg. https://www.bloomberg.com/news/articles/2024-03-19/microstrategy-owns-about-1-of-all-bitcoin-with-latest-purchase-mstr

Shin, D., & Rice, J. (2022). Cryptocurrency: A panacea for economic growth and sustainability? A critical review of crypto innovation. *Telematics and Informatics*, *71*, 101830. DOI: 10.1016/j.tele.2022.101830

Shi, Y., Tiwari, A. K., Gozgor, G., & Lu, Z. (2020). Correlations among Cryptocurrencies: Evidence from Multivariate Factor Stochastic Volatility Model. *Research in International Business and Finance*, *53*, 101231. DOI: 10.1016/j.ribaf.2020.101231

Shukla, S. (2022). UN Says Crypto Use in Terror Financing Likely Soaring. Bloomberg, October 31

Silahli, B., Dingec, K. D., Cifter, A., & Aydin, N. (2021). Portfolio Value-at-Risk with Two-SidedWeibull Distribution: Evidence from Cryptocurrency Markets. *Finance Research Letters*, *38*, 101425. DOI: 10.1016/j.frl.2019.101425

Silfversten, E., Favaro, M., Slapakova, L., Ishikawa, S., Liu, J., & Salas, A. (2020). *Exploring the use of Zcash cryptocurrency for illicit or criminal purposes*. RAND Europe. https://www.rand.org/content/dam/rand/pubs/research_reports/RR4400/RR4418/RAND_RR4418.pdf

Singh, S., Hosen, A. S., & Yoon, B. (2021). Blockchain security attacks, challenges, and solutions for the future distributed iot network. *IEEE Access : Practical Innovations, Open Solutions*, *9*, 13938–13959. DOI: 10.1109/ACCESS.2021.3051602

Singh, S., Singh, M., & Attri, S. (2025a). Mapping stock market dynamics: A tripartite neural network approach using modified grid search for stock market prediction. *Expert Systems with Applications*, *278*(February), 127243. https://doi.org/10.1016/j.eswa.2025.127243

Singh, S., Singh, M., & Attri, S. (2025b). Dynamic volatility linkages among crude oil, exchange rate, interest rate, gold and equity markets: An empirical Asian perspective. *Managerial Finance*. Advance online publication. DOI: 10.1108/MF-01-2025-0016

Sisodia, H. (2024). Case Study on the Sand Dollar CBDC of the Bahamas: Lessons, Challenges, and Insights. In Kaur, G., Lekhi, P., & Popli, S. (Eds.), *Exploring Central Bank Digital Currencie: Concepts, Frameworks, Models and Challenges* (pp. 298–314). IGI Global. DOI: 10.4018/979-8-3693-1882-9.ch018

Smales, L. A. (2022). Cryptocurrency as an alternative inflation hedge? *Accounting and Finance*.

Smutny, Z., Sulc, Z., & Lansky, J. (2021). Motivations, barriers and risk-taking when investing in cryptocurrencies. *Mathematics*, *9*(14), 1–22. DOI: 10.3390/math9141655

Soltani, R., Zaman, M., Sampalli, S., & Joshi, R. (2022). Distributed Ledger Technologies and Their Applications: A Review. *Applied Sciences (Basel, Switzerland)*, *12*(15), 7898. DOI: 10.3390/app12157898

Sommer, R., & Paxson, V. (2010). Outside the Closed World: On Using Machine Learning for Network Intrusion Detection. *2010 IEEE Symposium on Security and Privacy*, 305-316. DOI: 10.1109/SP.2010.25

Soufaih, A. (2020). *Revolutionizing International Remittance Payments Using Cryptocurrency and Blockchain-based Technology Cryptocurrency and Blockchain-based Technology*. https://repository.upenn.edu/server/api/core/bitstreams/f4a63a05-8edf-4113-a9c2-e84797629a48/content

Sovbetov, Y. (2018). Factors influencing cryptocurrency prices: Evidence from bitcoin, ethereum, dash, litcoin, and monero. *Journal of Economics and Financial Analysis*, *2*(2), 1–27. DOI: 10.1991/jefa.v2i2.a16

Staff, C. (2024). *The Early Days of Crypto Exchanges*. Gemini. https://www.gemini.com/cryptopedia/crypto-exchanges-early-mt-gox-hack

Stinchcombe, A. L. (1965). Social structure and organizations. In March, J. (Ed.), *Handbook of Organizations* (pp. 142–193). Rand McNally.

Stosic, D., Ludermir, T. B., & Stosic, T. (2019). Exploring disorder and complexity in the cryptocurrency space. *Physica A*, *525*, 548–556. DOI: 10.1016/j.physa.2019.03.091

Stoyanova, M., Nikoloudakis, Y., Panagiotakis, S., Pallis, E., & Markakis, E. (2020). A Survey on the Internet of Things (IoT) Forensics: Challenges, Approaches, and Open Issues. *IEEE Communications Surveys and Tutorials*, *22*(2), 1191–1221. DOI: 10.1109/COMST.2019.2962586

Stuurman, K., & Lachaud, E. (2022). Regulating AI. A label to complete the proposed Act on Artificial Intelligence. *Computer Law & Security Review*, *44*, 105657. DOI: 10.1016/j.clsr.2022.105657

Stylianou, K., Spiegelberg, L., Herlihy, M., & Carter, N. (2021). Cryptocurrency competition and market concentration in the presence of network effects. *Ledger*, *6*, 1–20. DOI: 10.5195/ledger.2021.226

Su, J. (2023). Redirecting the herd: Informing cryptocurrency regulations through the lens of behavioral science. *Hastings Sci. & Tech. LJ*, *14*, 123.

Sukumar, S. (2023). Digital Forensics in The Dark. https://www.linkedin.com/pulse/digital-forensics-dark-sandhya-sukumar/

Sukumaran, S., Bee, T. S., & Wasiuzzaman, S. (2022). Cryptocurrency as an Investment: The Malaysian Context. *Risks*, *10*(4), 86. Advance online publication. DOI: 10.3390/risks10040086

Sumanov, V., & Polanski, S. (2023). Token Classification Framework by Consideration of Origins of Value and Mechanisms of Manifestation Thereof. Retrieved September 20, 2023, from https://github.com/powerpool-finance/powerpool-research/blob/main/Papers/Value_Capturing_Mechanisms_.pdf

Sun, X., Liu, M., & Sima, Z. (2020). A Novel Cryptocurrency Price Trend Forecasting Model Based on LightGBM. *Finance Research Letters*, *32*, 101084. DOI: 10.1016/j.frl.2018.12.032

Suratkar, S., Shirole, M., & Bhirud, S. (2020, September). Cryptocurrency wallet: A review. In *2020 4th international conference on computer, communication and signal processing (ICCCSP)* (pp. 1-7). IEEE. DOI: 10.1109/ICCCSP49186.2020.9315193

Surjandy, F., I. P., & Heykal, M. (2024). The Impact of Government Support Factor on The Use of Cryptocurrency. *2024 International Conference on ICT for Smart Society (ICISS)*, 1–6. DOI: 10.1109/ICISS62896.2024.10751216

Suryawanshi, S., Katkar, T., Ghute, Y., Kawase, P., & Sharma, P. (2023). Detection of Cyber Attacks and Network Attacks Using Machine Learning Algorithms. *Proceeding International Conference on Science and Engineering*. DOI: 10.52783/cienceng.v11i1.120

Su, T., Sun, H., Zhu, J., Wang, S., & Li, Y. (2020). BAT: Deep Learning Methods on Network Intrusion Detection Using NSL-KDD Dataset. *IEEE Access : Practical Innovations, Open Solutions*, *8*, 29575–29585. DOI: 10.1109/ACCESS.2020.2972627

Sutton, R. I. (1987). The Process of Organizational Death: Disbanding and Reconnecting. *Administrative Science Quarterly*, *32*(4), 542–569. DOI: 10.2307/2392883

Swaminathan, A., & Ramakrishnan, B., M, K., & R, S., (2022). Prediction of Cyberattacks and Criminality Using Machine Learning Algorithms. *2022 International Conference on Innovation and Intelligence for Informatics, Computing, and Technologies (3ICT)*, pp. 547-552. DOI: 10.1109/3ICT56508.2022.9990652

Swan, M. (2015). *Blockchain: Blueprint for a new economy*. O'Reilly Media.

Swati, J., Nitin, P., Saurabh, P., Parikshit, D., Gitesh, P., & Rahul, S. (2022). Blockchain based Trusted Secure Philanthropy Platform: Crypto-GoCharity. *6th International Conference on Computing, Communication, Control and Automation (ICCUBEA)*. Pune, India. DOI: 10.1109/ICCUBEA54992.2022.10011026

Taleby Ahvanooey, M., Zhu, M. X., Mazurczyk, W., Kilger, M., & Choo, K. K. R. (2021, December). Do dark web and cryptocurrencies empower cybercriminals? In *International Conference on Digital Forensics and Cyber Crime* (pp. 277-293). Cham: Springer International Publishing.

Tapscott, A., & Tapscott, D. (2016). *Blockchain Revolution: How The Technology beyond Bitcoin is changing Money*. Business, and the World, Portfolio Penguin.

Tapscott, A., & Tapscott, D. (2017). How blockchain is changing finance. *Harvard Business Review*, *1*(9), 2–5.

Tauda, G. A., Omara, A., & Arnone, G. (2023). Cryptocurrency: Highlighting the Approach, Regulations, and Protection in Indonesia and European Union. *Bestuur*, *11*(1), 1–25. DOI: 10.20961/bestuur.v11i1.67125

Tavares, Ricardo de Souza, João Frois Caldeira, and Gerson de Souza Raimundo Júnior. 2020. It's All in the Timing Again: Simple Active Portfolio Strategies That Outperform Naïve Diversification in the Cryptocurrency Market. Applied Economics Letters 29: 118–22.

Tayebi, S., & Amini, H. (2024). The flip side of the coin: Exploring the environmental and health impacts of proof-of-work cryptocurrency mining. *Environmental Research*, *252*, 118798. DOI: 10.1016/j.envres.2024.118798 PMID: 38555086

Thampanya, N., Nasir, M. A., & Toan, L. D. H. (2020). Asymmetric Correlation and Hedging Effectiveness of Gold & Cryptocurrencies: From Pre-Industrial to the 4th Industrial Revolution. *Technological Forecasting and Social Change*, *159*, 120195. DOI: 10.1016/j.techfore.2020.120195 PMID: 32834136

Thiveaud, J. M. (1999). Between myth and history, from electronic money to electronic wallets, e-cash, digicash, e-business.... *Revue d'Economie Financiere*, (53), 197–213.

Tolossa, D., and Khawrin, M. (2022). The opportunities and challenges of cryptocurrencies: a systematic review. Vidya-A journal of gujarat university, *1*(1), 48-53.

Tomić, N. (2020b). *Organizacija savremenog platnog prometa*. Kragujevac: Ekonomski fakultet Univerziteta u Kragujevcu

Tomić, N., Todorović, V., & Jakšić, M. (2017). Misuses of electronic payment systems, Contemporary Issues in Economics, Business and Management - EBM 2016, Stojanović-Aleksić, V. (ed.), Faculty of Economics University of Kragujevac, 245-253

Tomić, N., & Todorović, V. (2018). Challenges of transition to cashless society. In Babić, V. (Ed.), *Contemporary issues in Economics, business and management – EBM 2018* [proceedings of the international scientific conference]. Faculty of Economics.

Tran, A. B., Ouyang, M., Ma, X., & Yuan, M. L. (2019). Blockchain for IoT: The challenges and opportunities. *IEEE Internet of Things Journal*, *6*(2), 2521–2540.

Tran, V. D., Ata, S., Tran, T. H., Lam, D. K., & Pham, H. L. (2023). CrowdFund: CrowdFunding decentralized implementation on Ethereum blockchain. *Sustainability*, *15*(21), 15545. DOI: 10.3390/su152115545

Tredinnick, L. (2019). Cryptocurrencies and the blockchain. *Business Information Review*, *36*(1), 39–44. DOI: 10.1177/0266382119836314

Trucíos, C., Tiwari, A. K., & Alqahtani, F. (2020). Value-at-Risk and Expected Shortfall in Cryptocurrencies' Portfolio: A Vine Copula–Based Approach. *Applied Economics*, *52*(24), 2580–2593. DOI: 10.1080/00036846.2019.1693023

Tsuchiya, Y., & Hiramoto, N. (2021). How cryptocurrency is laundered: Case study of Coincheck hacking incident. *Forensic Science International. Reports*, *4*, 100241. DOI: 10.1016/j.fsir.2021.100241

Two Sigma. (2021). Risk analysis of crypto assets. https://www.twosigma.com/articles/risk-analysis-of-crypto-assets/

Tziakouris, G. (2018). Cryptocurrencies—A forensic challenge or opportunity for law enforcement? An Interpol perspective. *IEEE Security and Privacy*, *16*(4), 92–94. DOI: 10.1109/MSP.2018.3111243

U.S. Department of the Treasury. (2022). *Crypto-Assets: Implications for Consumers, Investors, and Businesses*. U.S. Department of the Treasury. https://home.treasury.gov/system/files/136/CryptoAsset_EO5.pdf

Ujjawal, A. (2024). *How does the Blockchain Work?* Geeksforgeeks. https://www.geeksforgeeks.org/how-does-the-blockchain-work/

Ulaşan, F. (2022). The Environmental Effects of Cryptocurrency Mining in the World. *Journal of Sustainable Economics and Management Studies*, *3*(1), 1–20.

Ullah, S., Attah-Boakye, R., Adams, K., & Zaefarian, G. (2022). Assessing the influence of celebrity and government endorsements on bitcoin's price volatility. *Journal of Business Research*, *145*, 228–239. DOI: 10.1016/j.jbusres.2022.01.055

Umar, M., Chi, W. S., Syed, K. A. R., & Xue, F. S. (2021). Bitcoin: A Safe Haven Asset and a Winner amid Political and Economic Uncertainties in the US? *Technological Forecasting and Social Change*, *167*, 120680. DOI: 10.1016/j.techfore.2021.120680

Umar, Z., & Gubareva, M. (2020). A Time–Frequency Analysis of the Impact of the Covid-19 Induced Panic on the Volatility of Currency and Cryptocurrency Markets. *Journal of Behavioral and Experimental Finance*, *28*, 100404. DOI: 10.1016/j.jbef.2020.100404 PMID: 32983899

Umar, Z., Jareño, F., & González, M. O. (2021). The Impact of COVID-19-Related Media Coverage on the Return and Volatility Connectedness of Cryptocurrencies and Fiat Currencies. *Technological Forecasting and Social Change*, *172*, 121025. DOI: 10.1016/j.techfore.2021.121025 PMID: 34658451

United Nations Development Programme. (2019). "Blockchain and Distributed Ledger Technology in the UN System." UNDP Report.

Urom, C., Abid, I., Guesmi, K., & Chevallier, J. (2020). Quantile Spillovers and Dependence between Bitcoin, Equities and Strategic Commodities. *Economic Modelling*, *93*, 230–258. DOI: 10.1016/j.econmod.2020.07.012

Urquhart, A. (2016). The inefficiency of Bitcoin. *Economics Letters, 148*, 80–82. DOI: 10.1016/j.econlet.2016.09.019

Uzougbo, N. S., Ikegwu, C. G., & Adewusi, A. O. (2024). International enforcement of cryptocurrency laws: jurisdictional challenges and collaborative solutions. *Magna Scientia Advanced Research and Reviews, 11*(1), 068-083.

Uzougbo, N. S., Ikegwu, C. G., & Adewusi, A. O.Ngozi Samuel UzougboChinonso Gladys IkegwuAdefolake Olachi Adewusi. (2024). Enhancing consumer protection in cryptocurrency transactions: Legal strategies and policy recommendations. *International Journal of Science and Research Archive*, *12*(01), 520–532. DOI: 10.30574/ijsra.2024.12.1.0801

Valeonti, F., Bikakis, A., Terras, M., Speed, C., Hudson-Smith, A., & Chalkias, K. (2021). Crypto Collectibles, Museum Funding and OpenGLAM: Challenges, Opportunities and the Potential of Non-Fungible Tokens (NFTs). *Applied Sciences (Basel, Switzerland), 11*(21), 9931. DOI: 10.3390/app11219931

van der Linden, T., & Shirazi, T. (2023). Markets in crypto-assets regulation: Does it provide legal certainty and increase adoption of crypto-assets? *Financial Innovation*, *9*(1), 22. DOI: 10.1186/s40854-022-00432-8 PMID: 36643685

Van Eck, N. J., & Waltman, L. (2017). Citation-based clustering of publications using CitNetExplorer and VOSviewer. [PubMed]. *Scientometrics*, *111*(2), 1053–1070. DOI: 10.1007/s11192-017-2300-7 PMID: 28490825

Van Hout, M. C., & Bingham, T. (2013). „Silk Road“, the virtual drug marketplace: A single case study of user experience. *The International Journal on Drug Policy*, *24*(5), 385–391. DOI: 10.1016/j.drugpo.2013.01.005 PMID: 23465646

Vasishth, S., Sharma, S. K., Nayyar, A. K., & Vijayakuamar, K. (2023). Impact of Elon Musk's tweets on the price of Dogecoin using Sentiment Analysis. *2023 International Conference on Advances in Computing, Communication and Applied Informatics (ACCAI)*, 1–8. DOI: 10.1109/ACCAI58221.2023.10199593

Venčkauskas, A., Grigaliūnas, Š., Pocius, L., Brūzgienė, R., & Romānovs, A. (2025). Machine Learning in Money Laundering Detection Over Blockchain Technology. *IEEE Access : Practical Innovations, Open Solutions*, *13*, 7555–7573. DOI: 10.1109/ACCESS.2024.3452003

Verma, K., & Jain, A. (2022). *What Is Digital Rupee? How Is It Different From Cryptocurrency?* Forbes Advisor.

Vinayakumar, R., Alazab, M., Soman, K., Poornachandran, P., Al-Nemrat, A., & Venkatraman, S. (2019). Deep Learning Approach for Intelligent Intrusion Detection System. *IEEE Access : Practical Innovations, Open Solutions*, *7*, 41525–41550. DOI: 10.1109/ACCESS.2019.2895334

Viroonluecha, P., & Kaewkiriya, T. (2018). Salary Predictor System for Thailand Labour Workforce using Deep Learning. DOI: 10.1109/ISCIT.2018.8587998

Vo, Au, Thomas A. Chapman, and Yen Sheng Lee. 2021. Examining Bitcoin and Economic Determinants: An Evolutionary Perspective. Journal of Computer Information Systems 62: 572–86.

Voshmgir, S., & Zargham, M. (2020). Foundations of Cryptoeconomic Systems. WU Vienna University of Economics and Business. Working Paper Series / Institute for Cryptoeconomics / Interdisciplinary Research No. 1.

Voshmgir, S. (2020). *Token Economy: How the Web3 reinvents the internet* (Vol. 2). Token Kitchen.

Vranken, H. (2017). Sustainability of bitcoin and blockchains. *Current Opinion in Environmental Sustainability*, *28*, 1–9. DOI: 10.1016/j.cosust.2017.04.011

Vukolić, M. (2017). Rethinking permissioned blockchains. In *Proceedings of the ACM Workshop on Blockchain, Cryptocurrencies and Contracts* (pp. 3-7). ACM. DOI: 10.1145/3055518.3055526

Walker, C. B. (2024). Going mainstream: Cryptocurrency narratives in newspapers. *International Review of Financial Analysis*, *94*, 103305. DOI: 10.1016/j.irfa.2024.103305

Wallace, B. 2011, "The Rise and Fall of Bitcoin," Wired, November 23, retrieved at https://www.wired.com/magazine/2011/11/mf_bitcoin

Waller, J. (2022). The US Dollar and Central Bank Digital Currencies, October, https://www.federalreserve.gov/newsevents/speech/waller20221014a.htm

Walton, A., & Johnston, K. (2018). *Exploring Perceptions Of Bitcoin Adoption : The South African Virtual Community Perspective*. 165–182. DOI: 10.28945/4080

Wang, Y., & Li, X. (2023). Privacy-Preserving Crypto Wallets for Enhanced Transaction Anonymity, arXiv preprint arXiv:2303.12940

Wang, G. J., Ma, X., & Wu, H. (2020). Are Stablecoins Truly Diversifiers, Hedges, or Safe Havens against Traditional Cryptocurrencies as Their Name Suggests? *Research in International Business and Finance*, *54*, 101225. DOI: 10.1016/j.ribaf.2020.101225

Wang, G. J., Xie, C., Wen, D., & Zhao, L. (2019). When Bitcoin Meets Economic Policy Uncertainty (EPU): Measuring Risk Spillover Effect from EPU to Bitcoin. *Finance Research Letters*, *31*, 489–497. DOI: 10.1016/j.frl.2018.12.028

Wang, H., & Gao, S. (2024). The future of the international financial system: The emerging CBDC network and its impact on regulation. *Regulation & Governance*, *18*(1), 288–306. DOI: 10.1111/rego.12520

Wang, J., Ma, F., Bouri, E., & Guo, Y. (2022). Which Factors Drive Bitcoin Volatility: Macroeconomic, Technical, or Both? *Journal of Forecasting*, •••, 1–19.

Wang, J.-N., Liu, H.-C., Lee, Y.-H., & Hsu, Y.-T. (2023). FoMO in the Bitcoin market: Revisiting and factors. *The Quarterly Review of Economics and Finance*, *89*, 244–253. DOI: 10.1016/j.qref.2023.04.007

Wang, J., & Ngene, G. M. (2020). Does Bitcoin Still Own the Dominant Power? An Intraday Analysis. *International Review of Financial Analysis*, *71*, 101551. DOI: 10.1016/j.irfa.2020.101551

Wang, P., Li, X., Shen, D., & Zhang, W. (2020). How Does Economic Policy Uncertainty Affect the Bitcoin Market? *Research in International Business and Finance*, *53*, 101234. DOI: 10.1016/j.ribaf.2020.101234

Wang, P., Zhang, H., Yang, C., & Guo, Y. (2021). Time and Frequency Dynamics of Connectedness and Hedging Performance in Global Stock Markets: Bitcoin versus Conventional Hedges. *Research in International Business and Finance*, *58*, 101479. DOI: 10.1016/j.ribaf.2021.101479

Wang, X., & Hui, X. (2024). Price-Volume Relationship in Bitcoin Futures ETF Market: An Information Perspective. *Discrete Dynamics in Nature and Society*, *2024*(1), 1–14. DOI: 10.1155/2024/8066742

Wang, Y., Xu, J., & Chen, B. (2022). "Duino Coin Mining Algorithm Analysis and Improvement," in *International Conference on High Performance Computing and Communications*, Springer, Cham, pp. 146-157.

Wang, Y., Xu, J., & Chen, B. (2022). Security Analysis of Duino Coin Smart Contracts. *International Journal of Software Engineering and Knowledge Engineering*, *32*(10), 1435–1457.

Ward, S. V. (2023, December 23). Bitcoin Fees Surge Reinforcing The Network's Antifragility. *Forbes*.

Ward, S. V. (2024, February 5). El Salvador Embraces Future With Bitcoin As Bukele Secures Historic Victory. *Forbes*.

Wasiuzzaman, S., & Pg Hj Ahmad, A. M. S. L. (2025). Perception towards government advisory, perceived risk and willingness to invest in cryptocurrency. *Journal of Economics and Business, 133*, 106208. DOI: 10.1016/j.jeconbus.2024.106208

Wątorek, M., Drożdż, S., Kwapień, J., Minati, L., Oświęcimka, P., & Stanuszek, M. (2021). Multiscale characteristics of the emerging global cryptocurrency market. *Physics Reports, 901*, 1–82. DOI: 10.1016/j.physrep.2020.10.005

Weatherford, J. (1997). *The history of money*. Crown Publisher Inc.

Weatherford, J. (1997). *The History of Money. From Sandstone to Cyberspace*. Crown Publishers.

Weber, M., Domeniconi, G., Chen, J., Weidele, D. K. I., Bellei, C., Robinson, T., & Leiserson, C. E. 2019. Anti-money laundering in bitcoin: Experimenting with graph convolutional networks for financial forensics. *arXiv preprint arXiv:1908.02591.*

Weber, I., Zhu, L., & Schmidt, C. (2016). A Data-Centric Perspective on Business Process Management in the Cloud. *Future Generation Computer Systems.*

Wendl, M., Doan, M. D., & Sassen, R. (2023). The environmental impact of cryptocurrencies using proof of work and proof of stake consensus algorithms: A systematic review. *Journal of Environmental Management, 326*, 116530. DOI: 10.1016/j.jenvman.2022.116530 PMID: 36372031

White, L. H. (2015). The market for cryptocurrencies. *The Cato Journal, 35*, 383.

Wilmott, P. (1998). *Derivatives: the theory and practice of financial engineering*. No Title.

Winnowicz, K., Au, C. D., & Stein, D. (2021). Crypto Regulation within the European Union. *Available atSSRN* 4194771.

Wiwoho, J., Trinugroho, I., Kharisma, D. B., & Suwadi, P. (2024). Islamic crypto assets and regulatory framework: Evidence from Indonesia and global approaches. *International Journal of Law and Management, 66*(2), 155–171. DOI: 10.1108/IJLMA-03-2023-0051

Woebbeking, F. (2021). Cryptocurrency volatility markets. *Digital Finance, 3*(3), 273–298. DOI: 10.1007/s42521-021-00037-3 PMID: 34368626

World Bank. (2018). "Remittance Prices Worldwide." World Bank Report.

World Bank. (2024, June 26). *Remittances Slowed in 2023, Expected to Grow Faster in 2024.*https://www.worldbank.org/en/news/press-release/2024/06/26/remittances-slowed-in-2023-expected-to-grow-faster-in-2024

Wronka, C. (2024). Crypto-asset activities and markets in the European Union: Issues, challenges and considerations for regulation, supervision and oversight. *Journal of Banking Regulation*, *25*(1), 84–93. DOI: 10.1057/s41261-023-00217-8

Wu, A. A., & Katz, J. (2023). *Competition and Speculation in Cryptocurrencies*. https://www.hbs.edu/ris/Publication%20Files/competition_speculation_78d8a8a7-4a79-4fc4-af7a-7c2a361fc80a.pdf

Wu, J. (2021). *Essays on Bitcoin and Cryptocurrencies*. https://scholarworks.wmich.edu/dissertations/3812

Wu, B., & Wu, B. (2023). Bitcoin: The Future of Money. In Wu, B., & Wu, B. (Eds.), *Blockchain for Teens* (pp. 77–134). Apress., DOI: 10.1007/978-1-4842-8808-5_3

Wu, C., Pandey, V., & Dba, C. (2014). The value of Bitcoin in enhancing the efficiency of an investor's portfolio. *Journal of Financial Planning*, *27*(9), 44–52.

Wu, R., Ishfaq, K., Hussain, S., Asmi, F., Siddiquei, A. N., & Anwar, M. A. (2022). Investigating e-Retailers' Intentions to Adopt Cryptocurrency Considering the Mediation of Technostress and Technology Involvement. *Sustainability (Basel)*, *14*(2), 641. Advance online publication. DOI: 10.3390/su14020641

Wu, W., Tiwari, A. K., Gozgor, G., & Huang, L. (2021). Does Economic Policy Uncertainty Affect Cryptocurrency Markets? Evidence from Twitter-Based Uncertainty Measures. *Research in International Business and Finance*, *58*, 101478. DOI: 10.1016/j.ribaf.2021.101478

Xiao, Z., Cui, S., Xiang, L., Liu, P. J., & He Zhang, H. (2023). The environmental cost of cryptocurrency: Assessing carbon emissions from bitcoin mining in China. *Journal of Digital Economy*, *2*, 119–136. DOI: 10.1016/j.jdec.2023.11.001

Xiong, X., & Luo, J. (2024). In Leonardos, S., Alfieri, E., Knottenbelt, W. J., & Pardalos, P. (Eds.), *Global Trends in Cryptocurrency Regulation: An Overview* (pp. 71–92). Springer Nature Switzerland., DOI: 10.1007/978-3-031-68974-1_4

Xu, J., & Feng, Y. (2023). Reap the Harvest on Blockchain: A Survey of Yield Farming Protocols. *IEEE Transactions on Network and Service Management*, *20*(1), 858–869. DOI: 10.1109/TNSM.2022.3222815

Xu, Q., Zhang, Y., & Zhang, Z. (2021). Tail-Risk Spillovers in Cryptocurrency Markets. *Finance Research Letters*, *38*, 101453. DOI: 10.1016/j.frl.2020.101453

Xu, X., Weber, I., Staples, M., Zhu, L., Bosch, J., Bass, L., Pautasso, C., & Rimba, P. (2017). A Taxonomy of Blockchain-Based Systems for Architecture Design. *2017 IEEE International Conference on Software Architecture (ICSA)*, 243–252. DOI: 10.1109/ICSA.2017.33

Yadav, S. P., Agrawal, K. K., Bhati, B. S., Al-Turjman, F., & Mostarda, L. (2022). Blockchain-based cryptocurrency regulation: An overview. *Computational Economics, 59*(4), 1659–1675. DOI: 10.1007/s10614-020-10050-0

Yaga, D., Mell, P., Roby, N., & Scarfone, K. (2019). Blockchain technology overview. *arXiv preprint arXiv:1906.11078.*

Yang, B., Sun, Y., & Wang, S. (2020). A Novel Two-Stage Approach for Cryptocurrency Analysis. *International Review of Financial Analysis, 72*, 101567. DOI: 10.1016/j.irfa.2020.101567

Yang, L., & Hamori, S. (2021). The Role of the Carbon Market in Relation to the Cryptocurrency Market: Only Diversification or More? *International Review of Financial Analysis, 77*, 101864. DOI: 10.1016/j.irfa.2021.101864

Yan, Y., Lei, Y., & Wang, Y. (2022). Bitcoin as a Safe-Haven Asset and a Medium of Exchange. *Axioms, 11*(8), 415. DOI: 10.3390/axioms11080415

Yao, S., Sensòy, A., Nguyen, D. K., & Li, T. (2024). Investor attention and cryptocurrency market liquidity: A double-edged sword. *Annals of Operations Research, 334*(1–3), 815–856. DOI: 10.1007/s10479-022-04915-w

Yen, K.-C., & Cheng, H.-P. (2021). Economic policy uncertainty and cryptocurrency volatility. *Finance Research Letters, 38*, 101428. DOI: 10.1016/j.frl.2020.101428

Yermack, D. (2015). Is Bitcoin a real currency? An economic appraisal. *Handbook of Digital Currency*, 31-43.

Yi, S., Xu, Z., & Wang, G. J. (2018). Volatility connectedness in the cryptocurrency market: Is Bitcoin a dominant cryptocurrency? *International Review of Financial Analysis, 60*, 98–114. DOI: 10.1016/j.irfa.2018.08.012

Yli-Huumo, J., Ko, D., Choi, S., Park, S., & Smolander, K. (2016). Where is current research on blockchain technology?—A systematic review. *PLoS One, 11*(10), e0163477. DOI: 10.1371/journal.pone.0163477 PMID: 27695049

Yue, Y., Li, X., Zhang, D., & Wang, S. (2021). How Cryptocurrency Affects Economy? A Network Analysis Using Bibliometric Methods. *International Review of Financial Analysis, 77*, 101869. DOI: 10.1016/j.irfa.2021.101869

Zarotiadis, G. (2014). Relieving Inflation or Palliative Self-destruction? *Journal of Stock & Forex Trading*, *3*(4), 4. DOI: 10.4172/2168-9458.1000133

Zarotiadis, G. (2023). Guilt Economics: Rediscovering the Civilizing Process. In *Handbook of Research on Socio-Economic Sustainability in the Post-Pandemic Era*. IGI Global., DOI: 10.4018/978-1-7998-9760-6.ch017

Zeng, H., & Ahmed, A. D. (2023). Market integration and volatility spillover across major East Asian stock and Bitcoin markets: An empirical assessment. *International Journal of Managerial Finance*, *19*(4), 772–802. DOI: 10.1108/IJMF-03-2021-0161

Zeng, T., Yang, M., & Shen, Y. (2020). Fancy Bitcoin and Conventional Financial Assets: Measuring Market Integration Based on Connectedness Networks. *Economic Modelling*, *90*, 209–220. DOI: 10.1016/j.econmod.2020.05.003

Zetzsche, D. A., Buckley, R. P., Arner, D. W., Didenko, A. N., & van Romburg, L. J. (2020). Sovereign digital currencies: The future of money and payments? University of Hong Kong Faculty of Law Research Paper, (2020/053), 23-30.

Zhang, D., Sun, Y., Duan, H., Hong, Y., & Wang, S. (2023). Speculation or currency? Multi-scale analysis of cryptocurrencies -The case of Bitcoin. *International Review of Financial Analysis*, *88*, 102700. DOI: 10.1016/j.irfa.2023.102700

Zhang, G. P. (2019). *Neural networks for time series forecasting with r: An intuitive step by step blueprint for beginners*. Createspace Independent Publishing Platform.

Zhang, P., Xu, K., & Qi, J. (2023). The impact of regulation on cryptocurrency market volatility in the context of the COVID-19 pandemic—Evidence from China. *Economic Analysis and Policy*, *80*, 222–246. DOI: 10.1016/j.eap.2023.08.015

Zhang, S., & Gregoriou, A. (2021). Cryptocurrencies in Portfolios: Return–Liquidity Trade-off around China Forbidding Initial Coin Offerings. *Applied Economics Letters*, *28*(12), 1–5. DOI: 10.1080/13504851.2020.1796908

Zhang, W., & Li, Y. (2020). Is Idiosyncratic Volatility Priced in Cryptocurrency Markets? *Research in International Business and Finance*, *54*, 101252. DOI: 10.1016/j.ribaf.2020.101252

Zhang, X., Li, Y., & Wang, Y. (2022). Duino Coin Mining Hardware Design and Optimization. *Journal of Low Power Electronics and Applications*, *12*(4), 34.

Zhang, X., Li, Y., & Wang, Y. (2023). Economic Analysis of Duino Coin Mining Profitability. *Journal of Financial Technology*, *12*(3), 182–201.

Zhang, Y., Wen, Y., Chen, Y., & Li, J. (2019). Blockchain based cloud manufacturing: A case study of 3D printing service. *Robotics and Computer-integrated Manufacturing*, *56*, 335–344.

Zhao, K., Huang, C., & Zhang, W. (2021). "Market Data Analysis and Prediction for Optimal Coin Switching," arXiv preprint arXiv:2106.12961, 2021.

Zhao, Y., Sun, J., & Li, X. (2021). "Security Analysis of Duino Coin Mining Protocols," in *Proceedings of the 2021 IEEE International Conference on Blockchain and Cryptocurrency (ICBC)*, IEEE, 2021, pp. 1-7.

Zhao, K., Dong, G., & Bian, D. (2023). Detection of Illegal Transactions of Cryptocurrency Based on Mutual Information. *Electronics (Basel)*, *12*(7), 1542. Advance online publication. DOI: 10.3390/electronics12071542

Zheng, Z., Xie, S., Dai, H., Chen, X., & Wang, H. (2017). An Overview of Blockchain Technology: Architecture, Consensus, and Future Trends. *2017 IEEE International Congress on Big Data (BigData Congress)*, 557–564. DOI: 10.1109/BigDataCongress.2017.85

Zheng, Z., Xie, S., Dai, H.-N., Chen, W., Chen, X., Weng, J., & Imran, M. (2020). An Overview on Smart Contracts: Challenges, Advances and Platforms. *Future Generation Computer Systems*, *105*, 475–491. DOI: 10.1016/j.future.2019.12.019

Zhou, X., Liang, W., Shimizu, S., Ma, J., & Jin, Q. (2021). Siamese Neural Network Based Few-Shot Learning for Anomaly Detection in Industrial Cyber-Physical Systems. *IEEE Transactions on Industrial Informatics*, *17*(8), 5790–5798. DOI: 10.1109/TII.2020.3047675

Zhuk, A. (2024). Crypto-anarchy: a paradigm shift for society and the legal system. *Journal of Computer Virology and Hacking Techniques*, https://doi.org/.DOI: 10.1007/s11416-024-00525-1

Zohren, S., & Roberts, S. (2018). Blockchain for financial market infrastructures. *Annual Review of Financial Economics*, *10*(1), 311–328.

About the Contributors

Eduardo Tome B Econ, M Econ, PhD is an active researcher and teacher in the domain of the economics of human resources. He also plays an important role in the network of research active European academics in his field of study. To date he has had 64 papers published in peer-reviewed journals which he has authored or co-authored and 116 papers in peer-reviewed conference proceedings. He has also authored 15 book chapters. He has co-edited two books in IGI, He is a member of the Editorial Board of several peer-reviewed Journals. He has received several Honours, among two Prizes for Scientific Achievement. Eduardo Tome teaches a variety of subjects on both undergraduate and post graduate programs. He is also active as a supervisor where he works with undergraduates, master students and PhD students. He is noted for his success with both masters and doctoral students. He also lectures on a PhD programme. He is equally comfortable teaching in both Portuguese and English. He can also speak, read and write in French and Spanish. Long before Covid-19 he used online platforms (emails, Moodle, Blackboard, Skype, etc) as a complementary form of communication with students and colleagues, a situation that has been made essential after the pandemic. Eduardo Tome has a significant presence among the academic community in general and especially those interested in intangibles. Since 2009, he has organized well-attended international conferences for his university on themes such as knowledge management, human resource development, and intellectual capital. With friends he created the TAKE conference, which has been held every year since 2016., with the exception of 2020. The conferences enlarged the external focus and international relationships of his activities. All conferences resulted in spin-offs such as special issues of journals. These event have brought both prestige and financial rewards to the university . Currently he is a member of GOVCOPP of UnIversidade de Aveiro, Intrepid of UTAD and teaches at Univerisidade Lusofona

***

Arohi Anand's educational background includes a Ph.D. in Economics, which she completed in 2022 at Patna University. Her doctoral thesis, titled "Analyzing Financial Market Volatility (2000-2010): A Case Study of India," demonstrates her expertise in the field. She also obtained her Master of Arts (M.A.) degree in Economics from Patna University in 2013, specializing in Monetary Economics at Magadh Mahila College in Patna. In addition to her academic pursuits, Dr. Arohi Anand has made significant contributions to the field through her published works. She has authored several books, including "An Introduction to Applied Mathematics for Economics," "Decisions that Changed India," "Transforming Indian Economy," "Economics for Managers," "Principles of Business Economics," and "The Tech Side of Money: An Introduction to the World of FinTech." These publications have been released by renowned publishing houses such as Kindle Publishing, Notion Press, and Cogent Publishing, and they cover a wide range of economic topics.

Manmeet Kaur Arora is a Research Scholar at the School of Law, Sharda University, Greater Noida. She is a graduate of Law and has completed her Master's in Law from Amity University, Noida. Manmeet Kaur is a qualified Company Secretary Executive Programme. She has over 8+ years of Industry Experience and 1 year of experience as an Associate at a reputed IPR Law Firm. Manmeet Kaur has attended 20+ National & International Conferences, Webinars, Seminars, Symposiums, and Paper Presentations and participated in 5+ Faculty Development programs. She has over 50+ publications in various esteemed Journals and Books. She is active at the Family Dispute Resolution Clinic, Meditation Centre, Greater Noida. Manmeet Kaur has a keen interest in the areas of Corporate Law, Intellectual Property Rights, Insolvency, Artificial Intelligence, Machine Learning, and Blockchain Technology.

Shradha Attri, a Research Scholar at the Central University of Himachal Pradesh, is pursuing a Ph.D. in Finance. Her research interests lie in Decentralized Finance, Cryptocurrency, Blockchain, Forecasting, Econometrics Modelling, Time Series Analysis, and Behavioral Finance, Shradha's research aligns at the intersection of finance and emerging technologies. Her commitment to advancing academic knowledge is evident through innovative methodologies and a keen understanding of market dynamics. Shradha aims to contribute valuable insights to the academic and research community, showcasing a passion for exploring the evolving landscape of finance and technology.

Mitrashis Basu Roy enjoys the thought of being able to influence the whole world while sitting in a room was an idea that fascinated me as a child. Prof. Roy has expanded their fields of interest to include entrepreneurship and investing. With the recent boom in fintech and ed-tech start-ups, Mitrashis is interested in blockchain implementation techniques and machine learning and aims to contribute to these growing fields. Prof. Roy is currently learning various skills such as C++, python, and Front-end development, so that the idea from childhood could become a reality. Mitrashis is confident about their level of proficiency in MS Excel, HTML, CSS, Java (intermediate), is a critical thinker, and a good communicator who can get along with people very easily. Prof. Roy is confident about public speaking skills having participated in various debate/theatre programs throughout school life.

Komal Bhardwaj is currently working at the Maharishi Markandeshwar Institute of Management, Maharishi Markandeshwar University as Assistant Professor of Finance. She has a rich experience of more than eight years of teaching in the field of management. She has a research experience in the areas of assets pricing, derivatives, option pricing and study on stock volatility. Her research interest includes consumer behaviour, investments, corporate governance, and assets liability management. She also worked as a Thesis supervisor for a program called upgrad-LJMU MBA at upgrade education private limited. Arshan Bhullar is working as an Assistant Professor at the MBA Department, Chandigarh School of Business, CGC Jhahjeri, Mohali. She is specialised in the area of marketing. She has interest in the diverse areas of strategic marketing, marketing research, product and brand management, and consumer behaviour. She is actively involved in writing, teaching, and research in the diverse areas of business management.

Saurabh Chandra is an accomplished legal scholar and currently serves as an Associate Professor & Assistant Dean at the School of Law, Bennett University, India. With a robust academic foundation, he earned his Bachelor of Arts and Bachelor of Laws (B.A. LL.B.) from the prestigious Aligarh Muslim University (A.M.U.). He further specialized in Business Laws, completing his Master of Laws (LL.M.) at the renowned National Law School of India University (NLSIU), Bangalore. Dr. Chandra's academic journey culminated in a Doctorate in Law (Ph.D.) from the esteemed National Law University (NLU) Delhi. In addition to his impressive legal education from some of India's most prestigious institutions, Dr. Saurabh Chandra also holds a master's degree in Management with specialization in Human Resources in Management and another in Journalism and Mass Communication. With 16 years of teaching experience, he has established himself as an expert in Business and Corporate Laws, with numerous publications to his credit. Dr. Saurabh Chandra is a distinguished expert in Business and Corporate Laws, with a profound understanding of the intricate legal frameworks that govern the business world. His expertise is complemented by a robust portfolio of scholarly publications, which underscores his commitment to advancing knowledge in his field. Throughout his career, Dr. Chandra has consistently produced high-impact research that addresses critical issues in Business and Corporate Law. His publications are widely recognized for their depth of analysis, innovative perspectives, and practical relevance. He has contributed extensively to leading journals, where his work has often set new standards for legal scholarship. His publications not only reflect his scholarly rigor but also his dedication to addressing contemporary challenges faced by businesses and policymakers. By bridging the gap between theoretical insights and real-world applications, Dr. Chandra's work serves as a valuable resource for academics, legal practitioners, and industry professionals alike. Dr. Chandra brings a wealth of experience in Academic Administration, having successfully held various key administrative positions. His diverse qualifications and extensive experience make him a distinguished figure in the academic and legal communities.

Lakshmi D is presently designated as a Senior Associate Professor in the School of Computing Science Engineering and Artificial Intelligence and Assistant Director, at the Centre for Innovation in Teaching & Learning (CITL) at VIT Bhopal. From 2016 to 2021 served as an Educational Research Officer, at Vishnu Educational Development and Innovation Centre (VEDIC) Shri Vishnu Educational Society, Hyderabad She has 26 years of teaching experience. She has addressed innumerable guest lectures, acted as a session chair, and was invited as a keynote speaker at several international conferences. She has conducted FDPs that cover approximately ~1,00,000 plus faculty members including JNTU, TEQIP, SERB, SWAYAM, DST, AICTE, MHRD, ATAL, ISTE, Madhya Pradesh Government-sponsored, MALVIYA MISSION TEACHER TRAINING, Central University of Gujarat and self-financed workshops across India as well as Misamis University, Philipines on Artificial Intelligence in Education: The Future and Futuristic Perspectives both theory and practical sessions. The other titles such as Modern Tools and Software in Teaching Learning Practices, Outcome Based Education, Scientific Educational Practices, Flipped Learning, Blended Learning, Activity Based Learning, Marching towards Quality and Excellence in Higher Educational Institutions, NEP 2022, Emotional Intelligence, Python Essential, Data Analytics, IoT, Machine Learning, Deep Learning, Cyber Security, AR/VR in Medicine, Architecture and Military Applications Instructional Strategies, Assessment techniques, Research Writing, etc. She has 20 international conference presentations, and 70 international journal papers and book chapters inclusive of SCOPUS & SCI. A total of 20 SCOPUS-indexed book chapters. A total of 24 patents are in various stages and 18 patents have been granted at both national and international levels. She was appointed as an external examiner for several Ph.D candidates at reputed universities. Under her supervision, one scholar has completed a Ph.D. at Annamalai University. One scholar is pursuing a Ph.D. right now at VIT Bhopal University. She has won three Best Paper awards at international conferences, one at the IEEE conference and another one at EAMMIS 2021 (First European, Asian, Middle Eastern North African Conference on Management & Information Systems). She received two awards in the year 2022 on the eve of Teacher's Day 1. Kamal Sharma Award of Academic Excellence - 2022 from Lexicon Group of Institutions, Pune for the Engaged Pedagogies. from the virtual ceremony. 2. Bharat Academic Excellence "UttamaAdyapika" Award from Braino Vision. She published a book on "Theory of Computation" in 2003, "Leading Education in the Age of Disruption" in 2021, and "Smart Cities: Disruptive Technologies Driving the Force", in 2023. In the last three editions, she acted as a SPOC for KAVACH and the Smart India Hackathon. She has created 15 hours of the high-quality "Python Essentials" online course at VITyarthi Online Learning Platform. She has 11 SCOPUS Indexed book edits with three CRS Press, Taylor, and Francis, four IGI Global, and two IEEE Rivers.

Reena Dogra is an Assistant Professor in the Department of Economics at Himachal Pradesh University, Shimla. Her areas of Interest include Agricultural Economics, Population Studies, and Public Finance.

Gurwinder Dua is an Assistant Professor at Post Graduate Government College - 11, Chandigarh.

Ramy El-Kady is a full criminal law professor at the Police Academy and holds the position of department chair of criminal law. He was rewarded with the State Encouragement Award in Legal and Economic Sciences, Citizenship and Human Rights Branch, on the topic of "the right of persons cooperating with justice for protection in international conventions and national legislation. He graduated from the Police College in 1999. He obtained a postgraduate diploma in criminal sciences and public law, which is equivalent to a master's degree in criminal law, in 2003. He received a PhD in criminal law from the Faculty of Law, Cairo University, on the topic of (Mediation as an Alternative to a Criminal Case: A Comparative Study. He currently teaches criminal law subjects to college students. He supervised numerous studies submitted for doctoral degrees and higher diplomas and authored a host of research in the criminal law field. He has previously judged multiple research papers in a number of refereed regional scientific journals. He published a host of research in refereed and indexed periodicals and took part in a number of international and local conferences and symposia.

Sanjeev Gupta, Ph.D., is a distinguished Professor and Dean at the Central University of Himachal Pradesh, India. He specializes in FinTech, Data Science, Forecasting, Applied Econometrics, and Digital Finance, with a focus on emerging technologies like Artificial Intelligence, Blockchain, IoT, CBDC, and

Cryptocurrency. A prolific researcher, Professor Gupta has numerous publications in leading journals, reflecting his expertise in finance and technology. His commitment to advancing knowledge and fostering academic excellence makes him a significant contributor to the academic community.

Santos Andrés Gutiérrez Figueroa has a Doctor by the University of Salamanca with the thesis Civil liability for improper use of industrial design 2007, supervised by Dr. Eugenio Llamas Pombo, Dr. Manuel Antonio Domínguez García.

Animesh Karn is an Assistant Professor at Amity School of Economics, Amity University Jharkhand. He teaches mathematical economics, inferential statistics, and behavioral economics. With over 18 years of teaching experience, he has taught at various institutions including ICFAI School of Marketing Studies, Hyderabad, Usha Martin Academy, Chandigarh, and St. Xavier's College, Patna. An alumnus of the Banaras Hindu University, Varanasi, he has authored books on mathematical economics, managerial economics, and the Indian economy. Animesh is an expert in econometrics and quantitative techniques. He has extensive research experience in education economics, leadership management, and environmental economics. His research interests include institutional economics, public policy, behavioral finance, and contract laws. He advocates using technology in education and skilling students with open-source tech like R, Python, and LaTeX. Animesh is a respected and approachable teacher, known for his innovative teaching methods and dedication to providing the best education possible to his students.

Christian Kaunert is Professor of International Security at Dublin City University, Ireland. He is also Professor of Policing and Security, as well as Director of the International Centre for Policing and Security at the University of South Wales. In addition, he is Jean Monnet Chair, Director of the Jean Monnet Centre of Excellence and Director of the Jean Monnet Network on EU Counter-Terrorism.

Aprajita Kimta is a PhD Research Scholar in the Department of Economics at Himachal Pradesh University, Shimla. She obtained her postgraduate studies at Himachal Pradesh University in 2020 and is currently pursuing a Ph.D. as a Research Scholar in the Department of Economics at the same university.

Sahil Lal is a Research Scholar at School of Law, Sharda University. He pursued his graduation from National Law University, Lucknow and completed his Master's in Law from Gujarat National Law University, Gandhinagar. Sahil has completed a certificate course on 'AI & Law' from Lund University, Sweden and on 'Cyber Law' from Indian Law Institute, New Delhi. Sahil Lal is a qualified UGC-NET & JRF candidate. He has a 10+ year Industry Experience and is an active member of Family

Dispute Resolution Clinic, Mediation Center, Greater Noida. Sahil has attended 20+ International & National Conferences along with Paper Presentation and has also participated in more than 5+ Faculty Development Programme. Mr. Sahil has more than 50+ publications in various esteemed Journals & Books. Mr. Sahil has a keen interest in area of Artificial Intelligence, Machine Learning, Robotics, Block-Chain Technology and Intellectual Property Rights.

Asaf Levi has a PhD from the Universidad Rey Juan Carlos with the thesis Uncertainty and complex dynamics in econophysics 2019. Directed by Dr/a. Miguel Ángel Fernández Sanjuán. He has experience in the development of mathematical models, computational models, predictive models based on machine learning and agent-based models (ABM's), market research and economic programs. I have collaborated with startups, foundations and private companies in the development of innovative products and services and their introduction to the market. He directs the Digital Lab, the faculty's digital laboratory, and is a Principal Investigator (PI) in the research group The Company of the Future.

Nagalingayya M is working as an Associate Professor in the Dept. of Computer Science and Engineering. He completed her Ph.D. in the Faculty of Computer and Information Engineering, Sharanbasva University, India in the year 2023. He received her M.Tech degree in CSE from VTU India in the year 2013. B.E. in ISE from VTU, India in the year 2008. He has 14 years of experience in Teaching and Research from Reputed Engineering Colleges.

Natchimuthu comes with 17+ years of experience in Teaching and Research. Currently, he is working as an Associate professor at the Department of Commerce, CHRIST (Deemed to be University). Natchimuthu has a PhD from Bharathiar University, Coimbatore India and has Master of Philosophy and Master of Commerce degrees from Madurai Kamaraj University, India. His research interest lies in the field of Financial Econometrics and particularly in the area of Volatility estimation and Machine Learning. Dr Natchimuthu has published research papers in Scopus-indexed and other international Journals. His recent publications include "Volatility spill over among metals", "Calendar anomalies in Indian stock market" and "Is gold price leveraged in India?".

Maicol Ochoa Arrellano has a Doctor by the Universidad Carlos III de Madrid with the thesis Sobre expectiles, generalizaciones y algunas aplicaciones en análisis multivariante 2022, supervised by Dr. Ignacio Cascos Fernández. As a mathematician with more than fifteen years of teaching experience, I have acquired solid knowledge and skills in solving complex problems of different kinds, with a special interest in topics such as Fundamental Mathematics, Probability Theory, Pure and Applied Statistics, as well as some applications to Data Analysis, Economics, Management and Quantitative Finance. I am committed to continuous growth and learning, and always looking for a better version of myself, I am convinced that there is no better way to learn something than teaching it. Hence, I am entirely available not only to share the knowledge I already have but also to face the challenge of learning about new topics.

Bhimaraya Patil is working as an Associate Professor in the Dept. of Computer Science and Engineering. He completed her Ph.D. in the Faculty of Computer and Information Engineering, VTU, India in the year 2023. He received his M.Tech degree in CSE from VTU India in the year 2013. B.E. in CSE from VTU, India in the year 2009. He has 14 years of experience in Teaching and Research from Reputed Engineering Colleges.

Jean-Michel Rocchi had his first successes as a senior banker who financed LBO transactions (Elior, Générale de Santé,..). He then managed funds in Luxembourg, Switzerland and Dubai. He has taught Finance at Paris Dauphine and Neoma BS and has written more than twenty economic and financial books published in France and the United States. Jean-Michel Rocchi is an expert in financial engineering and private equity with more than $5bn in deals advised or financed in Europe. He also has extensive experience in IPOs with €10bn of money-in and money-out advised transactions on the stock markets in Paris, London and Brussels.

Michel Ruimy is an economist and consultant at Levy Capital Partners. He has written numerous books and articles on economics and finance, which he teaches at various universities and grandes écoles (Sciences Po, Paris, ESCP, etc.). He is regularly called upon by the media, both television and print, for his analysis of the economic and financial situation. Michel Ruimy is director of the SPAK think tank where he oversees social issues and macroeconomics.

Garima Sehrawat is working as an Assistant Professor at the Maharishi Markandeshwar Institute of Management, Maharishi Markandeshwar University. She has a rich experience of more than five years of teaching in the field of Management. She has interest in the diverse areas of agri business, finance and consumer behaviour. She has published several research papers and presented them at prestigious national and international conferences.

Preety Sharma is an Assistant Professor at MM Institute of Computer Technology, Maharishi Markandeshwar University, Mullana.

Bhupinder Singh working as Professor at Sharda University, India. Also, Honorary Professor in University of South Wales UK and Santo Tomas University Tunja, Colombia. His areas of publications as Smart Healthcare, Medicines, fuzzy logics, artificial intelligence, robotics, machine learning, deep learning, federated learning, IoT, PV Glasses, metaverse and many more. He has 3 books, 139 paper publications, 163 paper presentations in international/national conferences and seminars, participated in more than 40 workshops/FDP's/QIP's, 25 courses from international universities of repute, organized more than 59 events with international and national academicians and industry people's, editor-in-chief and co-editor in journals, developed new courses. He has given talks at international universities, resource person in international conferences such as in Nanyang Technological University Singapore, Tashkent State University of Law Uzbekistan; KIMEP University Kazakhstan, All'ah meh Tabatabi University Iran, the Iranian Association of International Criminal law, Iran and Hague Center for International Law and Investment, The Netherlands, Northumbria University Newcastle UK,

Sachin Singh is a Senior research fellow at the Central University of Himachal Pradesh, India, and is currently pursuing a Ph.D. in Finance. His research interests lie at the confluence of finance and cutting-edge technologies, specifically focusing on Stock Markets, Time series analysis, Econometrics Modelling, Forecasting, Machine Learning, and Deep Learning applications. Sachin is committed to advancing the understanding of financial markets through innovative methodologies, leveraging his expertise in quantitative analysis and predictive modelling. With a passion for exploring the intricate relationships within financial systems, he aspires to contribute novel insights that bridge the realms of academia and real-world financial practices.

Kavitha T is working as a Professor in the Dept. of Computer Engineering. She completed her Ph.D. in the Faculty of Information and Communication Engineering, Anna University Chennai, India in the year 2014. She received her M.E. degree in Systems Engineering and Operations Research from Anna University, Chennai India in the year 2006. B.E. in Electronics and Communication Engineering from Bharathidasan University, India in the year 2000. She has 21+ years of experience in Teaching and Research from Reputed Engineering Colleges. She is Anna University and VTU recognized supervisor for guiding Ph.D. and M.S(by Research) Programme. Under her guidance, a scholar completed a Ph.D. at Anna University. She has received Funds from different agencies like ISTE-SRM, VTU-TEQIP, IE, VTU, AICTE-ISTE, and AICTE to organize FDP, workshops, Training, and conferences. She is also a Mentor for the projects who got funds from VTU and KSCKT.

Nidhiya Maria Thomas is a research scholar at the Department of Commerce at CHRIST (Deemed to be University). She is also an ACCA affiliate. Her research interest lies in the field of finance, especially in the crypto market.

Nenad Tomić currently works at the Faculty of Economics, University of Kragujevac. Nenad does research in Electronic Payment Systems and Financial Economics.

Index

A

B

D

E

F

H

I

J

L

M

O

P

R

www.ingramcontent.com/pod-product-compliance
Lightning Source LLC
LaVergne TN
LVHW080351011026
849161LV00009B/2260